Anxiety disorders in children and adolescents

Anxiety disorders are among the most prevalent mental health problems in childhood. In this timely book, an international team of psychiatrists and psychologists review the most recent theoretical and empirical developments in the field and indicate how these may inform research and clinical practice.

Following a historical introduction, chapters review conceptual and management issues, including cognitive, neurobiological, learning and developmental processes, and the influence of the peer group and family. Phenomenology, classification and assessment are covered, as are clinical course, intervention and outcome, with attention to both pharmacological and psychosocial treatment approaches.

For clinicians and researchers this is an authoritative guide to the understanding and assessment of anxiety disorders in the young, and will appeal to all mental health professionals involved with

Wendy K. Silv   nd Family Psychosocial Research

Philip D. A. T   DATE DUE   lescent Psychiatry Curium and Pr   ty.

Cambridge Child and Adolescent Psychiatry

Child and adolescent psychiatry is an important and growing area of clinical psychiatry. The last decade has seen a rapid expansion of scientific knowledge in this field and has provided a new understanding of the underlying pathology of mental disorders in these age groups. This series is aimed at practitioners and researchers both in child and adolescent mental health services and developmental and clinical neuroscience. Focusing on psychopathology, it highlights those topics where the growth of knowledge has had the greatest impact on clinical practice and on the treatment and understanding of mental illness. Individual volumes benefit both from the international expertise of their contributors and a coherence generated through a uniform style and structure for the series. Each volume provides firstly an historical overview and a clear descriptive account of the psychopathology of a specific disorder or group of related disorders. These features then form the basis for a thorough critical review of the etiology, natural history, management, prevention and impact on later adult adjustment. Whilst each volume is therefore complete in its own right, volumes also relate to each other to create a flexible and collectable series that should appeal to students as well as experienced scientists and practitioners.

Already published in this series:

Anxiety disorders in children and adolescents

Research, assessment and intervention

Edited by

Wendy K. Silverman

and

Philip D. A. Treffers

CAMBRIDGE
UNIVERSITY PRESS

PUBLISHED BY THE PRESS SYNDICATE OF THE UNIVERSITY OF CAMBRIDGE
The Pitt Building, Trumpington Street, Cambridge, United Kingdom

CAMBRIDGE UNIVERSITY PRESS
The Edinburgh Building, Cambridge CB2 2RU, UK
40 West 20th Street, New York, NY 10011-4211, USA
10 Stamford Road, Oakleigh, VIC 3166, Australia
Ruiz de Alarcón 13, 28014 Madrid, Spain
Dock House, The Waterfront, Cape Town 8001, South Africa

http://www.cambridge.org

First published 2001

Printed in the United Kingdom at the University Press, Cambridge

Typeset in Dante MT 11/14pt [VN]

A catalogue record for this book is available from the British Library

Library of Congress Cataloguing in Publication data
Anxiety disorders in children: research, assessment, and intervention/edited by
Wendy K. Silverman and Philip D. A. Treffers.
    p.   cm. – (Cambridge child and adolescent psychiatry)
Includes index.
ISBN 0 521 78966 4 (pbk.)
1. Anxiety in children.   2. Anxiety in adolescence.   3. Child psychotherapy.
4. Adolescent psychotherapy.   I. Silverman, Wendy K.   II. Treffers, Ph. D. A.
III. Cambridge child and adolescent psychiatry series

RJ506.A58 A585 2000
618.92'85223 – dc21   00-033696

ISBN 0 521 78966 4 paperback

Every effort has been made in preparing this book to provide accurate and up-to-date information which is in accord with accepted standards and practice at the time of publication. Nevertheless, the authors, editors and publisher can make no warranties that the information contained herein is totally free from error, not least because clinical standards are constantly changing through research and regulation. The authors, editors and publisher therefore disclaim all liability for direct or consequential damages resulting from the use of material contained in this book. Readers are strongly advised to pay careful attention to information provided by the manufacturer of any drugs or equipment that they plan to use.

Contents

Contributors

Frits Boer
Leiden University Medical Centre
Academic Centre for Child and Adolescent
Psychiatry Curium
Endegeesterstraatweg 27
2342 AK Oegstgeest
The Netherlands

Steven L. Berman
Child and Family Psychosocial
Research Center
Department of Psychology
Florida International University
University Park
Miami, FL 33199, U.S.A.

Graham C. L. Davey
Psychology Group
School of Cognitive and Computing Science
University of Sussex
Brighton BN1 9QH, U.K.

Andy P. Field
Psychology Group
School of Cognitive and Computing Science
University of Sussex
Brighton BN1 9QH, U.K.

Antonio C. Fonseca
Department of Psychology
University of Coimbra
Coimbra, Portugal

Avigdor Klingman
University of Haifa
Faculty of Education
Mount Carmel
Haifa 31905, Israel

Annette M. La Greca
Department of Psychology
University of Miami
PO Box 249229
Coral Gables, FL 33124, U.S.A.

Ingeborg Lindhout
Leiden University Medical Centre
Academic Centre for Child and Adolescent
Psychiatry Curium
Endegeesterstraatweg 27
2342 AK Oegstgeest
The Netherlands

Katharina Manassis
Department of Psychiatry
Hospital for Sick Children
Toronto, Ontario M5G 1X8
Canada

John S. March
Department of Pediatric Psychiatry
Duke University Medical Center
PO Box 3527
Durham, NC 27710, U.S.A.

Jon M. McClellan
Department of Psychiatry and Behavioral
Sciences
University of Washington
Seattle, WA 98195, U.S.A.

Jaap Oosterlaan
Department of Clinical Neuropsychology
Free University
De Boelelaan 1105
1081 HV Amsterdam
The Netherlands

Lars-Göran Öst
Department of Clinical Psychology
Stockholm University
S-1-1069 Stockholm
Sweden

Sean Perrin
Institute of Psychiatry
De Crespigny Park
Denmark Hill
London SE5 8AF, U.K.

Pier J. M. Prins
Department of Clinical Psychology
University of Amsterdam
Roeterstraat 15
1018 WB Amsterdam
The Netherlands

Floyd R. Sallee
Pediatric Psychopharmacologic
Research Center
Department of Psychiatry
University of Cincinnatti
Cincinnatti, OH 45267, U.S.A.

Berend M. Siebelink
Leiden University Medical Centre
Academic Centre for Child and Adolescent
Psychiatry Curium
Endegeesterstraatweg 27
2342 A K Oegstgeest
The Netherlands

Wendy K. Silverman
Child and Family Psychosocial
Research Center
Department of Psychology
Florida International University
University Park
Miami, FL 33199, U.S.A.

Patrick Smith
Institute of Psychiatry
De Crespigny Park
Denmark Hill
London SE5 8AF, U.K.

Saundra L. Stock
Department of Psychiatry and
Behavioral Sciences
University of Washington
Seattle, Wa., U.S.A.

Philip D. A. Treffers
Leiden University Medical Centre
Academic Centre for Child and Adolescent
Psychiatry Curium
Endegeesterstraatweg 27
2342 AK Oegstgeest
The Netherlands

Frank C. Verhulst
Department of Child and
Adolescent Psychiatry
Sophia Children's Hospital
Erasmus University
Postbus 2060
3000 CB Rotterdam
The Netherlands

John S. Werry
University of Auckland
Department of Psychiatry
19 Edenvale Crescent
Mount Eden
Auckland 3
New Zealand

P. Michiel Westenberg
Department of Developmental and
Educational Psychology
Leiden University
Wassernaarseweg 52
2300 RB Leiden
The Netherlands

William Yule
Institute of Psychiatry
De Crespigny Park
Denmark Hill
London SE5 8AF, U.K.

Preface

The production of this volume was prompted by the international research conference on anxiety disorders in children and adolescents, held in Leiden, The Netherlands, May 15 and May 16, 1997, under the auspices of Curium, Academic Centre of Child and Adolescent Psychiatry, Leiden University, the Section of Child and Adolescent Psychiatry, Netherlands Psychiatric Association, and the Netherlands Institute for Postgraduate Studies. With the exception of chapters 1, 5, 11, and 15, the chapters in this volume began as papers presented at the conference. Each of these however has been extensively revised or fully rewritten, partly in response to feedback from the editors. The other chapters were specially invited contributions (except for chapter 1 which was written by the editors) intended to balance the thematic organization of the book.

As the programme committee for the conference and the editors of this volume, it was a privilege for us to work with such a distinguished group of scholars. In our view, each contributor successfully met the challenge of analysing and synthesizing the particular literature relevant to their chapter. As a consequence, each chapter represents an excellent treatise of a topical area. As a corpus of work, the volume thus provides for a thorough and complete summary of current issues and perspectives about anxiety disorders in children, and therefore advances our understanding about anxious children.

We believe it is important and useful to have a volume that provides this type of integrative summary of the various literatures relevant to anxiety and its disorders in children and adolescents because these literatures have grown considerably in recent years. Because of this growth, it has become increasingly difficult to keep up with the knowledge base. To move forward even more in knowledge development, however, we believe it is important to bring the various literatures together in a systematic way. Hence, a main goal of this volume is to bring together the various literatures most pertinent to anxiety and its disorders in children in order to build upon the current knowledge base in this area. This goal is accomplished by having each chapter cover a particular area (e.g. classification and assessment, psychopharmacology, cognition, peer influences) and present a consolidated and integrative picture of this area.

Because of the breadth of the topic areas covered and the scholarly manner in which each is handled by the contributors, the volume is likely to appeal to advanced students in psychology and psychiatry, as well as researchers and practitioners who are interested in learning more about anxiety and its disorders in children, from a variety of perspectives. The chapters contained herein also will hopefully set the stage for improved clinical research and practice with anxious children and their families for the future.

This book was the product of the efforts of many people. As we have noted, we are particularly appreciative of the chapter authors for each of their fine contributions. They accepted our suggestions for revisions willingly and were prompt (usually!) in providing us with final drafts. We appreciate, as well, their patience as the process proceeded from conference to book. We were aided in this volume by the staff of Cambridge University Press, particularly Jocelyn Foster who initiated the project with us and Pauline Graham who completed the project. We also appreciate the thoughtful comments that Dr Ian Goodyer, editor of the *Cambridge Monographs in Child and Adolescent Psychiatry*, gave us on our initial outline which helped to shape the final version of the text that you are now reading. Perhaps even more importantly, we appreciate his giving us the 'green light' to proceed with this project.

Finally, Wendy Silverman would like to thank her students at Florida International University in Miami for their willingness and eagerness to assist her with all her various endeavours, including this book. Armando A. Pina particularly deserves thanks for managing many of the administrative details involved in putting together a text of this sort. She also is grateful to Leiden University for her appointment in 1997 as a visiting professor of medicine. In addition, Wendy would like to thank, as always, her husband, Efraim Ben-Zadok, and her two children, Daniel and Rachel. For this project, they provided not just their usual emotional support, but physical support as well – they spent 1997 in Leiden with her while she was working on both the conference and the conceptual planning of this book with Philip.

Philip Treffers would like to thank Paul Engelen, the manager of the research conference in 1997, and Jerry O'Connor who was of great help with the translation of an initial version of the first chapter. He also is grateful to Leiden University for the appointment in 1997 of Wendy Silverman as a visiting professor. This resulted in collaboration on not just this volume, but on other childhood anxiety research projects. Philip's thanks to his wife, Ietje, and children, Milena, Hedda and Jakob, go without saying.

Wendy K. Silverman and Philip D. A. Treffers

13 July 1999

Anxiety and its disorders in children and adolescents before the twentieth century

Philip D. A. Treffers and Wendy K. Silverman

Fear is, I think, the greatest mental suffering for children.

George Sand (1854–1855)

Introduction

Little Hans and little Albert are so well-known that one might easily get the impression that Freud (1909) and Watson (Watson & Rayner, 1920) were the first to 'discover' anxiety and its disorders in children. This impression is likely to be reinforced by a reading of the contemporary child psychiatry and psychology literatures. These literatures are basically characterized by an absence of *any* mention about the existence of anxiety and its disorders as phenomena that existed in childhood prior to the year 1900. Klein & Last (1989) are among the few contemporary authors to note that anxiety and its disorders in children were mentioned by others as existing before this time period (they refer to Kraepelin (1883) and Emminghaus (1887) as the first authors to report anxiety states in children and adolescents).

In this first chapter, we present a historical perspective of anxiety and its disorders in childhood and adolescence in terms of how they were viewed in psychiatry and psychology prior to the twentieth century. We chose to focus our attention on this time period because we were more interested in exploring 'uncharted waters' than charted waters. That is, as noted, we believe most readers are already generally familiar with the main developments that occurred during the twentieth century (e.g. Little Hans and Little Albert). Most readers also are generally familiar with the Kraepelin approach to psychiatric classification which laid the foundation for current classification schemes (e.g. Diagnostic and Statistical Manuals; American Psychiatric Association, 1987, 1994) and International Statistical Classification of Diseases and Related Health Problems (World Health Organization, 1992), and how the anxiety disorders were classified with each version (for example Silverman, 1993; Werry, 1994).

As far as we know, however, there has never been a scholarly attempt made to chart the history of psychiatric and psychosocial approaches to anxiety and anxiety disorders in children and adolescents prior to the twentieth century. Even in publications on the history of child and adolescent psychiatry (e.g. Parry-Jones, 1994) anxiety disorders are only sparsely mentioned. In this chapter then, using primary sources wherever possible, we trace the way anxiety and anxiety disorders in children have been described and explained in the literature prior to the twentieth century. By so doing, the historical record is thus being preserved – something that we believe is important to do as we are of the view (held by many) that our futures *are* generally better off when they are informed by our pasts.

The general line of development is as follows: Until the nineteenth century anxiety in children was a focus of attention mainly in the field of education. At the beginning of the nineteenth century – the period in which psychiatry developed into an independent discipline – anxiety in children was primarily regarded as a 'vulnerability factor', which could later lead to the development of psychiatric problems. In the second half of the nineteenth century the contours of child and adolescent psychiatry became clearly defined. During this period, anxiety in children acquired the status of a psychiatric symptom and 'disorder'.

In the review that follows, which has no pretensions to exhaustiveness (though we tried our best to be as comprehensive as possible), we hope to shed light on the early history of conceptualizations of anxiety and its disorders in youth. In so doing, the review touches on conceptualizations of child and adolescent psychiatric disorders in general. We present these conceptualizations, because they appear relevant for anxiety disorders, which as such were described for the first time in the second half of the nineteenth century. Also worth noting is that during the times when these writings appeared, it was customary to use the masculine 'he', or 'his' only. To keep the original flavour of the writings we therefore retained this usage.

Educational and medical literature up to the nineteenth century

The first set of writings that we could locate where mention was made of anxiety in children was in Hippocrates' (460–370 BC) *Aphorisms*. In his *Aphorisms*, Hippocrates reported fears as being among the illnesses of newborns and infants, as well as aphtae (i.e.), vomiting and night fears (*Aphorisms* 24). Hippocrates, we do not believe, would have predicted that at least two millennia would pass before anxiety in children would again come to be regarded as an 'illness'.

It was not until the Middle Ages that anxiety in children was again the focus of attention, this time in educational circles. Numerous 'books of nurture' for parents and children remain from the Middle Ages. Wardle (1991) reported that on the basis of such 'books of nurture' he was able to isolate descriptions of 108 separate behavioural and emotional problems, including timidity, school refusal and anxiety.

The impression given by Ariès (1960) and DeMause (1974) in their historical accounts of childhood and childrearing during the Middle Ages is unrelentingly sombre. Child abuse and infanticide were present on a large scale. Others (Kroll & Bachrach, 1986; Pollock, 1983; Shahar, 1990) have presented a more nuanced picture. For example, on the basis of extensive source research, Shahar (1990) concluded that in the Middle Ages, authors of medical works, 'like most didactic writers, favour[ed] essentially lenient education and granting the child freedom to act in accordance with his natural tendencies' (Shahar, 1990, p. 98).

This does not mean that there were no 'harsh' measures used in child-rearing, such as physical punishment and 'frightening'. DeMause (1974) and Shahar (1990) provide examples of the use of fearsome masked creatures or drawings as childrearing techniques during this time. It is unlikely, though that such practices were widespread, bearing in mind that approaches to childrearing in the Middle Ages varied considerably, depending in large part on the period and the region. 'Frightening' one's children could be a necessity in childrearing, especially where religious education was involved – as fear was an important concept within the context of religious education. As a consequence, it is understandable that parents strictly adhered to the mores of the day, especially in times when 'non-adherence to the teachings' was severely punished by the religious authorities. Still the following conclusion drawn by Shahar (1990) probably represents a reasonably accurate summary statement about the Middle Ages' views of childrearing:

Since fear and dread cause melancholy, one should refrain, when rearing a child, from angering or saddening him. Nor should one act with excessive merriment. Everything should be done with moderation and in the proper proportion. (Shahar, 1990, p. 98)

In terms of care, in the Middle Ages the care of children with disorders was mainly in the hands of the church. Beek (1969), in his description of psychiatry in the Middle Ages, reported that different regions had a different saint as patron of one or more illnesses. The patron saint for epilepsy also was patron saint for childhood convulsions, fears and children's development in general. However, not only the clergy, but also doctors were involved in treating illness in children and adolescents: there are numerous sources in Middle Ages

literature which could be regarded as the 'first paediatric publications', such as
'The Boke of Children' by the father of English paediatrics, Thomas Phaer
(1545). In these publications sleep disorders, nightmares, enuresis, hysteria and
melancholia were treated (see reviews by Ruhräh (1925) and Demaitre (1977)).
One of the few publications in which 'fear' in children was addressed is the
treatise on stammering by the Italian doctor Hieronymus Mercurialis (1583) in
De Morbis Puerorum. In Mercurialis' view, the basic cause of stammering was
'natural humidity', because 'a tongue that is soft or too moist or weak on
account of the humidity of the muscles cannot be impelled vigorously enough
against the teeth . . .' (p. 227). The reason for stammering, in his opinion, could
often be found in 'affections of the mind'. One of these affections was fear, as 'is
both clear from experience and confirmed by Aristotle and Galen . . .' (p. 227).
In the treatment of stammering, Mercurialis pleaded for trepidation as an
effective remedy against an excess of humidity: 'Trepidation [in Greek
"agonia"] exists when men who are about to attack some great thing fear; and
this kind of fear is greater than fear so-called [in Greek "phobos"]'. In trepidation 'just as in shame the parts around the breast and face grow warm, as is
discerned from the redness, so, says he [Aristotle], to those in trepidation comes
a heat around the breast and around the face . . .' and 'it is not to be doubted
that there may also be removed that excessive humidity' (p. 234). Mercurialis
thus gave a physical explanation for stammering, although the brain as yet
played no role.

Mercurialis also cited 'fear' as one of the causes of stammering. This is
probably the reason why Walk (1964) summarized Mercurialis' conclusions as
follows: 'therapy . . . consists in driving out the emotion – usually fear, and
perhaps conceived as unconscious – supposed to be at the root of the trouble,
by an opposing one' (p. 754). It seems to us that this is too far-reaching an
interpretation of Mercurialis' struggle with dryness and humidity.

The sixteenth century stands to a large extent in the shadow of witch
burning, which also counted psychiatrically disturbed children as its victims.
The Dutchman Johann Weyer, the father of modern psychiatry (Stone, 1973),
and one of the first authors in child psychiatry played an important role in
bringing the care of mental illness into the domain of doctors and away from
the clergy. In the seventeenth century, the idea that psychiatric disturbances
were caused by satanic forces lost ground. Although the Englishman, Robert
Burton, in his famous dissertation on melancholy, named 'the power of Divels'
as one of the causes of melancholy (Burton, 1621), he adopted a 'multi-causal
position', pointing to the role of inheritance, which was also manifested in the
workings of the mind:

That other inward inbred cause of Melancholy, is our temperature [temperament] in whole or part, which wee receive from our parents (. . .) Such as the temperature of the father is, such is the sonnes; and looke what disease the father had when he begot him, such his son will have after him . . . Now this doth not so much appeare in the composition of the Body . . . but in manner and conditions of the Minde . . . (pp. 96–97)

In addition, Burton identified education as a cause of melancholy:

Parents and such as have the tuition and oversight of children, offend many times in that they are too sterne, always threatning, chiding, brawling, whipping, or striking; by meanes of which their poore children are so disheartned & cowed that they never have any courage, or a merry houre in their lives, or take pleasure in any thing. (. . .) Others againe in that other extreame doe as much harme . . . Too much indulgence causeth the like . . . (p. 97)

At the close of the eighteenth century, the article, 'On the Different Species of Phobia' was published, written by the American, Benjamin Rush (Rush, 1798). In this ironic essay Rush defined phobia as 'a fear of an imaginary evil, or an undue fear of a real one' (p. 177). He also referred to phobias in children, citing for example Thunder phobia as one type ('This species is common to all ages, and to both sexes: I have seen it produce the most distressing appearances and emotions upon many people' [p. 179]) and Ghost phobia ('This distemper is most common among servants and children . . .' [p. 180]).

Rush's writing contains, to our knowledge, the first written description of phobic anxiety in children. In 1812, Rush's *Medical Inquiries and Observations, upon the Diseases of the Mind* was published. The wide fame this book enjoyed was probably due to a section on depression, in which Rush stated that '. . . depression of mind may be induced by causes that are forgotten, or by the presence of objects which revive the sensation of distress with which it was at one time associated, but without reviving the cause of it in the memory' (p. 46). The book also contained an extensive discussion of fear. In the section, 'On Fear', Rush wrote: 'There are so much danger and evil in our world, that the passion of fear was implanted in our minds for the wise and benevolent purpose of defending us from them' (p. 325). Rush distinguished between 'reasonable' objects of fear, such as death, and 'unreasonable' objects of fear, such as 'thunder, darkness, ghosts, speaking in public, sailing, riding, certain animals, particularly cats, rats, insects, and the like' (p. 325).

Rush also offered several remedies for the fears found in childhood that, while innovative for the day, sound quite familiar to contemporary readers. For example, Rush's remedy for the fear of death was not to talk about it: 'Boys obviate fear in like manner, by silence in passing by a grave-yard, or by conversing upon subjects unconnected with death' (p. 328).

As regards remedies for unreasonable objects of fear, Rush focused on the importance of education and early preventive measures: 'The fear which is excited by darkness may easily be overcome by a proper mode of education in early life. It consists in compelling children to go to bed without a candle, or without permitting company to remain with them until they fall a sleep' (p. 321). And the 'fear from certain animals and insects, may all be cured by resolution. It should be counteracted in early life' (p. 332).

Finally, the foreshadowing of learning theory, as discussed by Field and Davey (chapter 8, this volume), also can be seen in Rush's closing paragraph on fear:

Great advantages may likewise be derived for the cure of fear, by a proper application of the principle of association. A horse will seldom be moved by the firing of a gun, or the beating of a drum, if he hear them for the first time while he is eating; nor will he start, or retire from a wheelbarrow, or a millstone, or any object of that kind, after being once or twice fed upon them. The same law of association may be applied in a variety of instances to the human mind, as well to the prevention, as cure, of fear. (p. 333)

The first half of the nineteenth century

The contours of child and adolescent psychiatry

In the nineteenth century, a distinction was increasingly drawn between idiocy and psychiatric disturbances in children. A growing number of short descriptions of children with 'moral insanity' (where 'moral' may usually be interpreted as 'psychic') appeared. These include statements by the Frenchman, Esquirol, who is regarded as the most important psychiatrist of the first decades of the nineteenth century. Views on psychiatric disturbances in youth were still largely influenced by ideas from adult psychiatry, however. Overall, little attention was paid during this period to anxiety and its disorders.

Causes of psychiatric disturbance in children and adolescents

There was general agreement that inheritance played an important role in psychiatric problems. Adams (1814) showed a remarkable appreciation of the nuances involved. 'Madness', he claimed, 'as well as *gout*, is never *hereditary*, but in *susceptibility*'. When a disposition was involved, only a trivial cause was needed to elicit the mental irritation for the outbreak of the disease: 'But when the susceptibility amounts only to a *predisposition*, requiring the operation of some external cause to produce the disease, there is every reason to hope, that the action of the disease may be for the most part much lessened, if not prevented altogether' (Adams, 1814; p. 692). Esquirol (1838), similarly, re-garded heritability as the most general cause to mental illness. In Esquirol's opinion, the disease could nevertheless be transferred in another way, from the mother to the child; that is, mothers who experienced strong emotions during pregnancy had children who at the slightest cause could become insane. Esquirol cited the French Revolution as an example of a time when this was a common phenomenon.

A relation was drawn also between insanity and upbringing. The English-man, James Parkinson (1807), in his short paper on the excessive indulgence of children, illustrated the far-reaching effects that education and inconsistent childrearing style could have:

On the treatment the child receives from his parents during the infantine stage of his life, will, perhaps, depend much of the misery or happiness he may experience, not only in his passage through this, but through the other stages of his existence. (p. 468)

The view that schooling – if begun too early or if too intensive – could be harmful to mental health also was popular in the nineteenth century (e.g. Adams, 1814). Esquirol (1830) regarded excessive study as one of the causes of the supposed increase in diseases of the mind: 'The advance of civilization leads to a multiplicity of the insane' (p. 332). He was later more nuanced in his view, remarking that 'it is not civilization, that we are to accuse, but the errors and excesses of all sorts, which it enables us to commit' (Esquirol, 1838, p. 42). Jarvis (1852) linked the presumed increase in mental illness in this period to 'the improvements in the education of children and youth': 'Thus they task their minds unduly, and sometimes exhaust their cerebral energies and leave their brains a prey to other causes which may derange them afterwards' (p. 358).

Masturbation was another factor that was increasingly cited as a cause of psychiatric symptoms in both adults and youth (Hare, 1962; Neuman, 1975). The explanation offered by Griesinger (1861) on the link between masturbation and psychiatric symptoms was both succinct and 'state of the art':

As to the more intimate foundation of mental diseases in childhood, they appear to depend in part on an original irritability of the brain (often hereditary), or produced and maintained by injudicious treatment (intimidation, ill-treatment of mind, intellectual over-extertion, dissipation), partly on deeper organic disease originating spontaneously, or after injuries of the head (. . .); they often proceed from sympathetic irritation of the brain transmitted from the genital organs (onanism, approach and entrance of puberty). (pp. 143–4)

(In 1845 the first edition was published of *Die Pathologie und Therapie der Psychischen Krankheiten*, by Wilhelm Griesinger. Our quotation comes from the second edition published in 1861, in which the section on psychiatric disturbances in children is considerably more extensive.)

Assumptions about the limited prevalence of child psychiatric disturbances

In the first half of the nineteenth century, numerous authors discussed causes of the supposed limited prevalence of psychiatric disturbances in children. The French phrenologist Spurzheim (1818), for example, attributed the limited prevalence to 'the extreme delicacy of their [children's] cerebral organization which would tend not to tolerate a serious illness without total loss of psychical faculties, or without grave danger to life itself' (p. 114).

Esquirol (1838) also believed that mental illness had limited prevalence in childhood, 'unless at birth the child suffers from some vice of conformation or convulsions, which occasion imbecility or idiocy' (p. 33). Although Esquirol had this view, he described a number of exceptions. Unlike Spurzheim, Esquirol regarded the limited prevalence of psychiatric disturbances in children as being due to the absence of passions in children:

Infancy, exempt from the influence of the passions, is almost a stranger to insanity; but at the epoch of puberty, the sentiments, unknown until this period, cause new wants to arise. Insanity then appears, to trouble the first moments of the moral existence of man. (Esquirol, 1838, p. 46)

The important role which Esquirol (1838) ascribed to the passions in psychiatric problems is clear in the following statement: 'One of the moral causes pointed out by Pinel, and which is frequently met with in practice, is the conflict which arises between the principles of religion, morality, education and the passions' (p. 47). Internal conflict as a cause of mental illness had made its debut!

The German physician, Griesinger (1861), also believed that insanity seldom occurred before puberty: '. . . the mobility of this age does not allow single insane ideas to become persistent and systematised, as at a late period' (p. 143). Paradoxically, in his opinion, as in Esquirol's, still almost all forms of insanity did occur in children, be it by way of exception.

Course of the illness

Occasionally a writer commented on the course of psychiatric illness in children. Adams (1814) suggested that some disturbances were 'phase-related': 'Sometimes we find the disease cease, as the changes of the constitution during that period are compleated' (p. 692). Esquirol (1838) approached the subject from a retrospective perspective: 'Almost all the insane, presented before their sickness, certain functional changes, which extended back many years, even to earliest infancy' (p. 54). Griesinger (1861), on the other hand, took a prospective approach: 'Also after recovery such patients are much disposed to relapse; their mental health continues in danger during the whole of their lives, or they occasionally become, without being actually insane, owing to an unfavorable change in their whole character, useless for the world' (p. 144). Commenting on the influence of mental disorders on the psychological development of the child in general, Griesinger claimed: 'It is a general essential characteristic of the mental disorders of childhood that they limit further mental development' (p. 143).

Anxiety

Anxiety did not occupy a prominent place in the literature on child and adolescent psychiatry in the first half of the nineteenth century. A number of authors, including Esquirol (1838), emphasized that the upbringing of children should not be fearful. Esquirol referred to strong impressions as a cause of disturbances in children, describing the intense fears that could be aroused. He did not regard the fear itself as a disturbance, but fear could form the basis of a mental illness that could arise later, at puberty. Esquirol (1838) described several cases to illustrate this view, including a 3-year-old boy who was:

frightened at the bears, exhibited (. . .) as a curiosity. From that time, he was subject to frightful dreams, and at seventeen years of age, he was seized with mania. A girl, six years of age, sees her father massacred, and has since been subject to panic terrors. At fourteen (. . .) she becomes a maniac. She wishes to rush upon every body. The sight of a knife or a weapon, or of many men assembled, excites her to the most violent fury. (p. 50)

Anxiety was thus viewed by Esquirol as a vulnerability, that is, as a point from which psychopathology could develop. Griesinger (1861) referred to anxiety in relation to melancholy in children in a similar way: 'Simple melancholic states also present themselves, whose foundation is a general feeling of anxiety' (p. 143). Griesinger was only one step away from the generalized anxiety disorder!

The second half of the nineteenth century

The birth of child and adolescent psychiatry as a discipline

Although small in number, the pages in Griesinger's handbook devoted to psychiatric disturbances in youth served as the impetus for a growing number of case studies, articles, and chapters on the topic in the second half of the nineteenth century. In these decades child and adolescent psychiatry began to acquire the form of a specific discipline. Authors were generally familiar with the work of their predecessors, which they used as a springboard for their own ideas. Articles appeared in which current knowledge was systematically ordered. The British doctor Charles West, regarded as the founder of modern paediatrics, had a central place in all these developments. It is likely that West was a source of inspiration for Maudsley, who, in 1867, published *The Physiology and Pathology of the Mind*. This handbook contained a separate chapter on child and adolescent psychiatry. (Wardle (1991) reports a detailed publication on child psychiatry, by a 19-year-old medical student, Chrichton-Browne (1860). Wardle assumes that Maudsley was familiar with the publication. Unfortunately, the authors were unable to locate it.) Less well known, but intriguing is an article on 'Moral Insanity' by the American psychiatrist, Savage (1881).

Another landmark in the history of child psychiatry was a comprehensive chapter by the German psychiatrist Hans Emminghaus devoted entirely to child and adolescent psychiatry, which appeared in an 1887 handbook on paediatrics. A monograph by the Frenchman Moreau (de Tours) (1888) followed a year later. In 1890, the American, Spitzka, included a chapter on 'insanity' in a paediatrics manual. This was followed by another comprehensive publication by Manheimer (1899): *'Les troubles mentaux de l'enfance'*.

Based on our reading of these publications, we offer the following general summary. First, views on the causes of psychiatric problems in children and adolescents began to be more finely differentiated. The importance attached to hereditary factors, referred to by Manheimer as the 'cause of causes', continued to be strong. However, in views on the contribution of hereditary factors, the emphasis shifted away from the hereditary determination of illness to the hereditary determination of temperament. For example, in terms of a 'nervous temperament' or a 'neuropathic temperament', almost all of the authors treated heredity not as a single entity but in relation to environmental influences. Only in exceptional cases was the influence of heredity as such inescapable, for example when the mother was mentally ill during pregnancy (e.g. Savage, 1881).

In addition, an illness in one of the parents (e.g. lead poisoning, alcoholism, syphilis) (Clevenger, 1883), drunkenness in the parents at conception (Manheimer, 1899), illness in the mother during pregnancy and obstetric complications (e.g. use of forceps) (Clevenger, 1883) were described as causes of child psychiatric problems. Under the influence of developments in paediatrics, the number of descriptions of psychiatric disturbances in relation to paediatric illnesses increased (Cohn, 1883; Emminghaus, 1887).

Intensive schooling continued to be regarded as a factor contributing to mental illness: 'Education conducted with school honors as the object to be worked for, causes mental overstrain, and is a potent exciting cause'

(Clevenger, 1883, p. 600) (cf. Hurd, 1894; Manheimer, 1899). Likewise for upbringing: 'Insanity in children [is] practically always hereditary, though bad bringing up might largely conspire with [the] original tendency to produce the result' (Albutt, 1889, p. 131).

In this period, there were two authors who we believe were far ahead of their time in terms of their ideas about the interaction between parents and child in relation to child psychiatric problems: West and Savage. Many of their views foreshadow a number of the ideas expressed by Boer and Lindhout (chapter 10, this volume). West's (1860, 1871) fame was partly due to his description of 'the contribution of the parents' in the continuation of 'feigned diseases' (we would probably today speak of somatoform disorders in these cases), and to his recognition of the inability of the parents of these children to provide limits. Perhaps even more advanced was Savage's (1881) hypothesis that 'parental style' was partially influenced by the temperament of the child:

I would most emphatically state my belief that very many so-called spoiled children are nothing more or less than children who are morally of unsound mind, and that the spoiled child owes quite as much to his inheritance as to his education. In many cases, doubtless, the parent who begets a nervous child is very likely to further spoil such child by bad or unsuitable education. (p. 148)

As in the first half of the nineteenth century, masturbation was often cited in the second half of the century as a cause of psychiatric problems in youth. An independent disorder was even suggested, namely 'masturbatory insanity' (Maudsley, 1868), which refers probably to hebephrenic dementia praecox or schizophrenia (Hare, 1962). A few decades later, however, authors began to have reservations about the feasibility of a relation between masturbation and mental illness. The German doctor Cohn (1883) remarked that 'onanism in a moderate degree is such a widespread ill, especially during puberty, that if it really did have a seriously dangerous influence, the number of mentally ill would take on enormous proportions' (p. 41). At the end of the nineteenth century authors began to expressly avoid a too rigorous position on the matter (e.g. Maudsley, 1895). In the United States, however, the 'masturbatory hypothesis' continued to hold ground for a long time (Hall, 1904; Spitzka, 1890).

Anxiety and anxiety disorders in child and adolescent psychiatry

Charles West's *On the Mental Peculiarities and Mental Disorders of Childhood* can be seen as revolutionary: in this essay he gave a central position to the experiential world of the child, and, in particular, to the 'imagination' (West, 1860). He illustrated his claims with a realistic description of the experience of anxiety in children:

> The child lives at first in the external world, as if it were but a part of himself, or he a part of it . . . The child who dreads to be alone, and asserts that he hears sounds or perceives objects, is not expressing merely a vague apprehension of some unknown danger, but often tells a literal truth. The sounds have been heard; in the stillness of its nursery, the little one has listened to what seemed a voice calling it; or, in the dark, phantasms have risen before its eyes, and the agony of terror with which it calls for a light, or begs for its mother's presence betrays an impression far too real to be explained away, or to be suitably met by hard words or by unkind treatment. (p. 133)

It is likely that Moreau de Tours' (1888) later description of childhood anxiety was inspired by West's writings, as was Maudsley:

> It is difficult for grown-up persons, unless perchance helped by a hateful memory of their own terrors in childhood, to realise the terrible agonies of fright and anguish, which seize some nervous children when they are alone in the dark, or are left by themselves in a large room, or have to pass a room or closet of which they have conceived some formless dread, or are sent alone on a strange errand. (Maudsley, 1895, p. 370)

To our knowledge, Strack's (1863) was the first description of a 13-year-old girl in whom anxiety ('precordial anxiety') was brought to the fore as a psychiatric symptom. A number of other case studies followed in which anxiety was a prominent symptom of the children (King, 1880; Savage in the discussion of Albutt, 1889; Von Rinecker, 1876). (In scientific literature in these days it was usual to publish the papers in journals, with a report of the discussion by the audience.)

As far as we could surmise, Emminghaus (1887) was the first to suggest a relation between anxiety and temperament characteristics – a prelude to the 'behavioural inhibition' concept described by Oosterlaan (chapter 3, this volume). He wrote of 'fearfulness and anxiety as individual predispositions to emotional disorders . . .' (p. 53). Fright, which he regarded as the most common psychic cause of mental disturbances, only led to mental illness if such a predisposition was present. Maudsley (1895), too, drew links between anxiety in children and a 'neuropathic temperament':

> One little creature used to shriek in an ecstasy of fright whenever another child or dog approached it in the street, yet exulted with a frenzy of delight in a strong wind, no matter how violent; another would go straight up to any strange dog which it met and take instant hold of it, without the least apprehension, never coming to harm by its fearless behaviour. (p. 370)

In his systematic discussion of symptomatology in child psychiatry, *Anomalies of the Feelings*, Emminghaus (1887) also became the first to afford anxiety (*Angor*) a significant role in mental illness. He regarded anxiety, cowardice and nervousness as pathological only 'if they were present as new behaviour in the child in addition to other signs of a psychic disorder . . .' (p. 70). One symptom of anxiety was 'fear of being alone, especially in the dark, of sleeping alone'. This fear, which mainly occurred in young children, by such events as hearing terrifying stories by servants, could continue through childhood. Emminghaus (1887) called anxiety 'practically the most common elementary, psychic symptom', because it was characteristic of so many diseases, including 'both organic and functional brain diseases' (p. 70). Emminghaus further noted that milder forms of anxiety in children could be manifested in a number of forms, consisting mainly of impulsive actions, such as apparently cheerful whistling, the imitation of animal noises, naughty behaviour, and over-affectionate behaviour, especially towards the mother. He called these types of behaviour 'the masks of anxiety', a concept derived from a publication by the adult psychiatrist Dick (1877). Dick's statement that anxiety 'could hide behind a thousand masks', led Emminghaus to the astute observation that 'accurate evidence for this will probably be difficult to produce' (p. 72).

Finally, Emminghaus (1887) referred to 'spontaneous anxiety', which, he said, arose without any recognizable cause, and in the absence of any psychic indications. In describing this form of anxiety, which in his opinion was always pathological, he probably gave the first description of a panic attack. Maudsley (1895) also described panic attacks in adolescents:

. . . singular nervous crises which befall persons who cannot cross an open place or square, being seized with an overwhelming panic of impotence at the bare thought or attempt to cross . . . a reeling of thought and feeling, an indescribable anguish, as if the foundation of self were sinking away . . . (pp. 409–10)

Maudsley (1895) also described adolescents with obsessive-compulsive symptoms:

These are they who, sensible in other respects and able to do their daily work in the world, are still haunted with urgent impulses to think, do, or say something ridiculous, obscene, or dangerous, and are in a perpetual fever of nervous apprehension and distress in consequence. (p. 407)

Maudsley (1895) attributed both panic attacks and obsessive-compulsive symptoms to 'self-abuse' in adolescents who had a 'high-strung neurotic temperament'; at the same time though he was able to place the role of masturbation within a reasonable better perspective: 'To conclude self-abuse to be the exciting cause in every case would be to conclude wrongly and to do wrong to the sufferer' (p. 411).

Other opinions also were formulated on the pathogenesis of panic disorders. Emminghaus (1887) took as his starting point the notion of the adult psychiatrist Arndt (1874), that the feeling of anxiety could be traced to an abnormal movement of the heart, which, due to abnormally sensitive sensory nerves, was able to be perceived and brought to consciousness. Emminghaus argued differently, claiming that heart activity could remain unchanged with anxiety, and that sometimes anxiety could occur with heart disease, and sometimes not. He had no doubt that the root cause of anxiety lay in processes in the cerebral cortex. Maudsley (1895), taking a comparable standpoint, and foreshadowing some of the cognitive views discussed by Prins (chapter 2, this volume), formulated a type of 'cognitive hypothesis' about panic attacks:

a disorganisation of the muscular sense, whereby the special mental forms or intuitions required to inform the proper purposive movements are rendered impossible. The mind being thus unable to form its fit grasps or apprehensions of the environment might naturally reel in impotent alarm, transferring its subjective disorder to the external world . . . (p. 411)

Finally, Emminghaus (1887) and Maudsley (1895) described the simultaneous occurrence of melancholic and anxiety symptoms:

. . . children of four or five years, sprung from a very neurotic stock, may have fits of moaning melancholy and apprehensive fears which, but for their neuropathic inheritance, might seem quite out of keeping with their tender age and to be inexplicable aberrations of nature. (Maudsley, 1895, p. 379)

In melancholic adolescents also

. . . morbid suspicions and fears ensue: fears and fancies of having done something wrong or of being suspected of wrong-doing, of not being loved by parents, of being disliked and spoken ill of by companions, of being watched and followed in the streets (. . .) (Maudsley, 1895, pp. 393–4).

Classification

The professionalization taking place in the field of child and adolescent psychiatry also was evident in the first attempt at classification (Cohn, 1883; Emminghaus, 1887; Maudsley, 1867; Moreau de Tours, 1888). Anxiety disorders were included for the first time in the classificatory system of child psychiatry of Cohn (1883). In Cohn's system obsessive-compulsive disorders were given a relatively minor place. Under the heading 'real psychoses', beside categories such as melancholy and mania, Cohn included the category 'madness' ('Verrücktheit'), which referred to delusional disorders. Obsessions and compulsive behaviour were seen as an 'abortive form' of these disorders.

Moreau (de Tours) (1888), in his 'Etude des formes' (under 'Exaltation psychique', which was part of 'Formes purement morales') gave anxiety the status of a disorder: 'Like all psychic disturbances, and in certain cases, anxiety must be regarded as a real sickness' (p. 191). The 'spores of devastation [of anxiety attacks in children] may remain up to an advanced age, and sometimes throughout the person's entire life (p. 192).

Treatment

In terms of intervention, the main method that was advocated was phar-macotherapy. For example, the persistent anxiety attacks of the girl described by Strack (1863) disappeared after a lengthy treatment with opium. Von Rinecker (1876) treated his patient with cannabis. His experiences led him to conclude that 'Indian hemp as a medicinal remedy has a future in psychiatry' (p. 565). Occasionally, an anxiety disorder necessitated residential treatment. In this regard Clevenger (1883) reported the case of a 10-year-old boy who was admitted to an asylum for 'pyrophobia'. Manheimer (1899) presented the most detailed description of the time of treatment. He mentioned pharmacological remedies (as linden-blossom tea and orange-blossom water, hypnotics, the various bromides, ether syrup, laurel cherry water, belladonna tincture, chloral and trional) and hydrotherapy (e.g. tepid baths, or bran baths, preferably just before retiring). He also pointed out that psychological treatment – verbal suggestion, reasoning ('*raisonnement*'), and persuasion – can be effective, as well as hypnotic suggestion in severe cases.

Contributions from psychology and other sciences

In his *Historical introduction to modern psychology* Murphy (1949) concluded that the final decades of the nineteenth century witnessed the appearance of the first systematic and serious publications in the field of child psychology. Interest in child development was strongly influenced by Darwin's theory of evolution. In 1877, Darwin published the observations he had made 37 years earlier on one of his children. On the basis of his observations on fear he remarked:

> May we not suspect that the vague but very real fears of children, which are quite independent of experience, are the inherited effects of real dangers and abject superstitions during ancient savage times? It is quite conformable with what we know of the transmission of formerly well-developed characters, that they should appear at an early period of life, and afterwards disappear. (p. 5)

Darwin had a strong influence on Preyer, whose publication, *Die Seele des Kindes* (The Mind of the Child) (1892), described development during the early years of life. In the section on fear (*Furcht*) Preyer reflected on why young children were afraid of unfamiliar things: 'Why is it that many children are afraid of cats and dogs, before they are aware of the dangerous qualities of these animals?' (p. 104). (It is interesting that Tiedemann (1787), in his first known 'baby biography' ('*Beobachtungen über die Entwickelung der*

Seelenfähigkeiten bei Kindern') made no mention of anxiety.) Following Darwin, Preyer attributed the many fears of children to an 'inherited fearfulness', or an 'inborn memory', a kind of an ethological explanation. Sully (1895) did not share this viewpoint of an 'inborn memory'. In regard to his observation that very young children were generally afraid of noises, he took a physiological viewpoint, describing this fear as 'an organic phenomenon, with a sort of jar to the nervous system' (p. 197). Later in development, he argued, the fear of visual impressions arose, but this was 'Called forth by the presentation of something new and strange, especially when it involves a rupture of customary arrangements' (p. 199). In his referral to the balance between fear and curiosity Sully adopted a 'modern' ethological approach: 'It is only (. . .) when attachment to human belongings has been developed, that the approach of a stranger, especially if accompanied by a proposal to take the child, calls forth clear signs of displeasure and the shrinking away of fear' (p. 201). However, 'the most prolific excitant of fear, the presentation of something new and uncanny, is also provocative of another feeling, that of curiosity, with its impulse to look and examine' (p. 224).

Shortly before the turn of the century, two pioneers in psychological research, Alfred Binet and Stanley Hall, conducted several studies on anxiety in children (Binet, 1895; Hall, 1897). The studies were mainly based on information obtained from a large number of checklists, whose respondents included for the most part teachers (Binet), and children and young adults (Hall) about sources of children's anxiety. Seen through modern glasses the methodology of these studies is of course very 'loose'. Binet (1895) sent about 250 questionnaires to teachers – not at random but only to an 'élite' of the most intelligent and diligent teachers. He also interviewed acquaintances and observed the children in their families and his own family. Hall (1897) published a 'syllabus' in several educational journals. To give an example of his material ('the records of the chief fears of 1,701 people', p. 151) the next quote is illustrative: 'Miss Lillie A. Williams, head of psychology at the Trenton, N.J., Normal School, sent reports by 461 persons, of which 118 were original, 163 reminiscence, 75 hearsay. The reminiscences averaged six or seven pages of note paper each. The other 105 were compositions on their fears, past and present, by girls from 5 to 18' (p. 150).

More important than the actual results of these studies were the conclusions they led to and the ideas they generated. Both Binet and Hall noted individual differences among children in the degree to which they developed anxious behaviour. In regard to the heritability of anxiety, Binet concluded that 'it is difficult to reach a conclusion':

. . . there have been various examples reported of anxious parents having children who are just as anxious as the parents. In the absence of careful observation these reports do not prove much because it is possible that the parents have transferred their own characteristics to their children by means of another route than inheritance, for example through upbringing. (Binet, 1895, p. 244)

Binet discussed in detail the anxiety resulting from poor treatment by parents and how parents may react to their child's anxiety, emphasizing the importance of instilling self-confidence in children. In contrast, Hall (1897) claimed that 'a childhood too happy and careless and fearless is a calamity so great that prayer against it might stand in the old English service book beside the petition that our children be not poltroons' (Hall, 1897, p. 243).

Hall explained the capacity for fear in evolutionary terms: 'As infants, although they cannot speak, yet, unlike apes, have a capacity to be taught language, so we must assume the capacity to fear or to anticipate pain, and to associate it with certain objects and experiences, as an inherited *Anlage*, often of a far higher antiquity than we are wont to appeal to in psychology' (p. 245). He placed the anxiety study in the context of 'exploring feeling, instinct and the rich mines of unconsciousness just opening' (p. 246). And '. . . the full scope of the more basal fears rarely come to expression in consciousness, but only partial aspects of them' (p. 247).

The above quotation reflects Hall's strong interest in the ideas of European psychiatrists such as Charcot, Bernheim and Janet (Ross, 1972), who also were all sources of inspiration for Freud. In 1909, at the invitation of Hall, Freud made a visit to the United States. In the same year, with the publication of Little Hans, an influential chapter was added to the literature on anxiety disorders in children.

Concluding comments

Before the nineteenth century, relatively little attention was paid to fear and anxiety in children in the psychological and medical literature. This lack of attention was probably related in part to the high degree of social cohesion that existed prior to the nineteenth century, with religion playing a particularly prominent role. This social cohesion also helped to contribute to enhanced feelings of self-confidence and certainty among individuals. The emphasis on individualization that followed from the industrial revolution – which took place during the course of the nineteenth century – contributed however to heightened sensibilities concerning anxiety. A generalized image of the self disappeared, and individual experience received a new meaning: experienced reality was also reality. It was in this climate that Kierkegaard, in 1844, published his essay 'The Concept of Anxiety'. The emphasis on individual experiences was reflected as well in how anxiety began to be viewed with respect to mental health: articles appeared in which anxiety as a symptom or disorder was the focus (Flemming, 1848).

In the medical literature on childhood anxiety, West (1860) describing anxiety from the perspective of the individual child, constituted a turning point. The fact that anxiety was now 'discovered' in children, was probably also related to rising concern about the position of the child. One avenue of expression for this concern was in legislation in the area of child labour (Parry-Jones, 1994). The increasing attention for the position of children also was reflected in the establishment of children's hospitals. In 1863 the first case study report of a nonphobic anxiety disorder in a child was published (Strack, 1863).

In the last decades of the nineteenth century tremendous strides forward were made with respect to thinking about anxiety. Concepts that had been touched on by individual authors in previous centuries – heredity and temperament, upbringing, masturbation, learning at school, and life events – became the subject of careful and systematic thought. Also, thinking about these concepts began to move away from relatively simple views to more complex views – views in which the complex interplay of the various concepts was emphasized. For example, anxiety and its disorders began to be viewed as the result of the interaction between life events and temperamental factors (e.g. Emminghaus, 1887).

In other respects too behaviour was increasingly approached in a scientific way. Ideas on the 'pathogenesis' of anxiety disorders were a prelude to the first scientific conceptualizations of the emotions (e.g. James, 1884). Another example of a scientific approach is the development of the first systems of diagnostic classification in psychiatry, and child and adolescent psychiatry. In the descriptions of anxiety disorders, phobias can be recognized as well as indications of generalized anxiety disorders and avoidance disorders. It is notable that in the literature prior to 1900 there were no strong indications of separation anxiety disorders. Bowlby (1973) pointed out that Freud's first mention of separation anxiety disorder was not until 1905; and it was not until 1926 that he devoted systematic attention to the subject. Bowlby further pointed out that Freud (1909) gave little consideration to the 'true' fear of Little Hans, namely, that his mother might desert the family.

Only about half a century after its entrance in psychiatry and psychology, anxiety became a central concept in psychoanalytic theory, which influenced psychiatry and psychology in the twentieth century deeply for decades. In psychoanalytic theory interest in manifest anxiety largely receded into the background: The interest was especially in anxiety as the supposed mediator for psychopathology in general. In the words of Klein (1981): 'The predominant American psychiatric theory in 1959 was that all psychopathology was secondary to anxiety, which in turn was caused by intrapsychic conflict' (p. 235).

Since the '60s of the twentieth century, with the emergence of scientific research in psychopharmacology, neurobiology and behavioural sciences interest in observable anxiety and anxiety disorders returned. It is fascinating that after such a long interruption the 'old' issues (e.g. the significance of heredity, temperament, upbringing), have been put back on the scientific agenda by these disciplines. Thus, insofar areas of scientific attention are inspired by world views (Reese & Overton, 1970), it would seem that our world views in about 100 years have changed less than one might suspect. However, there are some important differences that have come about. The view of masturbation as a 'cause' of psychopathology has been abandoned totally, as has the view that learning at school contributes to the occurrence of psychopathology.

Moreover, 'newer' concepts or issues appear to have come more to the forefront in the last decades of the twentieth century. For example, the meaning of 'cognition' in emotion and in emotional disorders, touched upon at the end of the nineteenth century, was articulated much more in the last decades. Bowlby took up the thread of ethology, and placed the significance of experiences in early childhood for later development in a completely different perspective than had been done by Freud. Thinking in terms of causality made room for transactional or contextual processes. Further, the context has been extended to include not only familial but also the child within the context of his or her peer group.

The chapters that thus follow in this book touch on all of these issues and concepts. Although the specific issues and concepts that are discussed are quite different, as is the author(s)' description of the meaning and significance of the various issues and concepts, there is something that is common across the chapters. Namely, each chapter provides an illustration of how the issues and concepts represent a broadening of views about anxiety that have occurred over the last 150 years. So in contrast to the insular beginnings that we saw with respect to thinking about anxiety, the area of anxiety disorders in children has been modified to incorporate new findings and to take into account factors and forces that shape anxiety and its disorders across multiple levels. The subsequent chapters are a reflection of this trend – a trend that will undoubtedly be even more prominent in the twenty-first century.

REFERENCES

Adams, J. (1814). *A Treatise on the Supposed Hereditary Properties of Diseases, Particularly in Madness and Scrofula*. London: Callow. [In Hunter & Macalpine, 1963, pp. 691–2.]

Albutt, C. (1889). Insanity of children. *Journal of Mental Science*, **35**, 130–5.

American Psychiatric Association (1987). *Diagnostic and Statistical Manual of Mental Disorders* (3rd edn revised) (DSM–III–R). Washington, DC: American Psychiatric Association.

American Psychiatric Association (1994). *Diagnostic and Statistical Manual of Mental Disorders* (4th edn) (DSM–IV). Washington, DC: American Psychiatric Association.

Ariès, Ph. (1960). *Centuries of Childhood*. Harmondsworth: Penguin Books, 1979.

Arndt (1874). Ueber den melancholischen Angstanfall. *Allgemeine Zeitschrift für Psychiatrie*, **30**, 88–99.

Beek, H. H. (1969). *De Geestesgestoorde in de Middeleeuwen; Beeld en Bemoeienis*. Haarlem: De Toorts.

Binet, A. (1895). La peur chez les enfants. *L'Année Psychologique*, **2**, 223–54.

Bowlby, J. (1973). *Separation; Anxiety and Anger*. London: The Hogarth Press and the Institute of Psycho-Analysis.

Burton, R. (1621). *The Anatomy of Melancholy, What it is. With all the Kinds, Causes, Symptomes, Prognostickes, and Several Cures of it*. Oxford: Cripps. [In Hunter & Macalpine, 1963, pp. 94–9.]

Clevenger, S. V. (1883). Insanity in children. *American Journal of Neurology and Psychiatry*, **2**, 585–601.

Cohn, M. (1883). Ueber die Psychosen im kindlichen Alter. *Archiv für Kinderheilkunde*, **4**, 101–7.

Crichton-Browne, J. (1860). Psychical diseases of early life. *Journal of Mental Science*, **6**, 284–320.

Darwin, C. (1877). A biographical sketch of an infant. *Mind*, **7**, 285–94. [In *Dev. Med. Child Neurol.* (1971) **13**, Supplement no. 24, pp. 3–8.]

Demaitre, L. (1977). The idea of childhood and child care in medical writings of the Middle Ages. *Journal of Psychohistory*, **4**, 461–90.

DeMause, L. (1974). The evolution of childhood. In *The History of Childhood*, ed. L. deMause, pp. 1–73. London: Souvenir Press.

Dick (1877). Die Angst der Kranken. *Allgemeine Zeitschrift für Psychiatrie*, **33**, 230–5.

Emminghaus, H. (1887). Die psychischen Störungen des Kindesalters. In *Handbuch der Kinderkrankheiten*, ed. C. Gerhardt, pp. 1–294. Tübingen: Laupp.

Esquirol, J. E. D. (1830). Remarques sur la statistique des aliénés. *Annales de Hygiène*, **4**, 332–59.

Esquirol, J. E. D. (1838) *Des Maladies Mentales, Considérées sous les Rapports Médical, Hygiénique et Médico-légal*. Bruxelles: Tircher. [Mental Maladies, A treatise on Insanity. New York: Hafner, 1965.]

Flemming, C. F. (1848). Ueber Precordialangst. *Allgemeine Zeitschrift für Psychiatrie*, **5**, 341–61.

Freud, S. (1909). Analysis of a phobia in a five-year-old boy. In *The Standard Edition of the Complete Works of Sigmund Freud*, 7th edn, Vol. 10, pp. 5–149. London: The Hogarth Press and the Institue of Psycho-analysis, 1975.

Griesinger, W. (1861). *Die Pathologie und Therapie der Psychischen Krankheiten*. Stuttgart: Krabbe. [Mental Pathology and Therapeutics, reprint of the 2nd edn, 1861, New York: Hafner.]

Hall, G. S. (1897). A study of fears. *American Journal of Psychology*, **8**, 147–249.

Hall, G. S. (1904). *Adolescence*. New York: Appleton.

Hare, E. H. (1962). Masturbatory insanity: the history of an idea. *Journal of Mental Science*, **108**, 2–25.

Hippocrates (460–370BC). *Aphorismes*, traduit par E. Littré. Paris, 1844.

Hunter, R. & Macalpine, I. (1963). *Three Hundred Years of Psychiatry 1535–1860*. London: Oxford University Press.

Hurd, H. M. (1894). Some mental disorders of childhood and youth. *Boston Medical and Surgical Journal*, **131**, 281–5.

James, W. (1884). What is an emotion? *Mind*, **9**, 188–205.

Jarvis, E. (1852). On the supposed increase of insanity. *Journal of Insanity*, **8**, 333–64.

Kierkegaard, S. (1844). *The Concept of Anxiety: a Simple Psychologically Orienting Deliberation on the Dogmatic Issue of Heredity Sin*. Princeton, NJ: Princeton University Press, 1980.

King, W. P. (1880). Case of morbid juvenile pyrophobia caused by malarial toxhaemia. *The Alienist and the Neurologist*, **1**, 345–7.

Klein, D. F. (1981). Anxiety reconceptualized. In *Anxiety: New Research and Changing Concepts*, eds. D. F. Klein & J. Rabkin, pp. 235–63. New York: Raven Press.

Klein, R. G. & Last, C. G. (1989). *Anxiety Disorders in Children*. Newbury: Sage Publications.

Kraepelin, E. (1883). *Compendium der Psychiatrie*. Leipzig: Ambr. Abel.

Kroll, J. & Bachrach, B. (1986). Child care and child abuse in early medieval Europe. *Journal of the American Academy of Child Psychiatry*, **25**, 562–8.

Manheimer, M. (1899). *Troubles Mentaux de L'enfance; Précis de Psychiatrie Infantile Avec les Applications Pédagogiques et Médico-légales*. Paris: Société d'Editions Scientifiques.

Maudsley, H. (1867). *The Physiology and Pathology of the Mind*. London: MacMillan & Co.

Maudsley, H. (1868). Illustrations of a variety of insanity. *The Journal of Mental Science*, **14**, 149–62.

Maudsley, H. (1895). *The Pathology of Mind: a Study of its Distempers, Deformities, and Disorders*. London: MacMillan and Co.

Mercurialis, H. (1583). *De Morbis Puerorum*. Venice. [In Ruhräh, 1925, pp. 221–36.]

Moreau (de Tours), P. (1888). *La Folie Chez les Enfants*. Paris: Baillière.

Murphy, G. (1949). *Historical Introduction to Modern Psychology, Revised Edition*. New York: Harcourt, Brace and Company.

Neuman, R. P. (1975). Masturbation, madness, and the modern concepts of childhood and adolescence. *Journal of Social History*, **8**, 1–27.

Parkinson, J. (1807). *Observations on the Excessive Indulgence of Children, Particularly Intended to Show its Injurious Effects on their Health, and the Difficulties it Occasions in their Treatment during Sickness. Medical Admonitions to Families*, 5th edn. London: Symonds.

Parry-Jones, W. Ll. (1994). History of child and adolescent psychiatry. In *Child and Adolescent Psychiatry*, 3rd edn, ed. M. Rutter, E. Taylor & L. Hersov, pp. 794–812. Oxford: Blackwell Scientific Publications.

Phaer, Th. (1545). *The Boke of Children*. [In Ruhräh, 1925, pp. 147–95.]

Pollock, L. A. (1983). *Forgotten Children. Parent-child Relations from 1500–1900*. Cambridge: Cambridge University Press.

Preyer, W. (1892). *Die Seele des Kindes; Beobachtungen über die geistige Entwicklung des Menschen in den ersten Lebensjahren.* Leipzig: Th. Grieben's Verlag.

Reese, H. W. & Overton, R. B. (1970). Models of development and theories of development. In *Life-span Developmental Psychology: Theory and Research*, ed. L. R. Goulet & P. B. Baltes, pp. 115–45. New York: Academic Press.

Ross, D. (1972). *G. Stanley Hall: the Psychologist as Prophet.* Chicago: Chicago University Press.

Ruhräh, J. (1925). *Pediatrics of the Past.* New York: Hoeber.

Rush, B. (1798). On the different species of phobia. *The Weekly Magazine of Original Essays, Fugitive Pieces, and Interesting Intelligence*, **1**, 177–80.

Rush, B. (1812). *Medical Inquiries and Observations upon the Diseases of the Mind.* Philadelphia: Kimber & Richardson. [New York, Hafner Publishing Inc., 1962.]

Sand, G. (1854–1855). *Histoire de ma Vie.* Paris: Gallimard, 1970.

Savage, G. H. (1881). Moral insanity. *Journal of Mental Sciences*, **27**, 148–55.

Shahar, S. (1990). *Childhood in the Middle Ages.* London: Routledge.

Silverman, W. K. (1993). DSM and the classification of anxiety disorders in children and adults. In *Anxiety across the Lifespan: A Developmental Perspective on Anxiety and the Anxiety Disorders*, ed. C. G. Last, pp. 7–36. New York: Springer.

Spitzka, E. C. (1890). Insanity. In *Cyclopaedia of the Diseases of Children, Medical and Surgical, vol. IV*, ed. J. M. Keating, pp. 1038–53. Philadelphia: Lippincott.

Spurzheim, G. (1818). *Observations sur la Folie ou sur les Dérangements des Fonctions Morales et Intellectuelles de L'homme.* Paris: Treuttel et Würtz.

Stone, M. H. (1973). Child Psychiatry before the Twentieth Century. *International Journal of Child Psychotherapy*, **2**, 264–308.

Strack (1863). Seelenstörung bei einem Kinde. *Correspondentzblatt für Psychiatrie*, pp. 76–8.

Sully, J. (1895). *Studies of Childhood.* London: Longmans & Green.

Tiedemann, D. (1787). *Beobachtungen über die Entwicklung der Seelenfähigkeiten bei Kindern.* Altenburg: Oskar Bonde, 1897.

von Rinecker (1876). Ueber irresein der kinder. *Allgemeine Zeitschrift für Psychiatrie*, **32**, 560–5.

Walk, A. (1964). The pre-history of child psychiatry. *British Journal of Psychiatry*, **110**, 754–67.

Wardle, C. J. (1991). Historical influences on services for children and adolescents before 1900. In *150 Years of British Psychiatry, 1841–1991*, eds. G. E. Berrios & H. Freeman, pp. 279–93. London: Gaskell.

Watson, J. B. & Rayner, R. (1920). Conditioned emotional reactions. *Journal of Experimental Psychology*, **3**, 1–14.

Werry, J. S. (1994). Diagnostic and classification issues. In *International Handbook of Phobic and Anxiety Disorders in Children and Adolescents*, eds. T. H. Ollendick, N. J. King, & W. Yule, pp. 21–42. New York: Plenum Press.

West, C. (1860). On the mental peculiarities and mental disorders of childhood. *Medical Times & Gazette*, Feb. 11 1860, 133–7.

West, C. (1871). *On some Disorders of the Nervous System in Childhood.* London: Greens & Co.

World Health Organization (1992). *International Statistical Classification of Diseases and Related Health Problems, 10th revision.* Geneva: WHO.

2

Affective and cognitive processes and the development and maintenance of anxiety and its disorders

Pier J. M. Prins

Introduction

The cognitive view of childhood anxiety assumes that anxiety is mediated by distorted and maladaptive cognition. Although research examining these cognitive mediational processes in children is limited, the evidence that childhood anxiety is associated with distorted cognition is growing. Cognitive variables thought to be involved in the development and maintenance of anxiety include negative cognition, worrying, causal attributions and biased attention and memory processes. The majority of studies on cognition and childhood anxiety has focused on the valence and content of cognition.

Several reviews of the research literature concluded nearly a decade ago that the understanding of cognitive disturbances in anxious children was limited and only beginning to emerge (Francis, 1988; Kendall & Chansky, 1991). Particularly, three issues were then considered to be in need of increased research attention: the cognitions of clinically anxious children, a comparative analysis of cognitive assessment measures and cognitive coding systems, and the relationship of anxious children's cognitions to adaptive and maladaptive functioning. The past years have witnessed an increase in research attention with respect to these issues.

Although childhood anxiety researchers have begun to document the importance of cognitive factors in understanding and treating childhood anxiety disorders (Kendall, 1994; Vasey & Daleiden, 1996), the level of complexity apparent in adult models (see Mathews & MacLeod, 1994) remains lacking in the child domain. Moreover, much of the existing theorizing is extended from clinical and experimental observations with adults, such as Beck's cognitive theory of anxiety. Generally, anxious children presumably judge threats as more serious and underestimate their coping ability, are characterized by a perceived lack of control over threat, and tend to report more catastrophizing thoughts than nonanxious children. Moreover, anxious children's self-talk is negatively valenced and of negative content.

The recent cognition and childhood anxiety literature is guided by several cognitive hypotheses and more or less elaborated cognitive models such as the 'distortion-deficiency' distinction, the content-specificity hypothesis, the States of Mind model, and the information processing perspective. Most of the empirical research on childhood cognition and anxiety to date is aimed at a test of these models.

In this chapter I present a selective review of recent research related to these cognitive hypotheses and models. First, I focus on the cognitive–behavioural approach and the information processing approach to childhood anxiety. I then discuss some cognitive–developmental aspects of anxiety-related cognition, the typical patterns of cognition in anxious children, and, finally, the development of an anxious cognitive style. The cognitive–behavioural treatment literature for childhood anxiety is not reviewed in this chapter, but rather is covered in chapter 14, this volume. I conclude this chapter by highlighting some areas that require particular research attention in future work.

Cognitive approaches to childhood anxiety

A generally accepted, multicomponent view of the etiology of anxiety disorders in children includes biological, cognitive and behavioural components. Dysfunctional anxiety in this model is considered a self-perpetuating cycle of elevated biological response to stress, debilitated cognition, and avoidance of stressful circumstances (e.g. Albano, Chorpita & Barlow, 1996). Cognition in this model is part of a complex process and is assumed to play a role in the etiology and maintenance of anxiety.

Two major cognitive approaches toward childhood anxiety and anxiety disorders include cognitive–behavioural theories and the information processing perspective. Both can be traced back to the pioneering work of Beck, who described anxious cognitive processing as heightened perceived threat and a decreased estimation of coping ability. Both approaches emphasize negative threat-related thoughts, and biases in cognitive processes such as attention, memory, thinking and making judgements. Considered broadly, the main difference between the two seems more methodological than theoretical: the cognitive–behavioural approach relying on self-report methodologies, and the information processing approach using experimental methods for studying anxiety-related cognition in children.

The information-processing perspective focuses on how affective information is cognitively processed by anxious children. It uses experimental tasks such as 'probe detection tasks' and emotional Stroop tasks to study cognitive processes, such as attention and memory in anxious children. This methodology allows the researcher to directly measure cognitive processes, instead of indirectly through self-report measures. An elaboration of the information processing perspective on childhood anxiety has recently been published by Daleiden & Vasey (1997). Generally, studies using this approach show that selective attention mechanisms influence children's processing of threatening information and may play an important role in the regulation and dysregulation of childhood anxiety (Dalgleish et al., 1997; Vasey, El-Hag & Daleiden, 1996). Future research is needed that examines the extent to which cognitive biases reflect an innate predisposition or exposure to chronically threatening environments, and whether the existence of such biases serves as a risk factor for chronic anxiety problems (Vasey, 1993). Because of space limitations and because most research on cognition and childhood anxiety has been based on the cognitive–behavioural theory, I concentrate in the present chapter on this approach.

The cognitive–behavioural theory emphasizes the role played by negative or maladaptive belief systems in the onset and course of anxiety disorders. They distinguish between four elements of cognition for the purpose of understanding the development of childhood anxiety. Each or all of these components may become dysfunctional and may precipitate the expression of psychopathology. First, cognitive structures or schemas are considered to guide the processing of information. Dysfunctional schemas are core, generalized beliefs that provide the basis for biased interpretations of external events. The second element relates to cognitive content, which is the information that is stored in schemas. The third element refers to cognitive operations, which transform environmental input and infer meaning from it. Distorted cognitive operations refer to processes of biased interpretation of external events (e.g. catastrophizing: anticipating the worst possible outcome for an event; or overgeneralization: taking one single event as representative of all others). Finally, the fourth element of cognition is the cognitive products, such as conscious thoughts and images. Negative thoughts or self-talk represent the outcomes of distorted cognitive processes.

Like schema-based theories of adult anxiety, the cognitive–behavioural theory of childhood anxiety assumes that anxiety disorders result from the chronic overactivity of schemas organized around themes of threat or danger.

These overactive schemas are presumed to focus processing resources on threat-relevant information in a chronic and disproportionate manner (Kendall & Ronan, 1990).

Particularly important in the cognitive–behavioural theory of child anxiety is the distinction between 'cognitive deficits' versus 'cognitive distortions' (Kendall, 1993). Cognitive deficits signify the lack or insufficient use of an adaptive cognitive skill or activity. Examples include a lack of planning or verbal mediation. Alternatively, cognitive distortion refers to cognitive processes that are biased or erroneous, and therefore yield dysfunctional and maladaptive thoughts and images. Examples include a tendency to selectively attend to signals of threat or interpret ambiguous events as threatening. Important distortions in childhood anxiety are described by Kendall (1993) and include misperception of environmental demands, excessive self-criticism, undervaluation of one's abilities, and excessive self-focused attention.

Cognitive development and anxiety-related cognition in children

Consideration of cognitive developmental factors that exert a significant influence on the content and functional value of anxiety-related cognition in children has been emphasized by various authors (Beidel, 1993; Vasey, 1993). Developmental factors have implications for how anxiety can be cognitively expressed, how children may mediate anxiety through their own thinking, and how children learn to cognitively cope with anxiety. Generally, children are thought to become capable of mediating severe anxiety through cognition as the relevant cognitive operations and structures develop.

Vasey (1993), for example, illustrated this point with regard to childhood worrying. Worrying is a cognitive process involving thoughts and images related to possible negative or threatening outcomes. It is predominantly anticipatory and self-referent in nature and is characterized by catastrophic thinking. As children grow older, they develop the ability to imagine and anticipate on events that are going to happen. This implies the capacity to go beyond what is merely observable and to consider what is merely possible. Thus, being able to conceptualize the future implies that children can make themselves anxious through their own cognitions. Worry-mediated anxiety should become increasingly prevalent as children develop in their abilty to conceptualize elaborate sequences of negative consequences. Vasey suggested that both the increase of overanxious disorder with age, and the increasing role of worry in anxiety as children develop may be considered supportive of this hypothesis. However, most children will not develop problems with pervasive worry just because they become capable of considering an infinite variety of catastrophic outcomes. Anxiety-supporting cognitive deficits and distortions must also be present (Vasey, 1993).

Another example of the potentially important role of development in the expression of anxiety is the hypothesis that spontaneous panic attacks will be rare or nonexistent prior to adolescence. According to the cognitive model of panic children lack the ability to make the internal, catastrophic attributions (i.e. thoughts of losing control, going crazy or dying) characteristic of panic. Therefore, children will not show panic attacks (Nelles & Barlow, 1988). In a recent study, however, children's cognitive interpretations of panic symptoms were examined and no clear support for this hypothesis was found. Children as young as 8 years of age were able to attribute external, somatic symptoms to internal, catastrophic cognitions (Mattis & Ollendick, 1997).

Both cognitive process and content appear sensitive to developmental changes. Brown et al. (1986) found that catastrophizing thoughts were fairly common in anxious children, aged 8–18, and also that the frequency of these thoughts rarely decreased with age. On the other hand, the frequency of coping cognitions increased with age primarily because of children's increased use of positive self-talk.

The association between age and the valence of self-statements is not yet clear. Some studies suggest that negative and positive self-statements do not vary as a function of age (Laurent & Stark, 1993); other studies have found significant increases in positive cognitions across the ages of 8 to 18 years (Brown et al., 1986). More research on this issue is needed to determine whether positive and negative self-statements vary as a function of development.

The content of children's anxiety-related cognition differs across age and appears to be related to developments in social–cognitive domains. Vasey (1993), for example, described research showing that the content of children's worries follows a progression from physicalistic (related to physical properties of the situations, to external bodily consequences, and to the possibility of punishment and other external sanctions) to psychological and abstract threats (anticipation of psychological consequences, such as shame, guilt or lack of personal integrity). There is an increase in fear of psychological distress and increases in academic and social fears as children become preadolescents.

Part of the experience of anxiety in children is related to the children's (mis)perceptions of their coping abilities. Coping with anxiety or affective self-regulation requires metacognitive skills, such as the ability to accurately label and monitor one's ongoing affective state. Anxiety thus may be related to deficits in metacognitive skills. If metacognitive deficits characterize anxious children (as they do impulsive children, for example), it is important to determine whether they reflect general delays in their metacognitive development or deficits that are specific to the regulation of anxiety and related cognitions. Also, such deficits may produce anxiety or be a product of it. It is possible that anxiety may interfere with children's abilities to apply otherwise intact metacognitive abilities and strategies (Vasey, 1993).

Patterns of cognition in anxious children

An extensive research tradition exists that focuses on the valence and content of anxious children's cognition. Anxious and anxiety-disordered children have been found to show characteristic patterns of cognition.

Negative cognition

High test-anxious children tend to show higher rates of cognitive errors, such as catastrophizing, overgeneralizing, personalizing and selective abstraction (Leitenberg, Yost & Carroll-Wilson, 1986), a higher level of negative self-evaluative thoughts (e.g. 'I am too dumb for this'), and more off-task thoughts than low test-anxious children (King et al., 1995; Prins, Groot, & Hanewald, 1994; Zatz & Chassin, 1985).

Similar associations have been found with dental-anxious children. Children high in dental anxiety reported greater proportions of negative self-statements related to the threat of pain and to escape from the situation, than children low in dental anxiety prior to a dental procedure (Prins, 1985). In another study, I examined the self-statements of children involved in an anxiety-provoking diving task (Prins, 1986). Again, high test-anxious children reported self-statements that were preoccupied with the threat of being hurt. They perceived the situation as more dangerous than it actually was ('Oh, I'll fall hard', 'Maybe my head will hit the bottom').

This pattern of negative cognition also has been reported for high trait anxious children (Fox, Houston & Pittner, 1983; Houston, Fox & Forbes, 1984), for a group of nondiagnosed community children showing negative affect (i.e. children who score high both on a measure of anxiety and depression; see Ronan, Kendall & Rowe, 1994), for social phobic children (Beidel, 1991), and for children diagnosed with anxiety disorders (Kendall, 1994). These studies show that childhood anxiety is associated with a cognitive bias of threat and negativity. Furthermore, recent studies provide initial evidence that anxious children have cognitive biases toward hostility (Bell-Dolan, 1995) and social-evaluative threat as well (Chansky & Kendall, 1997).

Positive cognition

Interestingly, no clear relationship has been found between anxiety and positive cognition. Some studies have found that low anxious children compared with high anxious children reported more positive cognition, such as on-task cognition, positive self-evaluation and coping thoughts (Zatz & Chassin, 1983, 1985); others have not found such a relation. Positive self-statements, for example, were not related to test anxiety in nonreferred fifth and sixth graders (Prins et al., 1994), to trait anxiety in fourth graders (Fox et al., 1983; Houston et al., 1984), to the anxiety of children performing an anxiety-provoking diving task (Prins, 1986), nor to anxiety in 5–11-year-old children receiving surgery (Brophy & Erickson, 1990).

The same pattern of findings has been reported with clinical samples. No difference in positive cognition was noted between anxiety-disordered and clinic-referred children, although a greater frequency of negative cognition was noted (Kendall & Chansky, 1991). Similarly, with a clinical sample of anxiety-disordered children, Treadwell & Kendall (1996) found in a recent study that negative but not positive cognition was significantly related to anxiety. This lends support to what Kendall (1984) has called the 'power of non-negative thinking', which refers to the fact that negative self-talk as opposed to positive self-talk is related to emotional disorder. For both children and adults it is the lower frequency of negative thoughts as opposed to the presence of positive ones that appears to be related to psychological health.

Ratio positive–negative self-statements

Healthy psychological functioning, it has been suggested, is not characterized by individual frequencies of positive and negative self-statements, but by an optimal balance of positive and negative self-talk. It is assumed, in the adult literature, that a specific proportion of negative to positive self-statments accounts for optimal emotional adjustment, and that dysfunction occurs when this ratio shifts (Schwartz & Garamoni, 1989). The States of Mind (SOM) model assumes that a balance of approximately 2:1 between positive and negative self-statements underlies optimal adjustment whereas significant deviations from this ratio underlie maladjustment. This optimal balance is reflected in what has been referred as the 'golden section' hypothesized proportion of 0.62 (Schwartz & Garamoni, 1989).

The SOM model proposes five categories representing specific ratios of positive self-statements divided by positive plus negative self-statements. First, the positive dialogue is defined by a ratio wherein positive cognitions are represented at a 'set point' of 0.62 (i.e. 62% positive thoughts and 38% negative thoughts) with a range from 0.56 to 0.68, and presumably associated with good coping and psychological adaptation. Second, the internal dialogue of conflict has a set point of 0.50, ranges from 0.45 to 0.55, and is associated with worry, mild anxiety and depression. Third, the negative dialogue is characterized by a ratio of 0.38 and a range of 0.32 to 0.44, and is associated with moderate anxiety or depression. Fourth, the negative monologue is characterized by ratios less than 0.32, which is associated with severe psychopathology. Fifth, the positive monologue, at the other extreme, is defined by a SOM ratio greater than 0.68, and is hypothesized to be characteristic of excessive optimism and mania. Studies with adult samples have consistently shown that the more negative SOMs (i.e. the dialogue of conflict, the negative dialogue and the negative monologue) are associated with increasingly severe psychopathology, whereas control groups are characterized by SOMs in the positive dialogue range (Michelson, Schwartz & Marchione, 1991).

The SOM model and anxious children's self-talk

Extension of the SOM model to children may enhance the understanding of the etiology of childhood maladjustment, such as anxiety and its disorders. To date, however, only a few studies have addressed the SOM model as it applies to children's self-talk (Daleiden, Vasey, & Williams, 1996; Prins & Hanewald, 1997; Ronan & Kendall, 1997; Treadwell & Kendall, 1996). Prins & Hanewald (1997) found some support for the SOM model in nonreferred test-anxious children. Two methods of assessing cognition, thought listing and self-statement questionnaire approaches, in 60 high, 128 moderate and 98 low test-anxious fifth and sixth graders, were investigated under naturalistic test-taking conditions. Because the number of positive self-evaluative thoughts that children listed on the thought listing was too small for analysis, the SOM scores were calculated on the positive and negative self-evaluation scores of the endorsement measure. The results showed that the SOM ratios significantly differentiated the high, moderate and low test-anxious groups and increased with a decrease in level of test anxiety. The SOM ratio of the high anxious children, however, did not fall within the hypothesized categories (i.e. the negative dialogue; negative monologue). The range for this group coincided with the range of the internal dialogue of conflict category.

Treadwell & Kendall (1996) also found limited support for the SOM model as applied to a sample of anxiety-disordered children. The SOM ratio for both anxiety-disordered children and normal controls fell within the same category (positive dialogue).

Clearly, more research is needed to assess the usefulness of the SOM model for understanding the role of cognition in anxiety-disordered children. Three issues have been emphasized by Kendall & Chansky (1991), that need to be examined to validate the SOM model with children. The first issue relates to whether the set point value of the positive dialogue (0.62) from which the other point predictions (ratios) are derived, is valid for children. SOM values identified for adults may be inappropriate for children, because children may hold excessively positive or optimistic views of themselves and the world (Kendall & Chansky, 1991).

The second issue relates to the appropriateness of available methods for measuring children's SOM ratios, and how cognitions are coded. SOM ratios may vary depending on the method of assessing positive and negative cognitions. Evidence from adults indicates that production methods yield lower SOM ratios than endorsement methods (Glass & Arnkoff, 1997). With a sample of nonclinic test-anxious children Prins & Hanewald (1997) found that, relative to a self-statement questionnaire measure, a thought listing procedure underestimated positive and coping cognition. In fact, the number of positive thoughts on thought listing was too small to allow calculating a SOM ratio based on thought-listing scores.

With regard to the issue of coding, there clearly is a lack of consistency in definitions of categories/codes of cognition, which may affect ratio data. While many studies use a positive/negative dichotomy, others employ different categories. For example, Houston et al. (1984) used categories such as 'preoccupation' (e.g. 'I'm feeling sort of scared about this, I'm nervous') and 'analytic attitude' (e.g. 'I think this is very interesting'). The categories used in Houston et al. (1984) would be subsumed under the rubric of negative and positive thoughts, respectively. In other studies, categories such as on-task, off-task, and coping have been used (e.g. Prins et al., 1994). This lack of uniformity in coding schemes needs to be resolved because it hinders generalizability across studies. Consensus about which coding scheme to adopt may be reached by using schemes that are theory-driven, consistent with previous research and relevant for the specific population as well.

Finally, a third issue relates to the various factors that may affect SOM-ratios. Research suggests that SOM ratios differ depending on the focus of the cognitions assessed such as self-statements that are either self-referential or not self-referential. For example, in a study examining various methods of cognitive assessment, Daleiden et al. (1996) found that self-referent SOM ratios were significantly higher than other-referent ratios for all methods.

The content-specificity hypothesis

Recently, there has been an increase in studies examining cognitive distortion in clinical samples of anxiety-disordered children. These studies are less concerned with assessing thoughts in specific stressful situations and how these thoughts affect behaviour, but more with the specificity of anxious children's cognition. The cognitive content specificity hypothesis states that each type of psychopathology has unique cognitive products or content. Depressed patients, for example, report automatic thoughts that involve themes of loss or failure, are absolute, past oriented and negative ('I'm worthless'), whereas anxious patients report thoughts that are relative, future oriented, and have a danger theme, harm and threat ('Something awful is going to happen') (Kendall & Ingram, 1987).

There is a growing number of empirical studies demonstrating the specificity of various dysfunctional cognitive styles for different childhood disorders, such as depression, anxiety and externalizing problems (see Ambrose & Rholes, 1993; Jolly, 1993; Leung & Wong, 1998). The evidence for cognitive specificity in anxiety, however, is mixed. For example, Laurent & Stark (1993) found in a sample of nonreferred elementary schoolchildren with diagnosable anxiety disorder and/or depressive disorder similar levels of anxious self-talk in the anxious, anxious and depressed, and depressed groups. Further, test-anxious and depressed children reported significantly greater depressotypic self-statements than normal children (Leitenberg et al., 1986). These results support the hypothesis that anxiety and depression may be manifestations of a similar underlying construct, negative affectivity (Watson & Clark, 1984). Thus, research is needed to determine whether cognitive symptoms unique to the experience of anxiety can be identified in children with other problems, such as depression.

It should be noted that various factors may moderate the relationship of specific cognitive content and type of psychopathology. Ambrose & Rholes (1993), for example, examined threat and loss cognitions and symptoms of depression and anxiety in a nonclinical sample of children and adolescents (fifth, eighth, and eleventh graders). Using self-report measures of anxiety and depression, such as the Children's Depression Inventory (CDI; Kovacs, 1979), the Cognitions Checklist and the State-Trait Anxiety Inventory for Children (STAIC; Spielberger, 1983), they found a progressive diminishment of the relationship of threat cognition to anxiety symptoms as threat cognitions reached higher levels and a progressive increment in the relationship of threat to depressive symptoms. These results indicate that at very high levels perceived threat becomes partially equivalent to perceived loss, leading to a shift from anxiety to depressive symptom formation. These findings need to be replicated with other age groups and symptom measures, before they can be generalized.

The study of Leitenberg et al. (1986) supported the notion that anxious children are more likely to exhibit catastrophizing cognitions. However, these were not specific to anxiety. For depressed children and children with low self-esteem catastrophizing cognitions were equally common. In other words, valence has been clearly related to high anxiety, but content less so.

Finally, Kendall & Ingram (1987) noted that the distinguishing feature between the cognitions of anxiety and depression is not the content or frequency of the cognitions, but their form. Depressed individuals make negative declarative statements, whereas the negative cognitions of anxious individuals take the form of a question. Whether this also applies to children awaits further investigation.

The functional value of coping cognitions

Along with the valence and content of anxious children's cognitions, the assessment of how these cognitions may affect children's behaviour is an important area to study. Studies on the functional significance of cognition may further clarify the meaning of cognition in the development and maintenance of childhood anxiety. Coping cognition, for example, is considered to positively affect the behaviour of anxious children, but has also been found to interfere with anxious children's functioning. Thus, children's cognitions, even the ones with a positive content, may interfere with performance and behaviour. Vasey & Daleiden (1996) described two pathways of cognitive interference in anxious children. The first pathway relates to attentional processes early in the information-processing sequence, that may evoke, maintain, or intensify children's anxiety, and may produce cognitive interference in several ways. The second pathway relates to cognitive attempts by anxious children to cope with the anxiety-provoking situation and with anxiety itself. These attempts consume processing resources, and may interfere with the task at hand. Here, the second pathway is discussed, because it is linked to coping cognition.

Cognitive assessment research investigating the role of positive and negative cognition in samples of high and low anxious children, has shown that high anxious children compared to low anxious children not only report more negative cognition, but also significantly more coping self-talk (Kendall & Chansky, 1991; King et al., 1995; Prins et al., 1994; Warren, Ollendick & King, 1996; Zatz & Chassin, 1985). Low anxious children may not require coping self-statements for effective performance, while high anxious children may be attempting to cope with the threatening aspects of the situation.

Moreover, Zatz & Chassin (1985) found that this coping self-talk, defined as cognitive attempts to control anxiety and mind wandering, was negatively related to the task performance of high test-anxious children and appeared to interfere with effective task performance. Similarly, in a previous study, the self-talk of 8–12-year-old children was examined during a stressful situation in the swimming pool, and it was found that coping self-talk was associated with reduced performance quality (Prins, 1986).

The results of the Zatz & Chassin (1985) study were replicated by Prins et al. (1994). High test-anxious children, compared to low anxious children, reported more coping thoughts, which, again, were negatively related to task-performance. The high frequency of self-reported coping thoughts, however, appeared to depend on the assessment method used. We found that on an endorsement method children reported a substantive amount of coping thoughts, while on a thought listing procedure they did not list coping cognition to any appreciable degree (Prins & Hanewald, 1997).

Several hypotheses have been offered in the literature to account for the negative relation between coping self-talk and task-performance. The negative nature of the coping self-talk (e.g. 'I don't have to get upset') may have sensitized children to the unpleasantness of the anxiety-arousing situation (Kendall, Howard & Epps, 1988). Second, excessive self-talk, even when positive in nature, may interfere with performance on active tasks such as tests, by distracting resources from task-relevant processing (Fox & Houston, 1981). Third, coping self-talk may not have been effective because of the preponderance of off-task and negative evaluative thoughts which characterize these children (Zatz & Chassin, 1985). Finally, high anxiety may result both in coping cognition and in debilitated performance, without any causal connection between the two (Prins et al., 1994).

Based on their findings, Zatz & Chassin concluded that coping self-talk does not appear to facilitate performance, but, instead, may produce cognitive interference. The implication from a treatment perspective would be that therapy would be better aimed at controlling or eliminating negative thinking, rather than assuming that increasing positive or task-facilitating thoughts will necessarily reduce anxiety (King et al., 1995; Zatz & Chassin, 1985). It is possible, however, as Spence (1994) pointed out, that increasing positive or coping self-statements may be an appropriate short-term treatment strategy, as a means of inhibiting negative cognitions, rather than being an end in itself.

Moreover, Vasey & Daleiden (1996) noted that cognitive assessment research provides little information about the relation between coping cognition and task performance, because the statistical tests necessary to separate the influence of coping self-talk from the effects of negative self-statements were not reported. Examining this relation is vital because coping self-talk is presumably a self-regulatory response to negative thoughts and appears to be positively correlated with such thoughts.

In a recent study, we tried to determine whether anxious children's coping self-talk makes a unique contribution to debilitated performance (Prins & Hanewald, 1999). To answer that question, the facilitating role of coping cognition should be assessed while controlling for the influence of negative thoughts, such as off-task and negative self-evaluative thoughts. It was suggested by Vasey & Daleiden (1996) that coping thoughts may indeed be independently negatively correlated with performance, but the correlation might instead be zero or even positive. A positive partial correlation could occur if coping self-talk actually serves to suppress what would otherwise be an even stronger negative correlation between performance and distracting negative thoughts.

We found that the relationship between coping self-talk and task-performance of high test-anxious children changed when the effects of negative cognition were controlled. This indicated that the negative association between the coping self-talk and task performance of high anxious children, which has been reported in assessment research, is confounded by negative cognition, such as negative self-evaluative thoughts and off-task thoughts. The findings of this study show that the coping self-talk of high anxious children was not a predictor of task-performance. Further, we found no support for the suggestion that coping cognition actually serves to suppress the negative impact of negative cognition on performance.

Our findings were consistent with the hypothesis that high anxiety may result both in coping cognition and debilitated performance, without any causal connection between the two. In other words, our data did not support the suggestion from cognitive assessment studies that coping cognition interferes with improved task performance. The suggestion from assessment studies that it is of little use to train anxious children in coping self-talk (King et al., 1995; Zatz & Chassin, 1985) contrasts with the findings from treatment studies, that show that both clinically referred and nonreferred anxious children can benefit from a training in the use of coping self-talk (Kendall, 1994; Rudolph, Dennig & Weisz, 1995). This suggests that to increase coping self-talk may be an appropriate short-term treatment strategy.

Nevertheless, one may still question the use of training children in coping self-talk, because we found that coping self-talk and performance were unrelated. Part of the discrepancy between assessment and intervention research with regard to the functional value of coping self-talk may stem from mistakenly equating the type of coping thoughts in assessment studies with the type in which children have been trained in intervention studies. The self-talk of anxious children may appear coping in nature (when rated by others in assessment studies), but at the same time may not be functional with respect to behaviour in terms of reducing stress and improving performance. Coping self-talk in treatment studies may be more specific or strategic (i.e. inspiring an action, whether cognitive or behavioural), and may be, as a result, more functional than the natural coping cognition which children report in assessment research (see Kendall & Chansky, 1991; Prins, 1988). Perhaps, anxious children in assessment research may not know how and when to use coping self-talk, or they may not believe in their coping self-talk.

Questions regarding the functional value of coping self-talk should directly be tested in intervention research. Whether increases in self-talk result in positive changes in anxiety is the question that must be tested in future intervention studies. A good example of the sort of study that is necessary to resolve questions regarding the functional value of self-statements is the study by Treadwell & Kendall (1996). In this study the impact of treatment on the internal dialogue of anxiety-disordered children (8–13-year-olds) was examined. Results indicated that negative (but not positive) self-statements significantly improved after treatment, and were positively related to treatment outcome.

Worry in children

Worrying is a cognitive process with negatively valenced thoughts and images related to potential threats and dangers (Borkovec, 1985). As part of the cognitive component of anxiety, worries are thought to play an important role in the development and maintenance of anxiety disorder in both adults (Barlow, 1988) and children (Silverman, LaGreca & Wasserstein, 1995; Vasey, Crnic & Carter, 1994). In particular, excessive and intrusive worrying is a core component of the DSM–IV diagnostic criteria for generalized anxiety disorder and separation anxiety disorder. Little research has been devoted to children's worries (Henker, Whalen, & O'Neil, 1995; Kendall & Chansky, 1991; Perrin & Last, 1997; Silverman et al., 1995). Specifically, few studies have addressed the content or frequency of worries in samples of children diagnosed with anxiety disorders. Much of the available information is based on studies of nonreferred children (see for a review Silverman et al., 1995). In a sample of nonreferred children between 7 and 12 years of age, Silverman et al. found that more than two-thirds of the sample reported at least one worry, primarily those involving health, school performance and personal harm. The most intense or frequent worries involved safety and personal injury. Based on self-report measures of anxiety, participants classified as 'high-anxious' reported a significantly greater number of worries and areas of worry, as well as more frequent or intense worrying. In all, the literature supports the notion that children do worry and this worry may be related to increased anxiety in the child.

While worry is common even among normal children, excessive worry is typical of several anxiety disorders. Distinctions between adaptive and maladaptive worrying are not yet well understood. Is worrying a clinically meaningful index of anxious cognition, because of specific content, number of worry-issues, frequency, intensity, interference or controllability? Does clinically relevant worry involve an excess of the same process found in normal people, or are there qualitative differences in cognitive and affective domains (Henker et al., 1995)?

Studies of anxiety-disordered children may shed more light on the clinical meaningfulness of children's worries. Perrin & Last (1997) administered a 31-item worry measure to referred children (between 5 and 13 years of age) with anxiety disorders or attention-deficit hyperactivity disorder, and to non-referred, never psychiatrically ill controls. Results found that children with anxiety disorders reported more frequent worrying, but not more types of worries. Infrequent worrying about a variety of issues was common to both psychiatrically ill and normal children. Infrequent worrying may not be a clinically meaningful index of anxious cognition. This study suggested that worries are common to children who have or do not have anxiety disorder. However, worries specific to the child's anxiety disorder distinguished them from their counterparts without anxiety disorder. Thus worries appear to play some role in the etiology of severe anxiety. Interestingly, in the same study total number of worries and total number of intense worries were significantly related to trait anxiety, and much less with state anxiety. Thus, worry seems clinically meaningful for trait but not for state anxiety.

Development of an anxious cognitive style in children

Cognitive behavioural theories assume that dysfunctional schemas are formed in early childhood. The development of negative cognition and its impact on the child's emotion and behaviour has been related to specific parent–child interactions. Many cognitive distortions of children, such as negative self-evaluations, or the overestimation of threat and danger are assumed to be learned through interactions within the family. Barrett et al. (1996) studied the extent to which family interactions influenced children's interpretations of ambiguous situations and their coping behaviour. High anxiety in children was associated with more parental negative feedback about possible physical and social threat and dangers. These specific parent–child interactions may result in a certain 'anxious cognitive style', which is characterized by a tendency to overestimate threat and danger. Similar associations have been found with children of agoraphobic parents (Capps et al., 1996).

These studies lend support to the notion that the 'socialization' of anxiety is, in part, based on the transmission of information processing styles in the children's early environment. Low perception of control, for example, has been suggested as the core feature of anxiety (Barlow, 1988). Early experiences with uncontrollability are therefore seen as an important factor in the development of childhood anxiety, and parents are considered to play a crucial role in this developmental process. Three parenting mechanisms, which may play a role in influencing the degree of cognitive biases in children, have been suggested by Chorpita, Albano & Barlow (1996). First, parents may 'prime' the activation of cognitive structures related to threat by exposing the child to their anxious ideas. In the adult literature, state anxiety, stress and other transient variables have been suggested as moderators of the relation of trait anxiety to cognitive biases. Consistent with this evidence, it may be possible that transitory influence from parents might similarly affect processing phenomena in children. Cognitive structures related to threat may be more easily or more continuously activated in anxious individuals when primed by previous exposure to threatening words. The other two mechanisms concern the influences of modelling, and the parent's rewarding of anxious cognition in their child.

The experience of anxiety is in part the result of children's low estimations of their coping ability. As I have discussed earlier, the regulation of anxiety requires meta-cognitive skills. Social factors appear to play an important role in the development of meta-cognitive skills. Children's cognitive processes are initially regulated via the efforts of parents and teachers. External control of the child's solving of academic or life problems gradually develops into conscious self-regulation. Similarly, emotion is initially regulated by others but gradually becomes self-regulated. For example, young children tend to be unskilled at self-distraction and therefore are reliant upon their parents to supply distractors for them. However, as they mature, children typically learn increasingly effective self-distraction skills (Vasey, 1993).

Important to further study is the question by what means/mechanisms parents convey a cognitive vulnerability to their children. A study by Kortlander, Kendall & Panichelli-Mindel (1997) provides some answers. Parental behaviour may be linked to the development of anxiety through cognitive factors (e.g. maternal expectations) that may relate to such parenting behaviours as overprotection and excessive control. With reference to the development of anxiogenic cognition in children, it is important to examine if parents themselves exhibit cognitive processing styles that are associated with anxiety (e.g. heightened perception of threat and estimation of low coping when thinking about their children in potentially stressful situations). Because some parents of anxious children believe something harmful might happen to their child, they might become overprotective and/or exhibit anxious behaviour themselves. Such parental behaviour would contribute to the child's development of a perception of danger and low coping, either through an internalization of parental fears about what might happen or through a process of parental modelling of anxious behaviour. Parental beliefs are important forces in the development of children's own beliefs (Kortlander et al., 1997).

A necessary condition for cognitive transmission of anxiety to take place is whether cognitive distortions in parental beliefs can be established. Kortlander et al. (1997) found that mothers' expectations of their anxious child's coping were more negative, although not very much lower, than the expectations of mothers of normal children. They expected their children to be less able to make themselves feel comfortable, and were less confident in their children's abilities to perform task-related behaviour. These lowered expectations for coping may relate to protective parenting which may maintain anxious behaviour and cognition in children.

Models of the maintenance of anxiety stress the importance of perceptions of threat and control over potential danger (e.g. Rapee, 1991). Excessive protection from a parent may help to provide information to the child that the world is a dangerous place and may also reduce the child's opportunities for learning otherwise. Thus, excessive parental control should be especially associated with higher levels of anxious behaviour and cognition (Rapee, 1997).

Conclusion

Cognition is an important aspect of childhood anxiety. The research into this area has received increasing attention during the past decade. Many important issues on various aspects of children's anxious cognition have been unearthed and discussed, which provide a solid and inspiring basis for future studies. Despite that, research in the area of cognition and childhood anxiety has been characterized by lack of consistency in methods and theory. Further, this review indicates that there is an overall and continuing need for more studies with samples of clinically referred, anxiety-disordered children.

One of the primary objectives in the area of cognition and childhood anxiety, already emphasized a decade ago by Kendall & Chansky (1991), should be the standardization of cognitive assessment measures. Content and functional meaning of self-statements, for example, have been found to depend on the cognitive assessment measure used. Type of measure appears to be associated with amount and type of reported cognition. Also the time of measuring cognition, before, during or after an anxiety-provoking event appears important and influences the result of the cognitive assessment (see Prins & Hanewald, 1997). Studies comparing different cognitive measures and coding systems with clinical samples of anxiety-disordered children are therefore needed to generate consistency among cognitive assessment studies.

An important limitation of the cognitive–behavioural theory of childhood anxiety pertains to tests of its etiological assumptions. There is an assumption that distorted cognition leads to (i.e. causes) maladaptive behaviour, such as anxiety. Although there is research support for faulty cognition as a concomitant of anxiety, evidence for the causal hypothesis is presently mixed and equivocal. The information available is generally of a correlational nature and it cannot automatically be assumed that cognitive distortions cause certain anxiety disorders. The possibility remains that some cognitive correlates result from the anxiety disorder. Furthermore, the possibility of circular relationships exists, whereby particular styles of cognitive processing result from overt behaviour patterns and emotions and in turn serve to maintain maladaptive behaviour and emotions (Spence, 1994).

Clearly, more studies on the specific role of cognitive distortion in the onset and maintenance of childhood anxiety are needed. This implies the incorporation of other research strategies. For example, there is a need for studies that use experimental manipulations in which anxious children are instructed to think or not think certain thoughts, followed by observations of the effects on the children's functioning. The need to examine the impact of cognitive variables as a complement to the more typical correlational methods, such as how an anxiety diagnosis correlates with scores on a self-statement inventory, is underscored and will be equally important for cognitive child anxiety research addressing issues of onset and maintenance of anxiety.

Little research has examined the question of the relationship between measures of cognitive products and cognitive structures such as memory bias, selective attention or responses on the Stroop colour naming task. This is an important area to study because changes in conscious thoughts may ultimately impact core cognitions. Individuals may not differ on self-statement subscale scores, but they may differ on information processing tasks (Glass & Arnkoff, 1997).

Finally, the need for developmentally oriented research should be stressed. Studies investigating cognitive–developmental factors that contribute to the mediating role of cognition in childhood anxiety disorders seem warranted (see Vasey, 1993). Also, more research into the development and transmission of anxious cognitive style in children is needed in order to help further clarify the role of cognitive processes in the development of anxiety and its disorders.

REFERENCES

Albano, A. M., Chorpita, B. F. & Barlow, D. H. (1996). Childhood anxiety disorders. In *Child Psychopathology*, ed. E. J. Mash & R. A. Barkley, pp. 196–242. New York: Guilford Press.

Ambrose, B. & Rholes, W. S. (1993). Automatic cognitions and the symptoms of depression and anxiety in children and adolescents: An examination of the content-specificity hypothesis. *Cognitive Therapy and Research*, **17**, 1–20.

Barlow, D. H. (1988). *Anxiety and its Disorders: The Nature and Treatment of Anxiety and Panic*. New York: Guildford Press.

Barrett, P. M., Rapee, R. M., Dadds, M. R. & Ryan, S. M. (1996). Family enhancement of cognitive style in anxious and aggressive children. *Journal of Abnormal Child Psychology*, **24**, 187–203.

Beidel, D. C. (1991). Social phobia and overanxious disorder in school age children. *Journal of the American Academy of Child and Adolescent Psychiatry*, **30**, 545–52.

Beidel, D. C. (1993). Developmental issues in measurement of anxiety. In *Anxiety across the Life Span*, ed. C. G. Last, pp. 167–203. New York: Springer.

Bell-Dolan, D. J. (1995). Social cue interpretation of anxious children. *Journal of Clinical Child Psychology*, **24**, 1–10.

Borkovec, T. D. (1985). Worry: A potentially valuable concept. *Behaviour Research and Therapy*, **23**, 481–2.

Brophy, C. J. & Erickson, M. T. (1990). Children's self-statements and adjustment to elective outpatient surgery. *Developmental and Behavioral Pediatrics*, **11**, 13–16.

Brown, J. M., O'Keefe, J., Sanders, S. H. & Baker, B. (1986). Developmental differences in children's cognitions in stressful and painful situations. *Journal of Pediatric Psychology*, **11**, 343–57.

Capps, L., Sigman, M., Sena, R. & Henker, B. (1996). Fear, anxiety, and perceived control in children of agoraphobic parents. *Journal of Child Psychology and Psychiatry*, **17**, 445–52.

Chansky, T. E. & Kendall, P. C. (1997). Social expectancies and self-perceptions in anxiety-disordered children. *Journal of Anxiety Disorders*, **11**, 347–63.

Chorpita, B. F., Albano, A. M. & Barlow, D. H. (1996). Cognitive processing in children: Relation to anxiety and family influences. *Journal of Clinical Child Psychology*, **25**, 170–6.

Daleiden, E. L. & Vasey, M. W. (1997). An information-processing perspective on childhood anxiety. *Clinical Psychology Review*, **17**, 407–29.

Daleiden, E. L., Vasey, M. W. & Williams, L. L. (1996). Assessing children's states of mind: A multitrait, multimethod study. *Psychological Assessment*, **8**, 125–34.

Dalgleish, T., Taghavi, R., Neshat-Doost, H., Moradi, A., Yule, W. & Canterbury, R. (1997). Information processing in clinically depressed and anxious children and adolescents. *Journal of Child Psychology and Psychiatry*, **38**, 535–41.

Fox, J. E. & Houston, B. K. (1981). Efficacy of self-instructional training for reducing children's anxiety in an evaluation situation. *Behaviour Research and Therapy*, **19**, 509–15.

Fox, J. E., Kent Houston, B. & Pittner, M. S. (1983). Trait anxiety and children's cognitive behaviors in an evaluative situation. *Cognitive Therapy and Research*, **7**, 149–54.

Francis, G. (1988). Assessing cognitions in anxious children. *Behavior Modification*, **12**, 267–80.

Glass, C. R. & Arnkoff, D. B. (1997). Questionnaire methods of cognitive self-statement assessment. *Journal of Consulting and Clinical Psychology*, **65**, 911–27.

Henker, B., Whalen, C. K. & O'Neil, R. (1995). Worldly and workaday worries: Contemporary concerns of children and young adolescents. *Journal of Abnormal Child Psychology*, **23**, 685–702.

Houston, B. K., Fox, J. E. & Forbes, L. (1984). Trait anxiety and children's state anxiety, cognitive behaviors, and performance under stress. *Cognitive Therapy and Research*, **8**, 631–41.

Jolly, J. B. (1993). A multi-method test of the cognitive content-specificity hypothesis in young adolescents. *Journal of Anxiety Disorders*, **7**, 223–33.

Kendall, P. C. (1984). Behavioral assessment and methodology. In *Annual Review of Behavior Therapy: Theory and Practice*, ed. G. T. Wilson, C. M. Franks, K. D. Braswell & P. C. Kendall, Vol. 9, pp. 39–94. New York: Guilford Press.

Kendall, P. C. (1994). Treating anxiety disorders in children: results of a randomized clinical trial. *Journal of Consulting and Clinical Psychology*, **62**, 100–10.

Kendall, P. C. (1993). Cognitive-behavioral therapies with youth: Guiding theory, current status, and emerging developments. *Journal of Consulting and Clinical Psychology*, **61**, 235–47.

Kendall, P. C. & Chansky, T. (1991). Considering cognition in anxiety-disordered children. *Journal of Anxiety Disorders*, **5**, 167–85.

Kendall, P. C., Howard, B. L. & Epps, J. (1988). The anxious child: cognitive–behavioral treatment strategies. *Behavior Modification*, **12**, 281–310.

Kendall, P. C. & Ingram, R. (1987). The future for cognitive assessment of anxiety: Let's get specific. In *Anxiety and Stress Disorders: Cognitive Behavioral Assessment and Treatment*, ed. L. Michelson & L. M. Ascher, pp. 89–104. New York: Guilford Press.

Kendall, P. C. & Ronan, K. (1990). Assessment of children's anxieties, fears and phobias: Cognitive-behavioral models and methods. In *Handbook of Psychological and Educational Assessment of Children*, Vol. 2, *Personality, Behavior and Context*, ed. C. R. Reynolds & R. W. Kamphaus, pp. 223–44. New York: Guilford Press.

King, N. J., Mietz, A., Tinney, L. & Ollendick, T. H. (1995). Psychopathology and cognition in adolescents experiencing severe test anxiety. *Journal of Clinical Child Psychology*, **24**, 49–54.

Kortlander, E., Kendall, P. C. & Panichelli-Mindel, S. M. (1997). Maternal expectations and attributions about coping in anxious children. *Journal of Anxiety Disorders*, **11**, 297–315.

Kovacs, M. (1979). *Children's Depression Inventory*. Pittsburgh: University of Pittsburgh.

Laurent, J. & Stark, K. D. (1993). Testing the cognitive content-specificity hypothesis with anxious and depressed youngsters. *Journal of Abnormal Psychology*, **102**, 226–37.

Leitenberg, H., Yost, L. W. & Carroll-Wilson, M. (1986). Negative cognitive errors in children: questionnaire development, normative data and comparisons between children with and without self-reported symptoms of depression, low self-esteem and evaluation anxiety. *Journal of Consulting and Clinical Psychology*, **54**, 528–36.

Leung, P. W. L. & Wong, M. M. T. (1998). Can cognitive distortions differentiate between internalising and externalising problems? *Journal of Child Psychology and Psychiatry*, **39**, 263–9.

Mathews, A. & MacLeod, C. (1994). Cognitive approaches to emotion and emotional disorders. *Annual Review of Psychology*, **45**, 25–50.

Mattis, S. G. & Ollendick, T. H. (1997). Children's cognitive responses to the somatic symptoms of panic. *Journal of Abnormal Child Psychology*, **25**, 47–57.

Michelson, L. K., Schwartz, R. M. & Marchione, K. E. (1991). States of mind model: Cognitive balance in the treatment of agoraphobia. *Advances in Behaviour Research and Therapy*, **13**, 193–213.

Nelles, W. B. & Barlow, D. H. (1988). Do children panic? *Clinical Psychology Review*, **8**, 359–72.

Perrin, S. & Last, C. G. (1997). Worrisome thoughts in children clinically referred for anxiety disorder. *Journal of Clinical Child Psychology*, **26**, 181–9.

Prins, P. J. M. (1985). Self-speech and self-regulation of high- and low-anxious children in the dental situation: An interview study. *Behaviour Research and Therapy*, **23**, 641–50.

Prins, P. J. M. (1986). Children's self-speech and self-regulation during a fear-provoking behavioral test. *Behaviour Research and Therapy*, **24**, 181–91.

Prins, P. J. M. (1988). Efficacy of self-instructional training for treating children's dental fear. *Child and Family Behavior Therapy*, **10**, 49–67.

Prins, P. J. M., Groot, M. J. M. & Hanewald, G. J. F. P. (1994). Cognition in test-anxious children: The role of on-task and coping cognition reconsidered. *Journal of Consulting and Clinical Psychology*, **62**, 404–9.

Prins, P. J. M. & Hanewald, G. J. F. P. (1997). Self-statements of test-anxious children: Thought-listing and questionnaire approaches. *Journal of Consulting and Clinical Psychology*, **65**, 440–7.

Prins, P. J. M. & Hanewald, G. J. F. P. (1999). Coping self-talk and cognitive interference in anxious children. *Journal of Consulting and Clinical Psychology*, **67**, 435–9.

Rapee, R. M. (1991). Generalized anxiety disorder: A review of clinical features and theoretical concepts. *Clinical Psychology Review*, **11**, 419–40.

Rapee, R. M. (1997). Potential role of childrearing practices in the development of anxiety and depression. *Clinical Psychology Review*, **17**, 47–67.

Ronan, K. & Kendall, P. C. (1997). Self-talk in distressed youth: States-of-Mind and content specificity. *Journal of Clinical Child Psychology*, **26**, 330–7.

Ronan, K., Kendall, P. C. & Rowe, M. (1994). Negative affectivity in children: Development and validation of a self-statement questionnaire. *Cognitive Therapy and Research*, **18**, 509–28.

Rudolph, K. D., Dennig, M. D. & Weisz, J. R. (1995). Determinants and consequences of children's coping in the medical setting: Conceptualization, review, and critique. *Psychological Bulletin*, **118**, 328–37.

Schwartz, R. M. & Garamoni, G. L. (1989). Cognitive balance and psychopathology: Evaluation of an information processing model of positive and negative states of mind. *Clinical Psychology Review*, **9**, 271–94.

Silverman, W. K., La Greca, A. M. & Wasserstein, S. B. (1995). What do children worry about? Worries and their relations to anxiety. *Child Development*, **66**, 671–86.

Spence, S. H. (1994). Practitioner review: cognitive therapy with children and adolescents: From theory to practice. *Journal of Child Psychology and Psychiatry*, **35**, 1191–228.

Spielberger, C. D. (1983). *The State-Trait Anxiety Inventory for Children (STAIC)*. Palo Alto, CA: Consulting Psychologists Press.

Treadwell, K. R. H. & Kendall, P. C. (1996). Self-talk in anxiety-disordered youth: States of Mind, content specificity, and treatment outcome. *Journal of Consulting and Clinical Psychology*, **64**, 941–50.

Vasey, M. W. (1993). Development and cognition in children: The example of worry. In *Advances in Clinical Child Psychology*, Vol. 15, ed. T. H. Ollendick & R. J. Prinz, pp. 1–39. New York: Plenum Press.

Vasey, M. W., Crnic, K. A. & Carter, W. G. (1994). Worry in childhood: A developmental perspective. *Cognitive Therapy and Research*, **18**, 529–49.

Vasey, M. W. & Daleiden, E. L. (1996). Information processing pathways to cognitive interference in childhood. In *Cognitive Interference: Theories, Methods, and Findings*, ed. I. G. Sarason, G. R. Pierce & B. R. Sarason, pp. 117–38. Hillsdale, NJ: Lawrence Erlbaum Associates.

Vasey, M. W., El-Hag, N. & Daleiden, E. L. (1996). Anxiety and the processing of emotionally threatening stimuli: Distinctive patterns of selective attention among high- and low-test-anxious children. *Child Development*, **67**, 1173–85.

Warren, M. K., Ollendick, T. H. & King, N. J. (1996). Test anxiety in girls and boys: A clinical-developmental analysis. *Behaviour Change*, **13**, 157–70.

Watson, D. & Clark, L. A. (1984). Negative affectivity: The disposition to experience aversive emotional states. *Psychological Bulletin*, **96**, 465–90.

Zatz, S. & Chassin, L. (1983). Cognitions of test-anxious children. *Journal of Consulting and Clinical Psychology*, **51**, 526–34.

Zatz, S. & Chassin, L. (1985). Cognitions of test-anxious children under naturalistic test-taking conditions. *Journal of Consulting and Clinical Psychology*, **53**, 393–401.

3

Behavioural inhibition and the development of childhood anxiety disorders

Jaap Oosterlaan

Children differ in their initial reactions to novel circumstances. Some children show a propensity to react consistently to novelty and unfamiliarity with initial restraint and avoidance. These children are referred to as temperamentally behaviourally inhibited. In this chapter, the suggestion is explored that behavioural inhibition (hereafter called inhibition) may predispose a child to the development of anxiety disorders. After reviewing research on the temperamental quality of inhibition, three areas of research are described that bear on the relation between inhibition and childhood anxiety disorders. First, studies are described which have examined the hypothesized predictive relation between temperamental inhibition and anxiety disorders. Second, the Behavioural Inhibition System (BIS; Gray, 1987, 1988, 1991) is proposed as a plausible neuropsychological substrate for the predictive association between temperamental inhibition and childhood anxiety disorders. Specifically, it is suggested that an overactive BIS seems to underlie the temperamental quality of inhibition as well as pathological anxiety. Third, research is reviewed which bears on the overactive BIS hypothesis for childhood anxiety disorders.

The literature on the relation between temperamental inhibition and anxiety disorders has been reviewed by others (Biederman et al., 1995; Pollock et al., 1995; Rosenbaum et al., 1993; Turner, Beidel & Wolff, 1996). This chapter reviews the more recent findings and focuses in particular on childhood anxiety disorders. Further, the chapter attempts to link the literature on the temperamental construct of inhibition with the notion of the BIS.

Inhibition as a temperamental construct

Inhibition may be defined as a temperamentally based predisposition of children to react consistently to novel and unfamiliar events, both social and nonsocial, with initial restraint and avoidance together with signs of wariness and fear (Reznick et al., 1992). In response to encounters with unfamiliar objects, people and situations, these children show a tendency to become quiet, cease activity, retreat, and seek proximity to a familiar person. Uninhibited children show the opposite behavioural pattern. Inhibited and uninhibited behaviour have been regarded as early manifestations of adult introversion and extroversion, respectively (Broberg, Lamb & Hwang, 1990; Kagan, 1989a; Matheny, 1989; Robinson et al., 1992). The concept of temperamental inhibition shows considerable overlap with notions such as withdrawn, shy, fearful, timid, unsociable, vigilant and cautious (Gersten, 1989).

Studies investigating the temperamental trait of inhibition in children have mostly relied on direct observations in laboratory situations. Different situations have been used to study inhibition across development. For example, 4-month-old infants have been studied for inhibition using visual stimuli and auditory stimuli presented in increasing intensity (Snidman et al., 1995). Children of about 2 years have been observed for their interaction with a strange adult and for their response to presentation with a robot (Reznick et al., 1989). Studies of older children have typically used social situations to elicit inhibited behaviour, for example a play group consisting of same sex and age peers (Kagan, 1989a).

The resultant measures of temperamental inhibition are approximately normally distributed. Studies have selected the top and bottom parts of the distribution to represent inhibited and uninhibited children, respectively. Among studies, the percentage of children classified as inhibited varies between the top 10–40% of the distribution (Kagan, Reznick & Gibbons, 1989; Scarpa et al., 1995). It is noted in passing, however, that there is debate about whether the concept of inhibition should be approached dimensionally or categorically (Kagan & Snidman, 1991b; Reznick et al., 1989). According to the dimensional approach, inhibition refers to a continuous trait such that any child can be ordered on a continuum or dimension that ranges from extremely inhibited to extremely uninhibited behaviour. Such an approach makes definitions of inhibited and uninhibited behaviour arbitrary. In contrast, according to the categorical approach, children who display inhibited or uninhibited behaviour represent qualitatively distinct groups. In favour of the latter view, some physiological correlates of inhibition show a noncontinuous distribution (Kagan et al., 1989; Kagan, Reznick & Snidman, 1987, 1988; Kagan & Snidman, 1991b; Snidman et al., 1995).

The most extensive research conducted on the temperamental quality of inhibition in childhood, has been the longitudinal research begun by Garcia-Coll and continued by Kagan and colleagues (for critical reviews see Rothbart

& Mauro, 1990; Turner et al., 1996; also see Gersten, 1989; Kagan, 1989*a,b*; Kagan et al., 1987, 1988). These investigators have prospectively studied inhibition in two samples of inhibited and uninhibited children. One sample was studied from 21 months onward, the second from 31 months onward. Both samples were studied through to 7.5 years of age.

Findings indicated moderate stability of temperamental inhibition over time and cross-situational consistency for widely varying contexts, including the laboratory, the school and the home. Kagan (1989*b*) claimed that three-quarters of the children classified as either inhibited or uninhibited in their second year of life, exhibited signs of this classification through their 8th year. This finding is remarkable given the differences in the indices of inhibition used across follow-up. However, results also suggested that inhibition is not an irreversible attribute.

Several studies have essentially replicated these results using samples of temperamentally inhibited and uninhibited children (Kagan & Snidman, 1991*b*; Kagan, Snidman & Arcus, 1992; Mullen, Snidman & Kagan, 1993; Snidman et al., 1995) as well as nonselected samples (Asendorpf, 1990; Broberg et al., 1990; Kagan et al., 1989; Matheny, 1989; Reznick et al., 1989; Robinson et al., 1992; Scarpa et al., 1995). Together these studies span the age range of 0 to 11 years of age. Stability of inhibition is higher in children who demonstrate extremely inhibited or extremely uninhibited behaviour than in nonselected samples.

Several studies have found that more girls than boys show temperamentally inhibited behaviour (Reznick et al., 1989; Robinson et al., 1992; Scarpa et al., 1995). Moreover, girls were found to be overrepresented in children who remain consistently inhibited over time (Scarpa et al., 1995). Probably, these findings reflect prevailing sex-role stereotypes of girls expected to be more inhibited and boys expected to display less inhibited behaviour. Two studies with infants, however, have failed to find gender differences (Broberg et al., 1990; Kagan & Snidman, 1991*a*).

Results of studies with twins indicate that there is an important genetic influence on temperamental inhibition in samples of 1- to 2.5-year-old children (DiLalla, Kagan & Reznick, 1994; Emde et al., 1992; Matheny, 1989; Robinson et al., 1992). Heritability reflects the extent to which the observed variance in inhibition can be attributed to genetic influences. Twin studies use monozygotic twin pairs, who are genetically identical, and dizygotic twin pairs, who on average share half the genetic material passed to them from their mother and father. An estimate of heritability (h^2) can be obtained by doubling the difference between the correlations for inhibited behaviour in monozygotic twins and in dizygotic twins.

Estimates of heritability in nonselected samples range from $h^2 = 0.42$ (Robinson et al., 1992) to $h^2 = 0.70$ (DiLalla et al., 1994), indicating modest to high genetic influence. Findings suggest that heritability may be particularly salient for extremely temperamentally inhibited and uninhibited behaviour (DiLalla et al., 1994; Robinson et al., 1992). Studies have also found evidence for substantial genetic contributions to continuity and change in inhibited behaviour over time, and to stability across situations. That is, monozygotic twins showed greater similarity in changes in inhibited behaviour over time and across situations than dizygotic twins (Matheny, 1989; Robinson et al., 1992).

Kagan and colleagues (Kagan et al., 1987, 1988) have suggested that extreme temperamentally inhibited behaviour may be related to enhanced excitability of the limbic system, and especially the amygdala and hypothalamus. On the basis of this hypothesis, inhibited children are expected to show greater reactivity in the systems that are controlled by these structures. Three such systems are: the sympathetic nervous system, the reticular formation with its projections to the skeletal muscles, and the hypothalamic-pituitary-adrenal axis.

Findings with temperamentally inhibited children have yielded support for increased reactivity in the sympathetic nervous system. Compared with uninhibited children, inhibited children demonstrate higher and more stable heart rates, as well as larger heart rate accelerations, larger diastolic blood pressure, larger pupillary dilation, and higher levels of norepinephrine to specific challenges. Furthermore, inhibited children evidence greater skeletal muscle tension and higher levels of salivary cortisol. These results support the idea of increased activity in the reticular formation and the hypothalamic-pituitary-adrenal axis, respectively (Kagan et al., 1987, 1988, 1989).

Evidence for greater sympathetic reactivity has also been found in infants who showed signs indicative of temperamentally inhibited behaviour at age 4 months. Specifically, these children showed greater sympathetic reactivity in the cardiovascular system 2 weeks before birth and at later follow-up assessments compared with infants who did not show evidence of inhibition (Kagan, 1997; Kagan & Snidman, 1991b; Snidman et al., 1995).

To summarize, temperamental inhibition can already be observed in infants and seems to be fairly stable over the years of childhood. This behavioural tendency seems to be under powerful genetic control and is associated with specific physiological correlates, such as increased sympathetic reactivity.

Temperamental inhibition: a precursor of (childhood) anxiety disorders?

In this section, studies investigating the hypothesized predictive relation between temperamental inhibition and anxiety disorders are reviewed. Table 3.1 summarizes the pertinent studies in terms of aim of the studies, subjects, results and methodological issues. Six of the studies used a cross-sectional design; three studies reported a longitudinal investigation of inhibited children. With the exception of the Reznick et al. (1992) and Caspi et al. (1996) studies, all research has been conducted by Kagan and colleagues.

Kagan and colleagues have utilized two different samples. The first sample (here referred to as the clinical sample) consisted of 56 children in the age range of 2 to 7 years, who were stratified into four groups: 13 children had a parent with panic disorder and agoraphobia (PDAG), 10 children had a parent with major depressive disorder (MDD), 20 children had a parent with a combination of PDAG and MDD, and 13 children had a parent neither diagnosed with PDAG, nor with MDD (non-PDAG/non-MDD group). Children from the clinical sample were classified either as inhibited or as not-inhibited and have been involved in different studies, including a 3-year follow-up study (Biederman et al., 1993).

The second sample comprised children from the two cohorts of children described earlier (see p. 47) who were characterized as inhibited or uninhibited at 21 or 31 months of age and followed longitudinally to age 7.5 years (here referred to as the nonclinical sample). Note that the definition of children without inhibition differed for the clinical and nonclinical samples. In the nonclinical sample, children were selected for not being inhibited (i.e. these children demonstrated the opposite behaviour to unfamiliarity compared with inhibited children). In contrast, in the clinical sample, this group comprised children who did not show inhibited behaviour to unfamiliarity rather than uninhibited behaviour. Hence, these children were labelled not-inhibited.

The first study that investigated the association between temperamental inhibition and anxiety disorders is the study by Rosenbaum et al. (1988). These authors argued that, if inhibition reflects a predisposition for anxiety disorders, inhibition would be more prevalent in children at risk for these disorders than in children who are not at risk. Using the previously described clinical sample, it was found that children at risk for anxiety disorders (i.e. those with a parent in the PDAG or PDAG + MDD group), demonstrated higher rates of inhibition than children not at risk (i.e. children with a parent in the non-PDAG/non-MDD group).

In a subsequent study, Biederman et al. (1990) investigated whether inhibited

Table 3.1. Evidence for the link between temperamental inhibition and childhood anxiety disorders

Study	Aim	Subjects	Results	Comments
Rosenbaum et al. (1988)	Examined whether inhibition is more prevalent in children at risk for PDAG (i.e. children with a parent having PDAG) as compared with children not at risk for PDAG.	*Rosenbaum et al. clinical sample*[a] 2- to 7-year-old children of parents diagnosed with: (a) PDAG (*n* = 13), (b) MDD (*n* = 10), (c) PDAG and MDD (*n* = 20), and (d) non-PDAG/non-MDD (*n* = 13; parents or siblings of these children were in treatment for various disorders).	Children of parents with PDAG and children of parents with PDAG + MDD were more likely to be inhibited than children in the non-PDAG/non-MDD group. The MDD group did not differ from the other groups.	Cross-sectional design. Since the MDD group did not differ from the PDAG and the PDAG + MDD group, the results do not support a specific relationship between PDAG and inhibition. Since other disorders than PDAG and MDD were not assessed, it is unclear whether inhibition is associated with other disorders than PDAG and MDD.
Biederman et al. (1990)	Examined whether inhibited children have an increased risk for anxiety disorders compared with children who are not inhibited.	*Rosenbaum et al. clinical sample*[a] 4- to 7-year-old children categorized as: (a) inhibited children (*n* = 18), and (b) not-inhibited children (*n* = 12). Added to these groups was (c) a group of 4- to 10-year-old normal control children (*n* = 20). *Kagan et al. nonclinical sample* 7- to 8-year-old children categorized at 21 months of age as: (a) inhibited (*n* = 22, including 7 boys), and (b) uninhibited (*n* = 19, including 9 boys).	*Rosenbaum et al. clinical sample* Compared with normal control children, inhibited children had higher rates of multiple psychiatric disorders, multiple anxiety disorders, oppositional defiant disorder, and overanxious disorder. No differences were found between inhibited and not-inhibited children. *Kagan et al. non-clinical sample* Inhibited children had higher rates of phobic disorders, and lower rates of oppositional defiant disorder than uninhibited children.	Cross-sectional design. Limited assessment of psychopathology. Rates of illness are reported as lifetime prevalences. Definition of children without inhibition differed for the two samples. In the clinical sample, children did not meet criteria for inhibition, while in the nonclinical sample, children were selected for being uninhibited.

Study	Aims	Sample	Results	Comments
Rosenbaum et al. (1991)	Examined whether parents and siblings of inhibited children have an increased risk for anxiety disorders compared with parents and siblings of uninhibited and normal children.	*Kagan et al. non-clinical sample* Parents and siblings of 7- to 8-year-old children categorized at 21 months of age as: (a) inhibited (parents: $n = 40$, including 19 men; siblings: $n = 28$, including 18 boys), and (b) uninhibited (parents: $n = 35$, including 17 men; siblings: $n = 17$, including 9 boys). Also studied were parents and siblings of 4- to 12-year-old normal control children (parents: $n = 35$, including 15 men; siblings: $n = 27$, including 19 boys). Mean age of parents was 39 years. Mean age of siblings was 9 years.	Compared with parents of uninhibited and normal control children, parents of inhibited children had higher rates of multiple anxiety disorders, any childhood anxiety disorder and continuing anxiety disorder. These results were accounted for by higher rates of social phobia, avoidant disorder and overanxious disorder in parents of inhibited children. The rate of multiple childhood anxiety disorders was higher in parents of inhibited children than in parents of uninhibited children. Parents of uninhibited children had higher rates of MDD than parents of normal control children. No differences were noted for siblings.	Cross-sectional design. Rates of illness are reported as lifetime prevalences. Limited assessment of psychopathology. Contrasting results reported by Rosenbaum et al. (1992).
Hirshfeld et al. (1992)	Examined whether children who remain consistently inhibited over time have a higher risk for anxiety disorders in themselves and in their relatives than children who do not remain consistently inhibited over time.	*Kagan et al. nonclinical sample* 7.5- to 8-year-old children categorized as: (a) stable inhibited ($n = 12$, including 2 boys), (b) unstable inhibited ($n = 10$, including 5 boys), (c) stable uninhibited ($n = 9$, including 7 boys), and (d) unstable uninhibited ($n = 10$, including 2 boys) based on assessments at age 21 months, age 4 and 7 years. At the time these children were 10 years old, their parents ($n = 75$) and siblings ($n = 45$) were studied[b].	Stable inhibited children had higher rates of any anxiety disorder, multiple anxiety disorders and phobic disorders compared with children who were not stably inhibited. Stable uninhibited children had higher rates of oppositional defiant disorder than children who were not stably uninhibited. Compared with parents of children who were not stably inhibited, parents of stably inhibited children had higher rates of multiple childhood anxiety disorders, avoidant disorder in childhood and continuing anxiety disorder. Siblings of stable inhibited children had higher rates of multiple anxiety disorders than siblings of children who were not stably inhibited. Unstable inhibited children did not differ from stable and unstable uninhibited children, neither did their parents, nor their siblings.	Cross-sectional design. Rates of illness are reported as lifetime prevalences. Limited assessment of psychopathology.

Table 3.1. (*cont.*)

Study	Aim	Subjects	Results	Comments
Reznick et al. (1992)	Examined the relation between retrospective self-report of inhibition and adult mental health.	*Study 1*[b] Undergraduate students (*n* = 98, including 38 men). *Study 2*[b] Undergraduate students (*n* = 76, including 27 men). *Study 3*[b] Undergraduate students (*n* = 153, including 77 men). *Study 4* Adults diagnosed with: (a) panic disorder (*n* = 27, including 8 men), (b) depression (*n* = 24, including 6 men), and (c) normal controls (*n* = 32, including 11 men).	*Study 1 and 2* Self-reported childhood inhibition correlated positively (*r* = 0.44–0.47) with self-reported mental health problems (ever having used psychopharmacological medication, been diagnosed as having depression or an anxiety disorder). *Study 3* Self-reported childhood inhibition correlated positively with self-reported state anxiety (*r* = 0.37), and depression (*r* = 0.22). This association was mediated by those subjects who continued to be inhibited through adulthood. *Study 4* Both the panic disorder and depression group reported more childhood inhibition than normal controls. The panic disorder group reported more childhood inhibition than the depression group.	Cross-sectional design. Retrospective self-report of inhibition threatens validity of measurement of inhibition. Assessment of psychopathology limited to internalizing psychopathology (anxiety and depression).

Study	Objective	Sample	Results	Comments
Rosenbaum et al. (1992)	Examined whether inhibited children with multiple anxiety disorders have a greater familial loading for anxiety disorders (manifested by multiple anxiety disorders in the parents) than inhibited children without anxiety disorders, and children neither inhibited nor having an anxiety disorder.	*Rosenbaum et al. clinical sample* Parents of 4- to 7-year-old children categorized as: (a) inhibited children with multiple anxiety disorders (n = 8, including 4 men), (b) inhibited children without anxiety disorders (n = 28, including 14 men) and (c) children who were neither inhibited nor had anxiety disorders (n = 24, including 12 men). Mean age of parents was 37 years. *Kagan et al. nonclinical sample* Parents of 7- to 8-year-old children categorized at 21 months of age as: (a) inhibited children with multiple anxiety disorders (n = 8, including 4 men), (b) inhibited children without anxiety disorders (n = 32, including 17 men) and (c) children who were neither inhibited nor had anxiety disorders (n = 35, including 18 men). Mean age of parents was 40 years.	*Rosenbaum et al. clinical sample* Parents of inhibited children with multiple anxiety disorders had higher rates of multiple adulthood anxiety disorders, PDAG and PDAG + MDD than the other two groups of parents. No differences were noted between parents of inhibited children without anxiety disorders and parents of children who were neither inhibited nor had anxiety disorders. No group differences were noted for MDD. *Kagan et al. nonclinical sample* Parents of inhibited children with multiple anxiety disorders had higher rates of multiple childhood and adulthood anxiety disorders, continuing anxiety disorder, social phobia and comorbid social phobia + MDD than the other two groups of parents. No differences were noted between parents of inhibited children without anxiety disorders and parents of children who were neither inhibited nor had anxiety disorders. No group differences were noted for MDD.	Cross-sectional design. Rates of illness are reported as lifetime prevalences. Assessment of psychopathology in children limited to anxiety disorders. Assessment of psychopathology in parents limited to anxiety disorders and MDD. The lack of differences between parents of inhibited children and parents of children who were neither inhibited nor had anxiety disorders, contrasts with the findings of Rosenbaum et al. (1991).
Biederman et al. (1993)	Examined whether inhibited children and uninhibited children differed for the rates of psychiatric disorders at 3-year follow-up.	*Rosenbaum et al. clinical sample* 2- to 7-year-old children categorized as: (a) inhibited children (n = 26, including 18 boys) and (b) not-inhibited children (n = 17, including 10 boys). *Kagan et al. nonclinical sample* 7- to 8-year-old children categorized at 21 months of age as: (a) inhibited (n = 18, including 6 boys) and (b) uninhibited (n = 15, including 7 boys).	Analyses were conducted on the combined sample only. Compared with children who were not inhibited, inhibited children had higher rates of multiple psychiatric disorders, multiple anxiety disorders, avoidant disorder, separation anxiety disorder and agoraphobia at follow-up. Stable inhibited children had higher rates of anxiety disorders than non-stable inhibited children, both at baseline and at follow-up. Among those children without a disorder at baseline, at follow-up inhibited children had higher rates of multiple anxiety disorders, avoidant disorder, and separation anxiety disorder than uninhibited children.	Longitudinal design. Rates of illness are reported as lifetime prevalences. Assessment of psychopathology limited to anxiety disorders. Definition of children without inhibition differed for the two samples. In the clinical sample, children did not meet criteria for inhibition, while in the nonclinical sample, children were selected for being uninhibited.

Table 3.1. (*cont.*)

Study	Aim	Subjects	Results	Comments
Schwartz, Snidman & Kagan (1996)	Examined whether inhibited children and uninhibited children differed for self-reported and parent-reported psychopathology at 10- to 11-year follow-up.	*Kagan et al. nonclinical sample* 13-year-old children categorized at either 21 or 31 months of age as: (a) inhibited ($n = 44$, including 20 boys) or (b) uninhibited ($n = 35$, including 16 boys).	Children categorized as uninhibited at 21 months of age, scored higher than children classified as inhibited on scales measuring externalizing symptomatology, delinquent behaviour, aggressive behaviour and attention problems. Parental ratings agreed with these self-report findings for externalizing symptomatology and aggressive behaviour. Children categorized as uninhibited at 31 months of age, scored higher than children classified as inhibited for self-reported attention problems and parent-reported externalizing symptomatology and aggressive behaviour. For none of the scales, groups scored within the clinical range.	Longitudinal design. Reports of psychopathology were calculated across the last 6 months.
Caspi et al. (1996)	Examined whether behavioural styles were linked to psychiatric disorders at 18-year follow-up.	A representative sample of 21-year-old subjects categorized at age 3 as: (a) undercontrolled ($n = 94$), (b) inhibited ($n = 73$), (c) confident ($n = 268$), (d) reserved ($n = 142$) and (e) well-adjusted ($n = 375$)[b].	Inhibited and uninhibited subjects were compared with well-adjusted subjects. Undercontrolled and inhibited subjects were at increased risk for psychiatric problems. Groups did not differ for the rates of anxiety disorders. Undercontrolled subjects were more likely to meet diagnostic criteria for antisocial personality disorder, and to be involved in crime. Inhibited subjects were more likely to meet diagnostic criteria for depression. Both groups were more likely to attempt suicide, and both groups had alcohol-related problems.	Longitudinal design. Rates of illness were calculated across the last 12 months.

PDAG = panic disorder and agoraphobia; MDD = major depressive disorder; Continuing anxiety = a childhood and adulthood anxiety disorder in the same individual; Multiple anxiety disorders = two or more anxiety disorders in the same individual (the rationale of studying the presence of multiple anxiety disorders is to increase the specificity of determining the presence or absence of an anxiety disorder); Multiple psychiatric disorders = four or more psychiatric disorders in the same individual (the rationale of studying the presence of multiple psychiatric disorders is to increase the specificity of determining the presence or absence of psychopathology).
[a]Gender distribution was not reported. [b]Age distribution was not reported.

children have an increased risk for anxiety disorders compared with children not classified as inhibited. This study used the nonclinical sample, the clinical sample and a group of normal control children. The results showed that inhibited children indeed had an increased risk for childhood anxiety disorders.

In a third study, Rosenbaum et al. (1991) reasoned that, if inhibition is linked with a familial predisposition to anxiety disorders, parents and siblings of inhibited children should be at increased risk for anxiety disorders. Using the nonclinical sample, it was found that parents of inhibited children had higher rates of anxiety disorders than parents of children who are uninhibited and parents of normal control children. However, similar differences were not noted for siblings.

Not all inhibited children develop anxiety disorders. Hirshfeld et al. (1992) argued that, if inhibition reflects an enhanced vulnerability to develop anxiety disorders, children who remain consistently inhibited over time would have a greater risk for anxiety disorders than children who fail to do so. In addition, they hypothesized that, if inhibition is an expression of a familial predisposition, the relatives of children who remain consistently inhibited over time should show a higher prevalence of anxiety disorders than the relatives of children who do not remain consistently inhibited over time. Using children from the nonclinical sample, both hypotheses were supported: children who remained inhibited over a period of 5 years were more likely than other children to have anxiety disorders themselves and to have relatives with an anxiety disorder. No such differences were noted between children who did not remain consistently inhibited over time and children classified as (consistently) uninhibited.

In a subsequent study, Rosenbaum et al. (1992) hypothesized that the risk for anxiety disorders in inhibited children should be greater in those children who have in addition parents with anxiety disorders than in children whose parents do not have anxiety disorders. To test this hypothesis, Rosenbaum et al. stratified children from both the clinical and the nonclinical sample into three groups on the basis of the presence or absence of inhibition and anxiety disorder. In an attempt to increase the specificity of the diagnosis of anxiety disorders, this diagnosis was made only if diagnostic criteria for two or more anxiety disorders were met on a structured diagnostic interview. Thus, three groups were included in the Rosenbaum et al. study: (1) inhibited children with anxiety disorders, (2) children who manifested inhibition alone, and (3) children with neither inhibition nor anxiety disorders. These three groups were compared for the presence or absence of anxiety disorder in their parents.

The results showed that parents of inhibited children with anxiety disorders had higher rates of anxiety disorders than the other two groups of parents. No differences were noted between parents of inhibited children without an anxiety disorder and parents of children who were neither inhibited nor had an anxiety disorder. Parental anxiety disorders may thus help to identify those inhibited children at increased risk to develop anxiety disorders.

One of the studies that has yielded the most powerful support for inhibition as a predictor of later anxiety disorders is the longitudinal study by Biederman et al. (1993). In this study, inhibited children and children not classified as inhibited were followed for 3 years. Children came from both the clinical and nonclinical sample. At follow-up, inhibited children showed higher rates of anxiety disorders than not-inhibited children. Importantly, among inhibited children the rates of anxiety disorders increased from baseline to follow-up.

The most recent study by the Kagan group investigated parent- and self-reported psychiatric correlates at 10- to 11-years follow-up in the nonclinical sample (Schwartz, Snidman & Kagan, 1996). Based on the findings of previous studies (Biederman et al., 1990; Hirshfeld et al., 1992), it was hypothesized that inhibited children would show more internalizing symptoms, whereas uninhibited children were predicted to show more externalizing symptoms. In contrast to what was hypothesized, the two groups did not differ for internalizing symptoms. However, support was found for the hypothesis that uninhibited children would show more externalizing symptoms than inhibited children.

Besides Kagan and colleagues, only Reznick et al. (1992) and Caspi et al. (1996) have studied the hypothesized predictive association between inhibition and anxiety disorders. Reznick et al. studied undergraduate students and three groups of adults, including a panic disorder group, a depression group and a normal control group. Using a newly developed questionnaire, a retrospective self-report of childhood inhibition was obtained.

For the undergraduates, inhibition was associated with self-reported mental health problems (questions about whether they had ever used psychopharmacological medication, and whether they had ever been diagnosed as having depression or an anxiety disorder), and with self-reports of state anxiety and depression. The association with anxiety and depression was mediated by those subjects who continued to be inhibited through adulthood. Furthermore, it was found that adults with either panic disorder or depression reported more childhood inhibition than normal controls. However, the panic disorder group reported more childhood inhibition than the depression group. Thus inhibition was not specifically related to anxiety.

Caspi et al. (1996) reported a 18-year follow-up study of a large representative sample of children, known as the New Zealand, Dunedin cohort. On the basis of behavioural observations at age 3 years, these children were classified as either inhibited, uninhibited or well-adjusted. At age 21 years, inhibited and uninhibited children were compared with well-adjusted children for anxiety disorders, mood disorders, antisocial personality disorder and alcohol dependence. In contrast to what was hypothesized, groups did not differ for the rates of anxiety disorders. Inhibited children, however, were more likely to meet diagnostic criteria for depression. Uninhibited children (Caspi et al. used the notion 'undercontrolled'), were more likely to meet diagnostic criteria for antisocial personality disorder and to be involved in crime. Both groups were more likely to attempt suicide, and both groups had alcohol-related problems.

To summarize, although most studies support the idea that temperamental inhibition is a possible precursor for anxiety disorders, some studies have failed to do so. The risk for anxiety disorders seems to be most pronounced in children who remain consistently inhibited over time and in children who have parents with anxiety disorders. However, the present findings should be interpreted with caution for several reasons.

First, to investigate the role of temperamental inhibition as a precursor of anxiety disorders, a longitudinal design is needed. Other designs do not allow conclusions to be drawn about the direction of causation (i.e. whether inhibition really antecedes anxiety disorders). Only three of the eight studies employed a longitudinal design. Of these three studies, only one (Biederman et al., 1993) has yielded support for the hypothesis that inhibited children are at increased risk for anxiety disorders. Second, the results of these longitudinal studies seem to suggest that temperamental inhibition is only predictive of anxiety disorders across relatively short periods of time (Biederman et al., 1993), but not across relatively long periods of time (Caspi et al., 1996; Schwartz et al., 1996). Third, the studies by Kagan et al. have capitalized on the same samples and utilized relatively small groups.

Fourth, the full spectrum of psychiatric disorders was not assessed in any of these studies. Most studies have focused on the assessment of internalizing psychopathology, and on the assessment of anxiety disorders in particular. Where reported, the assessment of externalizing disorders was limited in nature, and in none of these studies was the possible presence of conduct disorder checked (Biederman et al., 1990; Caspi et al., 1996; Hirshfeld et al., 1992; Rosenbaum et al., 1991; Schwartz et al., 1996). Consequently, no clear conclusions can be drawn about the specificity of the relation between temperamental inhibition and anxiety disorders. Another drawback of the limited assessment of psychopathology is that the association between uninhibited behaviour and psychopathology remains largely unexplored. The available evidence suggests, however, that uninhibited behaviour is predictive of externalizing psychopathology. For example, Biederman et al. (1990) and Hirshfeld et al. (1992), studying the nonclinical sample, found that rates of oppositional defiant disorder (ODD) were higher in uninhibited children than in inhibited children. Schwartz et al. (1996) found that uninhibited children obtained higher self- and parent-reports of externalizing symptoms. In the Caspi et al. (1996) study, uninhibited children, compared with well-adjusted children, were more likely to meet diagnostic criteria for antisocial personality disorder and to be involved in crime.

Finally, studies differed in the time-window in which disorders were assessed. Six of the eight studies reported lifetime prevalences of disorders. Caspi et al. (1996) studied the rates of disorders across a period of 12 months, whereas Schwartz et al. (1996) used a time-window of 6 months. In the latter two studies, inhibited children were not found to be at increased risk for anxiety disorders. Thus the chance of finding support for the predictive association between temperamental inhibition and anxiety disorders could be related to the time-window in which disorders were assessed.

All in all, the current findings await replication and more attention should be devoted to the specificity of the association between temperamental inhibition and anxiety disorders.

Gray's neuropsychological conceptualization of inhibition: the Behavioural Inhibition System

This section attempts to link the literature on the temperamental construct of inhibition with the notion of the BIS (Gray, 1987, 1988, 1991). It is suggested that an overactive BIS is a plausible neuropsychological conceptualization of temperamental inhibition. Furthermore, the BIS offers one possibility to explain the predictive link between temperamental inhibition and anxiety disorders: activity in the BIS is associated with anxiety, and overactivity in this brain system is associated with pathological anxiety.

Extrapolating primarily from animal research, Gray has developed a neuro-psychological model of brain functioning (Gray, 1987, 1988, 1991). In this model, two primary and separate brain systems are distinguished that control behaviour: the BIS and the behavioural activation system (BAS). The BIS and the BAS each respond to a separate set of events with a specific set of behaviours. Both brain systems will be described briefly.

The BIS responds to three classes of stimuli: (1) novel stimuli, (2) signals of impending punishment, and (3) stimuli which signal nonreward, i.e. the omission of anticipated reward or the termination of reward. Signals of punishment and nonreward have also been referred to as threatening or aversive stimuli.

Activity in the BIS gives rise to three behavioural changes: (1) inhibition of all ongoing behaviour, (2) an increment in attention to the environment, such that more information is taken in, especially concerning novel features of the environment, and (3) an increment in the level of arousal, causing an increased readiness for action.

Much of the empirical evidence for the existence and the working of the BIS is derived from studies investigating the effects of anxiolytic drugs. These drugs have been found to antagonize the operation of the BIS. According to Gray, activity in the BIS is accompanied by anxiety and overfunctioning of the BIS results in pathological anxiety.

The core neurological structures that discharge the functions of the BIS are the septohippocampal system (septal area and hippocampus), the ascending noradrenergic fibres to the septohippocampal system that originate in the locus coeruleus, and the serotonergic afferents to the septohippocampal system originating in the median raphe in the brainstem. Other structures involved are the Papez loop, the entorhinal cortex which projects to the hippocampus, and the prefrontal cortex which projects to the entorhinal cortex and cingulate cortex.

The BAS is sensitive to signals of reward and stimuli that signal the termination or omission of punishment (i.e. appetitive stimuli). This brain system serves to maximize reward (by approach to reward) and to minimize punishment (by escape from punishment or active avoidance of punishment). Activity in the BAS is suggested to give rise to positive emotional states. The key anatomical structures that discharge the functions of the BAS are the basal ganglia, the dopaminergic fibres that ascend from the mesencephalon to innervate the basal ganglia, the thalamic nuclei closely linked to the basal ganglia, and similarly the neocortical areas closely linked to the basal ganglia.

To summarize briefly: In Gray's model, behaviour is explained in terms of the activity of two opposing brain systems, the BIS, which is sensitive to novel stimuli as well as to signals of punishment and nonreward (threatening or aversive stimuli), and the BAS, which is sensitive to signals of reward and nonpunishment (appetitive stimuli). The BIS serves to inhibit behaviour, whereas the BAS controls the activation of behaviour. There are reciprocally inhibitory links between the two brain systems: activity in each of the systems tends to suppress activity in the other.

According to Gray, individual differences in the strength of the BIS and the BAS, and their interaction, determine temperament. Gray uses the terms temperament and personality interchangeably. Individuals with high activity in the BIS would show high levels of inhibition, as well as enhanced sensitivity to novelty and threatening or aversive stimuli. In contrast, individuals with high activity in the BAS would show high levels of behavioural activation and increased sensitivity to appetitive stimuli. According to Gray, individual differences in the intensity of the functioning of the BIS correspond to differences in trait anxiety, such that high BIS activity corresponds with high levels of trait anxiety. Individual differences in the intensity of the functioning of the BAS correspond to differences in impulsivity, such that high BAS activity corresponds with high levels of impulsivity.

For the present discussion, it is important to emphasize that the BIS produces, amongst others, inhibition in response to novelty, i.e. the behaviours that characterize temperamental inhibition. In addition to inhibition, activity in the BIS is associated with anxiety, and overfunctioning of this brain system is linked with pathological anxiety. The BIS thereby provides a plausible neuropsychological basis for the predictive association between temperamental inhibition and childhood anxiety disorders.

From this the extrapolation of Gray's model to childhood anxiety disorders is straightforward, as has been noted by Quay (Quay, 1988a,b): These disorders may be traced back to overfunctioning of the BIS. Quay, however, has also used Gray's neuropsychological model for the explanation of two other major childhood psychopathological disorders: attention deficit hyperactivity disorder (ADHD) and conduct disorder. Specifically, Quay has suggested that ADHD reflects a persistently underactive BIS (Quay, 1988a,b, 1997). Children with conduct disorder were proposed to have an overactive BAS that dominates the BIS (Quay, 1988a,b, 1993).

Quay's model has stimulated research into the functioning of the BIS and the BAS in children with ADHD and conduct disorder (for review see Quay, 1993, 1997). However, few studies have explored the validity of the overactive BIS hypothesis in childhood anxiety disorders.

Evidence for the overfunctioning BIS hypothesis in childhood anxiety disorders

In this section, research will be reviewed which bears on the overactive BIS hypothesis for childhood anxiety disorders, including: (a) studies investigating inhibition, (b) a study investigating sensitivity to punishment and reward and (c) a study measuring salivary cortisol.

A series of studies has employed the so-called stop task (Logan & Cowan,

1984; Logan, Cowan & Davis, 1984) to investigate inhibition in diverse child psychopathological groups. Although the primary aim of these studies was to investigate inhibitory control in children with ADHD, children with other disorders, including children with anxiety disorders, were incorporated in these studies as comparison groups.

The stop task is purported to measure the ability to stop a current course of action and has been suggested as a direct measure of BIS functioning (Daugherty & Quay, 1991). Briefly, the stop task requires fast and accurate execution of a reaction time task. Occasionally, a stop signal is presented, which requires the child to inhibit the response. Stop signals are presented at different intervals before the subject's expected response. The shorter the interval, the more difficult it becomes to inhibit a response. Usually, the intervals are chosen such that the shortest interval will yield a probability of inhibition close to 0, whereas the longest interval will produce a probability of inhibition close to 1.

There are two main dependent measures in the stop task: (a) the inhibition function, which reflects the efficiency of the inhibitory mechanism controlling for between-subjects differences in the speed of responding, and (b) stop signal reaction time, which is an estimate of latency of the inhibitory process.

Due to their hypothetically overactive BIS, children with anxiety disorders are expected to display a particularly strong capability for inhibition in the stop task. From Quay's model, contrasting predictions could be made for children with ADHD and children with conduct disorder. Specifically, children with ADHD are expected to show inhibitory deficits due to their hypothetically underactive BIS (Quay, 1988a,b, 1997). In children with conduct disorder, the excessive BAS activity causes a strong tendency to activate behaviour that interferes with the capability for inhibition (Quay, 1988a,b, 1993). Thus, according to Quay, both ADHD and conduct disorder (CD) are associated with inhibitory deficits. However, the dysfunction underlying poor inhibition for these two groups of children is different.

In a recent meta-analysis of studies with the stop task (Oosterlaan, Logan & Sergeant, 1998), strong evidence was found for the existence of an inhibitory deficit in children with ADHD and CD: both groups had flatter inhibition functions than normal control children. The impairment in inhibition was traced back to a slow inhibitory process. These findings lend support for Quay's prediction that both ADHD and CD are associated with poor inhibition.

Four studies have investigated inhibitory control in children with anxiety using the stop task. In two of these studies (Daugherty, Quay & Ramos, 1993; Oosterlaan & Sergeant, 1996), no support was obtained for the hypothesis that anxiety disorders are associated with enhanced levels of inhibition. Daugherty et al. (1993) studied 9- to 13-year-old children, including a small group of anxious children ($n = 12$). Subjects were selected from regular schools on the basis of a single teacher questionnaire. Consequently, the level of impairment in their anxious children may have been insufficient to find evidence for strong inhibition. Oosterlaan & Sergeant (1996) studied children in the age range 6 to 12 years. In this study, a group of 20 anxious children participated (including 13 boys), consisting of children who obtained scores above the 95th percentile on at least two questionnaire measures of anxiety administered to the parent, the teacher and the child. However, these children also obtained elevated parent and teacher ratings of ADHD and CD symptoms. Because ADHD and CD are associated with inhibitory deficits, the presence of associated ADHD and CD symptoms may have attenuated the hypothesized enhanced levels of inhibition in these anxious children.

Two other studies have found some support for the hypothesis that anxiety disorders are associated with strong inhibition (Oosterlaan & Sergeant, 1998; Pliszka et al., 1997). Oosterlaan & Sergeant (1998) used a modification of the stop task that exerts particularly high demands on the inhibitory process (De Jong, Coles & Logan, 1995; Logan & Burkell, 1986). Four small groups of children were compared: 11 anxious children (six boys), 10 ADHD children (all boys), 11 disruptive children (nine boys), and 21 normal control children (15 boys). Subjects were in the age range 8 to 12 years. The anxious group consisted of children who obtained scores at or above the 95th percentile on at least two questionnaire measures of anxiety administered to the parent, the teacher and the child. It was found that anxious children showed better inhibition than normal children, but the two groups did not differ in their speed of the inhibitory process. However, ratings of anxiety, and ratings of ADHD and CD, differed in their association with the speed of the inhibitory process. Ratings of ADHD and CD correlated positively with the speed of the inhibitory process. In contrast, ratings of anxiety correlated negatively with the speed of the inhibitory process. That is, the higher the ratings of anxiety, the faster the inhibitory process.

Pliszka et al. (1997) used a stop task to examine the impact of co-existing overanxious disorder on inhibitory control in a predominantly male sample of 6- to 10-year-old children with ADHD. Interestingly, the presence of concurrent anxiety disorder was found to attenuate the inhibition deficit in children with ADHD. Children with ADHD and co-existing overanxious disorder had better inhibition functions and faster inhibitory processes than children with only ADHD. These results support indirectly the hypothesis that anxiety disorders are associated with enhanced inhibition.

A similar result has been obtained by Pliszka (1992). In this study, a task was used in which children had to react to different coloured shapes on a computer screen. However, when a blue square appeared on the screen, children had to inhibit their response. Three groups were studied: 58 children with ADHD, 34 children with ADHD and co-existing anxiety (child-reported overanxious disorder symptoms), and 12 normal control children. The majority of children in the three groups were boys (54, 29 and 9, respectively). Subjects were in the age range 6–12 years old. ADHD children were found to show inhibition deficits in comparison with normal controls. However, children with ADHD and co-existing anxiety did not differ from their normal peers. Interestingly, failures to inhibit correlated negatively with self-reported and parent-reported anxiety.

Further support for enhanced levels of inhibition in anxiety disordered children was obtained in a study by Werry, Elkind & Reeves (1987). In this study, 21 anxious children (nine boys), 39 ADHD children (32 boys) and 35 children with comorbid ADHD + CD (31 boys) were compared with matched normal control children. Subjects were in the age range 5 to 13 years. When asked to draw a line as slowly as possible, anxious children showed longer latencies than normal controls. Children with ADHD and children with comorbid ADHD + CD did not differ from their normal peers.

To summarize, the above studies yield some evidence for enhanced inhibition in children with anxiety disorders and children with high levels of anxiety, thereby supporting the overactive BIS hypothesis.

Another prediction that could be derived from the hypothesis of increased BIS functioning in children with anxiety disorders is that these children would show increased sensitivity to aversive stimuli compared with their normal peers. This prediction was tested in a study by Daugherty & Quay (1991). Daugherty & Quay compared five small groups of children for their sensitivity to punishment and reward: nine anxious children, nine ADHD children, 10 CD children, 10 children with comorbid CD + ADHD, and 15 normal control children (7, 2, 5, 5 and 7 boys, respectively). These children were selected from regular classes using teacher ratings. Children were in the age range of 8 to 12 years. Given their hypothetically overactive BAS, children with CD were predicted to show increased sensitivity to appetitive stimuli.

Children were tested with a task in which credits could be earned and lost, simply by opening doors that were displayed on a computer screen. In this task, the probability of winning a credit decreased by 10% with each succeeding set of 10 trials (from 90 to 0%), whereas there was a complementary increase in the probability of losing credits.

Children with CD (both the CD and the comorbid CD + ADHD group) opened more doors than anxious and normal control children. Moreover, the majority of children with CD kept responding even when the odds were turning and more credits were lost than earned. In contrast, the majority of anxious children quit the task too early. That is, anxious children stopped responding even though more credits were earned than lost. These findings support the hypothesis of increased sensitivity for reward in children with CD as well as the hypothesis of increased sensitivity for punishment in children with anxiety disorders (Quay, 1988a,b, 1993, 1997).

From the hypothesis that children with CD are characterized by both an overactive BAS and an underfunctioning of the BIS, it could be predicted that children with CD and co-existing anxiety disorder would be less impaired in their BIS functioning since anxiety is associated with overactivity in the BIS. This prediction was tested by McBurnett et al. (1991). Subjects were boys aged 8 to 13 years classified into four groups based on the presence or absence of CD and anxiety disorder (either separation anxiety disorder or overanxious disorder): 21 children with anxiety disorder, seven children with CD, 11 children with comorbid CD + anxiety disorder, and 28 children free from both CD and anxiety disorder. In this study, salivary cortisol was used as a measure of BIS functioning. Consistent with the hypothesis, children with both CD and co-existing anxiety disorder had higher levels of cortisol than children with CD alone. However, in the absence of CD, anxiety disorder was not clearly associated with higher levels of cortisol.

To summarize, studies investigating diverse correlates of BIS functioning generally support the overfunctioning BIS hypothesis for anxiety disorders. However, research is scarce and findings await replication.

Inhibition in childhood anxiety disorders: concluding remarks

This chapter began with a discussion of the research that has been conducted on the temperamental quality of inhibition in children. Temperamental inhibition was described as a fairly stable and heritable trait to react consistently to novelty and unfamiliarity with initial restraint and avoidance. For this trait, specific physiological correlates have been found, including increased sympathetic reactivity. Next, three areas of research were discussed that bear on the suggestion that inhibition may be a predisposing factor in the development of childhood anxiety disorders. First, both cross-sectional and prospective studies showed that temperamental inhibition predicts anxiety disorders. The risk for anxiety disorders seems to be most pronounced in children who remain consistently inhibited over time, and in children who have parents with anxiety disorders. Second, there seems to be one brain system that mediates the behaviours associated with temperamental inhibition, anxiety, as well as pathological anxiety: the BIS. An overactive BIS was put forward as a plausible neuropsychological substrate for the predictive link between temperamental inhibition and anxiety disorders. The core neurological structure that appears to discharge the functions of the BIS is the septohippocampal system. Third, studies of BIS correlates in anxiety-disordered children have supported the view that an overactive BIS is implicated in childhood anxiety disorders. All in all, there seems to be coherent evidence for a relation between inhibition and anxiety disorders in children. However, research is scarce and findings await replication.

Little is known about how temperamental inhibition may lead to the development of childhood anxiety disorders. Turner et al. (1996) have suggested four different pathways. One hypothesis is that inhibition is a genetically transmitted trait that, by interaction with environmental factors, may culminate in the development of maladaptive anxiety. A second possibility is that inhibition is an inherited predisposition that makes a child particularly prone to respond intensely to anxiety producing events. This may ultimately result in the development of maladaptive anxiety. Third, inhibition may be a manifestation of a more comprehensive personality or behavioural disposition that predisposes to anxiety disorders, such as trait anxiety, neuroticism, negative affect and introversion. Finally, Turner et al. (1996) have suggested an overfunctioning BIS as a pathway by which inhibition may lead to childhood anxiety disorders. In this chapter the latter possibility is elaborated upon (see Figure 3.1).

There is enough empirical evidence for the claim that some children have an inherited predisposition to react consistently with inhibition to situations of novelty and unfamiliarity. It is suggested that an overactive BIS is a plausible neuropsychological basis for this predisposition: the BIS produces, amongst others, inhibition in response to novelty, i.e. the behaviours that characterize temperamental inhibition.

For some children, the overactivity in the BIS may lead to the development of pathological anxiety. Specifically, it is suggested that the undue activity in the BIS causes increased sensitivity to novelty, as well as sensitivity to cues signalling punishment and nonreward. This, in turn, may initiate a process of conditioning that generates avoidant behaviours and the development of anxious behaviour. Ultimately this may lead to the development of pathological anxiety.

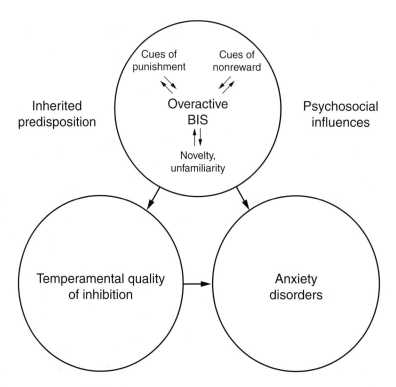

Fig. 3.1. Some children have an inherited predisposition to react consistently with inhibition to situations of novelty and unfamiliarity. For some children, this temperamental trait is found to be predictive of later anxiety disorders. It is suggested that an overactive behavioural inhibition system (BIS) mediates this predictive relationship. Psychosocial influences may strengthen or counteract the overactivity in the BIS.

Indeed, activity in the BIS is associated with anxiety, and chronic overactivity in this brain system is linked with pathological anxiety. The BIS thereby provides a plausible neuropsychological basis for the predictive association between temperamental inhibition and childhood anxiety disorders. Evidence supports the idea of an overfunctioning BIS in children with pathological anxiety.

It is clear that the association between temperamental inhibition and child-hood anxiety disorders is not deterministic. Not all inhibited children develop anxiety disorders, and children with an anxiety disorder may not have a history of inhibition. Some uninhibited children may even develop anxiety disorders (Biederman et al., 1990, 1993; Hirshfeld et al., 1992). Inhibition may be seen as one factor that predisposes to the development of anxiety disorders, or – if we assume that an overactive BIS underlies the temperamental trait of inhibition – as an indicator of an overfunctioning BIS which brings along an enhanced risk for the development of anxiety disorders. A variety of psychosocial influences may ultimately determine whether temperamental inhibition is followed by the onset of an anxiety disorder.

For example, environmental influences may strengthen or counteract the overactivity in the BIS. To illustrate, frequent experiences of being ignored (nonreward) or rejected (punishment) by peers may initiate a process of conditioning to these stimuli. This, in turn, may trigger BIS activity and lead to a vicious cycle with increasing levels of inhibition in situations with peers. Temperamentally inhibited children may be particularly prone to such a process of conditioning given their reluctance to engage in social interactions. Consistent with this reasoning, Asendorpf (1990) has reported a positive correlation between failed social interactions and inhibition. However, environmental influences may also counteract inhibition. Broberg (1993), for example, demonstrated that inhibited children in day-care facilities became less inhibited than children raised at home. It is important to note, however, that genetic factors seem to be much more powerful than environmental influences (Emde et al., 1992; Robinson et al., 1992).

In addition to environmental influences, cognitive influences may be important. For example, cognitive factors may distort the perception of stimuli that activate the BIS (e.g. going to school may be perceived as threatening by a child with separation anxiety disorder, whereas it may be perceived as fun by a normal developing child).

Extreme and persistent temperamental inhibition in childhood may indicate that a child is at risk for later anxiety disorders and thus may help identify children for preventive interventions. Longitudinal research is needed to study the transformation from temperamental inhibition to anxiety disorders. This kind of research would permit the study of factors that may protect against or further the development of anxiety disorders.

In addition, more attention should be devoted to the study of the specificity of the relationship between temperamental inhibition and childhood anxiety disorders. First, little is known about whether inhibition is linked with particular kinds of childhood anxiety disorders. Second, future research should address the issue of whether inhibition is specifically related to anxiety disorders or a risk factor for the broader class of internalizing disorders. Third, research on inhibition has largely ignored the possible association between uninhibited behaviour and the development of externalizing psychopathology. Finally, more research is needed to test the validity of the overactive BIS hypothesis for temperamental inhibition as well as for anxiety disorders.

REFERENCES

Asendorpf, J. B. (1990). Development of inhibition during childhood: Evidence for situational specificity and a two-factor model. *Developmental Psychology*, **26**, 721–30.

Biederman, J., Rosenbaum, J. F., Bolduc-Murphy, E. A., et al. (1993). A 3-year follow-up of children with and without behavioral inhibition. *Journal of the American Academy of Child and Adolescent Psychiatry*, **32**, 814–21.

Biederman, J., Rosenbaum, J. F., Chaloff, J. & Kagan, J. (1995). Behavioral inhibition as a risk factor for anxiety disorders. In *Anxiety Disorders in Children and Adolescents*, ed. J. S. March, pp. 61–81. New York: Guilford Press.

Biederman, J., Rosenbaum, J. F., Hirshfeld, D. R., et al. (1990). Psychiatric correlates of behavioral inhibition in young children of parents with and without psychiatric disorders. *Archives of General Psychiatry*, **47**, 21–6.

Broberg, A. (1993). Inhibition and children's experiences of out-of-home care. In *Social Withdrawal, Inhibition, and Shyness in Childhood*, ed. K. H. Rubin & J. B. Asendorpf, pp. 151–76. Hillsdale, NJ: Lawrence Erlbaum Associates.

Broberg, A., Lamb, M. E. & Hwang, P. (1990). Inhibition: Its stability and correlates in sixteen- to forty-month-old children. *Child Development*, **61**, 1153–63.

Caspi, A., Moffitt, T. E., Newman, D. L. & Silva, P. A. (1996). Behavioral observations at age 3 years predict adult psychiatric disorders. *Archives of General Psychiatry*, **53**, 1033–9.

Daugherty, T. K. & Quay, H. C. (1991). Response perseveration and delayed responding in childhood behavior disorders. *Journal of Child Psychology and Psychiatry*, **32**, 453–61.

Daugherty, T. K., Quay, H. C. & Ramos, L. (1993). Response perseveration, inhibitory control, and central dopaminergic activity in childhood behaviour disorders. *Journal of Genetic Psychology*, **154**, 177–88.

De Jong, R., Coles, M. G. H. & Logan, G. D. (1995). Strategies and mechanisms in nonselective and selective inhibitory motor control. *Journal of Experimental Psychology*, **21**, 498–511.

DiLalla, L. F., Kagan, J. & Reznick, J. S. (1994). Genetic etiology of behavioral inhibition among 2-year-old children. *Infant Behavior and Development*, **17**, 405–12.

Emde, R. N., Plomin, R., Robinson, J., et al. (1992). Temperament, emotion, and cognition at 14 months: The MacArthur longitudinal twin study. *Child Development*, **63**, 1437–55.

Gersten, M. (1989). Behavioral inhibition in the classroom. In *Perspectives on Behavioral Inhibition*, ed. J. S. Reznick, pp. 71–91. Chicago, IL: University of Chicago Press.

Gray, J. A. (1987). *The Psychology of Fear and Stress* (2nd edn). Cambridge, England: Cambridge University Press.

Gray, J. A. (1988). The neuropsychological basis of anxiety. In *Handbook of Anxiety Disorders*, ed. C. Last & M. Hersen, pp. 10–37. Elmsford, NY: Pergamon Press.

Gray, J. A. (1991). The neuropsychology of temperament. In *Explorations in Temperament: International Perspectives on Theory and Measurement*, ed. J. Strelau & A. Angleitner, pp. 105–28. London: Plenum Press.

Hirshfeld, D. R., Rosenbaum, J. F., Biederman, J., et al. (1992). Stable behavioral inhibition and its association with anxiety disorder. *Journal of the American Academy of Child and Adolescent Psychiatry*, **31**, 103–11.

Kagan, J. (1989*a*). The concept of behavioral inhibition to the unfamiliar. In *Perspectives on Behavioral Inhibition*, ed. J. S. Reznick, pp. 1–23. Chicago, IL: University of Chicago Press.

Kagan, J. (1989*b*). Temperamental contributions to social behavior. *American Psychologist*, **44**, 668–74.

Kagan, J. (1997). Temperament and the reactions to unfamiliarity. *Child Development*, **68**, 139–43.

Kagan, J., Reznick, J. S. & Gibbons, A. (1989). Inhibited and uninhibited types of children. *Child Development*, **60**, 838–45.

Kagan, J., Reznick, J. S. & Snidman, N. (1987). The physiology and psychology of behavioral inhibition in children. *Child Development*, **58**, 1459–73.

Kagan, J., Reznick, J. S. & Snidman, N. (1988). Biological bases of childhood shyness. *Science*, **240**, 167–71.

Kagan, J. & Snidman, N. (1991*a*). Infant predictors of inhibited and uninhibited profiles. *Psychological Science*, **2**, 40–4.

Kagan, J. & Snidman, N. (1991*b*). Temperamental factors in human development. *American Psychologist*, **46**, 856–62.

Kagan, J., Snidman, N. & Arcus, D. M. (1992). Initial reactions to unfamiliarity. *Current Directions in Psychological Science*, **1**, 171–4.

Logan, G. D. & Burkell, J. (1986). Dependence and independence in responding to double stimulation: A comparison of stop, change, and dual-task paradigms. *Journal of Experimental Psychology*, **12**, 549–63.

Logan, G. D. & Cowan, W. B. (1984). On the ability to inhibit thought and action: A theory of an act of control. *Psychological Review*, **91**, 295–327.

Logan, G. D., Cowan, W. B. & Davis, K. A. (1984). On the ability to inhibit thought and action: A model and a method. *Journal of Experimental Psychology*, **10**, 276–91.

Matheny, A. P. (1989). Children's behavioral inhibition over age and across situations: Genetic similarity for a trait during change. *Journal of Personality*, **57**, 251–35.

McBurnett, K., Lahey, B. B., Frick, P. J., et al. (1991). Anxiety, inhibition, and conduct disorder in children. II. Relation to salivary cortisol. *Journal of the American Academy of Child and Adolescent Psychiatry*, **30**, 192–6.

Mullen, M., Snidman, N. & Kagan, J. (1993). Free-play behavior in inhibited and uninhibited children. *Infant Behavior and Development*, **16**, 383–9.

Oosterlaan, J., Logan, G. D. & Sergeant, J. A. (1998). Response inhibition in ADHD, CD, comorbid ADHD + CD, anxious and normal children: A meta-analysis of studies with the stop task. *Journal of Child Psychology and Psychiatry*, **39**, 411–25.

Oosterlaan, J. & Sergeant, J. A. (1996). Inhibition in ADHD, aggressive, and anxious children: A biologically based model of child psychopathology. *Journal of Abnormal Child Psychology*, **24**, 19–36.

Oosterlaan, J. & Sergeant, J. A. (1998). Response inhibition and response re-engagement in ADHD, disruptive, anxious and normal children. *Behavioural Brain Research*, **94**, 33–43.

Pliszka, S. R. (1992). Comorbidity of attention-deficit hyperactivity disorder and overanxious disorder. *Journal of the American Academy of Child and Adolescent Psychiatry*, **31**, 197–203.

Pliszka, S. R., Borcherding, S. H., Spratley, K., Leon, S. & Irick, S. (1997). Measuring inhibitory control in children. *Developmental and Behavioral Pediatrics*, **18**, 254–9.

Pollock, R. A., Rosenbaum, J. F., Marrs, A., Miller, B. S. & Biederman, J. (1995). Anxiety disorders of childhood: Implications for adult psychopathology. *Psychiatric Clinics of North America*, **18**, 745–66.

Quay, H. C. (1988*a*). Attention deficit disorder and the behavioral inhibition system: The relevance of the neuropsychological theory of Jeffrey A. Gray. In *Attention Deficit Disorder: Criteria, Cognition, Intervention*, ed. L. M. Bloomingdale & J. A. Sergeant, pp. 117–25. Oxford: Pergamon Press.

Quay, H. C. (1988*b*). The behavioral reward and inhibition system in childhood behavior disorder. In *Attention Deficit Disorder: New Research in Attention, Treatment, and Psychopharmacology*, ed. L. M. Bloomingdale, pp. 176–85. Oxford: Pergamon Press.

Quay. H. C. (1993). The psychology of undersocialized aggressive conduct disorder: A theoretical perspective. *Development and Psychopathology*, **5**, 165–80.

Quay, H. C. (1997). Inhibition and attention deficit hyperactivity disorder. *Journal of Abnormal Child Psychology*, **25**, 7–13.

Reznick, J. S., Gibbons, J. L., Johnson, M. O. & McDonough, P. M. (1989). Behavioral inhibition in a normative sample. In *Perspectives on Behavioral Inhibition*, ed. J. S. Reznick, pp. 25–49. Chicago, IL: University of Chicago Press.

Reznick, J. S., Hegeman, I. M., Kaufman, E. R., Woods, S. W. & Jacobs, M. (1992). Retrospective and concurrent self-report of behavioral inhibition and their relation to adult mental health. *Development and Psychopathology*, **4**, 301–21.

Robinson, J. L., Kagan, J., Reznick, J. S. & Corley, R. (1992). The heritability of inhibited and uninhibited behavior: A twin study. *Developmental Psychology*, **28**, 1030–7.

Rosenbaum, J. F., Biederman, J., Bolduc-Murphy, E. A., et al. (1993). Behavioral inhibition in childhood: A risk factor for anxiety disorders. *Harvard Review of Psychiatry*, **1**, 2–16.

Rosenbaum, J. F., Biederman, J., Bolduc, E. A., Hirshfeld, D. R., Faraone, S. V. & Kagan, J. (1992). Comorbidity of parental anxiety disorders as risk for childhood-onset anxiety in inhibited children. *American Journal of Psychiatry*, **149**, 475–81.

Rosenbaum, J. F., Biederman, J., Gersten, M., et al. (1988). Behavioral inhibition in children of parents with panic disorder and agoraphobia: A controlled study. *Archives of General Psychiatry*, **45**, 463–70.

Rosenbaum, J. F., Biederman, J., Hirshfeld, D. R., et al. (1991). Further evidence of an association between behavioral inhibition and anxiety disorders: Results from a family study of children from a non-clinical sample. *Journal of Psychiatric Research*, **25**, 49–65.

Rothbart, M. K. & Mauro, J. A. (1990). Temperament, behavioral inhibition, and shyness in childhood. In *Handbook of Social and Evaluation Anxiety*, ed. H. Leitenberg, pp. 139–60. New York: Plenum Press.

Scarpa, A., Raine, A., Venables, P. H. & Menick, S. A. (1995). The stability of inhibited/ uninhibited temperament from ages 3 to 11 years in Mauritian children. *Journal of Abnormal Child Psychology*, **23**, 607–18.

Schwartz, C. E., Snidman, N. & Kagan, J. (1996). Early childhood temperament as a determinant of externalizing behavior in adolescence. *Development and Psychopathology*, **8**, 527–37.

Snidman, N., Kagan, J., Riordan, L. & Shannon, D. (1995). Cardiac function and behavioral reactivity in infancy. *Psychophysiology*, **31**, 199–207.

Turner, S. M., Beidel, D. C. & Wolff, P. L. (1996). Is behavioural inhibition related to anxiety disorders? *Clinical Psychology Review*, **16**, 157–72.

Werry, J. S., Elkind, G. S. & Reeves, J. C. (1987). Attention deficit, conduct, oppositional, and anxiety disorders in children. III. Laboratory differences. *Journal of Abnormal Child Psychology*, **3**, 409–28.

4

Psychosocial developmental theory in relation to anxiety and its disorders

P. Michiel Westenberg, Berend M. Siebelink &

Philip D. A. Treffers

We must advance beyond the simple 'stimulus charting' of fears in youth if we are to truly understand their significance in development and their long-term impact on adjustment

Ollendick, King & Frary, 1989, p. 26

Introduction

Epidemiological and clinical studies have indicated that the prevalence of the different anxiety disorders is related to age, and that the average age-at-intake and age-at-onset also differ for the various anxiety disorders. At the same time, however, virtually any anxiety disorder may occur in any age cohort. This chapter addresses the question whether the differences both between and within age cohorts may be explained in terms of general theories of psychosocial development.

The following age pattern was observed for nonphobic anxiety disorders (Kashani & Orvaschel, 1990; Last et al., 1987; Westenberg et al., 1999; see also American Psychiatric Association (APA), 1987, 1994): (a) separation anxiety disorder (SAD) occurs most frequently in childhood, (b) overanxious disorder (OAD) is most characteristic of adolescence and (c) panic disorder (PD) appears most frequent in late adolescence and (young) adulthood. Yet, SAD may also occur in adolescence, and PD may occur even in childhood (Ollendick, 1998). DSM–IV no longer includes OAD, and merged this classification with Generalized Anxiety Disorder (GAD; APA, 1994). However, the core criteria and the clinical features of OAD are highly similar to those in children with GAD (see APA, 1994). Tracey et al. (1997) observed that 'DSM–IV GAD criteria are identifying the same sample as the DSM–III–R OAD criteria' (p. 409).

A similar age pattern was observed for phobic anxiety disorders (Last et al., 1992; Öst, 1987; Sheehan, Sheehan & Minichiello, 1981; see also APA, 1987, 1994): (a) specific phobias (SP) occur at all ages, but retrospective studies indicate that animal phobias tend to begin in early to middle childhood, whereas (b) the natural and situational phobias tend to begin primarily during late childhood or early adolescence, (c) social phobia (SOP) is relatively rare in childhood and most frequently has its onset in middle to late adolescence and (d) agoraphobia (AG) is relatively rare until late adolescence and (young) adulthood. Social phobia and agoraphobia do occur in childhood and early adolescence, but less frequently (see also Öst, chapter 13, this volume).

Although age trends in the onset and prevalence of anxiety disorders are repeatedly observed and acknowledged, explanations are hardly ever offered except as post-hoc hypotheses. Existing explanations often revolve around the assumption that anxiety disorders are somehow related to the normal development of the child, or more specifically, to the normal development of fears and worries (Miller, Boyer & Rodoletz, 1990; Wenar, 1990). The literature reports age trends in the waxing and waning of regular fears and worries in children and adolescents (Angelino, Dollins & Mech, 1956; Bamber, 1979; Bauer, 1976; Croake, 1967; Derevensky, 1979; Maurer, 1965): (a) fears of animals, the dark and fantasized objects occur most frequently in children under 10 years of age, (b) fears of natural phenomena and other concrete situations (e.g. transportation devices) are reported most frequently in late childhood and early adolescence, (c) social fears are most prevalent in adolescence and (d) fears of failing personal standards and fears of negative emotional states are most characteristic of late adolescence and (young) adulthood.

These naturally occurring fears may be aligned with the various phobias: the natural fear of animals and the animal phobias are conceptually similar and are both linked to childhood, the regular social fears and the social phobias are conceptually similar and are both connected with adolescence, and so forth. But the presumed link between normally occurring fears and the phobias only suggests that the phobic anxiety disorders are extreme cases of normal fears. It does not explain why there should be a developmental pattern in the occurrence of normal fears in the first place. Age is an 'empty', nonexplanatory construct (Kazdin, 1989). Moreover, the developmental course of regular and specific fears cannot explain the age trends for the nonphobic anxiety disorders, which represent more pervasive mental states.

The converging age pattern of regular fears and anxiety disorders may be explained on the basis of general psychosocial development.

Psychosocial developments in the early years

Anxiety disorders in children and adolescents have been traced to psychosocial development in the early years. The two most prominent approaches are the psychoanalytic and attachment theories (see also Manassis, chapter 11, this volume).

The psychoanalytic approach offers a general theory of psychosocial development and a related theory about the development of anxiety and its disorders. On the basis of his therapeutic work with adult psychiatric patients, Freud formulated a number of ideas about the development of children and adolescents. He described the development of the sexual drive from oral, to anal, and phallic organizations, and the parallel development of object relations, in which the Oedipus complex assumes a prominent role (S. Freud, 1933). These developments were thought to occur during the first 5–6 years of the child's life.

Freud related the development of anxiety directly to the phase of the child's development: '. . . a particular determinant of anxiety (that is, situation of danger) is allotted to every age of development as being appropriate to it' (S. Freud, 1933, p. 88). Building on this assumption, Anna Freud formulated a developmental line of anxiety (A. Freud, 1966, 1970). She distinguished, in chronological order, the archaic fears of the infant (symbolically expressed in fear of the dark and strangers, for example), the separation anxiety of the symbiotic phase (symbolically expressed, for example, in fears of annihilation and helplessness), and the fear of loss of the object's love (symbolically expressed in fears of punishment, rejection and death, for example). In boys the phallic phase is characterized by castration anxiety (symbolically expressed, for example, in fears of mutilation, surgery and doctors). The relations with age-peers and going to school are connected with the fear of social disgrace. And finally, with the development of the super-ego arises the fear of the super-ego, expressed in terms of guilt.

A basic psychoanalytic assumption is that anxieties in children aged 6 years and beyond and anxieties in adolescents are almost invariably symbolic expressions of early fears. Fears are rooted in inner conflicts stemming from the first 5 or 6 years of life. Moreover, there is no one-to-one correspondence between the manifested fear and the underlying conflict: the same inner conflict may express itself in many different fears, and vice-versa, the same fear may represent different inner conflicts. In the words of Anna Freud (1970): '. . . almost any type of anxiety can find expression in almost any mental representation, or can remain free-floating and unattached' (p. 32).

Hence, the psychoanalytic theory of anxiety is limited to developments in early fears, and cannot explain further developments in the (expression) of anxiety and its disorders. It is unclear why the symbolic representation of anxieties would change across the life course.

Attachment theorists trace anxiety disorders in children and adolescents to an insecure attachment relation to one's primary caretakers in the first 2–3 years of life. Manassis (chapter 11, this volume) addresses the general relation between insecure attachment and the existence of anxiety disorders in children and adolescents. Here we will only address the possible connection between separation anxiety disorder in the early years and panic disorder–agoraphobia later in life.

Clinical observations led Bowlby (1973) to believe that agoraphobia could be seen as a disorder of anxious attachment caused by pathogenic family interaction patterns in early childhood. Similarly, Klein (1981) suggested a connection between a strong separation anxiety in the young child, as a consequence of insecure attachment, and agoraphobia in adulthood. De Ruiter & van IJzendoorn (1992) conducted a meta-analysis and found adults with agoraphobia to report more childhood separation anxiety disorder in comparison with nonpatients but not in comparison with 'neurotic control patients'. They argued that these findings indicated a nonspecific relation between anxious attachment in the early years and anxiety disorders later in life. Later studies reported no or only a small effect of anxious attachment on agoraphobia in adulthood (Lipsitz et al., 1994; Silove et al., 1995). The findings to date are supportive of de Ruiter & van IJzendoorn's (1992) argument for a nonspecific relationship between anxious attachment in the early years and 'neurotic problems' in adulthood (see also Shear, 1996; Thyer, 1993). Their argument resembles Anna Freud's line of reasoning that the same anxiety may be expressed in various ways. Insecure attachment may constitute a vulnerability toward developing an anxiety disorder later in life (Ollendick, 1998), but that life experiences and developmental level determine the specific outcome.

In sum, psychoanalytic and attachment theories may account for the early roots of vulnerabilities toward developing an anxiety disorder of some sort, but the specific type of anxiety disorder might be related to psychosocial developments beyond the early years.

Psychosocial development in childhood and adolescence

Several theories have been advanced to describe developments in childhood and adolescence, but none were explicitly meant to explain the development of emotional disorders such as anxiety. Widely known, studied and validated are Erikson's (1950) model of psychosocial development, Selman's (1980) developmental model of social cognition, Kohlberg's (1969) theory of the moralization of judgement, Damon's (1977) model of social understanding and Loevinger's

Table 4.1. Psychosocial development in childhood and adolescence: a stage-by-stage comparison

Ego Loevinger (1976)	Morality Kohlberg (1969)	Social Cognition Selman (1980)	Self Kegan (1982)	Altruism Krebs & van Hesteren (1994)
Symbiotic		Egocentric	Incorporative	Undifferentiated affective responsiveness
Impulsive	Punishment and obedience	Social informational	Impulsive	Egocentric accommodation
Self-protective	Naïve instrumental hedonism	Self-reflective	Imperial	Instrumental cooperation
Conformist	Good relations and approval	Mutual	Interpersonal	Mutual altruism
Self-aware[a]	Law and order	Social and conventional	Institutional	Toward conscientious altruism

[a]The four higher stages are characteristic of adulthood, are absent in childhood and are rare in adolescence.

(1976) model of ego development. The stages of these and other developmental models have been linked to one another, conceptually and empirically (Kegan, 1982; Krebs & van Hesteren, 1994; Kroger, 1989; Loevinger, 1976; Snarey, 1998). Despite the different topics and samples studied by the various authors, their stage models of development show a remarkable overlap (see Table 4.1 for a stage-wise comparison of some of these theories).

Loevinger understood the overlap between the various models as indicative of an organizing principle, 'ego'. Ego is the frame of reference through which we perceive the world and synthesize our experiences, manifesting itself in many of life's domains. Using James' distinction between I and Me, McAdams (1998) likened ego to I – the self-as-subject, whereas he assigned dispositional traits, personal concerns and life narratives to the Me – the self as object.

In search of ego, Loevinger (1976, 1993) captured the common ground of the various theories in her model of ego development, making it the prime candidate for exploring the developmental underpinnings of anxiety and its disorders in childhood and adolescence. Moreover, Loevinger's model is accompanied by an empirical method, a detailed scoring manual for the Washington University Sentence Completion Test (WUSCT; Hy Lê & Loevinger, 1996; Loevinger, 1985; Loevinger & Wessler, 1970). This measurement instrument has been widely used and validated (Borst & Noam, 1993; Carlson & Westenberg, 1998; Westenberg & Block, 1993; see also Westenberg, Blasi & Cohn, 1998a). The WUSCT allows for a direct empirical test of the relations between psychosocial development on the one hand and anxiety and its disorders on the other hand – regardless of the chronological age of the respondents.

Four levels of ego development are particularly relevant for the study of anxiety and its disorders in children and adolescents. A brief discussion of these levels is followed by an attempt to integrate them with regular fears and the anxiety disorders. The descriptions offered are based on a large-scale study of ego development in Dutch children, adolescents and young adults (age 8–25 years; $n = 2773$). This study was needed, as Loevinger's developmental model and method were based predominantly on research with (young) adults. On the basis of our findings, Loevinger's sentence completion test, scoring manual and descriptions of the earliest ego stages were modified to fit the development of children and adolescents (Westenberg, Treffers & Drewes, 1998c; Westenberg et al., 1998b).

Impulsive level

The lowest relevant level is the Impulsive level. This level is named 'Impulsive', because people at this level live by the moment of their immediate thoughts, feelings and wishes. They may display empathic impulses (e.g. jump to the rescue of others), but they may also display aggressive impulses. Aggression is mainly shown when dependency needs are frustrated: others are expected to take care of and protect them. Impulsive individuals feel generally vulnerable, and the vulnerability is aggravated by the lack of independent coping styles. They are generally docile: care-takers and other adults are expected to set the rules and to enforce them. Yet, impulses may override the generally docile attitude. They depend on others to curb their impulses, by immediate and personally enforced interventions.

Self-protective level

The next level is the Self-protective level. The central characteristic of this level is control. In contrast with the dependent attitude of the Impulsive individuals, Self-protective people want to be in charge of themselves, of other people and of situations. This need for control may be expressed in self-focused ways or in ways focused at other people: manipulation of one's own feelings (e.g. denial of hurt feelings or problems generally) is as typical as the manipulation of other people. Leading motives are the protection of one's own interests and a generally hedonistic attitude toward life. The Self-protective level is characterized by an opportunistic morality. The rules are played with and they try to get away with transgressions. The combination of a manipulative and opportunistic attitude makes them wary of other people. A lack of self-control and a lack of control over other people and situations is dreaded.

Conformist level

Instead of being geared toward the protection of one's self-interest, Conformist individuals are socially attuned. They try to meet the demands of their reference group, in terms of correct opinions, behaviour and appearance. They see and judge themselves through the eyes of others; the expectations of others are their own. When unable to meet social expectations or standards for achievement, they assume a self-blaming attitude. Dangers are not as much located outside oneself, as they were at the previous level, but are located within oneself. Relationships with other people are intrinsically valuable, and are characterized by reciprocity, equality and like-mindedness. Conformity not necessarily implies conventionality, but may also be expressed in adherence to the unconventional norms of one's own reference group.

Self-aware level

The external orientation of the Conformist person – to judge oneself through the eyes of others, is traded for an internal orientation toward personal feelings, thoughts and opinions. Self-aware people are focused at their own internal world, a world possibly different from the outside world. In case of a discrepancy between inner feelings and outer behaviour, inside is synonymous with 'true' while outside is synonymous with 'fake'. The inner world is passively observed: feelings and thoughts originate within oneself, are there without any effort, and cannot be changed. But while they are geared toward inner feelings and thoughts, they need the approval and mental support by others, leading to a complicated situation: the wish to be true to their own feelings and thoughts (e.g. they prefer to be sincere) may cause social disapproval and isolation. Good relations with other people are defined by a personal interest and acceptance of one's inner life. Self-aware is not synonymous with self-assured, but the latter is a central theme: self-assurance is valued, the lack thereof is considered problematic.

Ego development, fears and anxiety disorders: an integration

An integration of the findings on ego development, fears and anxiety disorders may be achieved on conceptual and empirical grounds. Part of the integration is based on direct empirical evidence we gathered in our own studies. Westenberg et al. (1999) found the expected relation between ego level and type of anxiety disorder: separation anxiety disorder was related to the Impulsive level, overanxious disorder was related to the Conformist level, regardless of age. These relations were controlled for socio-economic status and IQ.

In addition to the direct empirical evidence from our own studies, indirect evidence for relations among the three lines of research (i.e. ego development, normal fears and anxiety disorders) is accumulated by a host of other studies. For example, the presumed relation between the Self-aware stage of ego development, personal fears, panic disorder, and agoraphobia (see below), is supported by conceptual overlap, similar age trends for these four aspects, and the frequent comorbidity between agoraphobia and panic disorder.

The literature on regular fears, anxiety disorders and ego development may be integrated in terms of four clusters tied to four approximate age ranges. The presented age ranges refer to the period in which the corresponding developments are expected to peak. They do not imply that these developments never occur in younger or older subjects. Anxiety and its disorders may be related to psychosocial development, but the latter is only imperfectly related to age.

Cluster 1 (*c.* age 5–9)

The fear of fantasy objects and situations, fear of animals, specific phobias of the animal type, and separation anxiety disorder, all appear to be connected with the Impulsive stage of ego development. (See Table 4.2 for an overview.)

This cluster of fears and anxiety disorders highlights the combination of two central aspects of the Impulsive stage: vulnerability and dependency. The fundamental sense of vulnerability appears to be exacerbated by the inability to independently distinguish realistic from imaginary dangers. Aside from lacking independent means to effectively deal with threatening situations, other people have to determine whether a situation is dangerous in the first place. The presence of trusted elders is thus reassuring as they provide both reality-testing of and protection from potential dangers. The fear of animals is illustrative: elders are often the ones to determine which animal really is dangerous, and in which circumstance.

Because of the dual-dependency on elders, their greatest fear is to be without them, to be left to one's own very limited resources. To get lost or to lose one's

Table 4.2. Integration of age trends in the occurrence of regular worries and fears, in the onset and prevalence of anxiety disorders and phobias, and in the psychosocial development of children and adolescents

Age range	Normative fears[a]	Anxiety disorders[b]	Phobias[c]	Psychosocial development[d]

5–9	Fantasy fears
	  Non-existing objects
	  Unrealistic scenarios
	  Nightmares
	  Animals
		Separation anxiety disorder	Specific phobia (animal type)	Impulsive ego level

9–13	Concrete (physical) fears
	  Natural phenomena
	  Transportation devices
	  Accidents and injury
	  Molestation by others
		Avoidant disorder	Specific phobia (natural and situational type)	Self-protective ego level

13–17	Social fears
	  Adequacy of own
	    behaviour/appearance
	  School performance
	  Misfortune to others
	  Loss of friends/family
		Overanxious disorder	Social phobia	Conformist ego level

17–21	Personal fears
	  Loss of close
	    relationships
	  To be isolated/lonely
	  Negative emotional
	    states
	  Failing personal
	    standards/goals
		Panic disorder	Agoraphobia	Self-aware ego level

[a]The overview of the regular fears and worries is based on an extensive review of the literature (Drewes, 1996).
[b]The classification of the anxiety disorders is based on the DSM–III–R (APA, 1987).
[c]The classification of the phobias is based on the DSM–IV (APA, 1994).
[d]Level of psychosocial development is based on Loevinger's stage theory of ego development (Loevinger, 1976, 1993).

parents, are the most frightening prospects. That is why they may be worried about something happening to their parents, not because they feel for their parents, but because it would leave them unprotected.

The relative absence of fears of regular people (e.g. man-related dangers) is remarkable: one would expect that Impulsives fear physical harm inflicted by other people as much as they would fear physical harm inflicted by animals. A possible reason for this is that they depend on other people to take care of them. The trust in their care-takers is generalized to other people, particularly other adults. The child with a separation anxiety disorder appears to lack the transfer of trust to other adults. Another reason for not fearing other humans as much may lie in the familiar features of other people. The Impulsive person is focused on concrete-specific and physical features of people and situations: anything too discrepant from the physical norm is fear-provoking. Imaginary creatures are feared, because of their ugly and weird-looking features, as well as animals, because they are by definition different from people, especially the odd-looking insects and snakes. Dangerous people, such as burglars and other thugs, are imagined to be recognizable as such by their ugly faces, strange clothes, masks and weapons. But any person remotely resembling one's own kin is not feared. This inclination to trust familiar looking and sounding people makes many parents worry that their child will fall prey to the misleading charm of potentially harmful people. Adults realize the child's limited capacity to distinguish trustworthy from dangerous people, and his or her general incapability to distinguish real from imaginary dangers.

Cluster 2 (c. age 9–13)

The fears of natural phenomena and man-related dangers, specific phobias of the natural and the situational type, and a special type of social phobia, all appear to be connected with the Self-protective stage of ego development.

Two features of the Self-protective stage are highlighted in the corresponding fears: the importance of self-control and the general wariness about the intentions of other people. Children at this stage fear concrete physical damage directed to themselves, by other people, or other realistic dangers (i.e. realistic dangers in the Western world). Situations suggesting a lack of self-control are feared most intensely, such as enclosed spaces, heights or being abducted.

Many of the fears reflect the increased insight in the motives of other 'regular' people, who may have bad intentions, even though they may look harmless. The Self-protective person is aware of the difference between apparent and non-apparent intentions. The general wariness of other people's intentions may be turned into a constant suspicion and fear of others, culminating into a special form of social phobia, akin to avoidance disorder (APA, 1987; DSM–IV no longer includes avoidance disorder and considers it to be part of social phobia (APA, 1994)). The self-protective person fears social situations not because of the potential for criticism, ridicule and rejection, but because of the potential for physical harm.

Self-protective people appear to know the difference between imaginary and realistic dangers, and do not have to rely on elders to identify potential dangers. Nor do they depend on others to protect themselves from potential dangers: they either confront or avoid potentially dangerous situations.

Cluster 3 (*c.* age 13–17)

Social fears, social phobia and overanxious disorder all appear to be connected with the Conformist stage of ego development.

Social–evaluative fears and social phobia highlight key features of the Conformist stage: Conformists see themselves and judge themselves through the eyes of others, they try to meet the supposed demands of others, and reproach themselves if they cannot live up to whatever is expected from them.

The difference from the fears and anxiety disorders of the previous levels is twofold: the fears do not centre around physical harm but are social–evaluative in nature, and the danger does not reside in the outside world but is caused by one's own inability to meet social demands. Conformists are worried about not being able to live up to the expectations and demands of their parents, teachers or peers. Geared toward desired appearance, correct behaviour and expected level of performance, they are very concerned about the impression made on others.

The combination of constant alertness to the demands of the outside world with a self-blaming attitude may culminate in an overanxious disorder. Persons with an overanxious disorder constantly worry about the adequacy of their behaviour, appearance or performance. Moreover, just like regular Conformists, persons with overanxious disorder constantly seek reassurance from others and are also worried about the needs and welfare of other people.

Cluster 4 (*c.* age 17–21)

Personal fears, agoraphobia and panic disorder all appear to be connected with the Self-aware stage of ego development.

Personal fears are direct expressions of key concerns of the Self-aware person: the focus on internal states is reflected in the fear of negative emotional states (unhappiness, loneliness, depression), the focus on personal standards for achievement is reflected in the fear to fail one's own standards, the orientation on the future is reflected in the fear to fail life plans and goals, and the value put on close relationships to specific people is reflected in the fear to lose these relations.

The external orientation of the previous levels is exchanged for an internal orientation on own feelings and thoughts that may occur spontaneously, independent of external influences. This propensity toward spontaneously occurring sensations allows for the emergence of a panic disorder: the general fear of internal but unpleasant sensations may exacerbate into a full-blown panic disorder. Even fear itself may occur spontaneously, without any specific and external stimulus, and occur seemingly spontaneous.

The awareness of spontaneous and inner states (sensations, emotions, thoughts) is associated with a feeling of uniqueness, a feeling of being different from other people and of being isolated from the outside world. The feeling of being different and the importance of being true to oneself may lead to (the fear of) conflicts with other people, culminating in the fear of losing crucial relationships. This problem is experienced most acutely in the presence of other people: the perceived differences with others and the possibility for rejection are felt most intensely while in the presence of others. To be alone in a crowded place is to be faced with one's greatest fear: to be left alone, to be deserted, to be lonely. This fear is alleviated by being accompanied by a trusted person.

Discussion

Psychoanalytic and attachment theories describe the development of early fears, and may provide an explanation for the very early roots of anxiety disorders in children and adolescents. As far as the continuing changes in the expression or manifestation of anxiety and its disorders are concerned, one needs to take recourse to alternative theories of psychosocial development. The age data on the occurrence of regular fears and the prevalence of anxiety disorders appear to fit, both in terms of the fear content and in terms of empirical data, with psychosocial developments according to Loevinger's theory of ego development.

The presented overview suggests that the various nonphobic anxiety disorders are tied to specific levels of psychosocial development. For example, separation anxiety disorder (SAD) is an extreme version, or an anxious version of the Impulsive level. Many of the features of SAD are directly tied to the *modus vivendi* of the Impulsive stage, and are incompatible with the other stages of development. Hence, SAD is likely to disappear if the person advances to the next stage of development. That may be the reason why SAD is so rare among adolescents and is absent among adults (APA, 1994); the majority of adolescents and adults have moved beyond the Impulsive level. The same pattern appears present for the other nonphobic anxiety disorders: they are tied to a specific level of development, probably disappearing or being displaced by another anxiety disorder when moving to the next level of development.

The present data are insufficient to determine whether anxiety disorders hinder development to the next stage, or whether anxiety disorders are transformed into other anxiety disorders with development to the next level, or whether anxiety disorders dissipate with further ego development. Prospective studies have to be conducted to study the mutual impact of anxiety disorders and level of psychosocial development.

A slightly different pattern was observed for phobic disorders. Phobias appear to originate at particular stages of psychosocial development, but may persist while psychosocial development continues. For example, an animal phobia is most likely to develop during the Impulsive stage of ego development, but while the person continues to climb the ego development ladder, the animal phobia may persist. The same may happen with any other specific phobia, social phobia or agoraphobia. All phobias may persist while ego development continues.

The different developmental pathways for nonphobic anxiety disorders versus phobias are reflected in the different application of a specific DSM-criterion (APA, 1987, 1994): the awareness in the patient that the anxiety is irrational and too extreme. The classification of a nonphobic anxiety disorder never requires an awareness in the patient that the anxiety is irrational or too extreme. In contrast, the awareness-criterion is used in the case of adults with a specific or social phobia. Adults with these phobias are expected to be aware that the fear is too intense and irrational. This fits with the notion that phobias in adults have outlived the level of development at which they have come into existence. Over time, the discrepancy between the phobic fear and one's current level of development becomes sufficiently large to realize that the fear is irrational.

In contrast, the awareness criterion is not applied to children and adolescents with specific and social phobias. They are often unaware that their fear is irrational and too extreme, because it is not at odds with their current frame of reference. The only phobia for which the awareness criterion is not applied is agoraphobia. Adults with agoraphobia are not expected to see their fear as unnatural and too intense. This is consistent with the finding that many adults are and remain at the Self-aware level of ego development. It is the most frequent level among (young) adults in the U.S. (Holt, 1980; Westenberg & Gjerde, 1999), just as it is among young adults in the Netherlands (Westenberg et al., 1998b). The fear content of an agoraphobia is not at odds with the psychology of the Self-aware adolescent or adult.

The nonphobic anxiety disorder represents the more generic concerns and worries typical of a particular level of development, whereas the phobic fear represents a specific instance of this more generic concern. For example: the overanxious disorder represents the general concerns of Conformist persons, whether they are able to meet the demands and expectations of others. People with a social phobia, in contrast, are specifically worried about their performance in social situations, but they may not be worried about their competence in other areas.

Although the conceptual parallels and empirical connections are impressive, the overlap is not and cannot be perfect. The same anxiety may have different meanings just as different anxieties may have a similar meaning, depending on one's level of development. For example, a person with an overanxious disorder may not worry at all about social or competence issues, but may be worried sick about physical danger. The latter fears are expected to peak at the Impulsive or Self-protective level and not at the Conformist level of ego development. But that is, in fact, the contribution of the developmental context provided in this chapter: a developmental analysis of anxiety and its disorders provides insight into the meaning they have for individual people.

Developmental theories may provide insight into the type and meaning of an anxiety disorder, but they cannot explain the emergence of such disorders. The normal psychosocial development sketched in this chapter merely operates as a third factor, as a mediator between the personal (e.g. genetic) and environmental factors (e.g. life events): developmental level determines the general proclivity for developing a particular type of anxiety disorder or phobia. A person at the Impulsive level of ego development is more likely to develop separation anxiety disorder and not agoraphobia, whereas the opposite proclivity exists in the Self-aware person.

But even though a full-blown anxiety disorder may be due to other factors, the more generic version of the fear appears to be present irrespective of specific experiences, and the more generic version of the fear is tied to level of psychosocial development. The developmental perspective may be combined with the ethological viewpoint: the developmental pattern in the acquisition of normal fears suggests that some fears are more readily acquired during certain stages in development (see Johnson & Melamed, 1979). Within such periods one is particularly sensitive to certain environmental effects, whereas the same environmental events will not have any lasting effect during other stages of development. At the same time, 'phobias of traumatic origin do not have a characteristic age at onset' (APA, 1994, p. 408), and may develop at almost any age or stage of development.

Conclusion

The developmental analyses presented in this chapter shed light on the age trends in the onset and prevalence of anxiety disorders and phobias and provide the basis for the contention that the latter are related to normally occurring fears and worries. The analyses in this chapter also show that instead of a single anxiety disorder of childhood (APA, 1994), at least four types, consistent with the four clusters, need to be distinguished to account for the different manifestations of anxiety and its disorders in childhood and adolescence.

REFERENCES

American Psychiatric Association (1987). *Diagnostic and Statistical Manual of Mental Disorders* (3rd edn, revised) (DSM–III–R). Washington, DC: PA.

American Psychiatric Association (1994). *Diagnostic and Statistical Manual of Mental Disorders* (4th edn) (DSM–IV). Washington, DC: PA.

Angelino, H., Dollins, J. & Mech, E. V. (1956). Trends on the 'fears and worries' of school children as related to socio-economic status and age. *Journal of Genetic Psychology*, **89**, 263–76.

Bamber, J. H. (1979). *The Fears of Adolescents*. London: Academic Press.

Bauer, D. H. (1976). An exploratory study of developmental changes in children's fears. *Journal of Child Psychology and Psychiatry*, **17**, 69–74.

Borst, S. R. & Noam, G. (1993). Developmental psychopathology in suicidal and nonsuicidal adolescent girls. *Journal of the American Academy of Child and Adolescent Psychiatry*, **32**, 501–8.

Bowlby, J. (1973). *Attachment and Loss, Vol. 2, Separation: Anxiety and Anger*. New York: Basis Books.

Carlson, V. K. & Westenberg, P. M. (1998). Cross-cultural research with the WUSCT. In *Technical Foundations for Measuring Ego Development*, ed. J. Loevinger, pp. 57–75. Mahwah, NJ: Lawrence Erlbaum Associates.

Croake, J. W. (1967). Adolescent fears. *Adolescence*, **2**, 459–68.

Damon, W. (1977). *The Social World of the Child*. San Francisco: Josey Bass.

Derevensky, J.L. (1979). Children's fears: A developmental comparison of normal and exceptional children. *Journal of Genetic Psychology*, **135**, 11–21.

de Ruiter, C. & van IJzendoorn, M. H. (1992). Agoraphobia and anxious-ambivalent attachment: an integrative review. *Journal of Anxiety Disorders*, **6**, 365–81.

Drewes, M. J. (1996). *Sociaal-emotionele ontwikkeling en subjectieve angstbeleving (Social-emotional development and the subjective meaning of anxiety)*. Unpublished Master's Thesis, Leiden University, The Netherlands.

Erikson, E. H. (1950). *Childhood and Society*. New York: Norton.

Freud, A. (1966). *Normality and Pathology in Childhood*. London: The Hogarth Press and the Institute of Psychoanalysis.

Freud, A. (1970). The symptomatology of childhood; a preliminary attempt at classification. *The Psychoanalytic Study of the Child*, **25**, 19–41.

Freud, S. (1933). Anxiety and instinctual life. In *The Standard Edition of the Complete Works of Sigmund Freud*, 7th edn, Vol. 23, pp. 81–111. London: The Hogarth Press and the Institute of Psychoanalysis, 1975.

Holt, R. R. (1980). Loevinger's measure of ego development: reliability and national norms of male and female short forms. *Journal of Personality and Social Psychology*, **39**, 909–20.

Hy Lê, L. X. & Loevinger, J. (1996). *Measuring Ego Development*, 2nd edn. Mahwah, NJ: Lawrence Erlbaum Associates.

Johnson, S. B. & Melamed, B. G. (1979). The assessment and treatment of children's fears. In *Advances in Clinical Child Psychology*, Vol. 2, ed. B. B. Lahey & A. E. Kazdin, pp. 107–39. New York: Plenum Press.

Kashani, J. H. & Orvaschel, H. (1990). A community study of anxiety in children and adolescents. *American Journal of Psychiatry*, **147**, 313–18.

Kazdin, A. E. (1989). Developmental psychopathology: Current research, issues, and directions. *American Psychologist*, **44**, 180–7.

Kegan, R. (1982). *The Evolving Self: Problem and Process in Human Development*. Cambridge: Harvard University Press.

Klein, D. F. (1981). Anxiety reconceptualized. In *Anxiety: New Research and Changing Concepts*, ed. D. F. Klein & J. Rabkin, pp. 235–65. New York: Raven Press.

Kohlberg, L. (1969). Stage and sequence: The cognitive-developmental approach to socialization. In *Handbook of Socialization Theory and Research*, ed. D. A. Goslin, pp. 347–480. Chicago: Rand McNally.

Krebs, D. L. & van Hesteren, F. (1994). The development of altruism: toward an integrative model. *Developmental Review*, **14**, 103–58.

Kroger, J. (1989). *Identity in Adolescence: The Balance between Self and Other*. London: Routledge.

Last, C. G., Hersen, M., Kazdin, A. E., Finkelstein, R. & Strauss, C. C. (1987). Comparison of DSM–III separation anxiety and overanxious disorders: demographic characteristics and patterns of comorbidity. *Journal of the American Academy of Child and Adolescent Psychiatry*, **26**, 527–31.

Last, C. G., Perrin, S., Hersen, M. & Kazdin, A. E. (1992). DSM–III–R anxiety disorders in children: sociodemographic and clinical characteristics. *Journal of the American Academy of Child and Adolescent Psychiatry*, **31**, 1070–6.

Lipsitz, J. D., Martin, L. Y., Mannuzza, S., et al. (1994). Childhood separation anxiety disorder in patients with adult anxiety disorders. *American Journal of Psychiatry*, **151**, 927–9.

Loevinger, J. (1976). *Ego Development: Conceptions and Theories*. San Francisco: Josey-Bass.

Loevinger, J. (1985). Revision of the Sentence Completion Test of Ego Development. *Journal of Personality and Social Psychology*, **48**, 420–7.

Loevinger, J. (1993). Measurement of personality: True or false. *Psychological Inquiry*, **4**, 1–16.

Loevinger, J. & Wessler, R. (1970). *Measuring Ego Development: Construction and Use of a Sentence Completion Test*. San Francisco: Josey-Bass.

Maurer, A. (1965). What children fear. *Journal of Genetic Psychology*, **106**, 265–77.

McAdams, D. P. (1998). Ego, trait, identity. In *Personality Development: Theoretical, Empirical, and Clinical Investigations of Loevinger's Conception of Ego Development*, ed. P. M. Westenberg, A. Blasi & L. D. Cohn, pp. 27–38. Mahwah, NJ: Lawrence Erlbaum Associates.

Miller, S. M., Boyer, B. A. & Rodoletz, M. (1990). Anxiety in children – nature and development. In *Handbook of Developmental Psychopathology*, ed. M. Lewis & S. M. Miller, pp. 191–207. New York: Plenum Press.

Ollendick, T. H. (1998). Panic disorder in children and adolescents: New developments, new directions. *Journal of Clinical Child Psychology*, **27**, 234–45.

Ollendick, T. H., King, N. J. & Frary, R. B. (1989). Fears in children and adolescents: Reliability and generalizability across gender, age, and nationality. *Behavior Research and Therapy*, **23**, 19–26.

Öst, L. G. (1987). Age of onset in different phobias. *Journal of Abnormal Psychology*, **96**, 223–9.

Selman, R. L. (1980). *The Growth of Interpersonal Understanding: Developmental and Clinical Analyses*. New York: Academic Press.

Shear, M. K. (1996). Factors in the etiology and pathogenesis of panic disorder: revisiting the attachment-separation paradigm. *American Journal of Psychiatry*, **153**, 125–36.

Sheehan, D. V., Sheehan, K. E. & Minichiello, W. E. (1981). Age of onset of phobic disorders: a reevaluation. *Comprehensive Psychiatry*, **22**, 533–44.

Silove, D., Harris, M., Morgan, A., et al. (1995). Is early separation anxiety a specific precursor of panic disorder agoraphobia? A community study. *Psychological Medicine*, **25**, 405–11.

Snarey, J. (1998). Ego development and the ethical voices of justice and care: An Eriksonian Interpretation. In *Personality Development: Theoretical, Empirical, and Clinical Investigations of Loevinger's Conception of Ego Development*, ed. P. M. Westenberg, A. Blasi & L. D. Cohn, pp. 163–80. Mahwah, NJ: Lawrence Erlbaum Associates.

Thyer, B. A. (1993). Childhood separation anxiety disorder and adult-onset agoraphobia: review of evidence. In *Anxiety across the Lifespan: A Developmental Perspective*, ed. C. G. Last, pp. 128–47. New York: Springer.

Tracey, S. A., Chorpita, B. F., Douban, J. & Barlow, D. H. (1997). Empirical evaluation of DSM–IV generalized anxiety disorder criteria in children and adolescents. *Journal of Clinical Child Psychology*, **26**, 404–14.

Wenar, C. (1990). Childhood fears and phobias. In *Handbook of Developmental Psychopathology*, ed. M. Lewis & S. M. Miller, pp. 281–90. New York: Plenum Press.

Westenberg, P. M., Blasi, A. & Cohn, L. D. (ed.) (1998a). *Personality Development: Theoretical, Empirical, and Clinical Investigations of Loevinger's conception of ego development*. Mahwah, NJ: Lawrence Erlbaum Associates.

Westenberg, P. M. & Block, J. (1993). Ego development and individual differences in personality. *Journal of Personality and Social Psychology*, **65**, 792–800.

Westenberg, P. M. & Gjerde, P. F. (1999). Ego development during the transition from adolescence to young adulthood: A nine-year longitudinal study. *Journal of Research in Personality*, **33**, 233–52.

Westenberg, P. M., Jonckheer, J., Treffers, Ph. D. A. & Drewes, M. (1998b). Ego development in children and adolescents: Another side of the Impulsive, Self-protective and Conformist ego levels. In *Personality Development: Theoretical, Empirical, and Clinical Investigations of Loevinger's Conception of Ego Development*, ed. P. M. Westenberg, A. Blasi & L. D. Cohn, pp. 89–112. Mahwah, NJ: Lawrence Erlbaum Associates.

Westenberg, P. M., Siebelink, B. M., Warmenhoven, N. J. C. & Treffers, Ph. D. A. (1999). Separation anxiety and overanxious disorders: Relations to age and level of psychosocial maturity. *Journal of the American Academy of Child and Adolescent Psychiatry*, **38**, 1000–7.

Westenberg, P. M., Treffers, Ph. D. A. & Drewes, M. J. (1998c). A new version of the WUSCT: The sentence completion test for children and youths (SCT-Y). In *Technical Foundations for Measuring Ego Development*, ed. J. Loevinger, pp. 81–9. Mahwah, NJ: Lawrence Erlbaum Associates.

5

Neuropsychiatry of paediatric anxiety disorders

Floyd R. Sallee and John S. March

Introduction

Progress in the neurobiology of childhood anxiety has recently focused on the effects of rearing and environment in the progression of anxiety states. Convergence of evidence from both child studies of stress and trauma (Pfefferbaum, 1997; Pynoos, Steinberg & Wrath, 1995) as well as primate rearing and deprivation studies (Coplan et al., 1996; Higley, Suomi & Linnoila, 1992) illustrate that the effects of stress in the genesis of anxiety disorder can be profound. Anxiety disorders are now viewed from a developmental perspective (Ollendick, 1998; Rosenberg & Keshavan, 1998) in which an individual's history of exposure to threat and that threat's developmental and cognitive context are interwoven with internal factors (e.g. genetic and neurophysiological) as keys to the individual's 'stress-response system'. Later in this chapter, neuroanatomical and information processing models of panic and childhood obsessive–compulsive disorders (OCD) are discussed in their developmental context in order to shed light on both the development of anxiety disorder and its frequent association with comorbid conditions, such as attention-deficit hyperactivity disorder (ADHD), in child psychiatry. The implication is clear: anxiety disorders, now viewed across the life span (Ballenger, 1997; Lydiard & Brawman-Mintzer, 1997), require treatments that reflect both the developmental stage and context of anxiety disorder genesis and maintenance.

Our understanding of the neurobiology of anxiety has been propelled by new pharmacological therapeutic tools specific in their impact on certain central nervous system (CNS) receptors within the 'stress-response system'. New studies detail the efficacy of serotonin-selective reuptake inhibitors (SSRIs) in the treatment of OCD (March & Leonard, 1998), separation anxiety, panic and social phobia (Birmaher, Yelovich & Renaud, 1998). While treatment research advances slowly, progress in the origins and mechanisms of anxiety specific to childhood is also still quite limited. Much of the work described in this chapter deals with discoveries of underlying neurobiology either from the adult literature, or with childhood onset disorder studied in adult life (e.g. childhood onset post-traumatic stress disorder (PTSD)). Very few studies are available on anxious children or adolescents but work is advancing (March & Leonard, 1998; Pine et al., 1998). Childhood anxiety continues to be thought of as a risk factor or prodromal condition to fully expressed adult disorder (e.g. panic disorder and social phobia). The premise therefore of this chapter concerning neurobiology is that neural pathways involved in adult anxiety are reflected in childhood syndromes. Conversely, some provocative studies (Sallee et al., 1996) suggest that the onset of anxiety in childhood may differ in important respects from patterns anticipated from adult studies, which in turn necessitates therapeutic approaches that are specifically geared to children.

With respect to chemically addressed neuroanatomy, major neurotransmitter systems that appear to be involved in pathological anxiety include the GABAergic/glutamatergic, noradrenergic and serotonergic systems with recent evidence also suggesting involvement of neuropeptides cholecystokinin, neuropeptide Y and corticotropin releasing hormone. Recent advances with regard to their involvement in the pathophysiology of anxiety are briefly explored with emphasis to relevant work in the child literature where applicable. The neurobiological correlates of anxiety (Rogeness et al., 1990) in relationship to concepts of stress system homeostasis (Chrousos & Gold, 1992) is presented to elucidate sympathetic system vulnerability put forth by Kagan, Reznick & Snidman (1988) in 'behavioral inhibition'. This temperamental characteristic appears to be an index of biological vulnerability which under certain circumstances (e.g. separation–stress exposure) can contribute to anxiety disorder generation (Ollendick, 1998). The hypothalamic-pituitary axis and the locus coeruleus/sympathetic system appear to work in concert to provide homeostasis, the dysregulation of which is likely to manifest itself in anxiety states in children. We will explore in some detail two examples of childhood anxiety disorders (e.g. obsessive–compulsive disorder and panic disorder) where neurodevelopmental models provide a conceptual framework for approaching the challenges of the field.

The anatomically and chemically addressed 'stress-response system'

The anatomically addressed 'threat-response' apparatus of the brain is broadly termed the reticular activating system, but includes beyond brain stem arousal structures, such as the locus coeruleus, limbic and anterior temporal and septal-hippocampal systems, connections between pre-frontal and orbital frontal cortex and striatum and, most broadly, cortical and subcortical structures, such as the anterior cingulate, that mediate orienting and sustained attention. Similarly, chemically addressed components of this system include the locus coeruleus, the major noradrenergic component of the reticular activating system (RAS), dorsal raphe serotonergic neurons, and mesolimbic and mesocortical dopaminergic neurons. These anatomically and chemically addressed anatomic components together constitute the final common pathway of distress reflected in the emotion of anxiety (Perry, 1998). The limbic system of the developing brain is the emotion-processing circuit, which perceives anxiety (Davis, 1992). Its multiple interrelated areas such as the amygdala and hippocampus are involved in the perception of threat, association and generalization, as well as storage into memory of threat-related cues (Perry, 1998).

These interrelated structures mature functionally in a developmentally defined sequence. In a recent review of anxiety invoked in primates by social separation, Kalin (1993) describes the stages of an increasing fear response in young rhesus monkeys as vocalization and activation followed by a motionless 'freeze' to avoid detection, with hostile grimacing in its most extreme form. The ontogeny of these anxious responses (fully developed in 9–12-week animals) corresponds to the maturation of the stress-response system including the prefrontal cortex, amygdala and hypothalamus. An analogous time period in humans is 7–12 months when the prefrontal cortex activity increases and marked stranger anxiety is present. Kalin describes a similar maturational time frame for the hypothalamic region when after maternal separation corticotropin level increases are most profound at 9–12 weeks in rhesus. Each of these areas of the stress-response system have been examined in children but studies have mainly focused on brain stem arousal mechanisms, especially the locus coeruleus.

The locus coeruleus is a grouping of norepinephrine-containing neurons originating in the pons but projecting to all major brain areas. As such, the locus coeruleus functions as the general regulator of noradrenergic tone and activity. The locus coeruleus initiates and maintains the body's response to threat and plays a key role in the interpretation of incoming sensory information (Abercrombie & Jacobs, 1987). For example, suffocation cues (Klein, 1993), important in the carbon dioxide (CO_2) challenge paradigm of panic disorder, are interpreted by the locus coeruleus where rising CO_2 levels result in its increased neuronal discharge. These suffocation cues appear to be present in children with asthma, but are apparently missing in children with congenital central hypoventilation syndrome (Pine et al., 1994). Sensitivity to these cues and respiratory response may differentiate children with anxiety disorder, and separation anxiety in particular (Pine et al., 1998). Acute stress, in this example CO_2 challenge, results in increased release of catecholamine by the locus coeruleus throughout the brain and the rest of the body.

Hypothalamic and thalamic nuclei also play a role in the coordinated response to threat and serve to transmit arousal information from the reticular activating system (e.g. locus coeruleus) to limbic and cortical areas involved in sensory integration and perception. The thalamus has been hypothesized to play a role in the perception of anxiety (Castro-Alamancos & Connors, 1996), and hypothalamic nuclei mediate the neuroendocrine and neuroimmune response to stress. Hypothalamic neurochemistry is related to the behavioural fear repertoire as primates with relatively lower levels of cortisol 'freeze' for shorter periods compared to peers with higher levels of cortisol. These stress responses are heritable and by 5 months the young rhesus monkey stress responses mimic that of the mother both in duration of behaviour and corticotropin level. In children, those with high basal cortisol levels are likely to show greater behavioural inhibition in a novel situation (Kagan et al., 1988). The hypothalamic–pituitary axis has been extensively associated with stress, with cortisol identified as the 'stress' hormone along with cortisol-releasing hormone (CRH), implicated in the pathogenesis of panic disorder in man. Few anxiety patients exhibit nonsuppression of cortisol after dexamethasone (Coryell et al., 1989; Sheehan et al., 1986) but the response to CRH stimulation indicates a sensitized hypothalamic-pituitary axis (Yehuda et al., 1995). The link between the hypothalamic-pituitary axis and locus coeruleus is found in CRH stimulation of locus coeruleus activtiy (Owens & Nemeroff, 1991). Serotonin system modulation may also be involved as 5-HT1A agonist antianxiety drugs stimulate hypothalamic-pituitary axis activity and CRH release in particular.

Interestingly, findings from a rhesus separation anxiety model suggest involvement of the locus coeruleus/sympathetic system as well as the hypothalamic-pituitary axis stress response system (Chrousos & Gold, 1992) in modulating the effects of separation. Early postnatal handling and social isolation effect the HPA stress response by altering feedback mechanisms (e.g. glucocorticoid receptor) in the hippocampus and the frontal cortex (Meaney & Aitken, 1985). In the adult animal, environmental factors such as social rank work in concert with underlying neurobiology (temperament) to determine stress response (Sapolsky, 1990). In rhesus infants the interaction with a nuturing mother influences subsequent fear behaviours (Champoux, Higley & Suomi, 1997), as peer-raised animals have increased fear-related behaviours, higher cortisol and corticotropin, and increased alcohol consumption (Higley et al., 1991*a,b*) compared to maternal reared animals. Peer-only reared rhesus also have higher levels of cerebrospinal fluid (CSF) 5-HIAA and norepinephrine metabolite 3-methoxy-4-hydroxyphenylglycol (MHPG) than maternal reared animals. Upon separation, the MHPG concentration increases and remains elevated throughout the separation while 5-HIAA returns to baseline by 4 weeks.

Most of the naturalistic neurobiological data available in childhood anxiety deals with hypothalamic-pituitary axis involvement. Studies early in life in 1-year-old infants showing extreme distress when separated from their mothers demonstrate that urinary cortisol is elevated (Tennes, Downey & Vernadakis, 1977). In concert with this finding, it has been demonstrated that significant maternal deprivation stress early in life can promote changes in the hypothalamic-pituitary axis that persist into childhood (Ladd, Owens & Nemeroff, 1996). Furthermore, cortisol reactivity predicts anxiety and inhibition of social behaviour in school-aged populations (Tennes & Kreye, 1985). Salivary cortisol appears to be elevated in young children showing extreme inhibition in social situations, defined by Kagan et al. (1988) as 'behavioural inhibition'. Inhibited children had significantly higher cortisol levels than uninhibited children both in the home and in the laboratory. Kagan, Reznick & Snidman (1987) theorized that the hypothalamic-pituitary axis of inhibited children is tonically at a higher level of activity even in minimal stress situations. The opposite seems to be apparent for children who have been maltreated or traumatized (Hart, Gunnar & Cicchetti, 1995). Traumatized children exhibit reduced cortisol reactivity and fail to show elevations of cortisol in high social conflict situations as is found for normal children (Hart et al., 1995). Corticotropin-releasing hormone challenge in sexually abused children results in a blunted corticotropin (ACTH) (DeBellis et al., 1994). In contrast, depressed abused children seem to exhibit an augmented response of ACTH in response to CRH challenge (Kaufman et al., 1997), with augmented ACTH response to corticotropin-releasing hormone perhaps indicative of the effects of chronic ongoing stress rather than the effect of acute but remote trauma (Kaufman et al., 1997). The psychobiological effects of trauma in children are both developmentally and environmentally dependent. Though children with PTSD are prone to hypothalamic-pituitary axis dysregulation, factors such as (1) age at onset of abuse, (2) placement history, (3) present stressors and social supports and (4) family psychopathology are important contributing factors (Kaufman et al., 1997). Hypothalamic-pituitary axis dysregulation can occur in the context of comorbid anxiety states as well. For example, salivary cortisol was significantly elevated in conduct disordered children with comorbid anxiety disorder

(McBurnett et al., 1991) and anxiety symptoms exhibited a dose-response effect with increasing cortisol levels.

The limbic system, which as noted earlier includes anatomically or functionally related areas such as the amygdala, hippocampus, anterior cingulate and orbito-frontal cortex, is involved as a neuronal filter concerned with the interpretation of sensory information. In a manner analogous to the locus coeruleus which orchestrates arousal, the amygdala plays a central role in emotional processing of afferent and efferent connections involving sensory input, complex multisensory perceptions, cognitive abstractions and socially relevant stimuli (Perry, 1998; Selden et al., 1991). Functional imaging studies of anxiety disordered patients using provocation paradigms implicate the anterior paralimbic structures as key in symptomatic anxiety states (Rauch & Shin, 1997). Specific structures however are activated during provocation depending upon the underlying anxiety diagnoses. The caudate nucleus seems to be specifically activated with OCD symptoms while post-traumatic stress disorder may specifically activate the right amygdala and deactivate left-sided structures (Rauch & Shin, 1997). The hippocampus, another key limbic component, is involved in the storage and recall of cognitive and emotional memory (Selden et al., 1991). The hippocampus is sensitive to 'stress activation' such that the storage of certain types of cognitive information (e.g. verbal) is affected while nonverbal information is not altered. Recollections of traumatic experiences are often fragments of sensory components of the event with the capacity to 'tell' what is actually occurring much later (Van der Kolk, Burbridge & Suzuki, 1997). Cognitive distortions associated with the development of anxiety disorders (Pynoos et al., 1995) may be related to anxiety-induced disruptions of storage (often of sensory fragments with limited linguistic component) in hippocampal and related cortical association areas. This fragmentation appears to be independent of developmental stage or age at which the trauma occurs though very young children also have been theorized to form somatic more than linguistic memories (Siegel, 1995).

Stress has been shown to damage the hippocampus, with considerable evidence from both primate and rodent models of both functional (e.g. impaired learning and memory) and structural (e.g. reduced cell sprouting) damage (Sapolsky, 1996). The pyramidal hippocampal cells atrophy and neurogenesis shuts down in the dentate gyrus with repeated stress (McEwen, 1999). If stress is severe or prolonged, the pyramidal neurons die and the hippocampus atrophies. Presumably hippocampal damage occurs either by direct action of glucocorticoids, or indirectly through extracellular accumulation of excitatory amino acids such as glutamate (Bremner et al., 1996; Yehuda et al., 1995).

Neuroimaging studies of PTSD patients confirm a shrinkage of hippocampal volume with chronic stress (Bremner et al., 1995, Gurvits et al., 1996, Stein et al., 1997).

Perry (1998) argues for the sequential, use-dependent development of the brain which martials neuronal migration, differentiation, and processes of neurophysiological organization in response to the environment. Use-dependent development holds that the developing brain is extremely experience-sensitive. With the caveat that resiliency is poorly understood albeit critically important to understanding stress responsivity (Cicchetti et al., 1993), a corrolary assumption is that children exposed to traumatic experience should be expected to develop anxiety-regulation problems (Schwarz & Perry, 1994). Parenthetically, an environment which includes prenatal exposure to psychoactive drugs also might disrupt normal development, particularly in the stress-response system, hippocampal organization and hypothlamic-pituitary axis functioning (Perry, 1998). Animal studies have delineated exposure to certain stimulant drugs as an environmental stressor which may permanently impair the stress-response mechanism throughout life to both stress and stimulant drugs producing cross sensitization (Antelman & Chiodo, 1983). This may occur as a result of stimulant induced activation of the hypothalamic-pituitary axis through corticotropin releasing hormone and glucocorticoid hormones of the adrenal cortex (Kuhn & Francis, 1997). HPA activation can enhance stimulant sensitization as administration of CRH centrally enhances the loco-motor response to a single stimulant dose, while CRH antagonists retard the development of stimulant induced sensitization (Cador et al., 1993; Cole et al., 1990). It is believed that 'vulnerability' to stimulant administration can be predicted by magnitude of the HPA response to a novel stressor (Piazza & Le Moal, 1996). One theory suggests that reactivity of central CRH neurons to external events represents a critical factor in stimulant sensitization (Kuhn & Francis, 1997). If this were true then prenatally exposed children may, as a consequence of that exposure, have an altered responsivity to not only stress but to members of the stimulant drug class. Salivary cortisol levels in cocaine-exposed infants are normal under baseline conditions, but these infants are blunted in their cortisol response to stressful stimuli compared to controls (Magnano, Gardner & Karmel, 1992). Children at risk for substance abuse, with substance abusing fathers, also secrete less cortisol than controls before and after an anticipated stressor (Moss, Vanyukov & Martin, 1995). Children at risk for substance abuse appear to be cortisol hyporesponsive in contrast to shy and inhibited children who appear to hypersecrete cortisol in response stress (Kagan et al., 1988).

'Stress-response system' neurochemistry and pharmacotherapeutics

Noradrenergic system

The neurobiology of fear and anxiety to a large extent has focused on the noradrenergic system with much support from animal studies and animal models of anxiety (Redmond & Huang, 1979). Increased noradrenergic function has been associated with state anxiety measures in normal volunteers (Ballenger et al., 1984), and in panic patients (Ko et al., 1983). The locus coeruleus is the major nucleus for brain noradrenergic activity with overactivation a common pathway to a production of fear (Charney & Redmond, 1983). Preclinical and clinical studies (Charney & Heninger, 1986) suggest that dysregulation in the noradrenergic pathway is involved in the development of anxiety disorder.

The functioning of the noradrenergic system is highly regulated with important feedback monitoring attributed to the α_2-adrenergic autoreceptor. Central α_2-adrenoceptors have been investigated using peripheral markers such as the platelet indexed by tritiated ligands such as [H3]clonidine and [H3]yohimbine. Lowered α_2-adrenoceptor densities are found in platelets of panic-disordered patients (Cameron et al., 1990; Charney, Woods & Heninger, 1989), furthermore the [H3] clonidine determined Bmax for the platelet α_2-adrenoceptor appears to be associated with symptom severity in panic (Cameron et al., 1990). Subsensitivity of the post-synaptic α_2-adrenoreceptor has been implicated in panic, generalized anxiety disorder (GAD) and inferred from clonidine stimulated growth hormone release although other neurotransmitter systems are also involved (Uhde et al., 1992). Blunting of growth hormone release following clonidine challenge is one of the most robust and stable of findings in adult patients suffering from panic (Charney & Heninger, 1986), GAD (Abelson et al., 1991), social phobia (Tancer et al., 1993) and perhaps OCD (Brambilla et al., 1997). This subsensitivity is potentially the result of long-term locus coeruleus activity which, over time, leads to a downregulation of hypothalamic α_2-adrenergic postsynaptic receptors, which mediate growth hormone release. As shown in Figure 5.1, a recent study utilizing the clonidine challenge paradigm in children with anxiety disorder has failed to find growth hormone blunting and in fact has documented hypersecretion of growth hormone in comparison to normal controls (Sallee et al., 1996). Yohimbine, an α_2-adrenergic antagonist, increases release of norepinephrine in the hippocampus and increases the firing of the locus coeruleus. Yohimbine can produce both the behavioural and biological correlates of anxiety as well as induce panic attacks in patients with panic disorder. The quick onset and

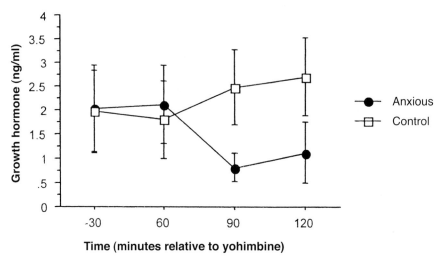

Fig. 5.1. Concentration-time curve of growth hormone in plasma (ng/ml) in anxious ($n = 17$) and control ($n = 15$) children in relationship to oral administration of yohimbine (5.4 mg) at time zero. RMANOVA demonstrates that growth hormone output is significantly lower for anxiety disordered compared to normal control subjects. Error bars are ± standard deviations with means plotted for each group.

limited duration of yohimbine effects on plasma levels of norepinephrine metabolite 3-methoxy-4-hydroxyphenylglycol (MHPG), diastolic blood pressure, and increased patient ratings of anxiety suggest that the sum total of effect is largely reflective of presynaptic norepinephrine activity. Yohimbine challenge in the same anxious child cohort increased anxiety ratings but did not produce panic (Sallee et al., unpublished data). Yohimbine in anxious children demonstrated blunting of GH, in concert with adult anxiety studies (Sallee et al., unpublished data; Figure 5.2).

The above adrenergic challenge outcomes in children, though somewhat incongruous with adult findings, may have implications for the development of anxiety disorder and its treatment in childhood. It might be that early in the course of anxiety disorder generation, sufficient exposure of the locus coeruleus to an overactive noradrenergic system has not yet led to post-synaptic α_2-adrenoceptor downregulation. This would suggest that therapies, directed at the presynaptic α_2-adrenoceptor, would be particularly effective in childhood anxiety and possibly preventative with respect to progression of disease. Positive reports are available regarding the utility of clonidine (α_2-adrenergic agonist) in the treatment of traumatized and abused children with PTSD symptoms (Donnelly, Amaya-Jackson & March, 1999). Furthermore, agents such as clonidine and guanfacine appear to prevent stress-induced cognitive

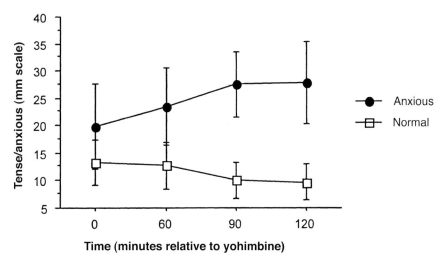

Fig. 5.2. Self-reported tenseness ratings, by visual analogue mood rating, over time in anxious ($n = 17$) and control ($n = 15$) children following 5.4 mg oral dose of yohimbine at time zero.

deficits particularly in working memory (Arnsten, 1999). Stress-induced cognitive effects can also be prevented by treatments that block either the D1 dopamine or α_1-adrenergic receptors (Arnsten, 1999). Unfortunately for paediatric psychopharmacology, neither of these intervention strategies are currently practical. There is a way however to alter dopamine availability indirectly, as serotonin can have a significant inhibitory effect on dopamine transmission. This strategy is now clinically useful in childhood anxiety, through increasing serotonin availability by using another SSRI (el Mansari, Bouchard & Blier, 1995; Kratchovil et al., 1999).

Serotonin

Serotonergic mechanisms have been implicated in the production of anxiety for GAD, panic disorder (Westenberg, den Boer & Kahn, 1987) and OCD (Stein & Uhde, 1995). Lines of evidence from animal (Chopin & Briley, 1987) and clinical studies indicate that the serotonin (5-HT) system plays an important role in the mediation of fear and anxiety (Heninger & Charney, 1988). In nonhuman primates, high CSF concentrations of serotonin metabolite 5-HIAA is associated with increased anxiety, fear and maternal separation (Higley & Suomi, 1989; Higley et al., 1992) and the turnover of monoamine neurotransmitters appears to be relatively stable and highly heritable (Higley et al., 1993). Evidence of such a role for 5-HT is indirect in childhood anxiety, stemming largely from treatment studies with SSRIs (DeVane & Sallee, 1996; Leonard et al., 1997; reviewed in Kratchovil et al., in press). Both open label (Apter et al.,

1994; Birmaher et al., 1994), and controlled trials of SSRIs support a role for 5-HT in childhood anxiety, particularly in OCD (Riddle et al., 1992, 1996). Evidence of developmental modulation of the 5-HT system includes: a decline of cerebrospinal concentrations of 5-HT metabolite 5-HIAA with age (Riddle et al., 1986), ontogenic changes in 5-HT receptor densities (Saxena, 1995) with specific nonlinear developmental changes in 5-HT_2 receptor (Biegon & Greuner, 1992), and decreases in neuroendocrine response to dl-fenfluramine challenge with age (McBride et al., 1990). As 5-HT neurotransmission decreases along an age continuum (Seifert, Foxx & Butler, 1980), and as decreased 5-HT turnover may be pivotal for the presence of anxiety, particularly OCD symptoms (Rosenberg & Keshavan, 1998), age of onset and its relationship to symptom severity should be developmentally determined (Rosenberg et al., 1997a).

Availability of 5-HT may also play a critical role in the response of OCD to serotonin transmission enhancement. Supportive evidence comes from an elegant treatment study of children with OCD (Swedo et al., 1992), which indicates that the more abnormal the CSF level of 5-HT metabolite 5-HIAA, the greater the patient's response to clomipramine treatment. Long-term (i.e. 2–7 year) prospective follow-up shows the prognosis of these very same OCD patients to be correlated with initial clomipramine response (Leonard et al., 1993). Leonard et al. (1993) speculate that pharmacotherapy may potentially improve long-term prognosis. These authors compared patients from an earlier study (Flament et al., 1990) who were largely untreated (28%) and exhibited greater symptom severity at follow-up compared to a largely treated group (96%), even though the two cohorts were indistinguishable in baseline severity and interim treatment interventions.

Commonly, the serotonergic dimension of childhood anxiety has been evaluated indirectly with peripheral blood markers, either whole blood 5-HT or platelet serotonin transporter (5HTPR) (Hanna, Yuwiler & Coates, 1995; Sallee et al., 1996). For example, childhood OCD is marked by reduced presynaptic 5HTPR capacity (Sallee et al., 1996), which should affect 5-HT turnover, and could lead to postsynaptic hypersensitivity. Indirect evidence of 5-HT hypersensitivity in children includes a positive correlation of OCD symptom severity and cerebrospinal fluid concentrations of 5-HT metabolite 5-hydroxyindoleacetic acid (5-HIAA) (Swedo et al., 1992).

In OCD adults, reduced postsynaptic 5-HT responsivity is hypothesized, based on challenge findings of prolactin (PRL) blunting in response to d-fenfluramine (Lucey et al., 1992; Monteleone et al., 1997a,b). Fenfluramine, a phenylethylamine derivative, potently releases presynaptic 5-HT and inhibits

5-HT uptake (Stein & Uhde, 1995), effectively impacting the entire 5-HT transmission system. Racemic fenfluramine has been used safely as a 5-HT challenge in children (Halperin et al., 1994, 1997). In racemic form, dl-fenfluramine also affects central noradrenergic and dopaminergic systems (Invernizzi et al., 1986) and is known to increase central availability for dopamine (Smith et al., 1997), though the PRL response is thought to be mediated by postsynaptic $5\text{-}HT_2 / 5\text{-}HT_{1c}$ receptor subtypes (Quattrome et al., 1983). Fenfluramine challenge differentiates childhood anxiety disorder from controls by reduced responsivity (e.g. lower self-rated anxiety and lower systolic blood pressure) in the anxious group (Sallee et al., unpublished data), but PRL response does not discriminate between groups. Only an OCD subgroup demonstrates an augmented PRL response (Sallee et al., unpublished data). In contrast, the adult literature reports selective anxiogenic effects of dl-fenfluramine (Targum, 1990) and a blunted PRL response in OCD specifically. Reconciling adult and child fenfluramine challenge data suggests that OCD may involve presynaptic dysfunction in children which could extend to postsynaptic disturbance over time in the adult. Some have advocated that studies closer to the onset of illness, often prior to treatment intervention, can give clarity to pathophysiology particularly in reference to OCD (Rosenberg et al., 1997a,b). Certainly adults with treatment-refractory illness typically report early onset of disease. Commonly many adults (65%) with a history of anxiety disorders have had two or more anxiety disorders as children and adults with panic disorder frequently report a history of childhood anxiety (e.g. separation anxiety) (Pollack et al., 1996).

Dopamine

The dopamine system plays a modulatory role with regard to the 'stress-response' system, often acting indirectly through serotonin pathways. There appears to be an inverse relationship between brain dopamine and serotonin, which is neurodevelopmentally based. In the prefrontal cortex, dopaminergic innervation in nonhuman primates changes dramatically during adolescence before stabilizing in the adult. In contrast, serotonergic innervation of the prefrontal cortex is fully developed much earlier in the life-cycle (Goldman-Rakic & Brown, 1982; Rosenberg & Lewis, 1994; Rosenberg & Keshavan, 1998). Specifically, the delicate balance between dopamine and serotonin is changing, producing a relative excess of dopamine transmission during the age of onset of certain anxiety disorders (e.g. OCD) (Rosenberg & Keshavan, 1998). In as far as increased activity of the direct basal ganglia pathway (Baxter et al., 1996) compared to the indirect pathway plays a major role in pathophysiology of disorders such as OCD, dopaminergic modulation can represent a therapeutic strategy (McDougle et al., 1990). Dopamine D1 receptor stimulation results in activation of the direct basal ganglia pathway while D2 stimulation inhibits the indirect pathway (Gerfen, 1992). Both of these actions would tend to exacerbate OCD symptoms resulting in increased intrusive thoughts and behaviours (D1 activation) and lessened ability to inhibit these intrusive thoughts (D2 activation). For this reason, dopamine blockade, particularly by mixed D1/D2 antagonists favouring D1 are used as adjunctive agents in treatment-resistant OCD (McDougle et al., 1990).

GABA-ergic/glutamatergic neurotransmission

Direct characterization of neurochemistry in childhood anxiety is limited but recent advances, particularly in OCD, have implicated the glutamatergic pathway by utilizing proton magnetic resonance spectroscopy (Moore et al., 1998). Glutamatergic pathways project from the medial prefrontal cortex to the anterior striatum, nucleus accumbens and substantia nigra providing a crucial modulatory role in the striatum. Stress is known to increase the release of excitatory amino acids such as glutamate, particularly in the prefrontal cortex and is thought to indirectly increase dopaminergic release, which feeds back ultimately to modulate glutamatergic transmission (Kalivas, Duffy & Barrow, 1989). Disruption of the glutamatergic pathway may also be the cause or the result of serotonin abnormalities in the caudate relative to OCD (Moore et al., 1998). Glutamatergic abnormalities may also underlie selective deficits in neurobehavioural response inhibition on oculomotor delayed response tasks in children with OCD, which suggests a maturation failure of the frontostriatal circuit (Rosenberg et al., 1997b). Glutamate, which appears to be in delicate balance with serotonin in the caudate, may provide a new therapeutic target for OCD treatment (Rosenberg & Keshavan, 1998).

Neuropeptides

Two important peptide modulators of anxious behaviour appear to be neuropeptide Y (NPY) and cholecystokinin (CCK). NPY is abundant in the hypothalamus, limbic system and cortex with a regulatory function implied in neuroendocrine and autonomic systems. Disturbed NPY transmission has been implicated in clinical symptoms of anxiety (Heilig & Widerlov, 1990). In rodents, central administration of NPY produces an anxiolytic effect. Modulation of anxiety in rodents has been achieved through use of an antisense oligodeoxynucleotide aimed at mimicking the NPY-Y1 receptor mRNA rendering these receptors nonfunctional (Wahlestedt & Reis, 1993). NPY-Y1 receptor binding was decreased by 60% while NPY-Y2 receptors were unaffected by antisense NPY Y1 mRNA. After two days of direct intracerebroventricular (i.c.v.) injection, rodents were tested using an elevated plus maze (a pharmacologically validated animal model of anxiety), with those antisense-treated animals sustaining a dramatic anxiolytic effect similar to that seen with benzodiazepines.

Another peptide that may play a role in anxiety is CCK-4 tetrapeptide (the active moiety of CCK). Recent challenge studies in humans (controls and panic patients) with parenteral CCK-4 has elicited panic in a dose-dependent fashion and can selectively differentiate panic patients from controls (Bradwejn, Koszycki & Shriqui, 1991). CCK functions both as a neurotransmitter itself and as a modulator for classical neurotransmitters such as dopamine, serotonin, GABA and excitatory amino acids. In the forebrain, CCK is localized in GABA neurons and its release is under tonic GABAergic control. Forebrain CCK receptor number correlates with anxiety states induced by anxiogenic β-carboline, or noncompetitive GABA antagonism causing an upregulation of CCK binding sites. CCK effects can also be blocked by 5-HT3 receptor antagonism and chronic imipramine treatment protects patients with panic disorder from the effects of CCK-4 challenge. Animal and human data point to CCK as an anticipatory stress modulator whose abnormal regulation may play a role in anxiety disorder. Lydiard et al. (1992) has reported decreased concentrations of cerebrospinal fluid CCK-8S in panic patients as compared to nonpanic patients and normal controls. Most direct investigation comes from the use of CCK-related peptides as challenge agents to induce anxiety states in patients and normal controls. From recent studies in patients with panic disorders, CCK-4 (25–50 µg) and CCK-5 (pentagastrin) (0.6 µg/kg) have consistently elicited panic-like symptoms under a challenge paradigm and in a dose-dependent fashion (Abelson & Nesse, 1990; Bradwejn et al., 1992). The attacks provoked by CCK-4 were rated by patients as very similar or identical to those experienced spontaneously. CCK-4 is a selective CCKB agonist thereby implicating these receptors in panic attack generation though CCKA may also be involved in animal models. Anxious monkeys who are more restless, submissive to threat, and excessively reactive to their environment are most sensitive to CCK-4 and react to lower doses than conspecifics, reacting to higher doses with frozen immobility, cowering and withdrawal.

Neuropeptides studied in child populations include CSF somatostatin (Kruesi et al., 1990). Somatostatin itself may stimulate serotonin release and somatostatin analogue 'Sandostatin' reduces panic-like attacks in patients with 'idiopathic flushing' (Abelson, Nesse & Vinik, 1990). Kruesi et al. (1990) found decreased somatostatin levels in disruptive behaviour disorders relative to OCD patients but a direct comparison to normal controls was not possible. Leckman et al. (1988) examined dynorphin A in Tourette disorder patients with comorbid OCD and found that dynorphin levels correlated with severity of OCD symptoms. Swedo et al. (1992) studied dynorphin A in CSF of children and adolescents with primary OCD. In contrast, these authors found no relationship between dynorphin A and OCD symptoms but a significant and negative association between arginine vasopressin concentration and OCD symptom severity. Dynorphin-related peptides may impact upon the hypothalamic-pituitary axis in that they are cotransmitters within populations of hypothalamic neurons secreting CRF. CRF and dynorphin-related peptides have reciprocal actions on the release of each other, with CRF stimulating dynorphin secretion and dynorphin inhibiting CRF release. Dynorphin 17 significantly inhibits the activating actions of CRF on the locus coeruleus (Overton & Fisher, 1989).

Models of childhood anxiety disorder

Panic disorder

Ollendick (1998) in a recent review highlights the varying clinical features of panic disorder expression in children and adolescents within the context of a developmental model. Drawing from the work of Clark (1986), based on the distinction between somatic and cognitive symptoms of panic, panic attacks are conceptualized to result from 'catastrophic misinterpretation' of bodily sensations. Shortness of breath, loss of control, shakiness are part of a vicious cycle that culminates in a panic attack and ultimately in panic disorder. Examples from Nelles & Barlow (1988), and Chorpita, Albano & Barlow (1996) argue that children's cognitive responses to somatic symptoms point to the external due to their inability for catastrophic misinterpretation, and illustrate the importance of cognitive development and context in internal attribution. Support for this comes from the construct of 'anxiety sensitivity' (fear of bodily sensations perceived as heralding a catastrophic event) potentially viewed as a risk factor for adult anxiety disorder. Anxiety sensitivity was surveyed using the child version of the Anxiety Sensitivity Index (Silverman et al., 1991) across ages 7–17 years amongst clinic-referred children. Evidence for anxiety sensitivity as such was only evident in children 12 years and older, clearly in concert with cognitive development (but see Weems et al., 1998).

Ollendick (1998) however reported a path-analytic evaluation of 649 unselected youth between the ages of 12–17 years, 16% of which reported at least one fully developed panic attack (King et al., 1997). Age was a key factor in panic group status and demonstrated a relationship to anxiety and fear. Though age was important, other factors such as self-reported anxiety, depression, fear and perceived home stress were also directly and positively related to panic attack group status (Ollendick, 1998).

In Mattis & Ollendick (1997*a*), cognitive responses to somatic symptoms of panic were elucidated in children 8, 11 and 14 years of age. In contrast to what would have been predicted based on Clark (1986), the majority (87%) at each age level reported psychophysiological conceptions for somatic symptoms of panic on the Conception of Illness Questionnaire. The final outcome of Mattis & Ollendick (1997*a*) was the demonstration that both younger and older (i.e. adolescent) children were able to interpret somatic symptoms of panic as signals of 'losing control', or 'going crazy'. Ollendick (1998) suggests that internal attributional style in response to negative outcomes and anxiety sensitivity are significantly predictive of internal catastrophic thoughts in children in a manner similar to that found for adolescents (Ollendick, 1998) and adults (Barlow, 1988).

Mattis & Ollendick (1997*b*) recently adapted the concept of biological vulnerability and Barlow's (1988) model of overreactivity to the stress of negative life events by focusing on the construct of temperament as the index of that vulnerability. Separation stress in their model provides the learned association between distress reactivity and interoceptive cues critical in the establishment of learned anxious apprehension over the possibility of future alarms. Ollendick (1998) noted that 'children who evince high distress reactivity combined with low self-regulatory ability (behaviorally inhibited children) and failure to regulate distress through caregiver contact (i.e. insecure-ambivalently attached children) are seen as most at risk for the experience of heightened distress reactivity from which escape is blocked, or at least made difficult' (p. 242). In the model, children who experience prolonged or heightened reactivity will conceptualize separation and its associated somatic alarms as frightening and would develop anxious apprehension concerning its recurrence and ultimately develop anxiety sensitivity. Hence, separation-anxiety per se can be viewed as a developmental way-station leading to panic disorder.

Obsessive–compulsive disorder

While controversies abound regarding the relationship between separation anxiety and panic disorder, many consider OCD the paradigmatic neuro-psychiatric disorder (for a comprehensive review see March & Leonard, 1998). Treatment with serotonin enhancing agents initially led to a neurobehavioural explanation for OCD in the form of the 'serotonin hypothesis' (reviewed in Barr et al., 1992). Later, phenomenological similarities between obsessive–compulsive symptoms (washing, picking and licking) coupled with studies of trichotillomania lead to the hypothesis that OCD is (in some patients) a 'grooming behaviour gone awry' (Swedo, 1989). Evidence favouring a neuro-psychiatric model of the etiopathogenesis of OCD includes: (1) family genetic studies suggesting that OCD and Tourette syndrome may in some, but not all, cases represent alternate expressions of the same gene(s), may represent different genes, or may arise spontaneously (Pauls et al., 1986); (2) neuroimaging studies implicating abnormalities in circuits linking basal ganglia to cortex (Rapoport, 1992; Rauch et al., 1994; Swedo et al., 1989b), with these circuits 'responding' to either cognitive–behavioural or pharmacological treatment with a SRI (Baxter et al., 1992); and (3) neurotransmitter and neuroendocrine abnormalities in childhood-onset OCD (Hamburger et al., 1989; Swedo & Rapoport, 1990).

Of these lines of evidence, the relationship between OCD and Tourette syndrome is particularly relevant (Cohen & Leckman, 1994). It is now well documented that there is an increased rate of tic disorders in individuals with OCD; the converse is also true (Pauls et al., 1995). Additionally, in systematic family genetic studies of probands with Tourette syndrome or other tic disorders, first degree relatives show an increased rate of both tic disorders and of OCD (Pauls et al., 1986). Similar findings are present in first degree relatives of OCD probands (Leonard et al., 1992). Interestingly, Pauls and colleagues note that early onset may indicate a greater degree of genetic vulnerability (Pauls et al., 1995).

OCD symptoms arising or exacerbating in the context of group A beta haemolytic streptococcal infection may define a singular subgroup of children with OCD (Allen, Leonard & Swedo, 1995). Obsessive–compulsive symptoms are not uncommon in paediatric patients with Sydenham's chorea, which represents a neurological variant of rheumatic fever. Moreover, when compared with non-choreic rheumatic fever patients, OCD is far more common when chorea is present than when absent (Swedo et al., 1989a). Resembling rheumatic carditis, Sydenham's chorea is believed to represent an autoimmune inflammation of the basal ganglia triggered by antistreptococcal antibodies (Kiessling, Marcotte & Culpepper, 1994. Thus Swedo and colleagues have theorized that OCD in the context of Sydenham's chorea may provide a medical model for the etiopathogenesis of OCD and tic disorders (Swedo et al., 1993). In this model, antineuronal antibodies formed against group A beta haemolytic streptococcal cell wall antigens are seen to cross-react with caudate neural tissue, with consequent initiation of OCD symptoms. In turn, this would suggest that acute onset or dramatic exacerbation of OCD or tic symptoms should prompt investigation of group A beta haemolytic streptococcal infection, especially since immunomodulatory treatments, including antibiotic therapies, may be of benefit to some patients (Swedo, Leonard & Kiessling, 1994).

In both instances – the relationship between OCD and Tourette syndrome and Paediatric Autoimmune Neuropsychiatric Disorder Associated with Strep (PANDAS) – one of the more striking findings over the past decade in adult and paediatric neuropsychiatry has been the repeated identification of abnormal information processing in cortico-striatal-thalamo-cortical (CSTC) circuitry both in OCD (Rapoport, Swedo & Leonard, 1992) and Tourette syndrome (Leckman et al., 1991). These hierarchically distributed neural networks (Mesulam, 1986) appear to modulate a wide range of domain-specific behaviours – including those mediated at the cortical level by supplementary motor, premotor, frontal eye fields, dorsolateral and orbitofrontal circuitry – such as the generation, maintenance, switching and blending of motor, mental, or emotional sets (Goldman & Selemon, 1990). CSTC computational functions are a property of the circuit as a whole and isolated from adjoining CSTC circuits; thus the behavioural/symptomatic consequences of dysregulation in CSTC circuits depends upon both lesion site and site-specific neurochemical factors (Goldman & Selemon, 1990). Because OCD at the symptomatic level is largely isolated from other areas of functioning – as illustrated, for example, by preservation of insight – it is generally assumed that neurocognitive 'overdrive' remains domain-specific as is the case for most operations within CSTC circuits, which operate in parallel (Saint-Cyr, Taylor & Nicholson, 1995).

The strongest evidence for CSTC involvement in OCD comes from imaging studies of OCD patients and controls using a variety of imaging methods (Baxter, 1992). With the caveat that inter-individual 'scatter' mandates cautious interpretation of the experimental data (Azari et al., 1993), studies in adults utilizing fluorodeoxyglucose positron emission tomographic (PET) scanning (Baxter et al., 1988) have found significant elevations in local cerebral glucose metabolic rates in the frontal cortex, orbital gyri and caudate nuclei of non-medicated OCD patients compared to depressed and normal controls (Baxter et al., 1988; Insel, 1992; Nordahl et al., 1989). Especially striking is the recent finding that these circuits are selectively activated in OCD adults presented with OCD-specific behavioural challenges (Rauch et al., 1994). Imaging studies more directly related to paediatric OCD also provide limited support for the proposed model. Luxenberg and colleagues found smaller caudate volumes on computerized tomography (CT) scans in 10 male adults with childhood onset OCD when compared to controls (Luxenberg et al., 1988). Swedo reported orbital frontal regional hypermetabolism and alterations in the left anterior cingulate in adults with childhood onset OCD (Swedo et al., 1989b). Interestingly, PET changes correlated positively with symptomatic improvement after both pharmacotherapy and behaviour therapy (Baxter et al., 1992; Schwartz et al., 1996). For both technical and ethical reasons, however, similar PET studies have yet to be done in young persons with OCD.

Understanding OCD at this level of analysis should help considerably to clarify taxonomic conundrums at the behavioural/symptomatic level (Enright & Beech, 1993; Yeates & Bornstein, 1994). For example, if tics, which usually are preceded by premonitory sensations, and compulsions, which usually are preceded by obsessional mental contents, can be represented at the level of functional neuroanatomy by hierarchically distributed neural networks linking basal ganglia to cortex (Cohen & Leckman, 1994), then the common clinical question 'Is it a complex tic or a tic-like compulsion?' will eventually yield to a scientific understanding of how cortico-striatal-thalamo-cortical circuits grade into each other as symptoms progress from OCD through comorbid OCD/Tourette syndrome to pure Tourette syndrome itself.

Baxter (1990) and others (Insel & Winslow, 1992; Modell et al., 1989; Rapoport, 1991) have integrated these findings into a model of OCD pathophysiology (Figure 5.3). In this model, OCD symptoms occur when an aberrant positive feedback loop develops in corticothalamic neuronal circuitry, which has been inadequately inhibited by ventromedial (limbic) portions of the striatum. Specifically, both ventral and dorsolateral frontal cortex provide direct (activitating) and indirect (inhibitory) input to the striatum, which in turn results in serial inhibition or disinhibition of associated thalamic relay nuclei. In OCD, a hypothesized imbalance in cortical output or in striatal inhibitory control or both leads to release of automatic obsessive (orbitofrontal) and compulsive (ventromedial striatum) behavioural routines, which in turn overpowers voluntary (indirect dorsolateral frontal cortex) control. From the point of view of the patient, Schwartz describes the resultant effect as an egodystonic failure to shift gears (Schwartz, 1996). In this model, serotonergic drug activity in OCD acts at direct circuit cortical and striatal targets to bolster inhibitory control, while cognitive-behavioural therapy acts primarily on the indirect circuit to moderate release of obsessive–compulsive symptomatology 'from the top down' (Baxter, personal communication, 1999). Interestingly, this model accounts for the failure of 'will' described by Janet (1903), namely deficient cortical inhibitory input (perceived by patients as weakened resistance

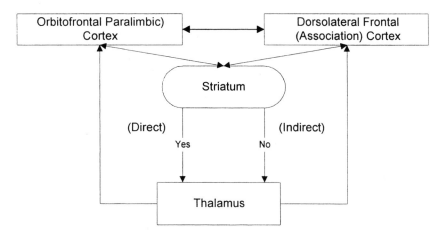

Fig. 5.3. CSTC neuronal circuitry.

to OCD) as seen in anxiety and depressive states, that Janet characterized as 'psychastenia' (Janet, 1903) and which some now associate with behavioural inhibition (Biederman et al., 1995). An experimental test of the hypothesis that SSRI and cognitive–behavioural therapy operate through different mechanisms is currently underway by the second author and others (David Rosenberg, Nili Benazon, personal communication, 1999).

Cognitive neuroscience as an integrative perspective

Despite these provocative neuroanatomical and neurochemical studies cited above as well as abundant data linking impairment in specific neurocognitive processes to paediatric emotional disorders (Harris, 1995; Rutter, 1999), the DSM–IV diagnostic criteria largely rely on behavioural symptoms (American Psychiatric Association, 1994). While this approach has advanced the cause of developmental neuropsychiatry by encouraging the formation of diagnostically homogeneous groups, underlying neuropsychological constructs are not well represented (Pennington & Welsh, 1995). Recent developments in the cognitive neurosciences, which have shown a remarkable ability to correlate functional neuroanatomy with CNS information processes (Gazzaniga, 1995), suggest a way out of this taxonomic conundrum, e.g. core neurocognitive processes, such as attention and fear and their interrelationship, inform most behavioural/symptomatic constructs (see for example Shaywitz & Shaywitz, 1991; Voeller, 1991) and so may provide one explanation for the extraordinary degree of comorbidity between neuropsychiatric disorders.

While neuropsychiatric disorders have been viewed neurocognitively as involving under- or over-allocation of attentional resources (Lorys-Vernon, Hynd & Lahey, 1990; Posner, 1993), it is critical to remember that allocation of CNS processing resources may be dysregulated at any of several information processing steps, including orienting of attention, sustained attention, visual-spatial-organizational skills, cognitive and/or behavioural inhibition and/or executive dysfunction (Hooper & March, 1995), each of which shares overlapping hierarchically distributed neural networks (Posner & Petersen, 1990). Note when engaging this issue that it is also crucial to avoid confusion over level of analysis (Fletcher & Taylor, 1984). Hence, although neurocognitive tests may both model symptomatic behaviour and reflect underlying CNS function, poor test performance does not permit inference of CNS dysfunction in the absence of experimental evidence linking different levels of analysis.

From the standpoint of paediatric neuropsychiatry, the contrast between ADHD and the anxiety disorders holds particular heuristic value. Anxiety disorders and ADHD contrast sharply in risk factors, developmental course and response to treatment. Curiously, however, these two apparently distinct psychopathological groupings, which together affect 10–15% of youths, share a high degree of comorbidity (Costello & Angold, 1995). Indeed, it is often difficult to determine whether the symptoms of restlessness, inattention and disorganization belong to one or the other of the disorders, which may imply that ADHD (as in selective attention to stimuli of more or less salience) and anxiety disorders (as in arousal effects on selective attention, especially to threat cues) share common underlying neurocognitive processes that result in comorbidity at the symptom level, while showing distinctive patterns at the neurocognitive level (Posner, 1993). For example, ADHD and anxiety disorders share inattentiveness and distractibility (cf. DSM–IV criteria), but one might hypothesize that ADHD children are distractible because their noradrenergically mediated automatic attention to sensory cues is underactivated, leading them to be underfocused; whereas pathologically anxious children are noradrenergically overactivated, causing high levels of vigilance to potentially threatening external cues. Although presenting behaviourally as 'distractible', highly anxious children might show highly efficient and precise automatic responses to sensory cues at the neurocognitive level, with ADHD the opposite. Behaviourally, both ADHD and anxiety-disordered children are easily disinhibited and therefore impulsive, but perhaps for quite different reasons. ADHD children could have low levels of response inhibition due to underactivation of response control mechanisms; whereas anxiety-disordered children under pressure might blur the distinction between target and nontarget stimuli, thus responding too often to both. In signal detection terms, children with ADHD have an altered response criterion bias, or beta-function, so that speed becomes more important than accuracy, while anxiety-disordered children have inefficient signal discrimination, or d-prime, so that anxiety is seen to interfere with distinguishing among a range of external cue characteristics. In both disorders the same neurocognitive systems are involved (arousal, activation, automatic and voluntary attention, vigilance), but take on different values (Epstein et al., 1997*a*,*b*).

While attention is a core component in the ADHD diagnostic (Barkley, Grodzinsky & DuPaul, 1992), numerous hypotheses regarding attentional dysfunction in ADHD have been proposed and later discarded (Conners et al., 1995). Current theories focus on dysregulation in short-term orienting of attention (Swanson et al., 1991) and vigilance or sustained attention. Attentional factors in anxiety-disordered adults are beginning to be explored along similar lines (Fox, 1994; McNally, 1995); however, much less has been done in the paediatric population (Harris, 1995). In a pioneering study, Pliszka compared children with non-anxious ADHD to children with comorbid ADHD and overanxious disorder and found that the combination of ADHD and anxiety disorder reduced the risk of comorbid conduct disorder, decreased impulsive responding on a continuous performance task, and produced sluggish reaction times on a Memory Scanning Test (Pliszka, 1989). This study suggests that arousal level, which by itself influences a wide range of primary attentional functions (McBurnett et al., 1991), may be a critical variable when interpreting the results of neurocognitive tests across different disorders.

At both the behavioural and neurocognitive levels (Conners & Weels, 1986; Hasher et al., 1991), the ability to inhibit cognitions and behaviours is a cardinal feature of attentional control mechanisms. Thus difficulty delaying impulsive responding (manifested as increased commission errors on a continuous performance task) has proven the most reliable finding in ADHD. In contrast, early investigations using negative priming models suggest that cognitive inhibitory mechanisms may be dysregulated in anxiety disorder (Fox, 1994). No paediatric negative priming studies have yet been published, but preliminary data from our laboratory suggest that negative priming effects do not discriminate anxiety disorder from ADHD (unpublished data).

Finally, CNS imaging technologies permit researchers to link brain structure to brain function, with magnetic resonance imaging and PET showing more utility for structural localization and event-related potentials showing more utility for understanding the temporal aspects of CNS information processing

(Pfefferbaum, Roth & Ford, 1995). PET studies are as yet impractical in most paediatric mental disorders, though studies in adults with childhood-onset disorders show some promise (Swedo et al., 1989*b*; Zametkin et al., 1990, 1993). In contrast, preliminary studies using event-related potentials indicate that ADHD exhibits electrophysiological markers of a disturbed attentional orienting system (Klorman, 1991). No quantitative electroencephalography event-related potential studies have yet been done in children with anxiety disorder, though such studies in anxious adults suggest overfocused sustained attention (Towey et al., 1994).

Conclusion

With the caveat that much more remains to be learned, it is likely that pathological anxiety in children and adolescents can usefully be represented as a heterogeneous collection of neurobehavioural disorders involving both disorder-specific and overlapping dysregulation in brain stem, limbic and cortico-striatal-thalamo-cortical circuits. In some patients with childhood-onset symptoms, OCD may represent an autoimmune illness related to rheumatic fever. In other patients, inherited temperamental vulnerability, e.g. behavioural inhibition, may predominate. In PTSD, catastrophic environmental stressors appear to trump both in-born vulnerabilities and weaker secondary adversities. For most patients, cognitive–behavioural psychotherapy alone or combined with pharmacotherapy with a SRI and perhaps a benzodiazepine – presumably acting directly on functional via chemically addressed neural circuits, perhaps through divergent mechanisms – defines the current treatment of choice (Kratchovil et al., in press). Conversely, given the limited availability of empirical data on the safety and efficacy of anxiolytic medications for paediatric indications, further systematic investigation should be a priority in treatment research in the anxiety disorders of children and adolescents. Such research should benefit materially from increased attention to the pathobiology of these syndromes.

Acknowledgements

This manuscript was supported in part by NIMH Grant 1 K24 MHO1557 (Dr. March) and by the Robert and Sarah Gorrell family.

For the reader interested in additional information, excellent reviews are now available covering the neuropsychiatry of paediatric mental illness (Coffey &

Brumback, 1998), paediatric anxiety disorders (Perry, 1998; Pine & Grun, 1999), paediatric OCD (March & Leonard, 1998), paediatric PTSD (Donnelly et al., 1999; Pynoos et al., 1997) and evolutionary biology as applied to the concept of mental illness in children and adolescents (Leckman & Mayes, 1998). Of interest also are more general reviews of the neurobiology of social anxiety disorder (Stein, 1998), generalized anxiety disorder (Connor & Davidson, 1998), post-traumatic stress disorder (Grillon, Southwick & Charney, 1996) and panic disorder (Goddard & Charney, 1997; Klein, 1996).

REFERENCES

Abelson J. L., Glitz, D., Cameron, O. G., Lee, M. A., Bronzo, M. & Curtis, G. C. (1991). Blunted growth hormone response to clonidine in patients with Generalized Anxiety Disorder. *Archives of General Psychiatry*, **48**, 157–62.

Abelson, J. L. & Nesse, R. M. (1990). Cholecystokinin-4 and Panic [Letter; Comment]. *Archives of General Psychiatry*, **47**, 395.

Abelson, J. L. Nesse, R. M. & Vinik, A. (1990). Treatment of panic-like attacks with a long-acting analogue of somatostatin. *Journal of Clinical Psychopharmacology*, **10**, 128–32.

Abercrombie, E. D. & Jacobs, B. L. (1987). Single-unit response of nor-adrenergic neurons in the locus coeruleus of freely moving cats, I: acutely presented stressful and nonstressful stimuli. *Journal of Neuroscience*, **7**, 2837–43.

Allen, A. J., Leonard, H. L. & Swedo, S. E. (1995). Case study: A new infection-triggered, autoimmune subtype of pediatric OCD and Tourette's syndrome. *Journal of the American Academy of Child and Adolescent Psychiatry*, **34**, 307–11.

American Psychiatric Association (1994). *Diagnostic and Statistical Manual of Mental Disorders* (4th revision) (DSM–IV). Washington, DC: APA.

Antelman, S. M. & Chiodo, L. A. (1983). Amphetamine as a stressor. In *Stimulants: Neurochemical, Behavioral, and Clinical Perspectives*, ed. I. Cresse, pp. 269–99. New York: Raven Press.

Apter, A., Ratzoni, G., King, R. A., et al. (1994). Fluvoxamine open-label treatment of adolescent inpatients with obsessive compulsive disorder or depression. *Journal of the American Academy of Child and Adolescent Psychiatry*, **33**, 342–8.

Arnsten, A. (1999). Development of the cerebral cortex: XIV. Stress impairs prefrontal cortical function. *Journal of the American Academy of Child and Adolescent Psychiatry*, **38**, 220–2.

Azari, N. P., Pietrini, P., Horwitz, B., et al. (1993). Individual differences in cerebral metabolic patterns during pharmacotherapy in obsessive–compulsive disorder: a multiple regression/discriminant analysis of positron emission tomographic data. *Biological Psychiatry*, **34**, 798–809.

Ballenger, J. C. (1997). Discussion and overview: What can we learn if we view panic disorder across the life span and across different presentations and contexts? *Bulletin of the Menninger Clinic*, **61**, A95–A102.

Ballenger, J. C., Post, R. M., Jimerson, D. C., Lake, C. R. & Zuckerman, M. (1984). Neurobiological correlates of depression and anxiety in normal individuals. In *Neurobiology of Mood Disorders*, ed. R. M. Post & J. C. Ballenger. Baltimore: Williams & Wilkins.

Barkley, R., Grodzinsky, G. & DuPaul, G. (1992). Frontal lobe functions in Attention Deficit Disorder with and without hyperactivity: A review and research report. *Journal of Abnormal Child Psychology*, **20**, 163–88.

Barlow, D. H. (1988). *Anxiety and its Disorders: The Nature and Treatment of Anxiety and Panic*. New York: Guilford Press.

Barr, L. C., Goodman, W. K., Price, L. H., McDougle, C. J. & Charney, D. S. (1992). The serotonin hypothesis of obsessive compulsive disorder: Implications of pharmacologic challenge studies. *Journal of Clinical Psychiatry*, **53**, 17–28.

Baxter, L. J., Schwartz, J. M., Bergman, K. S., et al. (1992). Caudate glucose metabolic rate changes with both drug and behavior therapy for obsessive–compulsive disorder. *Archives of General Psychiatry*, **49**, 681–9.

Baxter, L. J., Schwartz, J. M., Mazziotta, J. C., et al. (1988). Cerebral glucose metabolic rates in nondepressed patients with obsessive–compulsive disorder. *American Journal of Psychiatry*, **145**, 1560–3.

Baxter, L. R. (1990). Brain imaging as a tool in establishing a theory of brain pathology in obsessive–compulsive disorder. *Journal of Clinical Psychiatry*, **51** (2, Suppl), 22–5.

Baxter, L. R., Jr. (1992). Neuroimaging studies of obsessive compulsive disorder. *Psychiatric Clinics of North America*, **15**, 871–84.

Baxter, L. R., Saxena, S. Brody, A. L., et al. (1996). Brain mediation of obsessive–compulsive disorder symptoms: Evidence from functional brain imaging studies in the human and nonhuman primate. *Seminars in Clinical Neuropsychiatry*, **1**, 32–47.

Biederman, J., Rosenbaum, J., Chaloff, J. & Kagan, J. (1995). Behavioral inhibition as a risk factor. In *Anxiety Disorders in Children and Adolescents*, ed. J. March, pp. 61–81. New York: Guilford Press.

Biegon, A. & Greuner, N. (1992). Age-related changes in serotonin 5HT2 receptors on human blood platelets. *Psychopharmacology*, **108**, 210–12.

Birmaher, B., Waterman, G. S., Ryan, N., et al. (1994). Fluoxetine for childhood anxiety disorders. *Journal of the American Academy of Child and Adolescent Psychiatry*, **33**, 993–9.

Birmaher, B., Yelovich, A. K. & Renaud, J. (1998). Pharmacologic treatment for children and adolescents with anxiety disorders. *Pediatric Clinics of North America*, **45**, 1187–204.

Bradwejn, J., Koszycki, D., Payeur, R., Bourin, M. & Borthwick, H. (1992). Replication of action of cholecystokinin tetrapeptide in panic disorder: Clinical and behavioral findings. *American Journal of Psychiatry*, **149**, 962–4.

Bradwejn, J., Koszycki, D. & Shriqui, C. (1991). Enhanced sensitivity to cholecystokinin tetrapeptide in panic disorder: clinical and behavioral findings. *Archives of General Psychiatry*, **48**, 603–10.

Brambilla, F., Perna, G., Bellodi, L., et al. (1997). Noradrenergic receptor sensitivity in obsessive–compulsive disorders: I. Growth hormone response to clonidine stimulation. *Psychiatry Research*, **69**, 155–62.

Bremner, J. D., Krystal, J. H., Charney, D. S. & Southwick, S. M. (1996). Neural mechanisms in dissociative amnesia for childhood abuse: relevance to the current controversy surrounding the 'false memory syndrome'. *American Journal of Psychiatry*, **153** (7 Suppl), 71–82.

Bremner, J. D., Randall, P., Scott, T. M., et al. (1995). MRI-based measurement of hippocampal volume in combat-related posttraumatic stress disorder. *American Journal of Psychiatry*, **152**, 973–81.

Cador, M., Cole, B. J., Koob, G. F., Stinus, L. & Le Moal, M. (1993). Central administration of corticotropin releasing factor induces long-term sensitization to d-amphetamine. *Brain Research*, **606**, 181–6.

Cameron, O. G., Smith, C. B., Lee, M. A., Hollingsworth, P. J., Hill, E. M. & Curtis, G. C. (1990). Adrenergic status in anxiety disorders: Platelet Alpha2-Adrenergic receptor binding, blood pressure, pulse, and plasma catecholamines in panic and generalized anxiety disorder patients and in normal subjects. *Biological Psychiatry*, **28**, 3–20.

Castro-Alamancos, M. A. & Connors, B. W. (1996). Short-term plasticity of a thalamocortical pathway dynamically modulated by behavioral state. *Science*, **272**, 274–6.

Champoux, M., Higley, J. D. & Suomi, S. J. (1997). Behavioral and physiological characteristics of Indian and Chinese–Indian hybrid Rhesus macaque infants. *Developmental Psychobiology*, **31**, 49–63.

Charney, D. S. & Heninger, G. B. (1986). Abnormal regulation of noradrenergic function in panic disorders. *Archives of General Psychiatry*, **43**, 1042–54.

Charney, D. S. & Redmond, D. E. (1983). Neurobiologic mechanisms in human anxiety: Evidence supporting central noradrenergic hyperactivity. *Neuropharmacology*, **22**, 1531–6.

Charney, D. S., Woods, S. W. & Heninger, G. R. (1989). Noradrenergic function in generalized anxiety disorder: Effects of yohimbine in healthy subjects and patients with generalized anxiety disorder. *Psychiatry Research*, **27**, 173–82.

Chopin, P. & Briley, M. (1987). Animal models of anxiety: the effect of compounds that modify 5-HT neurotransmission. *Trends in Pharmacology*, **8**, 383.

Chorpita, B. F., Albano, A. M. & Barlow, D. H. (1996). Child anxiety sensitivity index: Considerations for children with anxiety disorders. *Journal of Clinical Child Psychology*, **25**, 77–82.

Chrousos, G. P. & Gold, P. W. (1992). The concepts of stress and stress system disorders: Overview of physical and behavioral homeostasis. *Journal of the American Medical Association*, **267**, 1244–52.

Cicchetti, D., Rogosch, F. A., Lynch, M. & Holt, K. D. (1993). Resilience in maltreated children: Processes leading to adaptive outcome. Special Issue: Milestones in the development of resilience. *Development & Psychopathology*, **5**, 629–47.

Clark, D. M. (1986). A cognitive approach to panic. *Behaviour Research and Therapy*, **24**, 461–70.

Coffey, E. & Brumback, R. (ed.). (1998). *Textbook of Pediatric Neuropsychiatry*. Washington, DC: American Psychiatric Association Press.

Cohen, D. J. & Leckman, J. F. (1994). Developmental psychopathology and neurobiology of Tourette's syndrome. [Review]. *Journal of the American Academy of Child and Adolescent Psychiatry*, **33**, 2–15.

Cole, B. J., Cador, M., Stionu, L., et al. (1990). Central administration of a CRF antagonist blocks the development of stress-induced behavioral sensitization. *Brain Research*, **512**, 343–6.

Conners, C., March, J. S., Erhardt, D. & Butcher, T. (1995). Assessment of attention-deficit disorders. *Journal of Psychoeducational Assessment*, **2**, 186–205.

Conners, C. & Weels, K. (1986). *Hyperactive Children: A Neuropsychosocial Approach*. Beverly Hills: Sage.

Connor, K. M. & Davidson, J. R. (1998). Generalized anxiety disorder: neurobiological and pharmacotherapeutic perspectives. *Biological Psychiatry*, **44**, 1286–94.

Coplan, J. D., Andrews, M. W., Rosenblum, L. A., et al. (1996). Persistent elevations of cerebrospinal fluid concentrations of corticotropin-releasing factor in adult nonhuman primates exposed to early-life stressors: Implications for the pathophysiology of mood and anxiety disorders. *Proceedings of the National Academy of Sciences, USA*, **93**, 1619–23.

Coryell, W. H., Black, D. W., Kelly, M. W. & Noyes, R. (1989). HPA axis disturbance in obsessive–compulsive disorder. *Psychiatry Research*, **30**, 243–51.

Costello, E. J. & Angold, A. (1995). Epidemiology. In *Anxiety Disorders in Children and Adolescents*, ed. J. S. March, pp. 109–124. New York: Guilford Press.

Davis, M. (1992). The role of the amygdala in conditioned fear. In *The Amygdala: Neurobiological Aspects of Emotion, Memory, and Mental Dysfunction*, ed. J. P. Aggleton, pp. 255–306. New York: Wiley-Liss.

DeBellis, M. D., Chrousos G. P., Dorn, L. D., et al. (1994). Hypothalamic-pituitary-adrenal axis dysregulation in sexually abused girls. *Journal of Clinical Endocrinology and Metabolism*, **78**, 249–55.

DeVane, C. L. & Sallee, F. R. (1996), Selective serotonin reuptake inhibitors in child and adolescent psychopharmacology: A review of published experience. *Journal of Clinical Psychiatry*, **57**, 55–66.

Donnelly, C. L., Amaya-Jackson, L. & March, J. S. (1999). Psychopharmacology of pediatric posttraumatic stress disorder [In Process Citation]. *Journal of Child and Adolescent Psychopharmacology*, **9**, 203–20.

el Mansari, M., Bouchard, C. & Blier, P. (1995). Alteration of serotonin release in the guinea pig orbito-frontal cortex by selective serotonin reuptake inhibitors. Relevance to treatment of obsessive–compulsive disorder. *Neuropsychopharmacology*, **13**, 117–27.

Enright, S. J. & Beech, A. R. (1993). Further evidence of reduced cognitive inhibition in obsessive–compulsive disorder. *Personality & Individual Differences*, **14**, 387–95.

Epstein, J. N., Conners, C. K., Erhardt, D., March, J. S. & Swanson, J. M. (1997a). Asymmetrical hemispheric control of visual-spatial attention in adults with attention deficit hyperactivity disorder. *Neuropsychology*, **11**, 467–73.

Epstein, J. N., Goldberg, N. A., Conners, C. K. & March, J. S. (1997b). The effects of anxiety on continuous performance test functioning in an ADHD clinic sample. *Journal of Attention Disorders*, **2**, 45–52.

Flament, M. F., Koby, E., Rapoport, J. L., et al. (1990). Childhood obsessive–compulsive disorder: A prospective follow-up study. *Journal of Child Psychology and Psychiatry*, **31**, 363–80.

Fletcher, J. M. & Taylor, H. G. (1984). Neuropsychological approaches to children: Towards a developmental neuropsychology. *Journal of Clinical Neuropsychology*, **6**, 39–56.

Fox, E. (1994). Attentional bias in anxiety: A defective inhibition hypothesis. *Cognition & Emotion*, **8**, 165–95.

Gazzaniga, M. (1995). *The Cognitive Neurosciences*. Cambridge: MIT Press.

Gerfen, C. R. (1992). The neostriata mosaic: Multiple levels of compartmental organization. *Trends in Neurosciences*, **15**, 133–9.

Goddard, A. W. & Charney, D. S. (1997). Toward an integrated neurobiology of panic disorder. *Journal of Clinical Psychiatry*, **58** (Suppl. 2), 4–11; discussion 11–12.

Goldman, R. P. & Selemon, L. D. (1990). New frontiers in basal ganglia research. Introduction [see comments]. [Review.] *Trends in Neurosciences*, **13**, 241–4.

Goldman-Rakic, P. S. & Brown, R. M. (1982). Postnatal development of monoamine content and synthesis in the cerebral cortex of rhesus monkeys. *Brain Research*, **25**, 339–49.

Grillon, C., Southwick, S. M. & Charney, D. S. (1996). The psychobiological basis of posttraumatic stress disorder. *Molecular Psychiatry*, **1**, 278–97.

Gurvits, T. G., Shenton, M. R., Hokama, H., et al. (1996). Magnetic resonance imaging study of hippocampal volume in chronic, combat-related posttraumatic stress disorder. *Biological Psychiatry*, **40**, 1091–9.

Halperin, J. M., Newcorn, J. H., Schwartz, S. T., et al. (1997). Age-related changes in the association between serotonergic function and aggression in boys with ADHD. *Biological Psychiatry*, **41**, 682–9.

Halperin, J. M., Sharma, V., Siever, L. J., et al. (1994). Serotonergic function in aggressive and non-aggressive boys with attention-deficit hyperactivity disorder. *American Journal of Psychiatry*, **151**, 243–8.

Hamburger, S. D., Swedo, S., Whitaker, A., Davies, M. & Rapoport, J. L. (1989). Growth rate in adolescents with obsessive–compulsive disorder. *American Journal of Psychiatry*, **146**, 652–5.

Hanna, G. L., Yuwiler, A. & Coates, J. K. (1995), Whole blood serotonin and disruptive behaviors in juvenile obsessive–compulsive disorder. *Journal of the American Academy of Child and Adolescent Psychiatry*, **34**, 28–35.

Harris, J. (1995). *Developmental Neuropsychiatry*. New York: Oxford University Press.

Hart, J., Gunnar, M. & Cicchetti, D. (1995). Salivary cortisol in maltreated children: Evidence of relations between neuroendocrine activity and social competence. *Development and Psychopathology*, **7**, 11–26.

Hasher, L., Stoltzfus, E. R., Zacks, R. T. & Rypma, B. (1991). Age and inhibition. *Journal of Experimental Psychology: Learning, Memory & Cognition*, **17**, 163–9.

Heilig, M. & Widerlov, E. (1990). Neuropeptide Y: An overview of central distribution, functional aspects, and possible involvement in neuropsychiatric illnesses. *Acta Psychiatrica Scandinavica*, **82**, 95–114.

Heninger, G. R. & Charney, D. S. (1988), Monoamine receptor systems and anxiety disorders. In *Psychiatric Clinics of North America Vol 11; Biologic Systems: Their Relationship to Anxiety*, ed. G. Winokur & W. Coryell, pp. 309–26. Philadelphia, PA: W. B. Saunders.

Higley, J. D., Hasert, M. F., Suomi, S. J. & Linnoila, M. (1991*a*). Nonhuman primate model of alcohol abuse: effects of early experience, personality, and stress on alcohol consumption. *Proceedings of the National Academy of Sciences, USA*, **88**, 7261–5.

Higley, J. D., Suomi, S. J. & Linnoila, M. (1991*b*). CSF monoamine metabolite concentrations vary according to age, rearing, and sex, and are influenced by the stressor of social separation in Rhesus monkeys. *Psychopharmacology*, **103**, 551–6.

Higley, J. D. & Suomi, S. J. (1989). Temperamental reactivity in nonhuman primates. In *Temperament in Childhood*, ed. D. Kohnstamm, J. E. Bates & M. K. Rothbart. Chichester: John Wiley & Sons.

Higley, J. D., Suomi, S. J. & Linnoila, M. (1992). A longitudinal study of CSF monoamine metabolite and plasma cortisol concentrations in young rhesus monkeys: effects of early experience, age, sex, and stress on continuity of interindividual differences. *Biological Psychiatry*, **32**, 127–45.

Higley, J. D., Thompson, W. W., Champoux, M., et al. (1993). Paternal and maternal genetic and environmental contributions to cerebrospinal fluid monoamine metabolites in Rhesus monkeys (*Macaca mulatta*). *Archives of General Psychiatry*, **50**, 615–23.

Hooper, S. R. & March, J. S. (1995). Neuropsychology. In *Anxiety Disorders in Children and Adolescents*, ed. J. S. March, pp. 35–60. New York: Guilford Press.

Insel, T. R. (1992). Toward a neuroanatomy of obsessive–compulsive disorder. *Archives of General Psychiatry*, **49**, 739–44.

Insel, T. R. & Winslow, J. T. (1992). Neurobiology of obsessive compulsive disorder. *Psychiatric Clinics of North America*, **15**, 813–24.

Invernizzi, R., Beretta, G., Garattini, S. & Samanin, R. (1986), D- and L-isomers of fenfluramine differ markedly in their interaction with brain serotonin and catecholamines in the rat. *European Journal of Pharmacology*, **120**, 9–15.

Janet, P. (1903). Les obsessions et al psychiatrie. (Vol. 1). Paris: Felix Alan.

Kagan, J., Reznick, J. S. & Snidman, N. (1987). The physiology and psychology of behavioral inhibition in children. *Child Development*, **58**, 1459–73.

Kagan, J., Reznick, J. S. & Snidman, N. (1988). Biological bases of childhood shyness. *Science*, **240**, 167–71.

Kalin, N. H. (1993). The neurobiology of fear. *Scientific American*, **268**, 94–101.

Kalivas, P. W., Duffy, P. & Barrow, J. (1989). Regulation of the mesocorticolimbic dopamine system by glutamic acid receptor subtypes. *Journal of Pharmacology and Experimental Therapeutics*, **251**, 378–87.

Kaufman J., Birmaher, B., Perel, J., et al. (1997). The corticotropin-releasing hormone challenge in depressed abused, depressed nonabused, and normal control children. *Biological Psychiatry*, **42**, 669–79.

Kiessling, L. S., Marcotte, A. C. & Culpepper, L. (1994). Antineuronal antibodies: tics and obsessive–compulsive symptoms. *Journal of Developmental and Behavioural Pediatrics*, **15**, 421–5.

King, N. J., Ollendick, T. H., Mattis, S. G., Yang, B. & Tonge, B. (1997). Nonclinical panic attacks in adolescents: Prevalence symptomatology, and associated features. *Behaviour Change*, **13**, 171–83.

Klein, D. F. (1993). False suffocation alarms, spontaneous panics, and related conditions: an integrative hypothesis. *Archives of General Psychiatry*, **50**, 306–17.

Klein, D. F. (1996). Panic disorder and agoraphobia: hypothesis hothouse. *Journal of Clinical Psychiatry*, **57** (Suppl 6), 21–7.

Klorman, R. (1991). Cognitive event-related potentials in attention deficit disorder. *Journal of Learning Disability*, **24**, 130–40.

Ko, G. N., Elsworth, J. D., Roth, R. H., Rifkin, B. G., Leigh, H. & Redmond, D. E. (1983). Panic-induced elevation of plasma MHPG levels in phobic-anxious patients. *Archives of General Psychiatry*, **40**, 425–30.

Kratchovil, C., Kutcher, S., Reiter, S. & March, J. S. (1999). Pharmacotherapy of pediatric anxiety disorders. In *Handbook of Psychotherapies with Children and Families*, ed. S. W. Russ & T. H. Ollendick, pp. 345–66. New York: Plenum Press.

Kruesi, M. J., Swedo, S., Leonard, H., Rubinow, D. R., et al. (1990). CSF somatostatin in childhood psychiatric disorders: A preliminary investigation. *Psychiatry Research*, **33**, 277–84.

Kuhn, C. & Francis, R. (1997). Gender difference in cocaine-induced HPA axis activation. *Neuropsychopharmacology*, **16**, 399–407.

Ladd, C. O., Owens, M. J. & Nemeroff, C. B. (1996). Persistent changes in corticotropin-releasing factor neuronal systems induced by maternal deprivation. *Endocrinology*, **137**, 1212–18.

Leckman, J. F., Knorr, A. M., Rasmusson, A. M. & Cohen, D. J. (1991). Basal ganglia research and Tourette's syndromes [letter]. *Trends in Neurosciences*, **14**, 94.

Leckman, J. F. & Mayes, L. C. (1998). Understanding developmental psychopathology: how useful are evolutionary accounts? [see comments]. *Journal of the American Academy of Child and Adolescent Psychiatry*, **37**, 1011–21.

Leckman, J. F., Riddle, M. A., Berrettini, W. H., et al. (1988). Elevated CSF Dynorphin a [1-8] in Tourette's Syndrome. *Life Sciences*, **43**, 2015–23.

Leonard, H. L., Lenane, M. C., Swedo, S. E., Rettew, D. C., Gershon, E. S. & Rapoport, J. L. (1992). Tics and Tourette's disorder: a 2- to 7-year follow-up of 54 obsessive–compulsive children. *American Journal of Psychiatry*, **149**, 1244–51.

Leonard, H. L., March, J., Rickler, K. C. & Allen, A.J. (1997). Pharmacology of the selective serotonin reuptake inhibitors in children and adolescents. *Journal of the American Academy of Child and Adolescent Psychiatry*, **36**, 725–36.

Leonard, H. L., Swedo, S. E., Lenane, M. C., et al. (1993). A 2- to 7-year follow-up study of 54 obsessive–compulsive children and adolescents. *Archives of General Psychiatry*, **50**, 429–39.

Lorys-Vernon, A. R., Hynd, G. W. & Lahey, B. B. (1990). Do neurocognitive measures differentiate Attention Deficit Disorder (ADD) with and without hyperactivity? *Archives of Clinical Neuropsychology*, **5**, 119–35.

Lucey, J. V., O'Keane, V., Butcher, G., Clare, A. W. & Dinan, T.G. (1992). Cortisol and prolactin responses to d-fenfluramine in non-depressed patients with obsessive-compulsive disorder. A comparison with depressed and healthy controls. *British Journal of Psychiatry*, **161**, 517–21.

Luxenberg, J. S., Swedo, S. E., Flament, M. F., Friedland, R. P., Rapoport, J. J. & Rapoport, S. I. (1988). Neuroanatomical abnormalities in obsessive–compulsive disorder detected with quantitative X-ray computed tomography. *American Journal of Psychiatry*, **145**, 1089–93.

Lydiard, R. B., Ballenger, J. C., Laraia, M. T., Fossey, M. D. & Beinfeld, M. C. (1992). CSF cholecystokinin concentrations in patients with panic disorder and in normal comparison subjects. *American Journal of Psychiatry*, **149**, 691–3.

Lydiard, R. B. & Brawman-Mintzer, O. (1997). Panic disorder across the lifespan: A differential diagnostic approach to treatment resistance. *Bulletin of the Menninger Clinic*, **61**, A66–A94.

Magnano, C. L., Gardner, J. M. & Karmel, B. Z.(1992). Differences in salivary cortisol levels in cocaine-exposed and noncocaine-exposed NICU infants. *Developmental Psychobiology*, **25**, 93–103.

March, J. S. & Leonard, H. L. (1998). Neuropsychiatry of pediatric obsessive compulsive disorder. In *Textbook of Pediatric Neuropsychiatry*, ed. E. Coffey & R. Brumback, pp. 546–62. Washington, DC: APA Press.

Mattis, S. G. & Ollendick, T. H. (1997a). Children's cognitive responses to the somatic symptoms of panic. *Journal of Abnormal Child Psychology*, **25**, 45–57.

Mattis, S. G. & Ollendick, T. H. (1997b). Panic in children and adolescents: A developmental analysis. In *Advances in Clinical Child Psychology*, ed. T. H. Ollendick & R. J. Prinz, pp. 27–74. New York: Plenum Press.

McBride, P. A., Tierney, H., DeMeo, M., Chen, J. S. & Mann, J. J. (1990). Effects of age and gender on CNS serotonergic responsivity in normal adults. *Biological Psychiatry*, **27**, 1143–55.

McBurnett, K., Lahey, B. B., Frick, P. J., et al. (1991). Anxiety, inhibition, and conduct disorder in children: II. Relation to salivary cortisol. *Journal of the American Academy of Child and Adolescent Psychiatry*, **30**, 192–6.

McDougle, C. J., Goodman, W. K., Price, L. H., et al. (1990). Neuroleptic addition in fluvoxamine-refractory obsessive-compulsive disorder. *American Journal of Psychiatry*, **147**, 652–4.

McEwen, B. (1999). Development of the cerebral cortex: XIII. Stress and brain development: II. *Journal of the American Academy of Child and Adolescent Psychiatry*, **38**, 101–3.

McNally, R. J. (1995). Automaticity and the anxiety disorders. *Behaviour Research and Therapy*, **33**, 747–54.

Meaney, M. J. & Aitken, D. H. (1985). The effects of early postnatal handling on hippocampal glucocorticoid receptor concentrations: temporal parameters. *Brain Research*, **354**, 301–4.

Mesulam, M. M. (1986). Frontal cortex and behavior. *Annals of Neurology*, **19**, 320–5.

Modell, J. G., Mountz, J. M., Curtis, G. C. & Greden, J. F. (1989). Neurophysiologic dysfunction in basal ganglia/limbic striatal and thalamocortical circuits as a pathogenetic mechanism of obsessive–compulsive disorder. *Journal of Neuropsychiatry and Clinical Neurosciences*, **1**, 27–36.

Monteleone, P., Catapano, F., Bortolotti, F. & Maj, M. (1997a). Plasma prolactin response to d-fenfluramine in obsessive–compulsive patients before and after fluvoxamine treatment. *Biological Psychiatry*, **42**, 175–80.

Monteleone, P., Catapano, F., DiMartino, S., Ferraro, C. & Maj, M. (1997b). Prolactin response to d-fenfluramine in obsessive–compulsive patients, and outcome of fluvoxamine treatment. *British Journal of Psychiatry*, **170**, 554–7.

Moore, G. J., MacMaster, F. P., Stewart, C. & Rosenberg, D. R. (1998). Case study: Caudate glutamatergic changes with paroxetine therapy for pediatric obsessive–compulsive disorder. *Journal of the American Academy of Child and Adolescent Psychiatry*, **37**, 664–7.

Moss, H. B., Vanyukov, M. M. & Martin, C. S. (1995). Salivary cortisol responses and the risk for substance abuse in prepubertal boys. *Biological Psychiatry*, **38**, 547–55.

Nelles, W. B. & Barlow, D. H. (1988). Do children panic? *Clinical Psychology Review*, **8**, 359–72.

Nordahl, T. E., Benkelfat, C., Semple, W. E., Gross, M., King, A. C. & Cohen, R. M. (1989). Cerebral glucose metabolic rates in obsessive compulsive disorder. *Neuropsychopharmacology*, **2**, 23–8.

Ollendick, T. H. (1998). Panic disorder in children and adolescents: New developments, new directions. *Journal of Clinical Child Psychology*, **27**, 234–45.

Overton, J. M. & Fisher, L. A. (1989). Modulation of central nervous system actions of corticotropin-releasing factor by dynorphin-related peptides. *Brain Research*, **488**, 233–40.

Owens, M. J. & Nemeroff, C. B. (1991). Physiology and pharmacology of corticotropin-releasing factor. *Pharmacological Research*, **43**, 425–73.

Pauls, D. L., Alsobrook, J. P., Goodman, W., Rasmussen, S., et al. (1995). A family study of obsessive–compulsive disorder. *American Journal of Psychiatry*, **152**, 76–84.

Pauls, D., Towbin, K., Leckman, J., Zahner, G. & Cohen, D. (1986). Gilles de la Tourette syndrome and obsessive compulsive disorder: evidence supporting a genetic relationship. *Archives of General Psychiatry*, **43**, 1180–2.

Pennington, B. F. & Welsh, M. (1995). *Neuropsychology and Developmental Psychopathology*. New York: John Wiley & Sons.

Perry, B. D. (1998). Anxiety Disorders. In *Textbook of Pediatric Neuropsychiatry*, ed. E. Coffey & R. Brumback, pp. 579–94. Washington, DC: APA Press.

Perry, B. D. & Pollard, R. (1998). Homeostasis, stress, trauma, and adaptation. A neurodevelopmental view of childhood trauma. *Child and Adolescent Psychiatric Clinics of North America*, **7**, 33–51, viii.

Pfefferbaum, A., Roth, W. T. & Ford, J. M. (1995). Event-related potentials in the study of psychiatric disorders. *Archives of General Psychiatry*, **52**, 559–63.

Pfefferbaum, B. (1997). Posttraumatic Stress Disorder in children: A review of the past 10 years. *Journal of the American Academy of Child and Adolescent Psychiatry*, **36**, 1503–11.

Piazza, P. V. & Le Moal, M (1996). Pathophysiological basis of vulnerability to drug abuse: Role of an interaction between stress, glucocorticoids, and dopaminergic neurons. *Annual Review of Pharmacology and Toxicology*, **36**, 359–78.

Pine, D. S., Cohen, P., Gurley, D., Brook, J. & Ma, Y. (1998). The risk for early-adulthood anxiety and depressive disorders in adolescents with anxiety and depressive disorders. *Archives of General Psychiatry*, **55**, 56–64.

Pine, D. S. & Grun, J. (1999). Childhood anxiety: integrating developmental psychopathology and affective neuroscience. *Journal of Child and Adolescent Psychopharmacology*, **9**, 1–12.

Pine, D. S., Weese-Mayer, D. E., Silvestri, J. M., Davies, M., Whitaker A. & Klein D. F. (1994). Anxiety and congenital central hypoventilation syndrome. *American Journal of Psychiatry*, **151**, 864–70.

Pliszka, S. (1989). Effect of anxiety on cognition, behavior, and stimulant response in ADHD. *Journal of the American Academy of Child and Adolescent Psychiatry*, **6**, 882–7.

Pollack, M. H., Otto, M. W., Sabatino, S., et al. (1996). Relationship of childhood anxiety to adult panic disorder: correlates and influence on course. *American Journal of Psychiatry*, **153**, 376–81.

Posner, M. I. (1993). Interaction of arousal and selection in the posterior attention network. In *Attention: Selection, Awareness and Control*, Vol. 436, ed. A. Baddeley, pp. 390–405. Oxford: Clarendon Press/Oxford University Press.

Posner, M. I. & Petersen, S. E. (1990). The attention system of the human brain. *Annual Review of Neuroscience*, **13**, 25–42.

Pynoos, R. S., Steinberg, A. M., Ornitz, E. M. & Goenjian, A. K. (1997). Issues in the developmental neurobiology of traumatic stress. *Annals of the New York Academy of Sciences*, **821**, 176–93.

Pynoos, R., S. Steinberg, A. M. & Wraith, R. (1995). A developmental model of childhood traumatic stress. In *Manual of Developmental Psychopathology: Risk, Disorder, Adaptation*, ed. D. Ciccheti & D. Cohen, pp. 72–95. New York: John Wiley & Sons.

Quattrone, A., Tedeschi, G., Aguglia, U., Scopacasa, F., Direnzo, G. F. & Annunziato, L. (1983). Prolactin secretion in man: a useful tool to evaluate the activity of drugs on central 5-hydroxytryptaminergic neurones. Studies with fenfluramine. *British Journal of Clinical Pharmacology*, **16**, 471–5.

Rapoport, J. L. (1991). Recent advances in obsessive–compulsive disorder [see comments]. *Neuropsychopharmacology*, **5**, 1–10.

Rapoport, J. L. (1992). Animal models of obsessive–compulsive disorder. *Clinical Neuropharmacology*, **15** (Suppl. 1, Pt A), 261A–262A.

Rapoport, J. L., Swedo, S. E. & Leonard, H. L. (1992). Childhood obsessive–compulsive disorder. *Journal of Clinical Psychiatry*, **56**, 11–16.

Rauch, S. L., Jenike, M. A., Alpert, N. M., et al., (1994). Regional cerebral blood flow measured during symptom provocation in obsessive–compulsive disorder using oxygen 15-labeled carbon dioxide and positron emission tomography. *Archives of General Psychiatry*, **51**, 62–70.

Rauch, S. L. & Shin, L. M. (1997). Functional neuroimaging studies in posttraumatic stress disorder. *Annals of the New York Academy of Sciences*, **821**, 83–97.

Redmond, D. E. & Huang, Y. H. (1979). Current concepts II. New evidence for a locus coeruleus-norepinephrine connection with anxiety. *Life Sciences*, **25**, 2149–62.

Riddle, M. A., Anderson, G. M., McIntosh, S., et al. (1986). Cerebrospinal fluid monoamine precursor and metabolite levels in children treated for leukemia: Age and sex effects and individual variability. *Biological Psychiatry*, **21**, 69–83.

Riddle, M. A., Claghorn, J., Gaffney, G., et al. (1996). A controlled trial of fluvoxamine for OCD in children and adolescents. *Biological Psychiatry*, **39**, 568 Abstract.

Riddle, M. A., Scahill, L., King, R. A., et al. (1992). Double-blind trial of fluoxetine and placebo in children and adolescents with obsessive–compulsive disorder. *Journal of the American Academy of Child and Adolescent Psychiatry*, **31**, 1062–9.

Rogeness, G. A., Javors, M. A., Maas, J. W. & Macedo, C. A. (1990). Catecholamines and diagnoses in children. *Journal of the American Academy of Child and Adolescent Psychiatry*, **29**, 234–41.

Rosenberg, D. R., Averbach, D. H., O'Hearn, K. M., Seymour, A. B. & Birmaher, B. (1997b). Oculomotor response inhibition abnormalities in pediatric obsessive compulsive disorder. *Archives of General Psychiatry*, **54**, 831–8.

Rosenberg, D. R. & Keshavan, M. S. (1998). A.E. Bennett Research Award. Toward a neurodevelopmental model of of obsessive–compulsive disorder. *Biological Psychiatry*, **43**, 623–40.

Rosenberg, D. R., Keshavan, M. S., O'Hearn, K. M., et al. (1997*a*). Fronto-striatal morphology of treatment-naïve pediatric obsessive compulsive disorder. *Archives of General Psychiatry*, **54**, 824–30.

Rosenberg, D. R. & Lewis, D. A. (1994). Changes in the dopaminergic innervation of monkey prefrontal cortex during late postnatal development: A tyrosine hydroxylase immunohis-tochemical study. *Biological Psychiatry*, **366**, 272–7.

Rutter, M. (1999). The Emanuel Miller Memorial Lecture 1998. Autism: two-way interplay between research and clinical work. *Journal of Child Psychology and Psychiatry*, **40**, 169–88.

Saint-Cyr, J. A., Taylor, A. E. & Nicholson, K. (1995). Behavior and the basal ganglia. *Advances in Neurology*, **65**, 1–28.

Sallee, F. R., Richman, H., Beach, K., Sethuraman, G. & Nesbitt, L. (1996). Platelet serotonin transporter in children and adolescents with obsessive–compulsive disorder or Tourette Syndrome. *Journal of the American Academy of Child and Adolescent Psychiatry*, **35**, 1647–56.

Sapolsky, R. M. (1990). A. E. Bennett Award Paper. Adrenocortical function, social rank, and personality among wild baboons. *Biological Psychiatry*, **28**, 862–78.

Sapolsky, R. M. (1996). Stress, glucocorticoids, and damage to the nervous system: The current state of confusion. *Stress*, **1**, 1–19.

Saxena, P. R. (1995). Serotonin receptors: Subtypes, functional responses and therapeutic relevance. *Pharmacology and Therapeutics*, **66**, 339–68.

Schwartz, J. (1996). *Brain Lock*. New York: Harper Collins.

Schwartz, J. M., Stoessel, P. W., Baxter, L. R., Jr., Martin, K. M. & Phelps, M. E. (1996). Systematic changes in cerebral glucose metabolic rate after successful behavior modification treatment of obsessive–compulsive disorder. *Archives of General Psychiatry*, **53**, 109–13.

Schwarz, E. D. & Perry, B. D. (1994). The post-traumatic response in children and adolescents. *Psychiatric Clinics of North America*, **17**, 311–26.

Seifert, W. E., Foxx, J. L. & Butler, I. J. (1980). Age effect on dopamine and serotonin metabolite levels in cerebrospinal fluid. *Annals of Neurology*, **8**, 38–42.

Selden, N. R. W., Everitt, B. J., Jarrard, L. E., et al. (1991). Complementary roles for the amygdala and hippocampus in aversive conditioning to explicit and contextual cues. *Neuroscience*, **42**, 335–50.

Shaywitz, B. & Shaywitz, S. (1991). Comorbidity: A critical issue in attention deficit disorder. *Journal of Child Neurology*, **5**, 13–20.

Sheehan, D. V., Claycomb, J. B., Surman, O. S., et al. (1986). Panic attacks and the dex-amethasone suppression test. *American Journal of Psychiatry*, **140**, 1063–4.

Siegel, D. J. (1995). Memory, trauma, and psychotherapy: A cognitive science view. *Journal of Psychotherapy Practice & Research*, **4**, 93–122.

Silverman, W. K., Flesig, W., Rabian, B. & Peterson, R. A. (1991). Childhood anxiety sensitivity index. *Journal of Clinical Child Psychology*, **20**, 162–8.

Smith, G. S., Dewey, S. L., Brodie, J. D., et al. (1997). Serotonergic modulation of dopamine measured with [11C]raclopride and PET in normal human subjects. *American Journal of Psychiatry*, **154**, 490–6.

Stein, M. B. (1998). Neurobiological perspectives on social phobia: from affiliation to zoology. *Biological Psychiatry*, **44**, 1277–85.

Stein, M. B., Hanna, C., Koverola, C., Torchia, M. & McClarty, B. (1997). Structural brain changes in PTSD. Does trauma alter neuroanatomy? *Annals of the New York Academy of Sciences*, **821**, 76–81.

Stein, M. B. & Uhde, T. W. (1995). Biology of anxiety disorders. In *Textbook of Psychopharmacology*, ed. A. F. Schatzburg & C. B. Nemeroff, pp. 501–21. Washington, DC: American Psychiatric Press.

Swanson, J. M., Posner, M., Potkin, S. G., Bonforte, S., et al. (1991). Activating tasks for the study of visual-spatial attention in ADHD children: A cognitive anatomic approach. *Journal of Child Neurology*, **6** (Suppl), S119–S127.

Swedo, S. E. (1989). Rituals and releasers: an ethological model of obsessive–compulsive disorder. In *Obsessive–Compulsive Disorder in Children and Adolescents*, ed. J. L. Rapoport, pp. 269–88. Washington, DC: American Psychiatric Press.

Swedo, S. E., Leonard, H. L. & Kiessling, L. (1994). Speculations on anti-neuronal antibody-mediated neuropsychiatric disorders of childhood. *Pediatrics*, **93**, 323–6.

Swedo, S. E., Leonard, H. L., Kruesi, M. J., et al. (1992). Cerebrospinal fluid neurochemistry in children and adolescents with obsessive–compulsive disorder. *Archives of General Psychiatry*, **49**, 29–36.

Swedo, S. E., Leonard, H. L., Schapiro, M. B., et al. (1993). Sydenham's chorea: Physical and psychological symptoms of St Vitus dance. *Pediatrics*, **91**, 706–13.

Swedo, S. E. & Rapoport, J. L. (1990). Neurochemical and neuroendocrine considerations of obsessive–compulsive disorder in childhood. In *Application of Basic Neuroscience to Child Psychiatry*, ed. W. Deutsch, A. Weizman & R. Weizman, pp. 275–284. New York: Plenum Press.

Swedo, S. E., Rapoport, J. L., Cheslow, D. L., et al. (1989a). High prevalence of obsessive–compulsive symptoms in patients with Sydenham's chorea. *American Journal of Psychiatry*, **146**, 246–9.

Swedo, S. E., Schapiro, M. B., Grady, C. L., et al. (1989b). Cerebral glucose metabolism in childhood-onset obsessive–compulsive disorder. *Archives of General Psychiatry*, **46**, 518–23.

Tancer, M. E., Stein, M. B., Black, B. & Uhde, T. W. (1993). Blunted growth hormone responses to growth hormone-releasing factor and to clonidine in panic disorder. *American Journal of Psychiatry*, **150**, 336–7.

Targum, S. D. (1990). Differential responses to anxiogenic challenge studies in patients with major depressive disorder and panic disorder. *Biological Psychiatry*, **28**, 21–34.

Tennes, K., Downey, K. & Vernadakis, A. (1977). Urinary cortisol excretion rates and anxiety in normal one-year-old infants. *Psychosomatic Medicine*, **39**, 178–87.

Tennes, K. & Kreye, M. (1985). Children's adrenocortical responses to classroom activities and tests in elementary school. *Psychosomatic Medicine*, **47**, 451–60.

Towey, J. P., Tenke, C. E., Bruder, G. E., et al. (1994). Brain event-related potential correlates of overfocused attention in obsessive–compulsive disorder. *Psychophysiology*, **31**, 535–43.

Uhde, T. W., Tancer, M. E., Rubinow, D. R., et al. (1992). Evidence for hypothalamo-growth hormone dysfunction in panic disorder: Profile of growth hormone (GH) responses to clonidine, yohimbine, caffeine, glucose, GRF and TRH in panic disorder patients versus healthy volunteers. *Neuropsychopharmocology*, **6**, 101–18.

Van der Kolk, B. A., Burbridge, J. A. & Suzuki, J. (1997). The psychobiology of traumatic memory: Clinical implications of neuroimaging studies. *Annals of the New York Academy of Sciences*, **821**, 99–113.

Voeller, K. K. (1991). What can neurological models of attention, intention, and arousal tell us about attention-deficit hyperactivity disorder? *Journal of Neuropsychiatry and Clinical Neurosciences*, **3**, 209–16.

Wahlestedt, C. & Reis, D. J. (1993). Neuropeptide Y-related peptides and their receptors – are the receptors potential therapeutic drug targets? *Annual Review of Pharmacology and Toxicology*, **33**, 309–52.

Weems, C. F., Hammond-Laurence, K., Silverman, W. K. & Ginsburg, G. S. (1998). Testing the utility of the anxiety sensitivity construct in children and adolescents referred for anxiety disorders. *Journal of Clinical Child Psychology*, **27**, 69–77.

Westenberg, H. G. M., den Boer, J. A. & Kahn, R. S. (1987). Psychopharmacology of anxiety disorders: On the role of serotonin in the treatment of anxiety states and phobic disorders. *Psychopharmacology Bulletin*, **23**, 145–9.

Yeates, K. O. & Bornstein, R. A. (1994). Attention deficit disorder and neuropsychological functioning in children with Tourette's syndrome. *Neuropsychology*, **8**, 65–74.

Yehuda, R., Keefe, R. S. E., Harvey, P. D., et al. (1995). Learning and memory in combat veterans with posttraumatic stress disorder. *American Journal of Psychiatry*, **152**, 137–9.

Zametkin, A. J., Liebenauer, L. L., Fitzgerald, G. A., et al. (1993). Brain metabolism in teenagers with attention-deficit hyperactivity disorder. *Archives of General Psychiatry*, **50**, 333–40.

Zametkin, A. J., Nordahl, T. E., Gross, M., et al. (1990). Cerebral glucose metabolism in adults with hyperactivity of childhood onset. *New England Journal of Medicine*, **323**, 1361–6.

6

Clinical phenomenology, classification and assessment of anxiety disorders in children and adolescents

Antonio C. Fonseca and Sean Perrin

A considerable number of measures for the evaluation of anxiety in childhood and adolescence are available, most of them developed over the last 20 years. Yet, the selection of measures that best meets the needs and characteristics of a given child can be quite a challenging task. It depends not only on the purpose of the assessment and the qualities of the instruments, but also on the assessor's conceptualization of childhood anxiety disorders. In a behavioural approach to anxiety, the aim of the assessment is to identify eliciting stimuli and target behaviours, and the emphasis will be placed on observational techniques and objective records. In a psychoanalytical approach, the assessment will try to elicit intrapsychic conflicts and will rely primarily on unstructured interviews and projective techniques. The aim of the cognitive approach will be to uncover attentional biases and the schemata underlying anxiety manifestations. The evaluation process may include attributional questionnaires and diaries of dysfunctional thoughts.

Whatever one's theoretical view, the assessment strategy also will greatly depend on the child's age, symptom profile, the sources of information available, and the settings where the assessment is to be done. Similarly, the choice of methods for gathering data depends to a great extent on the classification system used in the assessment of anxiety disorders. For instance, structured diagnostic interviews are particularly suited to categorical classification of anxiety disorders, while self-report or problem checklists are more suited to a dimensional approach to classification.

Thus, a full and accurate assessment of anxiety disorders in childhood and adolescence will require some understanding of the various etiological models or definitions of anxiety (cognitive, behavioural or analytic), the diagnostic classification system used, and the developmental appropriateness of certain anxiety symptoms. Accordingly, we begin this chapter with a brief review of these issues.

Basic issues

Definition and phenomenology

Anxiety can be defined as a set of emotional reactions arising from the anticipation of a real or imagined threat to the self. In the literature, other terms such as fear, avoidance reactions, or phobia also have been used to denote the same phenomenon. Although it is possible to find subtle differences among these terms, we use them interchangeably.

Although anxiety reactions may take various forms, generally they are organized around three main components: a motor response, a subjective or cognitive response, and a physiological response, each of these in turn encompass a greater number of reactions (Zinbarg & Barlow, 1996). At the motor level, and usually in the presence of the feared stimulus, anxiety can be characterized by escape or avoidance behaviours, restlessness (e.g. pacing, hand-wringing), clinging to caregivers/loved ones, and occasionally, stuttering. Complete immobility or urgent pleas for assistance may also be seen. At the cognitive level, anxiety is characterized by fearful apprehension, worries or distorted cognitions about one's performance or safety. Finally, at the physiological level, anxiety is defined by heightened autonomic arousal (e.g. increased heart rate, skin conductance and perspiration), which are often reflected in the self-report of multiple somatic complaints. There has been considerable debate recently about the validity of this tripartite model of anxiety, however, it remains the model upon which the DSM–IV anxiety disorders are organized (Zinbarg & Barlow, 1996).

It is important to note that mild to occasionally moderate levels of anxiety are considered part of normal human development and are likely to be adaptive (Marks, 1987). Indeed, a large number of cross-cultural studies (for reviews see King, Hamilton & Ollendick, 1988; Marks, 1987) have demonstrated a fairly stable pattern of fears that arise and subside during different stages of development. For example, as the senses develop in infancy, fears of loud noises, loss of support and high places are evident. As cognitive processes develop during the first year and a new awareness of the constancy of surroundings emerges (object constancy), so do fears of strangers and separation from caretakers (Crowell & Waters, 1990; Klein, 1994). Between the ages of two and six years, there is an increase in fears regarding animals, the dark, imaginary creatures, threats of danger or harm to the body, fire, ridicule, robbers and death (Gray, 1987). As the child continues to develop socially and cognitively, so do concerns regarding their performance and evaluation, with social anxiety being a primary feature of early adolescence (Kashani et al., 1989; Ost, 1987).

While fears and anxiety are a part of normal human development, they can become so intense as to severely affect the child's functioning and psychosocial development. In such cases, the anxiety may be viewed as 'clinically significant' and qualify for diagnosis. Data from epidemiological studies have consistently shown that anxiety disorders are one of the more common forms of psychopathology in childhood, with prevalence rates between 2.5% and 9% in the general population, and between 20 and 30% among clinically referred children (Anderson, 1994; Costello et al., 1988). In the general population, girls show a slightly higher risk for anxiety disorder than boys (Anderson, 1994). Among treatment seekers, anxiety disorders are more evenly distributed between the genders (Last et al., 1992).

While it is not clear whether all forms of anxiety disorders meet the criteria set forward by Wakefield (1992) (i.e. mental disorder as 'harmful dysfunction'), there is nevertheless a general consensus amongst researchers and clinicians regarding the distinction between normal and pathological anxiety. In contrast to normal anxiety, pathological anxiety is seen as being beyond that expected for the child's developmental level, disproportionate to the threat posed (e.g. extreme fear of the dark), severe (e.g. causing distress to the child), persistent and impairing one or more areas of functioning (e.g. school and relations with family or peers). Whether anxiety disorders as defined in our current classification systems are truly discontinuous or qualitatively different from normal anxiety is a question for further investigation.

In addition, there is considerable heterogeneity in the clinical presentation of specific anxiety disorders in childhood. For example, children with a simple phobia of the dark often differ not only in the nature and frequency of their symptoms, but also in their severity, developmental history, response to treatment and long-term outcome. As Barrios & O'Dell (1989) have said, there may be 'variation from child to child in the exact make up of the fear and anxiety reactions to the same stimulus, and variation within the same child in the exact make up of the fear and anxiety reactions to different stimuli' (p. 436).

Classification

To account for the diversity of anxiety symptoms people present with and to provide clear and simple guidelines to group them, several classification schemes have been proposed (Morris & Kratochwill, 1983). Two have been particularly influential both in clinical and research settings: the categorical approach and the dimensional approach.

In the categorical approach, the criteria used to define each disorder are primarily grounded on the opinions of expert committees and are subject to frequent changes. A disorder can be classified by the careful observation of symptoms or symptom clusters, before any actual cause is known. This approach is well illustrated in the successive editions of the *Diagnostic and Statistical Manual of Mental Disorders* (DSM; American Psychiatric Association, 1994) and in the *International Classification of Diseases* (ICD; World Health Organization, 1992). The underlying assumption of both DSM and ICD is that anxiety-disordered children differ qualitatively from those who do not have these conditions. It is an 'either-or' approach with no middle term.

DSM–IV (APA, 1994) lists only one anxiety disorder specific to childhood and adolescence: Separation Anxiety Disorder. Separation anxiety disorder's main features are excessive worry about separation from the home or major attachment figures, sleep disturbances and nightmares involving the theme of separation, crying and pleading when parents do leave, clinging to caregivers or persistent tracking of major attachment figures, disruptions in behaviour and/or somatic complaints during separation, persistent fears of being alone and avoidance of separation from caregivers (e.g. leading to school refusal). According to DSM–IV, the child must have at least three of eight separation anxiety symptoms; an onset of the disorder before age 18; duration of at least 4 weeks; clinically significant impairment in the child's functioning; all of which cannot be explained by the presence of other disorders (APA, 1994). The separation anxiety should be in excess of that expected given the child's developmental level. For example, one would expect a 2-year-old but not an adolescent to demonstrate anxiety on separation from caretakers.

The remaining anxiety disorders are listed in the adult section of DSM–IV but may be applied to children whenever they meet the appropriate diagnostic criteria (Rapoport & Ismond, 1996). These disorders include: panic disorder, agoraphobia, specific and social phobia, obsessive-compulsive disorder, posttraumatic stress disorder, acute stress disorder, generalized anxiety disorder, anxiety disorder due to a general medical condition, substance induced anxiety disorder and anxiety disorder not otherwise specified.

Compared with previous editions of the DSM, DSM–IV presents some important changes regarding the diagnosis of anxiety disorders in childhood and adolescence. Overanxious disorder and avoidant disorder were eliminated as separate categories in the child section of the manual, given their lack of reliability and validity, and included in the adult equivalents of these disorders – generalized anxiety disorder and social phobia, respectively. Separation anxiety disorder has remained largely unchanged in the various editions of the DSM.

In ICD–10, childhood anxiety disorders are listed under a general category of 'emotional disorders with onset specific to childhood' that, in addition to separation anxiety, also includes phobic anxiety disorder of childhood, social anxiety disorder of childhood and sibling rivalry disorder. As in DSM, phobic anxiety disorder is characterized by excessive fear of specific stimuli (e.g. animals or heights) and social anxiety disorder by persistent fears of strangers or social situations to a degree that is outside the normal limits for the child. Sibling rivalry disorder, which has no equivalent in the DSM, is characterized by marked and persistent competition with siblings for the parents' attention, and is associated with overt hostility and negative feelings towards other children in the family. There is also a category of mixed disorders of conduct and emotions which involves a combination of antisocial behaviours and emotional difficulties (e.g. anxiety and depression). Like DSM–IV, ICD–10 allows anxiety disorders listed in the adult section of the manual to be applied to children where appropriate. These include: phobic anxiety disorders, obsessive-compulsive disorder, adjustment reactions and other anxiety disorders.

Despite efforts to increase the similarity of DSM and ICD, important discrepancies remain, particularly as regards the number and characteristics of syndromes and the procedures for assigning diagnoses (Werry, 1994). For example, in DSM–IV the same child may receive several diagnoses, while in ICD–10 children who qualify for more than one diagnosis are classified 'mixed disorders of conduct and emotions'. The DSM is commonly used in North America and has inspired numerous research studies, while ICD–10 is popular in Western Europe and other countries affiliated to the World Health Organization and has had fewer investigations of its diagnostic categories.

Still, the overall approach to classification in both DSM and ICD is a categorical one and so both have been the subject to similar criticisms. A primary criticism of DSM and ICD is that there is not a great deal of evidence for the validity of several of the individual anxiety diagnoses. For example, in a recent study of clinically referred children, Steinhausen & Reitzle (1996) found little evidence supporting the existence of a separate category of mixed disorders of conduct and emotions (including anxiety) as defined in ICD–10, since this category shares most of its characteristics with pure conduct disorder. Similarly, empirical evidence is still scarce for several of the anxiety disorders listed in DSM–IV, and many of the criticisms made about previous editions (see Silverman, 1992; Werry, 1994) are still valid now. Another criticism is that there is insufficient evidence that the various anxiety disorders listed are truly distinct clinical entities (i.e. with varying patterns of familial aggregation, course and treatment outcome), rather than manifestations of a common underlying diathesis.

The developmental appropriateness of the anxiety criteria to children continues to be neglected in both systems, as youngsters are often diagnosed as anxiety disordered if they meet the same criteria as adults. Moreover, clusters of anxiety symptoms that are particular to childhood (e.g. school phobia, test anxiety, fears of medical settings, etc.) are not included in either system as independent diagnoses. Given these criticisms or limitations of the categorical approach, many researchers and clinicians often adopt an alternative or complementary approach – the dimensional view of childhood psychopathology.

In the dimensional approach, anxiety is seen to occur along a continuum of severity, rather than falling above or below a 'diagnostic threshold' or into discrete diagnostic categories. Further, the symptoms that constitute the anxiety disorder, as well as the threshold between normal and abnormal anxiety, are statistically derived from large samples, and are permitted to vary according to the individual's sex and age. As opposed to a committee of experts defining disorders, the dimensional approach consists of asking parents, teachers and children to complete a large number of questions about the child's behaviour, and then factor analysing the responses to derive severity levels and symptom clusters.

Following this strategy, several authors have consistently identified a factor or dimension of anxiety and related problems for boys and girls across different age levels and settings. For example, Quay (1979) found a factor of anxiety-withdrawal, characterized by 'feelings of tension, depression, inferiority and worthlessness, and behaviours of timidity, social withdrawal and hyper sensibility'. Similarly, Achenbach (1991a,b,c) found an 'anxious/depressed' factor derived from a variety of informants (e.g. parents and teachers) and across different settings (e.g. clinical or community samples), which includes symptoms such as 'crying a lot, fear of doing or thinking bad things, the need to be perfect, to be nervous and fearful, guilty and self-conscious, worrying, feeling sad, or to feel lonely and worthless'.

Compared to categorical diagnoses, the dimensional approach has some advantages: it is empirically based, more readily accounts for developmental changes, relies on less costly and easier to administer measures, provides normative data differentiated by gender and age level, and presents higher indices of reliability for the derived 'emotion' factor. Taken together, these qualities make the dimensional approach to classification of anxiety very useful as a screening procedure and for community surveys. However, it is less advantageous in detecting specific or uncommon clusters of symptoms (e.g. obsessive-compulsive and panic disorder) in the general population, and its clinical utility has yet to be fully demonstrated. The validity of the dimensional approach has also been questioned. In particular, it has been difficult to find a pure anxiety factor on dimensional questionnaires, or factors that fit the corresponding categories of DSM–IV or ICD–10 (i.e. those often seen in clinical populations). Also, in the dimensional approach, anxiety disorders are simply defined as deviations from population norms, not as a consequence of their associated level of impairment for a particular child.

In addition to dimensional and categorical approaches, several other strategies have been used in the classification of anxious disorders. Two good examples are classifications based on the nature of the eliciting stimuli and functional analytic techniques. The first strategy, which consists of classifying the fear or anxiety according to the eliciting stimuli, was largely employed in early studies (see Morris & Kratochwill, 1983) and may be useful for identifying treatment targets. However, it is limited by its use of seemingly endless lists of fears and anxieties (e.g. aquaphobia, mikrophobia, xenophobia, etc.), and its assumption of homogeneity within each particular category of fear when, in fact, there is considerable variety of symptom presentation within categories (Morris & Kratochwill, 1983).

The second strategy for classifying anxiety is the functional analytic approach, which also focuses on the eliciting stimuli but identifies specific target responses (behaviours) and their immediate consequences. It assumes that the same fear or anxiety response may develop and be maintained in various ways without resorting to pre-set diagnostic categories or dimensions. Kearney & Silverman (1990, 1996) have developed a scale specific to school refusal that relies on this functional analytic approach – the School Refusal Assessment Scale (SRAS). The SRAS allows the clinician to delineate the following functions of school refusal (the response): avoidance arising from specific fears of school, separation anxiety, or social–evaluative situations; attention-getting behaviours; and obtaining tangible rewards (e.g. access to TV programmes/ toys). In this way, the SRAS leads to a more accurate classification of school refusal as either an anxiety or behaviour problem, and to targeted intervention programmes for each case. Its clinical utility has been supported most recently in a small treatment study of school refusers ($n = 8$) by Kearney & Silverman (1999). Specifically, the authors found that treatment programmes developed around the function of the school refusal (i.e. prescriptive treatments) were superior to traditional treatment programmes (e.g. relaxation, cognitive therapy, contingency contracting) which were not based on the function of the school refusal behaviour (i.e. nonprescriptive treatments).

Another way of subdividing childhood anxieties and fears is based on the evolutionary significance of the feared stimuli. Seligman (1971) distinguishes between 'prepared' and 'unprepared' fear stimuli. Prepared fears (e.g. heights, snakes) are those which have obvious evolutionary value and are thought to be easier to develop and more difficult to treat. By contrast, unprepared fears (e.g. a fear of flowers or shoelaces) may be experimentally induced but are thought to be more difficult to acquire naturally and easier to treat. Although these two categories have good face validity, experimental support for this distinction is very limited and this approach has been the subject of much debate (Davey, 1992; Honeybourne, Matchett & Davey, 1993).

In summary, all of the above classification systems can be said to have strengths and weaknesses, and thus it may be difficult to decide upon which to use. The superiority of any one approach still requires a good deal of comparative research. In particular, it remains to be seen whether the dimensional or categorical approach is better at predicting external criteria for anxiety disorders in children, and which of these approaches is best at dealing with the considerable comorbidity found in anxious children. Also, as Kearney & Silverman (1996) have pointed out, the validity of any classification system must, in the main, lead to reliable methods of assessment and effective treatments for the anxiety problem in question. When more treatment trials begin to appear for childhood anxiety disorders derived from different classification systems, then the validity of the various classification schemes can be better evaluated. Nevertheless, the classification systems described above clearly show that anxiety is not a unidimensional construct and as such, a comprehensive assessment will require a detailed knowledge of its diverse manifestations and associated features.

Comorbidity

Comorbidity, or the co-occurrence of multiple anxiety disorders in the same child, is discussed in detail elsewhere in this book (see Verhulst, chapter 12, this volume). Briefly, most children who present to clinics with anxiety, are found to have multiple anxiety disorders, and somewhat less frequently depressive and behaviour disorders (Last et al., 1992). In some cases, the comorbid depressive or behaviour disorder may be the primary reason for clinical referral, even though the anxiety disorder is 'primary' in the sense that it appeared first and is of greater severity. In addition, anxiety (or depressive or behaviour) disorders may differ in etiology, course and treatment response according to whether they arise as an isolated disorder or coexist with other forms of psychopathology (Caron & Rutter, 1991; Rutter, 1997). These points raise important questions about the validity of the anxiety disorder criteria as defined in the prevailing classification systems (see Anderson, 1994; Brady & Kendall, 1992; Rutter, 1997), and have important implications for assessment.

Given the above, it would be sensible for the clinician to include behaviour and depression measures in any assessment package for anxious children. However, this may simply result in multiple diagnoses being assigned; diagnoses which may be of little clinical usefulness due to problems with discriminant validity and/or method artefact. These problems may be significantly reduced by broadband approaches that eliminate item and symptom overlap between scales and diagnostic categories. Examples of such an approach are the use of such constructs as Positive-Affectivity (PA) and Negative-Affectivity (NA). Numerous studies have shown both PA and NA to be dominant and relatively independent dimensions in individuals with emotional disorders, and to increase the accuracy of discrimination between depressive and anxiety disorders (Brady & Kendall, 1992).

One such measure specifically designed to assess these constructs in children is the Negative Affect Self-Statement Questionnaire (NASAQ; Ronan et al., 1994). The NASAQ was found to discriminate anxious/nonanxious children from depressed/nondepressed children in separate 7–10- and 11–15-year-old strata (Ronan et al., 1994). Also, it was found to be sensitive, and relatively specific, to the effects of an anxiety treatment (Ronan et al., 1994). While the results of this study are promising, studies of negative and positive affectivity in children are still quite scarce and the issue requires more attention before its clinical usefulness can be judged (Merrell, Anderson & Michael, 1997). In particular, it will be necessary for any measure capable of encompassing different psychopathological disorders to demonstrate its sensitivity to the developmental manifestations of these disorders.

A developmental approach to the assessment of anxiety disorders

Because anxiety disorders are prevalent across the lifespan, it is important to consider whether childhood anxiety disorders persist in both form and function into adulthood (i.e. developmental continuity), simply remit, or change into other disorders (i.e. developmental discontinuity). For example, is panic disorder in adulthood the outcome of childhood separation anxiety disorder? Such questions are important because if childhood anxiety disorders are transient childhood phenomena unrelated to adolescent or adult anxiety disorders, then they may be of low priority when it comes to allocating resources to their prevention or treatment.

At present, the available literature suggests that childhood anxiety disorders are not simply transient developmental phenomena of little clinical importance, but neither are they particularly stable over time. In other words, children may suffer for long periods with anxiety disorders, but not necessarily with the same anxiety disorder throughout. By way of example, Cantwell & Baker (1989) followed a large sample of children and adolescents seeking treatment from a community speech clinic, and found that 89% of those with an initial diagnosis of separation anxiety disorder, 75% with overanxious disorder, and 71% with avoidant disorder no longer met criteria for the same diagnosis at the end of a 3- to 4-year follow-up. However, at least 25% of these children presented with other anxiety disorders at the end of the follow-up.

Further to this point, Berg et al. (1989) observed important changes over time in children with obsessive-compulsive disorder. In their follow-up study of clinically referred young persons with OCD (aged 10 to 25 years), only 31% continued with the same diagnoses 2 years later, while 56% developed other anxiety and affective disorders. Likewise, Leonard et al. (1993) found, in a 2–7-year follow-up study of clinically referred young people (aged 10 to 24 years) with OCD, that only 43% continued with the same disorder, while 96% met criteria for other diagnoses at follow-up. Only 11% were completely symptom free. Similar findings have been reported elsewhere for clinically referred children with separation anxiety disorder, overanxious disorder and phobias (see Last et al., 1996).

These patterns of development are not exclusive to clinical samples. In community studies carried out in New Zealand, McGee et al. (1992) and Feehan, McGee & Williams (1993) reported that in a group of adolescents initially diagnosed with anxiety disorders, less than 40% continued with a diagnosis of anxiety 4 and 8 years later, while 7% met criteria for other disorders. Generally, changes in diagnostic status over time do not seem to be a uniform phenomenon across the different anxiety disorders. For instance, there is some evidence of an increase in overanxious disorder from childhood to adolescence but a decrease in separation anxiety in community samples (Costello et al., 1988; Velez, Johnson & Cohen, 1989).

More recently, Beidel, Fink & Turner (1996), in a community-based follow-up study of school children, found 33% of those with an initial diagnosis of social phobia still had the same diagnosis 6 months later, while 16% received the diagnosis of overanxious disorder. Amongst those initially diagnosed with overanxious disorder, 50% maintained the same diagnosis at the end of that period, while 25% were diagnosed with social phobia. These results must be interpreted with some caution as the follow-up period was very short (i.e. 6 months), and the number of children in each diagnostic category was quite small.

The findings from the above studies may be viewed as evidence of the poor reliability of the specific anxiety disorder categories. Alternatively, they may suggest that the categories are valid but that anxiety disorders are developmentally discontinuous (e.g. specific anxiety disorders are replaced with other distinct disorders over time). One could argue that the discontinuous hypothesis is more valid as it mirrors the developmental changes in anxiety seen in normal children (e.g. separation anxiety is replaced by more performance related concerns during the school years). Thus, it is not surprising that the prevalence of separation anxiety disorder decreases and overanxious disorder increases from childhood to adolescence in community samples (Costello et al., 1988; Velez et al., 1989).

The importance of age in the clinical presentation of children with anxiety disorders cannot be underestimated. For example, among school phobics, Kearney & Silverman (1996) have found that younger children often refuse to go to school to gain attention or proximity to caregivers while older children and adolescents may refuse school to avoid social evaluative situations. Also, there is some evidence of a relation between age and the coexistence of anxiety and depression. Comorbid cases tend to be older than children with only one of these disorders and anxiety generally precedes depression (King, Ollendick & Gullone, 1991).

One conclusion to be drawn from the above studies is that an accurate assessment of childhood anxiety must rely on measures that are sensitive to age and developmental changes. In this sense, age-downward extensions of instruments originally designed for adults may be misleading and, consequently, the utilization of adult criteria for anxiety with children and adolescents may also be of limited value. Thus, it behoves the assessor to consider whether the anxiety symptoms are deviant for the child's age, and to comprehensively assess the fears and anxieties most relevant to each age level. Likewise, any measures or interviews used to assess the child should take into account the child's cognitive ability and, in particular, their capacity to discriminate and verbalize complex feelings and emotions. As very young children may have limited verbal abilities or be quite shy, it may be necessary to rely on information from other sources, including parents, teachers, peers or other relevant figures.

Combining different types of information

It is now widely accepted that there are only modest levels of agreement amongst informants as regards the child's symptoms. In a meta-analytic review of the literature on this topic, Achenbach, McConaughy & Howell (1987) reported an average correlation of 0.20 between teacher and child reports, of 0.27 between parent and child reports, and of 0.59 between mothers' and fathers' reports for the child's symptoms. Also, inter-informant agreement will vary considerably according to the type of symptom assessed. For instance, Silverman & Rabian (1995) assessing the child/parent concordance rate on several symptoms of anxiety, found kappa values that ranged from −0.21 for 'somatic complaints' to 0.29 for 'self-consciousness'. In general, levels of informer agreement for internalizing symptoms are much lower than for externalizing symptoms (Sylvester, Hyde & Reichler, 1987).

However, low or modest levels of agreement among informants are not necessarily indicators of low levels of validity or reliability in the informant's reports. Rather, different informants observe the same behaviour in different contexts and from their own perspectives. Thus, teachers may provide a more accurate picture of anxiety in the child's adaptation to school, while youngsters are generally the best informers about their own subjective experience of anxiety. Moreover, levels of inter-informer agreement seem to vary according to the child's age. As noted by Tarullo et al. (1995), both mother–child and mother–father agreements were higher for pre-adolescent offspring than for adolescents. Therefore, relying solely on one informant may lead to an incomplete or inaccurate picture of the problem.

Given the need for multiple informants in the assessment of child anxiety, several strategies have been proposed for combining information from different informants with a view towards increasing diagnostic accuracy. Reich & Earls (1987) suggest relying on the child's report to delineate major symptoms, the adults' reports to assess severity, and in cases of parent–child discrepancies, to use teacher information to reconcile the two. Piacentini, Cohen & Cohen (1992) have suggested using composite scores that average the global ratings obtained from different informants, giving each informant's report equal weight. Alternatively, Rowe & Kandel (1997) have recommended that maternal ratings be combined with the child's self-ratings, but treating the father's report separately. Bird, Gould & Staghezza (1992) have suggested that data from all informants be combined according to a predetermined, complex algorithm that leads to the attribution of different weights to the various informants. Puig-Antich & Gittelman (1982) suggested that, in the case of parent–child discrepancies, the child be interviewed separately and asked to explain why the parents rated them in the manner they did. Still other authors have used more than one strategy simultaneously in the identification of problematic children (see McConaughy & Achenbach, 1994).

The above strategies can be grouped into two main categories: complex schemes in which different weights are assigned to different informants, and simple schemes that give equal weight to all sources of information. The question then arises as to which of these approaches will lead to the most accurate diagnostic picture. In one of the few studies to examine this issue, Piacentini et al. (1992) concluded that the simple (unweighted) scheme works as well or even better than complex (weighted) schemes in arriving at diagnoses. However, one should not forget that, although for clinical purposes it may be useful to amalgamate data from different informants, for research purposes it may be useful to keep them separate. Not doing so may obscure the fact that anxiety symptoms obtained from different informants also have different correlates. For instance, McConaughy & Achenbach (1994) found that the comorbidity rates between anxious/depressed and aggressive behaviours vary with the informant (e.g. parents, teachers and youth) and this information would be lost if different sources were combined.

As noted by Hinden et al. (1997), this variation in comorbidity rates as a function of informant, may reflect informant biases towards the child. Specifically, the particular perspective of an informant as a result of their relationship to the child and the context in which the informant is most likely to observe the child can lead to bias. Again, this underscores the need for multiple informants in the assessment of anxiety disorders. Regardless of the method used to resolve discrepancies amongst informants, a method should probably be agreed upon a priori. Rapee et al. (1994) found that clinicians, without instruction to do so, gave little credibility to the child's reports on the Anxiety Disorder Interview Schedule for Children, and tended to base their diagnostic decisions mainly on the information provided by parents. The above literature suggests that this may not be the optimum approach for arriving at accurate diagnoses of childhood anxiety disorders.

Assessment methods and instruments

Any comprehensive assessment of childhood anxiety disorders will require a large range of instruments and procedures, including diagnostic interviews, parent/teacher rating scales, children's self-reports, and direct observation or psychophysiological recordings (where possible). The number of measures available for this task is huge. Ten years ago, Barrios & Hartmann (1988) described 100 instruments used in the assessment of childhood anxiety, with most of them focused on the motor or behavioural component. Since then, several other techniques have been developed, keyed to the most recent theoretical developments in the study of anxiety and the many revisions of the DSM and ICD.

There are recent and extensive reviews of the available measures for childhood anxiety disorders (see Barrios & Hartmann, 1997; Bird & Gould, 1994; Silverman & Serafini, 1998; Stallings & March, 1995). This chapter will focus only on those most frequently used both for research and clinical purposes. Further, our review will be restricted to general self-report measures of anxiety and structured diagnostic interviews. The large number of research-based measures aimed at very specific types (e.g. obsessive-compulsive disorders, social anxiety, school refusal or dental phobias) or aspects of anxiety (e.g. physiological techniques), have been discussed in detail in several recent publications (see King, Ollendick & Yule, 1994), and are beyond the scope of this chapter.

Interviews

An unstructured clinical interview with the parent(s) and the child is perhaps the most commonly used method for assessing anxiety disorders. Unstructured interviews have the advantage of great flexibility, permitting a relationship of trust to be developed with the child and parent, while at the same time allowing for a wide range of issues to be assessed. Moreover, unstructured interviews provide an excellent opportunity to observe family interactions and, in particular, how they influence the child's problems. However, because the interviewer may not ask the same questions of all family members, there are likely to be considerable differences in the information obtained from each informant. In addition, family members may disagree with one another regarding the occurrence, nature and meaning of the same behaviour or emotion.

In order to overcome these shortcomings, structured and semi-structured diagnostic interviews have been developed to increase the accuracy and reliability of diagnosis in children. As such, structured interviews consist of a long series of standardized questions covering a large range of problems that are asked in the same predetermined order and which yield DSM, or less often, ICD diagnoses. Most have parent and child forms, thus providing the interviewer with a more complex picture of the child's difficulties and allowing for the comparison of information from different informants. The parent and child forms are generally identical except for changes in the phrasing of questions. Additionally, some will include visual prompts (e.g. fear thermometers, calendars, diaries) for use with younger children to elicit more accurate responses.

The most well researched structured interviews are the Schedule for Affective Disorders and Schizophrenia in School-Age Children (K-SADS; Puig-Antich & Chambers, 1978), the Diagnostic Interview for Children and Adolescents (DICA; Herjanic & Reich, 1982), the Child Assessment Schedule (CAS; Hodges et al., 1982), the Diagnostic Interview Schedule for Children (DISC;

Costello et al., 1984), the Anxiety Disorders Interview Schedule for DSM–IV: Child and Parent Versions (ADIS–C/P; Silverman & Albano, 1996; Silverman & Nelles, 1988), and the Child and Adolescent Psychiatric Assessment (CAPA; Angold & Costello, 1995).

The validity and reliability of these interviews have been analysed and discussed in several recent reviews (Hodges, 1993; Silverman, 1994) and can be summarized in the following way: they all use a structured or semi-structured format; have equivalent forms for parents and children; are able to generate diagnoses based on DSM criteria; allow for recording of the child's behaviour during interview; can be used across a wide age range; and cover most childhood disorders. Generally, structured interviews are quite diverse in their flexibility of presentation, the number of items included, the time required for administration, the rating format, the amount of training required for correct administration, and the attention paid to anxiety and related disorders.

For instance, the K-SADS starts in an unstructured format with some general questions about the reasons for referral and about the child's functioning across different settings. In the structured part of the interview, questions about specific symptoms relative to several disorders are presented. The answers to these questions are rated on a 0–3 scale. When there is a discrepancy in parent and child ratings, information from other sources may also be used to arrive at a diagnosis. The final diagnoses are derived from the parent and child ratings, clinician ratings and any additional, relevant sources.

One of the few interviews specifically designed to assess anxiety disorders in children and adolescents, the ADIS–C/P (Silverman & Albano, 1996; Silverman & Nelles, 1988) is now one of the best known and most widely used. Like other structured diagnostic interviews, it has parent and child versions. The interview follows a preset format, covers all of the anxiety disorders as defined in DSM–III–R (APA, 1987), and more recently in DSM–IV. The parent and child versions are administered separately, have slightly different coverage and provide two independent scores, that are then combined to arrive at a diagnosis. Each diagnosis is rated for severity and level of impairment, and detailed information can be collected on associated problems (e.g. somatization), precipitating events, and course of the disorder. Additionally, the ADIS–C/P includes questions that can help in a functional analysis of the child's anxiety symptoms.

The ADIS–C/P is widely used for research and clinical purposes, and has been shown to have satisfactory interrater and test-retest reliability. In a recent study with a clinic sample, Silverman & Eisen (1992) calculated test-retest reliabilities over a period of 10–14 days. Overall kappas for diagnosis were 0.76,

0.67 and 0.75 for the child, parent and composite scores. Reliability for specific anxiety disorders was somewhat lower but still satisfactory, ranging from 0.38 for overanxious disorder in a child version to 1.0 for simple phobias, both in the child and composite versions (Silverman & Nelles, 1988). Similar kappas for the individual anxiety disorders were reported by Rapee et al. (1994) in a large sample ($n = 161$) of anxiety-disordered children.

To conclude, the ADIS–C/P provides coverage of all the anxiety disorders and seems to fare better than other existing structured interviews in differentiating between the specific anxiety disorders. Of course, like most structured interviews it can take a long time to administer when the child meets criteria for multiple anxiety disorders. Some children may find it difficult to sit through the entire interview, necessitating breaks. Also, like most interviews, its diagnostic validity for younger children (e.g. those under 9–10 years) requires further investigation. As noted earlier by Edelbrock, Greenbaum & Conover (1985) early on, structured clinical interviews with children below 8 years of age may be extremely unreliable and data gathered by this method should be compared and complemented with those obtained through other procedures.

Self-report measures

Because many symptoms of anxiety are internal to the child, they may pass undetected by other people. As such, the information provided by the child about their feelings, perceptions or cognitions becomes of paramount importance in the assessment process. Some of the earliest studies on childhood anxiety relied exclusively on children's or adolescents' answers to a single question such as 'What do you fear the most?' or 'Which is the thing to be more afraid of?'. The answers obtained by this procedure could be subsequently subjected to statistical analysis of variable complexity (e.g. frequency tallies, factor analysis, analysis of correspondence), leading to the classification of fears and anxieties in various categories (Porter & Cattell, 1963).

Today it is more common to use standardized self-reports measures such as rating scales or questionnaires in the assessment of childhood disorders. Self-report measures appear in a great variety of formats: behaviour checklists, symptom checklists, personality questionnaires and anxiety rating scales.

One of the most widely used behaviour checklists is the Youth Self-Report Questionnaire (Achenbach, 1991a). This measure was designed to assess child and adolescent (11–18 years) problems as well as adaptive behaviours. Social competencies are assessed through eight items, in a separate section at the beginning of the checklist, and in 16 items from a larger problem section. The main section of the checklist includes 102 items focusing on various behaviour problems to which the child responds by circling 0 (not true), 1 (somewhat or sometimes true), and 2 (very true or often true). Principal component analyses of these items have consistently produced eight factors thought to reflect an equal number of statistically derived syndromes.

Of relevance here is the Anxious–Depressed Scale that includes such symptoms as crying, a fear of doing things wrong, a need to be perfect, feeling nervous, worrying and other related symptoms. A second subscale includes items relating to withdrawal. Through statistical analysis, it is possible to obtain one broadband internalizing score that is derived from both the Anxious–Depressed and Withdrawn Scales. This broadband measure has been shown to successfully discriminate between referred and nonreferred youngsters and has good test-retest reliability, although this varies according to age and gender. However, there are little data on the validity of the anxiety measure despite the widespread use of the Youth Self-Report. Likewise most of the other widely used checklists that contain some internalizing scale (e.g. Children's Personality Questionnaire – Porter & Cattell, 1963; Eysenck Personality Questionnaire – Eysenck & Eysenck, 1975) have not been fully tested in their ability to identify or discriminate amongst anxiety-disordered children. Thus, their usefulness in the assessment of anxiety disorder awaits verification.

In contrast to these general purpose checklists, self-report instruments specifically designed to assess children's fears and anxieties are widely available. One of the most widely used is the Fear Survey Schedule for Children (FSSC; Scherer & Nakamura, 1968). The FSSC was originally developed for children between 9 and 12 years of age, and consisted of 80 items rated on a 5-point scale. It was subsequently revised (FSSC–R; Ollendick, 1983) to more accurately assess fears across a wider age range (7 to 18 years). In this regard, the response format was changed to a 3-point scale (none, some and much) to help younger children. Studies in the United States and Australia (Ollendick, 1983; Ollendick, King & Frary, 1989) have found acceptable internal consistency, test-retest reliability, and validity for the FSSC–R. The total score on the FSSC–R is positively associated with total scores on other measures of trait anxiety and negatively related to measures of an internal locus of control and self-concept (Ollendick, 1983). The FSSC–R has been used in several cross-cultural studies of children's fears and anxiety (Dong, Yang & Ollendick, 1994; Fonseca, Yule & Erol, 1994) and has helped establish the similarity of childhood fears in China, Europe and the United States.

The FSSC–R was not designed for diagnostic purposes and its clinical utility was initially viewed as rather weak (Strauss et al., 1988). In particular, because fears are rather ubiquitous in children, it was found to have difficulty discriminating anxiety-disordered from normal children (Perrin & Last, 1992). Nonetheless, Last, Francis & Strauss (1989) found that by using a qualitative approach to the items, it could be used to distinguish amongst clinically referred children with separation anxiety disorder, overanxious disorder and school phobia. Likewise, Weems et al. (1999) found that both child and parent completed versions of the FSSC–R could reliably distinguish clinically referred children with specific and social phobias. Thus, the FSSC–R may be more useful in discriminating amongst anxiety disorders in clinic samples than as a measure of anxiety disorder in nonreferred children.

One of the most researched and frequently used trait measures of childhood anxiety is the revised version of the Children's Manifest Anxiety Scale (RCMAS; Reynolds & Richmond, 1978). The original CMAS was developed by Castaneda et al. (1956) and consisted of 53 items (42 anxiety and 11 lie-scale items). In order to facilitate its administration, improve its psychometric properties and provide new normative data, the CMAS was revised to include 37 items (28 Anxiety and 9 Lie items) suitable for children 6–19 years of age (Reynolds & Richmond, 1978). Children respond to each item in a yes/no format. The authors found three statistically derived factors on the scale: Physiological, Worry/Oversensivity and Concentration. However, subsequent studies failed to replicate this factor structure but supported its use as a global measure of trait anxiety (Lee, Piersel & Unruh, 1989; Wilson et al., 1990).

In numerous studies, the RCMAS has been shown to possess good test-retest reliability across different time periods. It also has good convergent validity, as reflected in the high correlations between the RCMAS and the Trait Anxiety scale but not with the State Anxiety Scale of the STAIC (Spielberger, 1973). Data on its discriminant validity are generally mixed, as it has been shown to discriminate anxiety-disordered and normal controls (Perrin & Last, 1992) but not anxiety-disordered from depressed children (Brady & Kendall, 1992) or children with attention deficit hyperactivity disorder (Perrin & Last, 1992).

The literature is replete with studies of revised versions of existing measures and new ones for anxiety. Most have only been used for research purposes, are not widely available, and are almost exclusively in English. More recently, several efforts have been made to develop self-report measures more closely aimed at assessing the different anxiety disorders as defined in DSM. One such measure is the Multidimensional Anxiety Scale for Children (MASC; March et al., 1997). The MASC includes 39 items scored on a 4-point scale, with factor analytically derived subscales (i.e. physical symptoms, social anxiety, separation anxiety and harm avoidance) which are invariant across gender and age levels. The MASC has good internal consistency, good test-retest reliability, satisfactory convergent validity (reflected in high correlation coefficients with the RCMAS), and good discriminant validity (reflected in its low correlation with the Children's Depression Inventory: Kovacs, 1992) (March et al., 1997).

Another new measure is the Screen for Child Anxiety Related Emotional Disorders (SCARED; Birmaher et al., 1997). The SCARED consists of 38 items (both for children and parents) rated on a 3-point scale. These items have been statistically grouped into five factors or subscales, including a general anxiety, separation anxiety, social phobia, somatic/panic and school phobia. Data on the psychometric properties of this measure come from one large study ($n = 341$) of clinically referred children and adolescents (aged 9–18 years) (Birmaher et al., 1997). The SCARED was shown to have good test-retest reliability and internal consistency, as well as satisfactory validity. In particular, the SCARED succeeded in differentiating not only anxious from nonanxious children but also amongst various types of anxiety disorders. Additional studies are needed to replicate these findings with both clinical and community samples.

One of the more recently developed, DSM-based anxiety measures is the Spence Anxiety Scale for Children (SCAS; Spence, 1997). The SCAS was developed specifically to reflect the recent changes introduced in DSM–IV for anxiety disorders. It consists of 45 items (38 anxiety items and 7 filler items) rated on a 0 (never) to 3 (always) scale. Factor analyses (exploratory and confirmatory) from a large community study with children aged 8–12 years, revealed five interpretable factors across genders, including panic-agoraphobia, social phobia, separation anxiety, obsessive-compulsive problems, generalized anxiety and physical fears. Additional analyses revealed satisfactory test-retest reliability and good convergent and discriminant validity (Spence, 1997). Like the MASC and the SCARED, data on its psychometric properties come from only one published study conducted in a normal population, thus its clinical utility requires further investigation.

Taken together, self-report measures constitute a rapid, flexible and cost- and time-efficient means of assessing children's levels of anxiety. In this sense, they are particularly useful as screening instruments at the beginning of the assessment process. They may be, however, difficult for use with younger children (below age 8) whose reading abilities can vary greatly as well as their capacity to describe their anxiety. While several of the earlier measures had limited discriminant validity, newer measures based on DSM–IV criteria appear more promising as screening devices for anxiety-disordered children of school age. Additional improvements in the clinical utility of self-report measures may result from the inclusion of items relating to the severity and associated impairment due to symptoms; the development of teacher and parent versions, and reduced item overlap with measures of separate constructs (e.g. depression and behaviour disorders).

Ratings by significant others

Questionnaires and checklists completed by parents, teachers and other significant adults have often been used for the assessment of childhood anxiety disorders. The rationale behind using parent/teacher ratings of the child's anxiety is that those adults who observe the child over a long period of time, across numerous settings and stages of development, are in an excellent position to give an account of the child's problems. Further, they are also the persons who generally refer children for assessment and often become closely involved in treatment.

One of the most widely used checklists of this type is the Child Behaviour Checklist (CBCL; Achenbach, 1991a,b), available in separate forms for parents and teachers. It was designed to assess, in a standardized format, the social competencies and behaviour problems of children and adolescents (4–18 years of age). As such, it includes questions about demographic characteristics, child competence in school and elsewhere, and a list of 118 specific problems, some related to anxiety (e.g. 'Is nervous', 'Fears going to school' or 'Shy and timid'). Parents or teachers indicate the degree to which the child shows each problem on a rating scale of 0 (not true), 1 (somewhat or sometimes true), or 2 (very true or often true).

Like the Youth Self-Report, the CBCL provides a global score, separate scores for internalizing and externalizing problems, and eight narrow-band scales, including an Anxious-Depressed Scale. Test-retest reliability coefficients are high for both girls (0.85) and boys (0.87) (Achenbach, 1991a). Some advantages of the CBCL over similar measures are that it has a large normative database, can discriminate gender and age levels (increasing its sensitivity to developmental factors), and has good psychometric properties demonstrated in large standardization samples. Furthermore, the existence of parallel forms for teachers (Teacher Report Form – TRF) and adolescents (Youth Self-Report Form – YSR) allows a comparative assessment by informant over a range of symptoms. The CBCL has been translated and standardized in several languages, which makes it particularly useful for cross-cultural studies (De Groot, Koot & Verhulst, 1995; Sergeant, 1995; Weisz & Eastman, 1994). As to its clinical utility, data are still scarce but encouraging. Gould, Bird & Jaramillo (1993) found low but significant correlations between the CBCL internalizing scales and DSM–III–R diagnoses of anxiety and depression in an epidemiological sample. Achenbach (1991*a*) also has reported high correlations between this scale and other measures of anxiety.

There are a number of other broadband measures of child psychopathology completed by parents and teachers that include some measure of anxiety. These include the Conner's Rating Scales (Goyette, Conners & Ulrich, 1978), the Revised Behaviour Problems Checklist (Quay & Peterson, 1987), and Rutter Scales (Rutter, 1967; Rutter, Tizard & Whitemore, 1970). All have equivalent forms for parents and teachers and have been extensively used in community studies (Boyle & Jones, 1985; Weisz & Eastman, 1994), and have good test-retest reliability (Bloete & Curfs, 1986; Elander & Rutter, 1996; Lahey & Piacentini, 1985). Data on interrater reliability in the previously cited studies are less favourable, and in particular, the evidence for reliability tends to be much weaker for their internalizing scales. Also, while measures like the Rutter Scales are good at screening for 'psychiatrically-ill' individuals in the general population (cf. Elander & Rutter, 1996), they are likely to be much weaker when it comes to screening for anxiety-disordered children. Their internalizing scales usually include only a small number of anxiety items, mixed in with items relating to depression, isolation and other emotional problems. Also they rely on adult ratings of the child's anxiety that are subject to certain biases (McGee et al., 1983; Moretti et al., 1985; Turner, Beidel & Costello, 1987).

Ratings by significant others play an important role in the assessment of childhood anxiety disorders. However, the available parent/teacher measures were not designed with anxiety disorders in mind and have not been fully evaluated as measures of anxiety. Moreover, it is important to remember that parental depression and anxiety can influence the parent's perception of their child's difficulties (McGee et al., 1983; Moretti et al., 1985). Thus, parent and teacher rating scales should only be used as part of a comprehensive package that includes direct assessment of the child.

Direct observation methods

The central feature of direct observation methods is their focus on anxious behaviours as they actually occur in vivo or in situ, with particular emphasis on their antecedents and consequences. Assessment of this antecedent-behaviour-consequence (A-B-C) relationship goes beyond the typical assessment of antecedent only (i.e. fear-items on the FSSC-R), to provide a truly ideographic view of the anxious child. Also, direct observations are generally more useful in the development of treatment interventions than responses on most questionnaires. Indeed, direct observation of anxiety, by either the child him or herself or another, forms the backbone of most cognitive–behavioural treatments for anxious children.

There are two main categories of direct observations, those that occur in natural settings and those set up by the clinician such as Behaviour Avoidance Tests (BATs). Under natural observation conditions, the clinician or the child monitors a target anxiety symptom for setting, frequency, duration and intensity over well-defined periods. Naturalistic observation is useful in the assessment of fears of dental surgery, separation anxiety, test anxiety, public speaking anxiety and many other situations. A typical example of this method is to have the child record his or her mood, thoughts and behaviours during particular intervals throughout the day in a diary.

Glennon & Weisz (1978) developed an observation method for separation anxiety among preschool children that involves rating the occurrence of 30 behaviours (e.g. physical complaints, avoidance of eye contact, using words such as afraid and scared) believed to reflect anxiety, while the child performs tasks in the presence and absence of the mother. Another standardized measure is the Direct Observation Form (DOF; see McConaughy, 1985) to monitor children's behaviour in the classroom as well as in other group settings. It involves writing a narrative of the child's behaviour as it occurs over 10-minute intervals at different times of the day. Drawing on this narrative, the observer rates the 96 behaviour problems using a 0 (not observed) to 4 (definitely occurred) point scale. Although it is considered a general observation measure, some of its items are directly related to anxiety and fears. The DOF is typically administered by a trained observer (other than a teacher/parent) for use in the classroom with children of any age (McConaughy, 1985).

In contrast to the above, Behaviour Avoidance Tests (BATs) use observational methods to directly assess the child's anxiety when confronted with the threat-related stimuli under controlled and standardized situations. For example, a BAT for a child with a specific spider phobia would consist of asking him or her to enter a room where a spider could be found in a cage, and register in detail their reactions. Several indices of anxiety can be derived with this strategy, including response latency, distance from feared objects, number of tasks performed, number of approach responses, physiological reactions, and other reactions believed to reflect anxiety. This technique may be very helpful to evaluate the effects of treatment for specific phobias, but its usefulness is rather limited when the fear-eliciting stimuli cannot be clearly defined (e.g. in cases of generalized anxiety disorder).

More recently, there have been some efforts to develop observational techniques that can account for the interactions of anxious children with other members of their family. Underlying this approach is the idea that parenting styles, family psychopathology and family interactions generally play an important role in the etiology and maintenance of childhood anxiety. A good example of this approach is the Family Anxiety Coding Schedule developed by Dadds et al. (Dadds, Rapee & Barrett, 1994; Dadds et al., 1996). This schedule was designed to register, in specified time periods, the anxious behaviours of the child and parents, as well as their mutual influences (defined in terms of antecedents and consequences). Each family member's utterance is coded for content (e.g. descriptions, questions, reassurances), process (e.g. to facilitate, to listen), and affect (e.g. anxious, happy, sad). One difference from other traditional methods of observation is that it focuses not only on the child's individual reactions but also on the interdependencies between several people's behaviour.

Generally speaking, direct observation has several advantages over self- and parent-reports of childhood anxiety disorders: greater objectivity and flexibility, and the selection of target behaviours for intervention. However, despite the increasing sophistication of direct observation methods (e.g. cameras, microphones, videotapes), it is obvious that many aspects of the child's anxiety remain inaccessible to the outside observer. Objective and detailed records of the frequency and duration of anxiety reactions do not necessarily provide relevant information on the child's subjective experience of feared events. Indeed, the same score on a given BAT may represent quite different levels of distress for different children (e.g. it is difficult to know if crying reflects anxiety, fear, aggressiveness, opposition or other emotional states). Also, there is not as yet sufficient empirical evidence that observational methods are any better able to discriminate between anxious and nonanxious children, or between various forms of anxiety disorders than questionnaires. Furthermore, observational methods can be perceived as intrusive by the children and the family, and can be costly. Additionally, naturalistic observations are unlikely to provide any useful data about anxiety symptoms that are of very low frequency. Still, if attention is paid to these limitations, observational techniques are an important part of the assessment process and integral to development of prescriptive treatments.

Issues for further research

Despite the increased efforts to develop better measures of anxiety in childhood and adolescence, a number of important issues still require further investigations. In concluding this chapter, we briefly mention three of them.

The first has to do with the cross-cultural validity of the instruments. With few exceptions, the instruments that we discussed above (which are amongst the most widely used for the assessment of anxiety disorders in many countries), were originally developed and validated in English-speaking countries. Naturally, their utilization in other cultures raises important questions since anxiety manifestations may be affected by cultural variations (Ollendick et al., 1989). For instance, are normative symptom data and diagnostic criteria equivalent across different ethnic groups? Is the content equivalence of questionnaires guaranteed in different cultures? Do questionnaires maintain the same factor structure when they are translated and used in different countries?

These issues have been addressed in a number of recent cross-cultural studies using both general purpose and specific measures of fear and anxiety (Fonseca et al., 1994; Weisz & Eastman, 1994). Generally, these studies show that the original factor structure of the measures is not always replicated in other countries. Differences from the original normative sample (USA) also have been found in the distribution of global scores and subscales scores in non-English speaking countries (Weisz et al., 1993). Still, there is considerable evidence for the cross-cultural generality of an anxiety dimension, particularly as measured by the CBCL.

Another interesting finding from cross-cultural studies is that the original composition of some instruments may not cover the most relevant fears and anxieties that children face in other cultures. For example, some of the most frequently endorsed fears on an adapted version of the FSSC-R completed by British, Portuguese and Turkish youngsters (e.g. fear of father dying, of being kidnapped, of separation from parents) are not included in the North American version of the scale (Fonseca et al., 1994). Likewise, Burnham & Gullone (1997) observed that one of the most frequently reported fears in Australian children, a fear of sharks, does not show up on the FSSC–R.

Cultural variations can also be found in the emphasis placed on anxiety. For example, Weisz et al. (1988) presented vignettes describing overcontrolled children (e.g. fearful, anxious, shy) to Thai parents and teachers, and found they considered childhood anxiety problems less serious or less unusual than American adults. Moreover, these cultural effects seemed to depend upon the educational level of the adults.

Taken together, these data show that there may be important differences in the way fears and anxieties manifest themselves (or are perceived) across different cultures and, as a result, the psychometric and diagnostic qualities of an instrument in a given culture are not guaranteed in another culture, even after a careful translation. To assess the cross-cultural validity of anxiety disorders it is necessary to have a good knowledge of what is expected of the children in each culture. As Canino, Bird & Canino (1997) recently pointed out, 'combining ethnographic and empirical approaches is essential to better define what constitutes a case, particularly when using a psychiatric nosology that may be over inclusive in diagnosing children and adolescent in the community' (p. 271).

Another issue awaiting further research is the comparative validity of the instruments now in general use. Until now there has been little effort to systematically compare the psychometric properties of the different instruments used to assess childhood anxiety. For instance, are structured interviews superior to standardized self-report measures? And if yes, for what? Are adults' ratings better than observational records? Within each category of measures, which has the best construct and incremental validity? Which measures/interviews can be used reliably with very young children?

It has been often assumed that structured interviews have greater validity than other measures, but no studies have as yet examined this issue with different anxiety disorders, and across different settings and age levels. Also, it is often mentioned that an adequate assessment of anxiety in childhood will require information from different sources, but it is not yet clear which informant is the best for each situation. This is particularly the case with young children. How do we reconcile parent–child disagreements about anxiety when the child is a 4-year-old?

Finally, an issue deserving greater attention in the assessment of childhood anxiety is the measurement of 'cognition'. Indeed, data from recent clinical and experimental studies suggest that memory and attentional biases for anxiety relevant stimuli may reflect an underlying predisposition to fearfulness, or explain why anxiety can be so persistent in the absence of real threats (Dalgleish, 1995; Ruitter & Brosschot, 1994). In order to measure these memory/attentional processes, several laboratory tasks have been developed, including various adaptations of the emotional Stroop task, dichotic listening task and attention deployment task (Vasey, 1996). One advantage of these tasks is that they are thought to tap into preconscious or pre-attentional cognitive processes (i.e. they are not directly accessible via self or outside observation) (Bell-Dolan & Wessler, 1994; Vasey, 1996). Their application to the assessment of child anxiety may one day provide an interesting complement to traditional measures of the cognitive component of anxiety (e.g. fears, worries and obsessions).

Conclusion

In this chapter, we have provided an overview of the phenomenology and classification of childhood anxiety, and described several methods and instruments currently used to assess anxiety. Anxiety was presented as tripartite in nature (i.e. fear/worry, avoidance and hyperarousal), and although this view is now being challenged in the literature, it remains the dominant influence on the characterization of anxiety disorders in the DSM. The limitations and strengths of the DSM and its 'all-or-none' approach were contrasted with those that place anxiety on a continuum with no clear cutoffs to indicate where clinical significance begins. We then discussed the various measures of anxiety, including structured interviews, adult ratings, child self-reports and direct observation methods. Our review focused mainly on the psychometric properties qualities of these instruments (e.g. reliability, validity), the diversity of symptoms that they are supposed to cover, the availability of adequate normative data and their clinical utility.

In addition, we discussed several basic issues involved in the utilization of these measures, with particular emphasis on the developmental aspects of anxiety, their relation to the various systems of diagnostic classification, the importance of integrating data from different sources and methods, and the potential effects of cultural factors in the evaluation of children with anxiety disorders.

It is apparent from our review of the literature that despite the important advances registered in childhood assessment during the last 20 years, the psychometric properties of the widely used anxiety scales and measures are uneven, their coverage is often rather limited, and their sensitivity to developmental aspects of anxiety remains rather poor. On the one hand, no single measure has succeeded to account for all the facets of anxiety and no definitive rule has been provided to integrate the information from different sources and instruments. On the other hand, some of the most commonly used measures of anxiety are not specific enough since they often fail to discriminate between different emotional disorders. Moreover, there are biases to be considered when weighing the information from multiple informants. Thus, we conclude that a comprehensive assessment should include several self-report measures for the child and a structured interview.

REFERENCES

Achenbach, T. M. (1991a). *Manual for the Youth Self-Report and 1991 Profile*. Burlington, Vermont: University of Vermont Department of Psychiatry.

Achenbach, T. M. (1991b). *Manual for the Child Behaviour Checklist/4–18 and 1991 Profile*. Burlington, Vermont: University of Vermont Department of Psychiatry.

Achenbach, T. M. (1991c). *Manual for the Teachers Report Form and 1991 Profile*. Burlington, Vermont: University of Vermont Department of Psychiatry.

Achenbach, T. M., McConaughy, S. H. & Howell, C. T. (1987). Child/Adolescent Behavioural and Emotional Problems: Implications of cross-informant correlations for situational specificity. *Psychological Bulletin*, **101**, 213–32.

American Psychiatric Association (1987). *Diagnostic and Statistical Manual of Mental Disorders* (3rd edn) (DSM–III). Washington, DC: APA.

American Psychiatric Association (1994). *Diagnostic and Statistical Manual of Mental Disorders* (4th edn) (DSM–IV). Washington, DC: APA.

Anderson, J. C. (1994). Epidemiological issues. In *International Handbook of Phobic and Anxiety Disorders in Children and Adolescents*, ed. T. H. Ollendick, N. J. King & W. Yule, pp. 43–66. New York: Plenum Press.

Angold, A. & Costello, E. J. (1995). A test-retest reliability study of child-reported psychiatric symptoms and diagnoses using the Child and Adolescent Psychiatric Assessment (CAPA–C). *Psychological Medicine*, **25**, 755–62.

Barrios, B. A. & Hartmann, D. P. (1988). Fears and phobias. In *Behavioral Assessment of Childhood Disorders*, ed. E. J. Mash & L. G. Tardal, pp. 196–262. London: Guilford Press.

Barrios, B. A. & Hartmann, D. P. (1997). Fears and anxieties. In *Behavioral Assessment of Childhood Disorders*, 3rd edn, ed. E. J. Mash & L. G. Tardal, pp. 230–327. London: Guilford Press.

Barrios, B. A. & O'Dell, S. L. (1989). Fears and anxieties. In *Treatment of Childhood Disorders*, ed. E. J. Mash & R. A. Barkeley, pp. 167–221. London: Guilford Press.

Beidel, D. C., Fink, C. M. & Turner, S. M. (1996). Stability of anxious symptomatology in children. *Journal of Abnormal Child Psychology*, **20**, 257–69.

Bell-Dolan, D. & Wesler, A. E. (1994). Attributional style of anxious children: Extensions from cognitive theory and research on adult anxiety. *Journal of Anxiety Disorders*, **8**, 79–96.

Berg, C. Z., Rapoport, J. L., Whitaker, A., et al. (1989). Childhood Obsessive Compulsive Disorder: A two year prospective study of a community sample. *Journal of the American Academy of Child and Adolescent Psychiatry*, **28**, 528–33.

Bird, H. R. & Gould, M. S. (1994). The use of diagnostic instruments and global measures of functioning in child psychiatry epidemiological studies. In *The Epidemiology of Child and Adolescent Psychopathology*, ed. F. C. Verhulst & H. M. Koot, pp. 86–103. Oxford: Oxford University Press.

Bird, H. R., Gould, M. S. & Staghezza, B. (1992). Aggregating data from multiple informants in child psychiatry epidemiological research. *Journal of the American Academy of Child and Adolescent Psychiatry*, **31**, 78–85.

Birmaher, B., Khertarpal, S., Brent, D., et al. (1997). The Screen for Child Anxiety Related Emotional Disorders (SCARED): Scale construction and psychometric characteristics. *Journal of the American Academy of Child and Adolescent Psychiatry*, **36**, 545–53.

Bloete, A. W. & Curfs, L. M. (1986). Use of the Conners Teachers Rating Scale in the Netherlands: Some psychometric data. *Nederlands Tijdschrift voor de Psychologie en haar Grensgebieden*, **41**, 226–36.

Boyle, M. H. & Jones, S. C. (1985). Selecting measures of emotional and behavioral disorders of childhood for use in general populations. *Journal of Child Psychology and Psychiatry*, **26**, 137–59.

Brady, E. U. & Kendall, P. C. (1992). Comorbidity of anxiety and depression in children and adolescents. *Psychological Bulletin*, **111**, 244–55.

Burnham, J. J. & Gullone, E. (1997). The Fear Survey Schedule for Children–II: A psychometric investigation with American data. *Behaviour Research and Therapy*, **35**, 165–73.

Canino, G., Bird, H. R. & Canino, I. A. (1997). Methodological challenges in cross-cultural research of childhood psychopathology. In *Evaluating Mental Health Services*, ed. C. T. Nixon & D. A. Northrup, pp. 259–76. London: Sage Publications.

Cantwell, D. P. & Baker, L. (1989). Stability and natural history of DSM–III childhood diagnoses. *Journal of the American Academy of Child and Adolescent Psychiatry*, **28**, 691–700.

Caron, C. & Rutter, M. (1991). Comorbidity in child psychopathology: Concepts, issues, and research strategies. *Journal of Child Psychology and Psychiatry*, **32**, 1063–80.

Castaneda, A., McCandless, B. R. & Palermo, D. S. (1956). The children's form of the Manifest Anxiety Scale. *Child Development*, **27**, 317–26.

Costello, E. J., Costello, A. J., Edelbrock, C. S., et al. (1988). DSM–III disorders in pediatric primary care: Prevalence and risk factors. *Archives of General Psychiatry*, **45**, 1107–16.

Costello, E. J., Edelbrock, C., Dulcan, M. K., Kalas, R. & Klaric, S. (1984). *Report on the NIMH Diagnostic Interview Schedule for Children (DISC)*. Washington, DC: National Institutes of Mental Health.

Crowell, J. A. & Waters, E. (1990). Separation anxiety. In *Handbook of Developmental Psychopathology*, ed. M. Lewis & S. Miller, pp. 209–18. New York, NY: Plenum Press.

Dadds, M. R., Barrett, P. M., Rapee, R. M. & Ryan, S. (1996). Family process and child anxiety and aggression: an observational analysis. *Journal of Abnormal Child Psychology*, **24**, 715–34.

Dadds, M. R., Rapee, R. M. & Barrett, P. M. (1994). Behavioral observation. In *International Handbook of Phobic and Anxiety Disorders in Children and Adolescents,* ed. T. H. Ollendick, N. J. King & W. Yule, pp. 349–64. New York: Plenum Press.

Dalgleish, T. (1995). Performance on the emotional Stroop in groups of anxious, experts, and control subjects: a comparison of computer and card presentation formats. *Cognition and Emotion*, **9**, 341–62.

Davey, G. C. L. (1992). Classical conditioning and the acquisition of human fears and phobias: a review and synthesis of the literature. *Advances in Behaviour Research and Therapy*, **14**, 29–66.

DeGroot, A., Koot, H. & Verhulst, F. (1995). Cross-cultural generalizability of the CBCL Cross-Informants Syndromes. *Psychological Assessment*, **6**, 225–30.

Dong, Q., Yang, B. & Ollendick, T. H. (1994). Fears in Chinese children and adolescents and their relations to anxiety and depression. *Journal of Child Psychology and Psychiatry*, **35**, 351–8.

Edelbrock, C., Greenbaum, R. & Conover, N. C. (1985). Reliability and concurrent relations between the Teacher Version of the Child Behaviour Profile and the Conners Revised Teacher Rating Scale. *Journal of Abnormal Child Psychiatry*, **13**, 295–304.

Elander, J. & Rutter, M. (1996). Use and development of the Rutter parents' and teachers' scales. *International Journal of Methods in Psychiatric Research*, **6**, 63–78.

Eysenck, H. J. & Eysenck, S. B. G. (1975). *Manual for Eysenck Personality Questionnaire*. London: Hodder & Stoughton.

Feehan, M., McGee, R. & Williams, S. M. (1993). Mental health disorders from age 15 to 18 years. *Journal of the American Academy of Child and Adolescent Psychiatry*, **32**, 1118–26.

Fonseca, A. C., Yule, W. & Erol, N. (1994). Cross-cultural issues. In *International Handbook of Phobic and Anxiety Disorders in Children and Adolescents,* ed. T. H. Ollendick, N. J. King & W. Yule, pp. 67–86. New York: Plenum Press.

Glennon, B. & Weisz, J. R. (1978). An observational approach to the assessment of anxiety in young children. *Journal of Consulting and Clinical Psychology*, **46**, 1246–57.

Gould, M. S., Bird, H. & Jaramillo, B. S. (1993). Correspondence between statistically derived behaviour problem syndromes and child psychiatric diagnoses in a community sample. *Journal of Abnormal Child Psychology*, **21**, 287–313.

Goyette, C., Conners, C. & Ulrich, R. (1978). Normative data on Revised Conners Parent and Teachers Rating Scales. *Journal of Abnormal Child Psychology*, **6**, 221–36.

Gray, J. A. (1987). *The Psychology of Fear and Stress,* 2nd edn. Cambridge: Cambridge University Press.

Herjanic, B. & Reich, W. (1982). Development of a structured psychiatric interview: agreement between child and parent on individual symptoms. *Journal of Abnormal Child Psychology*, **10**, 307–24.

Hinden, B. R., Compas, B. E., Holwell, D. C. & Achenbach, T. M. (1997). Covariation of the anxious-depressed syndrome during adolescence: Separating fact from artifact. *Journal of Consulting and Clinical Psychology*, **65**, 6–14.

Hodges, K. (1993). Structured interviews for assessing children. *Journal of Child Psychology and Psychiatry*, **34**, 49–68.

Hodges, K., McKnew, D., Cytryn, L., Stern, L. & Kline, J. (1982). The Child Assessment Schedule (CAS) Diagnostic Interview: A report on reliability and validity. *Journal of the American Academy of Child Psychiatry*, **21**, 468–73.

Honeybourne, C., Matchett, G. & Davey, G. C. L. (1993). Expectancy models of laboratory preparedness effects: A UCS-expectancy bias in phylogenetic and ontogenetic fear-relevant stimuli. *Behavior Therapy*, **24**, 253–64.

Kashani, J. H., Orvaschel, H., Rosenberg, T. K. & Reid, J. C. (1989). Psychopathology in a community sample of children and adolescents: A developmental perspective. *Journal of the American Academy of Child and Adolescent Psychiatry*, **28**, 701–6.

Kearney, C. A. & Silverman, W. K. (1990). A preliminary analysis of a functional model of assessment and treatment for school refusal behaviour. *Behavioural Modification*, **14**, 344–60.

Kearney, C. A. & Silverman, W. K. (1996). The evolution and reconciliation of taxonomic strategies for school refusal behaviour. *Clinical Psychology Science and Practice*, **3**, 339–54.

Kearney, C. A. & Silverman, W. K. (1999). Functionally-based prescriptive and nonprescriptive treatment for children and adolescents with school refusal behaviour. *Behavior Therapy*, **30**, 673–95.

King, N. J., Hamilton, D. I. & Ollendick, T. H. (1988). *Children's Phobias: A Behavioural Perspective*. New York: John Wiley & Sons.

King, N. J., Ollendick, T. H. & Gullone, E. (1991). Negative affectivity in children and adolescents: Relations between anxiety and depression. *Clinical Psychology Review*, **11**, 441–59.

King, N. J., Ollendick, T. H. & Yule W. (1994). *International Handbook of Phobic and Anxiety Disorders in Children and Adolescents.* New York: Plenum Press.

Klein, R. G. (1994). Anxiety disorders. In *Child and Adolescent Psychiatry: Modern Approaches,* 3rd edn, ed. M. Rutter & L. Hersov, pp. 351–74. Oxford: Blackwell Scientific Publications.

Kovacs, M. (1992). *The Children's Depression Inventory Manual.* North Tonawanda, NY: Multi-Health Systems.

Lahey, B. & Piacentini, J. C. (1985). An evaluation of the Quay-Peterson Revised Behaviour Problem Checklist. *Journal of School Psychology,* **23**, 285–9.

Last, C. G., Francis, G. & Strauss, C. C. (1989). Assessing fears in anxiety-disordered children with the Revised Fear Survey Schedule for Children (FSSC–R). *Journal of Clinical Child Psychology,* **18**, 137–41.

Last, C. G., Perrin, S., Hersen, M. & Kazdin, A. E. (1992). DSM–III–R anxiety disorders in children: sociodemographic and clinical characteristics. *Journal of the American Academy of Child and Adolescent Psychiatry,* **31**, 1070–6.

Last, C. G., Perrin, S., Hersen, M. & Kazdin, A. E. (1996). A prospective study of childhood anxiety disorders. *Journal of the American Academy of Child and Adolescent Psychiatry,* **35**, 1502–10.

Lee, S. W., Piersel, W. C. & Unruh, L. (1989). Concurrent validity of the physiological subscale of the Revised Children's Manifest Anxiety Scale: a multitrait-multimethod analysis. *Journal of Psychoeducational Assessment,* **7**, 246–54.

Leonard, H. L., Swedo, S. E., Lenane, M. C., et al. (1993). A two to seven year follow-up study of 54 obsessive compulsive children and adolescents. *Archives of General Psychiatry,* **50**, 429–39.

March, J. S., Parker, J. D. A., Sullivan, K., Stallings, P. & Conners, K. (1997). The Multidimensional Anxiety Scale for Children (MASC): factor structure, reliability and validity. *Journal of the American Academy of Child and Adolescent Psychiatry,* **36**, 554–65.

Marks, I. (1987). The development of normal fear: A review. *Journal of Child Psychology and Psychiatry,* **28**, 667–97.

McConaughy, S. H. (1985). Using the Child Behaviour Checklist and related instruments in school-based assessment of children. *School Psychology Review,* **14**, 479–94.

McConaughy, S. H. & Achenbach, T. M. (1994). Comorbidity of empirically based syndromes in matched general population and clinical samples. *Journal of Child Psychology and Psychiatry,* **35**, 1141–57.

McGee, R., Feehan, M., Williams, S. & Anderson, J. (1983). Prevalence of self-reported depressive symptoms and associated social factors in mothers in Dunedin. *British Journal of Psychiatry,* **143**, 473–9.

McGee, R., Feehan, M., Williams, S. & Anderson, J. (1992). DSM–III disorders from age 11 to age 15 years. *Journal of the American Academy of Child and Adolescent Psychiatry,* **31**, 50–9.

Merrell, K. W., Anderson, K. E. & Michael, K. D. (1997). Convergent validity of the Internalizing Symptoms Scale for Children with three self-report measures of internalizing problems. *Journal of Psychoeducational Assessment,* **15**, 56–66.

Moretti, M. M., Fine, S., Haley, G. & Marriage, K. (1985). Childhood and adolescent depression: Child-report versus parent-report information. *Journal of the American Academy of Child and Adolescent Psychiatry,* **24**, 298–302.

Vasey, M. W. (1996). Anxiety-related attentional biases in childhood. *Behaviour Change*, **13**, 199–205.

Velez, C. N., Johnson, J. & Cohen, P. (1989). A longitudinal analysis of selected risk factors for childhood psychopathology. *Journal of the American Academy of Child and Adolescent Psychiatry*, **28**, 861–4.

Wakefield, J. C. (1992). The concept of mental disorder: on the boundary between biological facts and social values. *American Psychologist*, **47**, 373–88.

Weems, C. F., Silverman, W. K., Saavedra L. S., Pina, A. A. & Lumpkin, P. W. (1999). The discrimination of children's phobias using the Revised Fear Survey Schedule for Children. *Journal of Child Psychology and Psychiatry and Allied Disciplines*, **40**, 941–52.

Weisz, J. R. & Eastman, K. L. (1994). Cross-natural research on child and adolescent psychology. In *The Epidemiology of Child and Adolescent Psychopathology*, ed. F. C. Verhulst & H. M. Koot, pp. 42–65. Oxford: Oxford University Press.

Weisz, J. R., Sigman, M., Weisz, B. & Mosk, J. (1993). Parent reports of behavioral and emotional problems among children in Kenya, Thailand, and the United States. *Child Development*, **64**, 98–109.

Weisz, J .R., Weiss, B., Walter, B. R., Suwanlert, S., Chaiyasit, W. & Anderson, W. W. (1988). Thai and American perspectives on over and undercontrolled child behaviour problems: exploring the threshold model among parents, teachers and psychologists. *Journal of Consulting and Clinical Psychology*, **56**, 601–9.

Werry, J. S. (1994). Diagnostic and classification issues. In *International Handbook of Phobic and Anxiety Disorders in Children and Adolescents*, ed. T. H. Ollendick, N. J. King & W. Yule, pp. 21–42. New York: Plenum Press.

Wilson, D., Chibaiwa, D., Majoni, C., Masukume, C. & Nkoma, E. (1990). Reliability and factorial validity of the Revised Children's Manifest Anxiety Scale in Zimbabwe. *Personality and Individual Differences*, **11**, 365–9.

World Health Organization (1992). *The International Classification of Mental and Behavioural Disorders: Clinical Descriptions and Diagnostic Guidelines*, 10th edition (ICD–10). Geneva: WHO.

Zinbarg, R. E. & Barlow, D. H. (1996). Structure of anxiety and the anxiety disorders: A hierarchical model. *Journal of Abnormal Psychology*, **105**, 181–93.

7

Friends or foes? Peer influences on anxiety among children and adolescents

Annette M. La Greca

Introduction

Youngsters' peer relationships and friendships play a critical role in their social/emotional development. From early childhood on, children spend a considerable amount of time with peers (Ellis, Rogoff & Cromer, 1981). For example, prior to the school years, children interact with peers in child care settings, playgroups or preschool programmes. By 6 to 7 years of age, children spend most of their daytime hours in school or play settings with classmates and friends; this trend continues, and accelerates, through adolescence (La Greca & Prinstein, 1999). It is in the context of these peer interactions that children learn how to share and take turns, how to interact with others on an equal basis, and how to place others' concerns before their own. Successful peer relations contribute in positive ways to the development of social skills and feelings of personal competence that are essential for adolescent and adult functioning (Ingersoll, 1989). Indeed, volumes have been written about the developmentally unique and essential social behaviours that develop in the context of children's peer interactions (Asher & Coie, 1990; Hartup, 1996; Newcomb, Bukowski & Pattee, 1993).

Children's peer relations also make a positive contribution to emotional adjustment and well-being. Supportive friendships serve a protective function, such as by moderating youngsters' reactions to disasters (La Greca et al., 1996; Vernberg et al., 1996), and lessening the impact of parental conflict (e.g. Wasserstein & La Greca, 1996). Furthermore, during adolescence, peer relationships are instrumental in facilitating adolescents' sense of personal identity and increasing their independence from family influences (Dusek, 1991; Ingersoll, 1989).

On the other hand, problematic peer relations are predictive of negative adjustment outcomes (see Parker & Asher, 1987). During middle childhood, for example, children who are disliked or excluded by their classmates often display high rates of internalizing difficulties, such as depression, anxiety and loneliness (Asher et al., 1990; La Greca & Stone, 1993; Strauss et al., 1988). Moreover, over time, problematic peer relations may contribute to serious mental health and academic adjustment problems. Investigators have found that preadolescent children who are actively rejected by their classmates display more mental health problems during late adolescence and early adulthood than their more accepted peers (Cowen et al., 1973). Findings such as these underscore the critical role of peer relations in social and emotional adjustment.

Brief overview of key concepts in peer relations

Children's peer relations have been most widely studied during middle childhood (ages 6 to 12 years). During this developmental period, children typically spend the school day in self-contained classrooms with a set group of classmates, although some youngsters may interact with peers in special educational settings (e.g. resource services for learning disabled youth, enhancement activities for gifted children). After school hours and on weekends, many children are involved in organized activities with peers (e.g. sports teams, dance, scouts, etc.), as well as in unstructured play activities with friends and neighbourhood youth. During the adolescent years, peer relations take on increasing prominence, importance and complexity. Most adolescents have a rich network of peer relations that includes their best friends, other close friends, larger friendship groups or cliques, social crowds, and even romantic relationships (Furman, 1989; Urberg et al., 1995).

In these social contexts, two aspects of peer relations are highly salient – youngsters' peer acceptance and their close friendships. Peer acceptance refers to the extent to which a child or adolescent is liked or accepted by the peer group (e.g. classmates). In contrast, friendships refer to close, supportive ties with one or more peers, and these friendships may occur within or outside the school setting (Furman & Robbins, 1985). Furman & Robbins (1985) emphasize that friendships and acquaintanceships serve different emotional needs; friendships provide youngsters with a sense of intimacy, companionship and self-esteem, whereas group acceptance may provide children with a sense of belonging or social inclusion. Thus, peer acceptance and friendships are related, but distinct. Both are critical for children's and adolescents' emotional health and psychological well-being.

Peer acceptance and rejection

Peer acceptance – or lack thereof – is an important marker for emotional difficulties. Although there are a variety of pathways by which children and adolescents can come to be rejected by peers (see La Greca & Prinstein, 1999), it is apparent that rejected youth are at risk for current and future psychological difficulties. Peer rejection appears to be relatively stable over time and resistant to change (Coie & Dodge, 1983). Furthermore, once children develop a negative reputation among their peers, it becomes exceedingly difficult to develop new friendship ties (Ladd, 1983). Not surprisingly, being rejected by one's peer group represents a significant source of stress for children and adolescents (Coie, 1990). Moreover, the withdrawal and social deficits that are often correlates of peer rejection represent potential antecedents for psychological disturbance (Newcomb et al., 1993).

Although peer acceptance is also important for adolescents, it may take on a somewhat different form, in that most adolescents are no longer spending the entire school day in self-contained classrooms with the same set of peers. Among adolescents, 'social crowds' represent a developmental outgrowth of the social status groups observed in the classrooms of preadolescent children. Crowd affiliations reflect the primary attitudes or behaviours by which an adolescent is known to his or her peers (Brown, 1989). The specific types of crowds adolescents identify appear to vary somewhat from early to late adolescence, although remarkable cross-setting consistencies have been observed. The most commonly identified crowds include: populars (or elites), brains, jocks, druggies or burnouts, loners, nonconformists, or special interest groups (e.g. drama, dance, band) (Brown & Clausen, 1986; Mosbach & Leventhal, 1988; Urberg, 1992). Some adolescents identify with more than one group (i.e. hybrids), and many consider themselves to be 'normals' or 'average'. However, adolescents from 'low status' peer crowds, such as burnouts, loners and nonconformists, may be rejected or excluded by peers, much in the way that rejected children are (La Greca & Prinstein, 1999). Thus, being rejected by classmates (for preadolescents) and belonging to low status peer crowds (for adolescents) may be a marker for negative or exclusionary peer experiences that could contribute to emotional distress and anxiety.

Close friendships

Although peer group acceptance is important, the ability to form and maintain close friendships also represents a critical social adaptation task (Parker & Asher, 1993a). Much of children's and adolescents' social lives revolve around dyadic or small group interactions with their same-aged friends (Parker &

Asher, 1993b). It is not surprising, then, that peers are significant providers of emotional support (e.g. caring, intimacy, validation) for children and adolescents, second only to the emotional support received from parents. Furthermore, peers serve as children's and adolescents' primary source of companionship (Berndt, 1989; Cauce et al., 1990; Furman & Buhrmester, 1985; Reid et al., 1989). In this context, the absence of close friendships, or having poor quality friendships, could be factors that contribute to internal distress and anxiety.

Although few normative data are available, existing findings suggest that most children and adolescents do have close friends. For example, among 9 to 12-year-olds ($n = 881$), Parker & Asher (1993a) found that 78% had at least one reciprocal 'best friend' in the classroom, and 55% had a 'very best friend'. Girls were more likely to have a best friend than boys (82% versus 74%, respectively); girls also had significantly more best friends than boys ($M = 1.54$ for girls; 1.35 for boys). Although few children were friendless, those who were reported significantly more loneliness and social dissatisfaction than those who had close friends (Parker & Asher, 1993a). Thus, children who have at least one close, mutual friendship appear to fare better emotionally than those who lack such personal ties.

Youngsters' friendships vary tremendously in the amount and type of support they provide, the degree to which conflict is present, and their level of reciprocity (Parker & Asher, 1993b). In particular, friendship qualities vary as a function of age and gender. Sharabany, Gershoni & Hofman (1981), for example, studied a large sample of children and adolescents. For same-sex friendships, findings revealed that several friendship qualities (sharing common activities, receiving help, and trust and sharing) did not vary with age, although frankness and sensitivity did show age-related increases. In addition, girls reported more giving and sharing, trust, and attachment in their same-sex friendships than did boys. Not surprisingly, Sharabany et al. also found that differences between same- and opposite-sex friendships were greatest for the younger children (i.e. preadolescents); fewer differences were apparent for adolescents. Intimacy and support from cross-sex friends showed a steady increase with age; in addition, adolescent girls generally rated their cross-sex friendships as more intimate than did boys.

In addition to the quality of a youngster's friendships, the *identity* of the friends appears to be important (Hartup, 1996). Children and adolescents typically choose as friends others who are similar to themselves (e.g. same age, same gender), who share common interests (e.g. play sports, listen to music), and who are fun to be with (Hartup, 1996; Parker & Asher, 1993b). This tendency to be friends with others who are similar has been referred to as homophily (Kandel, 1978). Homophily appears to be the result of both selection (i.e. youngsters seek out friends who are similar to themselves) and socialization (i.e. friends shape and reinforce similar attitudes and behaviours in each other) (Cohen, 1977; Kandel, 1978). Thus, one would expect, for example, that socially competent, well-adjusted children would have friends with similar qualities, but that problem youth might also have close friends with similar problematic behaviours. In fact, with respect to internalizing problems (e.g. anxiety, depression, social withdrawal) this appears to be the case. Specifically, among 14 to 18-year-olds, evidence suggests that adolescents tend to choose friends who possess similar levels of internal distress (see La Greca & Prinstein, 1999).

In general, one might expect that children and adolescents who do not have close friends, who experience problems in their close friendships, or whose friends have emotional problems, would themselves be at risk for problems such as loneliness, anxiety and internalized distress. Research in this area is just in its beginning stages. In the sections below, the potential role of social anxiety in understanding linkages between youngsters' peer relations and their psychosocial functioning are addressed.

Linkages between peer relations and poor adjustment: the potential role of social anxiety

Despite the emotional importance of youngsters' peer relations, little is known about the mechanisms that link poor peer relations with later maladjustment (Kupersmidt & Coie, 1990; Kupersmidt, Coie & Dodge, 1990). For this reason, investigators have begun to examine aspects of youngsters' affective experiences that may both result from problematic peer interactions and contribute to further social difficulties and subsequent maladjustment (Asher et al., 1990).

In this regard, social anxiety, particularly anxiety experienced in the context of peer relations, is a promising avenue of investigation. Social anxiety is one affective response that could result from poor peer relations, such as negative, aversive, or exclusionary experiences with peers. In turn, feelings of social anxiety may inhibit positive social interactions that are necessary for satisfactory social/emotional development. In this manner, social anxiety may play a substantial role in the development of socially withdrawn and avoidant behaviour, leading to missed opportunities for normal socialization experiences, as well as to further problems with peer relations. This bi-directional relationship between social anxiety and peer relations may help to explain linkages between problematic peer relations and later mental health problems. Certainly, social anxiety has long been recognized as an important factor for understanding adults' interpersonal behaviour and psychological functioning (Leary, 1983). For example, studies have demonstrated that socially anxious adults speak less frequently, are less likely to initiate interactions and are more likely to withdraw from anxiety-producing encounters than less socially anxious adults (Leary, 1983). Social anxiety is also likely to have a substantial effect on children's and adolescents' social interactions.

In fact, understanding children's peer relation problems and associated social anxiety may suggest one potential pathway for the development of certain anxiety disorders that have their onset in childhood or adolescence (DSM–III–R, American Psychiatric Association, 1987; DSM–IV, American Psychiatric Association, 1994). For example, social anxiety, in the form of excessive concerns about others' evaluations and avoidant social behaviour, is an essential feature of social phobia, the most common anxiety disorder among adults (Albano, Chorpita & Barlow, 1996), and recent work on the onset of social phobia suggests that 60% or more of the individuals who are seen for treatment report that their symptoms began in middle childhood or adolescence (Öst, chapter 13, this volume). Furthermore, an understanding of social anxiety in youth may aid in studying the etiological pathways for other disorders that are believed to have a substantial social component, such as eating disorders (Bulik et al., 1991) or alcohol abuse (Schneier et al., 1989).

Although potentially very important, the study of social anxiety among children and adolescents is in its very early stages. Until recently, a major obstacle to research in this area has been the absence of an accepted, well-validated measure for assessing youngsters' social anxiety. With this concern in mind, this paper describes the development of the Social Anxiety Scales for Children and Adolescents. Next, the chapter focuses on recent findings regarding the linkages between youngsters' social anxiety and their peer relations and emotional adjustment. Finally, emerging findings on linkages between social anxiety and clinically significant anxiety disorders among children and adolescents will be presented. Implications of the reviewed findings for research and practice will also be discussed.

Development of the Social Anxiety Scale for Children and Adolescents (SAS-A)

General conceptual background

The conceptual basis for the Social Anxiety Scales (SAS) was derived from two primary sources. Leary (1983) noted the importance of separately evaluating the 'subjective experience' of anxiety and 'behavioural consequences of anxiety', such as avoidance and behavioural inhibition. This distinction is important as some individuals who experience social anxiety function adequately in social settings, whereas others experience subjective distress and are socially avoidant.

This conceptual distinction is consonant with the work of Watson & Friend (1969) who identified two aspects of social anxiety in adults. One represents fear of negative evaluation (FNE) by others, also referred to as social evaluative anxiety. The second component is social avoidance and distress (SAD); that is, discomfort, distress, avoidance or inhibition experienced in the company of others. The initial goal of our work with children was to extend these concepts of social evaluative anxiety (or FNE) and social avoidance and distress (SAD) to a developmentally younger population.

Because adults are often poor informants for children's internalizing problems (La Greca, 1990), and because we were primarily interested in assessing youngsters' subjective experience of social anxiety, we developed a series of self-report measures. Our first efforts were to develop a measure of social anxiety that could be used with preadolescent children; this resulted in the development of the Social Anxiety Scale for Children (SASC; La Greca et al., 1988), and the more recent Social Anxiety Scale for Children – Revised (SASC-R; La Greca & Stone, 1993) which have been used in numerous studies to examine the role of social anxiety in children between the ages of 6 and 12 years (La Greca et al., 1988; La Greca & Stone, 1993; Silverman, La Greca & Wasserstein, 1995).

Recently, the SASC-R was modified for use with adolescents (La Greca & Lopez, 1998). This new instrument, the Social Anxiety Scale for Adolescents (SAS-A), builds on earlier work. As noted above, the SASC, SASC-R and SAS-A are all conceptually similar to social anxiety measures that have been developed for adults (Watson & Friend, 1969).

Both the SASC-R and the SAS-A have been translated into other languages, such as Spanish, German, Dutch and Turkish (see La Greca, 1998). Parent versions of these measures have also been developed. Each measure and its scoring is described in the Manual for the Social Anxiety Scales for Children and Adolescents (La Greca, 1998), which also contains recent normative and developmental information and a brief summary of findings on social anxiety in school-based and clinical populations.

Social Anxiety Scales: summary of psychometric studies
Overview of the measures

The Social Anxiety Scales (i.e. SASC-R and SAS-A) have been used with community samples of children (e.g. La Greca, Silverman & Wasserstein, 1998; Silverman et al., 1995), adolescents (Inderbitzen & Hope, 1995; Inderbitzen, Walters & Bukowski, 1997; La Greca & Lopez, 1998; Vernberg et al., 1992), and college-aged youth. These measures have also been used in clinical inpatient and outpatient settings (Ginsburg, La Greca & Silverman, 1997, 1998; Gonzalez et al., 1996; Kearney & Silverman, 1990, 1993), and with youth who have various medical conditions, such as cancer (Pendley, Dahlquist & Dreyer, 1997; Varni et al., 1995) arthritis and neurofibromatosis.

The SASC-R and the SAS-A are identical in format. They contain 18 items (plus 4 filler items) with similar content, each rated on a 5 point scale. Table 7.1 contains a selective listing of items from the two instruments.

Factor structure

The psychometric properties of the SASC-R and SAS-A are also quite similar. Studies of children (La Greca & Stone, 1993) and adolescents (La Greca & Lopez, 1998) have revealed three primary factors: FNE, SAD-New and SAD-General. Fear of Negative Evaluation (FNE; 8 items) reflects fears, concerns or worries regarding negative evaluations from peers. Two subscales emerged for Social Avoidance and Distress: SAD-New and SAD-General. SAD-New (6 items) reflects social avoidance and distress with new social situations or unfamiliar peers. The third factor, SAD-General (4 items), reflects more generalized or pervasive social distress, discomfort and inhibition (see Table 7.1). The discovery of an identical factor structure for social anxiety in studies with both school children and adolescents was important conceptually – in terms of providing evidence for developmental continuity of the construct of social anxiety. The similar factor structure of the SASC-R and SAS-A also provides a practical means of assessing social anxiety across a broad age range, and should facilitate developmental and longitudinal investigations of children's social and affective functioning.

Reliability

Various studies have examined the internal consistency, test-retest reliability and interscale correlations of the SASC-R and SAS-A (see La Greca, 1998, for details). Because of empirical and conceptual distinctions among the subscales,

Table 7.1. Sample items from the Social Anxiety Scales (SASC–R and SAS–A)

Fear of Negative Evaluation (FNE)

   I worry about being teased

   I worry about what other kids say about me

   I am afraid that others will not like me

Social Avoidance and Distress-New Peers / Situations (SAD-New)

   I feel shy around kids I don't know

   I get nervous when I meet new kids (people)

Social Avoidance and Distress-General (SAD-General)

   I feel shy even with peers I know well

   It's hard for me to ask others to do things with me

---

it is strongly recommended that subscales scores be used rather than a total score for the instrument.

Internal consistency

Across studies of the SASC-R and SAS-A, the FNE scale consistently has obtained the highest internal consistency (range = 0.80 to 0.91), followed by SAD-New (range = 0.66 to 0.87) and SAD-General (range = 0.69 to 0.78). This probably reflects, in part, the greater number of items for FNE, relative to SAD-New or SAD-General (see La Greca, 1998). For example, in a community sample of adolescents, La Greca & Lopez (1998) reported internal consistencies on the SAS-A of 0.91 for FNE, 0.83 for SAD-New and 0.76 for SAD-General; the internal consistency of the SAS-A subscales for a clinic-referred sample of adolescents with anxiety disorders was slightly higher (Ginsburg et al., 1997).

Test–retest

In general, high test-retest reliabilities have been obtained for the total SASC-R score (La Greca, 1998). Of the subscales, FNE and SAD-New tend to have higher retest reliabilities than SAD-General. For example, children between the ages of 8 and 12 years were administered the SASC-R and the Revised Children's Manifest Anxiety Scale (RCMAS) at two time points following Hurricane Andrew (La Greca et al., 1998). Over this 4-month interval, retest reliabilities were comparable for the SASC-R (0.70) and the RCMAS (0.72). The retest reliabilities for the SASC-R subscales were: 0.63 (FNE), 0.61 (SAD-New), and 0.51 (SAD-General; $Ps < 0.001$).

   Test-retest reliabilities over 2-month and 6-month intervals have been reported on the SAS-A for adolescents 13 to 15 years of age (Vernberg et al.,

1992). Over a 2-month interval, retest reliabilities were 0.78 for FNE, 0.72 for SAD-New and 0.54 for SAD-General ($Ps < 0.001$). Over a 6-month interval, retest reliabilities were 0.75 for FNE, 0.75 for SAD-New and 0.47 for SAD-General ($Ps < 0.001$).

Interscale correlations

Interscale correlations have revealed that the subscales of the SASC-R and SAS-A are related, but distinct. Interscale correlations have ranged between 0.45 and 0.59 for the SASC-R (La Greca & Stone, 1993), and between 0.52 and 0.67 for the SAS-A (La Greca & Lopez, 1998). Inderbitzen & Hope (1995) report correlations between 0.54 and 0.63 for adolescent boys, and between 0.53 and 0.60 for adolescent girls, on the SAS-A. Intercorrelations have tended to be higher in clinical samples (Ginsburg et al., 1997, 1998).

Demographic factors

Age/grade differences

Findings pertaining to grade or age effects suggest that younger children (approximately ages 7–10 years) report higher levels of social anxiety than older children (10–13 years), and that younger adolescents (12–15 years) report higher levels of social anxiety than older adolescents (16–18 years). More consistent age-related differences have been observed for the SAD subscales than for FNE. However, even when age or grade effects have been found, their magnitude has been relatively small (see La Greca, 1998).

Gender differences in social anxiety

Several studies have examined gender differences in social anxiety (Inderbitzen & Hope, 1995; La Greca et al., 1988; La Greca & Lopez, 1998; Vernberg et al., 1992). Whenever differences have been obtained, girls have been found to report higher levels of social anxiety than boys, especially for the social evaluative aspect of social anxiety (i.e. FNE). Although significant, the relative magnitude of these differences has been rather modest.

These findings are consistent with developmental data indicating that girls worry more than boys about peers' evaluations of them. For example, surveys have found that adolescent girls are more concerned than boys about others' judgements of their appearance and behaviour (Rosen & Aneshensel, 1976). Moreover, rates of internalizing problems have been found to be higher among girls than boys (Bernstein, Garfinkel & Hoberman, 1989; Kashani et al., 1989). Thus, girls may be more vulnerable than boys to feelings of social anxiety, and this may have implications for their social and emotional functioning.

Ethnicity

To date, few studies have evaluated ethnic differences in children's or adolescents' social anxiety. This is probably due to the relative 'newness' of this area of research. However, in the few samples for which ethnic differences were evaluated, ethnicity has not appeared to be a major factor in youngsters' reports of social anxiety (see La Greca, 1998, for more details).

Adults as reporters of youngsters' social anxiety

Parents

Parents are often a primary informant source for youngsters' psychosocial adjustment, even though they may be less useful informants for youngsters' internal states (Loeber, Green & Lahey, 1990). Data suggest that a cautious approach to the use of parents as informants for children's and adolescents' social anxiety is essential.

One recent study (La Greca & Shiloff, 1998) examined parent–adolescent agreement on social anxiety in a community sample of 250 adolescents, and also evaluated two factors that might moderate the degree of adolescent–parent agreement: gender, and adolescents' level of social anxiety.

Factor analysis of the parent-report version of the SAS-A yielded essentially the same three-factor structure as the adolescent report version and, in addition, the total SAS-A scores were not significantly different for the adolescent- and parent-reports. However, parent–adolescent agreement was modest, at best. In general, agreement was highest for FNE, followed by SAD-New and SAD-General; this sequence follows from the most observable items to the least observable or most subjective items.

Gender was one factor that moderated parent–adolescent agreement. Specifically, agreement was significantly higher for girls than for boys (on the FNE and the SAD-New subscales and on the total SAS-A). An additional factor associated with adolescent–parent agreement was the degree of social anxiety the adolescent reported. Adolescents with high levels of social anxiety (total SAS-A > 50) reported more agreement with their parents on the SAS-A ($r = 0.40$) than did adolescents with average ($r = 0.25$) or low scores (SAS-A < 28) ($r = 0.18$).

These findings suggest that parents may be more aware of social anxiety in their adolescent daughters than in their sons. It is possible that girls feel freer to express their feelings of social inhibition and discomfort with family members than do boys; this might account for the gender differences in adolescent–parent agreement. It may also be the case that parents expect girls to be more socially anxious than boys, and therefore are 'primed' to notice it more in their daughters than in their sons. Whatever the reason, it appears that parents may not be an accurate source for reporting adolescent boys' social anxiety. Nevertheless, adolescent–parent agreement was highest for the adolescents who reported high levels of social anxiety, regardless of gender, suggesting that the most socially anxious adolescents would not be 'missed' if their parents were the informant source for social anxiety. Together, these findings support the notion that adolescents are the best informants for social anxiety, and that caution should be taken if parents are to be a primary informant source, especially for boys.

Teachers

Teachers are another important informant source for children's adjustment; this is especially the case during the elementary school years (Loeber et al., 1990). However, work with preadolescent children suggests that teachers may not be accurate informants for children's social anxiety. On the other hand, in one study, peers' ratings corresponded better to children's self-reports of social anxiety than did teachers' ratings (Silverman & La Greca, 1992).

Specifically, Silverman & La Greca (1992) examined test anxiety and social anxiety in a community sample of 273 children (ages 7–13 years), who were evaluated using the Test Anxiety Scale for Children (TASC) and the SASC-R. Other measures included peer ratings of acceptance, rejection, behaviour problems and academic skills, based on traditional peer-nomination procedures, and teacher ratings of behaviour problems and academic skills (see La Greca & Silverman, 1993 for a detailed description of the measures). Children were classified as high test anxious if they met or exceeded clinical cutoffs for the TASC; children were classified as high socially anxious if they met or exceeded the cutoffs for the SASC-R. Very low scorers on the TASC and SASC-R were classified as non-anxious.

Of the 273 students, 25.6% were non-anxious, 18.5% were both test anxious and socially anxious (test/socially anxious), 4.8% were only socially anxious, and 3.7% were only test anxious. Comparisons of these subgroups were made using two factor MANOVAs (Test Anxiety × Social Anxiety). Findings revealed that teachers were not able to distinguish social anxiety among the children, but were good at identifying anxiety in test-anxious youth. Specifically, test-anxious children and test/socially anxious children were rated as more anxious in general, more inattentive, and as performing more poorly academically than non-test-anxious (non-anxious, socially anxious) children. Teacher ratings of conduct problems, positive social skills and social anxiety did not differentiate the groups. The findings suggest that teachers are primarily aware of anxiety in test-anxious youth.

In contrast to the teachers, peers appeared to be fairly good reporters of children's social anxiety. Specifically, socially anxious children and test-socially anxious children were rated by peers as being more anxious, more worried, more worried about what others think of them and as having more internalizing problems than non-anxious or test-anxious children. Socially anxious children were also significantly less well liked by peers than the non-anxious or test-anxious children; in fact, test-anxious children were the most well-liked by peers. Externalizing behaviour problems (e.g. fights, inattentive) and academic skills did not differentiate the groups based on peer ratings.

Until further research is conducted, it appears that substantial caution should be used when obtaining adult reports of children's social anxiety.

Linkages between peer relations and social anxiety: community studies

Problems with peer relations and friendships are believed to contribute to the development of feelings of social anxiety in children and adolescents. Social anxiety, in turn, may have a negative effect on subsequent social interactions of children and youth. Several studies have evaluated linkages between social anxiety and youngsters' interpersonal functioning with peers (Inderbitzen & Hope, 1995; Inderbitzen et al., 1997; La Greca & Lopez, 1998; La Greca et al., 1988; La Greca & Stone, 1993; Vernberg et al., 1992). In this regard, as mentioned near the beginning of the chapter, two specific aspects of interpersonal functioning are of interest: general levels of acceptance from peers and close friendships. Acceptance from peers generally provides youngsters with a sense of belonging, whereas close friendships provide children and adolescents with a sense of intimacy, companionship and emotional support (Berndt, 1982). Both aspects of interpersonal functioning are critical for social and emotional development (Hartup, 1996).

Peer group acceptance

Findings from several studies indicate that children who are rejected by peers, and those who are neglected or excluded from peer activities, report more social anxiety. In particular, studies have linked peer rejection with social evaluative anxiety, and peer neglect with both social evaluative anxiety and reports of social avoidance and inhibition. Specifically, La Greca and colleagues (La Greca et al., 1988; La Greca & Stone, 1993) found that peer-rejected children reported high levels of FNE relative to classmates, and socially neglected children reported both high levels of social evaluative anxiety and high levels of Social Avoidance and Distress (both SAD-New and SAD-General). It is interesting to note that rejected and neglected children do not necessarily report more general anxiety. In one study, children's reports on the Revised Children's Manifest Anxiety Scale did not differentiate children who were rejected or neglected by peers (La Greca et al., 1988).

The importance of peer group acceptance increases with age, and peaks in mid- to late-adolescence (Buhrmester & Furman, 1987). Consistent with these developmental patterns, evidence suggests that social anxiety relates in meaningful ways to adolescents' peer relations. In particular, peer exclusion and peer rejection have been linked with adolescents' social anxiety. Inderbitzen et al. (1997) found that adolescents who were neglected or rejected by peers reported significantly higher levels of social anxiety than those who were classified as average, popular or controversial (i.e. both liked and disliked). Specifically, in comparison to these last three groups, only rejected students evidenced significantly greater social evaluative concerns (i.e. high FNE scores). In addition, neglected and rejected youth reported more generalized social avoidance and distress (SAD-General) than the popular and controversial adolescents.

Interestingly, when the rejected adolescents were further classified into submissive-rejected and aggressive-rejected subgroups, findings revealed that the submissive-rejected subgroup reported significantly higher social anxiety than the aggressive-rejected subgroup. In fact, the submissive-rejected adolescents reported high levels of social evaluative concerns and high levels of generalized social avoidance. In contrast, the aggressive-rejected subgroup reported the lowest levels of social anxiety compared to other teens.

These findings are provocative, as they implicate peer experiences in the development of social anxiety. However, one drawback is that the data are correlational. Another study, by Vernberg and colleagues (1992) more clearly delineated linkages between problematic peer relations and subsequent feelings of social anxiety. Specifically, these authors evaluated social anxiety and peer relations among early adolescents who had recently relocated. In this short-term longitudinal study, teens who reported more peer rejection and exclusion during the fall increased in social evaluative anxiety (FNE) over the school year. In addition, peer exclusion contributed to significant increases in generalized social avoidance and distress (SAD-General). These data suggest that peer experiences play a causal role in the development of social anxiety. Interestingly, high levels of social anxiety in the autumn did not predict subsequent peer rejection, although it did have a later impact on close friendships (see the section below).

Also during the adolescent years, interest in romantic attachments and opposite-sex relations introduces a new dimension to social functioning; namely, the desire to be accepted as a romantic partner (Harter, 1988; Kuhlen &

Houlihan, 1965). One might expect social anxiety to be linked with lower perceptions of social acceptance and romantic appeal. In turn, feelings of social anxiety might limit adolescents' interactions with peers, and inhibit their dating and romantic attachments. La Greca & Lopez (1998) provided initial support for linkages between social anxiety and perceptions of romantic appeal. Specifically, in this study, high socially anxious adolescents reported lower social acceptance and romantic appeal than low socially anxious adolescents. Although the pattern of results was similar for girls and boys, the correlations were consistently stronger for girls.

Close friendships

In addition to peer group acceptance, close friendships represent a critical aspect of youngsters' interpersonal functioning. Close friendships with peers provide companionship, emotional support, intimacy and a means of expressing emotions and resolving conflicts (Berndt, 1982). Feelings of social anxiety – particularly generalized social avoidance and inhibition – could lead to disengagement from peer interactions (La Greca et al., 1988), and interfere with the development of close, supportive ties. Alternatively, youth who lack close friendships may be more vulnerable to feelings of social anxiety; that is, close friendships may protect children from feeling socially anxious.

Longitudinal work with early adolescents (Vernberg et al., 1992) provides support for this notion. Among seventh and eighth graders (i.e. 13–15-year-olds), high levels of generalized social avoidance and distress at the beginning of the school year predicted lower levels of intimacy and companionship in adolescents' close friendships months later; this was especially true for girls. These findings suggest that social anxiety interferes with adolescents' social functioning.

La Greca & Lopez (1998) further extended these findings by examining linkages between adolescents' social anxiety and their reports of the number of close friends, the quality of these friendships and their perceptions of competency in their close friendships. Compared to less socially anxious adolescents, those with higher levels of social anxiety reported having fewer close friendships, and perceived these relationships as less intimate and supportive. On the SAS-A, generalized social avoidance (SAD-General) was most strongly associated with the friendship variables. Although the overall pattern of results was similar for boys and girls, social anxiety generally was not significantly related to boys' close friendships, but was strongly linked to feelings of social anxiety for girls.

In summary, existing findings suggest that social anxiety may lead to impairments in adolescents' close friendships. In particular, generalized social inhibition may contribute to lower levels of closeness and companionship with peers, especially for adolescent girls.

Clinical levels of social anxiety

Research linking social anxiety with social dysfunction among clinical populations is in the very early stages; however, two lines of research are apparent. One has been efforts to develop cut-offs for clinical levels of social anxiety, based on normative data. A second line of inquiry has been to examine social anxiety among children and adolescents with clinically diagnosed anxiety disorders (Ginsburg et al., 1997, 1998), with the idea of evaluating social anxiety as a potential marker for social impairment among anxiety disordered youth. Both areas of work are reviewed below.

Determining clinical levels of social anxiety

In order to examine the potential utility of the SASC-R and SAS-A as tools for identifying clinical levels of social anxiety among community samples of adolescents, recent efforts have been directed at developing clinical cutoffs for the SASC-R (Silverman & La Greca, 1992) and the SAS-A (La Greca, 1998).

Children

Based on the work of Silverman & La Greca (1992), the following SASC-R cut-offs have been recommended for children: for girls, a SASC-R $\geq$ 54 is indicative of high social anxiety, and a SASC-R $\leq$ 40 is indicative of low social anxiety. For boys, a total SASC-R $\geq$ 50 is indicative of high social anxiety and a total SASC-R $\leq$ 36 is indicative of low social anxiety. Scores in between the cutoffs are considered to fall within the normal range (see La Greca, 1998 for more details).

Using these cutoffs, Silverman & La Greca (1992) identified high and low socially anxious children, and found that the high socially anxious children differed significantly from low-anxious children on all three of the SASC-R subscales ($Ps < 0.0001$); in fact, the magnitude of the difference between the high and low anxious groups was one to two standard deviations. Moreover, compared to low-anxious children, the high socially anxious children were rated by peers as being more anxious, more worried, more worried about what others think of them, and having more internalizing problems (e.g., feels worthless); high socially anxious children were also significantly less well liked by peers than the low socially anxious children. In contrast, externalizing behaviour problems (e.g. fights, inattentive) and academic skills did not differentiate the two groups of children based on peer ratings. Thus, children who exceed the recommended cutoffs for social anxiety do evidence more anxiety and social difficulties (as reported by peers) as well as greater difficulties in their peer acceptance.

Adolescents

For adolescents, total SAS-A scores above 50 may be a useful marker for clinically significant social anxiety among adolescents. Using data from a community sample, approximately 14% of the sample of 250 adolescents had SAS-A scores that exceeded the proposed clinical cutoff of 50 (La Greca & Lopez, 1998). The high socially anxious adolescents ($n = 36$) were compared with others whose scores were below the cutoffs ($n = 210$) on a battery of measures that assessed peer relations, friendships, self perceptions, social support and behavioural problems.

As can be seen from Table 7.2, high SA adolescents reported significantly more anxiety on each of the SAS-A subscales, and their parents also reported that their levels of social anxiety were higher than those of comparison youth. Moreover, high socially anxious adolescents, in comparison with other adolescents, reported significantly more rejection and exclusion experiences with peers; lower levels of social acceptance, romantic appeal, and support from classmates; fewer friends and less support and companionship from friends; greater loneliness; and higher levels of internalizing problems, especially anxiety/depression (on the Youth Self-Report). Parents of high socially anxious adolescents also rated their offspring as having significantly higher levels of anxiety/depression (on the Child Behavior Checklist), than did parents of comparison youth. In contrast, High socially anxious adolescents did not differ from other teens in terms of their perceived scholastic competence, their behavioural conduct, their overall Grade Point Average, or their externalizing behaviour problems (by self or parent report). Nor did high socially anxious youth differ from other adolescents in terms of perceived support from other adults, such as parents and teachers. In short, adolescents whose total SAS-A scores exceeded the proposed clinical cutoff differed from other adolescents in their social functioning and levels of anxiety, but not in their relationships with adults or in academic areas.

In summary, these data suggest that total SAS-A scores above 50 may be useful for identifying clinically significant levels of social anxiety in community samples of adolescents. Further replication and evaluation of this cutoff score in other samples of adolescents would be useful and desirable.

Table 7.2. Means (s.d) of high socially anxious and comparison adolescents: measures of social anxiety, self-perceptions, social support, friendships and behaviour problems

	High anxiety (SAS–A Total > 50)	Comparison (SAS–A Total < 50)	F value
n	36	210	
Social anxiety (SAS–A)			
Fear of negative evaluation	27.47 (5.1)	14.89 (4.5)	229.9***
Social avoidance and distress – new	22.39 (3.5)	14.16 (3.7)	155.9***
Social avoidance and distress –			
general	10.08 (3.9)	6.38 (2.2)	67.43***
Total score	59.94 (9.4)	35.43 (8.1)	269.9***
Parent SAS–A total score	45.11 (15.0)	36.33 (10.6)	17.92***
Self-perceptions (SPPA)			
Social acceptance	2.91 (0.7)	3.39 (0.5)	24.22***
Romantic appeal	2.43 (0.8)	3.03 (0.6)	28.18***
Scholastic competence	3.00 (0.6)	3.15 (0.6)	2.04
Behavioural conduct	2.99 (0.6)	3.06 (0.6)	0.53
Social support (SSSCA)			
Classmates	3.05 (0.7)	3.43 (0.5)	19.03***
Close friends	3.33 (0.8)	3.71 (0.5)	17.44***
Parents	3.19 (6)	3.42 (0.6)	5.34*
Teachers	3.00 (0.6)	3.04 (0.6)	0.11
Friendships			
No. of Friends (from YSR)	3.14 (0.8)	3.50 (0.6)	11.22***
Companionship (Adolescent			
Interview)	3.19 (0.9)	3.54 (0.7)	7.14**
Intimacy (Adolescent Interview)	3.68 (0.9)	3.98 (0.8)	4.43*
Behavior problems (YSR)			
Internalizing scale (raw score)	20.08 (9.2)	11.95 (7.0)	37.24***
Externalizing scale (raw score)	15.89 (7.6)	14.06 (6.9)	2.08
Internalizing – anxious/depressed	11.42 (6.0)	5.77 (4.2)	47.26***
Behaviour problems (CBCL)			
Internalizing scale (raw score)	9.67 (8.3)	7.04 (5.9)	5.27*
Externalizing scale (raw score)	7.81 (7.8)	7.06 (6.5)	0.38
Internalizing – anxious/depressed	5.03 (4.8)	2.90 (3.3)	11.05***

SAS–A = Social Anxiety Scale for Adolescents; SPPA = Self Perception Profile for Adolescents; SSSCA = Social Support Scale for Children and Adolescents; YSR = Youth Self Report; CBCL = Child Behavior Checklist.
*P < 0.05, **P < 0.01, ***P < 0.001.

Social anxiety among children and adolescents with anxiety disorders

Research has supported the use of the SASC-R and the SAS-A with anxiety-disordered youth (Ginsburg et al., 1997, 1998). Specifically, Ginsburg and colleagues (1998) examined the psychometric properties of the SASC-R in a large sample of children with anxiety disorders (n = 154), and also examined linkages between the children's social anxiety and their social–emotional functioning. The participants were children between the ages of 6 and 11 years, who were seen in a clinical setting for anxiety-disordered youth. Findings with the SASC-R revealed essentially the same three-factor structure that was evident in prior community samples. Furthermore, children with anxiety disorders who reported high levels of social anxiety on the SASC-R reported low levels of social acceptance and global self-worth and more negative peer interactions. Among the girls, those with higher levels of social anxiety were rated by their parents as having poorer social skills, particularly in the areas of assertive and responsible social behaviour. These findings suggested that social anxiety might be a marker for social impairment among anxiety-disordered youth, especially for girls. Moreover, the SASC-R might help to identify youth with social phobias, as children's reports of social anxiety were found to differentiate between the children who were diagnosed with simple phobias and those with simple phobia who also had a comorbid diagnosis of social phobia.

In addition to these findings with children, Ginsburg et al. (1997) provided data that support the validity of the SAS-A as a measure of social anxiety for adolescents with anxiety disorders. In this study, 70 adolescents (ages 12–17 years; 41% girls), who were evaluated at a university-based anxiety disorders clinic served as participants. The child and parent versions of the Anxiety Disorder Interview Schedule for Children (Silverman & Nelles, 1988) were used to determine adolescents' clinical diagnoses. The most prevalent primary diagnoses were simple phobia and social phobia (26%). Factor structure of the SAS-A yielded a three-factor solution (FNE, SAD-New, SAD-General) that closely approximated that of the SAS-A with a community sample of adolescents. Mean levels of overall social anxiety were higher for the anxiety-disordered youth (M = 43.6) than for the community sample reported by La Greca & Lopez (1998) (M = 39.1). Overall, these data supported the psychometric properties of the SAS-A with anxiety-disordered adolescents.

Of further interest, however, was the finding that SAS-A scores could discriminate adolescents with and without social phobia. Adolescents with a primary diagnosis of social phobia (n = 18) were compared to adolescents who did not have a primary or comorbid diagnosis of social phobia (n = 41). Adolescents with social phobia reported significantly higher levels of social anxiety (SAS-A total), social evaluative concerns (FNE) and discomfort around new and familiar peers (SAD-New and SAD-General) than adolescents diagnosed with other anxiety disorders ($Ps < 0.01$). In fact, the average level of social anxiety for the social phobia group exceeded the suggested clinical cutoff of 50.

Furthermore, among the clinic sample as a whole, social anxiety was linked with impairment in social functioning. Specifically, adolescents with anxiety disorders who reported higher levels of social anxiety also reported lower perceived social acceptance, lower self-worth, and less assertive social skills (as rated by their parents). In addition, the adolescents who reported high levels of social evaluative anxiety (FNE), reported significantly more negative peer experiences than those with fewer social evaluative concerns.

In summary, findings with clinical populations of children and adolescents with anxiety disorders are consistent with findings discussed earlier and derived from nonclinical samples (Inderbitzen et al., 1997; La Greca & Lopez, 1998; Vernberg et al., 1992). The data suggest that the SASC-R and the SAS-A may be good instruments for identifying social impairment among children and adolescents with anxiety disorders. Moreover, the two social anxiety scales may be useful tools for screening community samples in order to identify youngsters with socially based anxiety disorders, such as social phobia.

Conclusions

Summary of findings

In summary, the findings from studies of community samples of children and adolescents, as well as youth with clinically significant anxiety disorders, provide support for the utility of the SASC-R and the SAS-A for assessing social anxiety among children and adolescents. Both exploratory and confirmatory factor analyses have revealed essentially the same underlying factor structure for the SASC-R and the SAS-A (i.e. FNE, SAD-New and SAD-General). Such findings provide support for the developmental continuity of these three components of social anxiety from childhood through adolescence.

The availability of an instrument to assess social anxiety that has been validated across a wide age range (7 to 18 years of age) may facilitate developmental and longitudinal investigations of children's social and affective functioning. In particular, the SASC-R and the SAS-A may also prove useful for examining the onset and course of social phobia or other anxiety-related disorders that have substantial social components (e.g. eating disorders). To date, research into factors that may contribute to youngsters' anxiety disorders has focused largely on family and genetic factors (Black, 1995; Bruch, 1989; Weissman et al., 1984), as well as on temperament and biological predisposition (Kagan, Reznick & Snidman, 1987). In contrast, peer influences have been seriously neglected, despite findings that youngsters with clinically significant anxiety disorders are liked less by their peers and tend to be neglected by their classmates (Strauss et al., 1989). Thus, the SASC-R and the SAS-A may be useful tools for exploring the role of social anxiety as a mediator between poor peer relations and the development of clinically significant anxiety disorders in children and adolescents.

Based on existing findings, it appears that children and adolescents are the best informants for their experiences of social anxiety. Although parent reports may also be useful for identifying clinically significant social anxiety in adolescents, parents have been found to be less accurate in identifying low to moderate levels of social anxiety in their offspring. Moreover, parents (mostly mothers) were not especially good judges of social anxiety in their sons. Among preadolescents, teacher reports of social anxiety did not correspond to children's self-reports, and therefore, are not recommended for assessment at this time.

Consonant with findings that have been obtained for other internalizing problems, it appears that adult reports of social anxiety may be less useful than reports obtained directly from the children and adolescents themselves. In general, children and adolescents are considered to be the best informants for internalizing difficulties, relative to parents or teachers (Loeber et al., 1990), and findings with respect to youngsters' social anxiety are consistent with this perspective.

Across studies, perhaps most noteworthy were the findings linking children's and adolescents' social anxiety with problems in general peer acceptance (e.g., more aversive peer experiences, less acceptance and support from classmates). In addition, among adolescents, girls' social anxiety was linked with difficulties in close friendships (i.e. fewer friendships, and less intimacy and companionship in these friendships). If socially anxious children and adolescents perceive their general social acceptance to be low, as existing studies indicate, this may lead them to miss out on important socialization experiences and, over time, may contribute to impairments in social functioning. Consistent with this perspective, clinical reports suggest that about 70% of adults with social phobia report impairments in their social relationships (e.g. Turner et al., 1986), and epidemiological studies have shown that adults with social phobia are less likely to marry than normal controls (Schneier et al., 1992).

Research and clinical uses of the social anxiety scales

Given the conceptual and empirical distinctions among the social anxiety subscales of the SASC-R and SAS-A, it is generally recommended that subscale scores be used in research and clinical practice, rather than total scores. The one exception is that total scores may be useful for identifying clinical levels of social anxiety in youth (La Greca, 1998).

Overall, findings suggest that the SASC-R and SAS-A may be useful in several research and clinical contexts. Specifically, these include: screening children with high levels of social anxiety in community samples; identifying children with anxiety disorders who have impairments in their social functioning; measuring children's subjective distress and discomfort with peer interactions; and studying the onset and development of certain disorders that have a social anxiety component, such as social phobia, eating disorders and possibly generalized anxiety disorder. In addition, the SASC-R and SAS-A may be useful in longitudinal studies, given the broad age range that they span (7–18 years), and their similarity in content and conceptualization.

In clinical settings, the SASC-R and SAS-A may be useful for identifying high levels of social anxiety among clinically referred children and adolescents, and for identifying impairments in youngsters' social functioning and peer relations. It has not yet been determined whether scores on the SASC-R and SAS-A are sensitive to clinical interventions, and further investigation in this area would be highly desirable. Further, it should be noted that the Social Anxiety Scales were designed conceptually; they were not developed to 'map onto' specific DSM diagnoses. Thus, although the SASC-R and SAS-A are useful for screening purposes, other diagnostic tools will be needed to confirm specific clinical diagnoses (e.g. the Anxiety Disorders Interview Schedule; Silverman & Nelles, 1988).

Conceptual issues for further research

Several additional directions for future research are suggested from the present review. First, future studies might consider using short-term longitudinal methodologies, particularly during important social transition periods (e.g. school transitions, relocation), to further elucidate the causal pathways between social anxiety and social/emotional dysfunction. At the present time, it is difficult to determine whether feelings of social anxiety contribute to poor peer relations among children and adolescents, or whether poor peer relations lead to feelings of social anxiety. Most likely, being neglected or excluded from peer interactions represents a significant stressor for children and adolescents (Frankel, 1990), that leads to feelings of social apprehension, worry or distress (see Leary, 1990); these subjective feelings, in turn, may lead to behavioural avoidance of peers, and contribute to missed opportunities for normal socialization experiences, and eventually to clinical impairment. Further research of a longitudinal nature will be helpful in elucidating such etiological pathways.

Second, future work might also address reasons for the higher reported social anxiety among adolescent girls, and the stronger linkages between girls' social anxiety and impairment in their close friendships. Such findings are troubling, as they suggest that social anxiety may interfere substantially with girls' close interpersonal relationships. Intimacy and emotional support from close friends are salient features of adolescent girls' friendships (Berndt, 1982); thus, factors that interfere with the development of close, intimate friendships are especially important to understand. Kashani et al. (1989) observed that interpersonal anxiety appears to be a fact of life for adolescents at about the time when satisfaction with family decreases and peers become the focus of attention. Future efforts to elucidate linkages between social anxiety and adolescents' interpersonal functioning seem crucial, especially for girls.

Finally, additional attention should be given to the utility of the Social Anxiety Scales with anxiety-disordered youth. Findings now suggest that the SASC-R and SAS-A can discriminate between children and adolescents with and without social phobia, and that social anxiety may be a marker for social impairment among children and adolescents with clinically significant anxiety disorders. Thus, in the future, it would be useful to evaluate the sensitivity of the SASC-R and the SAS-A as screening tools for identifying children and adolescents with socially based anxiety disorders. In addition the sensitivity of the SASC-R and the SAS-A as measures of treatment-related changes in social anxiety would be important to examine.

Acknowledgements

Preparation of this manuscript was supported by a grant from the National Institute of Mental Health (RO1-MH48028) to the first author.

REFERENCES

Albano, A. M., Chorpita, B. F. & Barlow, D. H. (1996). Childhood anxiety disorders. In *Child Psychopathology*, ed. E. J. Mash & R. A. Barkley, pp. 196–241. New York: Guilford Press.

American Psychiatric Association (1987). *Diagnostic and Statistical Manual of Mental Disorders* (3rd edn revised) (DSM–III–R). Washington, DC: APA.

American Psychiatric Association (1994). *Diagnostic and Statistical Manual of Mental Disorders* (4th edn) (DSM–IV). Washington, DC: APA.

Asher, S. R. & Coie, J. D. (ed.) (1990). *Peer Rejection in Childhood*. New York: Cambridge University Press.

Asher, S. R., Parkhurst, J. T., Hymel, S. & Williams, G. A. (1990). Peer rejection and loneliness in childhood. In *Peer Rejection in Childhood*, ed. S. R. Asher & J. D. Coie, pp. 253–73. Cambridge: Cambridge University Press.

Berndt, T. J. (1982). The features and effects of friendship in early adolescence. *Child Development*, **53**, 1447–60.

Berndt, T. J. (1989). Obtaining support from friends during childhood and adolescence. In *Children's Social Networks and Social Supports*, ed. D. Belle, pp. 308–31). New York: John Wiley & Sons.

Bernstein, G. A., Garfinkel, B. D. & Hoberman, H. M. (1989). Self-reported anxiety in adolescents. *American Journal of Psychiatry*, **146**, 384–6.

Black, B. (1995). Separation anxiety disorder and panic disorder. In *Anxiety Disorders in children and adolescents*, ed. J. S. March, pp. 212–34. New York: Guilford Press.

Brown, B. B. (1989). The role of peer groups in adolescents' adjustment to secondary school. In *Peer Relationships in Child Development*, ed. T. J. Berndt & G. W. Ladd, pp 188–215. New York: John Wiley and Sons.

Brown, B. B. & Clausen, D. R. (1986, March). *Developmental changes in adolescents' conceptions of peer groups*. Paper presented at the biennial meeting of the Society for Research in Adolescence, Madison, WI.

Bruch, M. A. (1989). Familial and developmental antecedents of social phobia: Issues and findings. *Clinical Psychology Review*, **9**, 37–47.

Buhrmester, D. & Furman, W. (1987). The development of companionship and intimacy. *Child Development*, **58**, 1101–13.

Bulik, C. M., Beidel, D. C., Duchmann, E., Weltzin, T. E. & Kaye, W. H. (1991). An analysis of social anxiety in anorexic, bulimic, social phobic and control women. *Journal of Psychopathology and Behavioral Assessment*, **13**, 199–211.

Cauce, A. M., Reid, M., Landesman, S. & Gonzales, N. (1990). Social support in young children: Measurement, structure, and behavioral impact. In *Social Support: An Interactional View*, ed. B. R. Sarason, I. G. Sarason & G. R. Pierce, pp. 64–94. New York: John Wiley & Sons.

Cohen, J. (1977). Sources of peer group homogeneity. *Sociology of Education*, **50**, 227–41.

Coie, J .D. (1990). Toward a theory of peer rejection. In *Peer Rejection in Childhood*, ed. S. R. Asher & J. D. Coie, pp. 365–401. Cambridge: Cambridge University Press.

Coie, J. D. & Dodge, K. A. (1983). Continuities and changes in children's social status: A five-year longitudinal study. *Merrill-Palmer Quarterly*, **29**, 261–82.

Cowen, E. L., Pederson, A., Babijian, H., Izzo, L. D. & Trost, M. A. (1973). Long-term follow-up of early detected vulnerable children. *Journal of Consulting and Clinical Psychology*, **41**, 438–46.

Dusek, J. (1991). *Adolescent Development and Behavior*, 3rd. edn. Palo Alto, CA: Science Research Associates.

Ellis, S., Rogoff, B. & Cromer, C. C. (1981). Age segregation in children's social interactions. *Developmental Psychology*, **17**, 399–407.

Frankel, K. A. (1990). Girls' perceptions of peer relationship support and stress. *Journal of Early Adolescence*, **10**, 69–88.

Furman, W. (1989). The development of children's social networks. In *Children's Social Networks and Social Supports*, ed. D. Belle, pp. 151–72. New York: Academic Press.

Furman, W. & Buhrmester, D. (1985). Children's perceptions of the personal relationships in their social networks. *Developmental Psychology*, **21**, 1016–24.

Furman, W. & Robbins, P. (1985). What's the point: Issues in the selection of treatment objectives. In *Children's Peer Relations: Issues in Assessment and Intervention*, ed. B. H. Schneider, K. H. Rubin & J. E. Ledingham, pp. 41–56. New York: Springer-Verlag.

Ginsburg, G. S., La Greca, A. M. & Silverman, W. K. (1997, November). *The Social Anxiety Scale for Adolescents (SAS-A): Utility for youth with anxiety disorders*. Presented at the annual meeting of the Association for the Advancement of Behavior Therapy, Miami Beach, FL, November 1997. Available from authors.

Ginsburg, G. S., La Greca, A. M. & Silverman, W. K. (1998). Social anxiety in children with anxiety disorders: Linkages with social and emotional functioning. *Journal of Abnormal Child Psychology*, **3**, 175–85.

Gonzalez, K. P., Field, T. M., Lasko, D., La Greca, A. M. & Lahey, B. B. (1996). Social anxiety and aggression in behaviorally disordered children. *Early Child Development and Care*, **121**, 1–8.

Harter, S. (1988). *Manual for the Self Perception Profile for Adolescents*. Denver: University of Denver.

Hartup, W. W. (1996). The company they keep: Friendships and their developmental significance. *Child Development*, **67**, 1–13.

Inderbitzen, H. M. & Hope, D.A. (1995). Relationship of adolescent reports of social anxiety, anxiety, and depressive symptoms. *Journal of Anxiety Disorders*, **9**, 385–96.

Inderbitzen, H. M., Walters, K. S. & Bukowski, A. L. (1997). The role of social anxiety in adolescent peer relations: Differences among sociometric status groups and rejected subgroups. *Journal of Clinical Child Psychology*, **26**, 338–48.

Ingersoll, G. M. (1989). *Adolescents*, 2nd edn. Englewood Cliffs, NJ: Prentice Hall.

Kagan, J., Reznick, J. S. & Snidman, N. (1987). The physiology and psychology of behavioral inhibition in children. *Child Development*, **58**, 1459–73.

Kandel, D. (1978). Homophily, selection, and socialization in adolescent friendships. *American Journal of Sociology*, **84**, 427–36.

Kashani, J. H., Orvaschel, H., Rosenberg, T. K. & Reid, J. C. (1989). Psychopathology in a community sample of children and adolescents: A developmental perspective. *Journal of the American Academy of Child and Adolescent Psychiatry*, **28**, 701–6.

Kearney, C. A. & Silverman, W. K. (1990). A preliminary analysis of a functional model of assessment and treatment for school refusal behavior. *Behavior Modification*, **14**, 340–66.

Kearney, C. A. & Silverman, W. K. (1993). Measuring the function of school refusal behavior: The School Refusal Assessment Scale. *Journal of Clinical Child Psychology*, **22**, 85–96.

Kuhlen, R. G. & Houlihan, N. B. (1965). Adolescent heterosexual interest in 1942 and 1965. *Child Development*, **36**, 1049–52.

Kupersmidt, J. B. & Coie, J. D. (1990). Preadolescent peer status, aggression, and school adjustment as predictors of externalizing problems in adolescence. *Child Development*, **61**, 1350–62.

Kupersmidt, J. B., Coie, J. D. & Dodge, K. A. (1990). The role of poor peer relationships in the development of disorder. In *Peer Rejection in Childhood*, ed. S. R. Asher & J. D. Coie, pp. 274–305. Cambridge: Cambridge University Press.

La Greca, A. M. (1990). Issues and perspectives on the child assessment process. In *Through the Eyes of the Child: Obtaining Self-Reports from Children and Adolescents*, ed. A. M. La Greca, pp. 3–21. Boston, MA: Allyn & Bacon.

La Greca, A. M. (1998). *Manual for the Social Anxiety Scales for Children and Adolescents*. Available from Author, Miami, FL.

La Greca, A. M., Dandes, S. K., Wick, P., Shaw, K. & Stone, W. L. (1988). The development of the Social Anxiety Scale for Children (SASC): Reliability and concurrent validity. *Journal of Clinical Child Psychology*, **17**, 84–91.

La Greca, A. M. & Lopez, N. (1998). Social anxiety among adolescents: Linkages with peer relations and friendships. *Journal of Abnormal Child Psychology*, **26**, 83–94.

La Greca, A. M. & Prinstein, M. J. (1999). The peer group. In *Developmental Issues in the Clinical Treatment of Children and Adolescents*, ed. W. K. Silverman & T. H. Ollendick, pp. 171–98. Needham Heights, MA: Allyn and Bacon.

La Greca, A. M. & Shiloff, N. (1998, February). *Social Anxiety in Adolescents: Agreement between Parent and Teen*. Society for Research in Adolescence, San Diego, CA, February. Available from author.

La Greca, A. M. & Silverman, W. K. (1993). Parental bias in research participation. *Journal of Abnormal Child Psychology*, **21**, 89–101.

La Greca, A. M., Silverman, W. K., Vernberg, E. M. & Prinstein, M. J. (1996). Posttraumatic stress symptoms in children after Hurricane Andrew: A prospective study. *Journal of Consulting and Clinical Psychology*, **64**, 712–23.

La Greca, A. M., Silverman, W. K. & Wasserstein, S.B. (1998). Children's predisaster functioning as a predictor of posttraumatic stress following Hurricane Andrew. *Journal of Consulting and Clinical Psychology*, **66**, 883–92.

La Greca, A. M. & Stone, W. L. (1993). Social Anxiety Scale for Children – Revised: Factor structure and concurrent validity. *Journal of Clinical Child Psychology*, **22**, 17–27.

Ladd, G. W. (1983). Social networks of popular, average, and rejected children in school settings. *Merrill–Palmer Quarterly*, **29**, 283–307.

Leary, M. (1983). *Understanding Social Anxiety: Social, Personality, and Clinical Perspectives*. Beverly Hills, CA: Sage.

Leary, M. R. (1990). Responses to social exclusion: Social anxiety, jealousy, loneliness, depression, and low self-esteem. *Journal of Social and Clinical Psychology*, **9**, 221–9.

Loeber, R., Green, S. M. & Lahey, B. B. (1990). Mental health professionals' perceptions of the utility of children, parents, and teachers as informants on childhood psychopathology. *Journal of Clinical Child Psychology*, **19**, 136–43.

Mosbach, P. & Leventhal, H. (1988). Peer group identity and smoking: Implications for intervention. *Journal of Abnormal Psychology*, **97**, 238–45.

Newcomb, A. F., Bukowski, W. M. & Pattee, L. (1993). Children's peer relations: A meta-analytic review of popular, rejected, neglected, controversial and average sociometric status. *Psychological Bulletin*, **113**, 99–128.

Parker, J. G. & Asher, S. R. (1987). Peer relations and later personal adjustment: Are low-accepted children at risk? *Psychological Bulletin*, **102**, 357–89.

Parker, J. G. & Asher, S. R. (1993a). Friendship and friendship quality in middle childhood: Links with peer group acceptance and feelings of loneliness and social dissatisfaction. *Developmental Psychology*, **29**, 611–21.

Parker, J. G. & Asher, S. R. (1993b). Beyond group acceptance: Friendship and friendship quality as distinct dimensions of peer adjustment. In *Advances in Personal Relationships*, Vol. 4, ed. W. H. Jones & D. Perlman. London: Kingsley.

Pendley, J. S., Dahlquist, L. M. & Dreyer, Z. (1997). Body image and psychosocial adjustment in adolescent cancer survivors. *Journal of Pediatric Psychology*, **22**, 29–43.

Reid, M., Landesman, S., Treder, R. & Jaccard, J. (1989). 'My family and friends.' 6 to 12 year old children's perceptions of social support. *Child Development*, **60**, 896–910.

Rosen, B. C. & Aneshensel, C. S. (1976). The chameleon syndrome: A social psychological dimension of the female sex role. *Journal of Marriage and the Family*, **38**, 605–17.

Schneier, F. R., Johnson, J., Hornig, C. D., Liebowitz, M. R. & Weissman, M. M. (1992). Social phobia: Comorbidity in an epidemiological sample. *Archives of General Psychiatry*, **49**, 282–8.

Schneier, F. R., Martin, L. Y., Liebowitz, M. R., Gorman, J. M. & Fyer, A. J. (1989). Alcohol abuse in social phobia. *Journal of Anxiety Disorders*, **3**, 15–23.

Sharabany, R., Gershoni, R. & Hofman, J. (1981). Girlfriends, boyfriends: Age and sex differences in intimate friendship. *Developmental Psychology*, **17**, 800–8.

Silverman, W. K. & La Greca, A. M. (1992, February). *Screening for Childhood Anxiety: A Comparison of Test and Social Anxiety.* Paper presented at the Society for Research in Child and Adolescent Psychopathology, Sarasota, FL, February, 1992. Available from authors.

Silverman, W. K., La Greca, A. M. & Wasserstein, S. B. (1995). What do children worry about?: Worries and their relationship to anxiety. *Child Development*, **66**, 671–86.

Silverman, W. K. & Nelles, W. B. (1988). The Anxiety Disorders Interview Schedule for Children. *Journal of the American Academy of Child and Adolescent Psychiatry*, **27**, 772–8.

Strauss, C. C., Lahey, B. B., Frick, P., Frame, C. L. & Hynd, G. (1988). Peer social status of children with anxiety disorders. *Journal of Consulting and Clinical Psychology*, **56**, 137–41.

Strauss, C. C., Lease, C. A., Kazdin, A. E., Dulcan, M. K. & Last, C. G. (1989). Multimethod assessment of the social competence of children with anxiety disorders. *Journal of Clinical Child Psychology*, **18**, 184–9.

Turner, S. M., Beidel, D. C., Dancu, C. V. & Keys, D. J. (1986). Psychopathology of social phobia and comparison to avoidant personality. *Journal of Abnormal Psychology*, **95**, 389–94.

Urberg, K. A. (1992). Locus of peer influence: Social crowd and best friend. *Journal of Youth and Adolescence*, **21**, 439–50.

Urberg, K. A., Degirmencioglu, S. M., Tolson, J. M. & Halliday-Scher, K. (1995). The structure of adolescent peer networks. *Developmental Psychology*, **31**, 540–54.

Varni, J. W., Katz, E. R., Colegrove, R. Jr. & Dolgin, M. (1995). Perceived physical appearance and adjustment of children with newly diagnosed cancer: A path analytic model. *Journal of Behavioral Medicine*, **18**, 261–78.

Vernberg, E. M., Abwender, D. A., Ewell, K. K. & Beery, S. H. (1992). Social anxiety and peer relationships in early adolescence: A prospective analysis. *Journal of Clinical Child Psychology*, **21**, 189–96.

Vernberg, E. M., La Greca, A. M., Silverman, W. K. & Prinstein, M. J. (1996). Prediction of posttraumatic stress symptoms in children after Hurricane Andrew. *Journal of Abnormal Psychology*, **105**, 237–48.

Wasserstein, S. B. & La Greca, A. M. (1996). Can peer support buffer against behavioral consequences of parental discord? *Journal of Clinical Child Psychology*, **25**, 177–82.

Watson, D. & Friend, R. (1969). Measurement of social-evaluative anxiety. *Journal of Consulting and Clinical Psychology*, **33**, 448–57.

Weissman, M. M., Leckman, J. F., Merikangas, K. R., et al. (1984). Depression and anxiety disorders in parents and children. *Archives of General Psychiatry*, **41**, 845–52.

8

Conditioning models of childhood anxiety

Andy P. Field and Graham C. L. Davey

Little miss Muffet, sat on a tuffet
– Eating her curds and whey.
Down came a spider, that sat down beside her
and frightened miss Muffet away

Children seem particularly prone to fear, so much so that fear has been seen as a normal part of childhood development. It is documented in the research into childhood fear that during infancy children tend to fear stimuli within their immediate environment such as loud noise, objects and separation from a caretaker, but that as the child matures these fears adjust to incorporate anticipatory events and abstract stimuli (Campbell, 1986). Recent work has indicated that general fearfulness decreases as age increases and that this decrease continues at a fairly rapid rate until the beginning of adolescence (Gullone & King, 1997). Mild fears in children often appear and disappear spontaneously and follow a predictable course. For example, Bauer (1976) reported that younger children (4–8 years old) typically fear ghosts and animals whilst older children (10–12 years) are more likely to fear self-injury. These short-lived fears are part of a normal pattern of development, frequently have an obvious adaptive significance, and reflect the everyday experiences of the child. These normative fears are at their highest during the first 11–14 years of life but then stabilize, leaving only pervasive fears and phobias (Draper & James, 1985; Gullone & King, 1997). A phobia is a fear that is out of proportion to the demands of the situation that evokes it, it cannot be rationalized, is involuntary, and leads to avoidance of the situation (Marks, 1969). If children exhibit normal patterns of fearfulness then it seems likely that this early developmental period may be the origin of later adult phobia (in the sense that a normative fear may, for whatever reason, increase in magnitude and persist beyond its natural course). In this chapter we will explore the evidence that childhood experience has a bearing upon the acquisition of phobias and other anxiety disorders. A neoconditioning model is then described that attempts to explain what factors might determine which stimuli become the objects of phobic responding.

A profile of childhood fear: what do children fear?

There is evidence (cited above) that children experience general patterns of fear throughout their development. Some studies have looked specifically at the type of stimuli that children fear, but with conflicting results (see Ollendick, Hagopian & King, 1997 for a review). Silverman & Nelles (1989) investigated normative fear in 8–11-year-old children. They found that fears related mainly to physical injury and were highly stable over time, however, at follow-up there was a greater emphasis on fears related to psychic stress, criticism and failure. Ollendick & King (1991) used the Fear Survey Schedule for Children (FSSC-R) – a questionnaire that asks children to indicate on a three-point scale ('none', 'some' and 'a lot') how much they fear specific situations and stimuli – and found, over several studies, that children fear the following in rank order: (1) not being able to breathe; (2) being hit by a car; (3) bombing attacks; (4) getting burned by fire; (5) falling from a high place; (6) burglar breaking into the house; (7) earthquake; (8) death; (9) illness; and (10) snakes. However, these fears are clearly not independent because, for example, not being able to breathe, being hit by a car, bombing attacks, falling from a high place, illness and earthquakes may all potentially lead to death (a separately classified fear). Muris, Merckelbach & Collaris (1997a) found that when the FSSC-R was used on a sample of 9–13-year-olds, the rank order of their fears was quite similar to that of Ollendick & King (1991). However, Muris et al. (1997a) found quite different results when a free option method was employed in which the child was asked open-endedly what they feared most and then to describe various characteristics of their fear. The free option method revealed that fears of animals were the most frequent intense fears followed by fear of the unknown, fear of danger and death, medical fears and fear of failure and criticism. This study suggests that the research methodology employed can critically influence the rank order of children's fears (see also Muris et al., 1997b) and some have questioned the validity of the FSSC-R (see McCathie & Spence, 1991). Regardless of the differences resulting from methodology, it seems that the prominent clusters of childhood fears bear some intuitive relation to adult fears e.g. animal phobia, height phobia ('falling from a high place'), water phobia ('not being able to breathe'), necrophobia (fear of danger and death) and social phobias (fear of failure and criticism). However, although these normative fears bear obvious relations to adult phobias it is clearly not true that normative fears will necessarily develop into phobias. Nevertheless, this evidence provides a strong basis for assuming that the seeds of anxiety are sown in childhood. Interestingly, in preadolescence fears are solely death and injury related whereas adolescent fears incorporate more social fears such as fear of failure and rejection (Gullone & King, 1993, 1997).

Clearly children experience many normative fears and some of these fears bear some relation to common objects of phobia. However, the link between these preadolescent normative fears and phobic responding is illuminated by numerous retrospective studies of adult phobics. For example, Öst (1987) reported that for animal and blood-injection phobias the mean ages of onset were 7 and 9 years respectively. Other retrospective studies indicate that both height phobic (Menzies & Clarke, 1993*a*) and water phobic (Menzies & Clarke, 1993*b*) adults often report that they have had their fear for as long as they can remember. However, social phobias such as claustrophobia typically have much later ages of onset, for example, Öst (1987) reports a mean age of onset of 20. This fits with the pattern of normative fears exhibited by children in that normative fear of social situations increases with age (Gullone & King 1993, 1997) suggesting that normative fear could act as a predisposing factor to clinical fear or phobia (see Öst, chapter 13, this volume for details of onset work).

Finally, across a number of epidemiological studies, there is evidence of a prevalence rate from 5.7% to 17.7% of anxiety disorders in community samples of children and a prevalence rate of specific phobias from 2.6% to 9.1% (see Costello & Angold, 1995 for a review). Costello & Angold (1995) conclude that simple phobias and GAD are the most commonly diagnosed anxiety disorders occurring in around 5% of children whilst complex disorders such as social phobia, agoraphobia and OCD are much less common, occurring in below 2% of children.

How do children acquire phobias

Early models

As early as 1916 John Watson conceived that anxiety disorders could be understood in terms of conditioning theory. His latter empirical contribution with Rosie Rayner (e.g. Watson & Rayner, 1920) has gone down in psychological history as the 'little Albert' study. In this study, Watson & Rayner attempted to condition a 9-month-old child, Albert B, into fearing a white rat. They pretested Albert to ensure that he was not initially fearful of the rat (which acted as a conditioned stimulus, CS), and also established that he was fearful of a loud noise made by banging a claw hammer on an iron bar (which acted as an aversive unconditioned stimulus, UCS). Having established this, Albert was placed in a room with the rat and every time he touched the rat, Watson hit the iron bar, thus scaring the child. After several pairings of the rat with the loud noise, Albert began to cry when the rat was presented without the loud noise. Although Watson himself did not formulate a coherent theory of phobia acquisition, the implication from the study was that excessive and persistent fear (i.e. a phobia) could be acquired through experiencing a CS in temporal proximity to some fear-inducing or traumatic event. This overly simplistic model ignored the influence of previous experience with the CS and UCS and was reliant on contiguity between the CS and UCS rather than the predictive power of the CS.

Nevertheless, subsequent theorists have built upon this model to explain how phobias and avoidant behaviour might develop. Mowrer (1960) proposed a two-stage theory. In the first stage a person learns to associate a stimulus with an aversive outcome resulting in a conditioned fear response. In the second stage the person learns that avoiding the stimulus that evokes it can reduce the acquired fear response. This theory accounts for the persistent avoidance behaviour that phobics display. There are some studies that confirm that fear-inducing or traumatic experiences during childhood can lead to extreme and persistent fear. Dollinger, O'Donnell & Staley (1984) studied 29 children survivors of a severe lightning strike and found that these children showed more numerous and intense fear of thunderstorms, lightning and tornadoes than control children. Both of these studies support the idea that a single traumatic event can lead to intense fears of objects related to the trauma. In a similar study, Yule, Udwin & Murdoch (1990) studied 25 teenage girls who survived the sinking of the cruise ship *Jupiter*. Compared to control subjects of the same age, these girls showed an excess of fears relating to ships, water travel, swimming and water with this fear even generalizing to other modes of transport.

Criticisms of the early conditioning models

However, the simple conditioning models of Watson and Mowrer came under scrutiny in the 1970s when several shortcomings were identified (Rachman, 1977). There are five main criticisms of early conditioning models, which will be discussed with particular reference to childhood experiences:

Some phobics cannot remember an aversive conditioning experience at the onset of their phobia

It is clear that some phobics have no memory of an aversive conditioning event at the onset of their phobia. This is especially true of some animal phobics such as snake and spider phobics (Davey, 1992*b*) and height and water phobics (Menzies & Clarke, 1993*a,b*). This cannot simply be explained in terms of 'repression' of the traumatic memory because many other types of phobics, such as dental phobics (Davey, 1989) and dog phobics (DiNardo et al., 1988) can recall traumatic experiences in the etiology of their fear. In addition, for a particular feared stimulus some individuals may remember an associated traumatic event while others who fear the same stimulus have no such memory (Withers & Deane, 1995).

Not all people experiencing fear or trauma in a given situation go on to develop a phobia

Lautch (1971) showed that not all people who experience pain or a traumatic event whilst at the dentist go on to acquire a phobia. Likewise, most of us have experienced violent and scary thunderstorms yet are not phobic of these situations (Liddell & Lyons, 1978). Similarly, Aitken, Lister & Main (1981) showed that not all fliers who experience a traumatic flying accident go on to develop a fear of flying. The simple contiguity based model espoused by the early behaviourists simply does not have the power to predict when an individual will acquire a phobia and when they will not.

Incubation

Incubation (Eysenck, 1979) is a phenomenon where fear increases over successive non-reinforced presentations of the CS (for example, when a spider phobic subsequently comes into contact with spiders, each spider is unlikely to be paired with a traumatic event, yet the phobic becomes more fearful of spiders). An incremental-decremental conditioning model would predict that over non-reinforced presentations of the CS fear should extinguish.

Uneven distribution of fears

Pavlovian models of conditioning predict equipotentiality of stimuli which in this context simply means that all stimuli are equally likely to enter into an association with an aversive consequence. So, fears and phobias should be evenly distributed across stimuli and experiences (Seligman, 1971). This is clearly not the case because phobias of spiders, snakes, dogs, heights, water, death, thunder, and fire are much more prevalent than phobias of hammers, guns, knives and electrical outlets yet the latter group of stimuli seem to have a high likelihood of being associated with pain and trauma. Indeed, the literature on normative fears clearly demonstrates that there are common themes that appear in the fears of 'normal' children (Ollendick & King, 1991) across different countries (Burnham & Gullone, 1997; Gullone & King, 1992). Furthermore, attempts to replicate the 'little Albert' study have been successful when the CS had some biological relevance – Valentine (1946) conditioned a 2-year-old child to fear a caterpillar – but not when the CS was not ecologically significant – Bregman (1932) failed to condition a group of 1-year-old children to fear geometric shapes and cloth curtains. It seems therefore that some stimuli are more readily feared than others, yet early conditioning accounts cannot explain why this should be.

Fear acquired through observational learning

Rachman (1968) noted that fears can be acquired not only directly but vicariously and that stimuli are likely to develop fearful qualities through direct or vicarious association with a traumatic outcome. The notion that fears could be acquired through observing a stimulus and an aversive outcome was regarded by Rachman (1977) as a second route to learning.

In the light of these criticisms the simple conditioning model of phobias is clearly inadequate to explain the diversity of phenomena associated with phobias.

A contemporary conditioning model

Davey (1997) has proposed an updated model of fear acquisition based on recent developments in our understanding of human conditioning. To understand the model it is necessary to outline some of these advances.

What is learnt during conditioning?

It has been established that both animals and humans tend to learn associations between the CS and UCS during classical conditioning, and it is the association which mediates the CR (Rescorla, 1980). This is a crucial point because if a learnt phobic response is mediated by a CS–UCS association, then any factors which influence the strength of that association will also influence the magnitude of the conditioned fear response.

Factors affecting the strength of the CS–UCS association

It is now accepted that the strength of a CS–UCS association can be affected by many factors other than just experiencing CS–UCS pairings. In humans, these factors include: verbally and culturally transmitted information about the CS–UCS contingency (Dawson & Grings, 1968), existing beliefs and expectancies about the possible consequence associated with a particular CS (Davey, 1992a; Honeybourne, Matchett & Davey, 1993), and emotional reactions currently associated with the CS (Davey & Dixon, 1996). Davey (1997) has labelled these factors 'expectancy evaluations'.

Factors affecting the strength of CR

Finally, it has now been established that the strength of a CR can be radically influenced, not just by the strength of the CS–UCS association, but also by the way in which the individual evaluates the UCS. Davey (1997) refers to these factors as 'UCS revaluation processes'.

Expectancy evaluations

Figure 8.1 shows how Davey's (1997) model incorporates all of what is now known about the kinds of factors which influence the strength of association between a CS and UCS. Traditionally it was believed that it was simply the number of experienced CS–UCS pairings that had a bearing on the strength of association, however, it is now clear that many more factors come into play.

Situational contingency information

Although the number of experienced pairings of a CS and UCS does contribute to the strength of the CR, the correlation between CS and UCS is more important. So, conditioning depends upon how well a CS predicts the occurrence of the UCS (Alloy & Tabachnik, 1984). So, for example, a CS might be paired with a traumatic event on some occasions, but previously it could have been paired with other UCSs, or no UCSs at all, making the correlation between CS and UCS quite weak. An extreme example of this situation is when a CS has been experienced alone on many occasions, and is subsequently paired with a UCS. In this situation, it is much harder to learn an association between the CS and the new UCS than if there had been no previous CS-alone trials. This is known as latent inhibition and is an established feature of human conditioning (Siddle, Remington & Churchill, 1985). The implication here is that if an individual has had many trauma-free experiences with a stimulus, then it will be much harder to subsequently associate that stimulus with trauma. For example, if someone who has had a lot of 'friendly' contact with dogs encounters a dog that attacks or scares them, they are less likely to associate dogs with being scared than someone who has had little experience with dogs: because prior experience tells them that dogs do not generally attack

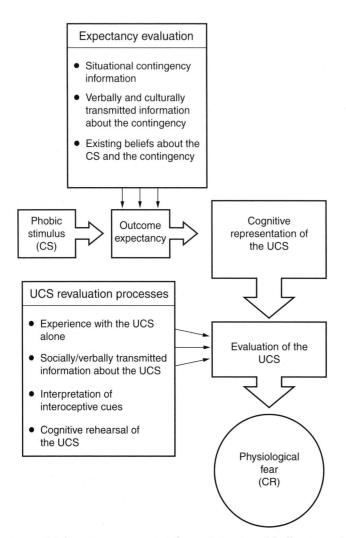

Fig. 8.1. Schematic representation of Davey's (1997) model of human Pavlovian conditioning (see text for details).

them. Therefore, early childhood experiences have some bearing on the ease with which a given stimulus is associated with trauma because the more fear-free contact a person has with stimuli the harder it will be for that person to associate those stimuli with fear. Hence, it should be more likely that an infant will associate a stimulus with fear or anxiety than a child will (because the infant has had less opportunity to experience that stimulus in the absence of fear or anxiety).

Verbally and culturally transmitted information

In laboratory conditioning experiments, merely informing subjects of the CS–UCS contingency can generate a CR prior to any CS–UCS pairings (Dawson & Grings, 1968). In addition, when subjects are misinformed about the contingencies, their conditioned responding complies with this false information and not the contingencies experienced by the subject (Deane, 1969). The implications of this are that an association between a stimulus and a traumatic event can be learned indirectly through observing someone else experiencing the contingency (vicarious learning), or by simply being informed about the contingency. This evidence is not incongruous with a conditioning model, however, there is little currently known about the strength or persistence of associations learned in this manner. All that is known is that they may be weaker and less resistant to extinction than situationally acquired associations (see Rachman, 1977) and that they seem to be mediated by the same mechanism that governs situational learning (Mineka & Cook, 1993).

Children clearly experience a great deal of culturally transmitted information about which objects might be scary and this information might not only guide their normative fears but also provide a basis for future phobias (Field, Argyris & Knowles, in press). For example, some nursery rhymes often transmit information about fearful objects: Little Miss Muffett was an exemplary spider phobic! Little Red Riding Hood was afraid of the 'big bad wolf' (fear of dogs), and the *Goosebumps* book series (popular in many countries such as the U.S. and U.K.) readily endorse ghosts and all things dead as being scary.

There is conflicting evidence as to the importance of direct conditioning experiences compared to so-called indirect pathways described above. Yule et al. (1990) reported data from a 'near miss' group of children who had wanted to go on a cruise ship that subsequently sank (see the earlier description of this study). These teenage girls displayed greater levels of anxiety and depression than a control group but did not show greater levels of specific fear to ships or related stimuli. This finding shows how vicarious experience can increase general fear levels but does not induce phobic levels of fear towards a particular stimulus (although the possibility remains that it may predispose a person to fearing that object at a later date). Ollendick & King (1991) asked children aged between 9 and 14 to indicate the origin of their fear for two common childhood fears – fear of snakes and not being able to breathe. They found that there were no differences between high- and low-fearful children when considering individual routes to fear. However, there were differences when comparing joint sources of fear-acquisition (specifically direct conditioning with vicarious learning, direct conditioning with information/instruction, and direct conditioning with both modelling and information/instruction). They concluded that extreme fear could not be attributed to a single pathway but a combination of sources. In addition, Muris et al. (1996) found evidence that fears reported by a group of children were a function of the degree to which their mothers expressed their own fears in front of them. However, Muris et al. (1997a) studied a similar age range of children and found much stronger evidence that direct conditioning is the dominant pathway to fear acquisition. In their study surprisingly few children attributed their fear to modelling and they concluded that modelling may have a role only in increasing general fearfulness, and not in the acquisition of specific fears.

Finally, Withers & Deane (1995) showed that subjects tended to ascribe their fear to direct conditioning when they could remember the onset of the fear (for both strong and moderate fears), but to indirect pathways (such as modelling and information) when they had no memory of onset. Withers & Deane concluded that when subjects have no memory of the onset of fear they are more likely to assume that they could not have experienced a direct conditioning episode otherwise they would have remembered it. This tends to suggest that retrospective studies on the onset of fear may underestimate the influence of direct conditioning experiences and this has serious implications for the conclusions that have been drawn from these studies.

Clearly, observational learning can influence levels of anxiety and probably contributes to the development of phobias and general anxiety in later life. Nevertheless, most of the recent work suggests that direct conditioning experiences have something of a larger role to play than they are given credit for.

Existing beliefs about the CS and the contingency

When subjects enter a conditioning episode they already hold a set of beliefs and expectancies about what is likely to happen during that episode. Often these prior expectancies are based on previous experiences with the events in the episode, or they are based on *ad hoc* judgements about the events.

There are many examples of such associative biases in covariation assessment studies where subjects are required to detect a correlation between events. Assessing the relationship between events seems to be influenced by both situational information (i.e. current information about the contingency) and prior expectations about the contingency (Crocker, 1981). In circumstances where situational information is unambiguous and prior expectations are low, humans can detect contingencies fairly accurately (Beach & Scopp, 1966) but there are a number of circumstances where situational information and expectancies give rise to a covariation bias, where perceptions of the existing relationship are distorted – usually in the direction of the prior expectation (Crocker, 1981).

This kind of covariation bias has also been found in situations where CS–UCS associations might be generated. Tomarken, Mineka & Cook (1989) exposed subjects to fear-relevant (i.e. spiders) and fear-irrelevant (i.e. flowers) stimuli that were followed by an electric shock, a tone or nothing. The relationship between the slides and the outcomes was completely random, yet subjects consistently overestimated the contingency between slides of fear-relevant stimuli and aversive consequences.

Davey (1992c) has shown in a number of studies that this tendency to overestimate the association between fear-relevant stimuli and aversive consequences is a pre-experimental expectancy bias rather than a computational bias that occurs during exposure to the stimulus. In a 'threat' conditioning procedure, where subjects were warned that they might receive shocks following some CSs but actually receive none, subjects began the experiment with significantly higher expectations that fear-relevant, rather than fear-irrelevant, stimuli would be followed by shock. Although this expectancy dissipated with continued nonreinforcement, it could be reinstated by a single CS–UCS pairing. This shows that individuals enter a conditioning episode believing that fear-relevant stimuli are more likely to have aversive consequences than fear-irrelevant stimuli. This speeds up the learning of associations between fear-relevant CSs and aversive UCSs, and makes them more resistant to extinction. These expectancy biases can be found in both phylogenetic (e.g. snakes, spiders) and ontogenetic (e.g. guns, electrical outlets) fear-relevant stimuli (Honeybourne et al., 1993) and can explain the rapid learning effects previously attributed to biological preparedness (Davey, 1995).

While expectancy biases clearly exist and can influence the rate at which a CS–UCS association is learned, it is not clear from where these biases originate. Davey & Dixon (1996) revealed that expectancy is correlated with estimates of how dangerous the CS is, judgements about the semiotic similarity between the CS and UCS, and the similarity of CS and UCS based on valence, arousal and anxiety.

What is clear from the recent literature is that prior expectancies about the outcome of conditioning can assist the learning of CS–UCS contingencies. These expectancies are especially associated with fear-relevant stimuli and are based on judgements about the nature of the CS and the features it has in common with the UCS. The judgements necessary to elicit these biases imply that there should be cultural differences in expectancy biases to fear-relevant stimuli, because different cultures have different values. The role of culturally transmitted information during childhood in creating these expectancies has yet to be explored, but intuitively it seems plausible that modelling and information from parents, siblings and friends will provide much of the impetus for these expectancy biases.

Emotions elicited by the CS

One important factor that affects UCS expectancy is the degree to which the CS already elicits fear or anxiety. For example, Diamond, Matchett & Davey (1995) presented spider phobics and nonphobics with slides of either spiders or kittens. UCS expectancy was measured using the threat-conditioning procedure described above. They found that the initial expectancy of shock following spiders was high in both sets of subjects, but the spider phobics' expectancy of shock following a slide of a spider was significantly higher than the nonphobics. Davey & Dixon (1996) also found that prior fear predicted variance in UCS expectancy independent of other factors (e.g. CS–UCS similarity). The obvious implication is that prior fear of a CS will hasten its association with aversive consequences, and will retard extinction of that association.

UCS revaluation processes

Davey has argued (1992a, 1997) that individuals have a cognitive representation of the UCS which is activated during conditioning through the CS–UCS association, and it is this representation that mediates the CR. Therefore, the strength or nature of the fear CR will be affected by any factor that changes information about the UCS that is contained within the UCS representation. For example, if the subject acquires information that a UCS is less aversive than they had previously conceived, this will result in the UCS representation mediating a substantially weaker CR next time the CS is encountered.

There are two important points regarding the UCS revaluation process in this model: (1) UCS revaluation can occur independent of changes in the strength of association which means that the strength of a fear CR can be influenced without subjects having to experience any CS–UCS presentations; and (2) there are differences between animals and humans because humans have the ability to symbolically represent information and communicate information between individuals. As such, there are considerably more factors that could affect UCS revaluation in humans than in other animals. Davey (1997) has identified five such factors.

Experience of the UCS alone

Post-conditioning experiences with the UCS alone can lead the UCS to be revalued – especially if these experiences lead the individual to perceive the

UCS as more or less aversive than it was during the conditioning event. There is evidence for this both from the laboratory, and from case histories.

Davey & McKenna (1983) found that UCS-alone trials that allowed subject's fear to habituate resulted in both a more favourable assessment of the UCS and a diminished CR when the CS was next presented. Conversely, the perceived aversiveness of a UCS can be inflated by subsequent experiences of a similar UCS of greater intensity. Often, the initial conditioning episode may be fairly unaversive (i.e. it evokes little anxiety), but subsequent experience with the UCS inflates the individual's evaluation of how aversive it is. As a result, subsequent encounters with the CS come to evoke much stronger and perceivable anxiety. For example, Davey, De Jong & Tallis (1993) report the case of L.L. who experienced mild anxiety in social situations which manifested itself through intestinal unease. On one occasion when L.L. was at home and not at all anxious similar symptoms of intestinal unease led to an uncontrollable attack of diarrhoea. From that moment on, L.L. catastrophically interpreted the symptoms of intestinal unease, that he regularly experienced in company, as a signal for losing control again and subsequently became extremely anxious and developed severe agoraphobic symptoms.

This evidence of UCS revaluation rules out the need to find specific traumatic conditioning events in a patient's history. In addition, UCS revaluation helps to explain how some individuals can experience a stimulus in the presence of a traumatic event yet not develop phobic symptoms – because the traumatic event is subsequently devalued.

Socially and verbally transmitted information about the UCS

Another way in which the UCS can be revalued is through socially or verbally transmitted information about the UCS. In the laboratory, it has been shown that if subjects are told that future presentations of the UCS will be more or less intense, and provided that they believe that information, then their evaluation of the UCS changes and this in turn affects the strength of the CR on subsequent CS presentations (Davey & McKenna, 1983). In addition, Davey et al. (1993) showed how verbally transmitted information can lead a UCS to be revalued. Client H.B. was a severe spider phobic. She had lived in Rio de Janeiro in Brazil during her childhood and once, at the age of 10 years, when she woke during the night a large tropical spider walked over her face. She reported being calm at the time, but when she told her parents about what had happened the next morning, they expressed extreme concern. From that moment on, H.B. was extremely frightened of spiders and exhibited severe phobic behaviour (Davey et al., 1993). This example demonstrates how verbally transmitted information about events during childhood can contribute to how a child perceives a conditioning event generally, or how they perceive the UCS specifically. This again demonstrates how important information from parents or caregivers can be in the development of anxiety.

However, it is worth noting that the contribution of verbally transmitted information appears to be asymmetric in that it seems relatively easy to elicit large increases in fear through verbally transmitted information, but extremely difficult to devalue the UCS in the same way (most clinicians will testify that telling a phobic that they have nothing to fear has little therapeutic value). It is unclear why this asymmetry exists but it may be that phobics give priority to contradictory forms of information that confirm their beliefs that the UCS is still aversive. Indeed, Martin, Horder & Jones (1992) found that children with a nonclinical fear of spiders had a bias towards processing spider-relevant words compared to a control group (but see Kindt, Bierman & Brosschot, 1997 for conflicting results). This suggests that phobic children may preferentially attend to fear-relevant information.

Another explanation of the asymmetry of verbally transmitted information is because of the perceived potential danger of interacting with a phobic stimulus: rather than trusting someone else's opinion phobics may require more direct evidence, such as actual experiences, to disconfirm their beliefs about the aversiveness of the UCS.

Interpretation of interoceptive cues

Many anxious people attend to their own bodily sensations and use these sensations as cues to possible threatening events or as a means of assessing the aversive nature of potentially aversive consequences (Valins, 1966). As such, a person's reaction to either a CS or UCS can act as an important source of information for evaluating the UCS. Studies on interoception have revealed three things: (1) when a CR is made more discriminable, by providing auditory feedback for changes in a skin conductance CR, subjects emit higher magnitude CRs and show relative resistance to extinction compared to subjects who have poor CR discrimination (Davey, 1987); (2) when subjects are led to believe that they are emitting a strong CR, even though they are not, they emit a stronger CR and exhibit a resistance to extinction compared to both attentional control subjects and subjects who falsely believe they are emitting a weak CR (Davey, 1987); and (3) subjects who are misinformed that they are emitting a strong UCR, emit a greater magnitude CR and show a greater resistance to extinction than subjects who believe they are emitting a weak UCR (Cracknell & Davey, 1988).

Davey (1992a, 1997) has argued that CR and UCR interoception influences

CR magnitude by influencing a person's evaluation of the UCS. Phobics may perceive a strong CR and attribute this to a fear of the forthcoming UCS – this inflates the aversiveness of the UCS which in turn activates a higher magnitude CR. Indeed, Davey & Matchett (1996) have found that subjects receiving false feedback gave higher aversiveness ratings of the UCS than other subjects. In addition, Arntz, Rauner & van den Hout (1995) asked anxiety patients and normal controls to rate the danger they perceived in a number of scenarios when information about objective safety-danger or anxious-nonanxious responding was systematically varied. Anxious patients inferred danger on the basis of information regarding anxious responding more than nonanxious subjects. These interoceptive cues could be one way in which UCS devaluation through socially communicated information is hindered, because phobic subjects may give precedence to their bodily sensations over mere verbal information.

Cognitive rehearsal of the UCS

Marks (1987) has provided evidence that individuals with anxiety disorders have a tendency to focus and rehearse the possible aversive consequences of phobic encounters, and this ruminative tendency may act to inflate their aversive evaluation of the outcome (UCS). So, for example, an agoraphobic may tend to focus in on the negative consequences of being in a social situation and then repeatedly think about those consequences such that their fear of social situations increases. Jones & Davey (1990) found that normal subjects asked to cognitively rehearse the UCS after conditioning produced larger magnitude CRs to subsequent presentations of the CS than did subjects who did not rehearse the UCS.

Whilst UCS rehearsal appears to at least maintain differential fear CRs, Davey (1992a) argued that there may be circumstances where persistent UCS rehearsal might enhance fear responding in a way that is characteristic of incubation. Davey & Matchett (1994) used a cued-UCS rehearsal procedure (Jones & Davey, 1990) on subjects with high or low levels of trait anxiety. They found that subjects with high levels of trait anxiety exhibited significantly greater magnitude CRs following UCS rehearsal than low anxiety subjects. These higher magnitude CRs were associated with higher levels of self-reported aversiveness of the rehearsal process. Additionally, they found that postrehearsal enhancement of the CR could be found in normal subjects who had undergone an anxious mood induction prior to the experiment.

This evidence is consistent with the hypothesis that increases in CR magnitude following UCS rehearsal result from the rehearsal process inflating the aversive evaluation of the UCS. However, this account fails to fully account for incubation, because there is no evidence that UCS rehearsal produces successive enhancements in fear responding. It could be that it is not UCS rehearsal per se that is a crucial factor, but rehearsal of catastrophic interpretations of possible UCSs. So, for example, spider phobics might not dwell directly on their fear or the CS (a spider), but on the possible outcomes of an encounter with the CS ('If I encountered a spider it might crawl up my leg'). The rehearsal of these possible consequences enhances fear both through rumination about that fear ('I would die of fright if a spider crawled up my leg') and through experiencing conditioning events in the mind (by imagining the spider crawling up their leg, phobics imagine the spider being paired with enhanced levels of fear). The former type of rehearsal may influence the evaluation of the UCS, whilst the latter form would influence the expectancy evaluation. This account can explain incubation: the phobic encounters their phobic stimuli (i.e. a spider), and experiences a fear CR that triggers a ruminative process in which both the encounter itself and possible catastrophic outcomes are rehearsed; these imagined events result in both rehearsal of the UCS ('If the spider had crawled up my leg I would have died of fright') which changes the evaluation of the UCS to become more aversive and also cognitive pairings of a 'worse case scenario' that may change the individual's expectancy of conditioning ('next time I encounter a spider I expect to suffer extreme anxiety because I did when I encountered the spider in my mind'). Therefore, when the phobic next comes into contact with the fear CS, fear has increased without having any direct exposure to the stimuli. The role of rumination in enhancing fear clearly needs empirical support but it potentially offers an explanation of how phobic responding might be maintained and enhanced over time.

Coping strategies that neutralize the UCS

One of the criticisms of conditioning theory is that not all people who experience traumatic events go on to develop phobias. It has already been intimated that some people may be capable of devaluing the traumatic event after experiencing it. One possible way of devaluing trauma is through coping strategies. Pearlin & Schooler (1978) identified three major types of coping with stressors. The first two coping styles closely resembled the problem- and emotion-focused coping identified by Lazarus & Folkman (1984), and the third related to strategies that function to control the meaning of the trauma. Pearlin & Schooler (1978) argued that the meaning of trauma could be controlled in at least three ways: (1) positive comparisons ('Lots of people experience similar stressful experiences'); (2) selective ignoring ('I'll try to forget this problem and look at the good things in life'); and (3) devaluing the importance of the trauma ('This problem is not worth getting upset about').

Subsequently, Davey (1993) identified a coherent neutralizing strategy label-led 'threat devaluation'. This construct was derived from the coping strategies identified by Pearlin & Schooler and functions to control the meaning of the trauma. The implication is that if individuals can devalue the impact of trauma through threat devaluation strategies, they should be significantly less likely to develop a phobia. Davey, Burgess & Rashes (1995) compared the coping strategies of simple phobics, panic disorder patients and normal controls and found that both the phobics and panic disorder patients differed from the normal controls by reporting greater use of avoidance strategies, and reduced use of threat devaluation strategies.

Davey et al. (1997) have refined the threat devaluation construct to identify seven factorially independent constructs that contribute to trauma devaluation: (1) downward comparison ('Other people are worse off than me'); (2) positive reappraisal ('In every problem there is something good'); (3) cognitive disen-gagement ('The problems involved in this situation aren't important enough to get upset about'); (4) optimism ('Everything will work itself out'); (5) faith in social support ('I know others who can help me through this'); (6) Denial ('I refuse to believe this is happening'); and (7) life perspective ('I can put up with these problems as long as everything else in my life is okay').

Davey et al. (1997) found that use of these strategies was positively corre-lated with measures of psychological health and inversely correlated with a variety of measures of psychopathology. In a prospective study these strategies could also predict future psychological health when existing levels of psycho-logical health were controlled for. These studies imply that the use of coping strategies may insulate the individual from developing anxiety following a traumatic event. In some instances this may account for why some individuals do not develop phobic reactions while others do (for example, at the dental surgery threat devaluers can reason that the pain experienced at the time is worth suffering because in the long term they will have healthy teeth).

Implications of the model

There are two implications of this conditioning model of phobias. First, phobic responding is not mediated only by strength of association: recent evidence has shown that performance factors, especially those related to the evaluation of the UCS, can have a dramatic effect on the strength and probability of phobic responding. Second, it is now clear that no direct conditioning experiences are necessary: an association between a neutral CS and an aversive outcome can be formed both through vicarious experience, and through associating a neutral CS with a fairly neutral UCS and then that UCS being revalued, at a later date, such that it becomes more aversive. This allows some of the criticisms of the early conditioning models to be answered.

Some phobics cannot recall an aversive conditioning event

This model predicts that direct conditioning events are not necessary for a phobia to develop. Far from indicating that some phobias are prewired, there is now substantial evidence that responding may be the result of a combination of sensory preconditioning and UCS inflation. So, the CS and UCS become associated while the UCS is perceived as nonaversive. Subsequently, the UCS is revalued in some way (either by verbal information, experience with a similar but more traumatic UCS, or through observation and reinterpretation of the UCS). This UCS inflation may not happen as a direct result of a single incident, but may gradually occur over time, as information is slowly acquired about the UCS. As such, a phobic may not recall a specific traumatic event simply because one never occurred: the phobia developed gradually over time.

Not all people who experience trauma develop a phobia

This neoconditioning model incorporates cognitive factors which could determine whether a person experiences a phobia as the result of trauma, or not. We have shown that coping strategies seem the most likely explanation of why some people can de-intensify the experienced trauma. However, another contributory factor could be the difference in how people interpret or perceive bodily sensations. Individuals who are 'keyed in' to their bodily sensations may perceive greater physical fear at times of trauma than those who are less sensitive to these cues.

Incubation

Although at present there is little empirical evidence for how incubation might operate, there is suggestive evidence that UCS rehearsal may be the first step to explaining incubation. The model incorporates the idea that UCS rehearsal may have a key role to play in an individual's evaluation of the UCS and that this, in turn, influences the strength of phobic responding. Empirical work needs to be done to ascertain whether UCS rehearsal can lead to successive increases in fear that would explain the incubation process.

The uneven distribution of fears

Far from being biologically predisposed to fear certain stimuli, this model suggests that people acquire expectancies about which stimuli will elicit fear responses. These expectancies are not just dependent on information about the existing contingency, but also verbally and culturally transmitted information. The origin of these biases may not be biological, but due to direct and vicarious conditioning experience, culturally determined beliefs and values which project the association of certain stimuli with fear (i.e. the association of spiders with fear in Western culture; Davey, 1994).

Fear acquired through observational learning

Observational learning is a key part of both the expectancy evaluation system, and the UCS revaluation system in this model. Information about which stimuli are likely to predict fear can be learned vicariously and incorporated into the individual's own expectancy system. In addition, the UCS can be revalued by observing others' reactions to the UCS and this in turn affects phobic responding.

Clinical implications and conclusions

This chapter has described how conditioning models of phobias have developed in recent years. Specifically, it has looked at the processes through which children might develop abnormal levels of anxiety towards stimuli. Through this model it is possible to develop therapeutic techniques to be implemented after traumatic disasters (such as the Jupiter sinking) that might help prevent anxious responding. In addition, if anxiety has already developed, the conditioning model suggests a number of areas that can be addressed for reducing anxious responding.

One of the important and novel features of the conditioning model outlined in this chapter is that it specifies a variety of processes that can modify the strength of the conditioned response (i.e. anxious or phobic responding). Each of these processes has implications for the potential treatment of anxiety and the amelioration of fearful responding. The traditional associative method of reducing conditioned responding has been through extinction. This involves the presentation of the CS in the absence of the UCS, so that the association between the two stimuli is broken, and this process gave rise to a whole range of influential exposure-based therapies including flooding, counter-conditioning and systematic desensitization. However, the processes concerned with UCS revaluation are potentially more important than those concerned with CS–UCS association in helping to reduce anxious responding. The present model assumes that the strength of the CR is mediated by how the individual evaluates the UCS: if the UCS is evaluated as aversive this will produce a strong fear response, if the UCS is evaluated as benign, a weak fear response results (cf.

Davey, 1997). Thus, any process that leads to the devaluation of the UCS has important therapeutic potential. In the therapeutic context, attempting to devalue the UCS is the same as attempting to convince the individual that the consequences (UCS) of interaction with the fear-evoking situation (CS) are not as dangerous or threatening as the individual believes. Some ways of devaluing the UCS that have been described in this chapter include (1) through verbal or socially transmitted information about the harmless nature of the UCS, (2) through direct experience of the harmless nature of the UCS (often obtained through direct exposure to the UCS under controlled therapeutic conditions – thus disconfirming their existing beliefs that the UCS is harmful or dangerous), (3) through the reinterpretation of bodily sensations as nonthreatening; this will eliminate beliefs that the UCS is dangerous that have been generated by interpretation of the CR as signalling threatening consequences, (4) preventing the rehearsal of the UCS while in an anxious state, and (5) by providing the individual with a range of appraisal strategies that will allow them to actively devalue the UCS when it is encountered.

At least some of these processes may be more successful than others when applied to the treatment of childhood anxieties. For example, it is becoming increasingly clear that the etiologies of childhood phobias can be grouped into three broad categories (King, Gullone & Ollendick, 1998): (1) those that have a clearly defined direct conditioning experience as the causal factor (e.g. dog phobia), (2) those that appear to have resulted from vicarious experiences such as observational learning and information acquired from others about the phobic object (e.g. the common fears discussed at the beginning of this chapter), and (3) those that appear to have no obvious onset factor but always seem to have been present (e.g. water phobia, height phobia). What still has to be established with these three etiology categories is whether anxious responding is maintained in each case by the child's belief that the consequences of contact with the phobic situation is dangerous, frightening or threatening (as is the case in adult phobic responding, e.g. Arntz et al., 1993; Thorpe & Salkovskis, 1995). If this is so, then the etiology of the problem becomes significantly less relevant to therapy, and therapy can proceed on the basis of eliminating dysfunctional outcome beliefs through UCS devaluation procedures.

Nevertheless, the processes by which the UCS became inflated in the first place (and thus generate anxious responding) can be important in determining what might be the most effective form of UCS devaluation. For example, in cases where UCS aversiveness has been generated by a direct conditioning episode (e.g. where a dog phobia has been generated by a dog bite), then exposure therapy may be sufficient enough to eliminate or disconfirm threatening outcome beliefs. This is because the original causal factor (being bitten by a dog) is not still present (i.e. as long as the child does not continue to be bitten or attacked by dogs following successful therapy, then the UCS will remain devalued). However, in phobias with different etiologies, different types of UCS devaluation strategy may be more appropriate. For instance, height phobia is closely associated with a tendency to detect bodily sensations and to misinterpret ambiguous bodily sensations as threatening (Davey, Menzies & Gallardo, 1998). Davey et al. (1997) have argued that height phobia may develop because of the individual's tendency to misinterpret bodily sensations as indicative of dizziness and nausea, and these may occur in situational circumstances which might lead the individual to associate these signs with an imminent catastrophic fall. This account is consistent with the fact that height phobia (as with water phobia in children) rarely has an etiology involving a recalled direct conditioning experience. If this account is correct, then in such circumstances it is important in therapy to address these inappropriate beliefs about the meaning of bodily sensations. If they are not addressed, then it is quite possible that exposure therapy alone will not be sufficient to prevent relapse. Devaluing the UCS by focusing on how aspects of the CR are being misinterpreted as threatening may be important in many childhood phobias where there is no evidence of direct or vicarious conditioning in the etiology of the disorder. This may be particularly pertinent in the case of childhood height and water phobia (King, Gullone & Ollendick, 1998).

REFERENCES

Aitken, R. C. B., Lister, J. A. & Main, C. J. (1981). Identification of features associated with flying phobias in aircrew. *British Journal of Psychiatry*, **139**, 38–42.

Alloy, L. B. & Tabachnik, N. (1984). Assessment of variation by human and animals: the joint influence of prior expectations and current situational information. *Psychological Review*, **91**, 441–85.

Arntz, A., Lavy, E., van den Berg, G. & van Rijsoort, S. (1993). Negative beliefs of spider phobics: a psychometric evaluation of the spider phobia beliefs questionnaire. *Advances in Behaviour Research and Therapy*, **15**, 257–77.

Arntz, A., Rauner, M. & van den Hout, M. (1995). 'If I feel anxious, there must be danger': ex consequentia reasoning in inferring danger in anxiety disorders. *Behaviour Research and Therapy*, **33**, 917–25.

Bauer, D. H. (1976). An exploratory study of developmental changes in children's fears. *Journal of Child Psychology and Psychiatry*, **17**, 69–74.

Beach, L. R. & Scopp, T. S. (1966). Inferences about correlations. *Psychonomic Science*, **6**, 253–4.

Bregman, E. (1932). An attempt to modify the emotional attitudes of infants by the conditioned response technique. *Journal of Genetic Psychology*, **45**, 169–96.

Burnham, J. J. & Gullone, E. (1997). The fear schedule for children – II: a psychometric investigation with American data. *Behaviour Research and Therapy*, **35**, 165–73.

Campbell, S. B. (1986). Developmental issues in childhood anxiety. In *Anxiety Disorders of Childhood*, ed. R. Gittelman, pp. 24–57. New York: Guilford Press.

Costello, E. G. & Angold, A. (1995). Epidemiology. In *Anxiety Disorders in Children and Adolescents*, ed. J. S. March, pp. 109–22. New York: Guilford Press.

Cracknell, S. & Davey, G. C. L. (1988). The effect of perceived unconditioned response strength on conditioned responding in humans. *Medical Science Research*, **16**, 169–70.

Crocker, J. (1981). Judgements of co-variation by social perceivers. *Psychological Bulletin*, **90**, 272–92.

Davey, G. C. L. (1987). An integration of human and animal models of Pavlovian conditioning: associations, cognitions and attributions. In *Cognitive Processes and Pavlovian Conditioning in Humans*, ed. G. C. L. Davey, pp. 83–114. Chichester: John Wiley & Sons.

Davey, G. C. L. (1989). Dental phobics and anxieties: evidence for conditioning processes in the acquisition and modulation of a learned fear. *Behaviour Research and Therapy*, **27**, 52–8.

Davey, G. C. L. (1992a). Classical conditioning and the acquisition of human fears and phobias: a review and synthesis of the literature. *Advances in Behaviour Research and Therapy*, **14**, 29–66.

Davey, G. C. L. (1992b). Characteristics of individuals with fear of spiders. *Anxiety Research*, **4**, 299–314.

Davey, G. C. L. (1992c). An expectancy model of laboratory preparedness effects. *Journal of Experimental Psychology: General*, **121**, 24–40.

Davey, G. C. L. (1993). A comparison of three cognitive appraisal strategies: the role of threat devaluation in problem-focussed coping. *Personality and Individual Differences*, **14**, 535–46.

Davey, G. C. L. (1994). The 'disgusting' spider: the role of disease and illness in the perpetuation of fear of spiders. *Society & Animals*, **2**, 17–25.

Davey, G. C. L. (1995). Preparedness and phobias: specific evolved associations or a generalized expectancy bias? *Behavioral and Brain Sciences*, **18**, 289–325.

Davey, G. C. L. (1997). A conditioning model of phobias. In *Phobias: A Handbook of Theory, Research and Treatment*, ed. G. C. L. Davey, pp. 301–22. Chichester: Wiley.

Davey, G. C. L., Burgess, I. & Rashes, R. (1995). Coping strategies and phobias: the relationship between fears, phobias and methods of coping with stressors. *British Journal of Clinical Psychology*, **34**, 423–34.

Davey, G. C. L., De Jong, P. J. & Tallis, F. (1993). UCS inflation in the aetiology of a variety of anxiety disorders: some case histories. *Behaviour Research and Therapy*, **31**, 495–8.

Davey, G. C. L. & Dixon, A. (1996). The expectancy bias model of selective associations: the relationship of judgements of CS dangerousness, CS–UCS similarity and prior fear to *a priori* and *a posteriori* co-variation assessments. *Behaviour Research and Therapy*, **34**, 235–52.

Davey, G. C. L. & Matchett, G. (1994). UCS rehearsal and the retention and enhancement of differential 'fear' conditioning: effects of trait and state anxiety. *Journal of Abnormal Psychology*, **103**, 708–18.

Davey, G. C. L. & Matchett, G. (1996). The effects of response feedback on conditioned responding during extinction: implications for the role of interoception in anxiety-based disorders. *Journal of Psychophysiology*, **10**, 291–302.

Davey, G. C. L., McDonald, A. S., Ferguson, C. E., O'Neill, A.-M., Shepherd, J. & Band, D. (1997). Cognitive neutralising strategies, coping and psychological health. Cognitive Science Research Paper, 483, University of Sussex.

Davey, G. C. L. & McKenna, I. (1983). The effects of postconditioning revaluation of CS1 and UCS following Pavlovian second-order electrodermal conditioning in humans. *Quarterly Journal of Experimental Psychology*, **35B**, 125–33.

Davey, G. C. L., Menzies, R. & Gallardo, B. (1998). Height phobia and biases in the interpretation of bodily sensations: Some links between acrophobia and agoraphobia. *Behaviour Research and Therapy*, **35**, 997–1001.

Dawson, M. E. & Grings, W. W. (1968). Comparisons of classical conditioning and relational learning. *Journal of Experimental Psychology*, **76**, 227–31.

Deane, G. E. (1969). Cardiac activity during experimentally induced anxiety. *Psychophysiology*, **6**, 17–30.

Diamond, D., Matchett, G. & Davey, G. C. L. (1995). The effect of prior fear levels on UCS-expectancy ratings to a fear-relevant stimulus. *Quarterly Journal of Experimental Psychology*, **48A**, 237–47.

DiNardo, P. A., Guzy, L. T., Jenkins, J. A., Bak, R. M., Tomasi, S. F. & Copland, M. (1988). Etiology and maintenance of dog fears. *Behaviour Research and Therapy*, **26**, 241–4.

Dollinger, S. J., O'Donnell, J. P. & Staley, A. A. (1984). Lightning-strike disaster: effects on children's fears and worries. *Journal of Consulting and Clinical Psychology*, **52**, 1028–38.

Draper, T. W. & James, R. S. (1985). Preschool fears: longitudinal sequence and cohort changes. *Child Study Journal*, **15**, 147–55.

Eysenck, H. J. (1979). The conditioning model of neurosis. *Behaviour and Brain Sciences*, **2**, 155–99.

Field, A. P., Argyris, N. G. & Knowles, K. A. (in press). Who's afraid of the big bad wolf: a prospective paradigm to test Rachman's indirect pathways in children. *Behaviour Research and Therapy*.

Gullone, E. & King, N. (1992). Psychometric evaluation of a revised fear schedule for children and adolescents. *Journal of Child Psychology and Psychiatry*, **33**, 987–98.

Gullone, E. & King, N. (1993). The fears of youth in the 1990s: Contemporary normative data. *Journal of Genetic Psychology*, **154**, 137–53.

Gullone, E. & King, N. (1997). Three-year follow-up of normal fear in children and adolescents aged 7 to 18 years. *British Journal of Developmental Psychology*, **15**, 97–111.

Honeybourne, C., Matchett, G. & Davey, G. C. L. (1993). An expectancy model of preparedness effects: a UCS-expectancy bias in phylogenetic and ontogenetic fear-relevant stimuli. *Behavior Therapy*, **24**, 253–64.

Jones, T. & Davey, G. C. L. (1990). The effects of cued UCS rehearsal on the retention of differential 'fear' conditioning: an experimental analogue of the worry process. *Behaviour Research and Therapy*, **28**, 159–64.

Kindt, M., Bierman, D. & Brosschot, J. F. (1997). Cognitive bias in spider fear and control children: assessment of emotional inference by a card format and a single-task format of the Stroop task. *Journal of Experimental Child Psychology*, **66**, 163–79.

King, N. J., Gullone, E. & Ollendick, T. H. (1998). Etiology of childhood phobias: current status of Rachman's three pathways theory. *Behaviour Research and Therapy*, **36**, 297–309.

Lautch, H. (1971). Dental phobia. *British Journal of Psychiatry*, **119**, 151–8.

Lazarus, R. S. & Folkman, S. (1984). *Stress, Appraisal and Coping*. New York: Springer.

Liddell, A. & Lyons, M. (1978). Thunderstorm phobias. *Behaviour Research and Therapy*, **16**, 306–8.

Marks, I. M. (1969). *Fears and Phobias*. New York: Academic Press.

Marks, I. M. (1987). *Fears, Phobias and Rituals. Panic Anxiety and their Disorders*. New York: Oxford University Press.

Martin, M., Horder, P. & Jones, G. V. (1992). Integral bias in naming of phobic-related words. Brief report. *Cognition and Emotion*, **6**, 479–86.

McCathie, H. & Spence, S. H. (1991). What is the revised Fear Survey Schedule for Children measuring? *Behaviour Research and Therapy*, **22**, 141–50.

Menzies, R. G. & Clarke, J. C. (1993*a*). The etiology of fear of heights and its relationship to severity and individual response patterns. *Behaviour Research and Therapy*, **31**, 355–66.

Menzies, R. G. & Clarke, J. C. (1993*b*). The etiology of childhood water phobia. *Behaviour Research and Therapy*, **31**, 499–501.

Mineka, S. & Cook, M. (1993). Mechanisms involved in the observational conditioning of fear. *Journal of Experimental Psychology: General*, **122**, 23–38.

Mowrer, O. (1960). *Learning Theory and Behaviour*. New York: John Wiley & Sons.

Muris, P., Merckelbach, H. & Collaris, R. (1997*a*). Common childhood fears and their origins. *Behaviour Research and Therapy*, **35**, 929–37.

Muris, P., Merckelbach, H., Meesters, C. & Van Lier, P. (1997*b*). What do children fear most often? *Journal of Behaviour Therapy and Experimental Psychiatry*, **28**, 263–7.

Muris, P., Steerneman, P., Merckelbach, H. & Meesters, C. (1996). Parental modelling and fearfulness in middle childhood. *Behaviour Research and Therapy*, **34**, 265–8.

Ollendick, T. H., Hagopian, L. P. & King, N. J. (1997). Specific phobias in children. In *Phobias: A Handbook of Theory, Research and Treatment*, ed. G. C. L. Davey, pp. 201–24. Chichester: John Wiley & Sons.

Ollendick, T. H. & King, N. J. (1991). Origins of childhood fears: an evaluation of Rachman's theory of fear acquisition. *Behaviour Research and Therapy*, **29**, 117–23.

Öst, L.-G. (1987). Age of onset in different phobias. *Journal of Abnormal Psychology*, **96**, 223–9.

Pearlin, L. I. & Schooler, C. (1978). The structure of coping. *Journal of Health and Social Behavior*, **19**, 2–21.

Rachman, S. (1968). *Phobias: their Nature and Control*. Springfield: Thomas.

Rachman, S. (1977). The conditioning theory of fear acquisition: a critical examination. *Behaviour Research and Therapy*, **15**, 375–87.

Rescorla, R. A. (1980). *Pavlovian Second-order Conditioning*. Hillsdale, NJ: Lawrence Erlbaum Associates.

Seligman, M. E. P. (1971). Phobias and preparedness. *Behavior Therapy*, **2**, 307–20.

Siddle, D. A. T., Remington, B. & Churchill, M. (1985). Effects of conditioned stimulus pre-exposure on human electrodermal conditioning. *Biological Psychology*, **20**, 113–27.

Silverman, W. K. & Nelles, W. B. (1989). An examination of the stability of mother's ratings of child fearfulness. *Journal of Anxiety Disorders*, **3**, 1–5.

Thorpe, S. J. & Salkovskis, P. M. (1995). Phobic beliefs: do cognitive factors play a role in specific phobias? *Behaviour Research and Therapy*, **33**, 805–16.

Tomarken, A. J., Mineka, S. & Cook, M. (1989). Fear-relevant selective associations and co-variation bias. *Journal of Abnormal Psychology*, **98**, 381–92.

Valentine, C. W. (1946). *The Psychology of Early Childhood*, 3rd edition. London: Methuen.

Valins, S. (1966). Cognitive effects of false heart-rate feedback. *Journal of Personality and Social Psychology*, **4**, 400–8.

Watson, J. B. (1916). Behaviour and the concept of mental disease. *Journal of Philosophy*, **13**, 589–97.

Watson, J. B. & Rayner, R. (1920). Conditioned emotional reactions. *Journal of Experimental Psychology*, **3**, 1–14.

Withers, R. D. & Deane, F. P. (1995). Origins of common fears: effects on severity, anxiety responses and memories of onset. *Behaviour Research and Therapy*, **33**, 903–15.

Yule, W., Udwin, O. & Murdoch, K. (1990). The 'Jupiter' sinking: effects in children's fears, depression and anxiety. *Journal of Child Psychology and Psychiatry*, **31**, 1051–61.

9

Traumatic events and post-traumatic stress disorder

William Yule, Sean Perrin and Patrick Smith

Introduction

Human beings have developed over the millennia by adapting successfully to their changing environments. We learn from experience. Through our senses, we constantly monitor and interact with our physical and social environments. Over the generations, mechanisms that have helped the species survive are coded into us. When we are threatened, we react in largely predictable ways. Such reactions have developed to protect us, but sometimes they can hinder adaptation. Strictly speaking, one should say that 'when we perceive that we are threatened . . .' because it is not only the external, objective nature of a threat that determines our reaction to it, but also the way we interpret the threat – the meaning it has for us, the subjective component.

In the past few years, the great strides in understanding and treating anxiety disorders that were achieved by the applications of learning theory and behaviour therapy (see Field & Davey, chapter 8, this volume), have been complemented and enhanced by similar strides coming from the application of findings from experimental cognitive psychology (see Prins, chapter 2, this volume). Rooted in models coming from information processing theories, these cognitive models have been applied to anxiety disorders in general (Brewin, 1988) and to the study of post-traumatic stress reactions in particular (Brewin, Dalgleish & Joseph, 1996; Joseph, Williams & Yule, 1997). This chapter will examine the role of traumatic events in the development of anxiety disorders, particularly post-traumatic stress disorder (PTSD), differentiating between single acute events and chronic and/or repeated ones. It will place the relationship between traumatic event and stress reaction within a developmental psychopathological context by looking especially at risk and protective factors in the etiology and maintenance of stress reactions.

Neurobiological aspects of reactions to stressors

We actively monitor our environment and adapt to the demand placed upon us. Much of this is done without conscious awareness. Information is taken in, processed and acted upon. When we are frightened or threatened, then our body prepares to, and often does, react before we are aware of the threat. The 'freeze, fight, flight' reaction has been well described. A series of changes occur almost automatically to prepare us to deal with the threat. These reactions are governed by a myriad of neurological, neurophysiological, neurochemical changes in many of the subsystems of the nervous system. They have been well described in relation to anxiety in general (Gray, 1987; see Sallee & March, chapter 5, this volume) and more specifically in relation to post-traumatic stress reactions (Bremner et al., 1995a,b, 1996a,b; Charney et al., 1993; Hagh-Shenas, Goldstein & Yule, 1999; McIvor, 1997).

Many interrelated brain systems are activated during stressful events, although their interrelationships are complex and poorly understood (Freidman, Charney & Deutch, 1995; Southwick et al., 1994). Three systems seem most relevant: the noradrenergic system, the hypothalamic-pituitary axis, and the endogenous opiates.

One widely held view is that the persistent symptoms of arousal so characteristic of many post-traumatic stress reactions reflect sympathetic nervous system dysregulation resulting from changes in the noradrenergic system (Southwick et al., 1994). During stressful events, central and peripheral levels of the neurotransmitter, norepinephrene, are increased and this leads to increases in heart rate and blood pressure, and the experience of fear. These changes appear to serve an adaptive function as they arouse the individual and activate centres of the brain that help to orient the person to external stimuli, help to engage in selective attention, and facilitate memory encoding of the event. Indeed, there is evidence that when an event is very sudden but also full of personal relevance, then a vivid, 'Flashbulb' memory may be laid down (Conway, 1995). However, repeated or uncontrollable stress may lead to chronic elevations in norepinephrene and alterations in norepinephrene receptors in the locus coereleus, resulting in the sort of persistent physiological arousal seen in PTSD (Southwick et al., 1994).

There is also increasing evidence that chronic or uncontrollable stress produces changes in activity of the corticotrophin releasing factor and the hypothalamic-pituitary-adrenal axis. The hypothalamic-pituitary axis system plays an important role in the whole stress response by releasing cortisol and adrenocorticotrophic hormone which assist in energy metabolism and tissue repair (Southwick et al., 1994).

Repeated or uncontrollable stress can cause the hypothalamic-pituitary axis system to become highly sensitized, leading to greater fluctuations in cortisol levels over a 24-hour period. Studies of combat veterans have reported decreased levels of urinary cortisol in those with PTSD compared with psychiatric and normal controls (Yehuda & McFarlane, 1995) and it has been suggested that the related changes in levels of glucocorticoids are associated with damage to the hippocampal region. In turn, such damage may underlie short-term memory impairments often reported in patients with PTSD.

Dysregulation of the hypothalamic-pituitary axis and noradrenergic systems may explain why individuals with PTSD frequently suffer from chronic levels of hyperarousal, hyperreactivity to trauma-related stimuli, emotional numbing, and difficulties with concentration and memory (including intrusive imagery). Put this way, PTSD is far from being 'a normal reaction to an abnormal event' but rather is a complex psychological and biological response to a trauma involving the phenotypic expression of vulnerabilities to the disorder (Yehuda & McFarlane, 1995). The reactions are only 'normal' in the sense that they are predictable and understandable, but many people who develop PTSD and other stress reactions take comfort in knowing even this.

Behavioural and psychological reactions to acute stress

When children are faced with a very frightening or even life-threatening situation, they may become very upset – crying, clinging, shaking with fear. If the upset is very great, they may go into shock and be largely unresponsive to outside stimulation for some time. These are normal reactions developed over generations as protective mechanisms. At times of danger, we need to be able to concentrate on what is threatening us to the exclusion of other, less relevant stimuli; we also need to be prepared to fight or flee. When the danger passes, a slow return to normality can usually be expected. But in some cases, such return to a normal state is elusive. Symptoms persist both day and night. This is when an adjustment reaction may develop into a PTSD.

Following a traumatic event, children often need to be close to their parents for comfort and reassurance. This clinginess is understandable, but often extremely irritating to parents who are not let out of sight for weeks. Even teenagers may need to be reassured at night and often regress to sharing the parental bed. But the most troublesome symptom from the child's point of view can be the intrusive images of the event. These can occur at any time, day or night and are notable for their vividness. Usually, the child 'sees' the event replaying over and over again, but this can be accompanied by repetitive memories in any of the sensory modalities – sound, smell, touch and motion. Occasionally, children will report that the experience is so vivid that they truly believe it is happening all over again. Such dissociative experiences are called flashbacks.

The intrusive images often come to the children as they are settling down for the night. So upsetting can they be that children will fight against sleep and try to stay awake. It is ironic that children who are extremely tired still try to remain awake with the obvious consequence that they become tired, irritable and unable to concentrate. The irritability can lead on to anger that can be difficult to deal with. Children develop fears, especially of stimuli that were present when the traumatic event happened. Thus, following the sinking of the cruise ship, *Jupiter*, teenagers reported a marked increase in fears of drowning, water in general, death and travel (Yule, Udwin & Murdoch, 1990). Following road traffic accidents, children are likely to find it difficult to get back into cars for some time. Obviously, these fears have a survival value, but when present in extreme, they can disrupt the child's and family's life.

In the immediate aftermath of an accident, children sometimes experience a great pressure to talk about what happened. Then, they often find it difficult to talk, especially with parents and friends. Anecdotally, many children report that they do not want to upset their parents when they talk about what happened and so they keep their feelings to themselves. In such circumstances, being able to talk to someone outside the family has obvious potential benefit.

Survivors have learned that life is very fragile. This can lead to a loss of faith in the future or a sense of foreshortened future. Their priorities change. Some feel they should live each day to the full and not plan far ahead. Others realise they have been overconcerned with materialistic or petty matters and resolve to rethink their values. Their 'assumptive world' has been challenged (Janoff-Bulman, 1985). Children have learned prematurely about their own mortality.

These sorts of symptoms were first officially recognized as forming a tripartite syndrome by the American Psychiatric Association in 1980 in DSM–III when the diagnostic label 'Post-traumatic stress disorder' (PTSD) was coined. Based on work with veterans of the Vietnam War, it was seen that what had variously been called nervous shock, railway spine, battle fatigue and so on consisted essentially of a group of three symptoms – intrusive and distressing recollections of the particular event, emotional numbing/avoidance and increased physiological arousal. At first, the applicability to children and adolescents was not clear, but by the time of the revisions DSM–III–R (1987) and

DSM–IV (1994) it was accepted that younger people could also develop PTSD. However, it must be emphasized that the application of the diagnosis was originally a downward extension from work with adults and considerable empirical study is still needed to pinpoint the nature and extent of stress reactions in children. Slightly different criteria for PTSD have been agreed by the World Health Organization in its official *International Classification of Diseases – Tenth Revision* (ICD–10; WHO, 1992).

Adolescent survivors report significantly high rates of depression, some becoming clinically depressed, having suicidal thoughts and taking overdoses in the year after a disaster. A significant number become very anxious after accidents, although the appearance of panic attacks is sometimes considerably delayed (Yule, Perrin & Smith, 1999). When children have been bereaved, they may need bereavement counselling.

Prevalence and incidence

The prevalence of PTSD among children in the community is unknown. There have been no large scale epidemiological investigations of the disorder to date. In a study of 386 older adolescents, Reinherz et al. (1993) found 6.3% met DSM–III–R lifetime criteria for PTSD. There have been several studies of the incidence of PTSD in children exposed to war, natural disaster, violent crime and sexual abuse ('at-risk' groups). The rates vary widely (from 0% to 100%), consistent with findings from studies of at-risk adults (Fairbank et al., 1995), and this is reflected in the estimates given for at-risk groups in DSM–IV (3–58%) (APA, 1994).

In one of the earliest studies, Terr (1979) reported that the incidence of psychic trauma was 100% in the 26 children involved in the Chowchilla bus-kidnapping. This rate was independent of the child's background and developmental history. Two additional studies provide estimates for PTSD among children exposed to civilian acts of violence. Pynoos et al. (1987) examined the occurrence of PTSD in 159 children one month after an attack by a sniper on their school playground. Seventy-seven per cent of the children under direct threat (i.e. those on the playground) had moderate or severe PTSD as measured on the PTSD Reaction Index. Moderate or severe PTSD were also high (67%) among children not exposed to the sniper but at the school on the same day (Pynoos et al., 1987). Schwarz & Kowalski (1991) assessed 64 preadolescent school children 6 months after a shooting spree by a woman in their school. Between 8% and 16% were reported to meet criteria for PTSD, depending on which version of DSM was used.

Five months after the sinking of the cruise ship, *Jupiter*, with over 400 British school children on board, Yule et al. (1990) studied self-reported fears, anxiety and depression in a party of 24 adolescent girls from one school. Yule (1992*a*) reported the data on 334 of the survivors, confirming the high scores on the Impact of Event Scale as well as increased fears. Around half of the survivors were found to meet criteria for a diagnosis of PTSD in the first year following the sinking. While there was a slow improvement in symptoms over the following 6 to 7 years, almost one in five of those who developed PTSD still met criteria 5 years after the sinking. Many others had anxiety or depression and so it was demonstrated that PTSD is not a transient disorder and it is associated with long-term morbidity in a sizeable minority of cases (Boyle et al., 1995).

Of 179 children aged 2–15 years who were examined 2 years after the Buffalo Creek disaster, 37% received probable PTSD diagnoses based on retrospective examination of records (Green et al., 1991). Milgram et al. (1988) observed a 40% prevalence rate for PTSD in children one month after a bus accident. Bradburn (1991) reported prevalence rates of 27% for moderate PTSD and 36% for mild PTSD in 22 children aged 10–12 years, some 6 to 8 months after the San Francisco earthquake. Shannon et al. (1994) reported an overall prevalence rate for PTSD of 5% in a sample of 5687 children nearly 3 months after Hurricane Hugo which struck South Carolina in 1989. Similarly, Garrison et al. (1993) reported current prevalence rates ranging from 1.5% to 6.2% one year after the hurricane in 11 to 17-year-olds.

A recent series of studies in the U.K. has established that around one-third of child survivors of road traffic accidents develop PTSD (Canterbury, Yule & Glucksman, 1993; DiGallo, Barton & Parry-Jones, 1997; Ellis, Stores & Mayou, 1998; Heptinstall, 1996; Mirza et al., 1998; Stallard, 1998).

From the above studies it can be seen that although reliable estimates of the population prevalence of PTSD in children and adolescents have not been established, with the use of better measures and agreed diagnostic criteria, a consensus is emerging that around a third of young people may develop PTSD following life-threatening accidents, with much higher rates following particularly stressful incidents, depending on the definition, criteria and measures used to diagnose PTSD.

Developmental aspects

Many writers agree that it is very difficult to elicit evidence of emotional numbing in children (Frederick, 1985). Some children do show loss of interest in activities and hobbies that previously gave them pleasure. Preschool children show much more regressive behaviour as well as more antisocial, aggressive and destructive behaviour. There are many anecdotal accounts of preschool children showing repetitive drawing and play involving themes about the trauma they experienced.

Although parents and teachers initially report that young children do not easily talk about the trauma, recent experience has been that many young children easily give very graphic accounts of their experiences and were also able to report how distressing the re-experiencing in thoughts and images was to them (Misch et al., 1993; Sullivan, Saylor & Foster, 1991). All clinicians and researchers need to have a good understanding of children's development to be able to assist them to express their inner distress.

Scheeringa et al. (1995) examined the phenomenology reported in published cases of trauma in infants and young children and evolved an alternative set of criteria for diagnosing PTSD in very young children. Re-experiencing was seen as being manifested in post-traumatic play; re-enactment of the trauma; recurrent recollection of the traumatic event; nightmares; flashbacks or distress at exposure to reminders of the event. Numbing was viewed to be present if one of the following was manifested: constriction of play; socially more withdrawn; restricted range of affect; loss of previously acquired developmental skill. Increased arousal was noted if one of the following was present: night terrors; difficulty getting off to sleep; night waking; decreased concentration; hypervigilance; or exaggerated startle response. A fourth subset of new fears and aggression was suggested and was said to be present if one of the following was recorded: new aggression; new separation anxiety; fear of toiletting alone; fear of the dark or any other unrelated new fear. To date, these altered criteria have not been tested against the traditional ones. Almqvist & Brandell-Forsberg (1997) provide evidence on how a standard set of play material can be used to obtain objective data on traumatic stress reactions from preschool children. Thus, one can anticipate a refining of criteria and methods of assessment of PTSD in preschool children in the next few years.

The nature of the traumatic event – the search for Criterion A

PTSD is classified as an anxiety disorder. While it is characterized by predominant symptoms of fear, avoidance and hyperarousal, it differs from other anxiety disorders in that it requires a definite event as a precipitant. Over the years, DSM has altered the criteria whereby the precipitating event may be regarded as traumatic. In DSM–III (APA, 1980), the criterion was 'The existence of a recognizable stressor that would evoke significant symptoms of distress in almost anyone'. Seven years later in the next revision, DSM–III–R (APA, 1987) formulates the first criterion to be met as: 'The person has experienced an event that is outside the range of usual human experience and that would be markedly distressing to almost anyone, e.g., serious threat to one's life or physical integrity; serious threat or harm to one's children, spouse, or other close relatives and friends; sudden destruction of one's home or community; or seeing another person who has recently been, or is being, seriously injured or killed as the result of an accident or physical violence'.

Clearly, clinical and research experience in the intervening years has clarified and elaborated the characteristics of the traumatic event, centring mainly on threat to the integrity of the individual. However, it remains unclear what was meant by 'outside the range of usual human experience'. For example, sadly many children are physically or sexually abused. Some go on to develop stress reactions. Given that abuse is so common, can it be said to be 'outside the range of usual human experience?' (McNally, 1993) Clearly not, and yet the children are still suffering. The definition did not take sufficient account of individual differences in response to apparently similar experiences. It did, however, admit that subjective interpretation of the event was important (March, 1993).

Leading up to the revision of DSM that became DSM–IV (APA, 1994), March (1993) posed four questions about the nature of the traumatic event that proved influential in determining the latest definition of Criterion A. Here, we will quote criterion A and then consider March's four questions in relation to evidence on stress reactions in children.

DSM–IV now states that 'The person has been exposed to a traumatic event in which both the following were present: (1) The person experienced, witnessed, or was confronted with an event or events that involved actual or threatened death or serious injury, or a threat to the physical integrity of self or others; (2) The person's response involved fear, helplessness, or horror. *Note:* In children, this may be expressed instead by disorganised or agitated behavior'.

Thus, DSM–IV focused in on the threat to the integrity of the individual, and that opened up much more explicitly the manner in which the individual perceives or interprets the threat. That is why it is always important to ask a child or adolescent whether they thought they, or other actors in the event, were going to die. DSM also recognized more explicitly than previously that the ways in which children manifest stress reactions may differ from adults.

March's four questions

To bring order into the literature on the nature of the stressor, March (1993) asked:

1. Do stressors demonstrate a quantitative (dose-response) effect?
2. Do specific stressor characteristics predispose to PTSD or are stressors equipotent with response varying as a function of intensity?
3. What is the evidence for subjective perception (i.e., the appraisal of threat) in the generation of PTSD?
4. Does the stressor criterion need to be specifically modified for children?

(March, 1993, pp. 38–9)

Let us consider March's (1993) conclusions to the questions he raised and elaborate upon them, where relevant, by reference to recent studies with children and adolescents.

Dose-response effects

These were reported in 16 of the 19 studies March examined. With many caveats, he concluded that the greater the severity of the stressful event, the more likely it was that survivors would develop PTSD. As far as children are concerned, it has been reported that within particular disasters there is evidence of a dose-response – or more specifically an exposure-response – relationship. Pynoos et al. (1987) reported the effects of a sniper attack on children in a Californian school. There was a clear relationship between the distance from the sniper (and hence the objective, personal danger) and later psychopathology, with some individual differences. In a systematic follow-up study, Nader et al. (1990) reported that 74% of the most severely exposed children in the playground still reported moderate to severe levels of PTSD, whereas only 19% of the unexposed children reported any PTSD. It is of note that in this study the lower the objective level of threat, the more other subjective factors entered the equation to produce stress reactions.

Pynoos et al. (1993) studied three large groups of children following the Armenian earthquake – one from a town at the epicentre where buildings were totally destroyed; one from a town on the periphery; and one from a city outside the affected area. Again, a very clear exposure-effect relationship was demonstrated.

Following Hurricane Hugo which struck South Carolina in 1989, Lonigan et al. (1991) reported PTSD prevalence rates of 5% in a no exposure group, 10% in a mild, 16% in a moderate, and 29% in a high exposure group of hurricane survivors, based on self-report data.

After Hurricane Andrew in 1992, Vernberg et al. (1996) studied the effects on 558 children. Using a specially developed Hurricane-Related Traumatic Experiences questionnaire and the children's own stress reaction ratings, they found that greater exposure to the hurricane was strongly associated with more PTSD symptoms.

Several investigations have examined the prevalence of PTSD among children exposed to war. Most have used self-completed questionnaires rather than individual diagnostic interviews. In general, early studies conducted in association with UNICEF in former Yugoslavia found not only high levels of traumatic stress symptoms, anxiety and depression while the fighting was still in progress, but also that the greater the level of exposure of children to war traumas, the higher their subjective distress (Stuvland et al., 1994). These findings have been confirmed and extended in a study of more than 3500 children in the Bosnian city of Mostar, conducted a few months after the Dayton agreement brought an uneasy peace to the region (Smith et al., 1996).

Type of stressor

With respect to civilian stressors, March concluded that '. . . threat to life, severe physical harm or injury, exposure to grotesque death, and loss and/or injury of a loved one are at least modestly correlated to the likelihood of developing PTSD . . .' (March, 1993, p. 46.) In general, the experience of a traumatic loss may trigger a grief reaction and is also associated with the onset of depression, whereas the experience of threat is more related to the onset of anxiety (Finley-Jones & Brown, 1981). As yet, there is little by way of specific data from studies of children to address this issue.

Subjective perception

Most studies of psychopathology following specific traumatic events report that only a minority of survivors go on to develop PTSD. The implication is that subjective factors must moderate the stress reactions. These subjective factors are both of a temperamental, biological nature and of individual differences in processing emotional reactions (Rachman, 1980). In adults, rape produces very high levels of psychopathology. In children, there is some retrospective information indicating that sexual abuse by fathers produces greater distress than that by strangers, with sexual abuse by peers carrying even less risk (McLeer et al., 1988).

In a 15-month follow-up of nearly 100 adolescent survivors of the sinking of the cruise ship, *Jupiter*, Yule, Bolton & Udwin (1992) reported that whilst 'objective' factors such as which part of the ship the children had been in at the point of impact and whether they saw the dead bodies of the rescuers, were not related to scores on intrusion, avoidance, depression or anxiety at 5 months post-accident, these objective factors did relate to the scores at 15 months. On the other hand, 'subjective' factors such as thinking they would die at the time, feeling terrified and feeling guilty were related to intrusion, avoidance and depression (but not to anxiety) at 5 months and also at 15 months.

Yule et al. (1990) presented evidence that there was a subjective exposure-effect relationship in so far as children who had experienced a school trip disaster were much more badly affected than children in the same school who had wanted to go on the cruise but had not obtained places compared to even less distress among children who had never wanted to go. In another study of a small sub-group of adolescents who survived that same ship disaster, Joseph et al. (1993) reported on the attributions of 16 adolescent survivors of the *Jupiter* sinking and found that more internal and controllable attributions were related to intrusive thoughts and feelings of depression one year after the accident.

Need for different stressor criterion in children

March (1993) acknowledged that there had been fewer studies of children when DSM–IV was being formulated, but concluded that there was a great need to incorporate an element of subjective perception within the stressor criterion as there seemed to be a greater and different range of reactions in children. He also noted the claim that parental symptoms could predict children's PTSD symptoms (Stoddard, Norman & Murphy, 1989). This latter point is contentious.

McFarlane et al. (1987) concluded that following bush fires, the level of mothers' reactions fully explained the level of psychopathology reported in their children. However, the mothers had rated both their own and their children's reactions. In our own studies of the effects of the war in Bosnia on children, we found that a proportion of the variance in children's reactions can be accounted for by the mothers' own reported mental health (especially when the mothers rate their children's mental health) but that when the children's own ratings of their stress reactions are used as the dependant variable, then the direct exposure to the traumatic events as measured by the War Trauma Questionnaire, accounts for the greatest percentage of the variance (Smith, Yule & Perrin, 1998).

Summary

It can be concluded from the above that in general, there is an exposure-effect relationship as far as children are concerned. Moreover, the nature of the stressor does matter, with incidents involving threat to life having greatest effects. Even so, as will be seen below in relation to incidence, there are wide individual differences in response to traumatic events. In part, these are related to biologically based individual differences and in part to the way in which the threat is perceived and blame is attributed. There is, as yet, no useful typology of stressors in relation to children but it is becoming increasingly clear that not all the effects experienced by children are mediated by the effects of trauma on their parents.

Single versus repeated or chronic stressors

Both DSM and ICD in different, and changing, ways discuss the nature of the event that gives rise to the stress reaction. Each concentrates on single, acute stressors such as an unexpected disaster or a violent attack each of which occurs in the context of ongoing normality. Naturally, as work on PTSD in children and adolescents began to appear, so people tried to extend the paradigm to help understand other experiences that affect children's development. Wolfe, Gentile & Wolfe (1989) were among the first to try to formulate the effects of child sexual abuse within a PTSD framework and this certainly helped to focus attention on aspects of the whole experience that were perhaps more amenable to intervention. Thus, by drawing attention to many of the avoidance behaviours, it was possible to think of desensitization and exposure treatments that might help alleviate some of the distress.

However, there are important differences between child sexual abuse and a one-off civilian disaster. In the first place, the latter happens in the context of ongoing normality. The threat comes out of the blue and the event is public. Thus the therapist or researcher can quickly gain a reasonably clear picture of what each survivor must have encountered during the event and so can guide the survivor in remembering what happened. By contrast, sexual abuse takes place in conditions of secrecy and shame, often with threats of violence should the child ever tell anyone else about it. Important details surrounding the violations are therefore private and not readily accessible to the investigator. Moreover, the abuse often occurs on many occasions over many years, and so it is difficult to focus on one particular incident when investigating cause-effect relationships in research or trying to help the victim relive the experiences in therapy.

Two other sorts of chronic stressors that affect children have been discussed in recent years, and each brings yet more variables into play. Worldwide concern was focused on the psychological effects on children following the

Chernobyl nuclear disaster in 1986. The World Health Organization has coordinated a number of studies of the health effects on children in Ukraine, Byelarus and Russia, and a number of local studies have also tried to assess the effects on psychological adjustment. The problem here is that while the acute stage of the disaster can be pinpointed, there has been continuing concern about the delayed effects of radiation to the extent that nine years later people in the affected areas still restrict children from playing outdoors and avoid eating mushrooms and other foods that are thought to be contaminated. Thus, there is a continuing, chronic level of stress and the symptoms displayed by the population affected appear to be much more expressed somatically than is found in 'classic' PTSD.

The other chronic stressor being investigated is that which occurs in war situations. UNICEF has been at the forefront of stimulating research into the effects of war on children, particularly the dreadful war in former Yugoslavia. Stuvland et al. (1994) used a version of the War Trauma Questionnaire and showed that children in Sarajevo had experienced very high levels of stressful events such as sniping and shooting. Over 50% of their large sample had seen dead people and in half the cases they had actually witnessed the killings. The level of exposure to war-related stress correlated highly with symptoms of PTSD reported on the Impact of Event Scale and with levels of depression reported on the Birleson (1981) scale. But again, it is difficult to disentangle the effects of the many other things that happen during a bloody war – the ethnic cleansing, the break-up of families, the forced move from home and school, the loss of parents and so on. Children take on adult roles prematurely and then find it difficult to adjust to more normal, more age-appropriate demands when they return to school after hostilities cease.

The debate about the different effects of single versus repeated stressors continues and the need to agree on a classification of stressors is clearly identified. Terr (1991) argued the need to distinguish what she termed Type I and Type II stressors – with greater dissociative symptoms being associated with the Type II, repeated stressors. Others, working with adults have argued the need to recognize a category called DESNOS – disorders of extreme stress not otherwise specified (Herman, 1992). As noted above, it is highly likely that different types of stressor will be associated with different psychological reactions, both in terms of severity and content. A better understanding of these links will lead to better assessment and intervention.

Risk and protective factors

Age

Age has been thought to be a factor in the development of PTSD. Indeed, DSM cited children as being at a high risk of psychopathology following a trauma. This seems to owe more to a particular theoretical view of child development than to any hard evidence. Age was not found to be related to Stress Reaction Index scores within the Armenian earthquake group (Pynoos et al., 1993). Indeed, it can be argued that developmental age in the sense of cognitive understanding could act in different ways – younger children may not fully appreciate the dangers they faced and so may be protected from strong emotional reactions (Keppel-Benson & Ollendick, 1993). This would imply that brighter children would be at an increased risk, and this does not appear to be the case by teenage years.

Gender

It is generally found that girls score higher than boys on self-report measures of anxiety, depression and stress reactions following a trauma (Gibbs, 1989; Lonigan et al., 1991; Pynoos et al., 1993; Yule, 1992a,b). There are only a few unexplained exceptions to this pattern of findings and, as always, it is far from clear whether these are culturally or biologically determined differences.

Ability and attainment

In general, higher ability is seen as a protective factor against developing psychopathology. The developmental concern around appraisal of the threat noted earlier complicates the issue. Early studies of *Jupiter* survivors indicated that high risk was associated with prior low pre-accident attainment (Yule & Udwin, 1991). There are now many individual case examples of children's educational careers being thrown off-course by the after-effects of traumas happening at crucial times, and there is also evidence that in general academic attainment falls for a while after a major trauma (Tsui, Dagwell & Yule, 1993).

Family factors

It has already been noted that children often try to protect their parents from learning about their reactions to a trauma for fear of upsetting the parents. Where parents have difficulty processing their own emotional reactions, they are less successful in helping their children (McFarlane, 1987). Families who had difficulty sharing immediate reactions had more problems later. While some authors argue that all of children's reactions to trauma are mediated by parental reactions, in our clinical and research experience this is far from the case. The evidence for there being direct effects on the children is overwhelming.

Pre-disaster functioning

La Greca, Silverman & Wasserstein (1999) evaluated 92 4th to 6th grade students 15 months prior to Hurricane Andrew striking southern Florida. While experiences during the hurricane were important determinants of immediate and longer term stress reactions, this unique longitudinal study found that higher anxiety levels, more attention problems and poorer academic attainment prior to the hurricane also significantly predicted stress reactions 3 months post-disaster. However, by 7 months, only anxiety level among the pre-disaster functioning measures remained as a significant predictor.

Treatment of PTSD

While there have been a number of single case reports of treatment of children suffering PTSD, as yet there are no accounts of randomized controlled studies. For the most part, treatment approaches are predominantly cognitive–behavioural and appear to consist of adaptations of approaches used with adults (Yule, 1991) (see also Klingman, chapter 16, this volume for prevention programmes in this area).

Critical incident stress

Debriefing techniques have been adapted for use with groups of children following a variety of traumas (Dyregrov, 1991). Such a structured crisis intervention approach was used with some children following the *Jupiter* sinking, with good effects on lowering the levels of intrusion and of fears (Yule & Udwin, 1991). Stallard & Law (1993) used two debriefing sessions to reduce distress in girls who survived a school bus crash.

Group treatments are obviously to be preferred as a first line of intervention when large numbers are involved. Gillis (1993) suggests that groups of 6 to 8 are optimum, and advises that separate groups should be run for boys and girls. However, different types of incident surely require different responses from professionals (Galante & Foa, 1986; Yule & Williams, 1990) and it is too soon to pontificate on what should be a standard approach.

March et al. (1998) have published one of the few outcome studies of a group treatment using a manualized approach. Seventeen children followed an 18-week group treatment based on cognitive–behavioural principles. Fourteen completed the course and of these, just over half no longer met criteria for a diagnosis of PTSD. Improvement continued to 6-month follow-up. Gains could be credited to the intervention because a multiple baseline across schools design was built in. Not only were there significant reductions in stress symptoms, but also improvements in depression, anxiety and anger. These results are encouraging, but 18 sessions seems very long compared with the 2 to 6 reported in clinic-based single case studies of EMDR and exposure.

Individual treatment centres mainly on cognitive–behavioural therapies that aim both to help the survivor make sense of what happened and to master their feelings of anxiety and helplessness. Drug treatments, as in the rest of child psychopathology in general, have limited applications at present. Asking children to draw their experiences can be useful in helping them recall both the event and the emotions associated with it (Blom, 1986; Galante & Foa, 1986; Newman, 1976; Pynoos & Eth, 1986) but merely drawing the trauma is not a sufficient therapy. A recent study from former Yugoslavia where great emphasis was placed on getting children to express their emotions through drawing found that 6 months after having had very structured sessions on drawing and other expressive techniques, there was no measurable change in children's adjustment on a range of self-report measures of stress reactions (Bunjevac & Kuterovac., 1994).

Saigh (1986) was one of the first to provide clinical evidence that, as Rachman (1980) had predicted, there were dangers in using standard systematic desensitization approaches as the length of exposure sessions may be too short to permit adequate habituation of anxiety. It should also be remembered that where children are frightened by the vividness of their memories then relaxation may only serve to intensify the vividness. The theoretical aspects of exposure therapy in treating PTSD in children are discussed elsewhere (Saigh, Yule & Inamdar, 1996) and other suggestions of techniques to promote emotional processing are described in Rachman (1980), Yule (1991), Richards & Lovell (1999) and Saigh (1992).

There is considerable interest in and scepticism about Eye Movement and Desensitization and Reprocessing (EMDR) treatment (Shapiro, 1991). To date empirical support for its use with children and adolescents is sparse (Muris et al., 1998) although claims for its value are being made on the conference circuit! As with all techniques that have no clear rationale, caution has to be exercised. However, if symptomatic relief can really be attained in a few brief sessions, then the approach needs to be carefully evaluated. Since there does seem to be a different quality to the memories of a trauma that appear at the same time to be locked in, vivid and unchangeable by merely talking about them, then any technique that will allow emotional processing to proceed must be examined.

Contingency planning

When trauma affects a large number of children at once, as in an accident at school, then a public health approach to dealing with the emergency is required (Pynoos, Goenjian & Steinberg, 1995). Schools need to plan ahead not only to deal with large scale disasters, but also to respond to the needs of children after threatening incidents that affect only a few of them. Thus, there are now a number of texts written especially for schools to help them develop contingency plans to deal with the effects of a disaster (Johnson, 1993; Klingman, 1993; Yule & Gold, 1993).

Final comments

After initial scepticism that children might develop PTSD (Garmezy & Rutter, 1985), there has been a rapid increase in the number of studies in this area (for reviews, see Pfefferbaum, 1997; Yule, 1999). There is widespread agreement that both single and multiple traumatic events can lead to PTSD in many children and adolescents exposed to them. There is also general agreement that the criteria in both DSM and ICD for diagnosing PTSD in young people are too narrow, and require adjustment to encompass the range of reactions shown, especially at the younger ages. Even so, it is now clear that a significant proportion of children exposed to a life threatening event will develop disabling stress reactions that may last over many years.

The fact that many of the children exposed to traumatic events do not develop PTSD indicates that there are significant individual differences that moderate the effects. These include temperamental and personality differences, family and social support, and attributional processes. As these are better explored and understood, they should have significant implications for better interventions (Joseph, Williams & Yule, 1997; Yule, 1999).

Advice on assessment and therapeutic intervention is now emerging (AACAP, 1998). Assessment needs to go beyond the use of self-report inventories, although these have an important role in screening following large scale disasters and war. It is vital that the young person is interviewed directly, together with family members and teachers (Pynoos & Eth, 1986).

Crisis and other early interventions through schools (Dyregrov, 1991; Klingman, 1993; Yule & Gold, 1993) is advised, but in view of the possibility that poor timing and poor techniques may add to the children's burden, more evaluation of different methods is needed. While variations on exposure treatment within a cognitive–behaviour therapy paradigm currently appear to be the most effective treatments, the reported success of EMDR in even fewer sessions challenges clinical researchers to provide better evidence for the efficacy and efficiency of all treatment methods.

REFERENCES

Almqvist, K. & Brandell-Forsberg, M. (1997). Refugee children in Sweden: Post-traumatic stress disorder in Iranian preschool children exposed to organized violence. *Child Abuse & Neglect*, **21**, 351–66.

American Academy of Child and Adolescent Psychiatry (1998). Practice parameters for the assessment and treatment of children and adolescents with posttraumatic stress disorder. *Journal of the American Academy of child Psychiatry*, **37**, (10 Supplement, 4S–26S).

American Psychiatric Association (1980). *Diagnostic and Statistical Manual of Mental Disorders* (3rd Edition) (DSM–III). Washington, DC: APA.

American Psychiatric Association (1987). *Diagnostic and Statistical Manual of Mental Disorders* (3rd Edition, Revised) (DSM–III–R). Washington, DC: APA.

American Psychiatric Association (1994). *Diagnostic and Statistical Manual of Mental Disorders* (4th Edition) (DSM–IV). Washington, DC: APA.

Birleson, P. (1981). The validity of depressive disorder in childhood and the development of a self-rating scale: A research report. *Journal of Child Psychology and Psychiatry*, **22**, 73–88.

Blom, G. E. (1986). A school disaster – intervention and research aspects. *Journal of the American Academy of Child Psychiatry*, **25**, 336–45.

Boyle, S., Bolton, D., Nurrish, J., O'Ryan, D., Udwin, O. & Yule, W. (1995). The Jupiter sinking follow-up: Predicting psychopathology in adolescence following trauma. Poster presented at Eleventh Annual Meeting of the International Society for Traumatic Stress Studies, Boston, 2–6 November 1995. Available from author.

Bradburn, L. S. (1991). After the earth shook: children's stress symptoms 6–8 months after a disaster. *Advances in Behaviour Research and Therapy*, **13**, 173–9.

Bremner, J. D., Krystal, J. H., Southwick, S. M. & Charney, D. S. (1995a). Functional neuroanatomical correlates of the effects of stress on memory. *Journal of Traumatic Stress*, **8**, 527–53.

Bremner, J. D., Krystal, J. H., Southwick, S. M. & Charney, D. S. (1996a). Noradrenergic mechanism in stress and anxiety: I. Preclinical studies. *Synapse*, **23**, 28–38.

Bremner, J. D., Krystal, J. H., Southwick, S. M. & Charney, D. S. (1996b). Noradrenergic mechanism in stress and anxiety: II. Clinical studies. *Synapse*, **23**, 39–51.

Bremner, J. D., Randall, P., Scott, T. M., et al. (1995b). MRI-based measurement of hippocampal volume in patients with combat-related posttraumatic stress disorder. *American Journal of Psychiatry*, **152**, 973–81.

Brewin, C. R. (1988). *Cognitive Foundations of Clinical Psychology*. Hove, UK: Lawrence Erlbaum Associates.

Brewin, C. R., Dalgleish, T. & Joseph, S. (1996). A dual representation theory of posttraumatic stress disorder. *Psychological Review*, **103**, 670–86.

Bunjevac, T. & Kuterovac, G. (1994). Report on the results of psychological evaluation of the art therapy program in schools in Hercegovina. Zagreb: UNICEF.

Canterbury, R., Yule, W. & Glucksman, E. (1993). PTSD in child survivors of road traffic accidents. Paper presented to Third European Conference on Traumatic Stress, Bergen, 6–10 June 1993. Available from author.

Charney, D. S., Deutch, A. Y., Krystal, J. H., Southwick, S. M. & Davis, M. (1993). Psychobiologic mechanisms of posttraumatic stress disorder. *Archives of General Psychiatry*, **50**, 294–305.

Conway, M. (1995). *Flashbulb Memories*. Hove, UK: Lawrence Erlbaum Associates.

DiGallo, A., Barton, J. & Parry-Jones, W. (1997). Road traffic accidents: Early psychological consequences in children and adolescents. *British Journal of Psychiatry*, 170, 358–62.

Dyregrov, A. (1991). *Grief in Children: A Handbook for Adults*. London: Jessica Kingsley Publishers.

Ellis, A., Stores, G. & Mayou, R. (1998). Psychological consequences of road accidents in children. *European Child and Adolescent Psychiatry*, **7**, 61–8.

Fairbank, J. A., Schlenger, W. E., Saigh, P. A. & Davidson, J. R. T. (1995). An epidemiologic profile or post-traumatic stress disorder: Prevalence, comorbidity, and risk factors. In *Neurobiological and Clinical Consequences of Stress: From Normal Adaptation to PTSD*, ed. M. J. Friedman, D. S. Charney & A. Y. Deutch. Philadelphia: Lippincott-Raven Publishers.

Finley-Jones, R. & Brown, G. (1981). Types of stressful life events and the onset of anxiety and depressive disorders. *Psychological Medicine*, **11**, 803–15.

Frederick, C. J. (1985). Children traumatized by catastrophic situations. In *Post-Traumatic Stress Disorder in Children*, ed. S. Eth & R. S. Pynoos, pp. 73–99. Washington, DC: American Psychiatric Press.

Freidman, M. J., Charney, D. S. & Deutch, A. Y. (1995). *Neurobiological and Clinical Consequences of Stress: From Normal Adaptation to Post-traumatic Stress Disorder*. Philadelphia: Lippincott-Raven.

Galante, R. & Foa, D. (1986). An epidemiological study of psychic trauma and treatment effectiveness after a natural disaster. *Journal of the American Academy of Child Psychiatry*, **25**, 357–63.

Garmezy, N. & Rutter, M. (1985) Acute reactions to stress. In *Child and Adolescent Psychiatry: Modern Approaches* (2nd Edition), ed M. Rutter & L. Hersov, pp. 152–76. Oxford: Blackwell.

Garrison, C. Z., Weinrich, M. W., Hardin, S. B., Weinrich, S. & Wang, L. (1993). Post-traumatic stress disorder in adolescents after a hurricane. *American Journal of Epidemiology*, **138**, 520–30.

Gibbs, M. S. (1989). Factors in the victim that mediate between disaster and psychopathology: A review. *Journal of Traumatic Stress*, **2**, 489–514.

Gillis, H. M. (1993). Individual and small-group psychotherapy for children involved in trauma and disaster. In *Children and Disasters*, ed. C. F. Saylor, pp. 165–86. New York: Plenum Press.

Gray, J. A. (1987). *The Psychology of Fear and Stress* (2nd Edn). Cambridge: Cambridge University Press.

Green, B. L., Korol, M., Grace, M. C., Vary, M. G., et al. (1991). Children and disaster: Age, gender, and parental effects on PTSD symptoms. *Journal of the American Academy of Child and Adolescent Psychiatry*, **30**, 945–51.

Hagh-Shenas, H., Goldstein, L. & Yule, W. (1999). Psychobiology of post-traumatic stress disorder. In *Post Traumatic Stress Disorder*, ed. W. Yule, pp. 139–60. Chichester: John Wiley & Sons.

Heptinstall, E. (1996). *Healing the Hidden Hurt: The Emotional Effects of Children's Accidents.* London: Child Accident Prevention Trust, 18 Farringdon Lane, London EC1R 3AU.

Herman, J. L. (1992). Complex PTSD: A syndrome in survivors of prolonged and repeated trauma. *Journal of Traumatic Stress*, **5**, 377–91.

Janoff-Bulman, R. (1985). The aftermath of victimization: Rebuilding shattered assumptions. In *Trauma and its Wake*, ed. C. R. Figley. New York: Brunner/Mazel.

Johnson, K. (1993). *School Crisis Management: A Team Training Guide.* Alameda, CA: Hunter House.

Joseph, S., Brewin, C., Yule, W. & Williams, R. (1993). Causal attributions and psychiatric symptoms in adolescent survivors of disaster. *Journal of Child Psychology and Psychiatry*, **34**, 247–53.

Joseph, S., Williams, R. & Yule, W. (1997). *Understanding Posttraumatic Stress: A Psychosocial Perspective on PTSD and Treatment.* Chichester: John Wiley & Sons.

Keppel-Benson, J. M. & Ollendick, T. H. (1993). Posttraumatic stress disorders in children and adolescents. In *Children and Disasters*, ed. C. F. Saylor, pp. 29–43. New York: Plenum.

Klingman, A. (1993). School-based intervention following a disaster. In *Children and Disasters*, ed. C. F. Saylor, pp. 187–210. New York: Plenum Press.

La Greca, A. M., Silverman, W. K. & Wasserstein, S. B. (1999). Children's predisaster functioning as a predictor of posttraumatic stress following Hurricane Andrew. *Journal of Consulting and Clinical Psychology*, **66**, 883–92.

Lonigan, C. J., Shannon, M. P., Finch, A. J., Daugherty, T. K. & Saylor, C. M. (1991). Children's reactions to a natural disaster: Symptom severity and degree of exposure. *Advances in Behaviour Research and Therapy*, **13**, 135–54.

March, J. S. (1993). What constitutes a stressor? The 'Criterion A' issue. In *Posttraumatic Stress Disorder: DSM–IV and Beyond*, ed. J. R. T. Davidson & E. B. Foa, pp. 37–54. Washington, DC: American Psychiatric Press.

March, J. S., Amaya-Jackson, L., Murray, M. C. & Schulte, A. (1998). Cognitive-behavioral psychotherapy for children and adolescents with posttraumatic stress disorder after a single-incident stressor. *Journal of the American Academy of Child Psychiatry*, **37**, 585–93.

McFarlane, A. C. (1987). Family functioning and overprotection following a natural disaster: The longitudinal effects of post-traumatic morbidity. *Australia and New Zealand Journal of Psychiatry*, **21**, 210–18.

McFarlane, A. C., Policansky, S. & Irwin, C. P. (1987). A longitudinal study of the psychological morbidity in children due to a natural disaster. *Psychological Medicine*, **17**, 727–38.

McIvor, R. (1997). Physiological and biological mechanisms. In *Psychological Trauma: A Developmental Approach*, ed. D. Black, M. Newman, J. Harris-Hendricks & G. Mezey, pp. 55–60. London: Gaskell.

McLeer, S. V., Deblinger, E., Atkins, M. S., Foa, E. B. & Ralphe, D. L. (1988). Post-traumatic stress disorder in sexually abused children: A prospective study. *Journal of the American Academy of Child Psychiatry*, **27**, 650–4.

McNally, R. J. (1993) Stressors that produce posttraumatic stress disorder in children. In *Posttraumatic Stress Disorder: DSM–IV and Beyond*, ed. J. R. T. Davidson & E. B. Foa, pp. 57–74. Washington, DC: American Psychiatric Press.

Milgram, N. A., Toubiana, Y., Klingman, A., Raviv, A. & Goldstein, I. (1988). Situational exposure and personal loss in children's acute and chronic reactions to a school bus disaster. *Journal of Traumatic Stress*, **1**, 339–532.

Mirza, K. A. H., Bhadrinath, B. R., Goodyer, I. & Gilmour, C. (1998). Post-traumatic stress disorder in children and adolescents following road traffic accidents – a preliminary study. *British Journal of Psychiatry*, **172**, 443–7.

Misch, P., Phillips, M., Evans, P. & Berelowitz, M. (1993). Trauma in pre-school children: A clinical account. In *Trauma and Crisis Management*, ed. G. Forrest. AACPP Occasional Paper.

Muris, P., Merckelbach, H., Holdrinet, I. & Sijsenarr, M. (1998). Treating phobic children: Effects of EMDR versus exposure. *Journal of Consulting and Clinical Psychology*, **66**, 193–8.

Nader, K., Pynoos, R. S., Fairbanks, L. & Frederick, C. (1990). Childhood PTSD reactions one year after a sniper attack. *American Journal of Psychiatry*, **147**, 1526–30.

Newman, C. J. (1976). Children of disaster: Clinical observation at Buffalo Creek. *American Journal of Psychiatry*, **133**, 306–12.

Pfefferbaum, B. (1997). Posttraumatic stress disorder in children: A review of the past 10 years. *Journal of the American Academy of Child Psychiatry*, **36**, 1503–11.

Pynoos, R. S. & Eth, S. (1986). Witness to violence: The child interview. *Journal of the American Academy of Child Psychiatry*, **25**, 306–19.

Pynoos, R.S., Frederick, C., Nader, K., et al. (1987). Life threat and posttraumatic stress in school-age children. *Archives of General Psychiatry*, **44**, 1057–63.

Pynoos, R.S., Goenjian, A., Karakashian, M., et al. (1993). Posttraumatic stress reactions in children after the 1988 Armenian earthquake. *British Journal of Psychiatry*, **163**, 239–47.

Pynoos, R. S., Goenjian, A. & Steinberg, A. M. (1995). Strategies of disaster interventions for children and adolesacents. In *Extreme Stress and Communities: Impact and Intervention*, ed. S. E. Hobfall & M. de Vries. Dordrecht, The Netherlands: Kluwer.

Rachman, S. (1980). Emotional processing. *Behaviour Research and Therapy*, **18**, 51–60.

Reinherz, H. Z., Giaconia, R. M., Lefkowitz, E. S., Pakiz, B. & Frost, A. K. (1993). Prevalence of psychiatric disorders in a community population of older adolescents. *Journal of the American Academy of Child Psychiatry*, **32**, 369–77.

Richards, D. & Lovell, K. (1999). Behavioural and cognitive behavioural interventions in the treatment of PTSD. In *Posttraumatic Stress Disorders*, ed. W. Yule, pp. 239–66. Chichester: John Wiley & Sons.

Saigh, P. A. (1986). In vitro flooding in the treatment of a 6-yr-old boy's posttraumatic stress disorder. *Behaviour Research and Therapy*, **24**, 685–8.

Saigh, P. A. (1992). The behavioral treatment of child and adolescent posttraumatic stress disorder. *Advances in Behaviour Research and Therapy*, **14**, 247–75.

Saigh, P. A., Yule, W. & Inamdar, S. C. (1996). Imaginal flooding of traumatized children and adolescents. *Journal of School Psychology*, **34**, 163–83.

Scheeringa, M. S., Zeanah, C. H., Drell, M. J. & Larrieu, J. A. (1995). Two approaches to the diagnosis of posttraumatic stress disorder in infancy and early childhood. *Journal of the American Academy of Child and Adolescent Psychiatry*, **34**, 191–200.

Schwarz, E. D. & Kowalski, J. M. (1991). Posttraumatic stress disorder after a school shooting:

Effects of symptom threshold selection and diagnosis by DSM–III, DSM–III–R, or proposed DSM–IV. *American Journal of Psychiatry*, **148**, 592–7.

Shannon, M. P, Lonigan, C. J., Finch, A. J., et al. (1994). Children exposed to disaster. I: Epidemiology of posttraumatic symptoms and symptom profiles. *Journal of the American Academy of Child and Adolescent Psychiatry*, **33**, 80–93.

Shapiro, F. (1991). Eye movement desensitization and reprocessing procedure: From EMD to EMD/R – a new treatment model for anxiety and related traumas. *Behavior Therapist*, **14**, 133–5.

Smith, P., Yule, W. & Perrin, S. (1998). Posttraumatic stress reactions in children and war: Risk and moderating factors. Poster presented to 14th Annual Meeting of the International Society for Traumatic Stress Studies, Washington, DC, November 1998. Available from author.

Smith, P., Yule, W., Perrin, S. & Schwartz, D. (1996). Maternal reactions and child distress following the war in Bosnia. Paper presented at the 12th Annual Convention of the International Society for Traumatic Stress Studies (November), San Francisco, CA. Available from author.

Southwick, S. M., Bremner, D., Krystal, J. H. & Charney, D. S. (1994). Psychobiologic research in post-traumatic stress disorder. *Psychiatric Clinics of North America*, **17**, 251–64.

Stallard, P. (1998). Presentation of symptoms in children. Paper presented to conference, Road Accidents and the Mind. Bristol, UK, September 1998.

Stallard, P. & Law, F. (1993). Screening and psychological debriefing of adolescent survivors of life-threatening events. *British Journal of Psychiatry*, **163**, 660–5.

Stoddard, F., Norman, D. & Murphy, J. (1989). A diagnostic outcome study of children and adolescents with severe burns. *Journal of Trauma*, **29**, 471–7.

Stuvland, R. et al. (1994). A UNICEF report on war trauma among children in Sarajevo. Zagreb: UNICEF.

Sullivan, M. A., Saylor, C. F. & Foster, K. Y. (1991). Post-hurricane adjustment of preschoolers and their families. *Advances in Behaviour Research and Therapy*, **13**, 163–71.

Terr, L. C. (1979). The children of Chowchilla. *Psychoanalytic Study of the Child*, **34**, 547–623.

Terr, L. C. (1991). Childhood traumas – An outline and overview. *American Journal of Psychiatry*, **148**, 10–20.

Tsui, E., Dagwell, K. & Yule, W. (1993). Effect of a disaster on children's academic attainment. Available from author.

Vernberg, E. M., La Greca, A. M., Silverman, W. K. & Prinstein, M. J. (1996). Prediction of posttraumatic stress symptoms in children after hurricane Andrew. *Journal of Abnormal Psychology*, **105**, 237–48.

Wolfe, V., Gentile, C. & Wolfe, D. A. (1989). The impact of sexual abuse on children: A PTSD formulation. *Behavior Therapy*, **20**, 215–28.

World Health Organization (1992). *The Tenth Revision of the International Classification of Diseases and Related Health Problems (ICD–10)*. Geneva: WHO.

Yehuda, R. & McFarlane, A. C. (1995). Conflict between current knowledge about posttraumatic stress disorder and its original conceptual basis. *American Journal of Psychiatry*, **152**, 1705–13.

Yule, W. (1991). Work with children following disasters. In *Clinical Child Psychology: Social*

Learning, Development and Behaviour, ed. M. Herbert, pp. 349–63. Chichester: John Wiley & Sons.

Yule, W. (1992*a*). Post traumatic stress disorder in child survivors of shipping disasters: The sinking of the 'Jupiter'. *Psychotherapy and Psychosomatics*, **57**, 200–5.

Yule, W. (1992*b*). Resilience and vulnerability in child survivors of disasters. In *Vulnerability and Resilience: A festschrift for Ann and Alan Clarke*, ed. B. Tizard & V. Varma, pp. 82–98. London: Jessica Kingsley.

Yule, W. (ed.) (1999). *Posttraumatic Stress Disorder*. Chichester: John Wiley & Sons.

Yule, W., Bolton, D. & Udwin, O. (1992). Objective and subjective predictors of PTSD in adolescents. Paper presented at World Conference of International Society for Traumatic Stress Studies, 'Trauma and Tragedy', Amsterdam, 21–6 June, 1992.

Yule, W. & Gold, A. (1993). *Wise Before the Event: Coping with Crises in Schools*. London: Calouste Gulbenkian Foundation.

Yule, W., Perrin, S. & Smith, P. (1999). PTSD in children and adolescents. In *Post Traumatic Stress Disorder*, ed. W. Yule, pp. 25–50. Chichester: John Wiley & Sons.

Yule, W. & Udwin, O. (1991). Screening child survivors for post-traumatic stress disorders: Experiences from the 'Jupiter' sinking. *British Journal of Clinical Psychology*, **30**, 131–8.

Yule, W., Udwin, O. & Murdoch, K. (1990). The 'Jupiter' sinking: Effects on children's fears, depression and anxiety. *Journal of Child Psychology and Psychiatry*, **31**, 1051–61.

Yule, W. & Williams, R. (1990). Post traumatic stress reactions in children. *Journal of Traumatic Stress*, **3**, 279–95.

10

Family and genetic influences: is anxiety 'all in the family'?

Frits Boer and Ingeborg Lindhout

Introduction

Anxiety disorders run in families. Children of anxious parents are prone to develop anxiety problems of their own, and parents of anxious children show more anxiety problems than parents of children without anxiety problems. This aggregation of anxiety in families can be due to common experiences as well as to common genes. Over the last two decades researchers have tried to disentangle the contributions of nature and nurture to the transmission of anxiety disorders. This chapter will review their research and their findings, as well as the new questions yielded.

The chapter has two sections. The first section, on the genetic contribution to anxiety in children, starts out with a brief review of the studies that have demonstrated that anxiety disorders aggregate in families. However, the studies show low specificity: children's anxiety disorders often do not coincide with those in the parents, and there appears to be overlap with other disorders, especially depression.

This is followed by a discussion of quantitative genetic studies, which addresses both genetic and environmental contributions to the transmission of anxiety disorders in families, and can shed light on questions of comorbidity. Most of this research has been conducted with adults, but findings from genetic research on anxiety disorders in children and adolescents are now emerging. These findings are both puzzling and intriguing – because different perspectives on the child's anxiety (parental report versus children's report) and different research designs (twin studies versus adoption studies) appear to yield contradictory findings.

The second section, on the contribution of family processes to anxiety in children, will commence with a brief overview of the contribution of family processes to the child's threat detection and the development of coping skills in normal development.

In describing the environmental contribution to etiology, we distinguish between two types of family processes: (1) harbouring threat and/or providing insufficient protection from it, (2) promoting threat sensitivity and/or impeding the development of coping skills. In reviewing studies on the role of parental rearing style, we note how our understanding of this phenomenon has changed: from a general characteristic of parents to a transactional process, with an important contribution from the child.

The genetic contribution to anxiety in children

Family studies

The familial prevalence of anxiety disorders can be studied 'top-down', by examining the children of anxiety-disordered parents, or 'bottom-up', by assessing parents and other relatives of children diagnosed as having an anxiety disorder (Last & Beidel, 1991). When it is not possible to interview all family members directly, as is often the case in studies with adult patients, information about some family members is obtained indirectly, from the patient or another relative. This procedure is known as the 'family history' method. In studies of child probands it is easier to approach all family members directly, a procedure called the 'family study' method. This last method provides the most reliable and complete information. We provide a short overview of both methods (for a review, see Last & Beidel, 1991).

In this section family studies are discussed in regard to questions of the prevalence of anxiety disorders. Some of these studies also have addressed the family processes that might contribute to the transmission of the anxiety disorders. We discuss those aspects in the second section, under the heading 'Parental anxious symptomatology'.

In a pioneering top-down study of 299 mothers with agoraphobia, employing the family history method, Berg (1976) found a prevalence of school phobia in the children (7% for children 7 to 15 years old, 15% when children 11 to 15 years old were considered separately), that he claimed was higher than would be expected in the general population. Another family history top-down study (Weissman et al., 1984) showed that children (aged 6 to 17 years; $n = 194$) whose parents suffered from depression plus an anxiety disorder had significantly more anxiety disorders ($n = 69$, prevalence: 16%) than children of normal controls ($n = 87$, prevalence: 2–3%) or of parents with depression only ($n = 38$, prevalence: 0%).

In a top-down study using the family study method, Turner, Beidel & Costello (1987) compared the offspring of anxious adults (agoraphobia or

obsessive-compulsive disorder) to three comparison groups: children of dysthymic parents, children of normal parents who were solicited as volunteers for
the study, and children of parents of a school 'normal' group. The children
were between the ages of 7 and 12 ($n = 59$). Turner et al. found that four of the
16 children (25%) of parents with an anxiety disorder met criteria for separation
anxiety, while two (13%) met criteria for overanxious disorder. Three of the 14
(21%) offspring of dysthymics met criteria for separation anxiety ($n = 1$),
overanxious disorder ($n = 1$), and social phobia ($n = 1$) respectively. Only one of
the 13 (8%) solicited normal parent offspring met DSM–III criteria with a
diagnosis of overanxious disorder, and none of the 16 (0%) children of parents
in the school normal group.

In a more recent study (Beidel & Turner, 1997) children (between the ages of
7 and 12 years; $n = 129$) of parents of four diagnostic groups (anxiety disorders
($n = 28$), depressive disorders ($n = 24$), mixed anxiety/depressive disorders
($n = 29$), and no psychiatric disorder ($n = 48$)) were assessed for overall psychopathology, including specifically the presence of anxiety disorders. The children
of the three 'high-risk' groups were significantly more likely to have a diagnosable disorder (including anxiety disorders) than offspring of normal parents
(40% versus 10%). However, this time no differences were found among the
children of the three parental diagnosis groups: children of depressed parents
were as likely to have an anxiety disorder as children of parents with a pure
anxiety disorder or a mixed anxiety/depressive disorder. There was the difference however that offspring of anxious parents were significantly more likely to
have only anxiety disorders (90% of those with diagnosable disorders), whereas
children from the other two groups of parental pathology exhibited a broader
range of psychopathology, e.g. major depressive episode or dysthymia (of
diagnosable disorders only 55% were anxiety disorders).

Other family studies of offspring of parents with panic disorder and agoraphobia with and without major depression (Biederman et al., 1991) and of
parents with social phobia (Mancini et al., 1996) demonstrated a higher prevalence of anxiety disorders (between 21% and 49%) than the 2% to 17% found in
epidemiological studies (Anderson et al., 1987; Kashani et al., 1990; McGee et
al., 1990), but often not the same anxiety disorder as the affected proband.

Bottom-up studies show a similar pattern: parents of children with an
anxiety disorder more often show anxiety disorders, but with little specificity of
the anxiety disorders involved (Berg, Butler & Pritchard, 1974; Last et al., 1991;
Messer & Beidel, 1994). An exception may hold for two disorders. Last et al.
(1991) found a trend for panic disorder to be more prevalent among relatives of
children with this disorder ($n = 39$, prevalence 10.8%) than relatives of

probands with anxiety disorder without panic disorder ($n = 235$, prevalence 3.9%), and a similar pattern for relatives of children with obsessive-compulsive disorder ($n = 47$, prevalence 6.7%), when compared with those of children with anxiety disorders without OCD ($n = 227$, prevalence 1.4%).

In summary, both top-down and bottom-up studies show an aggregation of anxiety disorders in families, but with minimal specificity. The lack of a specific relation between the disorders in the parents and those in the children could be due to differences in the nature of the child's anxiety disorder (Beidel & Turner, 1997). Because depression in children and adolescents is often preceded by anxiety, it could be that anxiety in the offspring of depressed parents represents a prodromal state for the later development of depression, whereas anxiety disorders in the offspring of anxious parents represent the early onset of anxiety disorders.

An important limitation of family aggregation studies is their inability to clarify these questions of comorbidity. Do we find this overlap between anxiety and depressive disorders because some of the genes which influence vulnerability to anxiety disorders also influence vulnerability to depression, or is it because familial–environmental factors predispose to both disorders, or, thirdly, because nonfamilial environmental factors (stressful events) predispose to anxiety as well as depression (Kendler et al., 1993b)? To address these questions, it is necessary to study the genetic contribution to the familial aggregation of anxiety disorders.

Genetic studies

Twin studies of adult anxiety disorders

Most of the knowledge about the genetic and environmental contributions to anxiety disorders in adults originates from a series of studies of a large group of female twins with a mean age of 30.1 (S.D. 7.6 years) in the North American state of Virginia (Kendler et al., 1987, 1992a,b,c, 1993a,b, 1995). These studies have demonstrated a genetic contribution to most anxiety disorders, varying from a modest size (30% to 35% explained variance in liability) for generalized anxiety disorder and phobia, to a moderate size (41% to 44% explained variance in liability) for panic disorder (Kendler et al., 1995). From a genetic perspective, anxiety disorders turn out not to be etiologically homogeneous. One genetic factor loads most heavily on phobia, panic disorder (and bulimia nervosa), while another genetic factor loads heavily on generalized anxiety disorder and major depression (Kendler et al., 1995).

The obtained patterns of comorbidity support an independent pathway (rather than a common pathway) model. Environmental risk factors produce a different pattern of comorbidity than genetic risk factors. The familial–environmental factor is not of substantial influence on the liability to develop an anxiety disorder or depression. Individual-specific environmental factors, however, appear to be major risk factors for all the disorders (although this may be somewhat inflated by unreliability of measurement).

Because the genes that influence vulnerability to major depression have the same effect on generalized anxiety disorder, and because familial environment plays no substantial role in their etiology, individual-specific experiences will decide whether somebody will suffer from generalized anxiety disorder or major depression (Kendler et al., 1992a). Life-event research supports this finding. In a study of an English inner-city population of working-class and single mothers at risk for both depression and anxiety conditions in adult life (because of adverse experiences in childhood), it appeared that the onsets of depression and anxiety were both provoked by life events. Whether depression or anxiety developed depended on the type of influence: loss (and lack of hope) tended to lead to depression, danger (and lack of security) to anxiety (Brown & Harris, 1993; Brown, Harris & Eales, 1993).

The independence of the genetic contributions to major depression and to phobias respectively is a relative one. When comorbidity occurs between major depression and a phobia, a modest proportion (25%) of it is caused by genetic factors that influence the liability to both disorders, while about 75% of the observed comorbidity is due to environmental risk factors shared by both syndromes (Kendler et al., 1993a).

How genetic and environmental influences differ in their respective contributions to different anxiety disorders, can be illustrated by Kendler et al.'s (1992b) study of four phobia subtypes: agoraphobia, social phobia, animal phobia and situational phobias. Genetic factors turned out to play a substantial, but by no means overwhelming role in their etiology: individual-specific environment accounted for approximately twice as much variance. However, these types of risk factors did not influence the pattern of subtypes of phobias in the same way. It appears that the subtypes of phobias can be placed along an etiologic continuum. At one end of this continuum lies agoraphobia, which has (1) the latest age at onset, (2) the highest rate of comorbidity, (3) the highest heritability, (4) the highest loading on the environmental common factor, (5) the least specific environmental influences, and (6) the lowest loading on the genetic common factor. Simple phobias (animal and situational) are at the other end of the continuum: (1) the earliest age of onset, (2) the lowest rates of comorbidity, etc., while social phobia lies intermediate between agoraphobia and the simple phobias.

The role of environmental experiences in simple phobias is often specific, for instance: having been locked in a dark closet, or bitten by the dreaded animal. The role of the environment in agoraphobia is not specific,· but consists of experiences that only influence the general level of phobia proneness (Kendler et al., 1992b).

Twin studies of childhood anxiety disorder

Quantitative genetic studies of anxiety (and other) disorders in children and adolescents have just been started (Eaves et al., 1997; Hewitt et al., 1997; Thapar & McGuffin, 1995). In the Virginia Twin Study of Adolescent Behavioral Development (Eaves et al., 1997; Hewitt et al., 1997) – a multiple phenotypic assessment of 1412 pairs of twins aged 8 to 16 years – the highest correlations were found between separation anxiety disorder and overanxious disorder. Separation anxiety disorder and overanxious disorder showed distinct time courses – symptoms of the former were more prevalent in younger children and those of the latter in older children, but their interfactor correlations were high enough to support the hypothesis that the same individuals may be vulnerable to separation anxiety disorder in early childhood, overanxious disorder in later childhood, and possibly to generalized anxiety disorder in adulthood.

Although few of the gender differences reached statistical significance in this study, the gender differences in the contribution of genes and environment to parental ratings of separation anxiety disorder were a marked exception to this general trend. The heritability estimate was effectively zero in boys and nearly 75% in girls in the data pooled across ages. This finding is similar to that obtained in an Australian study of adult twins, which also demonstrated a substantial genetic contribution to separation anxiety (reported retrospectively about their youth) in females, but not in males (Silove et al., 1995).

However the Eaves et al. (1997) findings regarding the heritability of separation anxiety disorder in girls were not replicated by the results derived from the interview with the child. This was also an important finding in an English twin study of childhood anxiety disorder. When the parent ratings were considered, anxiety symptoms appeared to be highly heritable with additive genes accounting for 59% of the variance. The results for the self-report obtained in an adolescent subsample were strikingly different: shared environmental effects rather than genetic factors appeared to be of primary importance (Thapar & McGuffin, 1995). These contradictory findings do not have to be interpreted as a sign of unreliability, because monozygotic twin correlations and test-retest reliability studies support at least moderate reliability of the adolescents' reports (Eaves et al. 1997). Parents and children have a different perspective on the child's behaviour and therefore may be rating different constructs (Hewitt et al., 1997). A possibility is that parents are rating more enduring traits, while the twins may be rating more acute, 'state' rather than 'trait' symptoms, which may be more influenced by shared environmental factors, such as school examinations (Thapar & McGuffin, 1995).

An adoption study of internalizing problems in young adolescents

A study of international adoptees in the Netherlands (van den Oord, Boomsma & Verhulst, 1994) yielded results that contrast sharply with those of twin studies. The sample in this study of 10- to 15-year-old international adoptees (mean age = 12.4 years; $n = 758$) comprised of a group of biological siblings (111 pairs), a group of nonbiological siblings (221 pairs) and a group of singletons (94). Parental ratings of children's problem behaviours were obtained with the Child Behavior Checklist (CBCL; Achenbach, 1991). Genetic influences were found to be substantial for Externalizing behaviours (explaining 65% of the variance) but unimportant for Internalizing behaviours (explained variance almost zero). The influence of shared environment was moderate, that of nonshared environment substantial. A partial replication of these results was obtained recently (Eley et al., 1998). Partial, because the adoptees in the second study were studied at a somewhat younger age (between 9 and 12), and because the second study was aimed specifically at depressive symptoms. The results were strikingly similar however, in showing negligible heritability (statistically nonsignificant), a modest influence of shared environment ($P < 0.05$), and a substantial influence of nonshared environment on the children's depressive symptoms ($P < 0.01$).

Van den Oord et al. (1994) used parental ratings in their study (recall that parental ratings yielded the highest contribution of heritability in the twin studies of childhood anxiety disorders), while Eley et al. (1998) used both parent and child ratings. After an extensive discussion of their findings Eley et al. concluded, 'In summary, we are left with no clear explanation of the discrepancy between the twin and adoption results. At the very least these findings raise doubt about genetic influence on depressive symptoms in middle childhood and warrant more than usual the maxim that more research is needed' (p. 342).

Only depressive symptoms were examined explicitly in the second study, so we need to be prudent in extrapolating this conclusion to anxious symptoms. These studies should also caution us to be careful in interpreting the findings of twin studies.

The nature of genetic transmission

One lesson to be learned from the research on adults is that the genetic contribution to anxiety disorders is probably not of a single nature. However, we know of only one aspect with sufficient empirical support, to be considered important in the genetic transmission of anxiety disorders in children: the neurophysiological and temperamental individual differences found with regard to what is called 'behavioural inhibition' (see Oosterlaan, chapter 3, this volume). Children with a stable inhibited temperament have a lower threshold for arousal in the amygdala and the hypothalamic circuits, and react with specific behaviours and sympathetic activation (Biederman et al., 1995; Kagan, 1994). Top-down studies show that the rates of behavioural inhibition are significantly higher in children of adults with panic disorder and agoraphobia, or with major depressive disorder, than in children of adults who are not psychiatrically ill. Bottom-up studies show that parents of inhibited children (compared with those of uninhibited and normal children) have significantly higher rates of social phobia, and histories of childhood anxiety disorders, or of a continuing anxiety disorder (Biederman et al., 1995).

So behavioural inhibition appears to be related not just to panic disorder in adults, but to social phobia as well. Some studies suggest that social phobia is familially distinct from panic disorder, although this may only be pertinent to discrete social phobias. Generalized forms of social phobia, social phobia associated with panic attacks, and social phobia occurring comorbidly with panic disorder, may have a common substrate vulnerability (Biederman et al., 1995).

As robust as these findings are, there continues to be debate about the exact nature of the relation between behavioural inhibition and the anxiety disorders. After a critical examination of the relevant literature, Turner, Beidel & Wolff (1996) suggested that behavioural inhibition is in particular associated with maladaptive social anxiety, and more likely is a genetically transmitted vulnerability, rather than a trait. This would mean that the early temperamental disposition by itself only minimally explains psychopathology, because it takes critical interactions with a host of environmental factors, which in turn are moderated by gender, age, social class and cultural context.

Somewhat more speculative, but heuristically important, Kovacs & Devlin (1998) advanced a specific temperament–personality characteristic in the research tradition of 'high negative emotionality' or 'negative affectivity' and proposed that this could be the genetic underpinning characteristic with special relevance for the development of anxiety and/or depressive disorders. This construct implies the inability to regulate negative emotion or mood, and to respond with particular sensitivity to negative life events. Kovacs and Devlin placed this construct within a developmental model, to be able to account for the chronology of disorders. Whereas genetic factors are believed to increase the risk for an anxiety or depressive disorder in a nonspecific manner, biological and cognitive mechanisms are thought of as complementary factors, that influence the probability of a disorder, or comorbid disorders to occur. Because there are constraints on the expression of a mood disorder at an early age, children before adolescence with negative emotionality will more easily develop an anxiety disorder. In some of them the anxiety disorder will be followed by a depressive disorder.

In summary, quantitative genetic research among adults strongly suggests a significant contribution of genetic factors to most anxiety disorders, although differing in size and not restricted to anxiety. The findings regarding children and adolescents are more inconsistent, not only depending on the informant, but also on the research approach chosen. We should avoid a simple extrapolation of the findings from research among adults to children and adolescents. We are not at all certain to what extent anxiety disorders of children are related to those in adults. Some researchers speculate that the separation anxiety disorder in children is an early manifestation of panic disorder in adolescents and adults (Abelson & Alessi, 1992), while overanxious disorder in children is now considered the early manifestation of generalized anxiety disorder in adults (American Psychiatric Association, 1994). Because panic disorder and generalized anxiety disorder in adults have different genetic backgrounds (Kendler et al., 1995), one would expect a distinction between separation anxiety disorder in children and the overanxious disorder. The preliminary findings in childhood genetic studies do not support this, however; instead separation anxiety disorder and overanxious disorder in children are highly correlated (Hewitt et al., 1997). These findings remind us of the possibility that genetic vulnerabilities are expressed differently in successive developmental stages, not only because of differences in biological and cognitive development, but also because of important changes in the interaction with the environment.

The contribution of family processes to anxiety in children

Because genetic factors play only a modest (although significant) role in the aggregation of anxiety disorders within certain families, the environmental contribution in the transgenerational transmission of anxiety disorders needs to be considered as well. This is often phrased as 'how do anxious parents pass on their anxiety to their children?', and has led to investigations of general familial factors, like the parental rearing style of anxious parents (Parker, 1983). We discuss this research in more detail in this section, but first we offer two caveats.

First, even though anxiety aggregates in families, not all anxiety-disordered children have anxious parents. If parents of children with an anxiety disorder have a rate of 40% anxiety disorders themselves (Last et al., 1991), more than one-half of the parents of anxious children do not. Therefore, in looking for possible environmental factors in families, we should not restrict ourselves to those derived from anxiety in the parent.

Second, a surprising finding from quantitative genetic research has been that shared family environment hardly seems to contribute to anxiety disorders. The (substantial) environmental contribution is almost completely unique, different for each child in the family. At first glance this seems to argue against the role of parental rearing style in the transmission of anxiety disorders – as rearing style is usually conceptualized as a general attitude of the parents, more or less the same for each child in the family. Because most of the empirical findings on the environmental contribution to anxiety disorders have been on rearing style, we will need to consider whether these divergent findings can be reconciled.

From the beginning of life fear and anxiety are emotions embedded within the primary relationships of the human being. Although these responses are innate, they are shaped within the family. One of the child's primary developmental tasks is learning to recognize danger, and learning how to cope with it. It has been Bowlby's (1973) important contribution to show that fear is not only related to actual danger, but to the absence of safety as well. In an analogy to the military commander who is expecting not only direct attack, but also trying to maintain open communication with his base as well, Bowlby distinguishes 'the threat from the front' from 'the threat from the rear'. This implies, in turn, that a child knows two sources of anxiety: real dangers and defection by the attachment figure. A combination of these two types of threats ('compound situations': a sudden noise and being alone) increases fear enormously.

Both forms of threat occur in families. In some families parental neglect is responsible for a 'threat from the rear', but when the neglect is accompanied by abuse, the rear becomes a second front: a source of threat within the family. Sometimes the subjective perception of the outside world as a threatening front, is not so much the reflection of objective danger, but the result of an amplification of threat, or of a feeling of helplessness in the face of it. Family processes can contribute to both.

The research findings with regard to these processes allow for a rough categorization of two types of families: (1) those harbouring threat and/or

providing insufficient protection from it, and (2) those promoting threat
sensitivity and/or impeding the development of coping skills

Families that harbour threat and/or insufficient protection from it

Although most clinicians will agree with Bowlby that parental neglect and/or
abuse are risk factors in the development of anxiety disorders, to our knowledge this has not been studied systematically in children – but some support can
be found in studies of adults.

An epidemiological study of 404 English working-class single mothers
showed a marked association of panic disorder, agoraphobia, generalized
anxiety disorder and social phobia with negative experiences in childhood
(parental indifference, sexual abuse or physical abuse) (Brown et al., 1993).
Other studies have found an association between panic disorder and the
experience of adversity in childhood (Faravelli et al., 1985; Raskin et al., 1982;
Tweed et al., 1989). Parental discord and a conflictual home atmosphere also
have been found to be associated with anxiety disorders (Kashani et al., 1990;
Laraia et al., 1994).

Indirect support also can be gained from attachment research. Children who
are confronted with threat within the family (for instance because a parent
shows frightening behaviour), often develop a disorganized attachment
(Schuengel, 1997). This type of attachment is a risk factor for the development
of a range of disturbances, including anxiety disorders (Manassis et al., 1994;
also see Manassis, chapter 11, this volume).

Families that promote threat sensitivity and/or impede the development of coping skills

Although the danger detection system in humans is biologically prepared, the
child does not enter the world with fixed notions of what is dangerous. That
would not be adaptive from a biological point of view, because it would not
leave room for the development of new reactions toward changed circumstances. It would also not be optimally adaptive for the child to have to discover by
trial and error which cues are dangerous and which are not. Therefore
information from significant others is included in the construction of the
distinction between safe and non-safe. Just watching another group member
reacting scared, can be enough to develop apprehension toward this trigger
('vicarious learning'), while noticing a calm and reassuring reaction in a trusted
fellow human being, can contribute to a lessening of fear ('social referencing').
Parents and older siblings may especially serve as models in these forms of
learning (Marks, 1987).

However, it is important to recognize the difference in learning by observation and through active investigation. If a child is able to approach and actively investigate a scary object (e.g. a moving toy), and is able to find out that it is not dangerous, he or she will be more reassured, than will be the case when he or she is able to see a trusted adult go through the same process (Marks, 1987). Research with monkeys has shown that the anxiety-reducing effects of such active control experiences are cumulative (Mineka, cited in Messer & Beidel, 1994).

This principle of active investigation is an important notion in the development of coping skills. There is, of course, a ceiling to this effect: when the somewhat scary object turns out to be really dangerous, the effect on the child will be opposite: it will be more fearful afterwards. To phrase it somewhat differently: exposure to stress of manageable proportions leads to anxiety reduction through habituation, while exposure to overwhelming stress can lead to a generalized heightened level of fear through sensitization.

What consequences for parenting can we distil from these principles? Ideally parents offer their child a realistic view of the world around in their assessment of danger and will model this view in their own behaviour. What will be manageable for the child, depends in part on the support he/she gets from the parents. Initially parents can provide opportunities for the development of coping skills by guided participation, letting the child manage, what he or she can (almost) manage him or herself, and providing protection when the burden is too heavy for the child. In later stages they will appeal to the child's autonomy.

Studies of parental rearing style

Parental rearing style has been studied systematically since the 1950s (Maccoby & Martin, 1983). By using the results of several factor analytic studies of parental characteristics, Schaefer (1959) demonstrated that the intercorrelations of a number of different variables can be ordered in a circumplex pattern with two major orthogonal dimensions: warmth versus hostility; and control versus autonomy. More than two factors have been proposed, as well as other definitions of these dimensions, but a large number of factor analytic studies in the decades since Schaefer's pioneering work have yielded two main factors. These two factors can be summarized by the terms rejection (with acceptance, warmth on one pole and rejection, criticism on the other) and control (protection versus promotion of autonomy) (Rapee, 1997).

Although, as Maccoby & Martin (1983) pointed out, such an orthogonal scheme is something of a Procrustean bed, much of the research conducted on child rearing and anxiety has been performed within this frame of reference, especially with questionnaires of perceived child rearing, that classify parental behaviour along these dimensions.

Work in a different research tradition, that of 'expressed emotion', has yielded similar dimensions. Expressed emotion is a summary measure of family affect, that was introduced in a study of relapse among schizophrenic patients (Brown, Birley & Wing, 1972). Expressed emotion refers to an index of particular emotions, attitudes and behaviours expressed by relatives, and derived from an interview procedure. Expressed emotion has the following components: (1) Critical comments, (2) Hostility, (3) Warmth, and (4) Emotional overinvolvement. The first three can easily be interpreted as lying on the 'rejection' dimension, while the last is akin to 'control' (protection). The similarity between dimensions of expressed emotion and those of parent rearing style should not surprise us, considering that expressed emotion has especially been measured in parents regarding their child, and as such may reflect child rearing attitudes.

In a study of 30 mothers with panic disorder and psychiatric controls and their 4- through 10-year-old children, Hirshfeld et al. (1997) found anxiety disorders in mothers to be positively associated with higher criticism (as a measure of expressed emotion) toward the child. Both the number of child diagnoses and the temperament of the child (the extent of the child's behavioural inhibition) interacted with the maternal anxiety in predicting higher criticism. The maternal criticism found in this study was not severe however and was characterized more by dissatisfaction than by clear hostility. These authors noted a possible contribution of the child to this phenomenon, by conceptualizing the maternal criticism as a response to taxing behaviour of the child, and as a contribution to heightened stress in the child, and thereby as a maintenance factor in the child's problematic behaviour.

A survey of 108 preadolescent children in a community sample, investigating the association between expressed emotion and psychiatric disorders (Stubbe et al., 1993) showed that the control-dimension 'emotional overinvolvement' was elevated in the parents of anxiety-disordered children.

Most of the studies on child rearing and anxiety disorders have been performed by the retrospective measurement of child rearing as perceived by adult patients. The most widely utilized in studies of anxiety have been the Parental Bonding Instrument (PBI; Parker, Tupling & Brown, 1979), and the Egna Minnen Beträffande Uppfostran (EMBU; 'Early memories of parental education'; Perris et al., 1980) (Gerlsma, Emmelkamp & Arrindell, 1990; Rapee, 1997). These questionnaires include the dimensions Affection and Control in their factor structure.

In a meta-analysis of five studies, with a total of 463 patients in the experimental groups, Gerlsma et al. (1990) found that adult phobics reported a parental rearing style characterized by less affection and more control. Studies of adults meeting diagnostic criteria for panic disorder or social phobia/avoidant personality disorder have demonstrated a similar recollection of childrearing patterns (Rapee, 1997).

This rearing style pattern contains elements from both types of family processes we discerned earlier. The perception of less parental affection could indicate a shortcoming in the provision of basic security, while the perception of more control might reflect a parental rearing style that does not leave the child enough room to develop coping skills.

A weakness of such retrospective studies is the difficulty in interpreting the findings: do the differences in retrospectively reported rearing style between anxiety-disordered adults and healthy controls reflect actual parental behaviour or is the recalled parenting a highly individual interpretation of the true events? Gerlsma et al. (1997) included family members (siblings and parents) in a study of recalled parental rearing style, and found that both parents and siblings had a less negative appraisal of the family than the patients. This could indicate that patients indeed had less favourable experiences than their siblings, or that patients are inclined to have more negative attributions (for instance in a process of scapegoating their parents for their own problems).

One way to distinguish between these possibilities is by studying actual, rather than recalled parental rearing behaviour. Preliminary results from a study of offspring of anxiety disordered parents (Boer, 1998) show that anxious parents themselves reported a somewhat less affectionate, and more controlling rearing style. Interestingly this was more so if they had a child with an anxiety disorder, than if their child had not (yet) developed such a disorder. This can be interpreted in two ways: only anxious parents with a less affectionate, more controlling parental style produce anxious children, or, only when an anxious parent has an anxious child, will she develop a less affectionate, more controlling rearing style. In other words, this raises the question of the child's contribution to this style of rearing.

The inclusion of siblings in Boer's (1998) study made it possible to investigate whether the reported parental style differed between anxious children and their nonanxious siblings. The results suggest it did: anxious children reported more maternal control, but their healthy siblings did not. The numbers in this study were very small however. A bottom-up study by the same team comprises a much larger number of children and siblings, and will allow the further investigation of this question.

Observational studies provide initial support for the impression that parents of anxious children have a more controlling style of childrearing. In a study of families with a child diagnosed with an anxiety disorder (Siqueland, Kendall & Steinberg, 1996) parents of anxious children were found to grant less psychological autonomy than the parents of control children. The anxiety-disordered children themselves rated their mothers and fathers as significantly less accepting than did control children. Recall that Stubbe et al. (1993) found emotional overinvolvement in the parents of anxiety-disordered children. Dadds et al. (1996) studied specific sequences of communication exchanged between parents and children (ages 7 to 14) in a discussion of ambiguous hypothetical situations. They found parents of anxious children ($n = 66$), to be less likely to grant and reward autonomy of thought and action than controls ($n = 18$). They also found that these parents influenced the child to be more cautious and to avoid taking a social risk, by modelling caution, providing information about risk, expressing doubt about the child's competency, and rewarding the child for avoidance by expressing agreement and nurturance when the child decides he would not join in with the other children. They referred to this as the FEAR effect (Family Enhancement of Avoidant and Aggressive Responses).

In summary, both retrospective and observational studies of child rearing behaviour of parents of anxious children show that parents are perceived as somewhat less affectionate and as providing more control. Most studies do not allow conclusions about the direction of effect, but most authors are keen to remind the reader to be cautious in making attributions about causality. As Dadds et al. (1996) noted, for example: 'It is likely that the parents are responding themselves to a sensitive child who has a history of fear and avoidance and much of their behaviour is just as "driven" by the child. Clearly, a model of reciprocal determinism should be embraced in which each person's behaviour is seen as interlinked, and the chances of blaming parents are minimized' (p. 733).

A prudent attitude in making causal attributions does not render the contribution of parental behaviour to anxiety disorders unimportant. Even if the parental behaviours are mainly the result of interactions with the child, once developed they may play an important part in the maintenance of the disorder.

Parental anxious symptomatology

Some studies of the offspring of anxiety-disordered patients have also addressed the family processes that might contribute to the transmission of anxiety disorders.

In a study of children of parents with respective panic disorder, agoraphobia with panic attacks, generalized anxiety disorder and a mixed group of phobias (Silverman et al., 1988) the occurrence of avoidance behaviour in the parents was found to be a stronger predictor of anxiety problems in the child than the frequency of parental panic attacks, which could be interpreted as a model of caution and fearfulness offered by the parent to the child. In addition, these researchers pointed out that agoraphobic parents who avoid a large number of different situations frequently develop a rule system, either implicit or explicit, focusing on phobic symptomatology. These rules tend to be rigid and ritualistic, sustaining the parent's avoidance behaviour.

In a study of children of agoraphobic parents the children did not differ from comparison children in their perceptions of danger in the outside world, but they did report considerably less control over negative events (Capps et al., 1996). The higher levels of anxiety found in these children seemed to stem from their perception of perceived control. The agoraphobic mothers reported more maternal separation anxiety with regard to their child, which negatively correlated with the children's perceived control. Although this may point toward parental behaviour impeding the development of autonomy in the child, a reverse direction of the effect has to be considered: when a child is more anxious, there may be a greater cause for the parent's anxiety about separation. Although living with an agoraphobic parent may provide a model of caution and fearfulness, the contribution to anxiety by a social phobic parent may be through teaching deficient social skills or social avoidance (Mancini et al., 1996).

Several studies indicate that parental anxious symptoms may serve as a source of threat itself. Turner et al. (1987) observed that children of anxiety-disordered parents, especially those experiencing panic, exhibited considerable concern about the welfare of their parent. And recall that Hirshfeld et al. (1997) found that anxiety-disordered mothers are more critical toward their child.

In summary, the findings of these studies of parents with severe anxious pathology, show comparable results with those of the parents of anxious children: a tendency to promote the threat perception of the children and to impede the development of coping skills. However, in these families of adult patients one finds more examples of 'threat within the family', with the disturbance of the parent as a source of fright for the child.

Again, these studies emphasize the interactive nature of the associations between parental and child characteristics. When we realize how a child can contribute to parental rearing behaviour, it is easier to reconcile the findings from the studies of parental rearing of anxiety-disordered patients with the findings from quantitative genetic research. It is probably not right to interpret the recollections of parental rearing by patients as the description of a familial environment factor, shared alike by all children in the family. It is a unique factor – not only because it reflects the perception of the rearing, rather than the objective interactions, but also because the rearing style of the parents is tailored to the specific child.

This nicely illustrates how nature can shape nurture. We can only begin to understand the contribution of family and genetic contributions to children's anxiety disorders when we are aware of their interplay.

Acknowledgements

The authors gratefully acknowledge the linguistic assistance of Martin Boer. The research by Frits Boer, Philip Spinhoven, Ingeborg Lindhout, Monica Markus, Sophie Borst and Thea Hoogendijk was supported by a grant from the Dutch National Fund for Mental Health (no. 4741).

REFERENCES

Abelson, J. L. & Alessi, N. E. (1992). Discussion of 'Child panic revisited'. *Journal of the American Association of Child and Adolescent Psychiatry*, **31**, 114–16.

Achenbach, T. M. (1991). *Integrative Guide for the 1991 CBCL/4-18, YSR, and TRF Profiles*. Burlington: Department of Psychiatry, University of Vermont.

American Psychiatric Association (1994). *Diagnostic and Statistical Manual of Mental Disorders* (4th edn) (DSM–IV). Washington, DC: APA.

Anderson, J. C., Williams, S., McGee, R. & Silva, P. A. (1987). DSM–III disorders in preadolescent children. Prevalence in a large sample from the general population. *Archives of General Psychiatry*, **44**, 69–76.

Beidel, D. C. & Turner, S. M. (1997). At risk for anxiety: I. Psychopathology in the offspring of anxious parents. *Journal of the American Academy of Child and Adolescent Psychiatry*, **36**, 918–24.

Berg, I. (1976). School phobia in children of agoraphobic women. *British Journal of Psychiatry*, **128**, 86–9.

Berg, I., Butler, A. & Pritchard, J. (1974). Psychiatric illness in the mothers of school-phobic adolescents. *British Journal of Psychiatry*, **125**, 466–7.

Biederman, J., Rosenbaum, J. F., Bolduc, E. A., Faraone, S. V. & Hirshfeld, D. R. (1991). A high risk study of young children of parents with panic disorder and agoraphobia with and without comorbid major depression. *Psychiatry Research*, **37**, 333–48.

Biederman, J., Rosenbaum, J. F., Chaloff, J. & Kagan, J. (1995). Behavioral inhibition as a risk factor for anxiety disorders. In *Anxiety Disorders in Children and Adolescents*, ed. J. S. March, pp. 61–81. New York: Guilford Press.

Boer, F. (1998). Anxiety disorders in the family: the contributions of heredity and family interactions. In *Emotionele Stoornissen en Somatoforme Stoornissen bij Kinderen en Adolescenten: de Stand van Zaken*, ed. Ph. D. A. Treffers, pp. 109–14. Leiden: Boerhaave Commissie.

Bowlby, J. (1973). *Attachment and Loss: Volume 2 – Separation*. London: The Hogarth Press and the Institute of Psychoanalysis.

Brown, G., Birley, J. & Wing, J. (1972). Influence of family life on the course of schizophrenic disorders: a replication. *British Journal of Psychiatry*, **121**, 241–58.

Brown, G. W. & Harris, T. O. (1993). Aetiology of anxiety and depressive disorders in an inner-city population. 1. Early adversity. *Psychological Medicine*, **23**, 143–54.

Brown, G. W., Harris, T. O. & Eales, M. J. (1993). Aetiology of anxiety and depressive disorders in an inner-city population. 1. Comorbidity and adversity. *Psychological Medicine*, **23**, 155–65.

Capps, L., Sigman, M., Sena, R. & Henker, B. (1996). Fear, anxiety and perceived control in children of agoraphobic parents. *Journal of Child Psychology and Psychiatry*, **37**, 445–52.

Dadds, M. R., Barrett, P. M., Rapee, R. M. & Ryan, S. (1996). Family process and child anxiety and aggression: an observational analysis. *Journal of Abnormal Child Psychology*, **24**, 715–34.

Eaves, L. J., Silberg, J. L., Meyer, J. M., et al. (1997). Genetics and developmental psychopathology: 2. The main effects of genes and environment on behavioral problems in the Virginia Twin Study of Adolescent Behavioral Development. *Journal of Child Psychology and Psychiatry*, **38**, 965–80.

Eley, T. C., Deater-Deckard, K., Fombonne, E., Fulker, D. W. & Plomin, R. (1998). An adoption study of depressive symptoms in middle childhood. *Journal of Child Psychology and Psychiatry*, **39**, 337–45.

Faravelli, C., Webb, T., Ambonetti, A., Fonnesu, F. & Sessarego, A. (1985). Prevalence of traumatic early life events in 31 agoraphobic patients with panic attacks. *American Journal of Psychiatry*, **142**, 1493–4.

Gerlsma, C., Emmelkamp, P. M. G. & Arrindell, W. A. (1990). Anxiety, depression, and perception of early parenting: A meta-analysis. *Clinical Psychology Review*, **10**, 251–77.

Gerlsma, C., Snijders, T. A. B., van Duijn, M. A. J. & Emmelkamp, P. M. G. (1997). Parenting and psychopathology: Differences in family members' perceptions of parental rearing styles. *Personality and Individual Differences*, **23**, 271–82.

Hewitt, J. K., Silberg, J. L., Rutter, M., et al. (1997). Genetics and developmental psychopathology: 1. Phenotypic assessment in the Virginia Twin Study of Adolescent Behavioral Development. *Journal of Child Psychology and Psychiatry*, **38**, 943–63.

Hirshfeld, D. R., Biederman, J., Brody, L., Faraone, S. V. & Rosenbaum, J. F. (1997). Expressed emotion toward children with behavioural inhibition: associations with maternal anxiety disorder. *Journal of the American Academy of Child and Adolescent Psychiatry*, **37**, 910–17.

Kagan, J. (1994). *Galen's Prophecy – Temperament in Human Nature*. New York: Basic Books.

Kashani, J. H., Vaidya, A. F., Soltys, S. M., Dandoy, A. C., Katz, L. M. & Reid, J. C. (1990). Correlates of anxiety in psychiatrically hospitalized children and their parents. *American Journal of Psychiatry*, **147**, 319–23.

Kendler, K. S., Heath, A. C., Martin, N. G. & Eaves, L. J. (1987). Symptoms of anxiety and symptoms of depression. *Archives of General Psychiatry*, **44**, 451–7.

Kendler, K. S., Neale, M. C., Kessler, R. C., Heath, A. C. & Eaves, L. J. (1992*a*). Generalized anxiety disorder in women. *Archives of General Psychiatry*, **49**, 267–72.

Kendler, K. S., Neale, M. C., Kessler, R. C., Heath, A. C. & Eaves, L. J. (1992*b*). The genetic epidemiology of phobias in women. *Archives of General Psychiatry*, **49**, 273–81.

Kendler, K. S., Neale, M. C., Kessler, R. C., Heath, A. C. & Eaves, L. J. (1992*c*). Major depression and generalized anxiety disorder. *Archives of General Psychiatry*, **49**, 716–22.

Kendler, K. S., Neale, M. C., Kessler, R. C., Heath, A. C. & Eaves, L. J. (1993*a*). Panic disorder in women: a population based twin study. *Psychological Medicine*, **23**, 397–406.

Kendler, K. S., Neale, M. C., Kessler, R. C., Heath, A. C. & Eaves, L. J. (1993*b*). Major depression and phobias: the genetic and environmental sources of comorbidity. *Psychological Medicine*, **23**, 361–71.

Kendler, K. S., Walters, E. E., Neale, M. C., Kessler, R. C., Heath, A. C. & Eaves, L. J. (1995). The structure of the genetic and environmental risk factors for six major psychiatric disorders in women. *Archives of General Psychiatry*, **52**, 374–83.

Kovacs, M. & Devlin, B. (1998). Internalizing disorders in childhood. *Journal of Child Psychology and Psychiatry*, **39**, 47–63.

Laraia, M. T., Stuart, G. W., Frye, L. H., Lydiard, B. & Ballenger, J. C. (1994). Childhood environment of women having panic disorder. *Journal of Anxiety Disorders*, **8**, 1–17.

Last, C. G. & Beidel, D. C. (1991). Anxiety. In *Child and Adolescent Psychiatry – A Comprehensive Textbook*, ed. M. Lewis, pp. 281–92. Baltimore: Williams & Wilkins.

Last, C. G., Hersen, M., Kazdin, A. E., Orvaschel, H. & Perrin, S. (1991). Anxiety disorders in children and their families. *Archives of General Psychiatry*, **48**, 928–34.

Maccoby, E. E. & Martin, J. A. (1983). Socialization in the context of the family: Parent–Child Interaction. In *Handbook of Child Psychology*, ed. E. M. Hetherington, pp. 1–101. New York: John Wiley & Sons.

Manassis, K., Bradley, S., Goldberg, S., Hood, J. & Swinson, R. P. (1994). Attachment in mothers with anxiety disorders and their children. *Journal of the American Academy of Child and Adolescent Psychiatry*, **33**, 1106–13.

Mancini, C., Van Ameringen, M., Szatmari, P., Fugere, C. & Boyle, M. (1996). A high-risk pilot study of the children of adults with social phobia. *Journal of the American Academy of Child and Adolescent Psychiatry*, **35**, 1511–17.

Marks, I. (1987). *Fears, Phobias, and Rituals*. Oxford: Oxford University Press.

McGee, R., Feehan, M., Williams, S., Partridge, F., Silva, P. A. & Kelly, J. (1990). DSM–III disorders in a large sample of adolescents. *Journal of the American Academy of Child and Adolescent Psychiatry*, **29**, 611–19.

Messer, S. C. & Beidel, D. C. (1994). Psychosocial correlates of childhood anxiety disorders. *Journal of the American Academy of Child and Adolescent Psychiatry*, **33**, 975–83.

Parker, G. (1983). *Parental overprotection: a Risk Factor in Psychosocial Development*. New York: Grune & Stratton.

Parker, G., Tupling, H. & Brown, L. B. (1979). A parental bonding instrument. *British Journal of Medical Psychology*, **52**, 1–10.

Perris, C., Jacobsson, L., Lindström, H., von Knorring, L. & Perris, H. (1980). Development of a new inventory for assessing memories of parental rearing behaviour. *Acta Psychiatrica Scandinavica*, **61**, 265–74.

Rapee, R. M. (1997). Potential role of childrearing practices in the development of anxiety and depression. *Clinical Psychology Review*, **17**, 47–67.

Raskin, M., Harmon, V. S., Peeke, H. V., Dickman, W. & Pinkser, H. (1982). Panic and generalized anxiety disorders. *Archives of General Psychiatry*, **39**, 687–9.

Schaefer, E. S. (1959). A circumplex model for maternal behavior. *Journal of Abnormal and Social Psychology*, **59**, 226–35.

Schuengel, C. (1997). *Attachment, Loss, and Maternal Behavior*. Doctoral dissertation. Leiden: University of Leiden.

Silove, D., Manicavasagar, V., O'Connell, D. & Morris-Yates, A. (1995). Genetic factors in early separation anxiety: implications for the genesis of adult anxiety disorders. *Acta Psychiatrica Scandinavica*, **92**, 17–24.

Silverman, W. K., Cerny, J. A., Nelles, W. B. & Burke, A. E. (1988). Behavior problems in children of parents with anxiety disorders. *Journal of the American Academy of Child and Adolescent Psychiatry*, **27**, 779–84.

Siqueland, L., Kendall, P. C. & Steinberg, L. (1996). Anxiety in children: perceived family environments and observed family interaction. *Journal of Clinical Child Psychology*, **25**, 225–37.

Stubbe, D. E., Zahner, G. E. P., Goldstein, M. J. & Leckman, J. F. (1993). Diagnostic specificity of a brief measure of expressed emotion: a community study of children. *Journal of Child Psychology and Psychiatry*, **34**, 139–54.

Thapar, A. & McGuffin, P. (1995). Are anxiety symptoms in childhood heritable? *Journal of Child Psychology and Psychiatry*, **36**, 439–47.

Turner, S. M., Beidel, D. C. & Costello, A. (1987). Psychopathology in the offspring of anxiety disorders patients. *Journal of Consulting and Clinical Psychology*, **55**, 229–35.

Turner, S. M., Beidel, D. C. & Wolff, P. L. (1996). Is behavioral inhibition related to the anxiety disorders? *Clinical Psychology Review*, **16**, 152–72.

Tweed, L. J., Schoenbach, V. J., George, L. K. & Blazer, D. G. (1989). The effects of childhood parental death and divorce on six-month history of anxiety disorders. *British Journal of Psychiatry*, **154**, 823–8.

van den Oord, E. J. C. G., Boomsma, D. I. & Verhulst, F. C. (1994). A study of problem behaviors in 10- 15-year-old biologically related and unrelated international adoptees. *Behavior Genetics*, **24**, 193–205.

Weissman, M. M., Leckman, J. F., Merikangas K. R., Gammon, G. D. & Prusoff, B. A. (1984). Depression and anxiety disorders in parents and children: results from the Yale Family Study. *Archives of General Psychiatry*, **41**, 845–52.

11

Child–parent relations: attachment and anxiety disorders

Katharina Manassis

Attachment theory provides an intriguing perspective on possible mechanisms for the development and maintenance of childhood anxiety disorders. Moreover, it is one of the better researched paradigms of parent–child relations, providing the opportunity to test these mechanisms empirically. Evidence linking attachment and childhood anxiety is reviewed to illustrate how attachment and other environmental factors can interact with temperament in the development of anxiety disorders. Such interactions may also contribute to the maintenance of anxiety over time, and to the considerable morbidity associated with childhood anxiety disorders. Informed by an understanding of these interactions, clinical suggestions for working with anxious children and their families are provided.

Attachment theory and anxiety

A brief review of attachment theory is presented below, and theoretical links to anxiety are described for behavioural, cognitive and emotional aspects of the theory.

Attachment theory postulates that to promote survival infants tend to behave in ways that enhance proximity to their caregivers, and caregivers tend to behave reciprocally (Bowlby, 1973). As a result of these tendencies, an interactive system focused on a specific caregiver, usually the mother, develops during the first year of life. When the infant has adequate proximity or contact with the caregiver for a given situation, attachment behaviours subside. When proximity or contact is inadequate, attachment behaviours escalate and compete with other behavioural systems, for example the exploratory system (Bowlby, 1973).

Using an experimental procedure involving two brief separations and reunions between parents and their 1-year-old infants (termed the 'strange situation procedure'), Ainsworth et al. (1978) were able to classify infant attachments as 'secure' (B classification) or 'insecure'. Secure infants were distressed when separated from their caregiver and responded positively when reunited with him or her. Insecure infants either showed minimal distress on separation and ignored the caregiver on reunion (termed 'insecure-avoidant' attachment, A classification) or showed high distress on separation and anger towards the caregiver on reunion (termed 'insecure-ambivalent/resistant' attachment, C classification). A later study identified one further group, termed 'insecure-disorganized' (D classification), that showed a variety of unusual responses to the strange situation procedure (Main & Solomon, 1986). Caregivers of secure infants were found to respond sensitively and predictably to their infants' expressions of distress, while caregivers of insecure infants did not (Ainsworth et al., 1978). Caregivers of avoidant, ambivalent/resistant and disorganized infants showed rejection or unavailability towards their infants, inconsistent or intrusive caregiving, and parenting affected by personal trauma or loss respectively (Ainsworth et al., 1978).

Infants of different attachment types are thought to develop different cognitions pertaining to interpersonal relationships and different ways of regulating affect. The cognitions are thought to be organized as 'Internal Working Models' (Main, Kaplan & Cassidy, 1985), defined as mental representations of the self, intimate others and the world, that guide appraisals of experience and guide interpersonal behaviour. Once organized, they are thought to function outside conscious experience and therefore be difficult to change. The nature of these models has been explored in adults using the Adult Attachment Interview (Main & Goldwyn, 1991), which examines how a discussion of one's attachment relationships affects the ability to maintain a coherent conversation. Using this interview, the following adult attachment types (with the corresponding infant–parent types in parentheses) have been elucidated: autonomous (secure), dismissive (avoidant), preoccupied (ambivalent/resistant) and unresolved (disorganized).

Given the caregiving styles associated with different attachment types, the content of the corresponding Internal Working Models has been inferred (Main & Goldwyn, 1991). Secure individuals see themselves as worthy and capable of eliciting needed care when distressed, others as trustworthy and protective, and the world as generally safe. Insecure avoidant individuals see themselves as unworthy and incapable of eliciting needed care when distressed, others as uncaring or indifferent, and the world as generally unsafe. By implication, self-reliance is very important to ensuring safety when threatened. Insecure ambivalent/resistant individuals see themselves as worthy and capable of eliciting needed care only under certain circumstances (largely dependent on the whims of the inconsistent caregiver), the caregiver as capable of giving love but frequently withholding it, and the world as unpredictable. By implication, the ability to maintain the caregiver's involvement is very important to ensuring safety when threatened. Disorganized individuals struggle to find ways of coping with emotionally wounded caregivers, typically by exhibiting caregiving or controlling behaviours towards them (Main & Solomon, 1986).

Infants of different attachment types also have been found to differ in their preferred means of regulating affect (Goldberg, McKay-Soroka & Rochester, 1994). Secure infants express all affects genuinely in response to situations, confident of others' caring responses. Insecure avoidant infants restrict expressions of distress, having experienced rejection in response to these in the past. Insecure ambivalent/resistant infants exaggerate expressions of distress, having learned that expressing distress persistently eventually pays off. Disorganized infants do not have a coherent strategy for regulating affect.

Using the above understanding of attachment theory and the various attachment types, links to behavioural, cognitive and emotional aspects of anxiety can be examined. Behaviourally, secure infants are more free to explore their environment than insecure infants (Bowlby, 1973). Confident in their caregivers' availability, their attachment system is only activated in truly dangerous situations. In non-dangerous situations, the attachment system is deactivated and the infant is free to explore, using the caregiver as a 'secure base'. Because insecure infants lack confidence in their caregiver's availability, their attachment system is chronically activated, even in situations with little danger, and exploration is curtailed. Such overly cautious behaviour is characteristic of anxious individuals, and resembles the 'behavioural inhibition' linked to anxiety disorders by temperament theorists (discussed below). Avoidance of new situations related to extreme caution also perpetuates anxiety, as it prevents the desensitization necessary to overcoming anxiety (Griest, Jefferson & Marks, 1991).

Cognitively, the separation distress experienced repeatedly by insecure infants is considered one of the earliest forms of anxiety (Sroufe, 1996). When this distress is internalized to form the internal working models described above, distorted cognitions that predispose to further anxiety may result. The models resulting from insecure attachment share a view of the self as incapable or unworthy of eliciting needed care, of the world as unsafe or unpredictable, and of others as untrustworthy (Main & Goldwyn, 1991). These cognitive distortions are found with greater frequency among anxious individuals than among nonanxious individuals (Beck et al., 1987). Chronic reliance on models based on insecure attachment may also contribute to the selective encoding of threatening information discovered among anxious adults (Macleod, 1991). Such models become self-perpetuating when individuals behave towards others as if their models were accurate. For example, a model based on avoidant attachment results in a perception of others as uncaring or indifferent. Therefore, an avoidant individual may manifest suspicious and emotionally distant responses to others when distressed. Such behaviour in turn elicits indifference or hostility from others, confirming the individual's perception of others as uncaring or indifferent. Thus, the cognitive models associated with insecurity may maintain anxiety.

Security of attachment has also been linked to affect regulation. Confident of maternal care, secure infants are open to appropriate negative feeling without being overly expressive (Shouldice & Stevenson-Hinde, 1992). Mothers of secure infants respond sensitively to both positive and negative affect (Goldberg et al., 1994) and secure adults are able to discuss emotions about intimate others freely without either restricting emotional content or losing track of the conversation (as their insecure counterparts do) (Main & Goldwyn, 1991).

Mothers of insecure avoidant infants respond preferentially to positive emotions, while those of insecure ambivalent/resistant infants respond preferentially to negative emotions (Goldberg et al., 1994), due to differences in their perceptions of emotional distress (Zeanah et al., 1993). Therefore, in order to ensure receiving care when distressed, avoidant infants minimize their displays of distress while ambivalent/resistant infants maximize it. In frightening situations, ambivalent/resistant infants thus show an exaggerated fear response, constituting overt anxiety. Avoidant infants do not display such overt anxiety, but do show elevated heart rates in frightening situations (Spangler & Grossman, 1993) indicating a high physiological fear response. The corresponding responses of disorganized infants have not been studied.

A further link between physiological arousal and security of attachment has been postulated by Kramer (1992), who reviewed evidence that secure attachment may influence neurotransmitter levels. Specifically, security may enhance the function of serotonin systems, one of the main systems involved in emotion regulation. Anxious individuals of all ages are thought to suffer from dysregulation of serotonin systems because serotonergic medications effectively reduce anxiety (American Academy of Child and Adolescent Psychiatry, 1997; Lydiard, Brawman-Mintzer & Ballenger, 1996).

In summary, the nature of their attachment relationships can influence infants' behavioural, cognitive, emotional and even physiological responses to frightening or distressing situations, thus increasing or decreasing their risk of developing anxiety disorders. Proposed links between attachment and anxiety disorders will be detailed later in this chapter (Cassidy, 1995; Manassis et al., 1994; Warren et al., 1997).

Attachment theory and anxious temperament

Temperament and attachment are both thought to contribute to the development of anxiety (reviewed in Manassis & Bradley, 1994). The concepts of behavioural inhibition, prone-to-distress temperament, temperament-attachment interaction, and the heritability of anxiety disorders are relevant to this discussion.

About 10% of toddlers (21 months of age or more) can be described as 'behaviourally inhibited', defined as 'tending to withdraw, to seek a parent, and to inhibit play and vocalization following encounter with unfamiliar people and events' (Kagan et al., 1990). Inhibition is demonstrated by measuring the child's responses to novel stimuli and new situations. Many behaviourally inhibited toddlers become less inhibited over time. As a group, however, they develop anxiety disorders at higher rates than children that are not inhibited (Biederman et al, 1990). The high levels of sympathetic arousal evident in inhibited children (Kagan, Reznick & Snidman, 1987) and high rates of inhibition among children of anxious parents (Manassis et al., 1995) suggest a temperamental basis for behavioural inhibition. A genetic basis for behavioural inhibition has been proposed by Suomi (1987) who selectively bred nonhuman primates that were either highly inhibited or highly uninhibited. He demonstrated behavioural and physiological differences between the two groups of offspring, consistent with their inhibited or uninhibited parentage.

Inhibited children often have histories of high levels of motor activity and high levels of crying in infancy (Arcus, 1991). These behaviours, termed 'prone-to-distress temperament', may affect attachment classification (reviewed in Goldberg, 1991). However, temperament per se does not appear to predict security. There is no association between parental reports of temperament and security of attachment (Sroufe, 1985). Also, security of attachment to the mother is independent of security of attachment to the father in most studies (Belsky & Rovine, 1987; Fox, Kimmerley & Schafer, 1991), suggesting that temperament is not critical in predicting attachment security.

In the development of anxiety, temperamental risk factors could thus operate independently of the predisposition to anxiety associated with insecure attachment. The heritability of anxiety disorders, however, must also be considered (Boer & Lindhout, chapter 10, this volume). Given the tendency for anxiety disorders to run in families, many infants with temperamental risk factors for anxiety are raised by caregivers who are anxious themselves. Mothers with anxiety disorders have been found to have high rates of insecure adult attachment, and the attachment relationships with their infants are also largely insecure (Manassis et al., 1994). Thus, among infants temperamentally vulnerable to anxiety, a greater than average number would be expected to have the additional risk factor of insecure attachment.

Early attachment may also influence observers' subsequent ratings of temperament. For example, due to his or her uncertainty about caregiver availability, a prone-to-distress infant that develops an insecure-ambivalent/resistant attachment would exhibit less and less exploratory behaviour over time. By age 21 months, when ratings of behavioural inhibition are possible, he or she might therefore appear to be more inhibited than a child who was securely attached.

In summary, although most studies suggest that temperament and attachment operate independently, interactions may occur in some cases due to shared temperament between parent and child and the effect of early attachment on later ratings of temperament.

Evidence for attachment–anxiety disorder links

There is considerable evidence linking security of attachment with favourable developmental outcomes, and insecurity of attachment with unfavourable developmental outcomes (reviewed by Main, 1996), but few of these studies specifically examined anxiety disorders. Before reviewing those that did, it is important to distinguish three terms used in the literature: anxious attachment, anxiety and anxiety disorder. Anxiety is an excessively fearful reaction relative to the degree of danger (Kaplan & Sadock, 1988). All people have such reactions occasionally, so they are not necessarily considered pathological. They become pathological, and are termed anxiety disorders, when they persist for longer periods of time and interfere with the individual's day to day functioning (American Psychiatric Association, 1994). Anxious attachment, by contrast, is synonymous with insecure attachment. It is considered within the norm and thus not pathological.

Three studies have examined the link between insecure attachment and anxiety disorders. Manassis et al. (1994) examined adult attachment and mother–child attachment in 20 mother–child dyads (children ages 18 to 59 months) in which the mothers suffered from anxiety disorders. The mothers all had insecure adult attachments, and 80% also had insecure attachments with their children.

Among the insecurely attached children, three of 16 met diagnostic criteria for anxiety disorders while none of the secure children did. Two had separation anxiety disorder (one with disorganized attachment, one with avoidant attachment) and one had avoidant disorder (with disorganized attachment). Insecure children also had higher internalizing scores on the Child Behavior Checklist

(Achenbach & Edelbrock, 1983) than secure children (Manassis et al., 1995).

Disorganized attachment predominated for both adult and mother–child attachment, indicating that many mothers' attachments were affected by unresolved trauma or loss (Manassis et al., 1994). When dyads classified as disorganized and mothers classified as unresolved were assigned their best alternate category and combined with the remaining three categories, a higher than expected rate of ambivalent/resistant attachment and a lower than expected rate of secure attachment were found (see Table 11.1). Small sample size and difficulties associated with measuring attachment and inhibition in children of varying ages were potential limitations of this study.

Warren et al. (1997) studied 172 adolescents aged 17.5 years who had participated in assessments of mother–child attachment at 12 months of age. Twenty-six met diagnostic criteria for anxiety disorders. More children with anxiety disorders were, as infants, classified as anxious/resistant and more children with other disorders were classified as avoidant. Anxious-resistant attachment doubled the risk of subsequently developing an anxiety disorder, and was a better predictor of adolescent anxiety disorders than either maternal anxiety or child temperament. The interaction between anxious-resistant attachment and one aspect of temperament (slow habituation to stimuli) further increased the risk of a subsequent anxiety disorder. Nevertheless, secure, insecure-avoidant, and insecure-resistant attachment were all represented among the adolescents with anxiety disorders (see Table 11.1). The insecure-disorganized classification was not yet available at the time of the attachment assessments.

Asking questions based on attachment theory, Cassidy (1995) found that adolescents and adults with generalized anxiety disorder reported more caregiver unresponsiveness, role-reversal/enmeshment, and feelings of anger/vulnerability toward their mothers than did controls. Although these reports closely resemble the descriptions of parents commonly provided by individuals with preoccupied adult attachment, formal assessments of adult attachment would be required to confirm high rates of preoccupation in this sample.

Studies linking attachment and subclinical anxiety will also be mentioned, because subclinical levels of anxiety have been associated with functional impairment in adults and school-aged children (Ialongo et al., 1995; Roy-Byrne et al., 1994), and have been associated with the subsequent development of anxiety disorders when occurring in preschool children (Biederman et al., 1990). Barnas, Pollina & Cummings (1991) found that female undergraduates who were insecurely attached were perceived by their friends as being more anxious than those who were securely attached. Crowell et al. (1991) found that

Table 11.1. Attachment distributions (%) in anxious versus normal samples

Sample	Attachment classification[a]		
	A	B	C
Manassis et al. (1994)			
1. Children of anxious mothers, $n = 20$	25	36	24
2. Anxious adults (female), $n = 18$	17	39	44
Warren et al. (1997)			
Anxious adolescents, $n = 26$	23	42	35
Ainsworth et al. (1978)			
Normative sample	22	66	12

[a]Attachment classifications: A = 'insecure-avoidant; B = 'secure';
C = 'insecure-ambivalent/resistant'.

behaviourally disturbed children whose mothers were classified as secure on the Adult Attachment Interview showed less self-reported anxiety and depression than those whose mothers were insecure-dismissing. Cassidy & Berlin (1994) reported increased fearfulness across several studies of insecure-ambivalent/resistant children. Calkins & Fox (1992) found insecure-ambivalent/resistant attachment at 14 months to be predictive of inhibited behaviour at 24 months. Manassis et al. (1994), however, found no relationship between attachment security and concurrent behavioural inhibition among young children of mothers with anxiety disorders.

Belsky & Rovine (1987) have suggested that the link between anxiety and attachment is best understood when the secure, ambivalent/resistant, and avoidant attachment categories are placed on a spectrum from those associated with the most overt distress (ambivalent/resistant) to those associated with the least overt distress (avoidant). Secures are in the middle of the spectrum, with some exhibiting relatively high distress and some exhibiting relatively low distress. Consistent with this suggestion, Stevenson-Hinde & Shouldice (1990) found that 2.5-year-old children who were either insecure-ambivalent/resistant or secure with relatively high distress showed higher indices of fear and separation distress than those in other attachment classifications.

In summary, insecure attachment has been consistently linked with both clinical and subclinical anxiety in a variety of age groups. The link may be even stronger in the presence of a temperamental vulnerability to anxiety, though the evidence is somewhat less conclusive on this point. Insecure-ambivalent/

resistant attachment and insecure-disorganized attachment have been associated with anxiety disorders by Warren et al. (1997) and Manassis et al. (1994) respectively. When insecure-disorganized subjects were assigned their best alternate classification, both of these studies found increased rates of insecure-ambivalent/resistant attachment and decreased rates of secure attachment among anxious subjects relative to a normative sample (see Table 11.1), but all attachment types were represented in the anxious groups. Thus, insecure attachment appears to be a risk factor (rather than a cause) in the development of anxiety disorders, and secure attachment may be protective. Given the small number of prospective studies, diverse definitions of anxiety used, and methodological limitations of some studies (for example, small sample sizes), replication of these findings is clearly indicated.

Other aspects of parenting linked to anxiety

The presence of an anxiety disorder in a parent has been linked to anxiety in children (Rosenbaum et al., 1988). A genetic basis for this link has been suggested as well as the fact that anxiety may influence parenting (see also Boer & Lindhout, chapter 10, this volume). Anxious parents could increase their children's risk of anxiety disorders by: (1) having difficulty modelling appropriate coping strategies; (2) reacting to their children's fears negatively because they represent an aspect of themselves which they would rather deny; or (3) becoming overly concerned about their children's anxiety, resulting in overprotection and thus reducing opportunities for desensitization. The latter two reactions are consistent with dismissive and preoccupied adult attachment types respectively. Anxious parents who are securely attached, however, may be able to empathize with their children's fears, resulting in the child feeling encouraged. Thus, the transmission of parental anxiety may depend on the interaction between attachment and parental psychopathology (Radke-Yarrow et al., 1995).

Rapee (1997) reviewed studies examining the influence of parenting style on the development of anxiety. A positive relation between parental rejection and control with later anxiety and depression was found with surprising consistency. Interestingly, adults with insecure-preoccupied attachments frequently report parental rejection and control (Main & Goldwyn, 1991), suggesting that parenting style may be related to adult attachment status. Caution is warranted, however, as many of these studies were based solely on anxious individuals' descriptions of their parents. These descriptions may be affected by the cognitive distortions associated with anxiety. Nevertheless, one recent study (Siqueland, Kendall & Steinberg, 1996) using observer ratings of parents still found parents of children with anxiety disorders to be less granting of psychological autonomy compared to controls.

No studies have related parenting style and the development of anxiety disorders prospectively. Therefore, it is unclear whether rejecting, overprotective parenting causes childhood anxiety or represents a common parental response to having an anxious child. For example, the parental frustration associated with repeatedly and unsuccessfully trying to get an anxious child to face a feared situation could result in some rejection of that child. Similarly, the anxious child's distress and pleas for reassurance could result in an underestimation of the child's competence, resulting in overprotection.

Factors affecting parental attachment security may indirectly affect the risk of an anxiety disorder in the child. For example, caregivers with few social supports (Jacobson & Frye, 1991) and high levels of life stress (Vaughn et al., 1979) have an increased risk of developing insecure attachments with their infants. Maternal depression has also been associated with an increased risk of insecure mother–child attachment (Kochanska, 1991). Thus, one would predict an increased incidence of childhood anxiety disorders in the presence of these factors. In addition, depressed mothers show less facilitation of their children's attempts to approach unfamiliar situations (Kochanska, 1991), thus reducing opportunities for desensitization in temperamentally vulnerable children.

The role of the marital relationship has received little attention in studies of childhood anxiety disorders, but presence of two parents has been found to reduce the risk of separation anxiety disorder (Last, Perrin & Hersen, 1992). The presence of two parents also allows one to compensate for parenting difficulties in the other, provided the marital relationship is supportive. Spouses may also ameliourate the effects of a child's insecure attachment with the primary caregiver (Fox et al., 1991).

Familial openness to outside influences, perhaps related to parental attachment status, can also affect the development of children's anxiety (Schneewind, 1989). For example, the opportunity to interact with peers enhances social skills (Rubin, 1982) and may thus protect children from social phobia. Given their diminished ability to trust others, parents with insecure adult attachments would be less likely to encourage their children to interact with peers than parents with secure adult attachments. Parental expectations based on cultural background, knowledge of child-rearing, and personal childhood experiences may also affect responses to children's fears, thus influencing the risk of anxiety disorders.

Possible mechanisms for the development and maintenance of childhood anxiety disorders

Descriptions of specific anxiety disorders do not imply any particular etiology, with the exception of post-traumatic stress disorder where a traumatic etiology is implied (American Psychiatric Association, 1994). The high comorbidity among anxiety disorders (Last et al., 1987) and the presence of similar physiological characteristics among individuals with various disorders has led some theorists to propose a single, temperamental etiology for all of them (Kagan et al., 1990). Temperament theories, however, do not account for the varied manifestations of anxiety in children and adults.

Attachment theory proposes that anxiety originates in an infant's uncertainty about caregiver availability, but responses to that uncertainty vary. These varied responses could account for the varied manifestations of childhood anxiety. However, because not all insecurely attached infants develop anxiety disorders, other risk factors must also play a role. For this discussion, it is assumed that insecure attachment contributes to at least some childhood anxiety disorders.

Within the framework of attachment theory, hypothetical links between different types of insecure attachment and different manifestations of anxiety can be made. In this framework, securely attached children could only develop anxiety disorders in the presence of high temperamental vulnerability (for example, severe, persistent behavioural inhibition resulting in social avoidance and eventually social phobia) or traumatic life events (for example, simple phobia of dogs after a dog bite, or post-traumatic stress disorder after a serious accident). Anxiety would be unlikely to persist, however, because securely attached children engage in more exploratory behaviour than insecure children (Ainsworth et al., 1978) allowing for desensitization, and are more likely to make appropriate requests for help than insecure children (Cassidy, 1995), creating opportunities to learn strategies for coping with anxiety.

A hypothetical pathway from avoidant attachment to anxiety would start with the child's perception of being rejected by the parent, resulting in excessive self-reliance (Main et al., 1985) and a decreased desire for social contact. Avoidance of social contact impairs the development of coping strategies for dealing with social situations and prevents desensitization to anxiety related to social situations (Griest et al., 1991). In temperamentally vulnerable individuals, these factors could result in a social phobia. Avoidantly attached individuals have also been found to restrict the expression of emotional distress, as expressions of distress tend to be disregarded by the parent (Goldberg et al., 1994). In the presence of temperamental vulnerability, the combination of excessive self-reliance and avoidance of negative affect can produce defences characteristic of obsessive-compulsive disorder (Kaplan & Sadock, 1988) or disavowal of emotional distress, resulting in its physical expression as somatoform symptoms. Anxiety in avoidant children could persist due to their difficulty asking for help when anxious, as they expect parental rejection when they express distress.

A hypothetical pathway from ambivalent/resistant attachment to anxiety can also be inferred. In this case, intermittent availability of the parent strongly reinforces attachment behaviour in the child (Main et al., 1985). A temperamentally vulnerable child would thus become preoccupied with obtaining the parent's comfort, reducing exploratory behaviour (Ainsworth et al., 1978). This process would reduce exposure to new situations that would otherwise desensitize the child to some forms of anxiety. Further, parents of such children may express frustration at the child's clinging (Manassis, 1996), thus increasing the child's sense of insecurity. In addition, the parent's selective attention to negative affect in ambivalent/resistant attachment (Goldberg et al., 1994) would reinforce it rather than reassuring the child. An escalating cycle of anxiety could thus develop between parent and child, with the child attempting to alleviate anxiety by being near the parent, but then experiencing parental hostility resulting in increased anxiety. Separation anxiety is a possible outcome. Anxiety could be maintained through preoccupation with obtaining parental comfort (reducing the opportunity to learn coping strategies and engage in desensitization) and exaggerated, overly dramatic displays of negative affect that fail to elicit reassurance from others.

In disorganized attachment, the child's caregiver has been psychologically affected by unresolved trauma or loss, and therefore provides the child with no consistent model for coping with distress (Main & Solomon, 1986). The children sometimes respond by being caregiving towards the caregiver, denying their distress to look after an emotionally unstable parent (Main & Solomon, 1986). This response could certainly contribute to anxiety. For example, the need to look after a physically or mentally ill parent at home has been cited as a frequent contributing factor to children's school phobia (Manassis, 1995), usually with associated separation anxiety. Anxiety could be maintained by the reduced acquisition of coping strategies and reduced opportunities for desensitization caused by excessive preoccupation with the caregiver's well-being.

The nature of the stresses that commonly trigger anxiety disorders could also differ depending on attachment type. As noted avoidant individuals use extreme self-reliance to allay anxiety when threatened. Such individuals would be expected to develop anxiety in response to events involving personal vulnerability or failure. On the other hand, ambivalent/resistant individuals use the ability to maintain emotional involvement with the caregiver to allay anxiety. Therefore, such individuals would be expected to be more stressed by events involving caregiver vulnerability or absence.

Differing parental attachment types could contribute to the maintenance of childhood anxiety. For example, an insecure-dismissive parent may consider a child's anxiety 'silly' or 'manipulative' while an insecure-preoccupied parent may see the same child as emotionally fragile, but difficult to manage (Manassis, 1996). In this situation, disagreements about how to respond to the child's anxiety can result in marital conflict that is anxiety-provoking to the child or in inconsistent management of the child's anxiety-related behaviours, resulting in treatment failure (Manassis, 1996).

Clinical and research implications

Attachment theory has implications for the prevention, assessment and treatment of childhood anxiety disorders. Intervening with parents and infants to reduce insecurity offers the hope of preventing some anxiety disorders. Lieberman, Weston & Pawl (1991) used infant–parent psychotherapy to improve the quality of attachment and social-emotional functioning in mothers and infants with insecure attachments and low socioeconomic status. Post-treatment, treated dyads were indistinguishable from secure controls. Erickson, Korfmacher & Egeland (1993) used an attachment-based preventive intervention with children of poor, young or poorly educated mothers. The treated mothers developed a better understanding of their babies' needs and showed less depression and anxiety than a control group. Similar interventions could be targeted to populations at risk for anxiety disorders (for example, behaviourally inhibited children with insecure attachments, or children of parents with anxiety disorders).

When intervening to prevent anxiety, the concept of sensitivity is important. Reliable, sensitive responses to infants' signals of distress foster the development of secure infant–parent attachments (Bowlby, 1973). In children predisposed to anxiety, this approach may seem to contradict the need to desensitize the child to frightening or distressing stimuli. In fact, overattentive parenting appears to perpetuate behavioural inhibition (Arcus, 1991). Sensitivity, however, does not imply extreme parental vigilance for any signal of infant upset or discomfort. Instead, the sensitive parent learns to 'read' his or her infant's signals accurately and intervenes only when the infant is significantly distressed. Thus, the infant learns to take minor upsets and discomforts in stride without parental help, but is confident of the parent's availability when he or she is genuinely distressed.

In the assessment of children with anxiety disorders, knowledge of how attachment can contribute to the development and maintenance of children's anxiety is helpful. Questions about the child's early temperament, parental response to it, and parents' own ways of coping with anxiety (often reflective of adult attachments) may elucidate the mechanisms predisposing a child to an anxiety disorder. Asking about attachment-related, anxiety-provoking events may reveal triggers for the onset of the disorder. Observing the family and considering possible attachment-related mechanisms that may perpetuate anxiety may provide clues about likely obstacles to treatment success.

In treating childhood anxiety disorders, attachment theory highlights the importance of parental involvement. Secure parent–child relationships may facilitate treatment, as the securely attached child is able to learn new coping strategies and engage in necessary desensitization confident of parental support. With minimal psychoeducation, secure parents can often coach their children in ways of better managing their anxiety, reducing the need for lengthy clinical interventions (Manassis, 1996). When longer therapeutic involvement is needed, treatment is more likely to succeed if the therapist can act as a secure base for the anxious child (Warren et al., 1997).

The high rate of disorganized attachment in anxious samples suggests that unresolved parental losses or traumas may need to be addressed in treatment. Similarly, the high rate of ambivalent/resistant attachment suggests a need to identify and address familial frustration with the anxious child.

Awareness of how insecure attachment can perpetuate anxiety may allow therapists to focus treatment on anxious children's coping styles (related to their internal working models), rather than just working towards symptom relief. Changing coping styles may ameliourate the recurrent exacerbations of anxiety symptoms that are common among anxious individuals (Bernstein & Borchardt, 1991), thus reducing long-term morbidity.

Attachment theory should not be used to assign blame to parents or other individuals in the anxious child's life. As a careful review of the evidence reveals, insecure attachment is only one of several risk factors for childhood anxiety disorders, and it frequently contributes to these disorders as a result of interactions with child temperament. Even if insecure attachment is thought to play a role in a particular child's anxiety, the processes that perpetuate maladaptive attachment-related behaviours and cognitions are largely outside the child's and parent's awareness. Finally, given the tendency for parents of children with emotional problems to blame themselves, it is more helpful to focus on what they can do to help the child, rather than blaming them further. When parents are encouraged to show empathy for their anxious child's distress but express confidence in his or her ability to face what is feared (an attitude characteristic of secure attachment relationships), they can facilitate their child's ability to overcome anxiety (Manassis, 1996).

Research is needed to clarify the interactions between temperament and attachment in the development of childhood anxiety disorders. The proposed links between specific attachment types and specific anxiety disorders also require empirical verification. The role of individuals outside the caregiver–child dyad (family members, peers, etc.) in the development of anxiety disorders must be clarified. Furthermore, all of these factors clearly interact with stressful life events and developmental changes, affecting the risk of anxiety disorders at various ages. Given all of the above, longitudinal studies are needed to accurately describe the development of various childhood anxiety disorders.

The effectiveness of attachment-based preventive interventions in samples at risk for childhood anxiety disorders should also be examined. Their potential for reducing parental anxiety (Erickson et al., 1993) suggests that they may be especially beneficial for children of anxious parents. Outcomes for anxious children receiving attachment-based treatments (i.e. those with high parental involvement and emphasis on changing coping styles) also require further study.

REFERENCES

Achenbach, T. M. & Edelbrock, C. (1983). *Manual for the Child Behavior Checklist and Revised Child Behavior Profile*. Burlington VT: University of Vermont Department of Psychiatry.

Ainsworth, M. D. S., Blehar, M. C., Waters, E. & Wall, E. (1978). *Patterns of Attachment: A Psychological Study of the Strange Situation*. Hillsdale, NJ: Lawrence Erlbaum Associates.

American Academy of Child and Adolescent Psychiatry (1997). Practice parameters for the assessment and treatment of children and adolescents with anxiety disorders. *Journal of the American Academy of Child and Adolescent Psychiatry*, **36**(10 Suppl.), 69S–84S.

American Psychiatric Association (1994). *Diagnostic and Statistical Manual of Mental Disorders* (4th Edition) (DSM–IV). Washington, DC: American Psychiatric Association.

Arcus, D. (1991). *The Experiential Modification of Temperamental Bias in Inhibited and Uninhibited Children*. Unpublished Doctoral Dissertation. Boston MA: Harvard University.

Barnas, M. V., Pollina, L. & Cummings, E. M. (1991). Life-span attachment: Relations between attachment and socioemotional functioning in adult women. *Genetic, Social, and General Psychology Monographs*, **117**, 175–202.

Beck, A. T., Brown, G., Steer, R. A., Eidelson, J. I. & Riskind, J. H. (1987). Differentiating anxiety and depression: A test of the cognitive content-specificity hypothesis. *Journal of Abnormal Psychology*, **96**, 179–83.

Belsky, J. & Rovine, M. (1987). Temperament and attachment security in the strange situation: An empirical rapprochement. *Child Development*, **58**, 787–95.

Bernstein, G. A. & Borchardt, C. M. (1991). Anxiety disorders of childhood and adolescence: critical review. *Journal of the American Academy of Child and Adolescent Psychiatry*, **30**, 519–32.

Biederman, J., Rosenbaum, J. F., Hirshfeld, D. R., et al. (1990). Psychiatric correlates of behavioral inhibition in young children of parents with and without psychiatric disorders. *Archives of General Psychiatry*, **47**, 21–6.

Bowlby, J. (1973). *Attachment and Loss: Attachment.* New York: Basic Books.

Calkins, S. D. & Fox, N. A. (1992). The relations among infant temperament, security of attachment, and behavioral inhibition at twenty-four months. *Child Development*, **63**, 1456–72.

Cassidy, J. (1995). Attachment and generalized anxiety disorder. In *Emotion, Cognition, and Representation: Rochester Symposium on Developmental Psychopathology VI*, ed. D. Cicchetti & S. Toth, pp. 343–70. Rochester, NY: University of Rochester Press.

Cassidy, J. & Berlin, L. J. (1994). The insecure/ambivalent pattern of attachment: theory and research. *Child Development*, **65**, 971–91.

Crowell, J. A., O'Connor, E., Wollmers, G. & Sprafkin, J. (1991). Mothers' conceptualizations of parent–child relationships: Relation to mother–child interaction and child behavior problems. *Development and Psychopathology (Special Issue: Attachment and developmental psychopathology)*, **3**, 431–44.

Erickson, M. F., Korfmacher, J. & Egeland, B. R. (1993). Attachments past and present: Implications for therapeutic intervention with mother–infant dyads. *Annual Progress in Child Psychiatry and Child Development*, pp. 459–76.

Fox, N., Kimmerly, N. L. & Schafer, W. D. (1991). Attachment to mother/attachment to father: a meta-analysis. *Child Development*, **62**, 210–25.

Goldberg, S. (1991). Recent developments in attachment theory and research. *Canadian Journal of Psychiatry*, **36**, 393–400.

Goldberg, S., MacKay-Soroka, S. & Rochester, M. (1994). Affect, attachment, and maternal responsiveness. *Infant Behavior and Development*, **17**, 335–40.

Griest, J., Jefferson, J. & Marks, I. (1991). *Anxiety and its Treatment.* Washington, DC: American Psychiatric Press.

Ialongo, N., Edelsohn, G., Werthamer-Larsson, L., Crockett, L. & Kellam, S. (1995). The significance of self-reported anxious symptoms in first grade children: prediction to anxious symptoms and adaptive functioning in fifth grade. *Journal of Child Psychology and Psychiatry*, **36**, 427–37.

Jacobson, S. W. & Frye, K. F. (1991). Effect of maternal social support on attachment: experimental evidence. *Child Development*, **62**, 572–82.

Kagan, J., Reznick, J. S., Snidman, N., et al. (1990). Origins of panic disorder. In *Neurobiology of Panic Disorder*, pp. 71–87. New York: Alan R. Liss Inc.

Kagan, J., Reznick, J. S. & Snidman, N. (1987). The physiology and psychology of behavioral inhibition in children. *Child Development*, **58**, 1459–73.

Kaplan, H. I. & Sadock, B. J. (1988). *Synopsis of Psychiatry* (5th edn). Baltimore, MD: Williams & Wilkins.

Kochanska, G. (1991). Patterns of inhibition to the unfamiliar in children of normal and affectively ill mothers. *Child Development*, **62**, 250–63.

Kramer, G. W. (1992). A psychobiological theory of attachment. *Behavioral and Brain Sciences*, **15**, 493–541.

Last, C. G., Hersen, M., Kazdin, A. E., Finkelstein, R. & Strauss, C. C. (1987). Comparison of DSM–III separation anxiety and overanxious disorders: demographic characteristics and patterns of comorbidity. *Journal of the American Academy of Child and Adolescent Psychiatry*, **26**, 527–31.

Last, C. G., Perrin, S. & Hersen, M. (1992). DSM–III–R anxiety disorders in children: Sociodemographic and clinical characteristics. *Journal of the American Academy of Child and Adolescent Psychiatry*, **31**, 1070–6.

Lieberman, A. F., Weston, D. R. & Pawl, J. H. (1991). Preventive intervention and outcome with anxiously attached dyads. *Child Development*, **62**, 199–209.

Lydiard, R. B., Brawman-Mintzer, O. & Ballenger, J. C. (1996). Recent developments in the psychopharmacology of anxiety disorders. *Journal of Consulting Clinical Psychology*, **64**, 660–8.

Macleod, C. (1991). Clinical anxiety and the selective encoding of threatening information. *International Review of Psychiatry*, **3**, 279–92.

Main, M. (1996). Introduction to the Special Section on Attachment and Psychopathology: Overview of the field of attachment. *Journal of Consulting and Clinical Psychology*, **64**, 237–43.

Main, M. & Goldwyn, R. (1991). Adult attachment classification system. In *Behavior and the Development of Representational Models of Attachment: Five Methods of Assessment*, ed. M. Main. Cambridge: Cambridge University Press.

Main, M., Kaplan, N. & Cassidy, J. (1985). Security in infancy, childhood and adulthood: A move to the level of representation. *Monographs of the Society for Research in Child Development*, **50** (1–2, Serial No. 209), 66–104.

Main, M. & Solomon, J. (1986). Discovery of an insecure-disorganized/disoriented attachment pattern. In *Affective Development in Infancy*, ed. T. B. Brazelton & M. Yogman. Norwood, NJ: Ablex.

Manassis, K. (1995). School refusal: How to address the underlying factors. *Canadian Journal of Diagnosis*, **12**, 55–68.

Manassis, K. (1996). *Keys to Parenting Your Anxious Child*. New York: Barron's Educational Series, Inc.

Manassis, K. & Bradley, S. J. (1994). The development of childhood anxiety disorders: Toward an integrated model. *Journal of Applied Developmental Psychology*, **15**. 345–66.

Manassis, K., Bradley, S., Goldberg, S., Hood, J. & Swinson, R. P. (1994). Attachment in mothers with anxiety disorders and their children. *Journal of the American Academy of Child and Adolescent Psychiatry*, **33**, 1106–13.

Manassis, K., Bradley, S., Goldberg, S., Hood, J. & Swinson, R. P. (1995). Behavioral inhibition, attachment and anxiety in children of mothers with anxiety disorders. *Canadian Journal of Psychiatry*, **40**, 87–92.

Radke-Yarrow, M., McCann, K., DeMulder, E. & Belmont, B. (1995). Attachment in the context of high-risk conditions. *Development and Psychopathology*, **7**, 247–65.

Rapee, R. M. (1997). Potential role of childrearing practices in the development of anxiety and depression. *Clinical Psychology Review*, **17**, 47–67.

Rosenbaum, J., Biederman, J., Gersten, M., et al. (1988). Behavioral inhibition in children of parents with panic disorder and agoraphobia. *Archives of General Psychiatry*, **45**, 463–70.

Roy-Byrne, P., Katon, W., Broadhead, W. E., Lepine, J. P. & Richards, J. (1994). Subsyndromal ('mixed') anxiety – depression in primary care. *Journal of General Internal Medicine*, **9**, 507–12.

Rubin, K. H. (1982). Social and social-cognitive developmental characteristics of young isolate, normal and sociable children. In *Peer Relationships and Social Skills in Childhood*, ed. K. H. Rubin & H. S. Ross, pp. 353–74. New York: Springer-Verlag.

Schneewind, K. A. (1989). Contextual approaches to family systems research: The macro-micro puzzle. In *Family Systems and Life Span Development*, ed. K. Kreppner & R. M. Lerner, pp. 197–221. Hillsdale, NJ: Lawrence Erlbaum Associates.

Shouldice, A. & Stevenson-Hinde, J. (1992). Coping with security distress: The Separation Anxiety Test and attachment classification at 4.5 years. *Journal of Child Psychology and Psychiatry*, **33**, 331–48.

Siqueland, L., Kendall, P. C. & Steinberg, L. (1996). Anxiety in children: Perceived family environment and observed family interaction. *Journal of Clinical Child Psychology*, **25**, 225–37.

Spangler, G. & Grossman, K. E. (1993). Biobehavioral organization in securely and insecurely attached infants. *Child Development*, **64**, 1439–50.

Sroufe, L. A. (1985). Attachment classification from the perspective of infant-caregiver relationships and infant temperament. *Child Development*, **56**, 1–14.

Sroufe, L. A. (1996). *Emotional Development*. New York: Cambridge University Press.

Stevenson-Hinde, J. & Shouldice, A. (1990). Fear and attachment in 2.5-year-olds. *British Journal of Developmental Psychology*, **8**, 319–33.

Suomi, S. J. (1987). Genetic and maternal contributions to individual differences in rhesus monkey biobehavioral development. In *Perinatal Development: A Psychobiological Perspective*, ed. N. A. Kresnegor, pp. 397–417. Orlando: Academic Press.

Vaughn, B., Egeland, B., Sroufe, L. A. & Waters, E. (1979). Individual differences in infant–mother attachment at 12 and 18 months: stability and change in families under stress. *Child Development*, **50**, 971–5.

Warren, S. L., Huston, L., Egeland, B. & Sroufe, L. A. (1997). Child and adolescent anxiety disorders and early attachment. *Journal of the American Academy of Child and Adolescent Psychiatry*, **36**, 637–44.

Zeanah, C., Benoit, D., Barton, M., Regan, C., Hirshberg, L. M. & Lipsitt, L. P. (1993). Representations of attachment in mothers and their one-year-old infants. *Journal of the American Academy of Child and Adolescent Psychiatry*, **32**, 278–86.

12

Community and epidemiological aspects of anxiety disorders in children

Frank C. Verhulst

Introduction

The epidemiological study of anxiety disorders in children involves individuals with anxiety disorders who receive treatment as well as individuals who do not receive treatment. (For brevity 'child' is used to include adolescent.) In this way it is possible to study relatively unselected samples. This is an advantage of epidemiological over clinical samples. Because there may be factors other than the psychopathological manifestation in itself that bring children into contact with mental health services, clinical samples may be highly selected. For example, we assessed the association between a large number of factors and mental health services use in a community sample (Verhulst & van der Ende, 1997). It was found that adverse family factors such as living in a one-parent family, changes in the family composition and problems in family functioning were strongly associated with mental health services use in addition to the level of psychopathology in the child. It was concluded that among referred children, those living under problematic family circumstances were over-represented, irrespective of the level of psychopathology.

Because epidemiological studies focus on the whole spectrum of problem behaviours, they provide information on quantitative and qualitative aspects of anxiety manifestations that are associated with maladaptive functioning. It may well be that certain anxiety phenomena that many children in the general population show to some degree are associated with rather undisturbed daily functioning, whereas other anxiety manifestations can be quite handicapping.

One of the first true epidemiological studies was the study by Lapouse & Monk (1958) who assessed the prevalence of parent-reported problems in a representative sample of 6–12-year-old children in Buffalo, New York. The high rates of fears and worries in this community sample casted doubt on the prevailing clinical opinion at that time that these problems indicate psycho-pathology. This study heralded a stronger community-based or norm-based attitude, and a growing awareness of the importance of factors that determine 'morbidity'.

By quantifying the deviation of certain behaviours from the norm, and by taking the level of handicap associated with certain behaviours into account, epidemiological studies can be of help to determine which behaviours can be regarded as normal and which behaviours can be regarded as pathological. For example, the DSM–IV (American Psychiatric Association, 1994) criteria for Separation Anxiety Disorder that should be met when this diagnosis is considered, require that the child shows developmentally inappropriate and excessive anxiety concerning separation. However, without normative data it is not possible to determine accurately whether or not certain behaviours should be considered developmentally inappropriate and excessive.

Epidemiological studies also made us aware that many children in the community with disorders that caused much suffering and maladjustment were left undetected and hence were not treated. Most general population studies showed that the majority of disordered children are not referred for professional help.

In this chapter, the prevalence of anxiety disorders both from a categorical-DSM as well as from a quantitative aspect is given, followed by cross-cultural comparisons. Because anxious and depressed affects are related, the issue of comorbidity between anxiety and depression is discussed.

Prevalence of categorical DSM diagnosis

The prevailing diagnostic system for which prevalence figures are available, is the Diagnostic and Statistical Manual for Mental Disorders (DSM). However, a problem with this system is the frequent changes of diagnostic criteria or even whole diagnostic categories from one edition to the other. There are no prevalence studies as yet that employed DSM–IV criteria; the most recent community studies with prevalence rates for anxiety disorders in children used DSM–III–R criteria (American Psychiatric Association,1987). Although there are numerous differences in the wording of diagnostic criteria across DSM–III–R and DSM–IV, the core concept of a number of diagnoses is comparable, including the diagnoses: Separation Anxiety Disorder, Specific or Simple Phobia, Social Phobia, Generalized Anxiety Disorder, Panic Disorder and Agoraphobia. The DSM–III–R diagnoses Avoidant Disorder and Overanxious Disorder that were specific to childhood or adolescence were not included in DSM–IV, although Overanxious Disorder can be regarded as closely related to Generalized Anxiety Disorder.

There are nine relatively large scale community surveys with adequate sampling and assessment methodologies that provide prevalences for anxiety disorders as defined by DSM–III (American Psychiatric Association, 1981) or DSM–III–R (Anderson et al., 1987; Bird et al., 1988; Cohen et al., 1993; Costello et al., 1996; Fergusson, Horwood & Lynskey, 1993; McGee et al., 1990; Velez, Johnson & Cohen, 1989; Verhulst et al., 1997; Whitaker et al., 1990).

Although largely comparable, there were differences across the studies with respect to assessment techniques and decision rules for making DSM diagnoses. One of the main differences between studies was the way information from different sources (parent, youth and teacher) was handled. Studies also differed with respect to the age of the children and the region where they lived. To enhance comparability with future studies, our own Dutch national survey used internationally available assessment procedures and scoring rules that are standardized and easily replicable (Verhulst et al., 1997). For more detailed discussion of the methodology of prevalence studies, see Verhulst (1995) and Verhulst et al. (1997).

In the majority of prevalence studies, the anxiety disorders were the most prevalent among all disorders.

Table 12.1 shows the prevalences for DSM–III and/or DSM–III–R anxiety disorders. Few studies reported prevalences for the full spectrum of anxiety disorders. Most studies reported prevalences for separation anxiety disorder, overanxious disorder, specific phobia and social phobia. Given the differences among studies we must be cautious to draw firm conclusions with respect to the prevalences. In an attempt to give rough estimates for disorders on which most studies reported, we looked at the median prevalence for each disorder, resulting in the following prevalences: separation anxiety disorder 3% (lower prevalence for adolescents versus younger children); overanxious disorder 3%; generalized anxiety disorder 2%; specific phobia 3%; social phobia 1% (higher prevalence for adolescents versus younger children).

There was a tendency for girls to have somewhat higher prevalences of anxiety disorders than boys. Adolescents tended to have higher prevalences of social phobia and lower prevalences of separation anxiety disorder than younger children.

Not every child with an anxiety disorder was severely handicapped in his or her daily functioning. In the Dutch prevalence study, 10.5% suffered from some kind of anxiety disorder based on the child interview. However, this prevalence figure dropped to 3.8% when only those individuals were counted who in addition to meeting DSM–III–R criteria for an anxiety disorder also showed

Table 12.1. Prevalence in percentage (with 95% confidence intervals in brackets) of anxiety disorders in community studies using DSM-III or DSM-III-R criteria

Study	Sample			Method		Prevalence of anxiety disorders								
	Size	Age	Method	Definition of disorder	Assessment methods	Separation anxiety disorder	Over-anxious disorder	Avoidant disorder	Generalized anxiety disorder	Specific (simple) phobia	Social phobia	Agoraphobia	Panic disorder	Any anxiety disorder
Anderson et al. (1987) Dunedin, New Zealand	792	11	Cohort born in one hospital; one stage	DSM-III criteria	Rutter Scale A; Rutter Scale B; DISC-C	3.5(1.2)	2.9(1.2)			2.4(1.1)	0.9(0.7)			
Bird et al. (1988) Puerto Rico, USA	777	4–16	Multistage probability sampling of households; two stage	DSM-III criteria, CGAS and severity rating by clinicians	CBCL and TRF in first stage; DISC-P and -C in second stage	4.7(0.9)				2.6(0.7)				
Cohen et al. (1993) New York State, USA	1495	10–20	Multistage random sample	DSM-III-R criteria	DISC-C and -P prevalence based on presence of symptom in parent or youth interview	6.1	11.3							
Costello et al. (1996) North Carolina, USA	4500	9, 11, 13	Multistage probability sampling of households	DSM-III-R criteria, and level of functioning	CBCL externalizing scale in first stage; CAPA in second stage (parent and child)	3.5(0.8)	1.4(0.5)		1.7(0.6)	0.3(0.1)	0.6(0.3)		0.0	5.7(0.0)
Fergusson et al. (1993) Christchurch, New Zealand	965	15	Cohort born in one area	DSM-III criteria met by abbreviated DISC	DISC-C abbreviated (only self-reported prevalences reported here)	0.5(0.4)	2.1(0.9)		4.2(1.3)	5.1(1.4)	1.7(0.8)			10.8(2.0)

Study	N	Age	Sample	Diagnosis	Instruments									
McGee et al. (1990) Dunedin, New Zealand	943	15	Cohort born in one hospital; one stage	DSM–III criteria met by abbreviated DISC responses	RBPC; open ended questions concerning global functioning; DISC-C abbreviated	2.0(0.9)	5.9(1.5)			3.6(1.2)		1.1(0.7)		
Velez et al. (1989) New York State, USA	776	11–20	Random sample in 1975, followed-up in 1983 and 1985	DSM–III-R	DISC-C and -P prevalence based on presence of symptom in parent or youth interview	5.1	2.7							
Verhulst et al. (1997) The Netherlands	780	13–18	Multistage probability sample of subjects from municipal birth registers; two stage	DSM–III criteria CGAS	CBCL, TRF, YSR in first stage; DISC-P and DISC-C in second stage (only DISC-C prevalence reported here)	1.4(1.8)	1.8(0.9)	1.4(0.8)	0.6(0.3)	4.5(1.5)	3.7(1.1)	0.7(0.4)	0.2(0.2)	10.5(2.1)
Whitaker et al. (1990) New Jersey, USA	5596	14-17	All 9–12 grade	DSM-III criteria students in one county; two stage	Author's constructed anxiety screening measures in first stage author's constructed child interview				3.7				0.6	

Instruments with abbreviations listed in the table: CBCL = Child Behavior Checklist (Achenbach, 1991b); CGAS = Children's Global Assessment Scale (Shaffer et al., 1983); DISC = Diagnostic Interview Schedule for Children (P = Parent version, C = Child version) (Shaffer et al., 1993); RBPC = Revised Behavior Problem Checklist (Quay & Peterson, 1983); TRF = Teacher's Report Form (Achenbach, 1991c); YSR = Youth Self-Report (Achenbach, 1991d); CAPA = Child and Adolescent Psychiatric Assessment (Angold et al., 1995).

probable general malfunctioning, and to 2.2% when only those were included who showed definite malfunctioning.

The most salient conclusion that can be drawn from the prevalence studies reviewed here, despite the great variation in methodology, is that anxiety disorders as defined by DSM–III or DSM–III–R are the most prevalent among disorders in children and adolescents. This finding combined with the finding that internalizing problems tend to be only slightly less persistent than externalizing problems across time (Verhulst & van der Ende, 1995), stresses the importance of both research and clinical attention to this domain of psychopathology.

Categorical versus quantitative-empirical diagnostic approaches

The prevalence studies discussed above reported prevalences of disorders as defined by the DSM. The DSM system is characterized by a categorical approach. The categorical approach typically employs categories that are scored 'present' versus 'absent' for each individual child. This approach starts with assumptions about the disorders that exist. Experts then formulate criteria for determining whether an individual has a particular disorder or not. The assumptions and criteria are based on accumulated clinical experience.

The quantitative approach is characterized by the use of standardized assessment procedures. Using these procedures to score problem behaviours of large samples of children, statistical procedures can be employed to identify syndromes of co-occurring problems. The scores obtained by an individual can then be used to determine how closely that individual's problems resemble each of the empirically derived syndromes. Also, the individual's scores can be compared with scores derived for large epidemiological samples indicating how much the individual's scores deviates from those of his or her sex- and age mates.

These two contrasting approaches are not mutually exclusive, as categorical diagnostic decisions can be based on quantitative data, for example by imposing cutoff points on a problem scale for determining which children can be regarded as disordered. Also, the quantitative approach does not assume that every disorder merely involves quantitative gradations along a particular dimension. On the contrary, because no one yet knows the true nature and boundaries of many child psychiatric conditions, quantitative methods can help to determine which problems are more effectively conceptualized as categorical, which are more effectively conceptualized as quantitative, and which require a mixture of categorical and quantitative concepts. Most likely the disorders that have the highest probability to be determined by single genes, or by known organic factors, will be candidates to be described best as categories, such as autism, Tourette's disorder, bipolar disorder or fetal alcohol syndrome. Disorders with risk factors that are polygenetically determined might be best described by continuous measures, such as most anxiety disorders, hyperactivity and depression in childhood.

A well-known exponent of the quantitative approach to assessment of child psychopathology is the Child Behavior Checklist (CBCL) and related instruments, the Teacher's Report Form (TRF) and the Youth Self-Report (YSR) (Achenbach, 1991b,c,d) as standardized procedures to obtain parents', teachers' and self-ratings respectively on children's problem behaviours.

Achenbach (1991e) has constructed eight so-called cross-informant syndromes that are similar on the parent, teacher and the self-report versions of the CBCL. The syndromes were empirically derived via factor analyses of scores obtained for large clinical samples. These syndromes were designated: Anxious/Depressed, Somatic Complaints, Withdrawn, Aggressive Behavior, Delinquent Behavior, Attention Problems, Thought Problems, and Social Problems. One of the striking features was that there were no separate Depression and Anxiety scales. Instead there was one scale designated as Anxious/Depressed comprising of items reflecting depressed affect (such as unhappy, sad, or depressed, and feels worthless or inferior), items indicative of anxiety (such as too fearful, or anxious, and nervous, highstrung or tense), and items reflecting either anxiety or depression, or both (such as cries a lot, and worries). Other items that might also be interpreted as anxiety and/or depression were part of other empirically derived syndromes such as Somatic Complaints and Withdrawn. Examples of such items are overtired, feels dizzy, headaches, nausea, and underactive, slow moving or lacks energy. The complete set of items of the Anxious/Depressed syndrome are listed in Table 12.2.

One way to test the validity of diagnostic constructs is to investigate whether disorders take the same form in samples differing in culture and language. In this way it is possible to investigate the intrinsic value of diagnostic constructs irrespective of the vicissitudes of language and other cultural factors.

Recently, we tested whether the cross-informant syndromes for the CBCL, TRF and YSR are applicable to CBCL problem scores derived for Dutch children using the CBCL (De Groot et al., 1994). In this study we used CBCL scores from parents of 4674 children aged 4–18 (2771 boys and 1903 girls) referred to 25 mental health services in The Netherlands. CBCLs were completed by the parents as part of the intake procedure. First, we determined the factor structure for the Dutch CBCL by performing exploratory factor analyses

Table 12.2. Items defining the Anxious/Depressed syndrome of the CBCL and related instruments (TRF and YSR)

Lonely	Suspicious
Cries a lot	Unhappy, Sad, Depressed
Fears impulses	Worries
Needs to be perfect	**Specific to YSR**
Feels unloved	Harms self
Feels persecuted	Thinks about suicide
Feels worthless	**Specific to TRF**
Nervous, tense	Overconforms to rules
Fearful, anxious	Hurt when criticized
Feels too guilty	Anxious to please
Self-conscious	Afraid of mistakes

CBCL = Child Behavior Checklist; TRF = Teacher's Report Form; YSR = Youth Self-Report.

on the CBCL scores of 2339 children constituting a derivation sample. The derivation sample consisted of half the sample and was randomly drawn from the total sample. The Dutch syndromes found by exploratory factor analyses were very similar in item composition to the American cross-informant syndromes. Of the 14 items constituting the American Anxious/Depressed scale, only one ('cries a lot') was not on the Dutch Anxious/Depressed scale. Reversely, of the 14 items constituting the Dutch Anxious/Depressed scale, only one ('easily jealous') was not on the American scale.

The American syndromes were used as a model with which to compare the Dutch syndromes. The Dutch children were scored separately on both the American and Dutch versions of each syndrome. Next, we computed correlations between the syndrome scores obtained when the Dutch children were scored on the American version of the syndrome and when they were scored on the Dutch version. The cross-national correlations between the Dutch and the American scales ranging from 0.82 to 0.99, with the Anxious/Depressed syndrome reaching the highest correlation of 0.99.

Next we tested both the Dutch exploratory syndromes and the original American cross-informant syndromes in a cross-validation sample consisting of the remaining 2335 Dutch clinically referred children. We used confirmatory factor analyses to test whether the Dutch exploratory syndromes fitted the scores of the Dutch children in the cross-validation sample better or more poorly than the American cross-informant syndromes. We used the Goodness-of-Fit and Adjusted Goodness-of-Fit indices as measures of the relative amount of variance and covariance accounted for by the model in the observed correlation matrix between the CBCL items. These measures can range from 0 to 1: the larger the value, the better the fit. Both the GFI and AGFI (0.885 and 0.878, respectively) were similar for the American and the Dutch models. The results indicated that both the Dutch and the American scales were supported by this procedure to the same degree.

The similarities between the Dutch and American CBCL syndromes, despite differences in language, culture, and mental health systems, supported the generalizability of the CBCL cross-informant syndromes across both countries.

A possible criticism to this approach may be that we used only parents as informants, and that the association between anxiety and depression is just an artefact as a result of the fact that parents are not able to separate problems indicative of anxiety and depression. We therefore employed a similar procedure for reports derived from teachers and youths themselves (TRF and YSR; De Groot, Koot & Verhulst, 1996). For the YSR we did not find separate Anxious/Depressed and Withdrawn syndromes for the Dutch sample. The Withdrawn syndrome contains many items indicative of depression, such as withdrawn, would rather be alone, underactive, and unhappy, sad, depressed. The combined Anxious/Depressed/Withdrawn syndrome correlated highly (0.95) with the American Anxious/Depressed syndrome. For the TRF the Anxious/Depressed syndrome could well be replicated in the Dutch sample correlating highly (0.92) with the American syndrome Anxious/Depressed.

The American–Dutch cross-cultural comparisons of empirically derived syndromes supported the finding that in large samples of clinically referred children, items indicative of anxiety and depression tend to co-occur rather than forming two separate syndromes of anxiety and depression.

The quantitative approach to the assessment of anxiety disorders has the advantage that it is closely linked to existing empirical information. Furthermore, a technical advantage which is especially relevant for researchers, is that quantitative information usually retains more statistical information than does categorical data. For the clinician, the categorical approach is more appealing as decisions with respect to individual patients need to be made. However, the dichotomy between the categorical or quantitative approach should not lead to a forced decision with respect to which approach is best under all circumstances. Both approaches can be combined and can form a fruitful strategy to enhance our knowledge.

Cross-cultural comparison of the CBCL Anxious/Depressed scale

To facilitate comparisons of mental health issues concerning anxiety disorders across cultures, assessment procedures that can be applied under diverse conditions and that can communicate useful information to mental health workers in different countries are necessary. Bird (1996) identified two main approaches in cross-cultural epidemiological research. One approach is to compare diagnoses based on DSM, and the other approach uses empirically based standardized assessment instruments to quantify informants' reports of behavioural/emotional problems. The methodologies with which the prevalences of DSM based anxiety disorders as listed in Table 12.1 were derived were so diverse that it is impossible to evaluate the differences in prevalences. Some studies combined parent and adolescent's self-report information, whereas others based their prevalences on only one informant; in some studies interviews were done on every subject, whereas others used a two-stage design with a screening phase followed by an interview phase; some studies pertained to populations from one relatively small area, whereas others obtained a nationwide sample. As Bird (1996) pointed out, the empirically based approach of the CBCL has generated direct comparisons of problem scores across studies and cultures in more standardized fashion than has the diagnostic approach of DSM.

Most cross-cultural studies have compared just two cultures (Verhulst & Achenbach, 1995). In a recent study, CBCL ratings for over 13 000 children from the general population aged 6–17 years from 12 cultures were systematically compared (Crijnen, Achenbach & Verhulst, 1997, 1999). Analyses were performed on CBCL ratings for children from Australia, Belgium, China, Germany, Greece, Israel, Jamaica, The Netherlands, Puerto Rico, Sweden, Thailand and the US. Analyses of variance (ANOVA) were performed to assess the differences in mean scores of the CBCL syndromes for the factors culture, sex and age. Separate analyses were performed for ages 6–11 (12 cultures), and ages 6–17 (nine cultures). We discuss here only the findings for the Anxious/Depressed syndrome. Differences in mean scores were expressed as effect sizes (ES) and evaluated according to Cohen's (1988) criteria as small, medium or large.

The culture ES for the Anxious/Depressed syndrome was small in the nine culture comparison and medium in the 12 culture comparison (5% and 9% ES respectively). Australia, Germany, Jamaica, The Netherlands and Sweden had lower mean scores on the Anxious/Depressed syndrome than the mean score across cultures, whereas Greece and Puerto Rico had higher mean scores. The scores for the other countries did not differ from the overall mean.

Age and sex had a small but significant effect on Anxious/Depressed syndrome scores with an ES < 1%. Girls had higher Anxious/Depressed scores than boys, and younger children had lower scores than older children.

Cross-cultural differences in prevalences such as we found among the 12 cultures, may reflect: (1) differences in true prevalence; (2) differences in methodology and language; and (3) cultural differences influencing adults' evaluation of children's problem behaviour and their propensity to report it. From our comparison it is not possible to tell which factors are responsible for the differences that we found. More research is needed to assess the origins of cross-cultural differences which may lead us to the origins of differences in the development of psychopathology.

Comorbidity between anxiety and depression: conceptual issues

The frequency with which anxiety and depressive features tend to co-occur, both in adult and child patients (Maser & Cloninger, 1990), have confronted clinicians and researchers with fundamental questions about psychiatric nosology, including whether or not anxiety and depression can really be regarded distinct disorders. The purpose of this section of the chapter was not to give a detailed overview of existing studies pertaining to the comorbidity between anxiety and depression in childhood. Instead, concepts, empirical findings and implications of comorbidity for anxiety and depression are considered.

There are a number of explanations for the coexistence of two or more disorders (Achenbach, 1991a; Caron & Rutter, 1991; Verhulst & van der Ende, 1993). A number of mechanisms may explain the existence of a true association, but there may also be factors operating that mimic a true association (Figure 12.1).

True associations
Two separate disorders
The first possibility is that there are two or more distinct disorders, each with a specific etiology. For instance, if the existence of disorder A does not protect an individual from having disorder B, the expected proportion of individuals with disorder A who also have disorder B will be equal to the population base rate of disorder B. The expected rate of comorbidity is obtained by multiplying the base rates for disorder A and B. If the observed rate of comorbidity is higher than the expected rate, it must be concluded that the two disorders are not

True association

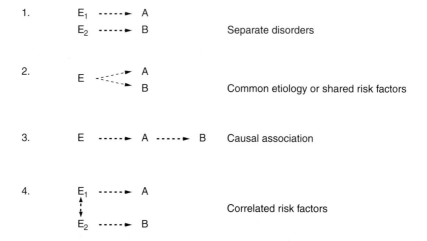

Artificial associations

1.   Treatment seeking factors

            Berkson's bias
            Referral bias

2.   Assessment artefacts

3.   Nosologic factors

            Artificial subdivision of syndromes
            Item overlap
            Variable expression
            Categorical versus quantitative perspectives

Fig. 12.1. Comorbidity: mechanisms that may explain a true association, and factors that may operate to mimic a true association.

distinct and that both disorders are associated. For example, the proportion of depressed individuals who also meet the criteria for anxiety disorders is much higher than the population base rates for anxiety disorders (McConaughy & Achenbach, 1994).

Common etiologies or shared risk factors

Two distinct disorders may be associated because they share etiologic factors. In other words, one etiologic factor is responsible for two distinct disorders. For example, family studies showed that the adult relatives of children with depression or anxiety disorders have high rates of psychiatric disorder (Weissman, 1990). So it may be that both depression and anxiety disorder are caused by the same underlying genetic or environmental factor.

Causal association

It is possible that disorder A creates a risk factor for disorder B. For example, it may be that prolonged anxiety increases the probability to become depressed, or alternatively, prolonged depression may lead to anxiety. In a longitudinal study, Kovacs & Paulauskas (1984) reported that 36% of children with a dysthymic disorder had a comorbid anxiety disorder. In the majority of cases the dysthymic disorder preceded the anxiety disorder. On the other hand, in some cases of major depressive disorder, the anxiety disorder preceded major depressive disorder.

Correlated risk factors

Because distinct etiologic factors may be correlated, it is possible that two distinct disorders, each related to one etiologic factor, will co-occur. If parental depression, alcoholism and marital breakdown are correlated, this may lead to comorbidity in offspring, with, for example, parental depression leading to depression in the offspring, and marital breakdown leading to conduct disorder.

Artificial associations

There are many possibilities why comorbidity can be regarded an artefact as a result of the way in which we assess and conceptualize psychopathology.

Treatment seeking factors

In case we study referred subjects, artificial comorbidity may result from treatment-seeking factors, such as referral bias (it is known, for example, that among children referred to mental health agencies, children who come from problematic families tend to be overrepresented) and Berkson's bias (a statistical phenomenon by which children with multiple disorders are more likely to be referred than children with one such condition because the probability of referral is related to the combined probabilities of referral for each condition separately) (Verhulst & van der Ende, 1993). Both factors are responsible for the fact that children with comorbid disorders have a greater probability to be referred for mental health services than children with single disorders. As a result, the level of comorbidity in referred samples is higher than that in general population samples (McConaughy & Achenbach, 1994).

Assessment artefacts

Comorbidity may result from artefacts in assessment procedures. For example, if an instrument for the assessment of anxiety contains items that are similar to those comprising an instrument for the assessment of depression, artificial association between anxiety and depression is the result. This is the case in child as well as adult psychiatry. For example, there is a clear overlap between items of the Hamilton Psychiatric Rating Scale for Depression, and the Hamilton Anxiety Rating Scale, both scales that are frequently used in adult psychiatry (Riskind et al., 1987).

Nosologic factors

Earlier it was stressed that there are two main diagnostic concepts: the categorical approach exemplified by the DSM, and the quantitative empirically based approach.

Both categorical and quantitative approaches can be employed for the study of comorbidity. From a categorical perspective it is assumed that if a child meets the criteria for two or more diagnoses, then the child has both or more disorders. From a quantitative point of view a child can obtain scores for multiple syndrome scales. This does not automatically imply that these children suffer from different and distinct, 'comorbid' disorders. Rather, the presence of high scores on multiple syndromes may reflect the fact that most disordered children show a variety of problem behaviours with either single or multiple etiologies. It is crucial that the variation in combinations and levels of children's problem behaviours are accepted as a reflection of the complexities of child psychopathology.

The comorbidity of depression and anxiety from a quantitative and categorical perspective

The categorical approach

The prevalence study of psychiatric disorder in Dutch children aged 13–18 years which was discussed above, also revealed that the most frequently occurring combination of diagnoses was of anxiety and mood disorders (Verhulst et al., 1997). Thirteen of the 17 subjects who met the criteria for a

DISC-P mood disorder (Shaffer et al., 1993), met the criteria for one or more other diagnoses as well. In nine cases (nearly 70% of the comorbid mood disorder cases) this was with an anxiety disorder. Of the 22 subjects who met criteria for DISC-C mood disorders (Shaffer et al., 1993), 10 met the criteria for one or more other diagnoses. In each of these 10 cases, the comorbid disorder included anxiety disorder. These results underscore the finding that mood and anxiety disorders tend to occur frequently together. If both disorders can be regarded as distinct from each other, this study's findings cast doubt on the ability of DSM–III–R criteria to distinguish both conditions.

The quantitative approach

The American–Dutch cross-cultural comparisons of empirically derived CBCL syndromes as discussed above, supported the finding that in large samples of clinically referred children, items indicative of anxiety and depression tend to co-occur rather than forming two discrete syndromes of anxiety and depression that can clearly be separated.

Both from a categorical and quantitative perspective, there is a clear association between anxiety and depression. As noted, it may be that assessment and diagnostic issues such as item overlap in assessment instruments or in diagnostic criteria (for example between DSM–III–R Overanxious Disorder and Major Depression) are responsible for the artificial association between anxiety and depression. Also it may be that DSM–III–R anxiety and depressive disorders are regarded as discrete, discontinuous categories, whereas, in reality, there is no clear categorical distinction between the two disorders in the first place. In that case, there seems to be comorbidity between two separate disorders where, in fact, there was no clear distinction between the two disorders in the first place.

However, these factors do not explain the clear association between anxiety and depression that we found in our research with the CBCL and related instruments, because there were no a priori assumptions about the composition of the syndromes. Instead, we empirically tested the covariation of problems reported for clinically referred children. The fact that our research replicated the finding for American samples in that both anxiety and depression items formed one syndrome rather than two separate syndromes, supported the view that anxiety and depression may be regarded as part of a broader construct of emotional distress. Some authors refer to the general mood state characterized by both anxiety and depression as 'negative affectivity' (King & Ollendick, 1991; Watson & Clark, 1984; Watson & Kendall, 1989). 'Negative affectivity' is characterized in adults by subjective feelings of nervousness, tension and worry, as well as feelings of anger, guilt, self-dissatisfaction, a sense of rejection and sadness. These subjective experiences are viewed as a pervasive disposition that can manifest itself in the absence of overt stress. The distinction between an anxiety and depression component is even more difficult for children than adults, because children differ from adults in their ability to experience cognitive features of emotions (Rutter, 1986).

The co-occurrence of problems of anxiety and depression does not automatically imply that some children cannot manifest primarily anxiety, or primarily depression. More research is needed to clarify whether anxiety and depression should be regarded as phenomena that are distinct from each other, or whether the relations between them are more complex. It may be that anxiety and depression are to be regarded as separate phenomena in certain developmental periods. Also, it is possible that certain rare and severe conditions such as panic disorder differ quantitatively as well as qualitatively from conditions which may be captured best as general affective disturbance. Because the evidence about how to regard childhood and adolescent affective disturbance is still far from conclusive, it is best to test the associations of a broad spectrum of anxiety and depression conditions assessed by both categorical and quantitative approaches, with possible etiologic factors, and with course and treatment response.

Research concerning anxiety and depression in children should take account of the fact that anxiety and depression tend to co-occur. The term 'comorbidity' is often held to reflect the existence of two distinct and unrelated factors, whereas many underlying factors other than the co-existence of two unrelated disorders can be responsible for the co-occurrence of anxiety and depression. Research which takes the co-occurrence of anxiety and depression into account may help us further in understanding this phenomenon.

Conclusion

Anxiety disorders are the most prevalent of disorders reported for children and adolescents in general population surveys. Depending on the definitions of disorders and assessment methodologies used, about 6–10% of children and adolescents from the general population suffer from some kind of anxiety disorder. This does not imply that all children with an anxiety disorder were handicapped in their everyday functioning. This was only true for about 2%.

Anxiety disorders were somewhat more prevalent in girls versus boys, and more prevalent in older versus younger children. Anxiety disorders were often accompanied by depressive manifestations. Both from a categorical as well as a quantitative perspective, anxiety and depression showed high levels of comorbidity. The fact that anxiety and depression are often not separable led a number of investigators to the view that anxiety and depression may be regarded as part of a broader construct of emotional distress, referred to as 'negative affectivity'.

In this chapter on the epidemiology of anxiety disorders emphasis was put on assessment and diagnostic issues. Knowledge on etiology, mechanisms and treatment of anxiety disorders can be improved if researchers and clinicians across countries agree upon assessment and diagnostic procedures that will facilitate comparisons. This will serve to assist the many children who suffer from an anxiety disorder and who need adequate treatment.

REFERENCES

Achenbach, T. M. (1991a). 'Comorbidity' in child and adolescent psychiatry: categorical and quantitative perspectives. *Journal of Child and Adolescent Psychopharmacology*, **1**, 271–8.

Achenbach, T. M. (1991b). *Manual for the Child Behavior Checklist/4-18 and 1991 Profile.* Burlington, VT: University of Vermont Department of Psychiatry.

Achenbach, T. M. (1991c). *Manual for the Teacher's Report Form and 1991 Profile.* Burlington, VT: University of Vermont Department of Psychiatry.

Achenbach, T. M. (1991d). *Manual for the Youth Self-Report and 1991 Profile.* Burlington, VT: University of Vermont Department of Psychiatry.

Achenbach, T. M. (1991e). *Integrative Guide for the 1991 CBCL/4-18, YSR, and TRF Profiles.* Burlington, VT: University of Vermont Department of Psychiatry.

American Psychiatric Association (1981). *Diagnostic and Statistical Manual of Mental Disorders* (3rd Edition) (DSM–III). Washington DC: APA.

American Psychiatric Association (1987). *Diagnostic and Statistical Manual of Mental Disorders.* (3rd Edition, Revised) (DSM–III–R). Washington, DC: APA.

American Psychiatric Association (1994). *Diagnostic and Statistical Manual of Mental Disorders (4th Edition) (DSM–IV).* Washington, DC: APA.

Anderson, J. C., Williams, S., McGee, R. & Silva, P. A. (1987). DSM–III diagnoses in preadolescent children. *Archives of General Psychiatry*, **44**, 69–76.

Angold, A., Prendergast, M., Cox, A., Harrington, R., Simonoff, E. & Rutter, M. (1995). The child and adolescent psychiatric assessment (CAPA). *Psychological Medicine*, **25**, 739–53.

Bird, H. (1996). Epidemiology of childhood disorders in cross-cultural context. *Journal of Child Psychology and Psychiatry*, **37**, 35–49.

Bird, H. R., Canino, G., Rubio-Stipec, M., et al. (1988). Estimates of the prevalence of childhood maladjustment in a community survey in Puerto Rico: the use of combined measures. *Archives of General Psychiatry*, **45**, 1120–6.

Caron, C. & Rutter, M. (1991). Comorbidity in child psychopathology: Concepts, issues and research strategies. *Journal of Child Psychology and Psychiatry*, **32**, 1063–80.

Cohen, J. (1988). *Statistical Power Analysis for the Behavioral Sciences*, 2nd edition. Hillsdale NJ: Lawrence Erlbaum Associates.

Cohen, P., Cohen J., Kasen, S., et al. (1993). An epidemiological study of disorders in late childhood and adolescence: I. Age and gender-specific prevalence. *Journal of Child Psychology and Psychiatry*, **34**, 851–67.

Costello, E. J., Angold, A., Burns, B. J., et al. (1996). The great smoky mountains study of youth. Goals, design, methods and the prevalence of DSM–III–R disorders. *Archives of General Psychiatry*, **53**, 1129–36.

Crijnen, A. A. M., Achenbach, T. M. & Verhulst, F. C. (1997). Comparison of problems reported by parents of children in 12 cultures: total problems, externalizing and internalizing. *Journal of the American Academy of Child and Adolescent Psychiatry*, **36**, 1269–77.

Crijnen, A. A. M., Achenbach, T. M. & Verhulst, F. C. (1999). Problems reported by parents of children in multiple cultures: The Child Behavior Checklist. *American Journal of Psychiatry*, **156**, 569–74.

De Groot, A., Koot, H. M. & Verhulst, F. C. (1994). Cross-cultural generalizability of the Child Behavior Checklist cross- informant syndromes. *Psychological Assessment*, **6**, 225–30.

De Groot, A., Koot, H. M. & Verhulst, F. C. (1996). Cross-cultural generalizability of the Youth Self-Report and Teacher's Report Form cross-informant syndromes. *Journal of Abnormal Child Psychology*, **24**, 651–64.

Fergusson, D. M., Horwood, J. & Lynskey, M. T. (1993). Prevalence and comorbidity of DSM–III–R diagnoses in a birth cohort of 15 year olds. *Journal of the American Academy of Child and Adolescent Psychiatry*, **32**, 1127–34.

King, N. J. & Ollendick, T. H. (1991). Negative affectivity in children and adolescents: Relations between anxiety and depression. *Clinical Psychology Review*, **11**, 441–59.

Kovacs, M. & Paulauskas, S. L.(1984). Developmental state and the expression of depressive disorders in children: An empirical analysis. In *Childhood Depression (New Direction for Child Development)*, ed. D. Cicchetti & K. Schneider-Rosen, No. 26, pp. 59–80). San Francisco: Josey-Bass.

Lapouse, R. & Monk, M. A. (1958). An epidemiological study of behavior characteristics in children. *American Journal of Public Health*, **48**, 1134–44.

Maser, J. D. & Cloninger, C. R. (ed.) (1990). *Comorbidity of Mood and Anxiety Disorders*. Washington, DC: American Psychiatric Press.

McConaughy, S. H. & Achenbach, T. M. (1994). Comorbidity of empirically based syndromes in matched general population and clinical samples. *Journal of Child Psychology and Psychiatry*, **35**, 1141–57.

McGee, R., Feehan, M., Williams, S., Partridge, F., Silva, P. A. & Kelly, J. (1990). DSM–III disorders in a large sample of adolescents. *Journal of the American Academy of Child and Adolescent Psychiatry*, **29**, 611–19.

Quay, H. C. & Peterson, D. R. (1983). *Interim Manual for the Revised Behavior Problem Checklist*. Miami: University of Miami.

Riskind, J. H., Beck, A. T., Brown, G. & Steer, R. A. (1987). Taking the measure of anxiety and depression validity of the reconstructed Hamilton Scales. *Journal of Nervous and Mental Disease*, **175**, 474–9.

Rutter, M. (1986). The developmental psychopathology of depression: Issues and perspectives. In *Depression in Young People: Development and Clinical Perspectives*, ed. M. Rutter, C. E. Izard & P. B. Read, pp. 3–30. New York: Guilford Press.

Shaffer, D. et al. (1983). A children's global assessment scale. *Archives of General Psychiatry*, **40**, 1228–31.

Shaffer, D., Schwab-Stone, M., Fisher, P., et al. (1993). The Diagnostic Interview Schedule for Children, Revised Version (DISC-R): I. Preparation, field-testing, interrater reliability, and acceptability. *Journal of the American Academy of Child and Adolescent Psychiatry*, **32**, 643–50.

Velez, C. N., Johnson, J. & Cohen, P. (1989). A longitudinal analysis of selected risk factors for childhood psychopathology. *Journal of the American Academy of Child / Adolescent Psychiatry*, **28**, 861–4.

Verhulst, F. C. (1995). A review of community studies. In *The Epidemiology of Child and Adolescent Psychopathology*, ed. F. C. Verhulst & J. M. Kook, pp. 146–77. Cambridge, MA: Oxford University Press.

Verhulst, F. C. & Achenbach, T. M. (1995). Empirically based assessment and taxonomy of psychopathology: cross-cultural applications. A review. *European Child and Adolescent Psychiatry*, **4**, 61–76.

Verhulst, F. C. & Van der Ende, J. (1993). Comorbidity in an epidemiological sample: A longitudinal perspective. *Journal of Child Psychology and Psychiatry*, **34**, 767–83.

Verhulst, F. C. & Van der Ende, J. (1995). The eight-year stability of problem behavior in an epidemiological sample. *Pediatric Research*, **38**, 612–17.

Verhulst, F. C. & Van der Ende, J. (1997). Factors associated with child mental health service use in the community. *Journal of the American Academy of Child and Adolescent Psychiatry*, **36**, 901–9.

Verhulst F. C., Van der Ende, J., Ferdinand, R. F. & Kasius, M. C. (1997). The prevalence of DSM–III–R diagnoses in a national sample of Dutch adolescents. *Archives of General Psychiatry*, **54**, 329–36.

Watson, D. & Clark, L. A. (1984). Negative affectivity: The disposition to experience aversive emotional states. *Psychological Bulletin*, **96**, 465–90.

Watson, D. & Kendall, P. C. (1989). Common and differentiating features of anxiety and depression: Current findings and future directions. In *Anxiety and Depression. Distinctive and Overlapping Features*, ed. P. C. Kendall & D. Watson, pp. 493–508. New York: Academic Press.

Weissman, M. M. (1990). Evidence for comorbidity of anxiety and depression: Family and genetic studies of children. In *Comorbidity of Mood and Anxiety Disorders*, ed. J. D. Maser & C. R. Cloninger, pp. 349–66. Washington, DC: American Psychiatric Press.

Whitaker, A., Johnson, J., Shaffer, D., et al. (1990). Uncommon troubles in young people. *Archives of General Psychiatry*, **47**, 487–94.

13

Onset, course, and outcome for anxiety disorders in children

Lars-Göran Öst and Philip D. A. Treffers

Onset of anxiety disorders in children

There has been relatively little research interest focused on the age of onset and precipitating factors regarding anxiety disorders in children. Relatively more research has been done on these issues for adults, and thus both bodies of research are summarized in this chapter.

Age of onset in children

Table 13.1 summarizes studies in which information concerning age of onset for various childhood anxiety disorders has been found. Separation anxiety disorder, avoidant disorder and simple phobia seem to have the earliest age of onset.

Especially relevant are the recent studies by Biederman et al. (1997) and by Wittchen, Reed & Kessler (1998). Biederman et al. (1997) charted the mean ages of onset of anxiety disorders among children with panic disorder and agoraphobia. They examined 472 consecutively referred children and adolescents via a structured diagnostic interview. These children and adolescents were referred to a paediatric psychopharmacology clinic that did not specialize in the treatment of any particular disorder. Among children with agoraphobia the earliest anxiety disorder to emerge was specific phobia, followed by avoidance disorder and separation anxiety disorder; each of these disorders preceded the onset of agoraphobia. Overanxious disorder, social phobia and obsessive-compulsive disorder tended to follow the emergence of agoraphobia. Children with panic disorder showed a similar course, but they showed slightly later ages at onset for all the disorders. Agoraphobia had an earlier age at onset than panic disorder. This last finding was confirmed in the community study by Wittchen et al. (1998). In this community study in 14–24-year-old adolescents, age of onset of both panic disorder and agoraphobia was much later than in the 4–18-year-old clinic population studied by Biederman et al. (1997).

Table 13.1. Mean age of onset of anxiety disorders in children and adolescents

Study/sample	Ages	Anxiety disorders							
		SAD	AVD	OAD	SP	SOP	AG	PD	OCD
Bolton et al. (1983); Clinic	12–18 years	—	—	—	—	—	—	—	11.9
Flament et al. (1988): Community	14–18 years	—	—	—	—	12.8	—	—	—
Last & Strauss (1989a); Clinic	mean 16.1 years	—	—	—	—	—	—	15.6	—
Last & Strauss (1989b); Clinic	6.5–17.6 years	—	—	—	—	—	—	—	boys: 9.5 girls: 12.6
Flament et al. (1990); Clinic	16–18 years	—	—	—	—	—	—	—	10.3
Riddle et al. (1990); Clinic	7–16 years	—	—	—	—	—	—	—	9.0
Last et al. (1992); Clinic	5–18 years	7.5	8.2	8.8	8.4	11.3	—	14.1	10.8
Rettew et al. (1992); Clinic	7–19 years	—	—	—	—	—	—	—	10.0
Keller et al. (1992); Community[a]	—	8.0	—	10.0	—	—	—	—	—
Leonard et al. (1993); Clinic	7–19 years	—	—	—	—	—	—	—	9.9
Giaconia et al. (1994); Community	18 years	—	—	—	6.7	10.8	—	—	—
Dummit & Klein (1994); Clinic[b]	mean 13.9	—	—	—	—	—	—	11.6	—
Hanna (1995); Clinic	7–18 years	—	—	—	—	—	—	—	10.0
Biederman et al. (1997); Clinic: PD									
Children with or without AG;	4–17 years	4.3	5.3	6.7	5.0	7.2	5.6	6.8	5.7
Children with AG	4–18 years	4.7	4.3	5.5	4.1	5.5	4.9	—	6.4
Wittchen et al. (1998); Community	14–24 years	—	—	—	—	—	12.6	14.5[a]	—
Wittchen et al. (1999); Community	14–24 years	—	—	—	—	boys: 11.5[c] girls: 12.5[c]	—	—	—

SAD = Separation anxiety disorder; AVD = avoidant disorder; OAD = overanxious disorder; SP = simple/specific phobia; SOP = social phobia; AG = agoraphobia; PD = panic disorder; OCD = obsessive-compulsive disorder.

[a]The sample was recruited for a study about the impact of parental affective illness in children.
[b]Based on reports in literature 1984–1990.
[c]DMS–IV social phobia, generalized type.
[d]Mean age at onset of PD with AG (the mean age at onset for PD without AG: 16.2 years).

There are no studies on post-traumatic stress disorder (PTSD) since the type of traumatic experiences that can lead to PTSD can occur at any time during the life of an individual, and there is no reason to assume that a certain age should confer a higher risk for being exposed to this type of event.

Age of onset in adults

Table 13.2 presents the age of onset data for various anxiety disorders in adult patients. It is obvious from this table that specific phobia is a heterogeneous diagnosis when it comes to onset age. Animal phobias have the earliest age of onset with a weighted mean of 8.6 years. The other types of simple phobias vary considerably, with blood-injury-injection phobia having a mean of 8.5 years, dental phobia 11.7 years, claustrophobia 20.2 years and situational phobias 27.3 years. Social phobia generally starts during the mid-late teens, with a mean onset age of 17.5 years. Agoraphobia is the anxiety disorder having the largest number of studies investigating age of onset. The means for the individual studies vary from a low of 19.7 years to a high of 32.0 years, with a weighted mean of 27.7 years. Thus, based on information from adults, agora-phobia usually starts during early adulthood. Panic disorder also has a rather variable mean onset age, and the weighted mean is 27.4 years. There are few studies that have described this variable in people with generalized anxiety disorder and the overall mean is 23.3 years. Finally, obsessive-compulsive disorder seems to start in the late teens with a weighted mean of 19.6 years. Some of the studies on obsessive-compulsive disorder found that males had a significantly earlier age at onset than females.

A tentative comparison of those anxiety disorders that are found both in the studies on children (Table 13.1) and adults (Table 13.2) indicates reasonable agreement regarding the rank order of age of onset.

Precipitating factors

Some research has been done regarding factors to which adult patients ascribe importance as a reason (perhaps the cause) for the start of their disorder. In agoraphobic patients Öst & Hugdahl (1983) found that 88% recalled various stressful events at the time of the onset for their agoraphobic problems. Most common of these were different kinds of somatic disorders, stressful working conditions, psychological stress in general, and problematic pregnancy or childbirth. Solyom, Ledwidge & Solyom (1986) compared three phobic samples and found similar proportions to have experienced life events during the 6 months preceding the onset of their phobias; agoraphobia 79%, social phobia 79% and simple phobia 61%.

Table 13.2. Age at onset for various anxiety disorders in adults

	n	% females	Mean (years)
Specific phobia: animal type			
Marks & Gelder (1966)	18	94	4.4
Öst (1987)	50	96	6.9
Himle et al. (1989)	25	100	12.8
Fredrikson et al. (1997)	158	100	8.9
Specific phobia: miscellaneous			
Marks & Gelder (1966)	12	75	22.7
Solyom et al. (1986)	72	78	12.8
Öst (1987) Claustro	40	90	20.2
Öst (1987) Dental	60	75	11.7
Himle et al. (1989) Situational	46	57	27.3
Himle et al. (1989) Choking	8	88	20.6
Himle et al. (1989) Blood	9	44	9.7
Öst (1992) Blood-injury	81	76	8.6
Öst (1992) Injection	59	65	8.1
Social phobia			
Marks & Gelder (1966)	25	60	18.9
Shafar (1976)	20	55	20.0
Amies et al. (1983)	87	40	19.0
Thyer et al. (1985)	42	52	15.7
Solyom et al. (1986)	47	47	16.6
Öst (1987)	80	65	16.3
Agoraphobia			
Marks & Gelder (1966)	84	87	23.9
Marks & Herst (1970)	1200	95	29.0
Berg et al. (1974)	786	100	26.0
Solyom et al. (1974)	43	95	19.7
Shafar (1976)	68	87	32.0
Buglass et al. (1977)	30	100	31.0
Burns & Thorpe (1977)	963	88	28.5
Sheehan et al. (1981)	100	85	24.1
Doctor (1982)	404	78	28.1
Amies et al. (1983)	57	86	24.0
Thyer et al. (1985)	115	81	26.5
Solyom et al. (1986)	80	86	24.5

Table 13.2. (*cont.*)

	n	% females	Mean (years)
Öst (1987)	100	87	27.7
Zitrin & Ross (1988)	77	70	25.4
Pollack et al. (1996)	194	59	29.1
Panic disorder			
Anderson et al. (1984)	48	71	22.8
Rapee (1985)	38	76	32.3
Roy-Byrne et al. (1986)	33	—	25.9
Yeragani et al. (1989)	35	60	14.2[a], 24.5[b]
Lelliot et al. (1989)	57	79	26.0
Noyes et al. (1992)	71	58	26.5
Starcevic et al. (1993)	54	56	34.7[c], 28.2[d], 24.4[e]
Battaglia et al. (1995)	231	75	29.1
Generalized anxiety disorder			
Anderson et al. (1984)	18	67	16.1
Rapee (1985)	48	58	25.7
Noyes et al. (1992)	41	78	23.6
Obsessive-compulsive disorder			
Rasmussen & Eisen (1990)	250	55	17.5[f], 20.8[g]
Ronchi et al. (1992)	131	54	19.6[f], 24.1[g]
Orloff et al. (1994)	85	59	17.2

[a]Patients having no loss; [b]Patients having severe loss; [c]No agoraphobia; [d]Mild agoraphobia; [e]Moderate/severe agoraphobia; [f]Males; [g]Females.

A few more studies on precipitating factors have been done on panic disorder. Roy-Byrne, Geraci & Uhde (1986) found that compared to controls panic disorder patients had experienced more life events that happened to them personally, reported greater subjective stress, and had a higher proportion of life events viewed as extremely uncontrollable and undesirable. Faravelli & Pallanti (1989) reported that during the year before the onset of the PD a higher proportion of panic patients than controls had at least one severe life event, one loss event, one threat event, and one adjustment event. Lelliot et al. (1989) found that 42% of their PD patients recalled a major negative life event the month before the first panic attack, and 74% ascribed this attack to various identifiable events or problems. Finally, Noyes et al. (1992) found that precipitating events were reported as often by panic disorder patients (69%) as generalized anxiety disorder patients (66%).

One childhood factor that has been specifically associated with panic disorder and agoraphobia in adults is separation anxiety (not necessarily full separation anxiety disorder). It is difficult to draw firm conclusions from these studies, however, as most of them lack a control or comparison group. Gittelman & Klein (1984) found that 50% of the adult panic patients had experienced separation anxiety during childhood. Raskin et al. (1982) reported that 35% of the patients with panic disorder and 25% of the patients with generalized anxiety disorder had experienced separation anxiety, while Noyes et al. (1992) found 28% and 20% for these two diagnoses. Thyer et al. (1985) reported that agoraphobia patients and simple phobia patients did not differ on a separation anxiety scale, and Thyer et al. (1986) found no difference between panic disorder and simple phobia on the same scale.

Other studies, however, have found separation anxiety to be associated with later panic disorder. Yeragani et al. (1989) reported that more panic disorder patients (30%) than major depressives (14%) and normal controls (3%) had experienced separation anxiety, and Battaglia et al. (1995) found a significant difference between patients with panic disorder (37%) and surgical patients (13%). The only study with a phobic comparison group finding a significant difference is Zitrin & Ross (1988). They found that among female patients, 48% of the agoraphobia patients compared to 20% of the simple phobia patients had experienced separation anxiety during childhood. However, among males the proportions were equal: agoraphobia patients 30% and simple phobia patients 35%. The conclusion that can be drawn is that the support for separation anxiety during childhood as a factor specifically linked to PD or AG in adults is generally uneven, and further research is needed. Particularly important would be to include comparison control groups in future studies.

Course and outcome of childhood anxiety disorders

With the exception of obsessive-compulsive disorder very little research has been done regarding the course and outcome of anxiety disorders in children. One reason for this is the difficulty in ascertaining the natural course. Basically, two types of studies can be found in the literature: epidemiological and clinical. The former is the result of a representative selection of the population of a certain age, and the purpose of the study is to investigate the prevalence of various psychiatric disorders. When the participants are reassessed a number of years later some of the previously diagnosed children will have obtained treatment, and some will not. This means that the researcher ends up with a sample of participants that varies considerably with respect to type and amount of treatment, if any, received. The clinical samples, on the other hand, consist of participants who have been referred for treatment due to an anxiety disorder(s). In this case, one would expect the patients to have received treatment, but this can also vary considerably (Last et al., 1996).

The ideal way to study natural course, from a methodological perspective, is to start with a sample of carefully diagnosed children with various anxiety disorders and then 'prevent' them from obtaining treatment for a certain time period (e.g. 5 years). Naturally, such a study would be ethically impossible, which means that the types of studies described above are the only ones available to yield information on these issues. Another methodological issue is whether the participants have been assessed at regular intervals during a follow-up period, or just at one point in time. The former methodology is rare (Last et al., 1996), but it gives more reliable information about recovery and relapse during the time period studied, compared to the latter form of studies which has to rely on retrospective information from the children or their parents.

Most of the studies conducted in clinical populations contain several methodological limitations that constrain the drawing of firm conclusions. These limitations include the relatively brief duration of time between the initial assessment and the post-assessment, the relatively small sample sizes and the failure of most studies (with exception of the Last et al. (1996) study) to include any comparison (i.e. non-anxiety-disordered) samples or nonpsychiatric control samples.

Anxiety disorders in general

A number of studies have not differentiated among the specific types of anxiety disorders. These studies are described in this section, followed by the studies of individual anxiety disorders (see also Kovacs & Devlin, 1998).

Rutter et al. (1976) reported from the large Isle of Wight study the follow-up of children from ages 10 to 14. About one-half of the children who had emotional problems (mainly anxiety disorders) at age 10 continued to have the same or similar problems when they were 14 years of age.

Cantwell & Baker (1989) reported the 4-year follow-up of the 151 children, who had received a DSM–III childhood psychiatric diagnosis, among 600 children who had presented for assessment of speech and/or language disorders at a community speech and hearing clinic. The anxiety disorders were grouped with affective disorder under the heading of emotional disorders. At the follow-up assessment, 34% of the 38 children were considered well, while 24% had the same disorder, and 42% had the developed some other type of disorder. The picture was different for the behavioural disorders where only 13% (of 64 children) were well, 55% had the same disorder, and 32% had developed other disorders.

Keller et al. (1992) studied the lifetime history of anxiety disorders in 275 children of parents with a broad range of affective disorders recruited for different research studies. Fourteen per cent ($n = 38$) of these children had a history of anxiety disorder fulfilling the DSM–III criteria for overanxious disorder ($n = 31$) or separation anxiety disorder ($n = 7$). At the time of assessment, 34% of these had remitted from their anxiety disorder. The mean duration of the children's anxiety disorder was 4 years, but the Kaplan–Meier life-table method indicated that the cumulative probability of having the disorder 8 years after onset was 46%.

McGee et al. (1992) studied a cohort of all children born at a certain hospital in Dunedin, New Zealand, during one year. They reported the DSM–III diagnoses in this large cohort at age 11 ($n = 925$) and age 15 ($n = 976$). The prevalence of disorders was 8.8% at age 11 and 19.6% at age 15, while the corresponding figures for anxiety disorders were 5.3% and 8.7%, respectively. In the total sample, 42% retained their disorder across the two assessments, and 81% of those with a disorder at age 15 did not have it at age 11.

Last et al. (1996) reported a follow-up of 102 anxiety-disordered children, 58 with attention deficit hyperactivity disorder, and 87 never psychiatrically ill, 3 to 4 years after their initial assessment at a childhood anxiety disorders specialty clinic. Overall, 82% of those with a primary, and 84% of those with a secondary anxiety diagnosis were recovered by the end of the follow-up. However, 8% relapsed after being recovered, and 30% developed a new psychiatric disorder during the follow-up period. Of those with an anxiety disorder, 36% were still psychiatrically disordered, and 53% of them retained their primary anxiety disorder.

To summarize the above studies, one can say that 34% to 54% of the subjects were considered well (free from psychiatric diagnoses) at follow-up, about 4 years after the initial assessment.

Separation anxiety disorder

Cantwell & Baker (1989) reported the 4-year follow-up data for 151 children who had presented for treatment at a speech/language clinic. Initially, nine children with a mean age of 3.6 years (range 2.4–6.6) fulfilled the DSM–III criteria for separation anxiety disorder. The assessment indicated that 44% of these children no longer fulfilled any diagnostic criteria, 11% still had separation anxiety disorder, while 44% had other disorders. Separation anxiety disorder had the highest recovery rate and the lowest stability of the anxiety disorders investigated in this study.

Keller et al. (1992) reported that four of the seven (57%) children with separation anxiety disorder in their study had remitted at the time of the assessment, but two of these developed another anxiety disorder after they were recovered from the separation anxiety disorder. McGee et al. (1992) found that separation anxiety disorder was the only anxiety disorder in their study that actually decreased from age 11 (1.9%) to age 15 (1.7%). In the previously mentioned study by Last et al. (1996) 96% of the children with separation anxiety disorder in their clinical sample were recovered by the end of the follow-up, and 25% had developed a new psychiatric disorder.

Avoidant disorder

In the previously described study by Cantwell & Baker (1989) 14 children had avoidance disorder, and at follow-up 36% were well, 29% had the same disorder, and 35% had developed some other disorder.

Overanxious disorder

In the Cantwell & Baker (1989) study only eight children were diagnosed with overanxious disorder, and four years later 25% of them were well, 25% had the same disorder, while 50% had developed other psychiatric disorders. A majority (82%) of the children in the Keller et al. (1992) study had overanxious disorder. However, the authors did not report the outcome for these children separately but in combination with the seven who had separation anxiety disorder. For the total sample the probability of still fulfilling diagnostic criteria 8 years after the onset was 46%.

McGee et al. (1992) found that the prevalence of overanxious disorder doubled, from 2.5% to 5.2%, between the ages 11 and 15. Last et al. (1996) reported that 80% of their patients with overanxious disorder recovered during the 3–4-year follow-up period, but fully 35% developed a new psychiatric disorder in the same interval. In this sample 20% still met criteria for over-anxious disorder at follow-up.

Specific phobias

Agras, Chapin & Oliveau (1972) reported the 5-year follow-up course of an epidemiological sample of 10 children and adolescents (under 20 years of age) and 20 adults, who had not obtained any treatment since the diagnosis of a specific phobia. Among the children 40% were symptom-free and 60% were improved, which was significantly better than the outcome for the adults (6% symptom-free, 37% improved, 20% unchanged and 37% worse). However, Ollendick (1979) has pointed out that a majority of the 'improved' children still had marked phobic problems at the follow-up assessment.

McGee et al. (1992) reported that the prevalence of specific phobias was 1.7% at 11 and 3.1% at 15 years of age. In general 42% had the same anxiety disorder at 15 years as they did at 11 years, but there is no specification as to the course of specific phobias. The previously mentioned study by Last et al. (1996) found that 69.2% of the children with a specific phobia in their clinical sample were recovered by the end of the follow-up, with 30.8% still meeting criteria. This was actually the lowest recovery rate among the six anxiety disorders studied. On the other hand, specific phobia had the lowest proportion of patients developing new psychiatric disorders (15%).

Obsessive-compulsive disorder

Warren (1960) published a 7-year follow-up study of 15 children and adolescents with 'obsessive-compulsive state' who received treatment at the Maudsley Hospital in London. Only two patients (13%) were free of psychiatric symptoms, 54% had mild to moderate symptoms, and fully 33% were still severely handicapped by their obsessive-compulsive disorder problems. Later studies seem to confirm this gloomy picture of the long-term outcome in children with obsessive-compulsive disorder. Hollingsworth et al. (1980) followed 10 out of 17 patients (59%) between 1.5 and 14 years after they first presented for treatment at the UCLA Neuropsychiatric Institute. Only three of the subjects (30%) were considered symptom-free, while seven still had obsessive-compulsive disorder problems, albeit at a less severe level.

Bolton, Collins & Steinberg (1983) presented a 1–4-year follow-up of 15 adolescents who had been treated with behaviour therapy at Maudsley Hospital. Thirteen (87%) were improved at follow-up. This group of patients were then followed 9 to 14 years after the initial treatment, and 57% were found to be improved, while 43% fulfilled the criteria for obsessive-compulsive disorder (Bolton, Luckie & Steinberg, 1995).

Berg et al. (1989) reported a 2-year follow-up of a community-based sample. The initial population consisted of all 9th to 12th grade pupils in a New Jersey county, and the study focused on the 59 who had obsessive-compulsive disorder (OCD) or an obsessive-compulsive spectrum disorder. Forty-five (76%) of the participants participated in the follow-up assessment and they were in the 16–21 age range. Of the 16 participants who initially fulfilled

DSM–III criteria for OCD, 31% still did so at follow-up, 25% had subclinical OCD, 12% had an obsessive-compulsive personality, 20% other diagnoses, while only 12% had no diagnoses. Of the 10 participants who initially had subclinical OCD, 10% fulfilled OCD criteria, 40% still had subclinical OCD, 30% had other diagnoses, and 20% had no diagnoses. Finally, of the 19 who had an obsessive-compulsive personality or other disorders with obsessive-compulsive features, 26% had developed OCD, 26% had subclinical OCD, while 37% still had the same diagnosis, and only 11% had no diagnoses. Overall, this means that only 13% had no psychiatric diagnoses, 36% had the same diagnosis as they did initially, 24% had a more severe disorder, while 27% had a less severe disorder.

Flament et al. (1990) described a 2–7-year (mean 4.4) follow-up of 25 out of 27 children (93%) who had been evaluated at the National Institute of Mental Health for a clomipramine treatment study. Twenty-three of the children had participated in the study, and received medication. Furthermore, 16 had obtained psychodynamic therapy and three behaviour therapy. The overall outcome was that 28% had no psychiatric symptoms, 68% had OCD, and 4% (1) had another diagnosis. In a sex- and age-matched control group comprising 23 subjects 65% had no psychiatric disorder, none had OCD, while 35% had other psychiatric diagnoses.

Leonard et al. (1993) reported the 2–7 year (mean 3.4 years) follow-up of 48 out of 54 (89%) children and adolescents who had received clomipramine treatment at the National Institute of Mental Health. At follow-up assessment, the patients had a mean age of 17.4 (range 10 to 24) years, and in the interim period 96% had received medication, 54% psychodynamic therapy, 33% behaviour therapy, and 20% family therapy. Twenty-three patients (43%) still met the DSM–III–R criteria for OCD, 18% had subclinical OCD, 28% had obsessive-compulsive features, while only 11% (six patients) had no obsessions or compulsions. However, only one-half of the group of patients in the 'no symptoms' category were medication-free and could be considered truly recovered.

Thomsen & Mikkelsen (1995) followed 23 children and adolescents with OCD 1.5–5 years after they had received treatment. About one-half of the group of patients still fulfilled the OCD diagnostic criteria and they had a high probability of comorbidity; anxiety, depression and tic disorder.

In the previously mentioned study by Last et al. (1996) 75% of the children with OCD in their clinical sample were recovered by the end of the follow-up, and 25% had developed a new psychiatric disorder.

Social phobia and panic disorder

Little is known about the course and outcome of social phobia and panic disorder in children and adolescents. In the clinical sample of Last et al. (1996), 23 children had social phobia and 10 had panic disorder according to DSM–III–R criteria. The recovery rate was 86% for social phobia and 70% for panic disorder. The proportion of patients who developed new psychiatric disorders during the 3–4-year follow-up period was 22% and 30%, respectively.

Summary

Keeping in mind the methodological constraints of most studies we can conclude that separation anxiety disorder seems the least stable of the anxiety disorders: the percentage still meeting criteria after follow-up is between 4.3% (Last et al., 1996) and 11% (Cantwell & Baker, 1989). Obsessive-compulsive disorder seems to be the most stable of the anxiety disorders: between 25% in the Last et al. (1996) study and 68% in the Flament et al. (1990) study. Across the various disorders the proportions of recovered patients are lowest in epidemiological, or other similar samples not receiving treatment (Berg et al., 1989; Cantwell & Baker, 1989), and highest in samples receiving cognitive–behavioural treatment (Bolton et al., 1995; Last et al., 1996). Last et al. (1996) found that 19% of the participants in their study continued to experience their previous primary anxiety disorder at the time of follow-up. In other words, the majority of the anxiety-disordered children were free from their initial anxiety disorder diagnosis. However, despite this, if the anxiety-disordered children were to receive another diagnosis for another disorder at follow-up, it tended to be an anxiety disorder. More specifically, 15.5% of the original sample had developed new anxiety disorders at the follow-up assessment point, versus 13.1% with a new depressive disorder and 7.1% with a new behaviour disorder.

Prediction of anxiety disorders in childhood

A small number of studies have investigated factors that may predict anxiety and other disorders from time 1 to time 2, or disorders, in general, at follow-up assessment.

McGee et al. (1992) divided their sample according to gender and the disorders into internalizing (anxiety and depression) or externalizing (particularly conduct and oppositional disorders). They found that for boys internalizing disorders (ID) at age 11 predicted externalizing disorders (ED) at age 15 (Odds ratio (OR) 5.8), but not internalizing disorders. However, externalizing disorders at 11 predicted externalizing disorders at 15 (OR 4.2), but not internalizing disorders. For girls, on the other hand, internalizing disorders at

11 predicted internalizing disorders at 15 (OR 6.2), but not externalizing disorders; and externalizing disorders at 11 did not predict either externalizing or internalizing disorders at 15. Furthermore, the background variables family disadvantage, reading disability, poor social competence and history of early behaviour problems did not alter the predictive relationship between disorders at 11 and 15 years of age.

Costello & Angold (1995) presented the same type of analysis between ages 7 to 11, initially, and 12 to 18 at follow-up for anxiety and depression diagnoses. For boys there was no significant prediction from childhood to adolescence. For girls on the other hand, both anxiety (OR 4.0) and depression (OR 8.0) in childhood predicted anxiety in adolescence, and depression in childhood predicted depression in adolescence (OR 21.1).

Offord et al. (1992) reported the 4-year follow-up of a randomized sample of all children 4 to 12 years of age from the census file in Ontario, Canada. A total of 881 (55% of those eligible) who had complete data sets were included in the analysis. The prevalence of emotional disorders was 10.8% in the initial analysis, and 9.7% four years later. Emotional disorders at the initial assessment were the strongest predictor of emotional disorders at follow-up (26%). However, those children who initially had conduct disorder or hyperactivity actually had somewhat higher proportions of emotional disorders at follow-up, 29% and 28%, respectively.

Last et al. (1996) used logistic regression analysis to assess the predictive power of age at intake, sex, history of depression, treatment after intake, family history of an anxiety disorder, age at onset of the first disorder, and severity of the anxiety disorder to recovery and development of new psychiatric disorders, respectively. None of these variables significantly predicted recovery. Regarding the development of new psychiatric disorders, the only significant predictor was treatment after intake. Those who received treatment were six times more likely to develop a new disorder during the 4-year follow-up period than those who did not get any treatment. The authors' interpretation of this finding is that the more disturbed children both seek treatment to a larger extent and run an increased risk of developing new psychiatric disorders.

In the Flament et al. (1990) follow-up study of children and adolescents with obsessive-compulsive disorder, correlational analysis was performed between baseline measures and outcome variables. Severity of obsessive-compulsive disorder symptoms, presence of neurological or neuropsychological impairment, a family history of depression and/or anxiety disorder were unrelated to outcome. Furthermore, neither the initial response to clomipramine treatment, nor any therapy during the follow-up period were related to long-term outcome.

Leonard et al. (1993) used multiple regression analysis to test the predictive power of five hypothesis-driven variables. The following three (out of five entered) variables significantly predicted OCD severity at follow-up: (1) OCD symptoms after completion of 5 weeks of clomipramine treatment, (2) parental Axis I disorder, and (3) lifetime history of tic disorder. Together these variables explained 31% of the variance in OCD scores at follow-up. In a subsequent exploratory regression analysis, 20 variables were included but the same three variables were the only significant predictors, explaining 62% of the variance in OCD scores.

The conclusion that can be drawn from prediction studies is that for girls but not for boys, internalizing disorders in childhood predict anxiety and depression in adolescence (Costello & Angold, 1995; McGee et al., 1992). The evidence that separation anxiety, especially in girls, leads to a higher risk for panic disorder with agoraphobia in adulthood (e.g. Black, 1995), is weak.

Risk for adjustment problems and disorders in adulthood

What will happen when children and adolescents with anxiety disorders reach adulthood? Will they 'grow out of it' or will they retain their disorder, perhaps in a more severe version? Few studies have reported a long-term follow-up of anxious children into adulthood. Ferdinand & Verhulst (1995) described an 8-year follow-up on 459 subjects (77%) who were 13 to 16 years of age (Time 1) when they were randomly selected from the population in Zuid-Holland (The Netherlands). At follow-up (Time 2) these subjects were 21 to 24 years old. The main comparison was based on Child Behavior Checklist data at Time 1 and the Young Adult Self-Report Form at Time 2. The syndromes designated as withdrawn, somatic complaints, and anxious/depressed constituted the internalizing scale, while delinquent behaviour and aggressive behaviour made up the externalizing scale. On the internalizing scale females had a significantly higher stability coefficient (0.38) than males (0.15), while the opposite was true for the externalizing scale; males 0.30, females 0.17. Of the 54 participants who had deviant scores on the internalizing scale at Time 1, 30% were still deviant, 46% had improved, while 24% had normal scores. Anxious/depressed syndrome at follow-up was significantly predicted by somatic complaints and anxious/depressed syndrome in adolescence. Finally, high scores on the anxious/depressed syndrome at Time 1 predicted more referrals to mental health services and generally poor outcome 8 years later (see Verhulst, chapter 12, this volume).

In the already mentioned Dunedin study, at 21 years old 195 of 389 cases with a psychiatric diagnosis had an anxiety disorder (Newman et al., 1996). Of these 65% had a history of anxiety disorder, 18.9% had a history of another psychiatric disorder and 19.5% had no history of previous disorder.

Last, Hansen & France (1997) presented an 8-year follow-up of the clinical sample described earlier (Last et al., 1996). Of the 118 eligible subjects, 101 (86%) were interviewed at a mean age of 21.9 years (range 18–26). There were 41 participants with anxiety disorders, 32 who were anxious-depressed, and 45 never psychiatrically ill (NPI). Variables of adult adjustment were assessed and the anxious group was to a significantly less extent living independently from their parents than the NPI group. However, the anxious-depressed group displayed more adjustment problems. Compared to the NPI group they had a significantly lower proportion of participants working or attending school, and higher proportions utilizing mental health services and reporting psychological problems. The anxious group also utilized mental health services less than the anxious-depressed group. Finally, an attempt was made to predict adjustment difficulties in the combined patient group using logistic regression analysis, but none of the child or parent variables emerged as a significant predictor. The conclusion that can be drawn from this study is that the young adults with a childhood anxiety disorder were doing as well as the NPI group, except when it came to leaving home. However, the participants who had a comorbid depressive disorder were doing poorly in many areas.

Pine et al. (1998) reported a 9-year follow-up of an epidemiological sample living in upstate New York. Of the initial 776 participants, 716 (92%) were assessed at a mean age of 22.1 (range 17 to 26 years). The proportion of participants fulfilling the respective DSM–III (Time 1) and DSM–III–R (Time 2) criteria were: major depression 3.2% and 8.2%, specific phobia 11.6% and 22.2%, social phobia 8.4% and 5.6%, overanxious disorder or generalized anxiety disorder 14.3% and 5.0%, and 'fearful spells' 21.4% and 1.7%. By using stepwise logistic regression analyses the prediction of adolescent onto adult disorders were examined while controlling for comorbidity in adolescence. The results showed that major depression in adulthood was predicted by overanxious disorder and conduct disorder in adolescence; specific phobia was only predicted by specific phobia; social phobia was predicted by social phobia and overanxious disorder; and generalized anxiety disorder was predicted by major depression, overanxious disorder and fearful spells. The conclusions drawn from this study are that an anxiety disorder during adolescence leads to a fairly high risk for anxiety disorders in adulthood, and that a large majority of the anxiety disorders in adulthood are preceded by anxiety or depression in adolescence.

The general conclusion that can be drawn from these studies is that anxiety disorders in childhood (with or without comorbid depression) lead to an increased risk of various adjustment problems and anxiety disorders in young adulthood.

Concluding comments

The above review of anxiety disorders in children and adolescents shows that these disorders start early in life. In Giaconia et al.'s (1994) study on the ages of onset of psychiatric disorders in adolescents, specific phobia had the earliest onset of all disorders, and also emerged earlier than other anxiety disorders. The stability of anxiety disorders is much higher than was hypothesized until recently. This can be considered an argument for the important contribution of constitutional (e.g. genetic) factors and/or information processing factors to the emergence and stability of anxiety disorders (e.g. Kovacs & Devlin, 1998). Anxiety disorders are however rather malleable: it is not uncommon that an anxiety disorder at a certain age has been 'substituted' for another anxiety disorder some years later. One possible explanation for this is that the expression of anxiety disorders changes in accordance with the level of socio-emotional development (see Westenberg, Siebelink & Treffers, chapter 4, this volume). Another explanation, not incompatible with the former, is that the presence of an anxiety disorder forms a risk for the development of another anxiety disorder (Kovacs & Devlin, 1998). Knowledge hereabout is still provisional: until recently it was thought that panic disorder was a risk factor for agoraphobia. Recent studies by Biederman et al. (1997) and Wittchen, Reed & Kessler (1998) suggest however, that agoraphobia usually emerges some years before panic disorder.

The presence of an anxiety disorder in childhood and/or adolescence leads to a greater risk of other adjustment and psychiatric problems in adulthood. One explanation for this finding could be that the same factors that underlie an anxiety disorder contribute to other psychiatric problems. This could include genetic factors (see Boer & Lindhout, chapter 10, this volume) and insecure attachment (see Manassis, chapter 11, this volume). Another explanation is that there is persistence of a disorder, which is comorbid with the anxiety disorder.

The identification of the risk factors and protective factors that determine the continuity or discontinuity of anxiety disorders in children remains one of the tasks of developmental psychopathologists in the twenty-first century.

Acknowledgement

Preparation of this chapter was supported by grant 12681 from the Swedish Medical Research Council.

REFERENCES

Agras, W. S., Chapin, H. H. & Oliveau, D. (1972). The natural history of phobias: Course and prognosis. *Archives of General Psychiatry*, **26**, 315–17.

Amies, P. L., Gelder, M. G. & Shaw, P. M. (1983). Social phobia: A comparative clinical study. *British Journal of Psychiatry*, **142**, 174–9.

Anderson, D. J., Noyes, R. & Crowe, R. R. (1984). A comparison of panic disorder and generalized anxiety disorder. *American Journal of Psychiatry*, **141**, 572–5.

Battaglia, M., Bertella, S., Politi, E., et al. (1995). Age at onset of panic disorder: Influence of familial liability to the disease and of childhood separation anxiety disorder. *American Journal of Psychiatry*, **152**, 1362–4.

Berg, C. Z., Rapoport, J. L., Whitaker, A., et al. (1989). Childhood obsessive compulsive disorder: A two-year prospective follow up of a community sample. *Journal of the American Academy of Child and Adolescent Psychiatry*, **28**, 528–33.

Berg, I. E., Marks, I. M., McGuire, R. & Lipsedge, M. (1974). School phobia and agoraphobia. *Psychological Medicine*, **4**, 428–34.

Biederman, J., Faraone, S. V., Marrs, A., et al. (1997). Panic disorder and agoraphobia in consecutively referred children and adolescents. *Journal of the American Academy of Child and Adolescent Psychiatry*, **36**, 214–23.

Black, B. (1995). Separation anxiety disorder and panic disorder. In *Anxiety Disorders in Children and Adolescents*, ed. J. S. March, pp. 212–34. New York: Guilford Press.

Bolton, D., Collins, S. & Steinberg, D. (1983). The treatment of obsessive-compulsive disorder in adolescence. *British Journal of Psychiatry*, **142**, 456–64.

Bolton, D., Luckie, M. & Steinberg, D. (1995). Long-term course of obsessive-compulsive disorder treated in adolescence. *Journal of the American Academy of Child and Adolescent Psychiatry*, **34**, 1441–50.

Buglass, D., Clarke, J., Henderson, A. S., Kreitman, N. & Presley, A. S. (1977). A study of agoraphobic housewives. *Psychological Medicine*, **7**, 73–86.

Burns, L. E. & Thorpe, G. L. (1977). The epidemiology of fears and phobias. *Journal of International Medical Research*, **5** (Suppl. 5), 1–7.

Cantwell, D. P. & Baker, L. (1989). Stability and natural history of DSM–III childhood diagnoses. *Journal of the American Academy of Child and Adolescent Psychiatry*, **28**, 691–700.

Costello, E. J. & Angold, A. (1995). Epidemiology. In *Anxiety Disorders in Children and Adolescents*, ed. J. S. March, pp. 109–24. New York: Guilford Press.

Doctor, R. M. (1982). Major results of a large-scale pretreatment survey of agoraphobics. In *Phobia: A Comprehensive Summary of Modern Treatments*, ed. R. L. DuPont, pp. 203–14. New York: Brunner/Mazel.

Dummit III, E. S. & Klein, R. G. (1994). Panic disorder. In *International Handbook of Phobic and Anxiety Disorders in Children and Adolescents*, ed. T. H. Ollendick, N. J. King & W. Yule, pp. 241–6. New York: Plenum Press.

Faravelli, C. & Pallanti, S. (1989). Recent life events and panic disorder. *American Journal of Psychiatry*, **146**, 622–6.

Ferdinand, R. F. & Verhulst, F. C. (1995). Psychopathology from adolescence into young adulthood: An 8-year follow up study. *American Journal of Psychiatry*, **152**, 1586–94.

Flament, M. F., Koby, E., Rapoport, J. L., et al. (1990). Childhood obsessive-compulsive disorder: A prospective follow up study. *Journal of Child Psychology and Psychiatry*, **31**, 363–80.

Flament, M. F., Whitaker, A., Rapoport, J. L., et al. (1988). Obsessive compulsive disorder in adolescence: An epidemiological study. *Journal of the American Academy of Child and Adolescent Psychiatry*, **27**, 764–71.

Fredrikson, M., Annas, P. & Wik, G. (1997). Parental history, aversive exposure and the development of snake and spider phobia in women. *Behaviour Research and Therapy*, **35**, 23–8.

Giaconia, R. M., Reinherz, H. Z., Silverman, A. B., Pakiz, B., Frost, A. K. & Cohen, E. (1994). Ages of onset of psychiatric disorders in a community population of older adolescents. *Journal of the American Academy of Child and Adolescent Psychiatry*, **33**, 706–17.

Gittelman, R. & Klein, D. F. (1984). Relationship between separation anxiety and panic and agoraphobia disorders. *Psychopathology*, **17**, 56–65.

Hanna, G. L. (1995). Demographic and clinical features of obsessive-compulsive disorder in children and adolescents. *Journal of the American Academy of Child and Adolescent Psychiatry*, **34**, 19–27.

Himle, J. A., McPhee, K., Cameron, O. G. & Curtis, G. C. (1989). Simple phobia: Evidence for heterogeneity. *Psychiatry Research*, **28**, 25–30.

Hollingsworth, C. E., Tanguap, P. E., Grossman, L. & Papst, P. (1980). Long-term outcome of obsessive compulsive disorder in childhood. *Journal of the American Academy of Child and Adolescent Psychiatry*, **19**, 134–44.

Keller, M. B., Lavori, P. W., Wunder, J., et al. (1992). Chronic course of anxiety disorders in children and adolescents. *Journal of the American Academy of Child and Adolescent Psychiatry*, **31**, 595–9.

Kovacs, M. & Devlin, B. (1998). Internalizing disorders in childhood. *Journal of Child Psychology and Psychiatry*, **39**, 47–63.

Last, C. G., Hansen, C. & Franco, N. (1997). Anxious children in adulthood: A prospective study of adjustment. *Journal of the American Academy of Child and Adolescent Psychiatry*, **36**, 645–52.

Last, C. G., Perrin, S., Hersen, M. & Kazdin, A. E. (1992). DSM–III–R anxiety disorders in children: Sociodemographic and clinical characteristics. *Journal of the American Academy of Child and Adolescent Psychiatry*, **31**, 1070–6.

Last, C. G., Perrin, S., Hersen, M. & Kazdin, A. E. (1996). A prospective study of childhood anxiety disorders. *Journal of the American Academy of Child and Adolescent Psychiatry*, **35**, 1502–10.

Last, C. G. & Strauss, C. C. (1989a). Panic disorder in children and adolescents. *Journal of Anxiety Disorders*, **3**, 87–95.

Last, C. G. & Strauss, C. C. (1989b). Obsessive-compulsive disorder in childhood. *Journal of Anxiety Disorders*, **3**, 295–302.

Lelliot, P., Marks, I., McNamee, G. & Tobeña, A. (1989). Onset of panic disorder with agoraphobia. *Archives of General Psychiatry*, **46**, 1000–4.

Leonard, H. I., Swedo, S. E., Lenane, M. C., et al. (1993). A 2- to 7-year follow up study of 54 obsessive-compulsive children and adolescents. *Archives of General Psychiatry*, **50**, 429–39.

Marks, I. M. & Gelder, M. G. (1966). Different ages of onset in varieties of phobias. *American Journal of Psychiatry*, **123**, 218–21.

Marks, I. M. & Herst, E. R. (1970). A survey of 1200 agoraphobics in Britain. *Social Psychiatry*, **5**, 16–24.

McGee, R., Feehan, M., Williams, S. & Anderson, J. (1992). DSM–III disorders from age 11 to age 15 years. *Journal of the American Academy of Child and Adolescent Psychiatry*, **31**, 50–9.

Newman, D. L., Moffitt, T. E., Caspi, A., Magdol, L., Silva, P. A. & Stanton, W. R. (1996). Psychiatric disorder in a birth cohort of young adults: prevalence, comorbidity, clinical significance, and new case incidence from ages 11 to 21. *Journal of Consulting and Clinical Psychology*, **64**, 552–62.

Noyes, R., Woodman, C., Garvey, M. J., et al. (1992). Generalized anxiety disorder vs. panic disorder. *Journal of Nervous and Mental Disease*, **180**, 369–79.

Offord, D. R., Boyle, M. H., Racine, Y. A., et al. (1992). Outcome, prognosis, and risk in a longitudinal follow up study. *Journal of the American Academy of Child and Adolescent Psychiatry*, **31**, 916–23.

Ollendick, T. H. (1979). Fear reduction techniques with children. In *Progress in Behavior Modification*, Vol. 8, eds. M. Hersen, R. M. Eisler & P. M. Miller, pp. 127–68. New York: Academic Press.

Orloff, L. M., Battle, M. A., Baer, L., et al. (1994). Long-term follow up of 85 patients with obsessive-compulsive disorder. *American Journal of Psychiatry*, **151**, 441–2.

Öst, L. G. (1987). Age of onset in different phobias. *Journal of Abnormal Psychology*, **96**, 223–9.

Öst, L. G. (1992). Blood and injection phobia: Background and cognitive, physiological, and behavioral variables. *Journal of Abnormal Psychology*, **101**, 68–74.

Öst, L. G. & Hugdahl, K. (1983). Acquisition of agoraphobia, mode of onset and anxiety response patterns. *Behaviour Research and Therapy*, **21**, 623–31.

Pine, D. S., Cohen, P., Gurley, D., Brook, J. & Ma, Y. (1998). The risk for early-adulthood anxiety and depressive disorders in adolescents with anxiety and depressive disorders. *Archives of General Psychiatry*, **55**, 56–64.

Pollack, M. H., Otto, M. W., Sabatino, S., et al. (1996). Relationship of childhood anxiety to adult panic disorder: Correlates and influence on course. *American Journal of Psychiatry*, **153**, 376–81.

Rapee, R. M. (1985). Distinction between panic disorder and generalized anxiety disorder: Clinical presentation. *Australian and New Zealand Journal of Psychiatry*, **19**, 227–32.

Raskin, M., Peeke, H. V. S., Dickman, W. & Pinsker, H. (1982). Panic and generalized anxiety disorders. Developmental antecedents and precipitants. *Archives of General Psychiatry*, **39**, 687–9.

Rasmussen, S. A. & Eisen, J. L. (1990). Epidemiology of obsessive compulsive disorder. *Journal of Clinical Psychiatry*, **51**, (suppl.), 10–15.

Rettew, D. C., Swedo, S. E., Leonard, H. L., Lenane, M. C. & Rapoport, J. L. (1992). Obsessions and compulsions across time in 79 children and adolescents with obsessive-compulsive disorder. *Journal of the American Academy of Child and Adolescent Psychiatry*, **31**, 1050–6.

Riddle, M. A., Scahill, L., King, R., et al. (1990). Obsessive compulsive disorder in children and adolescents: Phenomenology and family history. *Journal of the American Academy of Child and Adolescent Psychiatry*, **29**, 766–72.

Ronchi, P., Abbruzzese, M., Erzegovesi, S., Diaferia, G., Sciuto, G. & Bellodi, L. (1992). The epidemiology of obsessive-compulsive disorder in an Italian population. *European Psychiatry*, **7**, 53–9.

Roy-Byrne, P. P., Geraci, M. & Uhde, T. W. (1986). Life events and course of illness in patients with panic disorder. *American Journal of Psychiatry*, **143**, 1033–5.

Rutter, M., Tizard, J., Yule, W., Graham, P. & Whitmore, K. (1976). Isle of Wight studies, 1964–1974. *Psychological Medicine*, **6**, 313–32.

Shafar, S. (1976). Aspects of phobic illness: A study of 90 personal cases. *British Journal of Medical Psychology*, **49**, 221–36.

Sheehan, D. V., Sheehan, K. E. & Minichiello, W. E. (1981). Age of onset in phobic disorders: A reevaluation. *Comprehensive Psychiatry*, **22**, 544–53.

Solyom, L., Beck, P., Solyom, C. & Hugel, R. (1974). Some etiological factors in phobic neurosis. *Canadian Psychiatric Association Journal*, **19**, 69–78.

Solyom, L., Ledwidge, B. & Solyom, C. (1986). Delineating social phobia. *British Journal of Psychiatry*, **149**, 464–70.

Starcevic, V. Uhlenhuth, E. H., Kellner, R. & Pathak, D. (1993). Comorbidity in panic disorder: II. Chronology of appearance and pathogenic comorbidity. *Psychiatry Research*, **46**, 285–93.

Thomsen, P. H. & Mikkelsen, H. U. (1995). Course of obsessive-compulsive disorder in children and adolescents: A prospective follow up of 23 Danish cases. *Journal of the American Academy of Child and Adolescent Psychiatry*, **34**, 1432–40.

Thyer, B. A., Nesse, R. M., Cameron, O. G. & Curtis, G. C. (1985). Agoraphobia: A test of the separation anxiety hypothesis. *Behaviour Research and Therapy*, **23**, 75–8.

Thyer, B. A., Nesse, R. M., Curtis, G. C. & Cameron, O. G. (1986). Panic disorder: A test of the separation anxiety hypothesis. *Behaviour Research and Therapy*, **24**, 209–11.

Thyer, B. A., Parish, R. T., Curtis, G. C., Nesse, R. M. & Cameron, O. G. (1985). Ages of onset of DSM–III anxiety disorders. *Comprehensive Psychiatry*, **26**, 113–21.

Warren, W. (1960). Some relationships between the psychiatry of children and adults. *Journal of Mental Science*, **106**, 815–26.

Wittchen, H.-U., Reed, V. & Kessler, R.C. (1998). The relationship of agoraphobia and panic in a community sample of adolescents and young adults. *Archives of General Psychiatry*, **55**, 1017–24.

Wittchen, H.-U., Stein, M. B. & Kessler, R. C. (1999). Social fears and social phobia in a community sample of adolescents and young adults: Prevalence, risk factors and co-morbidity. *Psychological Medicine*, **29**, 309–23.

Yeragani, V. K., Meiri, P. C., Balon, R., Patel, H. & Pohl, R. (1989). History of separation anxiety in patients with panic disorder and depression and normal controls. *Acta Psychiatrica Scandinavica*, **79**, 550–6.

Zitrin, C. M. & Ross, D. C. (1988). Early separation anxiety and adult agoraphobia. *Journal of Nervous and Mental Disease*, **176**, 621–5.

14

Psychosocial interventions for anxiety disorders in children: status and future directions

Wendy K. Silverman and Steven L. Berman

Introduction

The clinical research literature on psychosocial interventions for use with anxiety disorders in children has made considerable advances in recent years in developing a solid knowledge base. The purpose of the present chapter is to review the status of the research literature in this area. In reviewing this literature, it shall become apparent that although considerable advances have been made, important issues remain. Thus, a second purpose of the chapter is to delineate a number of the main unresolved issues that would seem to be particularly important to resolve, or address, in future research efforts.

The particular type of psychosocial intervention that has received the most attention by child anxiety clinical researchers has been cognitive–behaviour therapy. Evidence for the efficacy of cognitive–behaviour therapy for use with anxiety disorders in children comes from case reports (Chiodos & Maddux, 1985; Eisen & Silverman, 1991), single case design studies (Eisen & Silverman, 1993, 1998; Kane & Kendall, 1989; Ollendick, 1995), and randomized clinical trials (Barrett, Dadds & Rapee, 1996; Cobham, Dadds & Spence, 1998; Kendall, 1994; Kendall et al., 1997; Silverman et al., 1999a,b). Because the case reports and single case designs have been summarized elsewhere (Morris & Kratochwill, 1998), and because the randomized clinical trials are most likely to inform future research efforts, the focus in this chapter is on the randomized trials.

The trials that are summarized all used rigorous methodological procedures, including the use of multisource assessments, structured diagnostic interviews, manualized treatments, treatment integrity checks and systematic follow-up procedures (see King & Ollendick, 1997; Silverman & Ginsburg, 1998). We begin by first summarizing clinical trials that have evaluated cognitive–behaviour therapy's efficacy using an individual child treatment format in comparison to a waitlist control condition. Within this summary are two trials that also examined whether the efficacy of the individual child treatment format could be enhanced through increased parental involvement. Next we summarize clinical trials that have evaluated cognitive behavioural therapy's efficacy using a group treatment format in comparison to a waitlist control condition. All the group treatment clinical trials included some degree of parental involvement. This is followed by a summary of two clinical trials that moved beyond the use of a waitlist control condition. The final section of the chapter delineates unresolved issues and suggests future research directions.

Empirical support for individual cognitive–behaviour therapy's efficacy (and for involving parents) relative to a waitlist control condition

Kendall (1994) presented the results of the first randomized clinical trial in which individual child-focused cognitive behavioural treatment (ICBT; n = 27) was found to be efficacious in reducing DSM–III–R anxiety disorders in children (aged 9 to 13 years) relative to a waitlist control condition (n = 20). Because the design and procedure of Kendall (1994) is the general prototype for the other clinical trials summarized in this chapter, the Kendall study is described in some detail.

Participants were children and parents who presented at a university-based childhood anxiety disorders specialty clinic. All children and parents were administered a comprehensive assessment battery which included a semi-structured interview, the Anxiety Disorders Interview Schedule for Children (ADIS-C/P; Silverman & Nelles, 1988) to derive DSM–III–R child diagnoses. In addition, a number of child and parent rating scales to assess anxiety and depressive symptoms, as well as several additional rating scales, were administered. Teacher ratings and behavioural observations (in the clinic setting) also were obtained. Children who met diagnostic criteria for overanxious disorder, separation anxiety disorder or avoidant disorder were selected to participate in the study, and were randomly assigned to either ICBT or a waitlist control condition.

The ICBT condition was 16 weeks in duration and involved cognitive (i.e. recognizing and clarifying distorted cognitions and attributions, devising coping plans, evaluating performance and administering self-reinforcement) and behavioural (i.e. in vivo exposures, relaxation training, contingent reinforcement) components. Following completion of ICBT, all the measures were readministered. The waitlist condition involved participants 'waiting' 8 weeks prior to receiving ICBT, much as they would wait in the case of limited availability of services. Subsequent to waiting, participants (children and parents) completed a 'post-wait assessment' which involved a re-administration of all the study's measures. After participating in the post-wait assessment, children received ICBT.

The findings revealed that children who received ICBT displayed significantly greater improvement compared to children assigned to the waitlist condition on most of the measures (i.e. significant time by condition interactions). Specifically, significant interactions were obtained for all the child and parent measures and on the behavioural observation measure. The only measure that failed to show a significant time by condition interaction was the teacher rating. As Kendall (1994) pointed out, however, teachers are more accurate in rating externalizing behaviour than internalizing behaviour in children, as the latter is often not as salient in the classroom. In addition to the improvements that were found on the child, parent and behavioural observation measures, improvement was evidenced by diagnostic recovery rate: 64% of the cases in the ICBT condition no longer met diagnostic criteria for an anxiety disorder at post-treatment; only one case (5%) in the waitlist control condition no longer met diagnostic criteria for an anxiety disorder. The efficacy of ICBT was further demonstrated in terms of continued improvement on the measures at 1-year follow-up (Kendall, 1994) and between 2 and 5 years (3.35 years average) follow-up (Kendall & Southam-Gerow, 1996).

In the Kendall & Southam-Gerow (1996) follow-up study, participants also were asked open ended as well as specific questions about the treatment they had received. In terms of the open ended questions, participants were asked what they recalled about treatment, what they felt was most important, and what they liked best. Fifty-three per cent of the participants recalled that they had 'dealt with fears and problems', 25% recalled that they had 'learned the FEAR steps', 25% recalled that they had 'in vivos', 19% recalled 'games and activities', and 17% recalled the therapeutic relationship. Rates of recall were higher when the participants were asked more specific questions about particular content areas of the treatment that were considered salient by the therapists (e.g. 24% recalled some part of FEAR steps and 39% reported having used them at one time). Interestingly, with respect to what participants felt was most important, the 'therapeutic relationship' was the most frequent response with 44% of the participants mentioning this factor. This was followed by 'dealt with their fears and problems' (39%), 'games and activities' (19%), and 'had in vivos' (17%).

Kendall et al. (1997) presented the results of a second randomized clinical trial. Once again, the efficacy of ICBT ($n = 60$) relative to a waitlist control condition ($n = 34$) was demonstrated in children (aged 9 to 13) with overanxious disorder, avoidant disorder or separation anxiety disorder. More specifically, significant time by condition interactions were found for most measures (i.e. child, parent and a behavioural observation measure). In terms of diagnosis, 71% of the ICBT cases no longer had their pre-treatment primary diagnosis as a primary diagnosis at post-treatment, and 53% no longer met diagnostic criteria for their pre-treatment primary diagnosis at all. This compared to only two cases (6%) in the waitlist condition that no longer met diagnostic criteria for their primary diagnosis at the post-wait assessment. Further, significant improvements were maintained at 1-year follow-up.

A clinical trial conducted in Australia by Barrett et al. (1996) provides further evidence for ICBT's efficacy ($n = 28$) relative to a waitlist control condition ($n = 26$) in reducing anxiety disorders in children with primary diagnoses of overanxious disorder, separation anxiety disorder and social phobia. Treatment sessions for the ICBT condition were 60 to 80 minutes in length and lasted for 12 weeks. The waitlist condition was similarly 12 weeks in length. In addition, whether ICBT's efficacy could be enhanced by parental involvement in the treatment was investigated by the inclusion of an additional experimental treatment condition, namely, cognitive–behaviour therapy (ICBT) plus 'family management' ($n = 25$). In this condition, the child was seen for ICBT for 30 minutes and 40 minutes were then spent with the child and his or her parents together. In these 40 minutes, emphasis was placed not only on providing child-focused cognitive–behavioural treatment but also on how parents interact with their children during displays of child anxiety, parental management of child emotional upsets, and communication and problem-solving skills.

Results indicated that across the two experimental treatment conditions (i.e. ICBT and ICBT plus family management), 69.8% of children no longer met diagnostic criteria for an anxiety disorder. This compares to only 26% of children in the waitlist condition. In addition, on all the child and parent rating scales, children in the two treatment conditions showed significant improvement relative to the children in the waitlist control condition. The only exception to this was the Revised Children's Manifest Anxiety Scale (Reynolds & Richmond, 1985) on which the control group also showed improvement. In addition to diagnostic recovery and self-rating scales, children's perceived threat interpretations and response plans to ambiguous hypothetical situations were assessed at pre- and post-treatment (and post-wait). For example, participants were asked: 'On the way to school you feel funny in the tummy. What do you think is happening? What would you do?' Children in both the ICBT and ICBT plus family management conditions displayed reductions in threat interpretation and avoidant responses; children in the waitlist condition remained the same from pre- to post-wait.

Follow-up assessment indicated that treatment recovery was maintained at 12 months. For example, 70.3% of children in the ICBT condition no longer met criteria for diagnostic status for an anxiety disorder. Children in the ICBT plus family management condition showed even greater improvement in diagnostic recovery (i.e. 95.6% of cases no longer met criteria for an anxiety diagnosis), as well as on many of the child and parent rating scales. Clinician's ratings and self-report measures also indicated greatest improvement from the ICBT plus family management condition. The findings of Barrett et al. thus provide further empirical evidence for the efficacy of ICBT in reducing anxiety disorders in children, and that ICBT's efficacy may be enhanced by involving parent(s) in the child's treatment (e.g. teaching parents ways to handle their children's anxiety problems).

Another study conducted recently in Australia provides additional evidence for the efficacy of ICBT as well as for the involvement of parents (Cobham, Dadds & Spence, 1998). In this study, however, parental involvement included not only parental management of the child's anxiety, but also parental management of their *own* anxiety. The potential utility of such an approach had been suggested by other investigators (Ginsburg, Silverman & Kurtines, 1995a) and is under investigation by our research group, in a current National Institute of Mental Health funded project. In the Cobham et al. (1998) study, 67 children (aged 7 to 14 years) with anxiety disorders (separation anxiety disorder, overanxious disorder, generalized anxiety disorder, simple phobia, social phobia or agoraphobia) were assigned to conditions according to parental anxiety level as measured by the State Trait Anxiety Inventory (Speilberger, Gorsuch & Lushene, 1970). More specifically, a parent score of 40 or above on the inventory was considered 'anxious', and a score below 40 was considered 'non-anxious'. Participants were then classified into groups based on one or both parent(s) scoring as anxious ($n = 35$) or neither parent scoring as anxious (i.e. nonanxious; $n = 32$). Within these two groups, participants were then randomly assigned to either ICBT or ICBT plus parental anxiety management. Total client contact time was about the same in the two treatment conditions, though ICBT plus parental anxiety management involved a greater number of sessions than the ICBT condition (ten 1 hour child sessions and four 1 hour parent sessions for ICBT plus parental anxiety management versus ten 1.5 hour sessions for ICBT).

In terms of the main findings, for children whose parents were in the nonanxious condition, 82% in the ICBT condition no longer met criteria for an anxiety disorder at post-treatment as compared to 80% in the ICBT plus parental anxiety management condition. However, for those children whose parents were anxious, only 39% in the ICBT condition no longer met criteria for an anxiety disorder. This compared to a 77% diagnostic recovery rate for those children with anxious parents in the ICBT plus parental anxiety manage-ment condition. In other words, ICBT was found to be highly efficacious for children with nonanxious parents. However, the addition of a parent anxiety management component to ICBT was important for diagnostic recovery for those children whose parents were anxious. In terms of follow-up, the above noted patterns were generally maintained at 6 and 12 months across most of the outcome measures.

A final piece of evidence for the efficacy of ICBT comes from a randomized clinical trial conducted in Australia that targeted school refusal behaviour (King et al., 1998). The study is relevant to this chapter given that the majority of children who display school refusal behaviour have a primary diagnosis of a phobic or anxiety disorder (Last & Strauss, 1990). King et al. (1998) evaluated the efficacy of a 4-week ICBT programme for school refusing children ($n = 17$; aged 5 to 15 years), relative to children who were assigned to a waitlist control condition ($n = 17$).

The findings indicated that children in the ICBT condition displayed signifi-cantly greater improvement than children in the waitlist control condition. This was true for most of the measures and indices, including attendance rates, and child, parent, teacher and clinician ratings. For example, in terms of perhaps the most important criterion, attendance rates, the mean percent of days present changed for the ICBT condition from 61% at pretreatment to 93% at posttreatment. Maintenance of therapeutic gains was demonstrated at a 3-month follow-up assessment point.

Overall, the studies summarized in this section provide empirical evidence for the efficacy of ICBT. The studies' findings further suggest that efficacy can be enhanced by involving parents in the treatment process (e.g. helping parents to manage their children's anxiety) and by targeting not only children's anxious symptoms but also parents', as necessary.

Empirical support for group cognitive behaviour therapy's efficacy (and for involving parents) relative to a waitlist control condition

Clinical researchers recently have begun to extend the knowledge base by evaluating the efficacy of cognitive–behaviour therapy when used in an alterna-tive intervention modality, specifically, 'group' cognitive–behavioural treatment (GCBT). There are several reasons why evaluating the efficacy of GCBT is important. These reasons have empirical, conceptual as well as practical significance. That is, empirical evidence that cognitive–behavioural treatment is efficacious when administered to an individual child does *not* necessarily mean that it is efficacious when administered to a group of children: it is important to demonstrate this empirically. This is because conceptually, it is possible to argue that group treatment might *not* be efficacious for a variety of reasons (e.g. the presence of other children may dampen the therapist–child relationship, may tax therapist resources, may create a context for negative modelling to occur). On the other hand, it is possible to argue that group treatment might *be* efficacious for a variety of reasons (e.g. the presence of other children may enhance the therapist–child relationship, may extend therapist resources, may create a context for positive modelling to occur). Thus, the question of the efficacy of group cognitive–behavioural treatment for children with anxiety disorders is important to answer on both empirical and conceptual grounds.

Evidence for the efficacy of a group modality also has considerable practical significance. It has, for example, practical significance for practitioners in the current context of the growth of HMOs, problems with third party payments, etc. In this context, there has been pressure mounting on practitioners to offer services that are not only efficacious, but also cost and time efficient (Kazdin, Siegel & Bass, 1990). Demonstrating that anxiety disorders in children can be reduced in a group format thus has important practical implications in that it serves to provide empirical evidence that practitioners *can* elect to work with this population via this cost and time efficient format. In addition, in the search for cost and time efficient interventions, demonstrating the efficacy of GCBT takes on further practical significance for families as children and their parents expend considerable time and energy in the treatment process at high financial cost (e.g. Kazdin, 1993).

Despite the empirical, conceptual and practical importance of developing and empirically supporting a group treatment format for use with children with anxiety disorders, research on group treatment for these disorders is sparse. The limited number of group treatment studies that exist were published prior to DSM–III and as a consequence, are not as methodologically refined with respect to measurement issues in general and the use of standardized diagnostic criteria in particular (e.g. see Ginsburg, Silverman & Kurtines, 1995*b* for review). Most of the early group treatment research consisted of evaluating systematic desensitization (i.e. relaxation training coupled with gradual counterconditioning procedures) in a group format to reduce test anxiety in school children (e.g. Barabasz, 1973; Deffenbacher & Kemper, 1974*a,b*; Mann & Rosenthal, 1969).

Recently however a clinical trials literature that shows similar quality in terms of its methodological rigour and measurement advances as found in the ICBT studies is emerging for GCBT. A recent study by Barrett (1998) in Australia represents the beginnings of the formation of such a literature. This study used structured interview procedures to assess diagnostic criteria, multi-source assessments, random assignment, manualized treatments and treatment integrity checks. Using a randomized clinical trials design, Barrett (1998) demonstrated that the GCBT condition ($n = 23$) was efficacious relative to a waitlist control condition ($n = 20$) in reducing children's anxiety disorders (i.e. overanxious disorder, separation anxiety disorder and social phobia) (aged 7 to 14 years). More specifically, results indicated that the percentage of children who no longer met DSM–III–R criteria for any anxiety disorder was significantly more for children in the GCBT condition (64.8%) than for children in the waitlist condition (25.2%). Barrett (1998) also included an additional parental involvement condition similar to that used in Barrett et al. (1996). That is, there was an experimental treatment condition in which children received not only cognitive–behavioural treatment but also parents received training in interacting with their children during displays of child anxiety, managing child emotional upsets and communicating and problem-solving skills ($n = 17$). Although results indicated that the additional parental involvement/training did not create a significant difference in recovery rate between the two treatment conditions at post-treatment, at 12-month follow-up, a significant difference was obtained with 64.5% of children in GCBT and 84.8% of children in GCBT plus parental involvement/training being diagnosis free.

Silverman et al. (1999) recently reported the results of another randomized clinical trial that provided further empirical evidence for the efficacy of GCBT to treat anxiety disorders in children. To establish the therapeutic efficacy of the intervention in maintaining as well as producing treatment gains, participants were randomly assigned to conditions with an assignment ratio of 2 to 1 (GCBT to control). Thus, of the 56 children (34 boys, 22 girls; 6–16 years old; average age 9.96 years) and parents who participated in the study, 37 (67%) of the participants were assigned to GCBT and 19 (33%) to the waitlist. Inclusion criteria were primary DSM–III–R diagnosis of either social phobia, overanxious disorder or generalized anxiety disorder. Children and parents attended separate but concurrent groups (conducted by two separate therapists). Parallel content was presented in the child and parent sessions (see Silverman & Kurtines, 1996*a* for details).

Findings indicated that GCBT was efficacious relative to the waitlist condition. For example, 64% of the cases in GCBT were recovered at post-treatment; only 12.5% were recovered in the waitlist condition. This pattern of improvement (from pre- to post-test) was also observed for the clinician ratings of severity, as well for the child- and parent-completed anxiety measures and additional parent ratings. In addition, using hierarchical linear models (Byrk & Raudenbush, 1987), the pattern for all the child- and parent-completed measures similarly indicated a continued reduction in degree and severity of anxious symptoms from post-treatment to 3-month follow-up, with improvement levelling off at that time but still being maintained at 6 and 12-month follow-up.

Flannery-Schroeder & Kendall (in press) provided further evidence for the efficacy of GCBT in treating children (aged 8–14 years) who met DSM–IV criteria for a primary diagnosis of generalized anxiety disorder, separation anxiety disorder or social phobia. The children met weekly in groups and the parents had occasional individual meetings with the therapists so that: therapists could learn more about the child's anxious behaviours and activities/ progress throughout the programme; and parents could be kept abreast of what was occurring in the child sessions. This study, which also included an ICBT condition ($n = 13$), showed that GCBT ($n = 12$) was generally comparable in efficacy to ICBT, and that both treatment conditions were superior to the waitlist control condition ($n = 12$).

Moving beyond the use of waitlist control designs

As we have noted, all of the clinical trials summarized in the preceding sections, both individual (Barrett et al., 1996; Kendall, 1994; Kendall et al., 1997; King et al., 1998) and group (Barrett, 1998; Cobham et al., 1998; Flannery-Schroeder & Kendall, in press; Silverman et al., 1999a), evaluated the efficacy of cognitive–behaviour therapy relative to a waitlist control condition. The waitlist design is widely used and controls for many of the challenges to internal validity, such as history, maturation and cohort effects (Campbell & Stanley, 1963). It is clear from these waitlist design studies that anxiety disorders in children do not improve with the passage of time. What is not clear from these studies, however, is how children in more active and credible control conditions would fare.

Two studies (Last, Hansen & Franco; 1998; Silverman et al., 1999b) recently examined this issue by using, not a waitlist condition as the comparison control, but an 'education support' condition. In both studies, education support was designed to match the experimental treatment conditions with respect to the organization, length of sessions, and duration of treatment. Education support also was designed to control for 'nonspecific' therapy effects (i.e. therapists' support, the client–therapist relationship) and for providing information about phobias and anxiety in a therapeutic context. In addition, although the education support conditions included sessions in which various treatment approaches for phobias and anxiety disorders (e.g. psychodynamic therapy, behaviour therapy) were explained to participants, in contrast to the experimental treatment conditions, education support did not contain therapist prescribed in-session or out-of-session exposures. Education support also did not contain therapists' prescriptions for any other behavioural or cognitive strategy.

Last et al. (1998) reported the results of a clinical trial of the efficacy of ICBT ($n = 32$) relative to education support ($n = 24$) in treating children and adolescents with school phobia (aged 6 to 17 years). Results indicated that both the ICBT and education support conditions were equally efficacious in returning children to school. Both conditions also were efficacious in reducing children's anxiety and depressive symptoms on self-rating scales. In addition, at the time of new school year re-entry, 40% of the treatment completers in ICBT reported having no difficulty returning to school the following school year, 30% were rated as having 'mild difficulty', 10% were rated as having 'moderate difficulty', and 20% were rated as having 'extreme difficulty'. For the education support condition, 52% of treatment completers were rated as having no difficulty returning to school the following school year, 19% were rated as having 'mild difficulty', 5% were rated as having 'moderate difficulty', and 24% were rated as having 'extreme difficulty'. In addition, at 4-week follow-up ($n = 29$), there were no significant differences between conditions as measured by school attendance. Across the ICBT and educational support conditions, 15 maintained their improvements, four continued to improve, two declined in attendance, and eight never improved from pre to post to follow-up.

A more recent study by Silverman et al. (1999b), provides additional support for the need to move beyond the use of waitlist controls and to begin to use other types of control conditions. Specifically, this study evaluated the efficacy of an individually focused exposure-based psychosocial intervention that used either cognitive or behavioural treatment procedures. For this study, children with phobic disorders and their parents were randomly assigned to one of three conditions, two experimental exposure-based treatment conditions: (1) contingency management, or (2) self-control; or (3) the comparison control condition, education support. In the contingency management condition procedures focused on modifying or rearranging parents' use of contingencies (e.g. reinforcement, extinction) as they relate to child phobic/avoidance behaviours. In the self-control condition, procedures focused on modifying or improving child self-regulation skills (e.g. self-observation, self-reward) as they relate to child phobic behaviours/avoidance behaviours. Hence these two conditions may be viewed as a 'dismantling' of the cognitive–behavioural 'package' used in ICBT (and GCBT).

A total of 104 children and their parents were recruited into the study, 54 were boys and 50 were girls (aged 6 to 16 years; average age = 9.83 years). All children met criteria for a primary DSM–III–R diagnosis for phobic disorder, with the majority meeting criteria for simple phobia ($n = 87$), and the remainder meeting criteria for social phobia ($n = 10$), and agoraphobia ($n = 7$), using the ADIS-C/P. Because a main goal of the study was to investigate the relative efficacy of contingency management and self-control, and because education support was primarily designed to serve as a comparison control condition, a strategy of proportional random assignment was used to maximize the size of the two experimental treatment condition samples. Thus, 41 children were assigned to the contingency management treatment condition, 40 to the self-control treatment condition and 23 to the education support control condition.

Outcome was evaluated in terms of diagnostic recovery rates and clinician, child and parent ratings. As expected, both experimental conditions produced significant treatment gains (time effects) and there were no significant differences between conditions. This was the case across all the main outcome measures across all sources. For example, both conditions produced significant treatment gains pre to post on the structured diagnostic measure and there were no consistent significant differences between the conditions over the multiple assessment periods (post-3-, 6-, 12-month follow-ups). In addition, results using hierarchical linear models showed that all the child and parent completed measures displayed a similar pattern of significant treatment gains pre to post and no significant interactions between the conditions over the multiple assessment points. The results thus indicated that both the contingency management and self-control conditions were efficacious in treating child phobias.

With respect to education support, the findings were similar to those obtained with the two experimental treatment conditions (i.e. contingency management and self-control). That is, a pattern of significant gains followed by maintenance was observed across all the indices of change and across all the child, parent and clinician ratings. Thus, all three conditions were similarly efficacious in improving phobic disorders in children.

Unresolved issues and future directions

The empirical studies reviewed in the preceding section provide evidence that cognitive behaviour therapy, used in either an individual or group treatment format, is efficacious in reducing anxiety disorders in children. The evidence from these studies further suggests that the efficacy of cognitive and behavioural treatment can be enhanced by involving parents (to work on managing their children's anxiety as well as the parents' own anxiety). Although the knowledge that has been garnered from these studies is considerable, there remain many unresolved issues that require addressing in future research. In this section, we highlight issues that we view as particularly important, and that are beginning to be investigated, either by ourselves or others.

Investigating education support and determining mechanisms of change

In both the Last et al. (1998) and Silverman et al. (1999b) studies, finding the education support comparison group to be efficacious was unexpected. It was unexpected because the education support condition was primarily designed to control for 'nonspecific' therapy effects (i.e. weekly meetings with a therapist who provided therapeutic support) and for providing information about phobias and anxiety in a therapeutic context. Moreover, the education support condition did not contain any in-session exposures or therapist-prescribed out-of-session exposures, or any other therapist-prescribed behavioural or cognitive strategy. As a consequence, a condition such as education support was expected to show little, if any, efficacy. The fact that it was found to be similarly efficacious as the experimental treatment conditions is intriguing.

Although the findings are intriguing with respect to the education support condition, speculation on their meaning and significance requires first that the findings be replicated and that their robustness under differing conditions be established. For example, both the Last et al. (1998) and Silverman et al. (1999b) studies targeted phobic disorders. It would seem worthwhile to investigate the efficacy of an education support condition relative to a treatment condition that targets both anxiety and phobic disorders. In addition, both Last et al. and Silverman et al. used individual treatment formats. Whether education support is also efficacious in a group treatment format would be useful to know.

That Silverman et al. (1999b) also found that both the contingency management and the self-control conditions were efficacious speaks more generally for the need for further research that systematically investigates potential variables that moderate or mediate positive outcome. Investigating this issue is important as a way to begin to determine the mechanism(s) of therapeutic change. For example, although contingency management, self-control conditions and education support in Silverman et al. (1999b) were all found to have high treatment credibility and to have been delivered with integrity, no direct effort was made to examine nonspecific therapy effects (e.g. therapist warmth and support), prescribed 'active' ingredients (e.g. number of in-session and out-of-session exposures in the contingency management and self-control conditions, changing of thoughts in the self-control condition, parental use of rewards in the contingency management condition), nonprescribed 'active' ingredients (e.g. self-directed out-of-session exposures in the education support condition, changing of thoughts in the contingency management condition, parental use of rewards in the self-control condition) that could account for the positive changes observed. Taken all together, it would seem important for future researchers to further investigate the role of credibility, nonspecific factors and utilization of intervention strategies (prescribed and nonprescribed) in child anxiety psychosocial interventions. We are beginning to launch another clinical trial to investigate these issues.

Predicting treatment outcome

As part of the effort to improve the overall efficacy of psychosocial interventions for use with children with anxiety disorders, it is important to determine predictors of treatment success or failure (Kazdin & Kendall, 1998). According to March & Curry (1998) knowledge of the variables that predict successful treatment outcome might lead to tailoring interventions that meet the specific set of circumstances for children and their families. Similarly, knowledge of the variables that predict poor treatment outcome might lead to further research into how treatment efficacy can be improved under those specific circumstances. Using childhood anxiety disorders as a case in point, March & Curry (1998) suggested a matrix of predictor variables worthy of investigation, including sociodemographics, severity of disorder, comorbidity, parental psychopathology and family functioning.

As far as we know, there have been no studies that have directly and systematically examined a wide range of potential predictors of treatment outcome for children with anxiety disorders. A small number of studies have attempted to identify specific predictors; however, they have had limited success. Kendall (1994), for example, examined children's perceptions of the therapeutic relationship and therapists' perceptions of parental involvement as predictors of successful treatment outcome. Neither variable was found to be related to outcome. Treadwell, Flannery-Schroeder & Kendall (1995) found that neither gender nor ethnicity were related to treatment outcome. Likewise, Kendall et al. (1997) found that age and comorbidity of diagnoses were both unrelated to treatment outcome. Barrett et al. (1996), on the other hand, found that both age and gender significantly interacted with treatment condition: younger children responded better than older children to ICBT plus the family management component than to ICBT alone, and girls responded better than boys to ICBT plus the family management component than to ICBT alone.

We (Berman et al., in press) recently systematically examined a full range of potential predictors of treatment outcome for anxiety disorders in children using the data from Silverman et al. (1999a,b). More specifically, we examined a number of sociodemographic and psychosocial variables that have been identified in previous child treatment research studies (not just childhood anxiety) (Brent et al., 1998; Kazdin, 1989, 1995; Kazdin & Crowley, 1997; Webster-Stratton, 1996; Webster-Stratton & Hammond, 1990), as well as variables that were relevant to the particulars of our clinical trials. These variables included: children's sociodemographics, diagnostic characteristics (e.g. number of diagnoses), treatment format (i.e. individual, group), child symptoms assessed from the perspective of the child and parent (e.g. anxiety, fear), parent symptoms and marital adjustment. The best predictor of treatment outcome was parental depression. Other parental symptoms (e.g. fear, hostility) and children's self-ratings of depression and trait anxiety also were significant predictors of treatment outcome. Predictors of outcome were not moderated by age, gender or treatment format.

It would seem important to have these findings replicated by other clinical researchers. If replicated, they would suggest several avenues by which psychosocial interventions for use with children with anxiety disorders might be modified to improve their efficacy. One avenue, for example, might be to target both depression and anxiety when both problems are comorbid in a child (Kendall et al., 1992). A second avenue, is one that we have already mentioned in this chapter; namely, the targeting of parental pathology as well as the child's. It also would seem important to extend the search for other theoretically or empirically relevant variables that may moderate treatment efficacy.

Prescribing treatments

Although randomizing treatment across participants is an excellent experimental mechanism to evaluate treatment effectiveness, clinical researchers are beginning to recognize the importance of matching or prescribing treatment to specific patient characteristics (e.g. Beutler, 1991; Kazdin, 1993; Kearney & Silverman, 1990; Ost, Jerremalm & Johansson, 1981; Ost, Johansson & Jerremalm, 1982). In treating generalized anxiety in children, for example, Eisen & Silverman (1993, 1998) provided preliminary evidence suggesting that a prescriptive approach may be useful. Using a multiple baseline design across participants, Eisen & Silverman (1998) systematically prescribed specific cognitive–behavioural interventions, cognitive therapy and relaxation training, to different problematic response classes (i.e. cognitive and somatic). Participants were four overanxious children (aged 8 to 12 years) who were randomly assigned to experimental and control conditions. Experimental participants received five weeks of prescriptive treatment (i.e. cognitive therapy for worry symptoms; relaxation therapy for somatic symptoms). Control participants, on the other hand, first received 5 weeks of nonprescriptive treatment (i.e. relaxation therapy for worry symptoms; cognitive therapy for somatic symptoms), followed by 5 weeks of prescriptive treatment. Children with a problematic response class that was primarily cognitive, responded most favourably to cognitive therapy; children with a problematic response class that was primarily somatic, responded most favourably to relaxation therapy.

Similar evidence for a functional approach to prescribing treatment has recently appeared for children with school refusal behaviour (Kearney & Silverman, 1990, 1999), a population which, as noted earlier, displays high rates of phobic and anxiety disorders (Last & Strauss, 1990). A functional approach emphasizes the identification of several 'motivating variables'. In terms of school refusal behaviour, Kearney & Silverman suggested that child refusal to attend school may be maintained by at least one of the following functions: (1) avoidance of stimuli provoking specific fearfulness or generalized anxiety, (2) escape from aversive social or evaluative situations, (3) attention-getting behaviour, analogous to traditional externalizing symptoms of separation anxiety, such as tantruming, and (4) positive tangible reinforcement analogous to truant behaviour, or preferring to stay home and play, or avoid school, for reasons other than fear or anxiety. The former two variables refer to school refusal behaviour controlled by negative reinforcement while the latter two are controlled by positive reinforcement. Identification of a child's motivating condition(s) for school refusal behaviour can be accomplished by using the School Refusal Assessment Scale (Kearney & Silverman, 1993). After such identification, a specific psychosocial intervention that 'fits' one of the four functional categories can be assigned and implemented, i.e. 'prescribed'.

Kearney & Silverman (1990) provided preliminary support for functionally based prescriptive treatment in six of seven cases of school refusal. Kearney &

Silverman (1999) provided incremental evidence for functionally based pre-scriptive treatment using a lagged, multiple baseline design study in eight children and adolescents. Functionally based prescriptive treatment was found to be more efficacious relative to nonprescriptive treatment in returning children to school and in reducing the children's internalizing and externalizing behaviour problems.

Despite the preliminary evidence for adopting an idiographic, prescriptive approach to treat anxiety disorders and/or school refusal behaviour in children, either through the identification of problematic response classes or motivating conditions, evidence is needed that the former is more efficacious than a nomothetic, statistically based approach (e.g. Barlow, Hayes & Nelson, 1984). Thus, it would seem important for future research to compare the relative efficacy of an idiographic, prescriptive approach to a 'cognitive behavioural package', similar to those used in the ICBT and GCBT studies. Examining this issue would be an important step toward helping children with anxiety dis-orders.

Involving peers

Peer relations play an extremely important role in children's social and emo-tional development. It is via peer interactions that children learn important social skills, such as how to share and take turns, how to interact with others on an equal basis, and how to place the concerns of others before their own (see La Greca, chapter 7, this volume). There is evidence that children with social phobia not only display significant impairment on a variety of paper-and-pencil measures but also have significantly poorer social skills than children without psychiatric disorders (Beidel, Turner & Morris, 1999; Spence, Donovan & Brechman-Toussaint, 1999). Problematic peer relationships (stemming in part from poor social skills) can contribute to phobic and anxiety disorders in children (Ginsburg, La Greca & Silverman, 1998).

It thus would seem important that as we look toward enhancing treatment efficacy for anxiety disorders in children that one important direction to take is the development of psychosocial interventions that include, not only the 'standard' cognitive–behavioural treatment procedures, but peer interactions and social skills training. This would seem particularly important to do in the context of working with social phobia in light of the evidence noted above. The group treatments described earlier are examples of such interventions.

Beidel and colleagues' (Beidel, Turner & Morris, 1994) Social Effectiveness Training for Children (SET-C) is another example. Designed specifically for use with children with social phobia, SET-C, is a 12-week intervention that contains two sessions per week. One session involves individualized exposure to social situations that provoke fear or anxiety in the child. The second session involves group social skills training. In addition, generalizability of the social skills training is paired with a peer generalization session where the socially phobic children have opportunities to interact with 'outgoing' peers in natural settings (bowling alleys, pizza parlours, museums). An evaluation of SET-C group has provided positive and encouraging evidence for its efficacy (Deborah Beidel, personal communication, June 21, 1999). It would seem important to further examine the efficacy of SET-C, and as is true with all the interventions discussed in this chapter, to begin to examine the issue of effectiveness.

Extending efficacy to effectiveness

Although the studies summarized in the beginning of this chapter provide evidence for the interventions' efficacy, it has been proposed by several authors that empirically supported treatments be used in community clinics (Weisz et al., 1995). This has been proposed because available evidence suggests that treatments received in community clinics are not effective (Weiss et al., 1999; Weisz et al., 1995). It has been argued therefore that the use of empirically supported treatments might improve the outcomes of clinic-referred youth. However, it remains an empirical question if the evidence based psychosocial interventions that have been described in this chapter also will 'work' (i.e. be 'effective') in clinic settings in light of the differences that exist in research versus community clinics (e.g. different therapists, conditions, clientele, etc.).

Weisz and his colleagues are currently investigating the clinical effectiveness of evidence based manualized psychosocial interventions as part of the Youth Anxiety and Depression Study at the University of California at Los Angeles, U.S. (Michael Southam-Gerow and John Weisz, personal communication, May 26, 1999). Relevant to this chapter, is their evaluation of ICBT for youth with anxiety disorders (e.g. Kendall, 1994). The Youth Anxiety and Depression Study will extend the findings of the efficacy studies by examining the effectiveness of ICBT with clinic-referred youth, treated in community clinics by clinic staff or clinic trainees (e.g. social work interns, psychology interns). About 260 youth (ages 8 to 15) who present at one of three large Los Angeles county community clinics and who are diagnosed with one of three anxiety disorders (separation anxiety disorder, social phobia or generalized anxiety disorder) are expected to participate. After completing an initial assessment, the treatment focus for the youth will be determined through the joint effort of the clinic, the project and the family.

Youth with anxiety as a primary problem will be assigned to the 'anxiety track' based on the youth's primary diagnosis at the intake interview (i.e. an anxiety disorder). Once assigned to the anxiety track, the youth will be randomly assigned to receive either the usual treatment in the clinic carried out by clinic staff or trainees supervised by clinic staff, or the manualized treatment, carried out by clinic staff or trainees trained to proficiency and supervised by experts in the programme. Staff and trainees will be randomly assigned to be either the usual care therapists or the manual group therapists. Client assessments will be carried out at four times: pre-treatment (intake), post-treatment, 15 months from intake and 2 years from intake. The assessments will include measures of (1) symptoms and diagnosis, (2) real-life functioning in social and school contexts, (3) consumer satisfaction and (4) system and service use (e.g. use of further mental health services) impact.

It will be several years before the findings of this study are available. When they are, they will provide important information about both the feasibility and generalizability of using empirically based, manualized, psychosocial interventions in community clinics.

Summary

This chapter reviewed the current status of the research literature on psychosocial interventions for use with children with anxiety disorders. The review indicates that considerable advances have been made in the knowledge base in terms of showing that cognitive–behavioural treatments, used in either an individual or group format, are efficacious in reducing anxiety disorders in children. That is, the treatments are more efficacious than not providing any treatment at all, i.e. a waitlist. Given the findings, however, that behavioural (i.e. contingency management) and cognitive (i.e. self-control) procedures were both efficacious in reducing children's phobic disorders (Silverman et al., 1999b) as well as the intriguing findings regarding education support (Last et al., 1998; Silverman et al., 1999b), in conjunction with the findings that participants felt that the therapeutic relationship was most important to their treatment (e.g. Kendall & Southam-Gerow, 1996), it is important that further work be done to examine 'what' it is about the current psychosocial interventions that lead to their efficacy in reducing children's phobias and anxiety disorders. Also important are further investigations into how efficacy can be enhanced (at post-treatment and at follow-ups) by involving others (e.g. parents, peers) in the treatment process (e.g. Barrett et al., 1996; Beidel et al., 1999).

Also important is to examine what it is about the children and families that lead them to use and/or benefit from the current interventions. The research on predictors of outcome provides some initial suggestions (Berman et al., in press). Future investigations on such issues as the role of credibility, nonspecific factors, and child (and parent) *actual* utilization of specific strategies included (or not included) in psychosocial interventions (e.g. cognitive, behavioural, education support, etc.) should further help inform us about this issue. Also of help will be further research on 'matching', or prescribing specific types of interventions to specific patterns of child/parent characteristics, such as problematic response classes or motivating conditions (e.g. Eisen & Silverman, 1998; Kearney & Silverman, 1999). Finally, as attention shifts from efficacy to effectiveness, the field is positioning itself as being even more likely to more fully help the children and families who present themselves for mental health services in the future.

REFERENCES

Barabasz, A. (1973). Group desensitization of test anxiety in elementary schools. *Journal of Psychology*, **83**, 295–301.

Barlow, D. H., Hayes, S. C. & Nelson, R. O. (1984). *The Scientist Practitioner: Research and Accountability in Clinical and Educational Settings*. New York: Pergamon Press.

Barrett, P. M. (1998). Evaluation of cognitive–behavioral group treatments for childhood anxiety disorders. *Journal of Clinical Child Psychology*, **27**, 459–68.

Barrett, P. M., Dadds, M. R. & Rapee, R. M. (1996). Family treatment of childhood anxiety: A controlled trial. *Journal of Consulting and Clinical Psychology*, **64**, 333–42.

Beidel, D. C., Turner, S. M. & Morris, T. L. (1994). *Social Effectiveness Therapy for Children: A Treatment Manual*. Charleston: Medical University of South Carolina.

Beidel, D. C., Turner, S. M. & Morris, T. L. (1999). Psychopathology of childhood social phobia. *Journal of the American Academy of Child and Adolescent Psychiatry*, **38**, 643–50.

Berman S. L., Weems, C. F., Silverman, W. K. & Kurtines, W. M. (in press). Predictors of outcome in exposure-based cognitive and behavioral treatments for phobic and anxiety disorders in children. *Behavior Therapy*.

Beutler, L. E. (1991). Have all won and must all have prizes? Revisiting Luborsky et al.'s verdict. *Journal of Consulting and Clinical Psychology*, **59**, 226–32.

Brent, D. A., Kolko, D. J., Birmaher, B., et al. (1998). Predictors of treatment efficacy in a clinical trial of three psychosocial treatments for adolescent depression. *Journal of the American Academy of Child and Adolescent Psychiatry*, **37**, 906–14.

Byrk, A. S. & Raudenbush, S. W. (1987). Application of hierarchical linear models to assessing change. *Psychological Bulletin*, **101**, 147–58.

Campbell, D. R. & Stanley, J. C. (1963). *Experimental and Quasi-Experimental Designs for Research*. New York: Rand McNally.

Chiodos, J. & Maddux, J. E. (1985). A cognitive and behavioral approach to anxiety management of retarded individuals: Two case studies. *Journal of Child and Adolescent Psychotherapy*, **2**, 16–20.

✕ Cobham, V. E., Dadds, M. R. & Spence, S. H. (1998). The role of parental anxiety in the treatment of childhood anxiety. *Journal of Consulting and Clinical Psychology*, **66**, 893–905.

Deffenbacher, J. L. & Kemper, C. C. (1974a). Counseling test-anxious sixth graders. *Elementary School Guidance and Counseling*, **7**, 22–9.

Deffenbacher, J. L. & Kemper, C. C. (1974b). Systematic desensitization of test anxiety in junior high students. *The School Counselor*, **21**, 216–22.

Eisen, A. R. & Silverman, W. K. (1991). Treatment of an adolescent with bowel movement phobia using self-control therapy. *Journal of Behavior Therapy and Experimental Psychiatry*, **22**, 45–51.

Eisen, A. R. & Silverman, W. K. (1993). Should I relax or change my thoughts?: A preliminary study of the treatment of Overanxious Disorder in children. *Journal of Cognitive Psychotherapy: An International Quarterly*, **7**, 265–80.

Eisen, A. R. & Silverman, W. K. (1998). Prescriptive treatment for generalized anxiety disorder in children. *Behavior Therapy*, **29**, 105–21.

Flannery-Schroeder, E. & Kendall, P. C. (in press). Group versus individual cognitive behavioral treatment for youth with anxiety disorders: A randomized clinical trial. *Cognitive Therapy and Research*.

Ginsburg, G. S., La Greca, A. M. & Silverman, W. K. (1998). Social anxiety in children with anxiety disorders: Relation with social and emotional functioning. *Journal of Abnormal Child Psychology*, **26**, 175–85.

Ginsburg, G. S., Silverman, W. K. & Kurtines, W. M. (1995a). Family involvement in treating children with phobic and anxiety disorders: A look ahead. *Clinical Psychology Review*, **15**, 457–73.

Ginsburg, G. S., Silverman, W. K. & Kurtines, W. M. (1995b). Cognitive-behavioral group therapy. In *Clinical Handbook of Anxiety Disorders in Children and Adolescents*, ed. A. R. Eisen, C. A. Kearney & C. E. Schafer, pp. 521–49. Washington, DC: American Psychological Association.

Kane, M. T. & Kendall, P. C. (1989). Anxiety disorders in children: A multiple baseline evaluation of a cognitive behavioral treatment. *Behavior Therapy*, **20**, 499–508.

Kazdin, A. E. (1993). Psychotherapy for children and adolescents: Current progress and future research directions. *American Psychologist*, **48**, 644–57.

Kazdin, A. E. (1995). Child, parent and family dysfunction as predictors of outcome in cognitive–behavioral treatment of antisocial children. *Behaviour Research and Therapy*, **33**, 271–81.

Kazdin, A. E. & Crowley, M. J. (1997). Moderators of treatment outcome in cognitively based treatment of antisocial children. *Cognitive Therapy and Research*, **21**, 185–207.

Kazdin, A. E. & Kendall, P. C. (1998). Current progress and future plans for developing effective treatments: Comments and perspectives. *Journal of Clinical Child Psychology*, **27**, 217–26.

Kazdin, A. E., Siegel, T. C. & Bass, D. (1990). Drawing on clinical practice to inform research on child and adolescent psychotherapy: Survey of practitioners. *Professional Psychology: Research & Practice*, **21**, 189–98.

Kearney, C. A. & Silverman, W. K. (1990). A preliminary analysis of a functional model of assessment and treatment for school refusal behavior. *Behavior Modification*, **14**, 340–66.

Kearney, C. A. & Silverman, W. K. (1993). Measuring the function of school refusal behavior: The school refusal assessment scale. *Journal of Clinical Child Psychology*, **22**, 85–96.

Kearney, C. A. & Silverman, W. K. (1999). Functionally-based prescriptive and nonprescriptive treatment for children and adolescents with school refusal behavior. *Behavior Therapy*, **30**, 673–95.

Kendall, P. C. (1994). Treating anxiety disorders in children: Results of a randomized clinical trial. *Journal of Consulting and Clinical Psychology*, **62**, 100–10.

Kendall, P. C., Flannery- Schroeder, E., Panichelli-Mindel, S. M., Southam-Gerow, M., Henin, A. & Warman, M. (1997). Therapy for youths with anxiety disorders: A second randomized clinical trial. *Journal of Consulting and Clinical Psychology*, **65**, 366–80.

Kendall, P. C., Kortlander, E., Chansky, T. E. & Brady, E. U. (1992). Comorbidity of anxiety and depression in youth: Treatment implications. *Journal of Consulting and Clinical Psychology*, **60**, 869–80.

Kendall, P. C. & Southam-Gerow, M. A. (1996). Long-term follow-up of a cognitive-behavioral therapy for anxiety-disordered youth. *Journal of Consulting and Clinical Psychology*, **64**, 724–30.

King, N. J. & Ollendick, T. H. (1997). Treatment of childhood phobias. *Journal of Child Psychology and Psychiatry and Allied Disciplines*, **38**, 389–400.

King, N. J., Tonge, B. J., Heyne, D., et al. (1998). Cognitive–behavioral treatment of school-refusing children: A controlled evaluation. *Journal of the American Academy of Child and Adolescent Psychiatry*, **37**, 395–403.

Last, C. G., Hansen, C. & Franco, N. (1998). Cognitive–behavioral treatment of school phobia. *Journal of the American Academy of Child and Adolescent Psychiatry*, **37**, 404–11.

Last, C. G. & Strauss, C. C. (1990). School refusal in anxiety-disordered children and adolescents. *Journal of the American Academy of Child and Adolescent Psychiatry*, **29**, 31–5.

Mann, J. & Rosenthal, T. L. (1969). Vicarious and direct counter conditioning of test anxiety in group desensitization. *Behaviour Research and Therapy*, **7**, 359–67.

March, J. S. & Curry, J. E. (1998). Predicting the outcome of treatment. *Journal of Abnormal Child Psychology*, **26**, 39–51.

Morris, R. J. & Kratochwill, T. R. (ed.) (1998). *The Practice of Child Therapy*. Boston: Allyn & Bacon.

Ollendick, T. H. (1995). Cognitive behavioral treatment of panic disorder with agoraphobia in adolescents: A multiple baseline design analysis. *Behavior Therapy*, **26**, 517–31.

Ost, L. G., Jerremalm, A. & Johansson, J. (1981). Individual response patterns and the effects of different behavioral methods in the treatment of social phobia. *Behaviour Research and Therapy*, **19**, 1–16.

Ost, L. G., Johansson, J. & Jerremalm, A. (1982). Individual response patterns and the effects of different behavioral methods in the treatment of claustrophobia. *Behaviour Research and Therapy*, **20**, 445–60.

Reynolds C. R. & Richmond B. O. (1985). *Revised Children's Manifest Anxiety Scale (RCMAS) Manual*. Los Angeles: Western Psychological Services.

Silverman, W. K. & Ginsburg, G. S. (1998). Anxiety disorders. In *Handbook of Child and Adolescent Psychopathology*, ed. T. H. Ollendick & M. Hersen, pp. 239–68. New York: Plenum Press.

Silverman, W. K. & Kurtines, W. M. (1996a). *Anxiety and Phobic Disorders: A Pragmatic Approach.* New York: Plenum Press.

Silverman, W. K. & Kurtines, W. M. (1996b). Transfer of control: A psychosocial intervention model for internalizing disorders in youth. In *Psychosocial Treatments for Child and Adolescent Disorders: Empirically Based Strategies for Clinical Practice*, ed. E. D. Hibbs & P. S. Jensen, pp. 63–81. Washington, DC: American Psychological Association.

Silverman, W. K., Kurtines, W. M., Ginsburg, G. S., Weems, C. F., Lumpkin, P. W. & Carmichael, D. H. (1999a). Treating anxiety disorders in children with group cognitive–behavior therapy: A randomized clinical trial. *Journal of Consulting and Clinical Psychology*, **67**, 995–1003.

Silverman, W. K., Kurtines, W. M., Ginsburg, G. S., Weems, C. F., Rabian, B. & Serafini, L. T. (1999b). Contingency management, self-control, and education support in the treatment of childhood phobic disorders: A randomized clinical trial. *Journal of Consulting and Clinical Psychology*, **67**, 675–87.

Silverman, W. K. & Nelles, W. B. (1988). The Anxiety Disorders Interview Schedule for Children. *Journal of the American Academy of Child and Adolescent Psychiatry*, **27**, 772–8.

Speilberger, C. D., Gorsuch, R. L. & Lushene, R. E. (1970). *Manual for the State-Trait Anxiety Inventory.* Palo Alto, CA: Consulting Psychologists Press.

Spence, S. H., Donovan, C. & Brechman-Toussaint, M. (1999). Social skills, social outcomes, and cognitive features of childhood social phobia. *Journal of Abnormal Psychology*, **108**, 211–21.

Treadwell, K. R., Flannery-Shroeder, E. C. & Kendall, P. C. (1995). Ethnicity and gender in relation to adaptive functioning, diagnostic status, and treatment outcome in children from an anxiety clinic. *Journal of Anxiety Disorders*, **9**, 373–84.

Webster-Stratton, C. (1996). Early-onset conduct problems: Does gender make a difference? *Journal of Consulting and Clinical Psychology*, **64**, 540–51.

Webster-Stratton, C. & Hammond, M. (1990). Predictors of treatment outcome in parent training for families with conduct problem children. *Behavior Therapy*, **21**, 319–37.

Weiss, B., Catron, T., Harris, V. & Phung, T. M. (1999). The effectiveness of traditional child psychotherapy. *Journal of Consulting and Clinical Psychology*, **67**, 82–94.

Weisz, J. R., Donenberg, G. R., Han, S. S. & Weiss, B. (1995). Bridging the gap between lab and clinic in child and adolescent psychotherapy. *Journal of Consulting and Clinical Psychology*, **63**, 688–701.

15

Pharmacological treatment of paediatric anxiety

Saundra L. Stock, John S. Werry and Jon M. McClellan

Introduction

Anxiety is a universal human experience associated with the anticipation of danger (Allen, Leonard & Swedo, 1995). It can be an adaptive trait which serves as a protective response to environmental stressors or potential threats. Children and adolescents typically experience anxiety at predictable points in their development as they attempt to negotiate normal developmental hurdles. Mastery of this anxiety and related fears gives rise to more adaptive defence mechanisms resulting in new areas of competency and a decrease in anxiety levels. However, if the anxiety is persistent, or causes intense distress, it may represent symptoms of psychiatric or other medical illnesses.

Anxiety generally presents as an uncomfortable emotional state associated with feelings of uneasiness and apprehension. Physical manifestations include palpitations, subjective shortness of breath, dizziness, tremor, flushing, perspiration and nausea. Anxious youth may also display other problems, including restlessness, decreased concentration, impulsivity, tantrums and aggression. An anxiety disorder is diagnosed when persistent, intense anxiety predominates, and is associated with significant impairment and distress. Anxiety disorders are the most prevalent psychiatric illnesses in children and adolescents. Symptoms of anxiety may be quite persistent and are associated with significant academic and social problems (Ialongo et al., 1994, 1995; AACAP, 1997). At least one-third of youth with one anxiety disorder have two or more anxiety disorders (AACAP, 1997). Anxiety disorders are also associated with mood and behaviour disorders, including major depression and attention-deficit hyperactivity disorder. Therefore, any child with significant anxiety symptoms needs to have a thorough psychiatric assessment. Treatment planning needs to account for both the primary anxiety problem, as well as other comorbid disorders.

The main focus of this review is the pharmacological treatment of anxiety. Medications may be used to treat anxiety whether or not it occurs as part of a distinct psychiatric condition. Sedative-hypnotic medications are the class of agents traditionally referred to as anxiolytics. However, other medications, including antidepressants, buspirone and antihistamines are also used to treat anxiety disorders. We will outline the indications, prescribing guidelines and pharmacology of these agents below.

Nonpharmacologic interventions, such as behavioural modifications (e.g. improved sleep hygiene, deep breathing, relaxation), are often effective in treating anxiety states and are generally preferred over medications when treating children and adolescents. Cognitive–behavioural therapy or other forms of psychotherapy also help reduce anxiety symptoms that occur as part of a psychiatric disorder. In general, medications are not recommended as the sole treatment of anxiety disorders, but rather are considered adjunctive agents to psychosocial interventions (AACAP, 1997).

Pharmacology

Prior to discussing specific agents, we will review pertinent issues and definitions related to the pharmacological properties of psychotropic agents.

Mechanisms of drug action

Psychotropic agents produce their effects via a multitude of complex biochemical mechanisms that influence neurochemical systems within the brain (Paxton & Dragunow, 1993). Specific issues related to the neurobiology of anxiolytic agents are reviewed below. Brain activity is dependent upon the electrical activity of nerve cells (neurons), and is regulated by processes which either increase (excitation) or decrease (inhibition) of neuronal firing. Neurotransmitters are specific chemicals produced and released by nerve cells that cause excitation or inhibition in other neurons. The space between nerve cells into which neurotransmitters are secreted is called the synapse. There are many chemicals that act as neurotransmitters, including dopamine, serotonin, norepinephrine and γ-aminobutyric acid (GABA). Hormones, including corticotrophin releasing factor (CRF), adrenocorticotropic hormone (ACTH) and cortisol, also act as neurotransmitters and influence central nervous system activity.

Psychotropic agents influence brain functioning by a variety of mechanisms (Paxton & Dragunow, 1993). Some drugs act by binding to receptor molecules located on the nerve cells that are specific for a neurotransmitter, and mimic (agonist) and/or block (antagonist) the effects of neurotransmitters. Other drugs work by interacting with enzymes or receptors that break down, or inactivate, certain neurotransmitters, leading to changes in brain concentrations of that agent. Finally, some drugs influence the functioning of nerve cell membranes and ion channels. Ion channels regulate the passage of specific ions (e.g. sodium, potassium, and calcium across the cell membrane which influence the nerve cells' electrical activity (the firing mechanism) and the release of neurotransmitters).

Neurochemical systems within the brain do not operate in isolation. Rather, they are highly interdependent and complex. Therefore, the effects of psychotropic agents are due both to their immediate neurochemical impact, as well to the resultant changes in other brain systems.

Pharmacokinetics

Pharmacokinetics refers to the study of how drugs vary in their concentration at different sites in the body over time. This process is dependent on drug absorption, distribution and elimination (Paxton & Dragunow, 1993). The amount of drug available to the body depends on the dose, how it was administered (e.g. by mouth versus intravenously), and how well it was absorbed. Distribution reflects where the drug concentrates in the body. Lipophilic agents are fat-soluble, and are widely taken up by tissues in the body; while lipophobic agents, which are not fat-soluble, are generally confined to the interstitial fluid surrounding cells. Finally, elimination refers to the process by which drugs are removed from the body. This generally involves either the excretion of the drug by the kidneys (renal elimination), or the transformation of the drug into another agent by the liver (hepatic transformation). If the chemical created by hepatic transformation also has psychotropic effects, that agent is referred to as an active metabolite.

Psychotropic agents may be used in single doses to achieve immediate, short-term effects. However, when using medications to treat psychiatric disorders, the goal is generally to maintain therapeutic blood levels over prolonged periods of time in order to achieve the desired treatment response (Paxton & Dragunow, 1993). A steady state is achieved when the amount of drug being administered equals the amount being eliminated, thereby maintaining constant blood levels. A drug's half-life is the amount of time required for the plasma concentration of the drug to be reduced by half. In general, a steady state is reached after taking a drug for the period of approximately 4–5 half-lives.

Pharmacokinetics in children and adolescents

The pharmacokinetic properties of psychotropic agents may vary between youth and adults (Paxton & Dragunow, 1993). For the purposes of this review, we will focus on those differences noted with children and adolescents, and not discuss issues related to infants.

Absorption

The rate of drug absorption in children and adolescents appears similar to that for adults (Paxton & Dragunow, 1993).

Distribution

The distribution of medications in the body is dependent on the relative ratios of body fat and water. Since children tend to have less fat in comparison to adults, fat-soluble drugs will not be as widely distributed (Paxton & Dragunow, 1993).

Elimination

Children have high rates of hepatic metabolism, and generally will eliminate drugs faster than teenagers and adults (Paxton & Dragunow, 1993). Therefore, the ratio of drug dose to body weight is often higher in children. Children may also require multiple doses throughout the day to maintain therapeutic blood levels.

Neurobiology

Much of what is known about the biology of anxiety is derived from studies of anxiolytic medications. Many neurotransmitter systems and brain structures are involved, although precisely how they exert their effects and which ones are involved in what circumstances remains unclear. An excellent review of the neurobiology of anxiety, by Longo (1998), is recommended for further reading.

GABA system and benzodiazepines

γ-aminobutyric acid (GABA) is the prominent inhibitory neurotransmitter in the central nervous system (CNS) (Longo, 1998). Benzodiazepines, the main class of anxiolytic drugs, bind to the benzodiazepine receptor which is located in close proximity to the GABA receptor. When a benzodiazepine binds to its receptor, it causes a structural change in the GABA receptor which increases its affinity for binding GABA. The GABA receptor, once activated, opens chloride ion channels in the membrane of the neuron thereby decreasing the excitability of that neuron. Presumably anxiety is decreased through this process.

There are two main types of GABA receptors, $GABA_A$ and $GABA_B$ (Longo, 1998). Benzodiazepine receptors are linked primarily to the $GABA_A$ receptor subtype. GABA receptors are located throughout the brain and are thought to be present on up to one-third of all CNS neurons. The inhibitory effects of GABA modulate a number of other neurotransmitter systems, and benzodiazepines have been shown to decrease serotonin turnover, noradrenergic activity and dopamine function (Longo, 1998).

The precise role of GABA and the benzodiazepine receptor in the modulation of human anxiety is unclear (Longo, 1998). In animal models, benzodiazepines have significant effects on anxiety behaviours. Rats placed into an unfamiliar environment generally exhibit an initial reduction in exploratory behaviour. However, when treated with a benzodiazepine, rats do not limit their exploration. This behavioural response is not noted with other sedating medications that do not affect GABA, such as opioid analgesics and neuroleptics. Barbiturates (another category of medication which impact the benzodiazepine receptor) produce disinhibition of behaviour only at doses that also produce ataxia and sedation (a kind of drunkenness), rendering them less useful for clinical application (Hobbs, Rall & Veroorn, 1996)

Until recently the presence of the benzodiazepine receptor in the CNS was a mystery since no naturally occurring endogenous benzodiazepine had been discovered. An endogenous neuropeptide which binds to the benzodiazepine receptor has now been identified. Diazepam-binding inhibitor binds to the benzodiazepine receptor and activates it (Roy et al., 1989). This causes an increase in anxiety, an action described as an inverse agonist. A naturally occurring benzodiazepine receptor agonist has not been discovered and the function of the diazepam-binding inhibitor is not clear. Medications like benzodiazepines likely affect the function of the diazepam-binding inhibitor in the brain.

Serotonergic system

Serotonin (5-HT) is believed to have a role in anxiety since a number of agents which modulate serotonin metabolism and release have anxiolytic properties. Serotonergic neurons are located in the dorsal raphe nuclei of the brainstem and have complex connections in the brain to areas that modulate other neurotransmitters, such as norepinephrine and dopamine (Longo, 1998). There are more than 15 serotonin receptor subtypes currently identified, several of which play a role in anxiety production. Serotonin receptors are also located in a number of areas in the body besides the brain. Therefore, serotonin can have widespread effects in the body including causing blood vessel dilation, increased gut motility and smooth muscle contraction.

A number of medications known to affect anxiety have actions at serotonin receptor sites. Buspirone affects 5-HT_{1A} receptors. Monoamine oxidase inhibitors (MAOIs), tertiary tricyclic antidepressants (TCAs) and trazodone inhibit 5-HT$_{2A}$ receptors. Additionally, the long-term administration of selective serotonin reuptake inhibitors (SSRIs) and MAOIs desensitizes 5-HT$_{2C}$ receptors (Lucki, 1996). Animal models have shown that ondansetron, a 5-HT$_3$ receptor antagonist, may have anxiolytic effects as well. Benzodiazepines have been found to reduce the release of serotonin in human and animal models (Pei, Zetterstrom & Fillenz, 1989).

Noradrenergic system

The locus coeruleus, which is located in the brain stem, is the predominant site of norepinephrine neurons in the CNS. The noradrenergic system is responsible for the 'fight or flight' response to aversive or threatening stimuli. It receives innervation from many different locations and systems in the brain which modulate the secretion of norepinephrine (Longo, 1998). For example, GABA neurons innervate the locus coeruleus and inhibit the release of norepinephrine, a process that can be enhanced by benzodiazepine administration.

The noradrenergic system may be responsible for many of the physical manifestations of anxiety. Symptoms such as palpitations, tachycardia and sweating can be meditated through β-1 receptor stimulation and can be inhibited through α-2 receptors. Excessive norepinephrine release has been associated with panic attacks and there is some postulation that anxiety symptoms may reflect a dysregulation in the inhibitory actions of the presynaptic α-2 autoreceptors.

Studies of the neurobiology of anxiety have shown altered physiological responses to a one time dose of clonidine (which stimulates the α-2 receptors) in adults with panic disorder and generalized anxiety disorder (Abelson et al., 1991; Charney & Heninger, 1986) indicating a prominent role for this system in anxiety production. A similar study done in children recently reported by Sallee et al. (1998) failed to show the same response to a clonidine challenge in children with anxiety disorders. These results could indicate a difference in the contribution of norepinephrine in the neurobiological underpinnings of childhood anxiety disorders as compared to adults.

Excitatory amino acids

Excitatory amino acid neurotransmitters may have a role in anxiety modulation through connections with the locus coeruleus and by achieving a homeostatic balance with the GABA inhibitory system (Longo, 1998). Glutamate is the primary neuropeptide mediating excitatory responses in the CNS. Glutamate receptors work through opening ion channels which are widely distributed throughout the brain. Glutamate receptors display a wide array of heterogeneity and may be responsible for differing effects produced by this excitatory amino acid.

One glutamate receptor that has been studied recently is the N-methyl-D-aspartate (NDMA) receptor. When glutamate binds to the receptor, calcium ions flow into the cell and cause excitation of the neuron (Longo, 1998). NDMA antagonists have been shown to have similar effects as alcohol, including changes in discriminative stimuli interpretation, anxiolysis and anaesthetic effects. NDMA antagonists can also lessen the severity of alcohol withdrawal induced seizures. One drug that acts at the NDMA receptor to decrease excitatory amino acid activity is acamprosate (Longo 1998). It has been used successfully in Europe to treat alcoholism and is currently undergoing trials for approval in the United States. It is unclear whether this drug has any benefit for anxiety disorders.

Neuroendocrine effects

Stress and anxiety have been shown to impact the hypothalamic-pituitary-adrenocortical axis, altering hormonal regulation (Leonard & Song, 1996). Corticotrophin releasing factor (CRF) secretion is increased at the hypothalamus under stressful conditions. The concentration of dopaminergic and serotonergic substances in rat brains are increased by acute administration of CRF. Subchronic treatment with CRF (a situation of simulated chronic stress) increased norepinephrine, dopamine and 5-hydroindoleacetic acid in the hypothalamus of rat brains (Longo, 1998).

CRF containing neurons are located in other areas of the brain as well. The amygdala has been implicated in a variety of psychiatric disorders, including depression and anxiety, and contains a high number of CRF secreting neurons and CRF receptors (Longo, 1998). The amygdala also has broad connections, both afferent and efferent, to other structures and neurotransmitter systems in the brain. Electrical stimulation of the amygdala and CRF injections in rat brains have both resulted in behavioural, neuroendocrine and autonomic changes similar to those observed during anxiety reactions and other fight or flight reactions (Gray & Bingaman 1996).

Other neuroendocrine systems may play a role in anxiety promotion or anxiety responses (Longo, 1998). Adrenocorticotropic hormone (ACTH) and cortisol (steroid) secretion is increased through CRF secretion and cortisol acts as a feedback messenger to the CNS at the hypothalamus and directly to the amygdala CRF secreting cells. Gonadal steroids may also be increased and feedback to the brain. Cholecystokinin has anxiogenic properties while neuropeptide Y and galanin have anxiolytic actions. Other hormonal mediators for anxiety are likely to be discovered in the future.

Anxiolytic agents

In these sections we will discuss the various classes of agents used to treat anxiety symptoms or disorders. The focus will be on the pharmacology, clinical indications, side-effects and other general issues relating to their paediatric use.

Sedative hypnotics

Before benzodiazepines appeared on the market in 1960, a number of agents were employed in treating anxiety and sleep difficulties (Werry & Aman, 1998), including ethanol, paraldehyde, chloral hydrate, barbiturates and meprobamate. Some of these agents are still used for sedation and amnesia before or during diagnostic and/or surgical procedures, or as antiepileptic agents (Hobbs et al., 1996). They also may be used as drugs of abuse. However, they are no longer indicated for anxiety disorders, especially in children, and will only be briefly reviewed here.

Pharmacology

All sedative hypnotics cause CNS depression, which may vary from mild sedation to impaired cognitive functioning, coma and death (Eisner & McClellan, 1998). Ethanol is a general CNS depressant and it exerts an inhibitory effect on all of the brain whereas other CNS depressants (such as benzodiazepines) are more selective in the types of cells they effect (i.e. GABA containing neurons). Barbiturates affect the GABA receptor, however in contrast to benzodiazepines, barbiturates can directly activate the GABA channel without the presence of GABA (Longo, 1998). Selective CNS depressants, such as benzodiazepines, are generally safer and may not proceed to coma unless combined with other CNS depressants, such as alcohol.

The different sedative hypnotics vary greatly in their length of action, but are all generally metabolized hepatically, with subsequent renal excretion, and therefore blood levels depend on the degree of distribution among various body tissues as well as the rate of metabolic degradation (Eisner & McClellan, 1998). Although alcohol generally suppresses CNS activity, at lower doses it may produce behavioural stimulation (Eisner & McClellan, 1998). Other sedative-hypnotics may also cause disinhibition and intoxication, making them potential substances of abuse. Barbiturates may produce a 'paradoxical reaction' in children, with noted extreme excitation and agitation. Long-term use of sedative-hypnotics may lead to physiological tolerance and dependence.

Benzodiazepines

Pharmacology

Benzodiazepines have largely replaced the other sedative hypnotics because of their safety profile. Overdoses of benzodiazepines are rarely lethal unless combined with other CNS depressants. Benzodiazepines exert their effects through the mediation of GABA receptors as described in the section on neurobiology. Benzodiazepine effects include sedation, hypnosis (induction of sleep), decreased anxiety, muscle relaxation and anticonvulsant effects (Hobbs et al., 1996).

Different benzodiazepines vary mainly in their potency and half-life (Table 15.1). Most benzodiazepines are quickly and completely absorbed after oral administration (Hobbs et al., 1996). Peak blood levels occur within 30 to 60 minutes. They are highly lipophilic and become distributed in fat stores over time. Intramuscular preparations are available, although lorazepam is the only benzodiazepine reliably absorbed. Some benzodiazepine can be given intravenously. However, this may produce a more rapid concentration in the brain, resulting in greater sedation or side-effects.

In general, children tend to metabolize medications in the liver faster than adults, while adolescents have physiology similar to adults. Most benzodiazepines are metabolized in the liver through the oxidative pathway (Hobbs et al., 1996). The exceptions to this are lorazepam, oxazepam and temazepam which are glucuronidated only. Most benzodiazepines have active metabolites (e.g. diazepam) and many metabolites have longer half-lives than the parent compound. Since studies of the half-life of a compound are generally done after a single dose, the true half-life after prolonged use is not well known. The actual duration of action may be longer than predicted by the parent compound's half-life alone, due to the accumulation of medication in the fat stores of the body. Lorazepam, oxazepam and temazepam have no active metabolites, which makes them better agents for patients with liver impairment or who are taking multiple medications that could affect metabolic pathways (Hobbs et al., 1996).

Clinical indications

There are no firmly established indications for using benzodiazepines in the treatment of psychiatric disorders in children and adolescents. They are primarily indicated for the short-term management of anxiety, seizures and

Table 15.1. Benzodiazepines

Compound	Half-life (hours)	Typical daily dose for children (mg/kg)	Approved indications (any age)
Alprazolam	12 ± 2	0.01–0.08	Anxiety, panic disorder
Clordiazepoxide	10 ± 3.4	0.2–0.5	Anxiety, alcohol withdrawal, pre-operative sedation
Clonazepam	2.3 ± 5	0.007–0.05	Seizure disorders
Clorazepate	2 ± 0.9	0.2–0.8	Anxiety, seizures, alcohol withdrawal
Diazepam	43 ± 13	0.07–0.5	Anxiety, muscle spasm, alcohol withdrawal, status epilepticus, pre-operative sedation
Estazolam	10–24	0.1–0.3	Insomnia
Flurazepam	74 ± 24	0.2–0.4	Insomnia
Lorazepam	14 ± 5	0.01–0.08	Anxiety, pre-operative sedation
Midazolam	1.9 ± 0.6	0.025–0.05 (IM or IV only)	Pre-operative sedation
Oxazepam	8 ± 2.4	0.1–1.7	Anxiety, alcohol withdrawal
Quazepam	39	0.1–0.2	Insomnia
Temazepam	11 ± 6	0.2–0.4	Insomnia
Triazolam	2.9 ± 1	0.002–0.007	Insomnia

Typical adult dose for adults converted to mg/kg by dividing by 70. Doses and indications for children and adolescents have not been established for most agents. The actual duration of action may be longer than predicted due to the presence of active metabolites. Half-lives usually established by single dose administration. Information for this table adapted from Werry & Aman (1998), Hobbs et al. (1996).

pre-operative sedation. Although benzodiazepines are occasionally used for treating anxiety disorders, agitation and sleep disturbances, their use is primarily justified on the basis of case reports, uncontrolled clinical impressions, and the adult literature (Werry & Aman, 1998). Caution must be taken before prescribing benzodiazepines to children and adolescents long-term for these issues. The risks and benefits must be carefully weighed, including the potential for tolerance and dependency (AACAP, 1997). The various potential indications for benzodiazepines in children are outlined below.

Anxiety disorders

Case reports suggest that benzodiazepines may help children and adolescents with anxiety disorders. In a study by D'Amato (1962), nine children (8 to 11 years old) with school phobia were treated with an open label trial of chlordiazepoxide at doses of 10 to 30 mg daily for up to 4 weeks. All children received psychotherapy concurrently and all were attending school within 2 weeks. A comparison group of 11 children receiving psychotherapy alone had only two of 11 return to school in 2 weeks. In a large open label trial, Kraft (1965) treated 130 children and adolescents with chlordiazepoxide (30 to 60 mg daily). Improvement was noted in 53 patients. There was heterogeneity of diagnoses and no systemic ratings were used. Finally, an open label study of alprazolam in 18 children and adolescents found some improvement for separation anxiety (0.5 mg to 6 mg daily; Kutcher et al., 1992). However, ratings by children and teachers were less favourable than those of parents and psychiatrists.

In contrast to these case-reports, the few double-blind placebo-controlled trials completed to date have not documented significant efficacy. Simeon et al. (1992) found no significant differences between alprazolam and placebo on clinical global ratings, in a double-blind placebo-controlled trial of 30 children and adolescents with avoidant or overanxious disorders. Similarly, Graae et al. (1994) found no significant differences in a double-blind crossover study comparing 4 week trials of clonazepam and placebo. Fifteen children, most with separation anxiety disorder, were studied. Although no significant effects were noted, nine of the 12 children treated with clonazepam were substantially improved at the end of the trial. The lack of significant effects reflects a high placebo response rate in children, which may be due to the supportive and psychoeducational interventions that are integral components of drug studies. Regardless, these few studies do not support using benzodiazepines as the primary treatment for youth with anxiety disorders (AACAP, 1997).

Sleep disturbances

Benzodiazepines are sometimes used to help with problems initiating or maintaining sleep. Children may have difficulty with sleep onset, sleep maintenance or parasomnias such as night terrors or somnambulism (Werry & Aman,

1998). Adolescents tend to have disturbances in their sleep-wake cycle. Although benzodiazepines do help initiate sleep, they also affect normal sleep architecture and may result in a subjective sense of being tired and/or irritable the following day (Werry & Aman, 1998). The effects of benzodiazepines on sleep architecture include a decrease in sleep latency, a decrease in the number of awakenings and decreased time spent in slow wave sleep (stages 3 and 4) (Dahl, 1992). The time from sleep onset to first REM episode is increased and the overall time spent in REM through the night is decreased. Benzodiazepines do not affect the nightly peaks of prolactin, growth hormone or luteinizing hormone.

Parasomnias like night terrors and somnambulism often occur sporadically and resolve spontaneously with time. Night terrors and somnambulism occur in 3% and 6% of children respectively (Anders & Eibens, 1997). Both occur during stage 4 sleep, and therefore may be suppressed by benzodiazepines. However, tolerance may develop, or the disorder may reoccur upon withdrawal of medication. Therefore, benzodiazepines are not generally used to treat these difficulties. Rather, reassurance and education is provided to the parents, with recommendations to avoid excessive daytime fatigue in the child, and to make the environment safe for sleep walkers. If benzodiazepines are to be used for treating problems with sleep onset, short acting agents are preferred. They have a rapid onset of action, and less potential for causing sedation and cognitive dysfunction the following day. Long acting agents may be useful for treating sleep difficulties associated with other anxiety problems. However, in general, the use of benzodiazepines, especially long-term, is discouraged. They are only indicated in severe cases to help facilitate a non-pharmacological treatment programme. For a more detailed review of pharmacological treatments of sleep disorders, see Dahl (1992).

Excited/aggressive states
Benzodiazepines have been successfully used in adults during excited states such as mania or schizophrenia (Werry & Aman, 1998). Although there are no studies addressing the use of benzodiazepines in youth with acute psychotic or manic episodes, clinically they are often helpful adjuncts to antipsychotic or mood-stabilizing agents. Since benzodiazepines can cause respiratory depression in combination with other sedating agents, care should be taken when administering benzodiazepines with other medications, or in the presence of alcohol or drugs.

Benzodiazepines are not recommended for treating aggression and/or behaviour problems in children and adolescents (Werry & Aman, 1998). Children may experience behavioural disinhibition with benzodiazepines (Coffey, Shader & Greenblatt, 1983). Furthermore, since aggression often occurs in the context of other disruptive or conduct problems, the possibility for abuse generally outweighs any potential short-term benefits.

Nonpsychiatric uses

Benzodiazepines have been used for their potential muscle relaxation effects. The muscle relaxation effects for most benzodiazepines have been overstated in the past. However, some benzodiazepines can result in decreased muscle tone and have been used to decrease rigidity in patients with cerebral palsy (Hobbs et al., 1996). Clonazepam, in particular, does cause muscle relaxation, but most other benzodiazepines do not. Tolerance to the muscle relaxant effects may occur, therefore short-term use with the lowest effective dose is recommended when prescribing for this purpose.

Benzodiazepines are used in the management of seizure disorders. Intravenous diazepam and lorazepam is indicated for the treatment of status epilepticus (Carpenter & Vining, 1993). Long acting oral benzodiazepines such as clonazepam can be used as adjunctive agents, with other anticonvulsants, for patients with difficult to control seizures.

Side-effects

Common side-effects of benzodiazepines include daytime sleepiness, poor concentration and decreased coordination (Coffey et al., 1983). Anterograde amnesia can occur after use of some benzodiazepines with short half-lives (e.g. triazolam). Other potential problems in children and adolescents include decreased performance on standardized tests of cognition and motoric skills, behavioural disinhibition and paradoxical reactions (Coffey et al., 1983).

The potential for tolerance, physical dependence and abuse are significant concerns (Werry & Aman, 1998). With tolerance, effects of the benzodiazepine may abate unless higher dosages are used. Physical dependence makes tapering the benzodiazepine necessary if used regularly for more than several weeks. Risks associated with benzodiazepine withdrawal include rebound anxiety and generalized seizures.

Benzodiazepines have a low lethality index, and are much better tolerated in an overdose situation than other sedative hypnotics. However, co-administration of benzodiazepines and other sedating agents can produce respiratory arrest. Flumazenil is a benzodiazepine receptor antagonist which can be administered intravenously (0.2 mg over 30 seconds) to reverse the effects of benzodiazepines (Hobbs et al., 1996). It has a half-life of 7 to 15 minutes and is

cleared by hepatic metabolism. Since its half-life is shorter than most benzodiazepines, additional doses may be necessary to prevent the effects of the
benzodiazepine from reemerging. Withdrawal seizures are possible when
patients have been taking benzodiazepines long-term. It does not reverse the
effects of other CNS depressants. It has not been studied for use in children or
adolescents.

Zolpidem

Zolpidem is a nonbenzodiazepine compound that acts on the GABA–benzodiazepine receptor complex in a fashion that is similar to the benzodiazepines
(Hobbs et al., 1996). It is more specific for CNS benzodiazepine receptors than
peripheral benzodiazepine receptors. It is used solely for hypnotic purposes at
this time and does not appear to have anxiolytic effects. It has a half-life of 2 to 3
hours. Zolpidem decreases sleep latency, but does not alter sleep architecture
like the benzodiazepines. Adverse reactions include daytime drowsiness, dizziness, headache and nausea. It has not been studied in children, nor is it
recommended at this time for the treatment of anxiety disorders.

Buspirone

Pharmacology

Buspirone is an azapirone and is chemically distinct from benzodiazepines
(Baldessarini, 1996). It does not interact with benzodiazepine or GABA receptors and therefore has no cross tolerance with benzodiazepines or alcohol.
Buspirone binds to 5-HT_{1A} receptors on serotonergic neurons and acts as a
partial agonist by stimulating the receptors on the presynaptic neuron and
blocking the stimulation of the postsynaptic neuron. Chronic administration
also causes a downregulation of 5-HT_2 receptors. The postsynaptic 5-HT_{1A}
receptors may affect anxiety through interactions with the hypothalamic-
pituitary-adrenal axis as well. Buspirone also has moderate affinity for
presynaptic D2 receptors and enhances dopamine synthesis and release
(Tunicliff et al., 1992). It is unclear if the effects on dopamine have any role in
decreasing anxiety.

Buspirone is rapidly absorbed and is 95% plasma protein bound. Peak levels
occur 40 to 90 minutes after oral administration with an average elimination
half-life of 2 to 3 hours (Baldessarini, 1996). Buspirone is metabolized in the
liver by oxidation with one active metabolite, 1-pyrimidinylpiperazine (1-PP).
The role of 1-PP in human pharmacokinectics appears to be minimal.

Clinical indications

Anxiety

Buspirone is used in adults for the short-term relief of anxiety, and to treat generalized anxiety disorder. The usual adult daily dosage is between 20 to 60 mg (60 mg is the maximum approved daily dose). The short half-life necessitates two or three times per day dosing schedules. Positive effects may not be noted until after 2 to 3 weeks.

Similar to many psychotropic agents, buspirone is not approved by the Food and Drug Administration (FDA) for use in individuals under 18 years of age. However, there are case reports describing the use of buspirone in children and adolescents with anxiety disorders, including generalized anxiety disorder, school phobia and social phobia. An open label trial in adolescents with generalized anxiety disorder or overanxious disorder showed a significant decrease in anxiety ratings after 6 weeks (Kutcher et al., 1992). Similarly, 13 children and adolescents with anxiety disorders had a decrease in anxiety symptoms on self, parent and teacher reports after 4 weeks of buspirone (Simeon et al., 1992). No double-blind placebo-controlled trials have been done to date.

Aggression/agitation

Anxiety disorders may be comorbid with disruptive behaviours and/or anxiety symptoms may be manifest as aggression or agitation. There are case reports noting the effectiveness of buspirone for agitation and aggression in individuals with developmental delays. The assessment of anxiety is particularly difficult in this population due to difficulties obtaining reports of subjective internal states.

Buspirone was reported to be helpful for treating anxiety, aggression and self-injurious behaviours in 14 developmentally disabled and mentally retarded adults (ages 18 to 63 years), using doses ranging from 15 to 45 mg/day (Ratey et al., 1989). The decrease in aggression was reported to be independent of anxiety. Realmuto, August & Garfinkel (1989) treated four autistic children with buspirone 5 mg three times daily with a resultant decrease in symptoms of hyperactivity in two of the children. No side-effects were noted. Pfeffer, Jiang & Domeshek (1997) treated 25 psychiatric inpatients, ages 5 to 12 years, in an open trial with buspirone for aggression over a 9-week period. Patients had a diagnosis of at least one disruptive behaviour disorder and were generally healthy without organic mental conditions. Patients received an average dose of 28 mg/day (maximum 50 mg/day). Patients showed improvement in standardized clinical measures of depression, aggression and global assessment of functioning.

No double-blind placebo-controlled trials have yet been performed. There-fore, while case-reports are encouraging, further study is needed before bus-pirone can be considered a first-line treatment for aggression and disruptive behaviour disorders in youth.

Side-effects
Common side-effects with buspirone include headache, nausea, dizziness, drowsiness and fatigue. Buspirone appears to be safe in overdose and does not cause physical dependence. Buspirone should not be administered with mono-amine oxidase inhibitors, since hypertension has been reported (Werry & Aman, 1998).

Dosages
Dosing guidelines for buspirone have not been established for children and adolescents. Coffey (1990) proposed starting at 2.5 to 5 mg in prepubertal children, then increasing by 2.5 mg every 2–3 days to a maximum of 20 mg/day. For adolescents, begin with 5 to 10 mg, then increase by 5 mg every 2–3 days to a maximum of 60 mg/day.

Antidepressants
Antidepressant medications are often used for the treatment of anxiety dis-orders in adults. The literature regarding safety, indications and efficacy for antidepressant medications is limited for children and adolescents. Few control-led studies have been conducted, however, case reports and clinical experience are abundant.

Selective serotonin reuptake inhibitors
Pharmacology
Selective serotonin reuptake inhibitors (SSRIs) inhibit the reuptake of serotonin into the nerve cell, thereby increasing levels of serotonin in the brain. SSRIs have demonstrated efficacy for a broad array of psychiatric disorders in adults including depression, dysthymia, panic disorder, obsessive-compulsive dis-order, social phobia and generalized anxiety disorder. The studies for use in children and adolescents are less extensive (AACAP, 1997).

Clinical indications
There are studies documenting the efficacy of SSRIs for obsessive-compulsive disorder in youth (AACAP, 1998a). Fluvoxamine and sertraline received FDA

approval for use in paediatric obsessive-compulsive disorder in 1997 (down to 8 and 6 years of age, respectively). Studies with fluoxetine and paroxetine for paediatric obsessive-compulsive disorder are ongoing (Riddle et al., 1992).

There are some studies supporting the use of SSRIs for the treatment of other anxiety disorders. An open label trial of fluoxetine in 21 children and adolescents diagnosed with separation anxiety disorder, social phobia or over-anxious disorder showed 81% had at least moderate improvement after 6 to 8 weeks of treatment (Birmaher et al., 1994). A 12-week double-blind, placebo-controlled trial of fluoxetine in 15 children with selective mutism demonstrated significant drug effects on parental rating scales of anxiety and mutism (Black & Uhde, 1994). Selective mutism has been conceptualized as a form of social phobia (Black & Uhde, 1994).

Side-effects
SSRIs are generally well tolerated by youth (AACAP, 1997). Potential side-effects include headache, nausea, diarrhoea or constipation, insomnia and an increase in anxiety or agitation. Some youth may develop significant agitation, motor restlessness or behavioural disinhibition (AACAP, 1997). SSRIs can also cause sexual dysfunction including decreased libido and anorgasmia which may be an important consideration when treating older sexually active adolescents.

SSRIs affect the P450 enzyme system in the liver which is responsible for the metabolism of many medications. Significant drug interactions can occur with medications such as tricyclic antidepressants, benzodiazepines, anticonvulsants, antihistamines and over the counter cough/cold preparations. The extent of these interactions varies for each SSRI. Overall, compared to tricyclic and MAOI antidepressants, SSRIs have the advantage of being better tolerated with fewer side-effects and relative safety in overdose.

Decision to use
In clinical practice, SSRIs are often used to treat childhood anxiety disorders, and anxiety symptoms related to other psychiatric problems, including depression and post-traumatic stress disorder (AACAP, 1998b) Commonly used SSRIs include fluoxetine, sertraline, paroxetine and fluvoxamine. Further studies are needed examining the efficacy of SSRIs in youth with anxiety disorders. In general, dosing guidelines have not been established for children (see Table 15.2 for typical dosages). Children tolerate the SSRIs well, often even at adult doses, although lower doses are generally used. There is some indication that higher doses may be necessary for treating obsessive-compulsive disorder as

Table 15.2. Use of medications for anxiety disorders

Medication	Anxiety disorders that medication may be useful in treating	Typical daily dose (mg/kg)	Pertinent side-effects and monitoring
Benzodiazepines	?Separation anxiety ?School phobia ?GAD ?Parasomnias	See Table 15.1	Sedation, tolerance and dependence, paradoxical disinhibition
Buspirone	GAD, ?School phobia ?Social phobia	0.2–0.85	Headache, nausea, dizziness
SSRIs			
Fluoxetine	OCD, ?Separation	0.5–1.0	Nausea, headache,
Sertraline	anxiety, ?school phobia,	1.5–3.0	insomnia, sexual
Paroxetine	?selective mutism,	0.25–0.7	dysfunction
Fluvoxamine	panic disorder	1.5–4.5	
TCAs (e.g. impramine, desipramine, amitriptyline)	?Separation anxiety, panic disorder	3–5 (1–3 for nortriptyline)	Anticholinergic effects, cardiac effects, sedation, weight gain, reports of sudden death on desipramine. Monitor baseline ECG
Clomipramine	OCD		and vitals
MAOIs	Panic disorder, ?social phobia	0.5–1.0	Dietary restrictions
Other antidepressants			
Mirtazapine	Anxiety associated with depression, ?anxiety	0.2–0.6	Somnolence, weight gain
Nefazodone	disorders, ?PTSD	4–8	Somnolence, dizziness
Trazodone		0.7–5.7	Risk of priapism
Buproprion		3–6	Risk of seizures, tremor
Venlafaxine		1–3	Weight loss, anxiety
β-blockers	?performance anxiety, ?GAD	2–8	Sedation, broncho-constriction

Table 15.2. Use of medications for anxiety disorders

Medication	Anxiety disorders that medication may be useful in treating	Typical daily dose (mg/kg)	Pertinent side-effects and monitoring
Antihistamines	?sleep onset difficulties	0.35–1.4	Sedation
Clonidine	?sleep onset problems, ?PTSD	0.001–0.004	Hypotension, sedation Monitor cardiac function
Neuroleptics	Agitated manic or psychotic states, anxiety related to psychosis	Varies with individual medication	Sedation, EPS, tardive dyskinesia

Table adapted from Biederman, Spencer & Wilens (1997). ECG = electrocardiogram; EPS = extrapyramidal symptoms; GAD = generalized anxiety disorder; MAOIs = monoamine oxidase inhibitors; OCD = obsessive-compulsive disorder; PTSD = post-traumatic stress disorder; SSRI = selective serotonin reuptake inhibitors; TCAs = tricyclic antidepressants. ? indicates diagnoses where clinical use is not supported by research data.

compared to other disorders. Given their relatively safe side-effect profile, and their documented efficacy for anxiety disorders in adults, it is reasonable to select an SSRI for youth with anxiety disorders if nonpharmacological psychosocial interventions have not been effective. Moreover, for obsessive-compulsive disorder, and possibly panic disorder, they are considered first-line treatments.

Tricyclic antidepressants (TCA)

Pharmacology

The name tricyclic antidepressant comes from the chemical structure of this class of agents, which have three rings of carbon as a common element. TCAs act primarily by blocking reuptake of various neurotransmitters at the synapse, including acetylcholine, norepinephrine, serotonin and dopamine (Biederman, Spencer & Wilens, 1997). The different TCAs vary in regard to their specificity for different neurotransmitter systems (e.g. clomipramine for serotonin).

Clinical indications

In adults, tricyclic antidepressants have documented efficacy for treating anxiety disorders. However, in children and adolescents, there is only a limited amount of research, some of which is contradictory. Imipramine was found to be effective for separation anxiety disorder and school phobia in a preliminary study by Gittleman-Klein & Klein (1971). Thirty-five children were treated with imipramine (100–200 mg/day) or placebo. Children treated with imipramine were more successful in returning to school than those receiving placebo (81% on imipramine versus 47% on placebo). However, three subsequent studies, including one by the same authors, failed to replicate these results (Berney et al, 1981; Bernstein, Garfinkel & Borchardt, 1990; Klein, Koplewitz & Kanner, 1992). In these studies, placebo was equally as effective as imipramine or other TCAs.

Clomipramine has demonstrated efficacy in treating paediatric obsessive-compulsive disorders in several studies (DeVeaugh-Geiss et al., 1992; Flament et al., 1985). This efficacy has not been found with other TCAs. In a 10-week double-blind crossover study comparing clomipramine to desipramine, clomipramine was superior for treating children and adolescents with obsessive-compulsive disorder (Leonard et al., 1989). The response rate for desipramine in this study was not greater than reported placebo response rates in other studies. At this time, clomipramine is the only TCA recommended for treating obsessive-compulsive disorder (AACAP, 1998a).

The effectiveness of TCAs for the treatment of other childhood anxiety disorders has not been studied. There are a few case reports suggesting that imipramine may be effective for panic disorder in children and adolescents (Black & Robbins, 1990). However, no controlled trials have been conducted.

Side-effects

Although generally well tolerated by youth, the side-effect profile of TCAs has been the focus of recent concern. Common side-effects include anticholinergic effects (e.g. dry mouth, constipation and sedation) and cardiovascular effects, including ECG changes, tachycardia, orthostatic hypotension and hypertension (Biederman et al., 1997). TCAs can also cause significant weight gain and can lower the seizure threshold potentially causing increased seizure frequency in susceptible patients. Of greater concern are the rare reports of sudden death, which primarily have been associated with desipramine (Biederman et al., 1997). Also, TCAs can be lethal in overdose and extreme caution should be used when dispensing to suicidal or impulsive patients.

Decision to use

Given their side-effect profile, and the lack of documented efficacy, TCAs are generally not considered the first agent of choice when treating anxiety disorders in children and adolescents. In clinical practice, TCAs may be used when anxiety symptoms from an anxiety disorder are prominent, and have not responded to other treatments. TCAs may also be considered in the presence of comorbid conditions for which they are also indicated (e.g. ADHD or enuresis).

The decision as to which TCA to use is generally based on side-effect profile and the patient's medication history. Other than clomipramine for the treatment of obsessive-compulsive disorder, the TCAs do not have documented superiority in efficacy in comparison to one another. However, given the reported cases of sudden death, many clinicians are no longer prescribing desipramine.

Obtaining informed consent from the parents/guardians and adolescents including the risk of cardiac problems, seizures and sudden death is essential. Family history of sudden death and cardiac problems should be obtained and documented. Due to the risk of cardiac problems which can be potentially fatal, certain monitoring steps have been recommended when prescribing a TCA (AACAP, 1997). These include obtaining a baseline ECG to rule out any type of pre-existing heart block as well as baseline blood pressure and pulse. The initial dose is generally 1 mg/kg/day in imipramine equivalents. Dosages are then gradually increased as tolerated. The typical target dose is 3 mg/kg/day (1.5 mg/kg/day for nortriptyline) divided into two or three doses per day with a maximum dose of 5 mg/kg/day (3 mg/kg/day for nortriptyline). A repeat ECG should be obtained at a dose of 3 mg/kg/day and with subsequent dose increases. Vital signs including orthostatic blood pressure and pulse should be monitored frequently during the initiation of TCA treatment. Drug levels do not need to be monitored regularly, however, it may be reasonable to check levels when planning dose changes at higher dose levels or when assessing side effects.

Monoamine oxidase inhibitors
Pharmacology

Monoamine oxidase inhibitors (MAOIs) interfere with neurotransmitter metabolism through blocking their breakdown by the enzyme monoamine oxidase. This results in increased levels of norepinephrine, serotonin and dopamine (Baldessarini, 1996). There are two classes of MAOIs based on structure. The hydralazine class contains phenelzine and isocarboxazid while tranylcypromine is a nonhydralazine, which is structurally related to stimulants.

Clinical indications

In adults, MAOIs have been found to be effective for depression and anxiety disorders especially panic disorder. There is also evidence that phenelzine may be useful in treating adults with social phobia (Liebowitz et al., 1992). There have been no controlled studies in children.

Side-effects and decision to use

MAOIs can cause positional blood pressure changes, drowsiness and weight gain. Some foods contain high levels of a substance (tyramine), which is usually broken down by monoamine oxidase. If tyramine is not metabolized it can cause dangerously high blood pressure, which sometimes result in heart attacks or stroke. Due to this, patients taking MAOIs have to follow a diet low in aged cheese and other foods. Drug interactions with a number of medications, including SSRIs, TCAs, meperidine and many over the counter cold preparations, can precipitate a hypertensive crisis. Therefore, due to the side-effect profile, dietary restrictions, the advent of newer safer medications, and the lack of efficacy data, MAOIs are not recommended as first line agents for anxiety disorders in children and adolescents. Their use should only be undertaken in children whose condition has been refractory to other treatments and who have close, reliable adult supervision available.

Other antidepressants

There are a number of antidepressants, many of which are newer, that do not fit into the categories of SSRIs, TCAs or MAOIs. These agents have demonstrated efficacy for depression in adults and many have been found to be useful in reducing the anxiety that is often associated with depression. Based on their pharmacology, it is possible to theorize that some may be useful in treating anxiety disorders. There are a few studies in adults with these medications. However, none of these agents have undergone study for the treatment of anxiety disorders in children and adolescents. These medications do not have approved dosing schedules for the paediatric population. See Table 15.2 for typical daily doses in mg/kg.

Mirtazapine is a newer antidepressant which is chemically distinct from SSRIs and TCAs. It affects both norepinephrine and serotonin levels through antagonism of central α_2 presynaptic autoreceptors and heteroreceptors on both norepinephrine and serotonin secreting cells (Stimmel, Dopheide & Stahl,

1997). This promotes the release of norephinephrine which subsequently increases serotonin release. It also blocks 5-HT$_2$ and 5-HT$_3$ receptors to prevent their stimulation by the increased serotonin levels. This action is thought to protect against some side-effects of increased serotonin levels such as nausea and sexual dysfunction. Common side-effects are somnolence, increased appetite, weight gain and dizziness. Mirtazapine is indicated for the treatment of major depression in adults. One study found that mirtazapine reduced anxiety associated with depression within one week of initiating treatment (Claghorn & Lesem, 1995). There are currently no studies of mirtazapine for use in treating anxiety disorders in adults or children.

Nefazodone is another structurally unique antidepressant that inhibits the reuptake of serotonin and norephinephrine. Common side-effects include positional blood pressure changes, somnolence, dry mouth, nausea, dizziness and constipation. It is reported to cause less sexual dysfunction problems than SSRIs which may be important in treating older sexually active patients. Nefazodone has demonstrated efficacy for the treatment of depression in adults. It is often used for depression that is accompanied by insomnia and/or anxiety. There is one study in adults for generalized anxiety disorder in which 15 of 21 felt they had significant improvement on nefazodone (Hedges et al., 1996). There are no studies in children for use in treating anxiety disorders.

Trazodone is structurally related to nefazodone. It inhibits serotonin reuptake and stimulates 5-HT$_1$ receptors as does its primary metabolite m-chlorophenylpiperazine (Baldessarini, 1996). It is a potent sleep-inducing agent and is sometimes used in low doses to help with sleep difficulties. Common side-effects are low blood pressure, dizziness, somnolence, nausea and headache. One serious potential side-effect is priapism which is a painful erection that may occur in the absence of sexual arousal. Priapism may need surgical intervention and can lead to permanent erectile dysfunction. Therefore use of trazodone in males should be cautious with informed consent of parents and adolescents. Trazodone is used to treat adults with depression, PTSD and sleep difficulties. There are no studies for use in children with anxiety disorders.

Buproprion inhibits the reuptake of neurotransmitters into the nerve cells with a stronger blocking effect on dopamine compared to its effects on norepinephrine and serotonin (Baldessarini, 1996). Common side-effects are agitation, dry mouth, headache, insomnia, constipation and tremor. One serious potential side-effect of buproprion is generalized seizures and therefore, it should not be used in patients with a seizure disorder. Patients with bulimia and anorexia were also found to have higher rates of seizures on buproprion. Seizures occur in 0.4% of patients taking buproprion which is four times greater than the general population. The risk for seizures increases with doses above 450 mg/day. Therefore the maximum daily dose is 450 mg/day with no individual dose exceeding 150 mg (Physicians' Desk Reference, 2000, pp. 1177–80). Buproprion is also available in a sustained release form which has slightly lower incidence of seizures, and can be given twice a day with a maximum daily dose of 400 mg/day. Buproprion is used to treat depression in adults and has been used to treat ADHD symptoms in children. There are no studies or reports for the treatment of anxiety disorders in children.

Venlafaxine inhibits norephinephrine and serotonin reuptake and is a weak inhibitor of dopamine reuptake as well (Baldessarini, 1996). Common side-effects are nausea, somnolence, nervousness or anxiety, decreased appetite, weight loss and headache. It can also cause increased blood pressure or decreased blood pressure. It has relatively few interactions with other medications. Venlafaxine has demonstrated efficacy in adults for treatment of depression. There is a small case series showing improvement in 5 of 10 adults with social phobia when treated with venlafaxine (Keck & McElroy, 1997). There are no studies in children or adolescents with anxiety disorders.

β-adrenergic blockers

β-adrenergic receptors mediate the 'fight or flight' reaction to stressful stimuli. They can be activated by the sympathetic nervous system or circulating catecholamines. Many physical symptoms of anxiety are expressed through noradrenergic stimulation. β-1 receptors are found mainly in the heart and brain while β-2 receptors are present in vascular tissue, airways and the gastrointestinal tract (Werry & Aman, 1998). β-adrenergic receptor blocking agents (β-blockers) interfere with the adrenergic response.

Pharmacology

A number of medications are classified as β-blockers (Hoffman & Lefkowitz, 1996). Their main uses are for cardiac conditions or hypertension. Some agents, such as propranolol, bind β-1 and β-2 receptors equally while other agents are more selective for β-1 receptors. Selective β-blockers include atenolol, metoprolol, esmolol and acebutolol. The lipid solubility varies for each medication. This may have some implications in drug selection for psychiatric conditions as the more lipophilic agents will penetrate the blood–brain barrier more readily. Propranolol and metoprolol are the most lipophilic while atenolol and nadolol are the least. The half-life for all β-blockers is relatively short (between 2 and 8 hours) necessitating multiple daily dosing schedules.

Side-effects

Potential side-effects include sedation, bronchoconstriction, bradycardia, hypo-tension, sexual dysfunction, nausea and hypoglycaemia (Werry & Aman, 1998). β-blockers are contraindicated in patients with asthma, diabetes, hyper-thyroidism and cardiovascular problems.

Clinical indications

β-blockers have been tried for a variety of anxiety states in adults, including performance anxiety, generalized anxiety disorder and panic attacks (Hayes & Schultz, 1987). Noyes (1982, 1988) found that β-blockers can limit the physical manifestations of anxiety when used to treat performance associated anxiety, however, their effects on the psychological aspects of anxiety are minimal. They are also used for treatment of akathisia and tremors.

Studies to establish the use of β-blockers in children with anxiety disorders have not been conducted. There are reports that β-blockers are helpful for episodes of aggression in children, primarily those with developmental disabili-ties and autism (Ratey et al., 1987). However, there are no controlled studies, and the case reports were confounded by the lack of standardized rating scales, and the concurrent use of other medications. Therefore, there is not sufficient evidence to document the efficacy of β-blockers for childhood psychiatric problems. Their use for anxiety in children and adolescents is only considered when other treatments have failed.

Antihistamines and anticholinergics

Historically, antihistamine medications have been used in paediatrics to treat sleep disturbances and fussiness in infants and children. Behavioural methods are preferred, however the short-term use of an antihistamine may be useful, especially in the context of a medical illness or an acute disturbance (Werry & Aman, 1998). The most commonly used agents are diphenhydramine, hy-droxyzine and promethazine (Biederman et al., 1997).

The mechanism for sedation is presumed to be through muscarinic receptors for acetylcholine or antihistamine receptors and likely produces a different quality of sleep from CNS depressants. Diphenhydramine has a short half-life (6 hours) which can reduce daytime sedation the next day. The other agents have a longer duration of action. Common side-effects are dry mouth, constipation and blurred vision. At higher doses or in overdose, the anticholinergic proper-ties can cause delirium or problems with memory.

There have been limited studies addressing their efficacy for childhood anxiety disorders. An early open trial with diphenhydramine conducted by Fish

(1960) on a heterogeneous patient population showed some efficacy for anxiety. A subsequent double-blind, placebo-controlled trial of diphenhydramine in a heterogeneous paediatric population did not support its use for anxiety (Korein et al., 1971). No recent studies have been conducted.

Clonidine

Pharmacology

Clonidine stimulates presynaptic α_2 receptors which results in a decrease in norepinephrine release and lower blood serotonin levels (Werry & Aman, 1998). Since it decreases arousal, some have hypothesized that clonidine may help decrease anxiety. There are reports of using clonidine in adults for conditions with high arousal states such as mania, aggression, panic attacks, post-traumatic stress disorder, and also for tic disorders (Werry & Aman, 1998).

For children and adolescents, there are a few studies that found clonidine helpful for Tourette's disorder and attention-deficit hyperactivity disorder (Hunt et al., 1990; Leckman et al., 1991). Clonidine has a short half-life of 2–3 hours and thereby requires multiple daily dosing, unless used solely as a sedative in the evening. Because of the need for frequent dosing and the possibility of rebound anxiety between doses, a related α_2 agonist, guanfacine, which has a longer half-life is sometimes considered instead of clonidine. Guanfacine has been studied by Hunt et al. (1995) for attention-deficit hyperactivity disorder, but no studies have been done for anxiety disorders. Further studies are needed to document the efficacy of α_2 agonists for the treatment of psychiatric disorders in children and adolescents including anxiety disorders.

Side-effects

Potential side-effects include hypotension and sedation (Cantwell, Swanson & Connor, 1997). The sedation may be problematic in youth, and care must be taken to ensure that any behavioural improvements noted are not simply due to tranquillizing effects. There also have been reports of adverse reactions to clonidine in combination with other medications, especially stimulants, including four cases of sudden death (Cantwell et al., 1997). Whether these cases were causally related to the use of clonidine is unclear. Cantwell et al. (1997) proposed guidelines for the use of clonidine in children and adolescents, including careful patient selection, routine monitoring of vital signs (baseline and every 4 to 6 weeks) and electrocardiogram (baseline and at maintenance dose).

Antipsychotic agents

Antipsychotic agents are primarily indicated for the treatment of psychotic disorders, i.e. schizophrenia, schizoaffective disorder and psychotic mood disorders. They also have utility for tic disorders, and organic brain syndromes. Inasmuch, they may provide some relief for anxiety symptoms associated with psychotic or confusional states. However, in these situations, the treatment of anxiety is generally considered secondary to the treatment of the primary thought disorder. Antipsychotic agents may also relieve anxiety symptoms associated with childhood anxiety disorders, in part due to their sedative properties. However, their side-effect profiles generally prohibit their use for anxiety problems. One possible exception is the use of antipsychotic medications to reduce the distress and dysfunction associated with severe obsessions and compulsions (AACAP, 1998a). However, these agents should only be used after other primary treatments for OCD have failed.

Pharmacology

There are several classes of antipsychotic agents (neuroleptics). They vary widely in their chemical composition and pharmacological actions. However, there are two broad classifications worth noting. Traditional antipsychotics (e.g. phenothiazines, butyrophenones) all produce some degree of dopamine blockade, which was the mechanism presumed responsible for their antipsychotic effects (Campbell et al., 1993). Their dopamine antagonism also produces extrapyramidal side-effects, including dystonias, rigidity, akathisia and tardive dyskinesia (McClellan & Werry, 1994).

Newer agents, described as 'atypical' (e.g. clozapine, respiradone, olanzapine) produce their antipsychotic effects via antagonism of serotonin receptors (although they also have some dopaminergic blockade). In general, these agents are better tolerated than traditional neuroleptics, and produce lower rates of extrapyramidal side effects. However, clozapine, which is the most effective antipsychotic agent for treating schizophrenia, rarely causes seizures and neutropenia (potentially life threatening low white blood cell counts) (McClellan & Werry, 1994). In general, all of the antipsychotic agents may cause sedation, cognitive blunting and weight gain. The risk for side-effects, and the lack of documented efficacy for anxiety disorders, generally precludes their use for anxiety in youth.

Self-medication

Patients suffering from anxiety symptoms or anxiety disorders may attempt to ameliorate their symptoms using nonprescription agents. These may include over the counter medications, herbal preparations or drugs of abuse. Commonly used herbal preparations include Vallerain root extract Kava Kava and melatonin. Many people feel that tobacco and marijuana help their symptoms and may develop patterns of abuse. It is important to enquire about nonprescription methods that patients are using or have tried for their symptoms.

Summary

Anxiety is a normal response to dangerous or novel situations. However, it may also be a symptom of psychiatric and other medical disorders. Anxiety disorders are the most commonly occurring psychiatric illnesses in children and adolescents. Anxiety symptoms are also associated with acute stressors, medical conditions or procedures, or agitated states. When anxiety is present and causing clinically significant distress or dysfunction, therapeutic intervention is warranted. Therefore, clinicians need to be familiar with the various types of anxiolytic agents available, as well as other nonpharmacological interventions.

The neurobiology of anxiety is complex, and involves multiple neurotransmitter and neuroendocrine systems, including GABA, norepinephrine and serotonin. Much of what is known about the neurobiology of anxiety is derived from the pharmacology of agents with anxiolytic properties. As a general rule, antianxiety agents tend to suppress central nervous system activity. However, the different medications all vary in their mode of action, and there is no single uniform mechanism by which these agents work.

Several agents are used to treat anxiety, including benzodiazepines, antidepressants and β-adrenergic blockers. Of these, the antidepressants are probably the most widely used in youth. At this time, there are very few studies examining the efficacy and safety of these agents in children and adolescents. Currently, SSRIs or clomipramine for the treatment of obsessive-compulsive disorder have the strongest scientific evidence supporting their efficacy. Otherwise, the rationale for using anxiolytic medications in youth is often based either on the adult literature, case reports or clinical experience. The choice of agent is dependent upon the specific indications, degree of impairment, side-effect profile and risk-benefit ratio. For most anxiety problems, nonpharmacological interventions, such as cognitive–behavioural therapies, family interventions or behavioural programmes, are the primary treatment, with medications being used as an adjunct in treatment resistant cases.

REFERENCES

Abelson, J.L., Glitz, D., Cameron, O. G., Lee, M. A., Bronzo, M. & Curtis, G. C. (1991). Blunted growth hormone response to clonidine in patients with generalized anxiety disorder. *Archives of General Psychiatry*, **48**, 157–62.

Allen, A. J., Leonard, H. & Swedo, S. (1995). Current knowledge of medications for the treatment of childhood anxiety disorders. *Journal of the American Academy of Child and Adolescent Psychiatry*, **34**, 976–86.

American Academy of Child and Adolescent Psychiatry (1997). AACAP official action: practice parameters for the assessment and treatment of children and adolescents with anxiety disorders. *Journal of the American Academy of Child and Adolescent Psychiatry*, **36**, 69S–84S.

American Academy of Child and Adolescent Psychiatry (1998*a*). AACAP official action: practice parameters for the assessment and treatment of children and adolescents with obsessive-compulsive disorder. *Journal of the American Academy of Child and Adolescent Psychiatry*, **37**, 27S–45S.

American Academy of Child and Adolescent Psychiatry (1998*b*). AACAP official action: practice parameters for the assessment and treatment of children and adolescents with posttraumatic stress disorder. *Journal of the American Academy of Child and Adolescent Psychiatry*, **37**, 4S–26S.

Anders, T. & Eibens, L. A. (1997). Pediatric sleep disorders: A review of the past 10 years. *Journal of the American Academy of Child and Adolescent Psychiatry*, **36**, 9–20.

Baldessarini, R. J. (1996). Drugs and the treatment of the psychiatric disorders. In *The Pharmacological Basis of Therapeutics*, 9th edn, ed. Goodman & Gilman, pp. 421–59. New York: McGraw–Hill.

Berney, T., Kolvin, I., Bhate, S. R., et al. (1981). School phobia: a therapeutic trial with clomipramine and short-term outcome. *British Journal of Psychiatry*, **138**, 110–18.

Bernstein, G. A., Garfinkel, B. D. & Borchardt, C. M. (1990). Comparative studies of pharmacotherapy for school refusal. *Journal of the American Academy of Child and Adolescent Psychiatry*, **29**, 773–81.

Biederman, J., Spencer, T. & Wilens, T. (1997). Psychopharmacology. In *Textbook of Child and Adolescent Psychopathology*, 2nd edn, ed. J. M. Wiener, pp. 779–812. Washington, DC: American Psychiatric Press.

Birmaher, B., Waterman, G. S., Ryan, N., et al. (1994). Fluoxetine for childhood anxiety disorders. *Journal of the American Academy of Child and Adolescent Psychiatry*, **33**, 993–9.

Black, B. & Robbins, D. R. (1990). Panic disorder in children and adolsecents. *Journal of the American Academy of Child and Adolescent Psychiatry*, **29**, 36–44.

Black, B. & Uhde, T. W. (1994). Treatment of elective mutism with fluoxetine: A double-blind, placebo-conrolled study. *Journal of the American Academy of Child and Adolescent Psychiatry*, **33**, 1000–6.

Campbell, M., Gonzalez, N. M., Ernst, M., Silva, R. R. & Werry, J. (1993). Antipsychotics (Neuroleptics). *Practitioner's Guide to Psychoactive Drugs for Children and Adolescents*, ed. J. S. Werry & M. G. Aman, pp. 269–96. New York: Plenum Medical.

Cantwell, D. P., Swanson, J. & Connor, D. F. (1997). Case Study: adverse response to clonidine. *Journal of the American Academy of Child and Adolescent Psychiatry*, **36**, 539–44.

Carpenter, R. O. & Vining, E. P. G. (1993). Antiepileptics (anticonvulsants). In *Practitioner's Guide to Psychoactive Drugs for Children and Adolescents*, ed. J. S. Werry & M. G. Aman, pp. 321–46. New York: Plenum Medical.

Charney, D. S. & Heninger, G. B. (1986). Abnormal regulation of noradrenergic function in panic disorders. *Archives of General Psychiatry*, **43**, 1042–54.

Claghorn, J. L. & Lesem, M. D. (1995). A double-blind study of Org 3770 in depressed outpatients. *Journal of Affective Disorders*, **34**, 165–71.

Coffey, B. J. (1990). Anxiolytics for children and adolescents: traditional and new drugs. *Journal of Child and Adolescent Psychopharmacology*, **1**, 57–83.

Coffey, B. J., Shader, R. I. & Greenblatt, D. J. (1983). Pharmacokinetics of benzodiazepines and psychostimulants in children. *Journal of Clinical Psychopharmacology*, **3**, 217–25.

Dahl, R. (1992). The pharmacologic treatment of sleep disorders. *Pediatric Psychopharmacology*, **15**, 161–78.

D'Amato, G. (1962). Chlordiazepoxide in the management of school phobia. *Diseases of the Nervous System*, **23**, 292–5.

DeVeaugh-Geiss, J., Moroz, G., Biederman, J., et al. (1992). Clomipramine hydrochloride in childhood and adolescent obsessive-compulsive disorder: a multicenter trial. *Journal of the American Academy of Child and Adolescent Psychiatry*, **31**, 45–9.

Eisner, A. & McClellan, J. (1998). Substances of abuse. In *Practitioner's Guide to Psychoactive Drugs for Children and Adolescents*, 2nd edn, ed. J. S. Werry & M. G. Aman, pp. 297–328. New York: Plenum Medical.

Fish, B. (1960). Drug therapy in child psychiatry: pharmacologic aspects. *Comprehensive Psychiatry*, **1**, 212–27.

Flament, M. F., Rapoport, J. L., Berg, C. J., et al. (1985). Clomipramine treatment of childhood obsessive-compulsive disorder. A double-blind controlled study. *Archives of General Psychiatry*, **42**, 977–83.

Gittleman-Klein, R. & Klein, D. F. (1971). Controlled imipramine treatment of school phobia. *Archives of General Psychiatry*, **25**, 204–7.

Graae, F., Milner, J., Rizzotto, L. & Klein, R. G. (1994). Clonazepam in childhood anxiety disorders. *Journal of the American Academy of Child and Adolescent Psychiatry*, **33**, 372–6.

Gray, T. S. & Bingaman, E. W. (1996). The amygdala: corticotropin-releasing factor, steroids and stress. *Critical Reviews in Neurobiology*, **10**, 155–68.

Hayes, P. E. & Schultz, S. C. (1987). Beta-blockers in anxiety disorders. *Journal of Affective Disorders*, **13**, 119–30.

Hedges, D. W., Reimherr, F. W., Strong, R. E., Halls, C. H. & Rust, C. (1996). An open trial of nefazodone in adult patients with generalized anxiety disorder. *Psychopharmacolgy Bulletin*, **32**, 671–6.

Hobbs, W. R., Rall, T. W. & Veroorn, T. A. (1996). Hypnotics and sedatives; ethanol. In *Goodman and Gilman's: The Pharmacological Basis of Therapeutics*, 9th end, ed. J. Hardman, pp. 361–96. New York: McGraw-Hill.

Hoffman, B. B. & Lefkowitz, R. J. (1996). Catecholamines, sympathomimetic drugs and adrenergic receptor antagonists. In *Goodman and Gilman's: The Pharmacological Basis of Therapeutics*, 9th end, ed. J. Hardman, pp. 212–16. New York: McGraw-Hill.

Hunt, R. D., Arnsten, A. F. & Asbell, M. D. (1995). An open trial of guanfacine in the treament of attention-deficit hyperactivity disorder. *Journal of the American Academy of Child and Adolescent Psychiatry*, **34**, 50–4.

Hunt, R. D., Capper, L. & O'Connell, P. (1990). Clonidine in child and adolescent psychiatry. *Journal of Child and Adolescent Psychopharmacology*, **1**, 87–102.

Ialongo, N., Edelsohn, G., Werthamer-Larsson, L., Crockett, L. & Kellam, S. (1994). The significance of self-reported anxious symptoms in first-grade children. *Journal of Abnormal Child Psychology*, **22**, 441–55.

Ialongo, N., Edelsohn, G., Werthamer-Larsson, L., Crockett, L. & Kellam, S. (1995). The significance of self-reported anxious symptoms in first grade: prediction to anxious symptoms and adaptive functioning in the fifth grade. *Journal of Child Psychology and Psychiatry*, **36**, 427–37.

Keck, P. E. & McElroy, S. L. (1997). New uses for antidepressants: Social Phobia. *Journal of Clinical Psychiatry*, **58**(suppl. 14), 32–6.

Klein, R. G., Koplewitz, H. S. & Kanner, A. (1992). Imipramine treatment of children with separation anxiety disorder. *Journal of the American Academy of Child and Adolescent Psychiatry*, **31**, 21–8.

Korein, J., Fish, B., Shapiro, T., Gerner, E. W. & Levidow, L. (1971). EEG and behavioral effects of drug therapy in children: chlorpromazine and diphenhydramine. *Archives of General Psychiatry*, **24**, 552–63.

Kutcher, S. P., Reiter, S., Gardner, D. M. & Klein, R. G. (1992). The pharmacotherapy of anxiety disorders in children and adolescents. *Psychiatric Clinics of North America*, **15**, 41–67.

Leckman, J. F., Hardin, M. T., Riddle, M. A., Stevenson, J., Ort, S. I. & Cohen, D. J. (1991). Clonidine treatment of Giles de la Tourette's Syndrome. *Archives of General Psychiatry*, **48**, 324–8.

Leonard, B. E. & Song, C. (1996). Stress and the immune system in the etiology of anxiety and depression. *Pharmacology, Biochemistry and Behavior*, **54**, 299–303.

Leonard H. L., March, J., Rickler, K. C. & Allen, A. J. (1997). Pharmacology of the selective serotonin reuptake inhibitors in children and adolescents. *Journal of the American Academy of Child and Adolescent Psychiatry*, **36**, 725–36.

Leonard, H. L., Swedo, S. E., Rapoport, J. L., et al. (1989). Treatment of obsessive-compulsive disorder with clomipramine and desipramine in children and adolescents. A double-blind comparison. *Archives of General Psychiatry*, **46**, 1088–92.

Liebowitz, M. R., Schneier, F., Campeas, R., et al. (1992). Phenelzine vs atenolol in social phobia. A placebo-controlled comparison. *Archives of General Psychiatry*, **49**, 290–300.

Longo, L. (1998). Anxiety: Neurobiologic underpinnings. *Psychiatric Annuals*, **28**, 130–8.

Lucki, I. (1996). Serotonin receptor specificity in anxiety disorders. *Journal of Clinical Psychiatry*, **57**(suppl. 6), 5–8.

McClellan, J. & Werry, J. S. (1994). Practice parameters for the assessment and treatment of children and adolescents with schizophrenia. *Journal of the American Academy of Child and Adolescent Psychiatry*, **33**, 616–35.

Noyes, R., Jr. (1982). Beta-blocking drugs and anxiety. *Psychosomatics*, **23**, 155–70.

Noyes, R., Jr. (1988). Beta-adrenergic blockers. In *Handbook of Anxiety Disorders*, ed. C. G. Last & M. Hersen, pp. 445–9. New York: Pergamon Press.

Paxton, J. W. & Dragunow, M. (1993). Pharmacology. In *Practitioner's Guide to Psychoactive Drugs for Children and Adolescents*, ed. J. S. Werry & M. G. Aman, pp. 23–56. New York: Plenum Medical.

Pei, Q., Zetterstrom, T. & Fillenz, M. (1989). Both systemic and local administration of benzodiazepine agonists inhibit the in vivo release of 5-HT in ventral hippocampus. *Neuropharmacology*, **28**, 1061–6.

Pfeffer, C. R., Jiang, H. & Domeshek, L. J. (1997). Buspirone in the treatment of psychiatrically hospitalized prepubertal children with symptoms of anxiety and moderately severe aggression. *Journal of Child and Adolescent Psychopharmacology*, **7**, 145–55.

Physicians' Desk Reference, 5th edn (2000). Buproprion, pp. 1301–4. Montvale, NJ: Medical Economics Company.

Ratey, J. J., Mikkelsen, E., Sorgi, P., et al. (1987). Autism: The treatment of aggressive behaviors. *Journal of Clinical Psychopharmacology*, **7**, 35–41.

Ratey, J. J., Sovner, R., Mikkelsen, E. & Chmielinski, H. E. (1989). Buspirone therapy for maladaptive behavior and anxiety in developmentally disabled persons. *Journal of Clinical Psychiatry*, **50**, 382–4.

Realmuto, G. M., August, G. J. & Garfinkel, B. D. (1989). Clinical effect of buspirone in autistic children. *Journal of Clinical Psychopharmacology*, **9**, 122–4.

Riddle, M. A, Scahill, L., King, R. A., et al. (1992). Double-blind, crossover trial of fluoxetine and placebo in children and adolescents with obsessive-compulsive disorder. *Journal of the American Academy of Child and Adolescent Psychiatry*, **31**, 1062–9.

Roy, A., Pickar, D., Gold, P., et al. (1989). Diazepam-binding inhibitor and corticotrophin-releasing hormone in cerebrospinal fluid. *Acta Psychiatrica Scandinavia*, **803**, 287–91.

Sallee, F. R., Richman, H., Sethuraman, G., Dougherty, D. Sine, L. & Altman-Hamamdzic, S. (1998). Clonidine challenge in childhood anxiety disorder. *Journal of the American Academy of Child and Adolescent Psychiatry*, **37**, 655–62.

Simeon, J. G., Ferguson, H. B., Knott, V., et al. (1992). Clinical, cognitive and neuropsychological effects of alprazolam in children and adolescents with overanxious and avoidant disorders. *Journal of the American Academy of Child and Adolescent Psychiatry*, **31**, 29–33.

Stimmel, G. L., Dopheide, J. A. & Stahl, S. M. (1997). Mirtazapine: an antidepressant with noradrenergic and specific serotonergic effects. *Pharmacotherapy*, **17**, 10–21.

Tunnicliff, G., Brokaw, J. J., Hausz, J. A., Matheson, G. K. & White, G. W. (1992). Influence of repeated treatment with buspirone on central 5-HT and dopamine synthesis. *Neuropharmacology*, **31**, 991–5.

Werry, J. S. & Aman, M. G. (ed.) (1998). Anxiolytics, sedatives and miscellaneous drugs. In *Practitioner's Guide to Psychoactive Drugs for Children and Adolescents*, 2nd edn, pp. 433–69. New York: Plenum Medical.

16

Prevention of anxiety disorders: the case of post-traumatic stress disorder

Avigdor Klingman

Introduction

This chapter deals with preventive intervention aimed at reactive psycho-pathology in children that arises as a result of exposure to traumatic events. Over the past decade awareness of the extent to which children and adolescents are exposed to traumatic experiences has increased. Such experiences include interfamilial violence, sexual abuse, neighbourhood/community/religious/political violence, war-related uprooting, terrorism encounters, natural disasters, technological disasters, fatal road accidents, terminal illness and death. Evidence suggests that most people will experience a traumatic event at some time during their lives, often while they are still quite young (Freedy & Hobfoll, 1995; Horowitz, 1996; Kilpatrick & Resnick, 1993; Leavitt & Fox, 1993; Meichenbaum, 1997; Saylor, 1993). Extremely stressful life events are now recognized as widespread, and our knowledge of reactions by children and adolescents to trauma has substantially increased (Leavitt & Fox, 1993; Van der Kolk, McFarlane & Weiseath, 1996; see Yule, Perrin & Smith, chapter 9, this volume). The frequency of traumatic events in the lives of children and young people is reason enough for the assertion that preventive measures (e.g. identification and early intervention) are critical.

Special attention is given in this chapter to trauma experienced collectively. Exposure to traumatic events often causes adverse stress reactions in children and adolescents, and many become preoccupied with their experiences and have involuntary intrusive memories. Most recover under favourable conditions. The extensive literature documents the typically short-lived negative response to natural and human-made disasters. In some instances, however, the transient stress reactions can develop into more severe chronic problems (Norris & Thompson, 1995). Those who do have difficulties in integrating the traumatic experience may develop specific patterns associated with pathological responses. The orientation underlying the preventive approach is that the observed symptoms are not genetically based but rather are due to the individual's inability or difficulty to come to terms with the real trauma. The trauma has overwhelmed the capacity for effectively coping (Van der Kolk et al., 1996). Traumatized young people can be incapable of finding flexible and adaptive solutions because the trauma keeps them rigidly fixated on the event. Thus, they are required to work through the issues of (1) regaining sense of safety in their life, and (2) completing the unfinished (past) event (e.g. giving it meaning, reframing personal attributions, dealing with avoidance of specific triggers of trauma-related emotions).

Terr (1991) has drawn an important distinction between Type I and Type II traumatic events. Type I is characterized as short-term, unexpected and more amenable to quick recovery, whereas Type II includes a series of traumatic events or an exposure to prolonged events that are likely to lead to complex reactions and poor recovery (Type I may, however, trigger or recapitulate an earlier history of victimization, fears of abandonment, and the like).

In the context of the present chapter, the potential 'clients' for Type I preventive intervention are: (1) children and educational/care systems at high risk of experiencing traumatic events, (2) groups of children who have been exposed to traumatic events and do not seek help but are proactively approached as part of a community-wide, post-disaster intervention, (3) individual children recently exposed to sudden, unpredictable stressors and/or victimizing experiences, who either initiate and seek help themselves or are referred for help by caretakers (e.g. parents, teachers), and (4) caretakers/care providers who may become, or are, vicariously traumatized and/or exhibit compassion fatigue (Klingman, 1993; Klingman, Sagi & Raviv, 1993; Meichenbaum, 1997).

The preventive interventions outlined in this chapter can be applied both directly (with the target population using one-to-one or group approaches) and indirectly in home and community settings. The latter influence individual children by changing their environments. Although the focus of this chapter is on prevention aimed at post-traumatic stress disorder, generalization to other anxiety disorders should be considered. Current data indicate that it is possible to screen child and adolescent populations and identify those with subclinical problems and to provide interventions that improve their adjustment (Beardslee, 1998; Buckner & Cain, 1998; Durlak & Wells, 1997). The brief discussions that follow do not constitute a comprehensive overview, but rather indicate the kinds of conceptualizations and basic interventions that are important in the prevention of post-traumatic stress disorder.

Trauma-related diagnostic categories

The trauma-related categories defined in the *Diagnostic and Statistical Manual of Mental Disorders* (DSM–IV) differ from other psychiatric diagnostic categories in that they include, beyond symptoms, a situational feature, i.e. occurrence of an acute / extreme life-threatening event outside the range of usual human experience (American Psychiatric Association, 1994).

A Post-traumatic Stress Disorder (PTSD) diagnosis requires that (1) the traumatic event is persistently re-experienced (i.e. intrusions), (2) stimuli associated with the trauma are avoided (including denial and numbing of responsiveness), (3) there are persistent symptoms of increased arousal absent before the trauma, and (4) associated symptoms persist for at least one month. When someone has symptoms resembling those of PTSD but is without known proximal identifiable stressors that preceded these symptoms, a very careful examination of the person's case history is required. If specific recent stressors (i.e. a traumatic event) accounting for the present symptoms are not uncovered, other diagnoses must be considered.

The DSM–IV does not differentiate between normal and pathological responses by the mere appearance of symptoms. Dissociation, distressing recollections of the event, repetitive child play and survivor's guilt in themselves may be considered adaptive coping aimed at making sense of what has happened and of what has been experienced.

After a traumatic event, most children report high levels of post-traumatic stress response symptoms, but this does not result in widespread diagnosable psychopathology, and the acute effects usually diminish over time. In general, younger children are affected more than older ones and adolescents, and those who exhibit the most pronounced symptoms of distress in the first few weeks appear to be at greater risk of developing subsequent clinical disorders (see reviews by Belter & Shannon, 1993; Vogel & Vernberg, 1993). Vulnerable children with pre-crisis personal, familial or cultural exposure are more likely to develop extreme, chronic psychopathology than are resilient children who are capable of recruiting the support they need or mobilizing personal resources to deal with the crisis on their own. Some evidence suggests that children are more vulnerable to less extreme stressors than those which may cause PTSD in adults (Meichenbaum, 1997).

Developmental considerations

Developmental considerations are of major importance. Children have special needs and vulnerabilities at various life stages that should be considered in developing and applying prevention measures. Unlike adults, children's abilities, repertoire of learned resourcefulness, and demands from others change over time. A major consideration in dealing preventively with children and adolescents following a traumatic experience is the developmental stage. Prevention must be developmentally sound both in identifying specific age-related responses and in providing age-appropriate interventions.

Eth & Pynoos (1985) and Keppel-Benson & Ollendick (1993) reported that children's symptoms vary across age groups. Preschoolers are more likely to show internalized behaviour (such as separation anxiety, somatic complaints); school-age children experience the more classic symptoms of PTSD (e.g. re-experiencing symptoms, avoidance, hyper-arousal) and decreased school performance; adolescents are most likely to exhibit both internalized and externalized behavioural extremes (e.g. decreased energy, greater dysphoria, aggressive behaviour, substance abuse). Both lack of progression along the continuum of development and developmental regression are important factors of distress, that vary across the age range.

The preventive conceptual model of intervention

Prevention is basically taking action to (1) prevent development of a problem, (2) identify problems early enough in their development, (3) reduce unnecessary suffering, and (4) utilize a myriad of interventions to restore, enhance, or promote resistance resources for at-risk populations. In the context of this chapter, prevention is directed at three major target populations: (1) children, (2) parents and significant others, and (3) key personnel in educational administrative roles (e.g. school staff). School setting, a hot-line, and the media have been proposed as optimum sites for organized prevention-oriented intervention (Klingman, 1993; Raviv, 1993).

Based on Caplan's (1964) conceptual model of primary, secondary, and tertiary levels of prevention, a five-level model has been developed: anticipatory, primary, early secondary, indicated (secondary), and tertiary interventions (Klingman, 1993, 1996).

Anticipatory guidance

Anticipatory guidance is an intervention initiated at the pre-impact level/stage. It entails planning for the impact, and it is implemented when there is ample time for it. This encompasses analysing past traumatic events and their impact, writing scenarios for simulation exercises, establishing organizational procedures for emergencies and coordination with community mental health services.

Primary preventive intervention

Primary preventive intervention is directed at the general population that is under extreme stress but not yet experiencing maladjustment, via educational, social and interpersonal action. Educational action includes provision of clear guidelines (to children, parents, teachers, etc.) and presentation of family media programmes to provide guidance on various psychological problems. Such programmes deal with family interactions and parent–child relationships in order to increase parents' sensitivity, openness, tolerance and flexibility in a specific situation; such programmes take holistic, educational, pluralistic and historical approaches. Social action mobilizes social support networks and includes the school organizational change so that it can effectively respond to the anticipated crisis course. Interpersonal action consists of the efforts directed toward crisis coping through both guidance and consultation for caregivers.

Early indicated (secondary) preventive intervention

Early indicated (secondary) preventive intervention involves mass screening aimed at early diagnosis and case finding and is initiated simultaneously with intervention at the primary prevention level. It is handled by service providers who have direct contact with the disaster site and is initially an organizational preventive intervention (OPI). Once identified, these cases are proactively approached using psychological first-aid for primary victims that include initiating psychological contact, exploring the dimensions of the traumatic event, assisting in taking concrete actions, and following up to check and evaluate progress (Slaikeu, 1984). The Institute of Medicine (1994) suggested that the term 'indicated preventive intervention' be used instead of the widely used 'secondary prevention intervention'.

Indicated (secondary) preventive intervention

Indicated (secondary) preventive intervention is activated once the immediate needs are met through primary prevention and the high-risk populations have been identified through early secondary prevention measures. This is based on more established patterns of help giving (e.g. school-based counselling) or treatment-based crisis intervention (e.g. out of school treatment). It seeks to intervene before a full-blown disorder develops. The expectation is that intervention during the early development of problems can be successful, and it can thus prevent the occurrence of later, more serious dysfunction. It is aimed at bringing the maladjustment under control rapidly, so that there is minimal impact on those affected and to prevent it from getting worse as well as to give support to afflicted individuals and their families.

Tertiary prevention

Tertiary prevention is applied after the crisis has been eased. It is meant to minimize the residual effects and to prevent relapse by stabilizing those who have experienced maladjustment, received treatment and are resuming regular activities (i.e. facilitating the re-integration of convalescing children).

It should be noted that preventive intervention levels are not mutually exclusive (for example, early indicated measures are taken while primary prevention is in progress). Although absolute distinctions between prevention levels are sometimes difficult to draw, they can be viewed along a continuum in terms of when intervention is offered in relation to problem development (Durlak & Wells, 1997).

Figure 16.1 shows the preventive model we have used in large-scale disasters (e.g. Klingman, 1987, 1996). It consists of four (A, B, C, D) intervention levels. Level A is anticipatory guidance, focusing on preparatory intervention with a community service or system (e.g. school), namely, organizational preventive intervention (OPI). Level B encompasses the trauma impact period and consists of primary prevention interventions (PPI) and early indicated (secondary) prevention intervention (EIPI) strategies (e.g. screening procedures; note the overlap of PP and ESP when activated simultaneously). Level C takes place later and involves crisis intervention methodology; thus, it is considered indicated (secondary) prevention intervention (IPI). It includes referrals of acute victims for clinic-based treatment when necessary, based on assessments made through ESPI and IPI. When children are treated for PTSD outside school, preventive efforts are targeted at the family (Family IPI). Level D is tertiary preventive intervention (TPI) involving school (staff, peers), the family, and the child himself or herself (e.g. relapse prevention). This is preventive in that it is especially applied in preparation for the child's return to school. It is a joint cooperative endeavour of the receiver in the school system (e.g. teachers, peers, administration), the mediator (e.g. a social worker, a school counsellor) and the clinician. It includes a two-way flow of information and on-going consultation (Figure 16.1; see arrows for TPI at level D) as a crucial element in the successful readjustment of the child. The measures range from recovery of previously held academic and social skills and competencies, through acquisition of new skills needed under the circumstances, to the modification of environmental characteristics shown to impede reintegration.

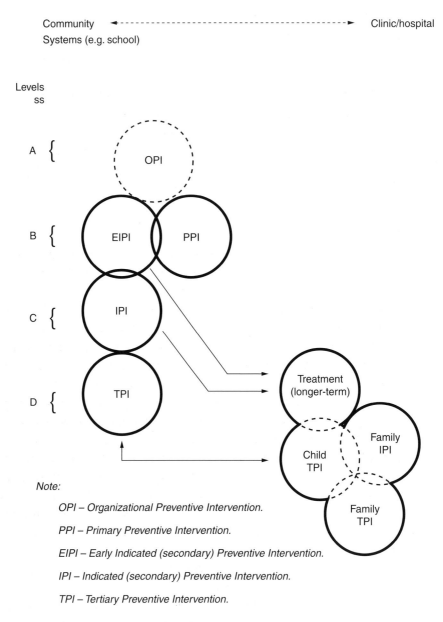

Fig. 16.1. Preventive community-wide intervention steps.

Preventive intervention principles

Based on long clinical experience, one unifying principle and five guiding intervention principles have been effective in prevention of PTSD. The latter five are (1) immediacy, (2) proximity, (3) expectancy, (4) community and (5) simplicity. The unifying principle is continuity. These are considered preventive in that they focus on the generic characteristics of stress response to trauma in the course of the particular crisis and in that the intervention is directed towards an adaptive resolution of the crisis (Klingman, 1996; Milgram & Hobfoll, 1986; Omer & Alon, 1994; Salmon, 1919).

Continuity principle

The continuity principle is proposed as a unifying guiding principle (Omer & Alon, 1994) within the preventive approach (Klingman, 1996). It stipulates that disaster situations cause extreme disruption to victims' lives, with major material, physical and/or psychological loss (Drabek, 1986; Hobfoll, Dunahoo & Monnier, 1995). Disruptions may shatter one's basic/fundamental schemata, such as beliefs in one's invulnerability, trust in people, and faith in the predictability, manageability and meaningfulness of the world (Alon & Levine Bar-Yoseph, 1994; Antonovski, 1990; Horowitz, 1986; Omer, 1994).

Preventive intervention (based on the continuity principle) is aimed at preserving and restoring functional, historical and interpersonal continuities (without which life may be intolerable) that have been disrupted as the result of the traumatic experience, whether at the level of individual, family, group, or community, and at all stages of the problem cycle. Indeed, at least part of the post-traumatic reactions are due to interruption of school work, changes in family routine roles, psychiatric or psychological labelling, and the suspension of habitual social and school roles and activities. Preservation of old roles, social support through social networks, and focusing on pre-traumatic personal resources are a few of the efforts included in this approach. For example, disaster mental health teams guided by the continuity principle, approach children in their respective schools. They help the school system regain learned resourcefulness, resume active roles, return quickly to routine functioning (however partial in view of the circumstances), and reach out to families to advise them on the proper versus the negative (situation-specific) reaction of children and on desirable ways of child coping they can encourage or reinforce. They also advise on how to open and maintain communication channels between the school and the existing, pre-crisis community services (Klingman, 1986).

Personal (i.e. historical) continuity is restored through the child's (age-appropriate) cognitive and emotional working through. The event is gradually processed and integrated into the child's perceived world so that (1) the child's life before the trauma, (2) the traumatic event itself, its meaning and the child's response to it and (3) the child's life after it become part of a meaningful continuum rather than remaining fragmented in disconnected segments. This is done through 'normalizing' the crisis situation and trying to preserve or restore personal identity awareness. It includes supplying basic (e.g. physical, medical) needs; disseminating information to orient the child about what has happened and what is happening, and what is currently being done regarding the event; acknowledging and sharing of cognitive and affective reactions; reframing the situation and the stress reactions as an expected 'normal' transitory process of adaptation; ascribing meaning to what has happened; clearly presenting positive expectations (without underestimating difficulties); clarifying the limited role of the helper and the expected limited course of the intervention.

Interpersonal continuity concerns establishing interpersonal support, preferably with peers and significant others. School group work is helpful in this respect. The restoration of social bonds is an important aspect of intervention, as is the enhancement of solidarity of the group. This provides the strongest protection against despair and the strongest antidote to traumatic experience.

Functional continuity means encouraging the child to act, first on a very simple/elementary level, gradually broadening the scope and complexity of assignments and functioning. Continuity is rehabilitated through relevant external action when the individual, the family, the peer group and the community system resume their previous routine tailored to the specific situation, in spite of the disturbance.

Organizational continuity is proposed as a most important prevention factor. The response of the community has a powerful influence on the ultimate resolution of a trauma. Restoration of the breach between a victim and the community depends on the community taking action to rebuild the survivor's sense of order and continuity.

Klingman (1993, 1996) described the appropriate role of the mental health professional responding to school organizational trauma-related emergencies. In this context, the child's school acts as major natural support system buffering the acute traumatic stress reaction. The key clients (e.g. the school principal and teachers) are not always capable of serving promptly as supporters. They are often inaccessible for direct intervention as they are overloaded with urgent and immediate operational emotional tasks. When accessible, they are often unable to be suitable collaborators (they may themselves encounter anxiety, be preoccupied with the safety of their own family, preoccupied with guilt for not being helpful, etc.) The major responsibility of the mental health professional is thus to serve the functioning parts of the organization. It includes those individuals and groups expected and able to continue with the operational tasks through educational (or re-educational) measures aimed at promoting change-ability within the system. The mental health professional becomes a facilitator who helps the school staff and administration realize their own potential, assisting them in probing and in processing geared to the immediate solution of problems and mitigation of difficulties. They are direct consultants and advisors who are also often required to make decisions, work at procedural rather than psychological solutions, and assume far greater responsibility than usual.

In contrast to the traditional clinical medical approach in which professionals alone are in a position to intervene, the preventive conceptual model, adhering to the unifying principle just described, entails proactively involving other caregivers to engage in, implement and initiate (or at least complement the expert's) work with the child. Every person, every event can become 'thera-peutic' if utilized to help individuals advance in the direction of 'bridging over some breach' (Alon & Levine Bar-Yoseph, 1994).

Five clinically derived intervention principles are applied to accommodate the unifying guiding principle: immediacy, proximity, expectancy, community and simplicity.

Immediacy
Immediacy means that the measures are taken as soon as possible after impact. This is in order to meet immediate needs (e.g. adequate food and drink, opportunity to ventilate feelings and talk) and circumvent difficulties, thus preventing hiatuses in living that would deepen the sense of disruption. It also entails treatment, if and when necessary, immediately upon detection.

Availability of immediate assistance to children in trauma is a fundamental aspect of indicated prevention, because they are highly suggestible and more receptive to help during the impact phase than they are in less turbulent times. Assistance during this period of flux and high motivation may have a greater impact than more prolonged intervention delivered in a less timely fashion (France, 1996; Puryear, 1979). The hours and the days after the traumatic event should be considered a key time for mental-health intervention (Gillis, 1993). The longer the children go unattended, the more likely it is that maladaptive responses will become more ingrained (Peterson, Prout & Schwarts, 1991).

Proximity

Proximity is the preference to intervene at, or as close as possible to, the scene of the traumatic experience (or where a breakdown has occurred). The preferred intervention is in the child's natural setting, so as to protect children's links with their interpersonal networks within which they usually live and function, namely, intervening in the natural setting as opposed to a remote protected environment.

Expectancy

Expectancy is communicating and conveying to the child, and his or her family, in a systematic and clear way that the child is expected (1) to recover, without underestimating difficulties and problems, and (2) resume, however gradually, prior, pre-crisis duties, activities and functioning. This expectancy should be conveyed by all who are in contact with the child as well as by those who are involved, when necessary, in treatment. Prompting and guiding the natural social support that promotes recovery through re-integration is a major task within the expectancy intervention.

Community

Community refers to promoting the resources in the child's familiar environment that can be mobilized to serve as effective support systems. This is done to retrain the child's feelings of belonging and relative stability, particularly through family members and significant others the child knew before exposure to the crisis event. Such resources are family, peer groups and key community figures (e.g. teachers, school counsellors, youth leaders and clergymen) in the natural setting.

Simplicity

Simplicity implies that intervention methods should be as simple as possible, swift and with clear goals aimed at normalization of stress reactions. Such features are provision of rest, opportunity for ventilation of feelings and simple forms of debriefing. For example, the debriefing process does not imply illness (i.e. it is preventive in nature) although it affords the opportunity for the identification of disorders if they exist (Lehman, 1993; Meichenbaum, 1997).

Child-focused preventive measures

Two major preventive methods have been employed with children, especially following large-scale disasters. These are stress inoculation and psychological debriefing.

Stress inoculation training

Stress inoculation training (Meichenbaum & Cameron, 1983) can be modified and utilized as a group procedure within anticipatory guidance. It was designed to provide participants with a sense of mastery over their stress by teaching a variety of coping skills and then providing an opportunity to practice them in a graduated ('inoculation') fashion, basically implemented in three phases: (1) conceptualization, (2) skills acquisition, consolidation and rehearsal and (3) application training (Meichenbaum, 1997). Stress inoculation training versions have been successfully implemented in the Israeli school system within anticipatory guidance intervention (e.g. Ayalon, 1983; Klingman, 1978). Ayalon (1983) reported a 'natural experiment' where an ultrasonic boom sent an entire school into shelter with 'panic' reactions, while a group of children who had completed a course of coping training (originally for shelling raids) and were equipped with alternative coping behaviours remained calm and organized.

Psychological debriefing

Psychological debriefing (Mitchell, 1983) is probably the most widely advocated early prevention intervention used to promote psychological processing of traumatic events (Bisson & Deahl, 1994; Dyregrove, 1989; Manton & Talbot, 1990). It is basically defined as a meeting with one or more people to review the impressions and reactions that survivors and other related people experienced during or after a traumatic incident (Dyregrove, 1989). It is a formalized structure of crisis intervention, usually (and preferably) carried out in groups and lasting from one extended single session to several sessions. It is designed to relieve and prevent trauma-related distress in a normal population relying on three therapeutic ingredients: (1) ventilation of feelings, (2) normalization of responses and (3) education about post-trauma reactions. It provides an opportunity for children to talk about their trauma-based/related feelings and experiences, clarify misconceptions, construct or reconstruct a clear picture of what actually happened, and feel a sense of communality and support with others who have shared the experiences. Children feel comforted by not being alone in their reactions and knowing that those feelings are legitimate and understandable. When psychological debriefing continues later on, it can do much to enhance children's sense of control (Gillis, 1993). Psychological debriefing is claimed to help process and assimilate distorted, fragmentary images and experiences into a broader whole. In this way the trauma becomes part of personal history, preventing the memories from having a separate, wounding existence (Mayhew, 1997).

Debriefing interviews have been conducted both in small groups and individually (Pynoos & Eth, 1986; Toubiana et al., 1988; Yule & Udwin, 1991). Yule (1993) suggested that 7 to 14 days after the event occurs are optimal, as most children are too numb to benefit from debriefing interviews within the first 48 hours. In contrast, others (e.g. Klingman, 1987; Pynoos & Eth, 1986; Toubiana et al., 1988) reported positive results from 2 hours to 48 hours after the traumatic event occurred (see also O'Hara, Taylor & Simpson (1994) and Stallard & Law (1993) for descriptions).

The role of parents and additional significant others

The immediate social environment is an important factor in individual outcomes, and children are considered particularly vulnerable to social mediators (Green & Solomon, 1995). The influence of parents and different significant others (e.g. peers, teachers) on symptoms and adjustment is a major consideration.

Children are dependent on adults, parents in particular; the younger the child, the greater the reliance on parental figures for stress-response cues, interpretation of the traumatic event, emotional security and structural stability. Children, like adults, need reconstruction of the sense of continuity. Because children are less familiar and less experienced than adults with the complex world around them, they rely on adults' appraisals of the traumatic situation. Adults are expected to communicate to them that the situation, or part of it, is under control (at least partially); that the child's response is proper under such unusual circumstances; that the child is not alone in the world; that the parents/significant others are available, empathic companions; and, that the adult is coping. In particular, the adults are expected to show confidence that things will improve and not to allow their responses to impair (at least some of) their prior routine activities; pre-crisis roles should (and are expected to) be gradually resumed.

The family provides the key site for reinstating a sense of safety and security. The behaviour of parents, siblings and peers during the impact stage may be even more critical for children's subsequent adjustment than their direct exposure to the event. In most cases, while the child experiences a traumatic event, other family members and significant people experience a wide range of anxiety-related reactions and undergo identical shock or are indirectly affected by various aspects of the event (perpetuated inside and/or outside the family). In such cases, children may observe maladaptive responses and/or emotional distress, conflicts, and other difficulties (e.g. economic) of their parents, and thus suffer (actual or perceived) loss of adult support just when they need it most. Parents are confused about how to respond properly to their child's reactions while having their own problems to solve.

Parental variables predict a child's or adolescent's adjustment to the trauma (Lyons, 1987; McFarlane, 1987; Milgram, 1989; Sullivan, Saylor & Foster, 1991). These parental variables have been found to strongly influence the longer-term PTSD symptoms in children (McFarlane, 1987): (1) separation from significant family members immediately after the adverse event, (2) mother's traumatic stress reaction level and the continuing maternal (but not paternal) preoccupation with the traumatic event and (3) deterioration of parental and/or family functioning.

A child in trauma imposes additional stress on parents. This can perpetuate and exacerbate dysfunctional family systems, engender stress in dysfunctional family members, and even hinder the preventive intervention or the therapeutic treatment with the affected child. The parents must first control their stress before seeking ways to help their child.

Parents emerge as a central mediating force by exacerbating or buffering the child's response (Bat-Zion & Levy-Shiff, 1993; Klingman, 1993), but may also proactively facilitate and provide a model for coping (e.g. Klingman, 1992). Family members can take an active part in preventing the development of the disorder, prompting spontaneous recovery, and/or take part in promoting recovery (when the child is in treatment) across the various levels of prevention by (1) detecting signs of traumatic stress in their children, (2) facilitating resolution of conflicts by reframing and perspective-taking, (3) exploring, discovering and prompting family members' strengths, (4) helping to find meanings and eventually develop a more optimistic vision of improved coping in case of relapse or the recurrence of a similar event, and (5) acting as co-therapists.

Therefore, any preventive intervention plan for children and adolescents must delve into the actual response and behaviour of the parents and other family members. Many therapists may still tend to ignore the many secondary adversities of children and their parents.

Three major strategies of guidance in this context are (1) debriefing, (2) telephone hotline, and (3) media education.

Didactic debriefing (Dunning, 1988) is often used as a primary and early secondary prevention. It focuses on provision of information about common psychological, behavioural and physical reactions. Parents' group didactic debriefing entails inviting them as normal people to review their thoughts and impressions with other normal people. This can be part of a school guidance programme concerning the child, presenting it as an expected prearranged process which can remove barriers (e.g. stigma, embarrassment) and thus allow the debriefing to become accepted as part of parenting responsibilities.

School-based intervention with parents is highlighted by Klingman (1993, 1996). Parents' concerns can be met through formalized in-school group meetings aimed at (1) presenting detailed information about what has happened, (2) delineating common child stress responses, (3) presenting preventive measures taken at school, (4) suggesting complementary (e.g. at-home) measures to the parents, (5) engaging the parents in their debriefing, (6) highlighting what children need from them (e.g. consistency of care, shared feeling, extra time, rebuilding belief in safety and trust) and (7) involving the parents in the dangers of being overprotective (with some modification, the same procedure should be conducted with the school staff). Another option is bringing parents and children together to share their feelings.

Hotline and media interventions are two unique forms of preventive intervention with parents. Both forms of intervention allow (1) placing a strong emphasis on prevention, (2) relatively easy access to parents and (3) extensive/mass use in a community-wide crisis situations. Media interventions belong to the category of primary prevention in that a targeted population is approached at the pre-impact stage and at impact before psychopathology arises. The hotline contains elements more similar to indicated (secondary) prevention for those individuals initiating calls when they have a need or problem.

The media (e.g. local radio, cable regional television channel) can become the central source of information, giving meaning to the chaos and calming fears. Mental health professionals can be interviewed as well as serve as media hotlines (providing answers to hundreds of parents and children questions called in to the station). Children's popular programmes can be adapted to focus on primary prevention by increasing parent's sensitivity, openness, tolerance and flexibility in their response to their children (for detailed descriptions and discussion see Raviv, 1993).

The telephone counselling service offers emotional first aid as well as consultation to callers on the basis of anonymous telephone interactions. Its unique features are high availability, anonymity of callers (and responders) and the fact that geographic barriers can be easily bridged (for characteristics of calls during war time, see Gilat, Lobel & Gil, 1998). It is interesting to note that reports from telephone hotlines show that in mass emergencies many of the parents who call about their child's symptoms move on to talk about their own adverse responses (Raviv, 1993). The use of hotlines by parents during crisis was studied by Blom (1986) and Klingman (1987), and was extensively elaborated by Raviv (1993).

Prevention of secondary victimization

The response and actions of community key figures and help-providers during and immediately after a traumatic event have the potential either to worsen or to improve the victims' coping. In addition to family and friends of the primary victims, other caregivers/interpersonal networks (e.g. teachers, school administration) may add considerable emotional upset that is often underestimated.

Caregivers in the emergency setting are often overwhelmed at first and have difficulties dissociating themselves from the many emotions affecting victims, and child victims in particular. They may become 'engulfed by anguish' experience 'identification with the perpetrator' (e.g. being judgemental with a rape victim) or develop 'bystander guilt' because of the extraordinary impact of the victim's experience. Sometimes they have to respond to the demands of numerous tasks under conditions of organizational confusion, a circumstance that may increase the stress they themselves experience (Klingman, 1986, 1987). Service providers frequently are traumatized by their disaster experience, especially those experiences relating to body recovery and identification, and work with grieving families; they are often referred to as 'hidden victims' (e.g. Raphael, 1984). This phenomenon is termed secondary catastrophic stress reactions, secondary victimization, vicarious traumatization, and it includes burnout, countertransference and compassion fatigue in those who treat the traumatized (Figley, 1995).

When caregivers do not understand and/or cannot contain their own reactions, they run the risk of becoming overprotective, thus 'disempowering' the victim, and eventually experience acute personal burnout. Caregivers should thus have a supportive context.

Prevention of secondary victimization may be initiated as anticipatory guidance. It consists of both personal and environmental-oriented interventions. Emergency workers and significant others who are expected to take responsibility/charge of child victims, and their families, need to develop personal guidelines that incorporate regular as well as certain, on-scene trauma-focused coping strategies. These include setting boundaries (time, work and personal) and obtaining peer and family support.

Stress inoculation training

Stress inoculation training (Meichenbaum & Cameron, 1983) versions and simulation methods (Klingman, 1982) were found effective strategies of choice. Klingman (1978) described an intervention with direct anticipation measures developed to prepare school children and staff to confront disaster to minimize the psychological damage. This intervention was tested in a day long simulation that included a prolonged stay in an underground shelter. Simulations that included the use of role-taking and role-playing by teachers with regard to anticipated school crisis (Klingman, 1982) and death in the school (Klingman, 1983) were useful. Preparatory training employing simulation withstood a 'trial by fire' in a community emergency, and proved valuable in changing attitudes and removing barriers between professional agencies (Ayalon, 1993).

Environmental intervention

Prevention via stress inoculation training is one component of secondary traumatization prevention. Environmental intervention is designed to complement stress inoculation training. It entails preparing and preplanning, information dissemination, educational procedures, media education, coalition building, and social activism, to exert a greater influence (e.g. Yassen, 1995), and instituting policies for preparing trauma workers and the educational system. In this context, school-oriented/based emergency manuals have been written as guides in drawing up a school plan to deal with a disaster should it occur. Many of the strategies suggested can be built into the curriculum of every school, so that by planning ahead for the short, medium and longer term, staff may be better prepared to cope with traumatic effects. In some cases (Klingman, 1998; Yule & Gold, 1993) a free copy of an emergency kit was mailed to schools. To minimize secondary victimization via anticipating/preventative community measures, interventions should be aimed at changing institutions, environments and individuals.

Critical incident stress debriefing

Debriefing the debriefers is a major indicated preventive intervention strategy to assist mental health personnel (Talbot, Manton & Dunn, 1992). One variant used for the prevention of secondary victimization is critical incident stress debriefing. It was developed as a group method to help rescue and health care workers to process and defuse their emotional reactions. This is done by means of educational, preventative and supportive processes in order to prevent unnecessary complications that follow from their exposure to the disaster (Curtis, 1995; Mitchell, 1983; Mitchell & Everly, 1995; Raphael et al., 1996). For mental health professionals, an ongoing supportive context combines supervisory relationship consultation and a peer support group that uses critical incident debriefing.

Case illustrations

Use of unifying principle in a 10-session indicated prevention format was illustrated by Alon & Levin Bar-Yoseph (1994). The event was a terrorist attack resulting in several deaths and injuries where several family members (father, mother, and two sons, aged 6 and 9) narrowly escaped death. The first session was held in the home of the wife's family of origin. The psychologist approached the municipal services and secured their intervention in aiding the family, which was suffering from a financial crisis. A debriefing session was held in which each family member recounted his or her action during and after the assault, revealing everyone's courage and resourcefulness. The next step was to help the children, while indirectly helping the parents by asking them to serve as coaches for the children between sessions, thus fostering vicarious learning as well as working at the resumption of habitual roles. Each of the ten sessions usually started with a joint family and therapist lunch (under the pretext that he came from a distant city and needed some refreshments), which reinforced family routine and cohesion. Then freedom of movement in the house was re-established with the children desensitized to the area in the house where they had met the terrorist. The family was then helped to resume work and study, the mother to regain her competence at home along with the children. A 2-year follow-up showed satisfactory adjustment.

In other cases, parents can implement preventive crisis intervention by themselves, with the psychologist serving as a guide and consultant. One such example (Klingman, 1992) is a 5-year-old child, who, after a near-miss experience of a missiles attack during the Gulf War, exhibited symptoms that could have further developed into full-fledged PTSD. One major problem was that the child aggressively rejected the use of the gas mask. The child was not considered to be harbouring any pre-crisis pathology. The parents' role was conceptualized as facilitating the child's recovery from the adverse experience. An interview with them centred on ventilation and classification of their feelings followed by discussion of the negative implications of their reaction at home. The parents were also given a review and analysis of behaviour, elaborating on the relevance of behavioural principles in dealing with noncompliance. They were then given action-oriented, didactic, step-by-step direct instructions for using a bibliotherapy-oriented story and a colouring booklet dealing with gas masks, missiles, the anxiety involved and coping behaviours. They were shown how to initiate cognitive–behavioural play sessions, taking specific themes from the previously read booklet followed by management procedures (i.e. desensitization and prompts).

The effectiveness of this short-term situation-specific intervention was evaluated using a multiple baseline single case study design. Results indicated the intervention as being successful in that substantial reduction for the aggressive and disruptive incidents was observed.

The case of Danny, a 12-year-old pupil, may illustrate another aspect of preventive intervention. He was on a school trip and witnessed the collision between one of the buses and a train. He did not appear at school the next day. The homeroom teacher immediately called Danny at home, and learned that he refused to go to school because he was afraid to board the bus to school. The school counsellor suggested that the homeroom teacher talk to Danny's parents as well. Talking with them, she found out that they tried hard to console him by preparing delicious food and buying him an expensive game he had especially wanted for a long time. They were very upset when they found out that all they did to console him increased his anguish. They were then advised how to respond differently and to take Danny to school.

Debriefing in school with Danny took place in the counsellor's office. When asked to refer to the tragic event by telling his story, he talked very little, did not show as much affect as expected, and made no effort to verify the condition of his best friend. He finally admitted being 'ashamed' to attend his friend's funeral, or visit any of the injured. As he found it difficult to participate in classroom activities, he was encouraged to join an art activity group instead. This group was especially set up for those pupils who could not remain in class (Klingman, Koenigsfeld & Markman, 1987).

The intervention as a whole included (1) screening for high-risk pupils, (2) reaching out by classmates and the teacher, (3) reducing sense of helplessness (by requiring Danny to go to school against his stated wish), (4) in-school debriefing session (where some abreaction was encouraged), (5) encouraging Danny to engage in a voluntary activity (in the school and in a group), (6) returning to regular class gradually and resuming, however partially, class activities and (7) return to boarding the school bus gradually (e.g. riding the bus first with a parent, later just being taken to the bus stop).

The cases presented here illustrate primary and indicated preventive interventions and strongly suggest that preventive intervention principles drawn in part from work with soldiers exposed to combat stress are applicable to children, families and organizations (i.e. school). Drawing upon much field experience in other types of disasters, our contention is that with some flexibility and adaptability these are sound, useful intervention principles.

Concluding remarks

It is difficult to definitely and conclusively demonstrate that a clinical disorder has not developed due to one or all prevention levels of intervention. However, research is beginning to articulate some specific etiologies and developmental courses of major behavioural and emotional difficulties leading to PTSD. Children's predisaster functioning, their level of exposure to the traumatic event and its aftermath, aspects of the recovery environment and learned resourcefulness can predict the emergence of severe lingering post-traumatic stress symptoms (La Greca et al., 1996; La Greca, Silverman & Wasserstein, 1998). Further research is necessary to better understand the factors that exacerbate or alleviate negative psychological effects of traumatic events, as well as to address different kinds of children, populations and related techniques.

Empowerment of victims and of the functioning parts in their surroundings (e.g. family, institutions, organizations and services) should become a major preventive effort. The primary and secondary victims must be, at least partially, the arbiters of their own recovery. Therefore, interventionists who adhere to the traditional medical model of treatment should (be aware and) adopt the fundamental principles outlined in this chapter and put them into practice.

Implementation of preventive measures depends largely on community attitudes and especially the attitudes of community leaders/key figures. It is the collective motivation of communities that determines whether preventive measures are planned and implemented. Community education is therefore an important endeavour for psychiatric and psychological services.

In this chapter, I have attempted to present and elucidate the important variables and key issues that have the potential of preventing PTSD in children and adolescents. The chapter is limited in its presentation of variables and methods of prevention intervention. I could only present and highlight the importance of the underlying principles and the crucial roles that parents, significant others and the community social/school system should play.

REFERENCES

Alon, N. & Levine Bar-Yoseph, T. (1994). An approach to the treatment of Post-Traumatic Stress Disorders (PTSD). In *The Handbook of Psychotherapy*, ed P. Clarkson & M. Pokorny, pp. 451–69. New York: Routledge.

American Psychiatric Association (1994). *Diagnostic and Statistical Manual of Mental Disorders* (4th edn). Washington, DC: APA.

Antonovski, A. (1990). Pathways leading to successful coping and health. In *Learned Resourceful-ness*, ed. M. Rosenbaum, pp. 31–63. New York: Springer Verlag.

Ayalon, O. (1983). Coping with terrorism. In *Stress Reduction and Prevention*, ed. D. Meichenbaum & M. E. Jarenko, pp. 293–339. New York: Plenum Press.

Ayalon, O. (1993). A community from crisis to change. In *Community Stress Prevention*, ed. M. Lahad & A. Cohen, pp. 69–83. Kiriat-Shmona: Community Stress Prevention Center.

Bat-Zion, N. & Levy-Shiff, R. (1993). Children in war: Stress and coping reactions under the threat of Scud Missile attacks and the effect of proximity. In *The Psychological Effects of War and Violence on Children*, ed. A. L. Leavitt & N. A. Fox, pp. 143–66. Hillsdale, NJ: Lawrence Erlbaum Associates.

Beardslee, W. R. (1998). Prevention and the clinical encounter. *American Journal of Ortho-psychiatry*, **68**, 512–20.

Belter, R. W. & Shannon, M. P. (1993). Impact of natural disasters on children and families. In *Children and Disaster*, ed. C. F. Saylor, pp. 85–104. New York: Plenum Press.

Bisson, J. I. & Deahl, M. P. (1994). Psychological debriefing and prevention of post-traumatic stress: More research is needed. *British Journal of Psychiatry*, **165**, 717–20.

Blom, G. E. (1986). A school disaster-intervention and research aspects. *Journal of the American Academy of Child Psychiatry*, **25**, 336–45.

Buckner, J. C. & Cain, A. C. (1998). Prevention science research with children, adolescents, and families: Introduction. *American Journal of Orthopsychiatry*, **68**, 508–11. Caplan, G. (1964). *Principles of Preventive Psychiatry*. New York: Basic Books.

Curtis, J. M. (1995). Elements of critical incident debriefing. *Psychological Reports*, 77, 91–6.

Drabek, T. E. (1986). *Human Systems Responses to Disaster: An Inventory of Sociological Findings*. New York: Springer.

Dunning, C. (1988). Intervention strategies for emergency workers. In *Mental Health Response to Mass Emergencies: Theory and Practice*, ed. M. Lystad. New York: Brunner/Mazel.

Durlak, J. A. & Wells, A. M. (1997). Primary prevention mental health programs for children and adolescents: A meta-analytic review. *America Journal of Community Psychology*, **25**, 115–52.

Dyregrove, A. (1989). *The Effect of Children's Trauma on the Helping Professional*. Paper presented at the Fourth Annual Meeting of the Society for Traumatic Stress Studies. Dallas, Tx.

Eth, S. & Pynoos, R. (ed.) (1985). *Post-traumatic Stress Disorders in Children*. Washington, DC: American Psychiatric Press.

Figley, C. R. (1995). Compassion fatigue as secondary traumatic stress disorder: An overview. In *Compassion Fatigue: Coping with Secondary Traumatic Stress Disorder in Those Who Treat the Traumatized*, ed. C. R. Figley, pp. 1–20. New York: Brunner/Mazel.

France, K. (1996). *Crisis Intervention: A Handbook of Immediate Person-to-Person Help*, 3rd edn. Springfield, IL: Charles C. Thomas.

Freedy, J. R. & Hobfoll, S. E. (ed.) (1995). *Traumatic Stress: From Theory to Practice*. New York: Plenum Press.

Gilat, I., Lobel, E. & Gil, T. (1998). Characteristic of calls to Israeli hot-lines during the Gulf War. *American Journal of Counseling*, **26**, 697–705.

Gillis, H. M. (1993). Individual and small-group psychotherapy for children involved in trauma and disaster. In *Children and Disasters*, ed. C. F. Saylor, pp. 165–86. New York: Plenum Press.

Green, B. L. & Solomon, S. D. (1995). The mental health impact of natural and technological disasters. In *Traumatic Stress: From Theory to Practice*, ed. J. R. Freedy, & S. E. Hobfoll, pp. 163–80. New York: Plenum Press.

Hobfoll, S. E., Dunahoo, C. A. & Monnier, J. (1995). Conservation of resources and traumatic stress. In *Traumatic Stress: From Theory to Practice*, ed. J. R. Freedy & S. E. Hobfoll, pp. 29–47. New York: Plenum Press.

Horowitz, F. D. (1986). *Stress Response Syndromes*. New York: Jason Aronson.

Horowitz, F. D. (1996). Developmental perspectives on child and adolescent posttraumatic stress disorder. *Journal of School Psychology*, **34**, 189–91.

Institute of Medicine (1994). *Reducing Risks for Mental Disorder: Frontiers for Preventive Intervention Research*. Washington, DC: National Academy Press.

Keppel-Benson, J. M. & Ollendick, T. H. (1993). Posttraumatic stress disorder in children and adolescents. In *Children and Disaster*, ed. C. F. Saylor, pp. 29–42. New York: Plenum Press.

Kilpatrick, D. & Resnick, H. (1993). Posttraumatic stress disorders associated with exposure to criminal victimization in clinical and community population. In *Posttraumatic Stress Disorders: DSM–IV and Beyond*, ed. J. Davidson & E. Foa, pp. 113–43. Washington, DC: American Psychiatric Press.

Klingman, A. (1978). Children in stress: Anticipatory guidance in the framework of the educational systems. *Personal and Guidance Journal*, **57**, 22–6.

Klingman, A. (1982). Persuasive communication in avoidance behavior: Using role simulation as strategy. *Simulation and Games*, **13**, 37–50.

Klingman, A. (1983). Simulation and simulation games as a strategy for death education. *Death Education*, **7**, 339–50.

Klingman, A. (1986). Emotional first aid during the impact phase of a mass disaster. *Emotional First Aid*, **3**, 54–60.

Klingman, A. (1987). A school-based emergency crisis intervention in a mass school disaster. *Professional Psychology: Research and Practice*, **18**, 604–12.

Klingman, A. (1992). The effect of parent-implemented crisis intervention: A real-life emergency involving a child's refusal to use a gas-mask. *Journal of Clinical Child Psychology*, **21**, 70–5.

Klingman, A. (1993). School-based intervention following a disaster. In *Children and Disaster*, ed. C. F. Saylor, pp. 187–210. New York: Plenum Press.

Klingman, A. (1996). School-based intervention following a disaster and trauma. In *Model Programs in Child and Family Mental Health*, ed. M. C. Robert, pp. 149–71. Hillsdale, NJ: Lawrence Erlbaum Associates.

Klingman, A. (1998). *Coping with Crisis in School: Emergency Manual*. Jerusalem: Psychological Service of Ministry of Education (In Hebrew).

Klingman, A., Koenigsfeld, E. & Markman, D. (1987). Art activity with children following disaster: A preventive oriented crisis intervention modality. *The Arts in Psychotherapy*, **14**, 153–66.

Klingman, A., Sagi, A. & Raviv, A. (1993). The effects of war on Israel children. In *Psychological Effects of War and Violence on Children*, ed. L. A. Leavitt & N. A. Fox, pp. 75–92. Hillsdale, NJ: Lawrence Erlbaum Associates.

La Greca, A. M., Silverman, W. K., Vernberg, E. M. & Prinstein, M. J. (1996). Symptoms of posttraumatic stress in children after Hurricane Andrew: A prospective study. *Journal of Consulting and Clinical Psychology*, **64**, 712–23.

La Greca, A. M., Silverman, W. K. & Wasserstein, S. B. (1998). Children's predisaster functioning as a predictor of posttraumatic stress following Hurricane Andrew. *Journal of Consulting and Clinical Psychology*, **66**, 883–92.

Leavitt, L. A. & Fox, N. A. (eds.) (1993). *The Psychological Effects of War and Violence on Children*. Hillsdale, N.J: Lawrence Erlbaum Associates.

Lehman, D. R. (1993). Continuing the tradition of research in war: The Persian Gulf War. *Journal of Social Issues*, **49**, 1–15.

Lyons, J. A. (1987). Posttraumatic stress disorder in children and adolescents: A review of the literature. *Journal of Developmental and Behavioral Pediatrics*, **8**, 349–56.

Manton, M. & Talbot, A. (1990). Crisis intervention after an armed hold-up: Guidelines for counselors. *Journal of Traumatic Stress*, **3**, 507–22.

Mayhew, G. (1997). Posttraumatic stress. In *The Gains of Listening: Prospectives on Counseling at Work*, ed. C. Feltham, pp. 200–19. Philadelphia: Open University Press.

McFarlane, A. C. (1987). Posttraumatic phenomena in a longitudinal study of children following a natural disaster. *Journal of the American Academy of Child and Adolescent Psychiatry*, **26**, 764–9.

Meichenbaum, D. (1997). *Treating Posttraumatic Stress Disorders: A Handbook and Practice Manual for Therapy*. New York: John Wiley & Sons.

Meichenbaum, D. & Cameron R. (1983). Stress inoculation training: Toward a general paradigm for training in coping skills. In *Stress Reduction and Prevention*, ed. D. Meichenbaum & M. E. Jaremko, pp. 115–59. New York: Plenum Press.

Milgram, N. A. (1989). Children under stress. In *Handbook of Child Psychopathology* ed. M. Hersen & T. H. Ollendick, pp. 399–418 New York: Plenum Press.

Milgram, N. A. & Hobfoll, S. E. (1986). Generalizations from theory and practice to war-related stress. In *Stress and Coping in Time of War: Generalizations from the Israeli Experience*, ed. N. A. Milgram, pp. 316–52. New York: Brunner/Mazel.

Mitchell, J. (1983). When disaster strikes: The critical incident stress debriefing process. *Journal of Emergency Medical Services*, **8**, 36–9.

Mitchell, J. & Everly, G. S. (1995). Critical Incident Stress Debriefing (CISD) and the prevention of work-related traumatic stress among high risk occupational groups. In *Psychotraumatology: Key Papers and Core Concepts in Post-traumatic Stress*, ed. G. S. Everly & J. M. Lating, pp. 267–80. New York: Plenum Press.

Norris, F. H. & Thompson, M. P. (1995). Applying community psychology to the prevention of trauma and traumatic life events. In *Traumatic Stress: From Theory to Practice*, ed. J. R. Freedy & S. E. Hobfoll, pp. 49–71. New York: Plenum Press.

O'Hara, D. M., Taylor, R. & Simpson, K. (1994). Critical incident stress debriefing: Bereavement support in schools – developing a role for LEA educational psychology service. *Educational Psychology in Practice*, **10**, 27–34.

Omer, H. (1994). *Critical Intervention in Psychotherapy: From Impasse to Turning Point*. New York: Norton.

Omer, H. & Alon, N. (1994). The continuity principle: A unified approach to treatment and management in disaster and trauma. *American Journal of Community Psychology*, **22**, 273–87.

Peterson, K. C., Prout, M. F. & Schwartz, R. A. (1991). *Posttraumatic Stress Disorder: A Clinician's Guide*. New York: Plenum Press.

Puryear, D. A. (1979). *Helping People in Crisis*. San Francisco, CA: Josey-Bass.

Pynoos, R. S. & Eth, S. (1986). Witness to violence: The child interview. *Journal of the American Academy of Child Psychiatry*, **25**, 306–15.

Raphael, B. (1984) Rescue workers: Stress and their management. *Emergency Response*, **1**, 27–30.

Raphael, B., Wilson, J., Meldrum, L. & McFarlane, A. C. (1996). Acute preventive interventions. In *Traumatic Stress: The Effect of Overwhelming Experience on Mind, Body and Society*, ed. B. A. Van der Kolk, A. C. McFarlane & L. Weiseath, pp. 463–79. New York: Guilford Press.

Raviv, A. (1993). The use of hotline and media interventions in Israel during the Gulf War. In *The Psychological Effects of War and Violence on Children*, ed. L. A. Leavitt & N. A. Fox, pp. 319–37. Hillsdale, NJ: Lawrence Erlbaum Associates.

Salmon, T. (1919). The war neurosis and their lessons. *New York State Journal of Medicine*, **109**, 933–44.

Saylor, C. F. (ed.) (1993). *Children and Disasters*. New York: Plenum Press.

Slaikeu, K. A. (1984). *Crisis Intervention: A Handbook for Practice and Research*. Boston, MA: Allyn & Bacon.

Stallard, P. & Law, F. (1993). Screening and psychological debriefing of adolescent survivors of life-threatening events. *British Journal of Psychiatry*, **163**, 660–5.

Sullivan, M. A., Saylor, C. F. & Foster, K. Y. (1991). Post hurricane adjustment of preschoolers and their families. *Advances in Behaviour Research and Therapy*, **13**, 163–71.

Talbot, A., Manton, M. & Dunn, J. (1992). Debriefing the debriefers: An intervention strategy to assist psychologists after a crisis. *Journal of Traumatic Stress*, **5**, 45–62.

Terr, L. C. (1991). Childhood trauma: An outline and overview. *American Journal of Psychiatry*, **148**, 10–20.

Toubiana, Y. H., Milgram, N. A., Strich, Y. & Edelstein, A. (1988). Crisis intervention in a school community disaster. Principles and practices. *Journal of Community Psychology*, **16**, 228–40.

Van der Kolk, B. A., McFarlane, A. C. & Weiseath, L. (ed.) (1996). *Traumatic Stress: The Effect of Overwhelming Experience on Mind, Body and Society*. New York: Guilford Press.

Vogel, J. & Vernberg, E. M. (1993). Children's psychological responses to disaster. *Journal of Clinical Child Psychology*, **22**, 454–84.

Yassen, J. (1995). Preventing secondary traumatic disorder. In *Compassion Fatigue: Coping with Secondary Traumatic Stress Disorder in Those Who Treat the Traumatized*, ed. C. R. Figley, pp. 178–208. New York: Brunner/Mazel.

Yule, W. (1993). Teaching-related disasters. In *Children and Disasters*, ed. C. F. Saylor, pp. 105–21. New York: Plenum Press.

Yule, W. & Gold, A. (1993). *Wise Before the Event: Coping with Crises in Schools*. London: Galouste Gulbenking Foundation/Turnaround Distribution.

Yule, W. & Udwin, O. (1991). Screening child survivors for post-traumatic stress disorders: Experiences from the 'Jupiter' Sinking. *British Journal of Clinical Psychology*, **30**, 131–8.

Index

Note: **bold** page numbers denote tables or figures; CAD is *childhood anxiety disorders*